Historical Linguistics

Historical Linguistics

R. L. Trask
Lecturer in Linguistics, University of Sussex

A member of the Hodder Headline Group
LONDON • NEW YORK • SYDNEY • AUCKLAND

First published in Great Britain in 1996
Third impression 1998 by Arnold
a member of the Hodder Headline Group
338 Euston Road, London NW1 3BH

Co-published in the United States of America by
Oxford University Press Inc.,
198 Madison Avenue, New York, NY 10016

British Library Cataloguing in Publication Data
A catalogue record for this book is available from the British Library

Library of Congress Cataloging-in-Publication Data
Trask, R. L. (Robert Lawrence), 1944–
A textbook of historical linguistics/R. L. Trask.
p.   cm.
Includes bibliographical references (p.) and index.
ISBN 0-340-66295-6. – ISBN 0-340-60758-0 (pbk.).
1. Historical linguistics.   2. Comparative linguistics.
I. Title
P140.T74 1996   96-17311
417.7-dc20   CIP

ISBN 0 340 60758 0

Typeset by J&L Composition Ltd, Filey, North Yorkshire
Printed and bound in Great Britain by J W Arrowsmith Ltd, Bristol

Contents

To the reader

The book in your hand is an introductory textbook of historical linguistics. It deals with the study of the histories and prehistories of languages, with the discovery of ancient connections between languages, and with the study of language change. Historical linguistics has existed as a scholarly discipline for over 200 years, and it was the first branch of linguistics to be placed on a firm scholarly footing; none the less, it is at present one of the liveliest and most engaging areas of linguistics. The subject has recently been revolutionized by the sociolinguistic examination of variation and change, and today, unlike our predecessors, we can watch a language changing in front of our eyes, or perhaps better hear it changing in front of our ears. Progress in other areas of linguistics, such as the study of typology and universals and the study of syntax, has had a profound effect on our discipline, by opening up new avenues for exploration. Our traditional links with archaeology have recently been renewed in dramatic fashion, and some of us are beginning to look at possible links with such unexpected fields as genetics and physical anthropology. In the last few years, exciting and controversial new hypotheses have turned up in the pages of our journals and attracted heated discussion. At the same time, new statistical and computational methods are being brought to bear on some of our outstanding problems. All of these developments are explained in the pages of this book.

The book is designed to be used with an instructor on a university course in the subject, but it can equally be read with pleasure and understanding by anyone interested in finding out something about how and why languages change, what the consequences of change are, and how we go about the business of uncovering the prehistories of languages and of families of languages.

To get the most out of this textbook, you will find it extremely helpful (and, if you're a student, essential) to consult certain reference books. Chief among these is the *Oxford English Dictionary*, the great dictionary of English which covers the last thousand years of the language. Most libraries will possess the *OED*, either on paper or on CD-ROM, and you should become familiar with it and learn how to use it. You will also find it useful to consult one of the etymological dictionaries of English: Onions (1966), Partridge (1966), or Klein (1971); your library will probably have at least one of these. It will not be necessary to consult etymological dictionaries of other languages, but, if you can read the relevant languages, you will find it illuminating to browse through Corominas and Pascual (1980) for Spanish (written in Spanish), Ernout and Meillet (1959) for Latin (written in French), Meyer-Lübke (1935) for the Romance languages (written in German), or Pokorny (1959) for Indo-European, the vast family to which English belongs (written in German). And, if your library has it, you should certainly become acquainted with Buck (1949), which is a treasure trove of information about the vocabularies of most of the major Indo-European languages; this book is written in English.

Every chapter in this book contains suggestions for further reading on the topics covered in that chapter, and you would be wise to chase up and read some of the books and articles suggested for those topics that particularly interest you. With just a few exceptions, all the references are to work written in English, and nearly all this work is reasonably easy to read.

To the teacher

This is a textbook of historical linguistics, designed to be used with a ten-week or fifteen-week course in the subject with university students meeting it for the first time. Students will need to have some background in basic descriptive linguistics: specifically, they will need some acquaintance with phonetics, with the (classical) phoneme concept, and with a little morphology. They will also require some grasp of traditional grammar, at least with the parts of speech and with notions like 'sentence', 'transitive verb', 'subordinate clause', and 'direct object'.

The book is as atheoretical as possible: absolutely no knowledge of contemporary theories of phonology or syntax is presupposed, and such theories are not introduced in the book. Some acquaintance with the notation of classical generative phonology will be helpful for Chapter 3, but is not essential. The only theories introduced here are theories of historical linguistics and of language change.

The organization is as follows. The book opens with a demonstration of the fact of language change, using data that will or may be familiar to the students. Next, it discusses lexical and semantic change, the types of change which are most readily visible. Succeeding chapters cover phonological change (syntagmatic and paradigmatic), morphological change, and syntactic change. Chapter 7 then addresses the consequences of language change, in the form of dialects and language families. With an understanding of language change and its consequences, students should then be ready to tackle the next two chapters, dealing with the principal historical methods and particularly with reconstruction. Chapters 10 and 11 deal with sociolinguistic issues, the first with the relation between variation and change, the second with contact, the birth and death of languages, and language planning. Chapter 12 examines a variety of issues in language and prehistory, including etymology and onomastics, connections with archaeology, and the recent statistical approaches. The final chapter addresses a number of recent and often controversial proposals in the field.

No attempt is made to cover every conceivable topic in historical linguistics. Instead, the book concentrates on presenting the most central issues as clearly and illuminatingly as possible, together with a representative sample of other topics which I consider particularly interesting. Abundant further reading is suggested for every topic discussed.

Especially in the earlier chapters, English data are used wherever possible, in order to encourage students to relate their own knowledge and experience to the content of the book. Some considerable use is also made of French, Spanish, German, and Italian, the second languages most likely to be known by English-speaking students. Exceptionally frequent are data from Basque, a language that rarely features in textbooks. But the book ultimately makes use of data from a wide range of Indo-European and non-Indo-European languages from all six inhabited continents and the Pacific. The ancient Indo-European languages figure less prominently here than in some other textbooks, but they are not neglected, and considerable attention is paid to Proto-Indo-European.

A prominent characteristic of this book is its insistence on combining the study of ancient languages with the study of contemporary change. So, a discussion of what happened in Latin or Old English centuries or millennia ago will frequently be found next to a discussion of what's going on in English or French at the moment. I believe strongly that students should grasp the idea that language change today is not significantly different from language change in the remote past: we may require different techniques for studying the two cases, but the phenomena are the same. Too many other textbooks, in my view, treat the study of historical linguistics as the study of mouldering museum pieces; I want the reader, once in a while at least, to read a paragraph and exclaim 'Hey – I know something about that!' I have therefore made every effort to avoid reducing students to passive spectators watching a train of dry facts parade majestically past their noses, and to persuade them instead that language change is something they are personally involved in.

Every chapter is accompanied by a set of original exercises. These are usually arranged from easiest to hardest and most time-consuming, so that instructors can select exercises according to the level of their course and the amount of time available.

The last four chapters are self-contained, and teachers will be able, if they like, to pick and choose among them according to the nature of the course they want to teach.

In comparison with most other textbooks, this one devotes an unusually large amount of space to etymology and onomastics, to the recent work on syntactic change, to the contribution of the sociolinguists, to language birth and death, to language planning, to the use of statistical methods, and to the controversial proposals of Joseph Greenberg, Luigi Luca Cavalli-Sforza, Johanna Nichols, Colin Renfrew, and the Nostraticists. It is further distinguished by its explicit discussion of how *not* to do historical linguistics. I would suggest that this book is slightly more demanding than Jeffers and Lehiste (1979), roughly comparable to Lehmann (1992) (from which it differs substantially in organization and coverage), and less demanding than Anttila (1988) or Hock (1986).

Those who have read the book in typescript have praised it for its organization, for its clarity, and for its engaging style. I hope that you will find the book satisfactory and that you will use it and continue to use it.

Acknowledgements

For helpful comments, advice, and suggestions on earlier drafts of some of the chapters, I am indebted to Richard Coates, Dorothy Disterheft, Alexis Manaster-Ramer, Caroline Walford, Roger Wright, and an anonymous reader. I am further indebted to David North for kindly allowing me to include some of his unpublished research, and to all those fellow linguists on the Linguist and HISTLING electronic discussion groups who provided advice and information. Finally, I am grateful to Hilary Walford for an outstanding job of copy-editing.

Abbreviations

A	adjective
Abs	absolutive case
Acc	accusative case
Act	active voice
AR	Allomorphy Rule (in Natural Morphology)
Arm	Armenian
Asp	aspect
Aux	auxiliary
Av	Avestan
B	Bizkaian dialect of Basque
BalSl	Balto-Slavic
Bq	Basque
c	percentage of shared cognates (in glottochronology)
C	Catalan
C	any consonant
CI	centralization index
cont	continuant
Cop	copula
CS	casual speech
Dat	dative case
DC	Déné-Caucasian
Decl	declarative particle
Det	determiner
Eng	English
Erg	ergative case
F	French
Fem	feminine (gender)
Fr	French
frict	friction
FS	formal speech
Fut	future tense
G	Gipuzkoan dialect of Basque

G	genitive noun phrase
Gen	genitive case
Ger	German
Ger	gerund
Gk	Greek
Gmc	Germanic
Go	Gothic
GVS	Great Vowel Shift
Hit	Hittite
HN	High Navarrese dialect of Basque
IE	Indo-European
Imperf	imperfect aspect
Indic	indicative mood
InIr	Indo-Iranian
Ir	Irish
It	Italian
Juss	jussive
L	Lapurdian dialect of Basque
Lat	Latin
Lith	Lithuanian
Masc	masculine (gender)
ME	Middle English
MHG	Middle High German
MPR	Morphophonological Rule (in Natural Morphology)
N	noun
Neg	negative
Neut	neuter (gender)
NM	Natural Morphology
Nom	nominative case
NP	noun phrase
Obj	object
Obl	oblique case
OCS	Old Church Slavonic
OE	Old English
OF	Old French
OHG	Old High German
OIr	Old Irish
ON	Old Norse
OSV	object–subject–verb word order
OV	object-precedes-verb word order
OVS	object–verb–subject word order
P	Portuguese
PAA	Proto-Afro-Asiatic
PAlt	Proto-Altaic
Part	participle
PD	Proto-Dravidian

Perf	perfect aspect
PGmc	Proto-Germanic
PIE	Proto-Indo-European
PK	Proto-Kartvelian
Pl	plural
PM	Proto-Mongolian
PN	Proto-Nostratic
Poss	possessive
Postp	postposition(al)
PP	prepositional phrase
PR	Phonological Rule (in Natural Morphology)
Prep	preposition(al)
Pres	present tense
Prop	proper-name marker
Prt	particle
PTg	Proto-Tungusic
PTk	Proto-Turkic
PU	Proto-Uralic
PWR	Proto-Western-Romance
r	glottochronological constant
Real	realis mood
Rom	Romansh
RPS	reading-passage speech
S	Spanish
Sard	Sardinian
Sg	singular
Sing	singular
Skt	Sanskrit
SOV	subject–object–verb word order
Sp	Spanish
Sub	subject
SVO	subject–verb–object word order
t	time-depth (in glottochronology)
TochB	Tocharian B
V	any vowel
Ved	Vedic Sanskrit
VO	verb-precedes-object word order
voi	voice
VOS	verb–object–subject word order
VSO	verb–subject–object word order
WLS	word-list speech
Z	Zuberoan dialect of Basque
1	first person
2	second person
3	third person

1

The fact of language change

1.1 *Boris Becker's observation*

In Britain today, the most usual everyday word for 'copulate' is *bonk*. No issue of a British tabloid newspaper is complete without a headline featuring 'bonking schoolgirls' or 'bonking vicars'. The word is inescapable. But it wasn't always like that.

In 1986 a sly reporter at Wimbledon asked the tennis player Boris Becker a question about 'bonking'. Becker famously replied, 'The word "bonking" is not in my dictionary.' This was hardly surprising: in 1986, the word 'bonk' wasn't in *anybody's* dictionary – at least, not in the relevant sense.

Today, everybody who's spent half an hour in Britain knows this word, presumably including Boris Becker, and, if you consult a good recent British dictionary of English, you will find the word entered there between 'bonito' (a type of fish) and 'bonkers' (meaning, of course, 'crazy'). But, if your dictionary is older than about 1987, you probably won't find it.

What conclusions can we draw? Well, one possible conclusion is that you need to buy a new dictionary. More importantly, though, we can conclude that a new word has entered English in the last few years. The word 'bonk' came into use only around 1985 or so, and the dictionaries picked it up a couple of years later. To put it another way, English has *changed* in this small respect: a few years ago this word didn't exist, but now it does.

This example is in no way unusual or remarkable: whether we are aware of it or not, English is changing all the time. New words are constantly coming into use, and not only new words, but also new pronunciations and even new grammatical forms. At the same time, old words, old forms, and old pronunciations are gradually dropping out of use.

Moreover, this constant change is not some new and alarming development. English, as we shall be demonstrating, has been changing throughout its history in the same sorts of ways, and the same is true of every other living language. One of the fundamental things you need to understand about languages is that they are always changing.

This book is about the study of language change. The first few chapters will discuss the different ways in which languages can and do change, and try to explain why some kinds of changes are more frequent than others. The next couple of chapters are devoted to the consequences of language change: what happens to languages after many generations of accumulated changes? After that, we turn to an examination of the methods that linguists have developed for studying change, both for uncovering changes that occurred long ago and for observing changes that are taking place now. Finally, we shall look at certain special cases and at some controversial new ideas that are currently stirring up some excited discussion in the field of historical linguistics.

1.2   *English then and now*

The language we now call English was introduced into Britain about 1500 years ago by invaders from the North Sea coast of the Continent. These invaders, commonly known as the *Anglo-Saxons*, were at first illiterate, but, within several centuries of settling in England, they had acquired the use of writing, and they began writing down all sorts of things in their English language: administrative records, historical chronicles, religious texts, and literary works. Very many of these texts survive today. Let's have a look at a passage from one of them. Here is a brief passage from the entry for the year 878 in the great historical document called the *Anglo-Saxon Chronicle*:

> Her . . . Ælfred cyning . . . gefeaht wið ealne here, and hine geflymde, and him æfter rad oð þet geweorc, and þær sæt XIIII niht, and þa sealde se here him gislas and myccle aðas, þet hi of his rice woldon, and him eac geheton þet heora cyng fulwihte onfon wolde, and hi þæt gelaston . . .

If you have never seen this kind of English before, you may be dumbfounded to be told that it is in fact English, and not Norwegian or Icelandic or something more exotic. But English it most certainly is, even though it is spectacularly different from the English we use now. We call this type of English **Old English**, and we can't read it without special study. Nevertheless, the people who spoke this language taught it to their children, who taught it to *their* children, who taught it to THEIR children, who . . . until it finally reached us, some eleven centuries later. But it has reached us in a very different state. So what happened?

Well, there was no one thing that happened. Like all languages that are spoken by people, English has been changing throughout its history. Eleven centuries is hardly more than forty generations, but all during those forty generations the language has been changing: a new word here, a new pronunciation there, a new grammatical form somewhere else, and . . . well, you see the result.

Let's look again at that passage, this time with a rough translation, or **gloss**, provided for each word:

Her . . . Ælfred cyning . . . gefeaht wið ealne here, and hine
Here   Alfred king   fought against whole army and it

geflymde,   and him æfter rad oð þet geweorc, and þær sæt
put to flight and it after rode to the fortress and there camped

XIIII niht,   and þa sealde se here him gislas   and myccle
fourteen nights and then gave the army him hostages and great

aðas, þet hi of his rice woldon,   and him eac geheton
oaths that they from his kingdom would [go] and him also promised

þet heora cyng fulwihte onfon wolde, and hi þæt gelaston . . .
that their king baptism receive would and they that did

And here is a translation into modern English:

Here King Alfred fought against the whole army, and put it to flight, and rode after it to the fortress, and there he camped for fourteen nights. And then the army gave him hostages and great oaths that they would depart from his kingdom, and they also promised that their king would receive baptism. And they did these things.

With this assistance, now let's see how much of the passage we can recognize as English. First, note that there are three unfamiliar letters in it. These letters were used by the Anglo-Saxon scribes but later dropped out of use. The two letters *thorn* (þ) and *eth* (ð) were used to write the sounds we now spell *th*, as in *think* and *then*, while *ash* (æ) was used to spell the vowel sound of *cat*. If you mentally replace these letters with *th* and with *a*, you may find that some words look a bit more familiar.

A few words are easy, especially the little grammatical ones: *her* is 'here', *and* is 'and', *æfter* is 'after', *þær* is 'there', *his* is 'his', *þæt* is 'that', and *him* is 'him' – at least sometimes! Only slightly harder are *cyning* and its contracted form *cyng* 'king', *rad* 'rode', *niht* 'nights', and *wolde*, *woldon* 'would'. And you have probably spotted that *sæt* is just our word 'sat'. Barely recognizable is *aðas* 'oaths', but, if you ignore the prefix *ge-*, you can see that *gefeaht* is the same word as our 'fought'. You may be startled to learn that the mysterious-looking *ealne* is just our word 'all' with a grammatical ending attached. Finally, that word *wið* is just our word 'with', but note that the word meant 'against' in Old English. The Old English word for 'with' was *mid*, which has completely disappeared except in the compound 'midwife' (literally, 'with-woman'); its job has been taken over by *wið*, which in turn has handed over its original meaning to yet another word, 'against'.

The rest of the passage, however, is very probably so much Martian as far as you're concerned. Part of the reason for that is that many of the other words in the passage have completely disappeared from the language and been replaced by other words which did not exist in Old English. The words used for 'army', 'kingdom', 'put to flight', 'fortress', 'baptism', and even 'they' have all disappeared in this way. The word *eac* 'also' has vanished too, but a trace of it remains in the name of what used to be *an eke-name* but is now *a nickname*.

A further source of strangeness is the unfamiliar word order: the passage has 'and it put to flight' instead of 'and put it to flight', 'it after rode' instead of 'rode after it', 'then gave the army him hostages' instead of 'then the army gave him hostages', and 'promised that their king baptism receive would' instead of 'promised that their king would receive baptism', among other curiosities. (If you have ever learned modern German or Dutch, some of these odd orders may look suspiciously familiar, for a reason to be explained in Chapters 7 and 8.)

Little words are sometimes unrecognizable: the passage has *him* or *hine* where modern English would have 'it'; the word for 'the' turns up as *þet* or *se*; *of* is used for 'from'. In one case (the phrase meaning 'fought against the whole army') the word for 'the' is missing altogether: clearly the rules for using this word were different in Old English. Other words have mysterious endings: 'would' is variously *wolde* or *woldon*, and the other verbs show these same endings; the words *mycel* 'great' and *ric* 'kingdom' appear as *myccle* and *rice; eall* 'all' appears as *ealne*. On the other hand, the word *niht* 'nights' has no ending at all.

Finally, though this is not so easy to see from a written text, the pronunciation of English has changed drastically. All those aitches in words like *gefeahte* 'fought', *niht* 'nights', and *fulwihte* 'baptism' were actually pronounced with a velar fricative, the loud, scrapy sound found in Scottish *loch* and German *ach*, and *niht* was pronounced with the vowel of *hit*. Indeed, the Old English *niht* sounded just about the same as modern German *nicht* 'not'. And almost all the vowel sounds were different from what you would guess from knowing modern English.

In short, then, English has changed beyond recognition in the space of forty generations or so. Since we are lucky enough to possess substantial written records in English from almost all periods since the English learned to write, we can see the changes showing up in our texts century by century and sometimes even decade by decade.

By the late Middle Ages, English had already undergone about five centuries of change from the time of the passage we've just examined, and it was beginning to look quite a bit more like modern English. Here is a passage from Chaucer's *Canterbury Tales*, published in the fourteenth century; unlike most of these tales, this one is in prose. The letter thorn is still in use here, though only for abbreviations. I have deliberately selected a passage which happens to be much easier than most passages from this period:

A yong man whilom called Melibeus myghty and riche bigat vp on his wif, þ^t called was Prudence a doghter, which þ^t called was Sophie. Vpon a day bifel þ^t he for his desport is went into the feeldes hym to pleye. His wif & eek his doghter, hath he laft inwith his hous, of which the dores weren faste yshette. Thre of his olde foos, han it espied, & setten laddres to the walles of his hous, and by wyndowes ben entred, &

betten his wif, & wounded his doghter with fyue mortal woundes in fyue sondry places. This is to seyn, in hir feet, in hir handes, in hir erys, in hir nose, and in hir mouth, and leften hir for deed & wenten awey.

This is much easier to understand than the Old English passage, but still very strange; we call the English of this period **Middle English**. You can probably cope with such unfamiliar spellings as *yong, riche, feeldes, pleye, thre, dores*, and *deed*, but you might have been troubled by *fyue* for 'five' or *erys* for 'ears'. There are not so many endings here as in the earlier passage, but there are still some: *weren* 'were', *yshette* 'shut', *han* 'have', *setten* 'set', *seyn* 'say', *wenten* 'went'. Only a few of Chaucer's words are now unfamiliar to us: *whilom* 'formerly' (or here, perhaps, 'once upon a time'), *inwith* 'inside', and of course *eek* 'also' (this is the same word as the *eac* of the earlier passage), while *desport* is now simply *sport*. The verbs *bigat* 'begat' and *bifel* 'befell' are now rather archaic, especially the first, though you might recall this one from the King James Bible.

The grammar and the word order are conspicuously more familiar than in Old English, but there are still surprises: 'his wife, that called was Prudence', 'a daughter, which that called was Sophie', 'he is went into the fields', '[they] have it espied', and others. And again, Chaucer's pronunciation, if we could hear it, would be largely unintelligible to us: the word *myghty* 'mighty' would sound rather like 'misty' spoken by someone with no teeth, and *feeldes* 'fields' rather like 'failed us', while Chaucer's *hous* 'house' would rhyme with our 'goose' and his *fyue* 'five' with our 'sleeve'.

It was not long after Chaucer's death in 1400 that the pronunciation of English vowels began to change to something approaching our modern vowel sounds, and many of the remaining grammatical endings began to disappear too. By the time of Shakespeare, in the late sixteenth century, the English of the day was beginning to become something that we can easily recognize as English. We call the language of this period **Early Modern English**; here is a sample taken from Shakespeare's play *As You Like It*, written around 1600. Orlando is speaking to Adam:

As I remember, Adam, it was upon this fashion bequeathed me by will but poor a thousand crowns; and, as thou sayest, charged my brother on his blessing, to breed me well; and there begins my sadness. My brother Jacques he keeps at school, and report speaks goldenly of his profit; for my part, he keeps me rustically at home, or, to speak more properly, stays me here at home unkept; for call you that keeping for a gentleman of my birth, that differs not from the stalling of an ox?

Even if you haven't read any Shakespeare before, you can understand almost all of this with little difficulty, but it still sounds very strange to our ears: we just don't *talk* like this. Things like 'upon this fashion', 'as thou sayest', 'report speaks goldenly of his profit', 'he . . . stays me here at home unkept', 'call you that keeping[?]', and 'that differs not' are all bizarre or impossible for us, even if they're not hard to understand.

By the eighteenth century, a hundred years or so after Shakespeare, several more generations of change had produced a form of English which scholars recognize as **Modern English** – that is, for purposes of classification, it is considered to be essentially the kind of English which we use now. But such classifications are, of course, no more than a convenience, and eighteenth-century English is still easily distinguishable from anything you will hear or read today. Here is a sample from the famous satirist Jonathan Swift; this is part of a letter he wrote in 1712 to the Earl of Oxford and Mortimer, a senior official in the British government. Swift was keenly aware of the ceaseless change in English which we have just been illustrating, and he didn't like it one bit, as you can see:

> My LORD, I do here, in the Name of all the Learned and Polite Perſons of the Nation, complain to your LORDSHIP, as *Firſt Miniſter*, that our Language is extremely imperfect; that its daily Improvements are by no means in proportion to its daily Corruptions; that the Pretenders to poliſh and refine it, have chiefly multiplied Abuſes and Abſurdities; and, that in many Inſtances, it offends againſt every Part of Grammar.
>
> I ſee no abſolute Neceſſity why any Language ſhould be perpetually changing; BUT what I have moſt at Heart is, that ſome Method ſhould be thought on for *aſcertaining* and *fixing* our Language for ever, after ſuch Alterations are made in it as ſhall be thought requiſite. For I am of Opinion, that it is better a Language should not be wholly perfect, than that it ſhould be perpetually changing; and we muſt give over at one Time, or at length infallibly change for the worſe:
>
> BUT where I ſay, that I would have our Language, after it is duly correct, always to laſt; I do not mean that it ſhould never be enlarged: Provided, that no Word which a Society ſhall give a Sanction to, be afterwards antiquated and exploded, they may have liberty to receive whatever new ones they ſhall find occaſion for:

The orthographic peculiarities (the long *s* and the numerous capital letters) were the fashion of the day, and had nothing to do with speech; the same is true of Swift's punctuation, which to our eyes is decidedly eccentric. You can see, though, why we call this Modern English, even if the style strikes us as stuffy and pompous now. But, style aside, this is still not quite the English we use now: the words 'ascertain', 'give over', and 'explode' clearly have meanings for Swift that they don't have for us; Swift refers to certain people as 'the pretenders to polish and refine it', which is not grammatical for us; similarly, he writes 'some method should be thought on' and 'I am of opinion', which are equally impossible for us.

Swift is here complaining about the constant changes in English, which he quite explicitly regards as largely a process of 'corruption'. He is proposing that something should be done about this, and that a body of people, an 'English Academy', should be set up to fix English once and for all, like a dead butterfly in a specimen box, after which nobody would be allowed to introduce any further changes at all, apart from the acceptance of an occasional new word which might be deemed necessary and allowable by the authorities.

Swift's hopes, of course, were not realized, and English has gone on changing, and it is still changing at this moment, as we have already seen and as we shall see below. In all likelihood, these processes of change will continue for ever, and the English-speakers of 500 years from now will find our English every bit as strange and difficult as we find Chaucer's English. Dedicated scholars will laboriously struggle to master that quaint and archaic form of the language, twentieth-century English, and they will instruct their handful of interested students in the black art of reading our books and magazines, and also of understanding the sound recordings which, unlike our ancestors, we shall be able to bequeath to them. Just as scholars today prepare specialist dictionaries to explain such obsolete Chaucerian words as *whilom* and *inwith*, future scholars will prepare dictionaries of obsolete and incomprehensible twentieth-century words like (perhaps) *cinema* or *exaggerate* or *beige*, or perhaps even *whale* or *train*.

Jonathan Swift is not alone in his dislike of this ceaseless change. Many other people have strong emotional reactions to language change. Let's see why.

1.3 *Attitudes to language change*

Language change is always with us, but, as we have just seen, some people take exception to this fact, and even complain that something should be done about it. Here is an example of something that has recently been upsetting quite a few of these people:

(1.1) Fortunately, I have a spare fan belt.
(1.2) Frankly, you ought to stop seeing Bill.
(1.3) Mercifully, the ceasefire appears to be holding.
(1.4) Undoubtedly, she has something up her sleeve.
(1.5) Hopefully, we'll be there in time for lunch.
(1.6) Honestly, you have no taste in clothes.

How do you feel about these sentences? Are they normal English or not? There is every likelihood that you find them perfectly normal, and very likely you're wondering what the point is of citing them here. In fact, five of them are probably perfectly normal for every English-speaker on the planet. But one of them is different.

The one that causes problems for some people is number (1.5). A small minority of English-speakers not only reject sentences like (1.5) but do so with steam coming out of their ears. The problem for such people is the way the word *hopefully* is used here. And they don't just dislike this use of *hopefully*: they're *infuriated* by it. Here is what Mr Philip Howard, a well-known writer on language, has to say about it: he describes this use of *hopefully* as 'objectionable', 'ambiguous', 'obscure', 'ugly', 'aberrant', 'pretentious', and 'illiterate'; finally, playing his ace, he asserts that it was 'introduced by sloppy American academics' (Howard 1977). In short, he really doesn't like it much.

Philip Howard is not alone in his dislike of this usage: many other writers have complained about it, often with similar bitterness. But why should a usage which seems so normal and unremarkable to most of the population attract such hostility from the rest?

All of the words set off by commas in my examples are instances of what linguists call **sentence adverbs**, but the key point is that, while the others have been in the language for several generations at least, *hopefully* began to be widely used as a sentence adverb only two or three decades ago. That is, this particular one happens to be a fairly recent innovation, just one more recent change in the long history of change in English.

Now the people who object to this use of *hopefully* are, almost without exception, middle aged or older. That is, they are people who had already been using English for several decades before this particular innovation became prominent. Moreover, they are also mostly people who are especially well educated, and who take a particular interest in the use of language. Such people are often very conservative in their view of language; they are perhaps particularly inclined to view any changes in the English they grew up with as instances of 'sloppiness' or 'corruption'. Younger speakers, in contrast, have grown up with this new usage, and they regard it as perfectly normal.

Now the conservative speakers do not object to the other sentence adverbs: nobody is complaining that, instead of *undoubtedly*, we should say *I do not doubt that*, or that, instead of *mercifully*, we should say *it is a mercy that*. It's only that recent introduction *hopefully* that they want to abolish in favour of *I hope that* or even the ghastly *it is to be hoped that*. But, quite apart from their curious desire to get rid of the brief and elegant *hopefully* in favour of a string of words, they've overlooked something. Recently the linguist Steven Pinker has pointed out an interesting fact about *hopefully*: it doesn't mean the same as *I hope that* (Pinker 1994: 382). Consider two more examples:

(1.7) I hope we'll be there in time for lunch, but I suspect we won't make it.

(1.8) Hopefully, we'll be there in time for lunch, but I suspect we won't make it.

The first of these is fine, but the second, I expect you'll agree, is not fine at all: it's very odd, almost incoherent. Why? Because *hopefully* seems to mean, not just *I hope that*, but rather something like *I hope and expect that*. That is, the word carries a clear sense of expectation, and hence the speaker of (1.8) is doing something perverse: she's simultaneously declaring that she expects to be in time and that she expects to be too late.

In spite of the vitriol which *hopefully* has attracted, then, this word provides us with a neat and elegant way of saying *I hope and expect that*, something which we couldn't say before without using a whole cumbersome string of words. To put it another way, the introduction of *hopefully* is not just a sloppy and meaningless deformation of the language, as the critics suggest: it has a *function*. It's *useful*. It can readily be regarded as one of those 'daily Improvements' which Jonathan Swift declared to be so rare in his letter.

Now I certainly am not going to suggest that every single change in language immediately results in improved communication: this is very far from being the case, as you will learn later in this book. But neither is it the case, as the critics often seem to maintain, that most changes represent nothing more than 'sloppiness' or 'corruption'. Indeed, a moment's thought suggests that such could hardly be the case: if the spectacular collection of changes which English has undergone in the last thousand years or so were really mostly just 'corruptions' of an originally unsullied tongue, then modern English would surely be so debased that we would hardly be able to use it at all. In fact, a few of the critics actually go so far as to maintain that this *is* the case, but they can't possibly be right. Such recent examples of English as the speeches of Winston Churchill, the novels of Ben Okri, the histories of Barbara Tuchman, and the essays of the medical scientist Lewis Thomas demonstrate that English today is just as fine a vehicle of expression as it ever was, and that all those centuries of 'sloppiness' and 'corruption' have had not the slightest deleterious effect.

Lest you suspect that my example of *hopefully* might be an atypical case, let's look at something quite different. Consider these examples:

(1.9)   My car is being repaired.
(1.10) My house is being painted.
(1.11) This problem is being discussed at today's meeting.

Anything strange here? I doubt it – I don't think there's an English-speaker alive who regards these as other than normal.

But it wasn't always so. Until the end of the eighteenth century, this particular construction did not exist in standard English, and an English-speaker would have had to say *My car is repairing*, *My house is painting* and *This problem is discussing at today's meeting* – forms which are absolutely impossible for us now. (For example, the seventeenth-century civil servant Samuel Pepys wrote in his famous diary the sentence 'I met a dead corpse of the plague, just carrying down a little pair of stairs', which is almost incomprehensible to us at first reading – we have to say *just being carried*.)

This curious (to us) construction was the only possibility in the eighteenth century, and, when a few innovating speakers began to say things like *My house is being painted*, the linguistic conservatives of the day could not contain their fury. Veins bulging purply from their foreheads, they attacked the new construction as 'clumsy', 'illogical', 'confusing', and 'monstrous'. But their efforts were in vain. Today all those who objected to the 'illogical' and 'monstrous' new form are long dead, and the traditional form which they defended with such passion is dead with them. The 'illogical' and 'monstrous' new form has become the only possibility, and even the most careful and elegant writer of English would not dream of trying to get away with the defunct older form. And you are probably marvelling at this eighteenth-century fury and wondering what all the fuss was about, just as the next generation will read in puzzlement about the attacks on *hopefully* and wonder what all the fuss was about.

Two thousand years ago Roman writers were making similarly hostile comments about the changes which were occurring in the spoken Latin of their day. Their dismay at the increasing 'corruption' of the language had, of course, no effect at all, and the increasingly 'corrupt' spoken Latin continued to change ('deteriorate') until it had developed into such modern forms as French, Spanish, and Italian. Naturally, the speakers of these languages do not regard them as corrupt, but as rich, beautiful, and expressive. More precisely, the linguistic conservatives in France, Spain, and Italy have great admiration for the language they grew up with, but they have some very harsh words for some of the things the young people seem to be saying these days. At every time, and in every place, there is a body of conservative opinion which holds that the language reached some kind of pinnacle of perfection a generation or so ago, and is now going rapidly downhill with all these 'ugly', 'sloppy', 'illiterate' new usages we keep hearing nowadays.

Nowhere is the effect of language change more apparent than in present-day French. Centuries ago, the French really did do for their language what Swift wanted done for English: they created a language academy, an august official body charged with making regulations for the proper use of French and staffed by distinguished (and often elderly) scholars of impeccable reputation. At frequent intervals the members of the French Academy meet to discuss things and to hand down solemn rulings about what French-speakers are allowed to say. Has this had the effect of freezing the French language into place, as Swift hoped?

Hardly. While written French, like most written languages, has remained rather conservative, spoken French has recently been changing as fast as any language on earth. Not long ago a friend of mine, after spending several years learning French in British schools, made his first visit to France. When he returned, he looked white and shaken, and he confided to me, 'You know, they don't speak French properly in France.'

The reality, of course, is that he had learned only the written language, and hence his exposure to the very different spoken form came as a shock. Here are some examples of contemporary French, taken from George (1993):

- 'Haven't you got ten francs?'
  Written: *Tu n'as pas dix francs?*
  Spoken: *T'as pas dix balles?*

- 'These clothes are very expensive.'
  Written: *Ces vêtements coûtent très chers.*
  Spoken: *Ces fringues coûtent la peau des fesses.*

- 'Finding a flat in the Invalides is not easy.'
  Written: *Trouver un appartement aux Invalides n'est pas facile.*
  Spoken: *Décrocher un appart aux Invaloches c'est pas évident.*
- 'My brother is very good at arithmetic.'
  Written: *Mon frère est très fort en arithmétique.*
  Spoken: *Le frangin, il est giga fort en cunu.*
- 'There's the woman whose bag was stolen.'
  Written: *Voilà la femme à qui on a volé le sac.*
  Spoken: *Vlà la meuf qui s'est fait péta son keus.*

Some of these spoken forms are used only by young people, while others are far more widespread, but all are typical of the sort of French you can expect to hear if you spend time in France – and, if you too have only ever learned written French, you may be just as bewildered as my friend. In written French, something may be *excellent*; in speech it is more likely to be *génial*, or *dément*, or *hypersensass*, or *mégafoutral*, or any of a dozen other things you won't have learned in your French class. Likewise, something really awful may be *mauvais* or *dégoûtant* in written French, but it will be *dégueulasse* (or more likely just *dégueu*) in speech, or something even less expected. A guy and a girl are *un mec* and *une nana*; the university is *la fac*; a fascist is *un facho*; a nudist is *un nunu*; someone who's not too bright is *pas très fu-fute*; a public toilet is *un pipi-room*; dreary modern architecture is *McDo* (from the name of a certain fast-food chain).

Whatever you may think of such French (and the members of the Academy mostly don't think much of it), this is the way the language is spoken, and telling the French that they're not speaking their language properly is not going to have much effect. If you want to learn French, you'll have to learn the French that people are speaking now, and not the French that was spoken a generation or two ago, just as a French-speaker learning English must learn to say *Bloody car won't start*, and not something like *I fear our motor car is declining to start.*

The changes in French are not just changes in words: there are also a number of grammatical changes in progress. If you know a little French, you will be able to spot, in my example sentences above, several striking differences in grammar between the written and spoken forms. And some of these grammatical changes are very substantial: you may have learned in school that 'John bought the car' is in French *Jean a acheté la voiture*, but what you're going to hear in France is far more likely to be something like *Jean, il l'a achetée, la bagnole* (literally, it would seem, 'John, he bought it, the car').

The French Academy has clearly had little success in maintaining a constant form of French. So what exactly is its function, apart from making its members feel important? Here is one case in which its decisions have had an effect. The traditional French form for 'the string bean' is *le haricot*, and this form was long required by the Academy. But almost everyone in France has for generations said *l'haricot*, in blissful defiance of the Academy's decisions. A few years ago, the Academy finally bowed to the inevitable and officially recognized *l'haricot* as a permissible alternative. Of course, the great majority who already said *l'haricot* didn't change their speech as a result, and neither did the small minority who had always said *le haricot*. What happened was this: formerly, a schoolteacher was allowed to box the ears of a child who said, or wrote, *l'haricot*; since the new ruling, schoolteachers aren't allowed to do that any more. So the Academy's role in life, it appears, is to decide when schoolchildren should have their ears boxed. It is scarcely likely that an English Academy, if we had ever bothered to create one, would have had any greater success in keeping the lid on change in English.

1.4   *The inevitability of change*

The lesson to be drawn from such observations is that language change is ceaseless and remorseless. Every language that is spoken continues to change, not just century by century, but day by day. The language that you speak is not just different from your parents' language: it's different from the language you were speaking last year or last week, even if you don't notice changes occurring on such a small time scale. In fact, most people don't notice the language changing at all: at best, they are merely aware that young people speak a little differently from the old folks. Even then, as we have already seen, if they draw any conclusion at all, that conclusion is likely to be that young people are 'lazy' or 'sloppy', and that they need to be taught how to speak the language 'properly'. Even those few who are perceptive enough to realize that the language is genuinely changing will often, like Jonathan Swift, regret this fact, and yearn for a world in which languages never change, or at least for one in which changes are carefully and thoughtfully introduced by suitable authorities after protracted deliberation. They can yearn all they like, but they're not going to get such a world.

But why? Why should language change be unavoidable? Isn't Jonathan Swift right in concluding that a fixed and carefully regulated language would be a great advantage? If the authorities could declare that a certain word must have a certain meaning, with no dissent allowed, wouldn't we all find it much easier to speak and write? Wouldn't we be free of the ambiguities and misunderstandings that not infrequently crop up when someone else's speech turns out to be slightly different from our own?

Fortunately, we're not likely ever to find out, because only in the brutal authoritarian world of Orwell's *1984* could anybody ever have the power to regulate language in such a way – and probably not even then. But we can ask a more promising question: why does language change?

Here I must admit at once that I can give you no simple answer. The causes of language change are many and various, and only some of them are reasonably well understood at present. One of those reasons, undoubtedly, is mere fashion. People like to change their speech in much the same way, and for the same reasons, as they change their hemlines or their neckties: they want to show that they are up to date and in the know about what's going on, and last year's speech can be every bit as embarrassing as last year's clothes or hair styles. This awareness of fashion is most noticeable among teenagers, for whom using this week's words is vital, since the alternative may be social ostracism. A mother who tries to win her teenage daughter's sympathy by using apparently trendy words like 'fab' or 'brill' may find that daughter helpless with laughter at hearing words which were passé when Noah reached dry land – even if she herself was using them a year ago.

But fashion certainly can't be the whole story, and there are many other reasons why languages change. In the next chapter we shall consider the most obvious type of language change, one in which fashion certainly does play a part, even if it's outweighed by other factors.

Further reading

There are very many books on the history of English. Among the better ones are Strang (1970),Williams (1975), Baugh and Cable (1993), Pyles and Algeo (1993). The very readable McCrum *et al.* (1992) concentrates on social factors in the development of English, as does Leith (1983), which, however, includes a great deal more in the way of linguistics. Freeborn (1992) is a coursebook with many dozens of exercises and samples of written English from all periods. Dillard (1992) is a linguistic and social history of American English.

Briefer accounts of the history of English can be found in several chapters of Crystal (1988), which is popular in style, and Bolton and Crystal (1987); glossy and popular, but well worth reading, is the first long section of Crystal (1995).

A particularly good introduction to Old English for linguistics students is Lass (1994), which requires some linguistic background and focuses on structure and change; it will not teach you to read Old English texts. (Your library will probably have a number of textbooks of Old English, if you would like to learn it.) Students with a particular interest in the Germanic languages (which include English) should read Robinson (1992).

L. Bauer (1994) is a readable study of change in contemporary English.

The observations on change in contemporary French are taken from George (1993); the same volume contains an article on the recent development of technical French (Noreiko 1993). Walter (1994) is a somewhat light-hearted account of the history of French and of current developments in it. Among the more readable books in English on the histories of other major European languages are Price (1971), Harris (1978) (syntax only), and Lodge (1993) (more sociolinguistic than linguistic) for French, Penny (1991) for Spanish, Maiden (1995) for Italian, Mattoso Camara (1972) for Portuguese, and

Lockwood (1965), Waterman (1966), Keller (1978) and C. J. Wells (1987) for German.

Exercises

Note: For these exercises, you will need to consult the *Oxford English Dictionary* and probably also a good etymological dictionary, as explained in *To the reader* at the beginning of this book.

Exercise 1.1

Certain English words have a decidedly strange spelling, with 'silent' letters included. Here are a few examples:

(a) *light, bright, sight, night* (silent *gh*)
(b) *knife, knee, knit, knot* (silent *k*)
(c) *write, wrong, wring, wrestle* (silent *w*)
(d) *walk, talk, folk, should* (silent *l*)
(e) *lamb, tomb, comb, bomb* (silent *b*)
(f) *castle, listen, rustle, fasten* (silent *t*)
(g) *ride, give, take, name* (silent *e*)

What do you suppose is the reason for this?

Exercise 1.2

Here are a few phrases from the passage quoted from Shakespeare's play *As You Like It* in the chapter. How would you express each of them in modern English?

(a) upon this fashion
(b) as thou sayest
(c) charged my brother . . . to breed me well
(d) report speaks goldenly of his profit
(e) he . . . stays me here at home unkept
(f) call you that keeping[?]
(g) that differs not . . .

Exercise 1.3

Here are some further quotations from Shakespeare's plays. What differences can you observe between Shakespeare's English and our own?

(a) Our remedies oft in ourselves do lie
    Which we ascribe to heaven.
(b) How now, wit! Whither wander you?

(c) Hath not old custom made this life more sweet
    Than that of painted pomp?
(d) A bloody deed! almost as bad, good mother,
    As kill a king and marry with his brother.
(e) All is not well; I doubt some foul play.
(f) But, soft! Methinks I scent the morning air.
(g) What do you read, my lord?
    [*addressed to Hamlet, who is reading a book*]
(h) The frame and huge foundation of the earth
    Shak'd like a coward.
(i) This was the most unkindest cut of all.
(j) 'Tis a naughty night to swim in.

Exercise 1.4

The following extract is taken from the Paston letters, the voluminous correspondence of the Paston family of Norfolk; it dates from 1476, just about the time that scholars consider that Middle English was giving way to Modern English. Translate it into modern English as best you can, and comment on any characteristics of the language that strike you. John Paston is writing to Margery Brews; the text has been modernized here in a few respects, and all of the numerous abbreviations of the original have been spelled out in full.

> Mastresse, thow so be that I, vnaqweyntyd wyth yow as yet, tak vp on me to be thus bold as to wryght on to yow wyth ought your knowlage and leve, yet, mastress, for syche pore seruyse as I now in my mind owe yow, purposyng, ye not dyspleasyd, duryng my lyff to contenu the same, I beseche yow to pardon my boldness, and not to dysdeyn, but to accepte thys sympyll bylle to recomand me to yow in syche wyse as I best can or may jmagyn to your most plesure. And, mastress, for sych report as I haue herd of yow by many and dyuerse persones, and specyally by my ryght trusty frend, Rychard Stratton, berer her of, to whom I beseche yow to geue credence in syche maters as he shall on my behalue comon wyth yow of, if it lyhe yow to lystyn hym. . . . Her I send yow thys bylle wretyn wyth my lewd hand and sealyd wyth my sygnet to remayn wyth yow for a wyttnesse ayenste me, and to my shame and dyshonour if I contrary it.

Exercise 1.5

Do the same with the following passage from the Prologue to Chaucer's *Canterbury Tales*. These lines were written in about 1387; the poet is apologizing for the apparent crudeness of some of the stories he is 'repeating':

> But first I pray yow, of youre curteisye,
> That ye n'arette it nat my vileynye,
> Thogh that I pleynly speke in this mateere,

To telle yow hir wordes and hir cheere,
Ne thogh I speke hir wordes proprely,
For this ye knowen al so wel as I,
Who so shal telle a tale after a man,
He moote reherce as ny as euere he kan
Eueriche a word, if it be in his charge,
Al speke he neuer so rudeliche or large,
Or ellis he moot telle his tale vntrewe,
Or feyne thing, or fynde wordes newe.

2

Lexical and semantic change

Undoubtedly the most conspicuous type of language change is the appearance of new words. When a new word appears in the language, there will be an occasion on which you hear it for the first time, and you may very well notice that you have just heard a new word and remember the occasion. Depending on your age, you may perhaps remember the first time you heard somebody mention *acid house*, or *chunnel*, or *glasnost*, or *floppy disc*, or *laser*; you may remember the first time President Lyndon Johnson spoke of the *escalation* of the war in Vietnam, or even the first time you heard the word *television*. I myself can clearly remember the first time I heard somebody use the word *rock'n'roll* to denote a new kind of music he was hoping to promote.

Apart from being conspicuous, the creation of new words is also exceedingly frequent. New words have been pouring into English throughout its history, and today the language is acquiring many hundreds, perhaps even thousands, of new words every year. One of the major tasks faced by lexicographers in preparing new editions of their dictionaries is to collect the thousands of new words which have appeared since their last edition, perhaps only three or four years earlier. Some dictionaries now come with cards tucked inside which invite readers to send in examples of new words they have come across, and one or two publishers even bring out annual volumes of new words. Where do all these new words come from?

There are, in fact, many different ways of acquiring new words, some of them exceedingly common, others rather unusual. In this chapter we will review these sources of new words, beginning with the simplest and most obvious source of all.

2.1 *Borrowing*

At present there are some 6000 different languages spoken on our planet, and every one of these languages has a vocabulary containing many thousands of words. Moreover, speakers of every one of these languages are in contact with neighbours who speak different languages; this is true today even for people living on remote Pacific islands on which they had previously been isolated for centuries. Consequently, everybody is in a position to learn some of the words used by their neighbours, and very frequently people take a liking to some of their neighbours' words and take those words over into their own language. So, for example, the word *glasnost* was taken into English from Russian a few years ago to denote the new political and social climate initiated by President Gorbachov in the former USSR, just as the Russians had earlier taken the word *vokzal* from English to denote a mainline railway station (at the time, Vauxhall Station in London was a particularly important station).

This process is somewhat curiously called **borrowing** – 'curiously', because, of course, the lending language does not lose the use of the word, nor does the borrowing language intend to give it back. A better term might be 'copying', but 'borrowing' has long been established in this sense. And words which are borrowed are called **loan words**.

Such borrowing is one of the most frequent ways of acquiring new words, and speakers of all languages do it. English-speakers have long been among the most enthusiastic borrowers of other people's words on earth, and many, many thousands of English words have been acquired in just this way. We get *kayak* from an Eskimo language, *whisky* from Scots Gaelic, *ukulele* from Hawaiian, *yogurt* from Turkish, *mayonnaise* from French, *algebra* from Arabic, *sherry* from Spanish, *ski* from Norwegian, *waltz* from German, and *kangaroo* from the Guugu-Yimidhirr language of Australia. Indeed, if you leaf through the pages of an English dictionary that provides the sources of words, you will discover that well over half the words in it are taken from other languages in one way or another (though not always by the sort of straightforward borrowing we are considering here).

Why should people be so eager to borrow somebody else's word? There are several reasons, but the simplest is that the word is the name of something genuinely new to speakers of the borrowing language. English-speakers had never seen kayaks, or skis, or ukuleles, or yogurt, before they encountered these things overseas and appropriated them along with their names.

Cases like *ski* and *yogurt* represent the most straightforward type of borrowing, but borrowing can be more complicated. We have just seen that Russian, instead of borrowing the English word *station* directly, borrowed the name of a particular English station and used it for any large station. Something similar happened with *kangaroo*: the Guugu-Yimidhirr word *gangurru* is in fact only the name of a particular species, the large black kangaroo, but English-speakers, never before having seen *any* kangaroos, simply took the word and applied it to all kangaroos.

Such misunderstandings and adjustments are very common. Our word *cafeteria* is borrowed from Spanish, but the Spanish word means 'coffee shop', while we have applied it to something very different. The English phrase *happy ending* has been borrowed into French, German, and Italian, but in the form *happy-end*, which doesn't exist in English, while English *footing* has been borrowed into French and Spanish, but only in the sense of 'jogging', which it doesn't have in English. It is even possible to 'borrow' a word which doesn't exist at all: English *nom de plume* 'pen name' is 'borrowed' from French, but no such word exists in French, in which the equivalent item is *nom de guerre*. English-speakers with a somewhat limited command of French were trying to borrow something from French, but got it wrong, and wound up inventing some fake French and borrowing that.

One of the finest examples of such confused borrowing occurs in a story told by the American linguist Charles Hockett. During the American occupation of the Philippines, at least one Filipino father named his son *Ababís*, after the patron saint of the USA. But no such saint exists. So what happened?

Before the American occupation, the Philippines were a Spanish colony, and Spanish was widely spoken. In Spanish, the word for 'saint', when it occurs in a male saint's name, is *San* – hence all those California place-names like *San Francisco*, *San José*, and *San Diego*. The father had noticed that American soldiers, in moments of stress, tended to call upon their saint by exclaiming *San Ababís!* – or something like that.

The case of *nom de plume* illustrates a further motivation for borrowing words. Why should English-speakers go to the trouble of trying to borrow a French word for something when English already had a perfectly good word with the same meaning: *pen name*? The reason is a simple one: prestige. For two or three centuries, before the rise of English earlier in the twentieth century, French was the most prestigious language in the European world. French was everywhere the language of diplomacy, of fine arts, of high culture generally – indeed, virtually the language of Western civilization. Consequently, many speakers of English (and of other languages) were eager to show off their command of this prestigious language by spattering their speech and writing with words and phrases borrowed from French. Why speak of a mere mishap or blunder when you can instead speak delightfully of a *contretemps* or a *faux pas*? Why describe someone as 'disreputable' or 'shifty' when you can make your own superiority so much more obvious by dismissing him as *louche*? No gentleman would dream of referring to a lady's 'bottom' or 'behind', when it is clearly so much more ladylike to have a *derrière*. And any class of person might possess composure or social graces, but surely only a true gentleman would exhibit *sang-froid* or *savoir-faire*.

French no longer enjoys quite the prestige it once did, but you may still know someone who cannot resist spattering his English speech with gallicisms like *au contraire*, *joie de vivre*, or *au naturel*. Not long ago, a well-known British journalist of courtly manners, needing a word to identify the prominent physical charms of a buxom young lady, found the entire vast repository of English words for mammary glands so obviously inadequate that he wound up referring ever so delicately to her *embonpoint*. This was a curious choice, since this French word, though it originally meant 'well developed', today means only 'stoutness', which is not exactly what the speaker was trying to convey – but presumably the whole point was merely to use a French word, rather than an English one, because French words are by definition more refined and elegant than our blunt and coarse English ones.

In fact, English has been borrowing French words in their thousands ever since the eleventh century, long before French had acquired the worldwide prestige which it later achieved. This was for a particular reason: in 1066 the French-speaking Normans conquered England, and for the next 200 years or so Norman French was the language of the ruling élite. Royalty and the aristocracy spoke French; the law spoke French; the upper echelons of the administration and the military spoke French. Consequently, Norman French words like *prince, duke, baron, judge, attorney, court, chancellor, bailiff, official, army, captain,* and *lieutenant* inevitably passed into English, displacing their native English equivalents, which passed out of use. (Remember the Old English word *here* 'army' in Chapter 1? This is now defunct, though it survives in the name of the English city *Hereford*, originally 'army-ford'.)

But it wasn't only these administrative words that were borrowed. Thanks to the vastly greater prestige of French, English-speakers eagerly borrowed almost any French words they could get their hands on, regardless of the fact that English in many cases already had perfectly good equivalents. Such Norman French words as *country, music, jewel, picture, beef, fruit, boil, courage, honour, virtue, pity, sentence, question, language, literature, fool, horrible, mirror, gentle, male, female,* even *face,* all came pouring into English, where they proved so popular that they drove the corresponding native words out of the language. Only a specialist scholar now knows that the English once said *to-come* instead of *arrive, learning-knight* instead of *apprentice, wrethe* instead of *support, wridian* instead of *flourish, anleth* instead of *face.*

One of the chief reasons that Old English texts are so difficult for us to read is that so many of the native English words used in those texts were later driven out of the language by borrowings from French. More than 60 per cent of the Old English vocabulary has disappeared, and the Norman Conquest is the greatest single reason for this. If William the Conqueror had been William the Defeated, this huge influx of French words might never have occurred, and English today might look a great deal more like Old English.

As you can see, English-speakers are still happily borrowing foreign words today: the recent frequency of the German words *deutschmark* and *Bundesbank* demonstrates the economic power of Germany, everyone has now heard of the Mexican rebels called the *zapatistas,* and the recent craze for things Japanese has brought *sumo, sushi,* and *karaoke* into our everyday speech. But perhaps we no longer borrow words so often for reasons of prestige – for English itself has become the most prestigious language on earth, and today English is primarily a donor language. Just as French words once poured into English, now English words are pouring into French, German, Spanish, Italian, and Japanese in vast numbers. Open any popular Italian or German or even Japanese magazine at random and you will find its pages spattered with English words: *superstar, top model, gadget, floppy disc, rockstar, hobby, T-shirt, massage parlour, mass media, status, fan, check-up, gentleman,* and hundreds of others. German computer magazines have columns called *Tips und Tricks*; Italian fashion magazines talk about the *look* and explain what's currently *in*. As always, some of the borrowings are a little unexpected: for example, the German word for 'contraceptive pill' is *Antibabypille*!

You might wonder how these English words are pronounced in German, Italian, or Japanese. This interesting question we shall examine in the next section. Before that, however, we note that new words can be formed in various ways by exploiting the resources of other languages without quite borrowing any words directly.

One way of doing this is to construct a calque. A **calque**, or **loan translation**, is a new word or phrase constructed by taking a foreign word or phrase as a model and translating it morpheme-by-morpheme. The Romans frequently used this technique to expand the vocabulary of Latin by appealing to the then more prestigious Greek. For example, the Greek word *sympathia* 'sympathy' consists of two morphemes: a prefix *syn-* 'with' and a stem *pathia* 'suffering'. The Romans rendered this with the Latin prefix *con-* 'with' and the stem *passio* 'suffering', obtaining the calque *compassio*, which therefore became the Latin word for 'sympathy'. Centuries later, the Germans in turn calqued the Latin word into German by using their preposition *mit* 'with' and the noun *Leid* 'grief', obtaining *Mitleid*, the German word for 'sympathy' or 'compassion'. If English had done the same, our word for 'sympathy' might now be **withgrief* (the asterisk marks a non-existent or impossible form), but we have, as usual, preferred merely to borrow directly, and so we have borrowed both *sympathy* from Greek and *compassion* from Latin. In the same way, Greek *poiotes* 'suchness' and *posotes* 'muchness' were calqued into Latin as *qualitas* and *quantitas*, respectively; in English, however, we have refrained from using the obvious calques *suchness* and *muchness*, and simply borrowed *quality* and *quantity* from Latin.

Very occasionally we do form calques in English: German *Übermensch* and *Weltanschauung* have been calqued into English as *superman* and *world-view*, and French *Ça va sans dire* has been calqued as *It goes without saying*. Mostly, though, English-speakers are not fond of calques: we prefer to borrow directly.

Another way of exploiting foreign languages is to pillage their vocabularies in order to extract morphemes which can then be imported and used as building blocks for constructing words in another language. Such building blocks are called **combining forms**, and English does this on a massive scale in order to create technical and scientific terms with combining forms extracted from Greek and Latin. Thus, Greek *thermos* 'heat' and *metron* 'measure' provide the combining forms for our word *thermometer*, literally 'heat-measure', and most European languages do the same: French *thermomètre*, Spanish *termómetro*, German *Thermometer*, Welsh *thermomedr*, Basque *termometro*, Turkish *termometre*, Russian *termometr*, Swedish *termometer*, and so on. Only Hungarian has defied this trend with its *hőmérő*, a calque constructed from the Hungarian words for 'heat' and 'measure'.

The overwhelming majority of our technical terms are constructed in this way: *microphone* (Greek 'small-voice'), *television* (Greek plus Latin 'far-seeing'), *carnivore* (Latin 'meat-eater'), *streptococcus* (Greek 'twisted-seed'), *bibliography* (Greek 'book-writing'), *astronomy* (Greek 'star-law'), *orthodontist* (Greek 'straight-teeth' plus *-ist*), *consanguineous* (Latin 'with-blood' plus *-ous*), *pharmacology* (Greek 'drug-word'), and *telecommunications* (Greek and Latin 'far-sharing'). The vast majority of such formations, of course, never existed in ancient Greek or Latin, and even the best-educated Roman would be utterly baffled by formations like the chemical name for aspirin, *acetylsalicylic acid*, which is literally 'vinegary-willowy sour-stuff'.

Some of these combining forms have become so familiar that we now happily attach them to almost anything, including native English words, producing things like *biodegradable*, *megastar*, *psychobabble*, *cyberpunk*, and *technospeak*. It appears that such elements are losing their purely technical status and coming to be regarded as everyday English morphemes. Only this morning I was reading a magazine article which sneered at computer addicts as *techno-anoraks*: the word *anorak* 'warm waterproof jacket' is a loan from Eskimo; in British usage, it has acquired the sense of 'nerd' (from the suggestion that nerds wear anoraks), and *techno-anorak* is perhaps the first Greek–Eskimo hybrid to appear in English – though I very much doubt that the writer of the article was aware that he was making this little bit of linguistic history. Indeed, it is possible that our long tradition of constructing our technical terms from Greek and Latin may be drawing to a close. The scientists of earlier generations were often well acquainted with the classical languages, but today's technical people rarely are, and in particular the people who have created our now vastly important computer industry know nothing of Greek or Latin. It is noticeable that technical terms in computing are never formed in the traditional Graeco-Latin manner, and Greek and Latin elements appear only occasionally and incidentally. Computer people prefer other devices for coining their technical terms: *RAM*, *screen saver*, *bus*, *graphics card*, *reboot*, *software*, *prompt*, *debug*, *bulletin board*, *mouse*, *floppy disc*, *pixel*, *modem*, *scroll bar*, *window*, *hard copy*, *browser*, *NAND gate*, *hacker*, *password*, *icon*, and, of course, the inimitable *WYSIWYG*. An earlier generation might have preferred *telecommunicator* to *modem*, or *manual selector* to *mouse*, but times have changed.

In a somewhat similar way, French-speakers have recently been coining both technical terms and everyday words by combining English elements either with French words or with other English words: *top modèle* 'super-model', *crack-pain* 'crispbread', *pipi-room* 'public toilet', *papy-boom* 'growth in the number of old-age pensioners', *perchman* 'boom operator', *tennis-woman* 'female tennis player', *baby-foot* 'table football', and *baby-star* 'child star'.

All languages borrow words, but it is notable that some types of words are borrowed more readily than others. For one thing, nouns are borrowed more often than verbs or adjectives. This occurs partly because nouns are far more numerous than other classes of words to begin with, partly because new things are more likely to be denoted by nouns than by other words, and partly because new nouns are often easier to accommodate within the grammatical system of the borrowing language.

For example, Turkish has borrowed heavily from its prestigious neighbour Arabic, but the verbal morphologies of Arabic and Turkish are so utterly different that there is no way an Arabic verb can be accommodated in Turkish: an Arabic verb has a root consisting entirely of consonants (like *ktb* 'write') and it is inflected by internal changes (*katab* 'he wrote', *kutib* 'it was written', *aktub* 'he's writing', and so on), while a Turkish verbal root always contains at least one vowel (like *yaz-* 'write') and is inflected by suffixation (*yazdı* 'he wrote', *yazıldı* 'it was written', *yazıyor* 'he's writing', and so on). Unable to borrow an Arabic verb directly, therefore, what Turkish does is to borrow the corresponding noun and combine this with a 'dummy' verb *etmek* 'do' to produce a verb which can be used in Turkish. Thus, the Arabic verbal noun *kabul* 'acceptance' is borrowed and used to form the compound verb *kabul etmek* 'accept'; *mukayese* 'comparison' yields *mukayese etmek* 'compare'; *ispat* 'proof' gives *ispat etmek* 'prove'; *teşkil* 'formation' yields *teşkil etmek* 'form'; and so on for many hundreds of such borrowings. Verbs are taken from other languages in the same way: the Persian noun *rija* 'request' gives the Turkish verb *rica etmek* 'request', the French participle *désinfecté* 'disinfected' yields *dezenfekte etmek* 'disinfect', and the English noun *knock-out* gives *nakavt etmek* 'knock (somebody) out' (in boxing).

Further, there is clear evidence that certain semantic classes of words are much less likely to be borrowed than other words. These are chiefly the items of very high frequency which we would expect to find in every language: pronouns, lower numerals, kinship terms, names of body parts, simple verbs like *go*, *be*, *have*, *want*, *see*, *eat,* and *die*, widespread colour terms like *black*, *white*, and *red*, simple adjectives like *big*, *small*, *good*, *bad*, and *old*, names of natural phenomena like *sun*, *moon*, *star, fire*, *rain*, *river*, *snow*, *day*, and *night*, grammatical words like *when*, *here*, *and*, *if*, and *this*, and a few others. Such words are often called the **basic vocabulary**, and the fact that they are rarely borrowed makes them of considerable importance in historical linguistics, as we will see later in the book. Note, however, that it is not actually impossible for such words to be borrowed: English has borrowed *face* and *river* from French and *give*, *sky*, and even the pronoun *they* from Old Norse; Latin borrowed the word **blancus* 'white' from a Germanic language (whence French *blanc*, Spanish *blanco*, Italian *bianco*); Turkish has borrowed *ve* 'and' from Arabic; younger speakers of Thai have reportedly borrowed the English pronoun *you* as a neutral term of address which allows a speaker to avoid the numbingly complex rules for addressing people in Thai; Swahili, formerly used as a trade language between Africans and Arabs, has borrowed the Arabic numerals for 'six', 'seven', and 'nine'; the two Basque words for 'leg', *zango* and *hanka*, are both borrowed from neighbouring Romance languages, and Basque *orain* 'now' is a loan from Latin with a Basque suffix. Still, the frequency of such borrowings is sufficiently low to make such basic words valuable in investigating the prehistories of languages.

2.2   *Phonological treatment of loans*

Every language has its own phonological system: its own collection of available speech sounds and its own rules for combining these sounds into pronounceable words. But the phonological systems of English, French, German, Italian, and Japanese are all rather different, and hence a loan word can be very difficult for speakers to pronounce. English does not have the nasal vowel of French *genre* or the front rounded vowel of German *Muesli*; Spanish does not allow the initial [st-] cluster of English *star* and *status*; French lacks (or used to lack) the velar nasal of English *camping*; Japanese allows neither the consonant clusters nor the final consonant of English *grapefruit* – yet all these words have been borrowed. How do they get pronounced?

Broadly speaking, there are two ways of dealing with this problem. First, if you have some idea how the word is pronounced in the donor language, you can try your best to reproduce that pronunciation in your own language, producing as a result something which is conspicuously foreign. Second, you can abandon such efforts and just pronounce the loan word as though it were a native word, following the ordinary phonological patterns of your language, and as a result changing the original pronunciation of the word, perhaps greatly. Both these approaches are widely used.

On the one hand, most English-speakers who use the word *genre* do their best to produce something approximating to the French pronunciation and wind up saying something like [ʒɑɹə], with a nasal vowel but often with an English /r/ instead of the French uvular /r/. On the other hand, nobody tries to pronounce *muesli* in a German way, as ['my:zli]: we all just say ['mju:zli] or ['mju:sli], with English sounds throughout. The choice is not predictable, but you are more likely to take the first option if you have some command of the lending language's pronunciation and if you consider the lending language to be prestigious. Lots of English-speakers know some French, especially in the academic circles in which the word *genre* is chiefly used, and French still retains some of its earlier prestige, so *genre* gets a French-type pronunciation. But few of us know much German, and German doesn't seem to enjoy the same *cachet* with us as French, and so *muesli* is simply anglicized.

Not all speakers will make the same choice. The English word *video* has been borrowed into Japanese, which has no /v/, and so many Japanese pronounce the word as *bideo*, with the nearest native equivalent, /b/, but others carefully pronounce the word with a /v/. Almost all of us pronounce the Spanish loan *guerrilla* just like *gorilla*, but there used to be a television newsreader who made a point of pronouncing it with a Spanish accent, trilled [r], palatal lateral, and all — an odd choice, because the word does not in fact mean 'guerrilla' in Spanish (it means 'guerrilla war'), and hence her attempts at accuracy were rather pointless. It is reported that the polyglot physicist Murray Gell-Mann always pronounces the name *Montreal* in an impeccable French manner, even in English, which to most people seems a quaint affectation.

On the whole, especially if the loans are few in number, or if they present formidable phonological difficulties, or if they quickly come into use as everyday words, we may expect speakers to prefer the second option, nativization. Thus, English *grapefruit* is borrowed into Japanese as *gureepufuruutsu*, which conforms perfectly to the phonological patterns of Japanese, and Mexican Spanish *juzgado* 'courthouse' was borrowed into American English as the famous *hoosegow* 'jail' of Western movies, with totally English phonology (in small Western towns, the courthouse and the jail were often in the same building).

It is, however, the first option which chiefly concerns us here. If a few English-speakers pronounce a few French loans in a more-or-less French manner, then such words are just oddities in English. However, if lots of us pronounce lots of French loans in the same way, something has happened to the phonological system of English.

Consider the case of English /v/. Old English had no phoneme /v/, though it did have /f/, which had a voiced allophone [v] between vowels, so that *ofer*, for example, was pronounced with [v] — as it still is today: this is the word we now spell *over*. Word-initially, however, /f/ could only be pronounced as voiceless [f], as it still is today in native words like *five*, *fish*, *friend*, and *fire*.

French, however, has both /f/ and /v/, both of which can occur in most positions, including word-initially. Many of the words borrowed into English from Norman French had initial /v/, and English-speakers obviously made an effort to pronounce this unfamiliar sound, because dozens of French words came into English with initial [v]: *very*, *vine*, *vinegar*, *voice*, *view*, *vicar*, *victory*, *venue*, *vault*, *vassal*, *value*, *villain*, *virgin*, *vowel*, and many others. As a result, English acquired a contrast between [f] and [v] which had not previously existed: contrasts like *few* and *view*, or *fine* and *vine*, became possible for the first time. Thus /v/ became a phoneme in English, and the phonological system of English was changed. Today /f/ and /v/ contrast in almost all positions: *fat* and *vat*, *rifle* and *rival*, *strife* and *strive*.

(In the same way, those Japanese-speakers who pronounce a [v] in English loans like *video* have acquired a new phoneme /v/, contrasting with native /b/.)

English has acquired another voiced fricative from French, the /ʒ/ of *beige*, but this time the process was rather more complicated. French has a front rounded vowel /y/ which English lacks, and, when English-speakers began borrowing French words containing this vowel, they could not pronounce it.

Instead, they replaced this awkward vowel with a sequence of English sounds: /ju:/. Hence the /ju:/ of words like *music* and *puny* represents an adaptation of French /y/. Now in many cases this French vowel followed the fricative /z/, and hence English has borrowed a number of French words with the sequence /zju:/ representing French /zy/: *measure, pleasure, treasure, leisure, azure,* and others. In these cases, however, there was a further change: the alveolar fricative /z/ merged with the following palatal glide /j/ to produce instances of the fricative [ʒ], instances which were not present in the original French words. As you can confirm, the pronunciation with /ʒ/ is now the only possibility for most of these words.

Much more recently, we have obtained new instances of /ʒ/ by borrowing French words containing it. When it occurs finally, there is a good deal of variation, and loans like *entourage, camouflage, garage, barrage, massage,* and *rouge* can be heard both with [ʒ] and with [dʒ]. You may find that you pronounce some of these with the fricative but others with the affricate, and you are likely to find that your friends differ from you on one or two of these. With very recent loans from French, however, there is a strong tendency to use the fricative, and words like *beige, luge, cortège, gigolo, collage, dressage,* and, of course, *genre* are almost always heard with [ʒ], though I have heard *gigolo*, at least, pronounced with [dʒ]. English has, therefore, if apparently somewhat reluctantly, acquired another voiced fricative from French.

Recently we have repaid the generosity of the French by providing them with a new phoneme. Until not long ago, the velar nasal /ŋ/ was absent from French, but French-speakers have shown a taste for borrowing English words containing the suffix *-ing*, and have now borrowed a sizeable number of these, though not always with the original meaning: *smoking* ('dinner jacket', from earlier English *smoking jacket*), *camping* ('campsite'), *footing* ('jogging', now increasingly replaced by *jogging*), *feeling* (in the musical sense of 'play with feeling', but also in the sense of 'instinct, intuition'), *living* ('living room'), *shopping, mailing* (in the sense of 'mail-shot'), *listing,* and others. The majority of speakers now pronounce such loans with [ŋ], and thus French has acquired an additional phoneme. Indeed, linguists have noted that *-ing* has actually now become a productive suffix in French, and French-speakers use it to coin new words which do not exist in English: *lifting* ('face-lift'), *zapping* ('compulsive channel-changing'), *brushing* 'blow-dry', *jogging* ('track suit'), and *caravaning* ('caravan park', 'trailer park').

Without introducing any new phonemes, lexical borrowing can also affect the phonotactics of the borrowing language. English has long had the consonant phoneme /ʃ/, usually spelled <*sh*>, as in *ship* and *fish*. Until recently, however, this /ʃ/ could not occur at the beginning of a word followed by any other consonant except /r/: hence we have words like *shrink, shred,* and *shrimp*, but no words with initial /ʃt-/, /ʃl-/, /ʃm-/, and so on. Now, though, as a result of loans from German and more especially from Yiddish, this situation has changed. The Yiddish-influenced English of the New York City area now contains dozens of words with these 'impossible' clusters: *schmuck, shlemiel, schlock, shlep, shtum, shtick, schmo, schnoz, spiel* (pronounced /ʃpiːl/), and many others. Many of these have passed into general currency in American English, and some of them have recently crossed the Atlantic to Britain, where they are reinforced by the German loans *schnapps, schnauzer, schnitzel,* and *schmaltz,* by the trade name *Schweppes,* and, of course, by the familiar term *schwa* from phonetics (a loan from Hebrew). As a result, the phonotactics of English now permit a whole series of initial clusters which were formerly impossible.

2.3 *Morphological treatment of loans*

We saw above that Turkish finds it awkward to borrow verbs directly and prefers to borrow nouns which are then turned into verbs with the 'dummy' verb *etmek*. This is, in fact, quite a common practice: Japanese borrows foreign verbs in the same indirect manner by taking over nouns and combining them with its verb *suru* 'do': hence the Chinese loan *benkyoo* 'study' produces the Japanese verb *benkyoo suru* 'study', and Japanese is full of verbs borrowed indirectly from English, like *hitto suru* 'make a hit', *doraibu suru* 'drive a car', *kisu suru* 'kiss', and *pasu suru* 'pass an exam'. Verbs like *etmek* and *suru* are sometimes called **light verbs**, meaning that they have little or no semantic content of their own and serve only to provide a usable verbal form of an item which carries the semantic content of a verb but which is formally a noun.

Even nouns may produce morphological complications for the borrowing language, however. In the majority of languages, nouns are inflected for number, and in many languages they are also marked for case and/or grammatical gender. Borrowed nouns must be fitted into all this morphology in one way or another, and the result may be disturbances to the borrowing language's morphology.

Consider first number. With just a handful of exceptions like *feet* and *children*, English nouns form their plural with an invariable suffix *-s*: *books, cars, discos, databases, CD-ROMs,* and so on for virtually every noun, old or new. With borrowed nouns, however, we agonize and vacillate. Many nouns borrowed from Greek and Latin have been taken over complete with their foreign plurals: hence *phenomena, indices, crises, formulae, cacti, bacteria,* and some dozens of others (or hundreds, if we count purely technical terms like *protozoa* and *hominidae*). Such un-English plurals disrupt the ordinary English morphology, and speakers often find them confusing and rearrange them in various ways. We formerly had singular *datum* and plural *data,* but the more frequent plural form just doesn't look like a plural to English eyes, and most speakers now treat *data* as a singular (as in 'This data is interesting'; compare the earlier 'These data are interesting', now confined to a handful of conservative speakers), and *data* now has no plural.

Something similar is perhaps happening with *criterion /criteria, phenomenon/ phenomena*, and *bacterium/bacteria*: very few of my students seem to be at all sure which form is the singular and which the plural, and use them the wrong way round as often as not: *this criteria, these phenomenon, a new bacteria.*

Confusion arises in other ways. The Greek word *syllabus* has a Greek plural *syllabontes* which is rarely used in English, but the model of Latin nouns like *radius/radii* has misled some speakers into creating a plural *syllabi*, which is now so frequent that it's recognized by most dictionaries. In the same way, the uncommon Latin loan *nexus*, whose Latin plural is *nexus*, has been given a surprising English plural *nexi* by some speakers, including even by a few linguists who use it as a technical term, and I have even seen the startling form *casi bellorum* used as the plural of *casus belli* 'cause of war', whose Latin plural is again just *casus belli.*

We borrow a few other foreign plurals, such as *cherubim* and *kibbutzim* (from Hebrew), *concerti* and *castrati* (from Italian), and *bureaux* and *beaux* (from French), but we don't always take over a foreign plural. Latin *circus*, Italian *pizza*, German *kindergarten*, Greek *daemon*, French *béret* and Eskimo *anorak* all just form regular English plurals in *-s*: nobody tries to use such plurals as **circus*, **pizze*, **kindergärten*, or **daemones*; the French plural happens to be *bérets* anyway, and how many of us have the faintest idea how to form a plural in Eskimo?

When the borrowing language has a large number of different ways of forming plurals, the problem becomes more acute. German, for example, has a wide variety of patterns for plurals: *Weg* 'way', plural *Wege*; *Mann* 'man', *Männer*; *Mensch* 'person', *Menschen*; *Uhu* 'eagle-owl', *Uhus*; *Lehrer* 'teacher', *Lehrer*; *Bruder* 'brother', *Brüder*; *Hand* 'hand', *Hände*; *Blume* 'flower', *Blumen*; *Buch* 'book', *Bücher*; *Mineral* 'mineral', *Mineralien*. Loan words have to be given some plural form or other, and German-speakers have made various decisions. Many loan words are stuck into one pattern or another in a seemingly arbitrary manner: *Tenor* 'tenor', *Tenöre*; *Film* 'film', *Filme*; *Ski* 'ski', *Skier*; *Pilot* 'pilot', *Piloten*; *Experte* 'expert', *Experten*; *Boxer* 'boxer', *Boxer*; *Fossil* 'fossil', *Fossilien*. By far the largest number of recent loans, however, take the *-s* plural: *Test, Bungalow, Teenager, Kiwi, Job, Schock* 'shock', *Kamera* 'camera', *Bar* (for drinks), *Lady, Party, Story, Ghetto, Kasino* 'casino', *Kommando* 'commando', *Hobby, Baby, Zebra, Hotel*, and hundreds of others all form *-s* plurals (*Tests, Bungalows, Teenagers*, and so on). This is slightly surprising, since the *-s* plural is one of the rarest patterns of all for native words: there are perhaps fewer than a dozen native words of any antiquity that form this kind of plural. Interestingly, the plural in *-s* is beginning to turn up in colloquial speech in native words which never used to have it, and one can hear things like *Mädchens* 'girls', *Fräuleins* 'young ladies' and *Onkels* 'uncles'. Perhaps these are the first signs that German may be going the same way English went many centuries ago: generalizing the once-obscure *-s* plural at the expense of a dozen other patterns. (Old

English was just like modern German in having many different ways of forming plurals.)

In German, the problem of dealing with loan words is made still more acute by the fact that the language has a case-system – and naturally different classes of nouns take different sets of case-endings. Table 2.1 shows just a few of the patterns which exist; the names of the cases are Nom(inative), Acc(usative), Gen(itive), and Dat(ive).

Loan words which take the -*s* plural are accommodated in an unexpected way: with just one exception, they simply don't take any case-endings, as shown in Table 2.2. The one exception is that certain nouns do take the genitive singular ending -*s*, even though this makes the genitive singular look just like all the plural forms.

In Russian, which has a substantially more complex case morphology than German (six cases and well over a dozen different patterns for forming them), most loan words are treated in the same way: they just don't take any case-endings at all.

A language with grammatical gender, like French, German, or Russian, has the additional problem of assigning loan words to a gender. French, which has only two genders, traditionally called 'masculine' and 'feminine', solves the

Table 2.1 Some inflectional patterns of German nouns

		Weg 'way'	*Bär* 'bear'	*Art* 'kind'	*Dach* 'roof'
Sg	Nom	*Weg*	*Bär*	*Art*	*Dach*
	Acc	*Weg*	*Bären*	*Art*	*Dach*
	Gen	*Weges*	*Bären*	*Art*	*Daches*
	Dat	*Weg(e)*	*Bären*	*Art*	*Dach(e)*
Pl	Nom	*Wege*	*Bären*	*Arten*	*Dächer*
	Acc	*Wege*	*Bären*	*Arten*	*Dächer*
	Gen	*Wege*	*Bären*	*Arten*	*Dächer*
	Dat	*Wegen*	*Bären*	*Arten*	*Dächern*

Table 2.2 The treatment of loan words in German

		Kamera 'camera'	*Test* 'test'
Sg	Nom	*Kamera*	*Test*
	Acc	*Kamera*	*Test*
	Gen	*Kamera*	*Tests*
	Dat	*Kamera*	*Test*
Pl	Nom	*Kameras*	*Tests*
	Acc	*Kameras*	*Tests*
	Gen	*Kameras*	*Tests*
	Dat	*Kameras*	*Tests*

problem in the simplest way possible: virtually all loan words are simply assigned to the masculine gender. Hence English loans like *look* (in the fashion sense), *western* (film), *zip* (zipper), *kiwi* (both the bird and the fruit), *strip-tease, week-end, cocktail, gin, bridge* (the card game), *bestseller, football, jazz, heavy-metal*, and hundreds of others are all masculine in French.

German has a third gender, the 'neuter', and German-speakers may assign a loan word to any of the three genders. Thus, *Jet, Cocktail, Bestseller*, and *Western* are masculine, *Cleverness, Yacht*, and *Lady* are feminine, *Bridge* and *Quiz* are neuter, while *Striptease, Yoghurt*, and *Curry* are masculine for some speakers but neuter for others. As you can see, there is some variation in gender assignment, but in most cases speakers quickly agree what the gender of a loan word should be, a fact which has puzzled some observers.

If the morphological mismatch between the lending and borrowing languages is greater still, the borrowing language may be obliged to indulge in some strenuous manœuvres in order to accommodate the loans. Swahili has eight genders, and the gender of a noun is regularly marked by one prefix in the singular and another in the plural: *mtu* 'person', plural *watu*; *mti* 'tree', *miti*; *kitu* 'thing', *vitu*; *jicho* 'eye', *macho*; *ulimi* 'tongue', *ndimi*, and so on. Loan words are fitted into this system in various ways. Many are put into the *ji-/ma-* gender, but without the singular prefix *ji-*. Hence, the Arabic loans *juma* 'week', *duka* 'shop', *waziri* 'vizier', and *kadhi* 'Islamic judge', and the English loan *boi* 'houseboy', are all treated as singulars lacking a prefix, and they form plurals *majuma, maduka, mawaziri, makadhi*, and *maboi*. However, the Arabic loan *walimu* happens to look like a plural of the *m-/wa-* gender, and so it is treated as a plural 'teachers', and given a singular in *m-*, but surprisingly *mwalimu* instead of the expected **mlimu*. On the other hand, the Arabic loan *kitabu* 'book' fits comfortably into the *ki-/vi-* class, and so it is given a Swahili plural *vitabu* (the Arabic plural is *kutub*), which makes the word unrecognizable to outsiders.

2.4 *Formation of new words*

Borrowing is very far from being the only way of obtaining new words. Languages can use their own resources to create new words, without appealing to other languages. There are many ways of doing this, some much commoner than others.

One very frequent technique is **compounding**: combining two (or more) existing words into a new word. Compounding is exceedingly common in English: at various times, English-speakers have created such compounds as *girlfriend, gingerbread, major-general, ice cream, table tennis, close-up, overturn, jetlag, hatchback, lipstick, soundproof, forget-me-not*, and the *drop-dead* of *a drop-dead blonde* (which means 'a stunningly beautiful blonde'). (Some of these are written with hyphens or white spaces, but they are still compounds.) Some other languages form compounds equally freely: Basque has compounds like *burubero* 'unreasonable, fanatical' (*buru* 'head' plus *bero* 'hot'), *joan-etorri* 'return trip, round trip' (*joan* 'go' plus *etorri* 'come'), *musu eman* '(to) kiss' (*musu* 'kiss' plus *eman* 'give'), and the delightful *eztabaida* 'argument, dispute', derived from the two complete sentences *Ez da! Bai da!* 'No, it isn't! Yes, it is!' German, as is well known, is something of a European champion in this respect. Our little word *lift* (as in 'Can you give me a lift home?') is rendered in German by the startling compound *Mitfahrgelegenheit*, literally 'with-travel-opportunity'). From *um* 'around' and *Welt* 'world' German forms *Umwelt* 'environment'; to this is added *Schutz* 'protection' to obtain *Umweltschutz* 'protection of the environment'; to this is added *Maßnahmen* 'measures' (itself a compound) to derive the formidable *Umweltschutzmaßnahmen* 'measures for the protection of the environment'. This is as far as things normally go in German, but German-speakers delight in coining such entertaining curiosities as the legendary *der Donaudampfschiffahrtsgesellschaftskapitän* 'the captain of the Danube Steamship Company' and *der Hottentottenpotentatentantenattentäter* 'the would-be assassin of the aunt of the Hottentot dignitary'.

Some other languages form compounds only with difficulty. French is one such. While English easily forms *country house*, French *campagne* 'country' and *maison* 'house' cannot be combined into **campagne-maison*, but only into *maison de campagne*, literally 'house of country'; similarly, English *table wine* is equivalent to French *vin de table*. The same is true of Spanish, on the whole, but Spanish does readily allow a type of compound which is very rare in English, as in *tocadiscos* 'record player', literally 'play-records', and in the American Spanish *robacarros* 'car thief', literally 'steal-cars'. The closest we have to this in English is the very rare pattern illustrated by *scarecrow* and *pickpocket*.

You will already have noticed that English forms many different types of compounds, but the majority of English compounds conform to certain rules. The chief rule is that the **head** of a compound is usually its final element. Thus, a *house cat* is a type of cat, and not a type of house, while a *cathouse* is a type of house (it's a brothel) and not a type of cat. Similarly, an *eyeliner* is a type of liner, not a type of eye, and *olive green* is a type of green, not a type of olive.

Some other languages have different rules. In Welsh, for example, the head comes first, and hence Welsh has compounds like *brws danedd* 'toothbrush' (from *brws* 'brush' and *danedd* 'teeth') and *jwg laeth* 'milk jug' (from *jwg* 'jug' and *llaeth* 'milk', with one of the famous Welsh consonant mutations). That is, Welsh compounds are **head-initial**, while English ones are head-final. Even compound verbs in English are **head-final**: when you *overturn* something, you are turning it in a particular way, and when you *babysit*, you are sitting in a particular way.

There are, however, exceptions. One type of exception is that presented by **dvandva compounds**, or **copulative compounds**. Here both members are equally heads: *Alsace-Lorraine*, *tragicomic*, and the American *panty-hose* (= 'tights'). This type of formation is rare in English, except in names of companies: *Cadbury-Schweppes*, *Rank-Hovis-McDougal*, *Metro-Goldwyn-Mayer*.

A far more frequent type of exception is provided by **exocentric compounds**, in which there is *no* head. A *hatchback* is not a type of back, but neither is it a type of hatch: it's a type of car, but the element *car* does not occur in the name. Similarly, a *skinhead* is a type of person, and so is a *highbrow* or a *redneck* or a *hard-hat* or a *Tarheel* (this last denotes a person from North Carolina). A *forget-me-not* is a type of flower, and a *hit-and-run* is a type of offensive play in baseball (these last two examples illustrate more complex and unusual patterns of compounding).

Sometimes a compound contains an affix in addition to its constituent words: *blue-eyed*, *long-legged*, *lived-in*, *outgoing*, *hard-liner*, *flat-earther*, *fast-acting*.

Even more frequent than compounding, and probably the single most important mechanism in the languages of the world for obtaining new words from native resources, is **derivation**. Derivation is the process of creating words by adding **affixes** (prefixes and suffixes) to existing words. Like many other languages, English has a large number of prefixes and suffixes used in this way: prefixes like *un-*, *pre-*, *dis-*, *re-*, *anti-*, *non-*, *con-*, *mini-*, *ex-*, *de-*, *step-*, *proto-*, and *counter-*; suffixes like *-ness*, *-ful*, *-ity*, *-less*, *-ly*, *-al*, *-ian*, *-esque*, *-ee*, *-er*, *-ese*, and *-ize*. To the adjective *happy* we can add the prefix *un-* to obtain a new adjective *unhappy*; to this we can add the suffix *-ness* to obtain the noun *unhappiness*. From *civil* we can variously derive *uncivil*, *civility*, and *civilize*; from this last we can further derive *civilization*. From *derive* itself we can successively obtain *derivation*, *derivational*, and the obscure technical linguistic term *transderivational*. (Note that there are usually clear rules governing the order of addition of affixes: neither **transderive* nor **trans-derivation* exists.)

Not all affixes are equally productive. The **productivity** of an affix is the degree of freedom with which it can be used to derive new words. The ancient English suffix *-th* is now totally unproductive: it occurs in a few old formations like *warmth* and *depth* (and, slightly disguised, in *height* and *weight*), but it can no longer be extended to other cases: things like **happyth* and **bigth* are impossible. The suffix *-dom* is chiefly found in a few old formations like *freedom* and *kingdom*, but it has never quite died out entirely: *stardom* is a recent formation, and we occasionally come across new instances of its use, like *gangsterdom*, *tigerdom*, and even *girldom*. The old suffix *-wise* was formerly unproductive and confined to a few cases like *clockwise* and *otherwise*, but it has recently become productive again, and such novelties as *moneywise*, *healthwise*, *profitwise*, *fitnesswise*, and even *clotheswise* are now probably familiar to you.

On the other hand, the prefix *re-* is very highly productive: *rewrite, repaint, rediscover, reroute, reschedule, rewrap, rethink, re-emerge, resolidify,* and other such verbs can be coined almost at will. The same is true of the suffix *-ness*: *blackness, manliness, separateness, inventiveness, salaciousness, obstructiveness* show that this suffix can be added to almost any adjective (though adjectives ending in *-ical* usually prefer *-ity*: *topicality,* not **topicalness*).

Most affixes are of intermediate productivity. Thus, for example, the prefix *pre-* turns up in recent formations like *pre-shrunk, prearrange, preassemble, precancerous, precensor, premix,* and *pre-Darwinian,* but there none the less seems to be something wrong with **pre-ride, *pre-interested, *pre-destroy,* and **pre-eliminate.* (***'Genghis had intended to raze the city, but, when he got there, he found it had been pre-destroyed by his rival.')

A sensational recent success story in English is the prefix *mini-.* Before 1960, this prefix did not exist at all (see below for its origin), but the single new creation *miniskirt* apparently caught the public imagination to such an extent that the prefix now turns up everywhere: we now encounter *mini-budgets, mini-successes, mini-microphones, minicomputers, minicars, mini-kilts,* and even *mini-wars.*

Over half a century ago, the linguists of the Prague School were arguing that the structure of any language is, at any given moment, a mixture of fully active and productive processes, the dead and dying remains of ancient processes now disappearing from the language, and the first glimmerings of new processes just beginning to come into existence. Nowhere is the truth of this view more evident than in word-formation, and most particularly in derivation.

Various other devices are used to coin new words in English and other languages. A rather subtle but very important one in English is **conversion**, also called **zero-derivation**. Conversion is the process of moving a word from one lexical category (part of speech) to another, with no affixation or other modification. For example, the adjective *brown* becomes a verb in *brown the meat*; the verb *drink* becomes a noun in *have a drink*; the noun *access* becomes a verb in computing locutions like *you can access that utility from the main menu*; the preposition and particle *up* becomes a verb in *up the ante* and a noun in *ups and downs*. This sort of thing happens all the time in English and has been going on for centuries. Most of us don't even blink the first time we hear someone refer to *a nasty* or *a dyslexic* or when someone talks about *leafleting a neighbourhood* or *networking a computer*, or perhaps even the first time we hear someone say *I have a long commute to work*. Conversion is frequent only in languages with very little morphology, like English; morphologically richer languages usually require some kind of affixation in order to change the class of a word.

Another increasingly frequent device is **clipping**: extracting a word from a longer word of the same meaning. Thus, *telephone* becomes *phone*, *brassière* becomes *bra*, *gymnasium* becomes *gym*, *hippopotamus* becomes *hippo*, *violoncello* becomes *cello*, *influenza* becomes *flu*, *head-shrinker* ('psychiatrist') becomes *shrink*, and *show business* becomes *show biz*; in French, *fast food* becomes *fast*, *pullover* becomes *pull*, *bulldozer* becomes *bull*, and *hardware* (in the computer sense) becomes *hard*. In some such cases, as with *cello* and *flu*, the clipped form has more or less completely replaced the original longer word. (Note that a clipped form is a real word, and **not** an abbreviation.) Sometimes a clipped form acquires a curious suffix, as in English *ciggy* 'cigarette', *nightie* 'nightgown', *ammo* 'ammunition', *goalie* 'goalkeeper', and *fresher* 'freshman', British English *turps* 'turpentine' and *starkers* 'stark naked', Australian English *umpy* 'umpire', and French *apéro* (for *apéritif*), *Amerlo* (for *Américain*), *facho* (for *fasciste*), and *blackos* ('black person'). Technical terms often exhibit unusual types of clipping, as in the British *polythene* (for *polyethylene*).

A sort of combination of compounding and clipping is **blending**, in which pieces of existing words are combined to make a new word. Classical examples are *motel* (*motor* plus *hotel*), *smog* (*smoke* plus *fog*), *brunch* (*breakfast* plus *lunch*), and *Oxbridge* (*Oxford* plus *Cambridge*); more recent ones include *heliport* (*helicopter* plus *airport*), *Eurovision* (*European* plus *television*), *breathalyser* (*breath* plus *analyser*), and *Chunnel* (*Channel* plus *tunnel*). Such formations are beloved of advertisers and journalists, who constantly create new blends, which usually have only a momentary existence: *sexsational*, *infotisement*, *rockumentary*, and the like. You will doubtless be dimly aware that several such **nonce formations** (as short-lived creations are called) slide past your eyes every day, though it is unlikely that most of them make any lasting impression on you.

Blends were widely used for official purposes in German during the Nazi era and in Russian during the Communist period: German *Gestapo* (for *Geheime Staatspolizei* 'Secret State Police') and Russian *Sovnarkom* (for *Soviet Narodnyx Komissarov* 'Council of People's Commissars').

Of particular linguistic interest is **back-formation**: the creation of a word by the removal of an *apparent* affix from another word. English has a number of agent nouns derived from verbs with the suffix *-er*: *writer* from *write*, *singer* from *sing*, *smoker* from *smoke*, and so on. At various times, we have acquired the nouns *pedlar* (an alteration of earlier *pedder*, from obsolete English *pedde* 'basket'), *editor* and *sculptor* (loans from Latin), and *burglar* and *lecher* (loans from Norman French). All these happen to end in a syllable that sounds just like *-er*, and hence English-speakers have removed this 'affix' from the nouns to create the verbs *peddle*, *edit*, *sculpt*, *burgle*, and *letch* (as in 'Mike is letching after Susie'). Similarly, the Latin name *pisa* for a certain vegetable and the Norman French name *cherise* for a certain fruit were borrowed into English as *pease* and *cherries*, respectively. Originally, these were uncountable nouns, like *spinach* and *fruit*, but they both happened to end in what *sounds* like an English plural suffix, and so speakers removed this 'suffix' to obtain the new singular forms *pea* and *cherry*. A more recent example of back-formation, familiar to fans of a certain cult TV show, is the verb *self-destruct*, back-formed from the compound noun *self-destruction* (note that no such verb as *destruct* exists in English). Other examples are *baby-sit* (from *baby-sitter*), *televise* (from *television*), and *double-glaze* (from *double-glazing*). An unusual case of back-formation involves the verb *orient* (as in 'to orient oneself'); this yields a noun *orientation*, by the regular rules, but British speakers have extracted from this noun a new verb *orientate*, and most Britons now say things like 'I couldn't orientate myself', which sound very odd to most other speakers.

In the same vein as back-formation, but more complex, is **reanalysis**: interpreting a word as having a structure which is not historically valid and hence obtaining a new morpheme for use in coining other words. The familiar *hamburger* takes its name from the German city of *Hamburg*, but, since the first syllable looks like the name of a kind of meat, we have reanalysed the word as a compound of *ham* plus *-burger*, and the new morpheme *-burger* is now used to derive names for all kinds of things in a bun: *cheeseburger*, *chickenburger*, *vegeburger*, and so on. Indeed, in Britain, things have gone so far that the original item is now commonly called a *beefburger*. A particularly amusing case of reanalysis involves the word *bikini*, the name of a bathing costume. This word is taken from the name of a Pacific atoll where some the earliest nuclear bomb tests were conducted, and it is thought to reflect the stunning impact of the scanty new costume at a time when bathing suits normally covered a great deal more skin than they do now. Now English has a prefix *bi-* meaning 'two', as in *bifocals* and *bilateral* – and the new costume consisted of two pieces. Consequently, when an even more shocking costume was introduced, consisting only of the bottom part of a bikini, some wags reanalysed the name *bikini* as containing the prefix *bi-*, and replaced this with the prefix *mono-*, meaning 'one', to name the microscopic new one-piece garment. The word *monokini* is still rather marginal in English, but it has become fully established in French.

Reanalysis is the origin of the prefix *mini-*, discussed above. English has long had the two words *miniature* and *minimum*, both derived from Latin; historically, these two words are not related at all, and their resemblance in form is purely an accident. But they both have meanings involving the sense of 'very small', and, around 1960, someone reanalysed them as though they both contained an element *mini-*, meaning 'very small'; this new morpheme was used to construct that pioneering word *miniskirt*, and the rest is history.

Even more dramatic than reanalysis is **folk etymology**: restructuring a word whose structure is opaque into something seemingly more transparent. A good example is *bridegroom*. English once had a word *guma*, meaning 'man', and this was compounded with *bryd* 'bride' to give *brydguma* – literally, 'bride-man'. With time, however, the word *guma* dropped out of the language, and *bridegoom* came to seem mysterious. As a result, the puzzling second element was altered to *groom* (a *groom* was a servant, though today the word normally just means somebody who looks after horses). We thus obtained *bridegroom*, in which the second element is at least familiar, if not obviously very sensible. In a similar way, the French loan *écrevisse* was folk-etymologized into *crayfish* – a crayfish is, of course, not a fish, but at least it lives in the water. My favourite example, though, comes from Basque. Spanish has borrowed the word *zanahoria* 'carrot' from Arabic, and the Spanish word has in turn been borrowed into Basque. There, however, it has been re-formed into *zainhoria*, which in Basque literally means 'yellow-root' (*zain* is 'root', *hori* is 'yellow', and -*a* is the Basque article). This is surely the most successful folk etymology of all time.

A device for coining words which has recently become very popular is the reduction of a long phrase or name to a few important letters, usually the first letters of the principal words in it. If the result can only be pronounced letter-by-letter, we call it an **initialism**; if it can be pronounced as a word, we call it an **acronym**. (Some people use the term 'acronym' for both cases.) Examples of initialisms are *FBI* (for *Federal Bureau of Investigation*), *BBC* (for *British Broadcasting Corporation*), *TNT* (for *trinitrotoluene*), *DJ* (for *disc jockey*), *GCHQ* (for *Government Communications Headquarters*), and *Ph.D.* (for *Philosophiae Doctor*, Latin for 'Doctor of Philosophy'). Examples of acronyms are *NATO* (for *North Atlantic Treaty Organization*), *radar* (for *radio detection and ranging*), *scuba* (for *self-contained underwater breathing apparatus*), *AIDS* (*acquired immune deficiency syndrome*), and, of course, *laser* (for *light amplification by the stimulated emission of radiation*); this last has inevitably given rise to the back-formed verb *lase*. Computer people are particularly fond of acronyms: *RAM* (for *random-access memory*), *ROM* (for *read-only memory*), *DOS* (for *disk-operating system*), and *WYSIWYG* (for *what you see is what you get*).

The growing use of initialisms and acronyms is hardly surprising: who in her right mind would prefer to recite on every occasion the full name of the *BBC*, or of *AIDS*, or of *RAM*? How many of us can even remember just what *DDT* stands for, or *UNICEF*, or even *laser*?

Variation in usage is possible. The military term *AWOL* (for *absent without leave*) is pronounced by some as an initialism, by others as an acronym, and the same is true of *UFO*. In English, *CIA* is an initialism, but, in Spanish, it's an acronym pronounced to rhyme with the Spanish word *día* 'day'.

Some recent formations are impossible to classify, since they combine features of blends with features of initialisms or acronyms and possibly other devices. The military are particularly fond of these hybrids, with their *CINCPAC* (*Commander-in-Chief in the Pacific*) and their *UNPROFOR* (*United Nations Protective Force*), but technical terms like *CD-ROM* show the same complexity.

To the great exasperation of manufacturers, trade names may become so successful that they pass into the language as generic terms for products. Once upon a time *aspirin*, *cellophane*, and *escalator* were all trade names, but now they are simply common nouns. The Hoover Company is not at all pleased to find *hoover* being used in Britain as another word for 'vacuum cleaner', nor are the manufacturers of Kleenex amused when people refer to all paper tissues as *kleenex*. Equally, the American manufacturers of Scotch Tape, the British manufacturers of Sellotape, and the Australian manufacturers of Durex are all appalled to find their trade names applied generically to sticky tape in their respective countries, and all manufacturers are prepared to go to legal and financial lengths to protect their brand names. Only a few years ago, the US courts stripped Parker Brothers of their copyright trade name *Monopoly*, ruling that the word had become a generic term for any board game. (As a keen game-player myself, I find this last ruling incomprehensible: who are all these dimwits who apparently can't tell Monopoly from Scrabble?)

Finally, one of the rarest of all ways of obtaining new words is simply to invent them, more or less out of thin air. The paragraph on the back of a book telling you how wonderful the book is and why you absolutely have to buy it didn't use to have a name in English; a publisher invited the American humorist Gelett Burgess to invent one, and he came up with the inspired creation *blurb*, which is now universally used. The word *nylon* (originally a trade name) was apparently also created in this way (the often-told story about New York and London appears not to be true). Some such formations may have a vague source: the Belgian chemist J. B. van Helmont invented the word *gas* by rearranging the Greek word *khaos* 'chaos' to his liking, and the Basque nationalist Sabino Arana, finding that Basque had only loan words for 'write', seized upon an archaic verb *iraatsi* 'carve' and twisted this around at his pleasure to produce *idatzi*, which is now the universal Basque word for 'write'.

This survey by no means exhausts all the possible ways of obtaining new words. If you do Exercise 2.3 below, you will come across some further devices, and the Further Reading will suggest some more comprehensive accounts of word-formation in English.

2.5 *Change in word-meaning*

In Chapter 1 we saw several examples of English words which have changed their meanings over the years. The word *with* meant 'against' in Old English; the word *cheer* meant 'state of mind' for Chaucer; even the eighteenth-century writer Swift used *ascertain* to mean 'fix, prevent from changing' and *explode* to mean 'drive out'.

Change in meaning is called **semantic change**, and it is just as common as other types of change. English words have been changing their meanings for centuries, and words are still changing their meanings today. Here are some examples.

Not so long ago, there was a clear difference in meaning between *uninterested* and *disinterested*: the first meant 'apathetic', while the second meant 'having nothing to gain or lose from any outcome'. Hence a judge presiding over a civil case was expected to be disinterested, but he certainly wasn't supposed to be uninterested. Today, however, many people use *disinterested* to mean exactly the same as *uninterested*: 'I'm disinterested in opera.' For such speakers, the word *disinterested* has changed its meaning; since they appear to be a majority, we may reasonably conclude that the word has changed its meaning in English, even though conservative speakers (like me) still find the new sense objectionable.

Another case is the verb *transpire*. This used to mean 'come to light', 'become known'. Thus, a sentence like 'It transpired that the councillors had been fiddling their expenses' meant 'It came to light that . . . '. But such sentences were easily misunderstood, and many people, on encountering them, took them to mean rather 'It happened that . . . '. Consequently, *transpire* is now commonly used to mean 'happen, occur', and now we often hear things like 'We don't know what transpired', meaning 'We don't know what happened', which would have been impossible not so long ago. The word *transpire* has also changed its meaning.

This last example illustrates one way in which the meaning of a word can change: it is commonly used in a context in which a different interpretation of the whole sentence is possible and reasonable. Something similar happened with *cheer*. This formerly meant 'state of mind', but its frequent occurrence in sentences like 'Be of good cheer' induced hearers to assume that the word meant specifically a *good* state of mind, and that is the only sense the word now has.

Misunderstandings are not necessary to bring about semantic change, however: words can change their meanings for any of a vast number of reasons. One very common reason is a change in the world.

For centuries, the word *tennis* denoted a racquet-and-ball game played on an enclosed court embellished with sloping roofs and various types of obstacles off which or through which the players hit the ball. In the late nineteenth century, another racquet-and-ball game was invented which was played on an open grass court, and this was dubbed *lawn tennis*. Within a few years, the new game had become vastly more popular than the old, and the name *lawn tennis* was quickly shortened to *tennis*. Today, any English-speaker hearing the word *tennis* immediately thinks of the game Steffi Graf plays, and the handful of enthusiasts for the older game have been obliged to give it a new name, *real tennis*.

(In North America, the same thing has happened to *hockey*: the newly invented ice version originally called *ice hockey* has completely eclipsed its older cousin, and a North American uses *hockey* for the ice game and *field hockey* for its grass counterpart. In Britain, where the grass version is still the more widely played one, this has not happened.)

Much the same has happened to our word *car*. This ancient word long denoted a cart or wagon pulled by animals. When self-propelled vehicles with their own engines were invented in the late nineteenth century, the obvious compound *motor car* was coined to denote one of these newfangled devices. Such was the success of the new invention, however, that the compound was soon shortened to *car*, and today no English-speaker who hears 'I've just bought a new car' is going to expect a shiny new oxcart with antilock brakes and a built-in cassette player.

Such examples represent one variety of what we call a **shift in markedness**: originally, the **unmarked** form of tennis was the variety played on an enclosed court, and the unmarked type of car was an oxcart, but the earlier **marked** varieties on grass and with a motor have now become the unmarked forms, while the old unmarked forms are now marked, and the language has been adjusted accordingly.

These relatively recent examples illustrate an important general point: sometimes we can understand the history of a word only by knowing something crucial about the society in which the word was formerly used. A famous example is the word *money*, which derives from the Latin word *monēta* 'coins, cash' (the Romans had no paper money). No problem there, but the Latin word had originally meant 'one who admonishes'. This seems an incomprehensible change, until we learn that a famous mint was located in the Roman temple of the goddess Juno, and that Juno was nicknamed *Monēta* 'the Admonisher'. A more recent example is the word *southpaw* 'left-handed person', which also seems mysterious at first, even though the use of *paw* for 'hand' is familiar enough. This usage derives from the American game of baseball, and it originally denoted a left-handed pitcher (the pitcher is the equivalent of the bowler in cricket). A baseball diamond is traditionally laid out so that the afternoon sun shines into the eyes of the fielding side, including the pitcher; the pitcher therefore faces west, and the south is on his left – hence the origin of the word.

An area in which semantic change is particularly rapid is that involving subjects which are **taboo** (that is, subjects on which complete frankness is socially unacceptable). In English, taboo subjects include (or have included) sex, reproduction, excretion, death, and the human body. Since taboos prohibit the use of plain language, speakers are constantly forced to resort to **euphemisms** (roundabout expressions which are socially acceptable); inevitably, the euphemisms themselves come to be regarded as blunt ways of speaking and have to be replaced by further euphemisms.

Consider copulation. The Latin word *copulate*, which originally meant only 'join together', itself originated as a euphemism for sexual activity, introduced to avoid the use of older English words which had come to seem unbearably crude. But *copulate* has now become unbearably crude in its turn: Jessica is hardly going to confide to her friends 'I'm copulating with Mike'. Only a few years ago she would not have said 'I'm having sex with Mike', though she might, if not too shy, have ventured 'I'm going to bed with Mike' or 'I'm sleeping with Mike', using one of our now-familiar euphemisms. Most likely, though, she would have contented herself with 'I'm seeing Mike' or 'I'm going out with Mike'. Such phrases could hardly seem more innocent or irrelevant, but everyone would have understood them, and friends would not have assumed that Jessica and Mike were enjoying regular Scrabble matches. But this particular taboo had recently been losing its force, and today Jessica will very likely just announce to her friends 'I'm shagging Mike', or something similar, depending on which particular blunt term is currently in vogue.

The act of love itself has become next to impossible to talk about in English: we can choose between obscure medical terminology or words which would get our faces slapped in some company, with little in between. As a result, speakers try desperately to find some word or phrase that will be readily understood without producing sniggers or glares, but no such word can be used for long. In the nineteenth century, the novelist Jane Austen could write of the very genteel Miss Anne Elliott and her haughty neighbour Captain Wentworth that 'they had no intercourse but what the commonest civility required'. The author would have been dumbfounded by the effect of this sentence on a modern reader; in her time, of course, the word *intercourse* meant nothing more than 'dealings between people'. In the twentieth century, however, the roundabout phrase *sexual intercourse* was created as a very delicate way of talking about copulation; this has now been shortened to *intercourse*, and this sexual sense is now so prevalent that we find it impossible to use the word in any other sense at all.

The effect of taboo can be very powerful. Several generations ago, the simple anatomical terms *leg* and *breast* came to be regarded as highly indelicate in American speech. The unacceptability of these words required euphemisms not only for talking about the human body but even for talking about roast chicken and Thanksgiving turkeys, with the result that Americans began to speak of *dark meat* and *white meat*, as they still do today, even though *leg* and *breast* have more recently lost their indelicate status. Similarly, the total unacceptability of *cock* in its anatomical sense has for Americans made the word unavailable for referring to a male chicken, and several euphemisms have been pressed into service, with *rooster* now having won out as the near-universal American word for the bird. Many Americans do not even know that *cock* is another word for a rooster. British speakers have not gone quite so far, but many now prefer the derivative *cockerel* for the bird.

Excretion is even worse. Our native English words for excretion are now widely regarded as crude to the point of obscenity, and even such Latinate words as *urinate* are too offensive for ordinary use, with the result that euphemisms come and go in this domain at a brisk pace. Our friend Jessica is not going to excuse herself by saying 'I have to urinate', nor, unless drunk, will she probably explain 'I have to piss'. Her mother might have said 'I have to powder my nose', or even 'I have to use the little girls' room', but these dated euphemisms are now no more than jokes. With people she doesn't know well, especially old people, Jessica will probably settle for something innocuous like 'Will you excuse me?' or 'I'll be back in a minute'. With close friends, though, she will very likely resort to nursery language (a common source of euphemisms) and announce 'I have to wee' – unless she's had a few drinks too many, in which case she may have few inhibitions about using more graphic language.

Taboo can apply in other areas of the vocabulary. The English word *bear* (the animal) is related to the colour term *brown* and originally meant merely 'the brown one', and the Russian word for 'bear', *medvedev*, means literally 'honey-eater'. In both languages these curious words completely replaced an earlier name for the bear, and it is thought that this happened because the original name became taboo: presumably the bear was regarded with such awe by our remote ancestors that they could not bring themselves to utter its name, and resorted instead to euphemisms. Southern European languages show something similar with foxes: earlier names for the fox have been frequently replaced by curious new terms, many of them derived from personal names. For example, in part of Spain the fox is called *el garcía*, from the familiar Spanish surname, and the standard French name for the animal is *renard*, derived from the personal name *Reginhard*.

Something of an extreme in tabooing is found in Australia. To begin with, every Australian language has a special **avoidance style** which must be used in the presence of certain relatives; these relatives always include a man's mother-in-law, and hence avoidance styles are sometimes called **mother-in-law language**. Mother-in-law language uses different words from ordinary speech: in this circumstance, the everyday words are taboo. In some languages, only certain words are tabooed and replaced; in others, the *entire* vocabulary of the everyday language is replaced by different words, even pronouns and numerals. So far, this has nothing to do with language change, but there's more. In all indigenous Australian languages, when a person dies, his name becomes taboo, and not just his name, but all words similar in sound to his name. For example, when a man named *Djäyila* died in 1975, the common verb *djäl-* 'want' became taboo in his community, and was replaced by *duktuk-*, apparently borrowed from a neighbouring language (native Australians are traditionally multilingual). Likewise, in about 1950 a man called *Ngayunya* died, and consequently the pronoun *ngayu* 'I' was tabooed in his community, and replaced by *nganku*, borrowed from the mother-in-law language; ten years later, another death made *nganku* itself taboo, and some speakers therefore revived *ngayu*, while others, with a knowledge of English, simply borrowed *mi* from English. (In Australia, obviously, speakers have no hesitation in borrowing even the most basic words when the need arises.) It must be an interesting experience being a child learning an Australian language: no sooner have you successfully learned a few hundred words, when the grown-ups change some of them, and refuse to let you use the words they were so happy to hear you using yesterday.

There is one type of euphemism which derives, not from taboo, but from a simple desire to be polite, and it involves the extension of a flattering word to cases where it is not literally appropriate. The English word *gentle* once meant 'of good birth', and hence a *gentleman* was a man who was well born, a man of quality. Over time, this word has come to be extended to any man, of whatever background, who is courteous and honourable, who knows how to behave in polite society, and this is still its most frequent sense. In some circumstances, however, it is extended further and applied to any man at all, as when you begin a speech with *ladies and gentlemen*, or when you say to a shop assistant *This gentleman is ahead of me*. The Spanish word *caballero* has had a similar history. Derived from *caballo* 'horse', it originally meant only 'horseman'. But, since only people of a certain social position could afford to own horses, *caballero* came to mean first 'knight, nobleman' and then 'man of quality, gentleman' (in the earlier English sense). Today, though, if you visit Spain, the first place you will encounter the word will almost certainly be in the form of *Caballeros* written on the door of a public toilet.

It is not always easy to understand why a word changes its meaning. The word *realize* formerly meant 'make real', and still sometimes does, as in *She finally realized her childhood ambition*. But the word has acquired two new senses: 'understand', as in *I realize that time is short*, and 'come to understand', as in *She suddenly realized that she had forgotten her keys*. It is not at all obvious how this change could have occurred, since the new senses actually require a different construction (a *that*-complement clause) from the old sense (a simple transitive construction). The change in meaning has been so dramatic that few people are now aware that *realize* is related to *real*.

Certain types of semantic change, while not always easy to understand, are so frequent that they are given specific names; among these are **generalization** (or **broadening**) and **specialization** (or **narrowing**). Generalization is the spread of meaning from a narrower to a broader class of things. The word *dog* once denoted only a particular type of canine, but now it is our generic term for all canines. Our word *arrive*, a loan from French, formerly meant 'come to shore', but now means more generally 'come (to a place)'. The Basque word *akats* formerly meant only 'nick, scratch', but today it is used to mean 'defect' (of any kind). Specialization is the opposite change. Formerly, *girl* meant 'young person (of either sex)', but now it denotes only a young female person. The word *deer* once meant 'animal (in general)', but can now be applied only to a cervine animal. The word *meat* formerly meant 'food' (as it still does in the archaic phrase *meat and drink*), but otherwise it now means only 'flesh food'. Curiously, specialization appears to be far more frequent than generalization.

Two other named types of semantic change are **melioration** and **pejoration**. Melioration is an 'improvement' in meaning. The words *queen* and *knight* formerly just meant 'woman' and 'boy', but today these terms are applied only to people occupying certain exalted positions. Pejoration is the opposite: the word *knave* also once meant only 'boy', but then came to be demoted to a term of abuse. All of the words *villain*, *churl*, and *boor* once meant merely 'farm-worker', but, no doubt because of the city-slicker's habitual contempt for his unsophisticated country cousin, all three have likewise become purely insults. Something similar is now happening to the word *peasant*: we can still refer to impoverished third-world farmers as 'peasants' without intending any slight, but we can equally say *You peasant!* when we want to insult someone. The word *mistress* was once a respectful term for addressing any woman, on a par with *mister* for men, but now it only means 'woman kept by a man for sexual purposes'; this change has left the old abbreviation *Mrs* in the embarrassing position of being an abbreviation for nothing.

This last example illustrates a fact about semantic change which feminists understandably find very annoying: words pertaining to women undergo pejoration far more frequently than do words pertaining to men. Consider a brief list of words for men and women which were once entirely parallel:

master	mistress
sir	madame
governor	governess
bachelor	spinster
courtier	courtesan
working man	working girl

In each case, the word denoting the woman now represents some position at least much less important than the male term (*governess*) and possibly insulting or humiliating (*spinster*); very often the female term now means something like 'woman available for sex'. Some words even have different senses when applied to men and to women. In American English, at least, when you describe a man as a *pro* you mean that he is experienced, competent, and reliable; when you describe a woman as a *pro* you mean she's a prostitute. The frequency of such developments is a clear reminder of the long-standing subordinate position of women in our society.

One of the commonest of all types of semantic change is **metaphor**: applying a word to something it does not literally denote in order to draw attention to a resemblance. Metaphor is so frequent that it might reasonably be taken as the paradigm type of semantic change.

Our word *head* originally just meant the part of the body on top of the shoulders. But, since this is both the highest part of the body and the part that is perceived as being in charge of the whole body, *head* has come to be used as a metaphor for all kinds of things and people that are high, in front, in charge, or just rather round: we speak of the *head* of a valley, the *head* of a nail, the *head* of a large corporation, the *head* of a flower, the *head* of a school, the *head* of a river, the *head* of a tape recorder, a *head* of garlic or cabbage, and so on. Even grammarians talk about the *head* of a construction. Body-part names are particularly subject to metaphorical use: we speak of the *eye* of a needle or of a hurricane, the *mouth* of a river, a cave, or a jar, a *hand* of bridge, a *neck* of land, the *foot* of a mountain, the *teeth* of a comb, and so on.

The Latin ancestor of our word *precocious* meant 'ripening early' and was applied to fruit; we have applied this term metaphorically to children who develop earlier than most. Our verb *govern* derives from a Latin verb that meant only 'steer' or 'pilot' (a boat); the metaphor here is obvious. The Romans themselves took their word *expressio* 'squeezing out', a word applied to activities like squeezing oil out of olives, and extended it meta-phorically to the 'squeezing out' of meanings from speech – hence our word *expression*, borrowed from Latin. Our word *field* originally denoted a fairly well-defined piece of land; today we commonly also use it metaphorically for a fairly well-defined area of activity: *She's a leading scholar in her field*. And any reader who has studied a little syntax will be familiar with the two types of metaphors used in describing sentence structures: arboreal ones like *tree*, *root*, *branch*, and *node*, and kinship terms like *mother*, *sister*, and *daughter*.

Almost any sort of resemblance, real or imagined, may cause a word to be pressed into service as a metaphor. An outstanding performer is a *star*; a person who publicly declares homosexuality *comes out of the closet*; small football teams facing powerful opponents are *minnows*; a defective car is a *lemon*; a political leader who no longer exercises effective power is a *lame duck*; an overwhelming winner has *demolished* or *shredded* the opposition; a terrified person is *petrified*; austere economic policies *bite*. A slovenly, a cunning, a rapacious, a capricious, or a timid person may be described as a *pig*, a *fox*, a *wolf*, a *butterfly*, or a *mouse*, reflecting the presumed character-istics of these creatures. The word *hot* can be applied to a currently fashion-able or successful performer, to stolen money or goods, to an intense shade of red or pink, to a bad-tempered argument or discussion, to a sexually inviting woman (there we go again!), to spicy food, to a hard-hit ball, to recent and dramatic news, to an exciting style of jazz, to a live electrical wire, to a recent trail left by a game animal or a fugitive, and doubtless to many other things; in each case, you can probably see the resemblance to heat which makes the metaphor possible.

Somewhat different from metaphor, but also common, are metonymy and synecdoche. **Metonymy** is the use of an attribute to denote the thing that is meant, as when we speak of the *crown* instead of the king (or the queen), when we say the *stage* to mean the theatrical profession, or when we say the *White House* to mean the American president – or, for that matter, when we say *anorak* to mean 'nerd'. Metonymy can be very deeply ingrained in our speech: if I say to you 'I have to hurry; I'm parked on a double yellow line', I certainly don't mean that *I* am parked illegally, but rather that my car is. A metonymy may persist long after its motivation is forgotten: everybody knows what a *red-light district* is, but few people realize that the name derives from the former practice of putting red lights in the windows of brothels to identify them. **Synecdoche** is the use of the whole to denote a part, or of a part to denote the whole. We say 'Ireland play Italy in the first round of the World Cup finals' when we mean only that the football teams representing those countries are meeting. On the other hand, we say *hands* to mean 'workers' or 'sailors', as in 'We need to hire more hands' or 'All hands on deck'.

Metonymy and synecdoche are pervasive in certain fields, such as politics and diplomacy, but they are not rare elsewhere. We say *Downing Street* for the British prime minister, *Brussels* for the administration of the EU, the *Quai d'Orsay* for the French foreign office, *Foggy Bottom* for the US State

Department, *Scotland Yard* for the metropolitan London police, *Anfield* for Liverpool Football Club, and *Washington* for the American government, all from their locations, though the London police have not actually been located in Scotland Yard for many years now.

Observe that, in many cases, a new meaning for a word may coexist happily with its older meanings. This does not always happen, however; in other cases the new meaning may completely displace an older meaning. This has happened, for example, with the words *with, cheer, ascertain,* and *explode,* discussed above, and the same thing is possibly going to happen with *disinterested.* In certain cases, a new meaning may drive out an older meaning very rapidly. This particularly happens when the new meaning is offensive, or at least capable of producing embarrassing misunderstandings if confused with the old meaning. We have already seen this with *intercourse,* whose new sexual sense has virtually driven the old neutral sense out of the language. The same has happened with *gay,* which formerly meant 'cheerful', but which has recently acquired the new sense of 'homosexual'. If somebody says to you *John is gay,* you are most unlikely to understand 'John is cheerful': the old meaning has become virtually unavailable. This phenomenon is sometimes called **interference**, but some linguists, with mock seriousness, invoke what they call **Gresham's law of semantic change**, which asserts 'Bad meanings drive out good' (the field of economics has a Gresham's law which declares 'Bad money drives out good'). Interference is, however, more general than this light-hearted 'law' would suggest. Old English had the two verbs *lætan* 'allow, permit' and *lettan* 'hinder, obstruct', and both of these developed into the modern form *let.* Having identical verbs meaning 'allow' and 'hinder' was obviously a serious nuisance, and so we have dropped the one meaning 'hinder'. Today the verb *let* means only 'allow', though the other verb barely survives as the related noun *let* 'obstruction', which is confined to legal language (*without let or hindrance*) and to certain sports, such as tennis and squash (a *let* is an obstruction of the serve or of a stroke).

You will note that my discussion of semantic change has been somewhat anecdotal, and you may be wondering whether there are any principles involved. Certainly there are some interesting observations to be made. One of these is the metaphorical use of body-part names, discussed above. Another is the curious tendency of words denoting parts of the face to 'move around': for example, Latin *maxilla* 'jaw' has become *mejilla* 'cheek', in Spanish, and English *chin,* Old Norse *kinn* 'cheek' and Old Irish *gin* 'mouth' all derive from the same source.

But there have, in fact, been some attempts at identifying general principles of semantic change. In a famous article in his 1926 book, the French linguist Antoine Meillet proposed three principles of semantic change. One of these is merely the occurrence of change in the world, which we have already discussed above with examples like *tennis* and *car.* A second is change in linguistic context. This includes the cases of taboo that we have already discussed, in which new euphemisms are pushed into contexts in which they did not formerly occur, while older terms became relegated to undeniably vulgar contexts. But it also includes other types of cases, such as the narrowing of *cheer* from 'state of mind' to 'good state of mind' as a result of its frequent occurrence together with adjectives like *good*.

Meillet's third principle is change resulting from borrowing, in those cases in which a loan word induces a shift in the meaning of an earlier word. Here is an example of what he means. The Basque colour term *urdin* formerly covered the whole range of colours distinguished in English as *green*, *blue*, and *grey*. But Basque has borrowed the words *berde* 'green' and *gris* 'grey' from the neighbouring Romance languages, and hence *urdin* is now restricted to about the same territory as English *blue*: the word has changed its meaning in response to the presence of loan words. This change has left some older formations isolated: a certain mushroom with a bright green underside is still called in Basque a *gibelurdin* (literally, it would now seem, 'blue-back'), and a common Basque word for 'old maid' is *mutxurdin* (literally, 'blue-cunt', but the Basque word is no more offensive than the English one). The word *urdin* can no longer be applied to things that are green or grey outside of cases like these.

More interesting, perhaps, is the recent work of Elizabeth Traugott (1982, 1989). Traugott suggests three tendencies in semantic change, slightly reworded here:

Tendency I: external descriptions of reality become internal descriptions of perceptions and evaluations. Cases like the semantic shift of *boor* 'farmer' to 'oaf' illustrate this tendency, as does the observation that English *feel*, which once meant only 'touch' (an external description), now denotes the perceptions of the person doing the touching.

Tendency II: external and internal descriptions become textual meanings – that is, they acquire meanings that give overt structure to discourse. English *while* formerly meant only 'period of time', as it still does in cases like *Wait for a while*. But it eventually acquired the discourse function of 'the period of time (during which something happens)', as in *While my wife was away, I lived on pizza*. Later still, it acquired the more abstract discourse function of 'although': *While she's very talented, she's somewhat careless.* English *but* originally meant 'on the outside (of)'; it acquired the sense of 'except for', which it still has in a few cases like *everything but the kitchen sink*; today, though, it mostly occurs with the discourse function of contrast: *It's perfect, but it's too expensive.*

Tendency III: meanings become increasingly based in the speaker's subjective beliefs and attitudes. Here are several examples. The word *apparently* originally meant 'openly, in appearance'. It then acquired a weak sense of evaluation: 'to all appearances'. In the nineteenth century, it acquired the strong sense of evaluation of evidence which it now has, as in *She is apparently determined to pursue this.* Similarly, *probably* once meant only 'plausibly, believably', but today it also expresses the speaker's evaluation of evidence: *She is probably going to be promoted.* The verb *insist* originally meant 'persevere, continue'. In the seventeenth century it acquired a new sense of 'demand', as in *I insist that you come home early.* A century later, it acquired the sense of 'believe strongly': *I insisted that a mistake had been made.*

What all three tendencies have in common is a movement away from the external and the objective toward the discourse-internal and the subjective. Traugott's observations suggest that such movement is a pervasive force in semantic change, and they further suggest that there are indeed important general principles of semantic change which we are only beginning to understand.

Further reading

There are many books on loan words in English; particularly detailed is Sheard (1966), while Manser (1988) is rather light-hearted. Most histories of English include chapters or sections on the same subject; try Strang (1970), Williams (1975), Baugh and Cable (1993), or Pyles and Algeo (1993). A classic book on contact between languages generally is Weinreich (1953).

Two readable books on English word-formation are Adams (1973) and L. Bauer (1983). An approachable but more linguistically demanding book on the English vocabulary generally, including both loan words and word-formation, is Katamba (1994).

It is more difficult to find detailed accounts of changes in meaning, but the four histories of English just cited all have something to say about it. Several other textbooks of historical linguistics have chapters or sections on semantic change which you might find it helpful to consult: Bynon (1977), Anttila (1988), Lehmann (1992), and especially the very large Hock (1986). Much more substantial accounts can be found in Stern (1931) and Ullmann (1961). Sommerfelt (1962) emphasizes the sociolinguistic aspect of semantic change.

I mention here for the first time a book which you should certainly get acquainted with if your interests lie chiefly in the Indo-European (IE) languages (the vast family of languages to which English belongs): Buck (1949). This book presents the words expressing a given meaning in dozens of IE languages, and it provides a wealth of data on semantic change and lexical replacement.

Exercises

Exercise 2.1

Consulting a dictionary which provides sources of English words, identify the language from which each of the following words is borrowed, and, if possible, the approximate time it was borrowed. In some cases, you may find that the word is taken *ultimately* from one language but *directly* from another: that is, it was borrowed from one language to another to another.

(a) soprano   (h) tulip
(b) coach   (i) tea
(c) palaver   (j) yacht
(d) sex   (k) sauna
(e) juggernaut   (l) caviar
(f) celery   (m) mustard
(g) lemon   (n) cinnamon

Exercise 2.2

A few of the very numerous derivational suffixes of Basque are illustrated below. In each case, identify as accurately as you can the function of each suffix. Ignore any phonological alternations.

(a) -te

negu	'winter'	*negute*	'wintertime'
legor	'dry'	*legorte*	'drought'
aintzina	'before'	*aintzinate*	'antiquity'
izotz	'ice'	*izozte*	'(a) frost'

(b) -keta

saldu	'sell'	*salketa*	'sale'
ibili	'go about'	*ibilketa*	'(a) walk'
garbitu	'(to) clean'	*garbiketa*	'clean-up'
ikasi	'(to) study'	*ikasketa*	'study(ing)'

(c) -gaitz

aldatu	'change'	*aldagaitz*	'invariable'
sinetsi	'believe'	*sinesgaitz*	'incredible'
barkatu	'forgive'	*barkagaitz*	'unforgivable'
ulertu	'understand'	*ulergaitz*	'incomprehensible'

(d) -kor

ahaztu	'forget'	*ahazkor*	'forgetful'
aldatu	'change'	*aldagaitz*	'variable'
hil	'die'	*hilkor*	'mortal'
eman	'give'	*emankor*	'fertile'

What do you suppose are the meanings of the following additional Basque words?

| *euri* | 'rain' | *eurite* | ? |
| *gose* | 'hungry' | *gosete* | ? |

zapaldu	'oppress'	*zapalketa*	?
erosi	'buy'	*erosketa*	?
ikusi	'see'	*ikusgaitz*	?
eskuratu	'obtain'	*eskuragaitz*	?
sinetsi	'believe'	*sineskor*	?
iragan	'pass'	*iragankor*	?

Exercise 2.3

None of the English words below is strictly a loan word; each has been either constructed from English elements or obtained in a slightly unusual way. Consulting a good dictionary where necessary, explain the origin or formation of each; comment on any unusual features and, if possible, on the degree of productivity of the pattern. Be alert; some of these have more complex origins than might at first seem to be the case.

(a) quixotic
(b) eco-friendly
(c) software
(d) ongoing
(e) carbon-date (*verb*)
(f) noodle western
(g) fattist
(h) magenta
(i) skyjack
(j) astronaut
(k) megalopolis
(l) she-goat
(m) see-through (blouse)
(n) cardigan
(o) nosebleed
(p) dreads (hairdo)
(q) callanetics
(r) vandal
(s) fax
(t) grok

Exercise 2.4

Choose two passages each of around 100 words from two very different sources – say, a chemistry textbook and a popular newspaper. Using a dictionary, find out the origin of each word. For each passage, classify the words by origin, using such categories as 'native English', 'Old Norse', 'Greek', 'Latin', 'French' and 'others' (some words may be difficult to classify, but do your best). Count the words in each category, and calculate the percentage of words in the passage from each source. IMPORTANT: Count each different word only once, no matter how many times it occurs. Compare the results for the two passages. What conclusions can you draw?

Exercise 2.5

Each of the following is a quotation from a piece of English written three or four centuries ago. In each one, the word in boldface has changed its meaning rather conspicuously since that time. Consulting a dictionary where necessary, identify the earlier meaning represented in the extract. Where possible, comment on why the meaning change might have occurred.

(a) Doth she not count her blest . . . that we have wrought so worthy a gentleman to be her **bride?**
[Shakespeare, *Romeo and Juliet*]

(b) Thus we **prevent** the last great day, and judge ourselves.
[Herbert, 'The Temple']

(c) The exception **proves** the rule.
[proverb]

(d) If I attain I will return and **quit** thy love.
[Arnold, 'The Light of Asia']

(e) My ships are safely come to **road**.
[Shakespeare, *The Merchant of Venice*]

(f) I dreamt a dream **tonight**.
[Shakespeare, *Romeo and Juliet*]

(g) So said he, and forebore not glance or **toy**, of amorous intent, well understood of Eve.
[Milton, *Paradise Lost*]

(h) This God is most mighty thing that may be, the most **witty** and most rightful.
[*Lay Folks' Catechism*]

Exercise 2.6

Each of the following Japanese words is a loan from English, and each has been modified to make it conform to the phonological structure of Japanese. Try to identify the English word which has been borrowed in each case. In the transcription used, $<j> = [d\ 3]$, $<y> = [j]$, $<sh> = [3]$ and $<ch> = [t\int]$; other symbols have approximately their usual phonetic values in the IPA. Here are a few examples to get you started: *jampaa* = 'jumper', *waffuru* = 'waffle', *miruku* = 'milk', *appuru pai* = 'apple pie'. Note that Japanese *u* and final *o* are rather weakly pronounced. What conclusions can you draw about the phonological system of Japanese?

(a) *aisu kuriimu*   (m) *purezento*
(b) *torakku*   (n) *firumu*
(c) *kompyuutaa*   (o) *burondo*
(d) *gaarufurendo*   (p) *herikoputaa*
(e) *uetto suutsu*   (q) *hambaagaa*
(f) *zuumu renzu*   (r) *yuu-taan*
(g) *nambaa pureeto*   (s) *sukaafu*
(h) *masukara*   (t) *teeburu*
(i) *tii-shatsu*   (u) *ai-rainaa*
(j) *basuketto booru*   (v) *doraiyaa*
(k) *saamosutatto*   (w) *shiito beruto*
(l) *eya-hosutesu*   (x) *erochikku*

Exercise 2.7

About 2000 years ago, an ancestral form of Basque, which I shall call *pre-Basque*, came into contact with Latin, and a large number of Latin words were borrowed into pre-Basque. Table 2.3 shows some examples. The Latin forms are cited in what scholars believe to have been the spoken Latin forms of the time; note that Latin <c> and <g> invariably represent [k] and [g]. The Basque forms are given in their modern standard form; note that Basque <z> represents a voiceless sibilant [s]. What would you suggest might have been true of the plosive system in pre-Basque?

Table 2.3

	Latin	Basque	Gloss
1.	*ballaena*	*balea*	'whale'
2.	*dominica*	*domeka*	(L) 'of the Lord', (B) 'Sunday'
3.	*domine*	*done*	(L) 'lord', (B) 'saint'
4.	*denariu*	*diru*	(L) 'denarius', (B) 'money'
5.	*granu*	*garau*	'grain'
6.	*gula*	*gura*	'desire'
7.	*gypsu*	*gisu*	'plaster'
8.	*pace*	*bake*	'peace'
9.	*pice*	*bike*	'pitch'
10.	*peccatu*	*bekatu*	'sin'
11.	*piper*	*biper*	'pepper'
12.	*tempora*	*denbora*	(L) 'times', (B) 'time'
13.	*causa*	*gauza*	(L) 'reason', (B) 'thing'
14.	*cella*	*gela*	(L) 'chamber', (B) 'room'
15.	*corpus*	*gorputz*	'body'
16.	*Iudaeu*	*judu*	'Jew'
17.	*lege*	*lege*	'law'
18.	*rege*	*errege*	'king'
19.	*ripa*	*erripa*	'slope'
20.	*rota*	*errota*	'mill'
21.	*auditu*	*aditu*	'heard'
22.	*saccu*	*zaku*	'sack'
23.	*succu*	*zuku*	(L) 'juice', (B) 'soup'
24.	*necatu*	*nekatu*	(L) 'killed', (B) 'exhausted'
25.	*sabbatu*	*zapatu*	(L) 'Sabbath', (B) 'Saturday'
26.	*abbas*	*apaiz*	(L) 'abbot', (B) 'priest'

3

Phonological change I: Change in pronunciation

All types of change in pronunciation are collectively known as **phonological change**, or, using a more traditional term, as **sound change**. Phonological change has been more intensively studied than any other type of language change; after nearly 200 years of scholarly investigation, we now know a great deal about the subject.

Here I find it convenient to divide the study of phonological change into two chapters, each looking at the subject from a different point of view. This first chapter deals with **syntagmatic change**: change in the sequence of speech sounds representing the pronunciation of a particular word, or, more accurately, of groups of similar words. The next chapter will then go on to consider the consequences of such change for the phonological system of an entire language.

As a result of this long tradition of study, syntagmatic changes have been classified into a number of different types, and these types have been given names in the form of technical terms. These several dozen terms you will have to learn, but fortunately the task is not difficult. The great majority of sound changes are phonetically natural: they are easy to understand in terms of the structure and movements of the speech organs, and the terms which label various types of change mostly reflect rather directly what the speech organs are doing.

3.1 The phonetic basis of phonological change

If you are reading this book, you should already know something about the organs of speech, about the ways in which they are used to produce speech sounds, and about the conventional system for classifying and labelling speech sounds. For our purposes, the key point to bear in mind is that the lips, the various parts of the tongue, the velum, the jaw, the larynx, and the glottis can be manipulated during speech in ways which are partly independent but also partly interrelated. For example, you can round your lips or not, regardless of what the tongue is doing, but you can't round your lips tightly and keep your jaw lowered at the same time, nor can you produce a trill with your tongue while your mouth is closed. You can produce a uvular plosive or a palatal lateral, but you can't do them one right after the other: the organs just can't be moved fast enough. Moreover, even a possible manœuvre is of little use if it produces no audible sound: you can certainly open your glottis, make an alveolar closure, lower your velum, and expel air through your nasal cavity, but the result will produce nothing that anyone can hear. A great deal of phonological change (though not all of it) can be readily understood in terms of these limitations.

When we speak, we produce a stream of **speech sounds**, or segments, one after the other. Thus, for example, our word *cleaned* is conventionally represented at the phonological level as a series of English phonemes /kli:nd/, and at the phonetic level by something with more detail included, such as [kʰli:nd]. In each case, the representation shows a series of segments. In fact, we know that these segments are more of a psychological reality than a physical one: physically, the various speech organs are all moving about at their own pace, and they do not all simultaneously and instantly jump from one configuration to another, as you move from one speech sound to the next. Instead, the organs spend a good deal of time moving away from one configuration and towards the next one, leaving and arriving at different times. When you say *cleaned*, for example, the velum is lowered to begin the nasalization required for /n/ well before the tongue is moved up to make the closure also required for that consonant, and the vibration of the vocal folds required for /d/ is stopped some time before the tongue stops making the closure for it.

In spite of such unsynchronized timings, our ears and brains still hear the individual segments which are 'supposed' to be there. All this being so, however, you might suspect that small changes in the movements of the speech organs, even small changes in timing, might have significant effects on what is heard, and you would be right: a great deal of phonological change derives merely from such small adjustments in the movements of the organs of speech.

3.2 *Assimilation and dissimilation*

One of the commonest types of sound change is **assimilation**: the process by which two sounds that occur close together in speech become more alike. This sort of change is easy to understand: moving the speech organs all over the place requires an effort, and making nearby sounds more similar reduces the amount of movement required, and hence the amount of effort. Here is a simple example: the spoken Latin word *nocte* 'night', pronounced [nokte], has become *notte* [notte] in Italian, which is a modern form of spoken Latin. The earlier [k] has turned into a [t] by assimilating to the following [t], thus reducing the amount of movement required. This is a case of **total assimilation**: the sound undergoing assimilation has become identical to the influencing sound. Most assimilations, however, are **partial assimilations**: the assimilated sound becomes only more similar, and not identical, to the influencing sound. For example, Basque has the words *lan* 'work' [lan] and *bide* 'way' [biðe]; these form a compound *lanbide* 'occupation, profession', which, in spite of its spelling, is pronounced [lambiðe], with a labial nasal. The nasal undergoes partial assimilation to the following labial plosive, but remains a nasal.

Both of these are also examples of **contact assimilation**, in which the two sounds involved are directly adjacent, but we also often encounter **distant assimilation**, in which the sounds in question are separated by other sounds. The ancestor of German had a noun *gast* 'guest' [gast], whose plural was **gastiz* [gastiz] (the asterisk in this case marks a form which is not recorded, but which linguists are sure must have existed). The back vowel in the plural underwent assimilation to the front vowel in the following syllable, producing **gestiz* [gestiz]. As a result of other, later, changes, the word comes into modern German as *Gast*, plural *Gäste* [gestə], in which the vowel [e] is written as <ä> in order to show the connection with the singular form. Another example of distant assimilation, this time total, is provided by the Latin word for 'five'. This was originally *[peŋkʷe], but the initial [p] underwent assimilation to the later plosive, yielding *[kʷeŋkʷe], which, after a later vowel change, produced the classical form *quīnque*.

All the examples we have seen so far involve the assimilation of an earlier sound to a later one; this very common type is called **anticipatory assimilation**, or sometimes **regressive assimilation**. But it's also possible for a later sound to assimilate to an earlier one, and then we speak of **perseverative assimilation** or **progressive assimilation**. For example, the Basque words for 'side' and 'sturdy' were originally *alte* and *sento*, respectively, and these are still the forms in the eastern dialects. In all other dialects, though, the words have become *alde* and *sendo*: the plosive has been assimilated in voicing to the preceding sonorant. Similarly, the pre-Icelandic words **munθ* 'mouth' and **gulθ* 'gold' have undergone total perseverative assimilation to yield the modern forms *munn* and *gull*.

(A cautionary note: while most linguists use the terms 'regressive' and 'progressive' as described here, more than a few use them exactly the other way round. I therefore advise you to avoid the use of these terms altogether: the terms 'anticipatory' and 'perseverative' are unambiguous and should be preferred.)

It is possible for assimilation to operate in both directions at the same time, and here we speak of mutual assimilation. For example, the Basque word for 'blind' is *itsu* in most dialects, but the Zuberoan dialect has *ütsü*, where <ü> represents a front rounded vowel. Here the vowel [i] has assimilated in rounding to the following [u], and that [u] has itself been assimilated in frontness to the preceding [i].

Any assimilation can therefore be classified as *partial* or *total*, as *contact* or *distant*, and as *anticipatory* (right-to-left), *perseverative* (left-to-right), or *mutual* (both directions at once). All possible combinations are found, though some are commoner than others. Thus, when the word *orangutan* is pronounced (as it often is) *orangutang*, we have an instance of distant total perseverative assimilation. The combination of Welsh *yn* 'in' with *Cymru* 'Wales' yields *yng Nghymru*, where the [n] of the preposition becomes [ŋ] before the velar plosive and the [k] of the noun becomes a *voiceless* velar nasal [ŋ̊] after the preceding nasal: an instance of partial contact mutual assimilation.

Specialists in particular languages sometimes give distinctive names to particular types of assimilation which are important in those languages. For example, the type of anticipatory vowel assimilation shown in the example of German *Gast/Gäste* above is very important in the Germanic languages, and it is called **umlaut** by specialists in Germanic. As far as possible, I'll try to avoid using such additional terms.

The opposite of assimilation is **dissimilation**: making sounds more different than they were before. Given what I have said about the naturalness of assimilation, you might wonder why dissimilation should ever occur at all. The explanation lies in what we might call the 'tongue-twister effect'. One reason why a tongue-twister is hard to say is that our speech organs can get weary of making the same sound (or very similar sounds) repeatedly. This effect occasionally shows up in ordinary speech. For example, the Latin word *arbor* 'tree' has become *árbol* in Spanish (another modern form of Latin), in which the second of the two [r] sounds has been dissimilated to an [l]. On the other hand, Italian *colonello* 'colonel' appears in Spanish as *coronelo*: this time the first of the two [l] sounds has been dissimilated to [r]. (Note that English, bizarrely, uses the Italian-type spelling but the Spanish-type pronunciation.) Dissimilation of liquid consonants is particularly common, but other types occur. Latin *anima* 'soul' has been taken into Basque as *arima*, with dissimilation of the first of the two nasals, and in Afrikaans, a distinctive offshoot of Dutch, Dutch [sxo:n] 'clean' has become [sko:n], in which the second of two fricatives has been dissimilated to a plosive. As you might expect, dissimilation is far less common than assimilation.

Certain changes can be equally regarded as assimilations and dissimilations, such as the change of Basque *ingiru* 'vicinity' (a loan from Latin *in gyru* 'around') into *inguru* (now the more widespread form), in which the medial [i] can be regarded either as dissimilating from the preceding [i] or as assimilating to the following [u].

3.3 *Lenition and fortition*

Another major class of changes is represented by **lenition**, or **weakening**, which affects only consonants. Consonants can be classified as stronger or weaker on several different scales; the symbol '>' here means 'is stronger than':

1. geminate > simplex
2. stop > fricative > approximant
3. stop > liquid
4. oral stop > glottal stop
5. non-nasal > nasal
6. voiceless > voiced

Each of these scales has a clear phonetic basis: the first four all reflect differing degrees of obstruction of the airflow in the mouth; the fifth reflects differing degrees of obstruction of the airflow through the nasal cavity; the last reflects differing degrees of distance from a vowel and often also differing degrees of tension in the speech organs. A 'weaker' consonant is thus one which involves less articulatory effort than a corresponding 'stronger' one, or which is generally less 'consonantal' and more 'vocalic'.

Naturally, speakers, being human, prefer to make less effort rather than more, and there is an understandable tendency for consonants to shift from left to right along one or another of these scales; this is what we call 'lenition'. Lenition processes are pervasive, but they occur above all between vowels. The passage from a vowel to a consonant and then back to a vowel again typically involves a great deal of movement of the speech organs, and leniting the consonant generally has the effect of reducing that movement. In effect, the consonant becomes more 'vowel-like', and this type of lenition can therefore be regarded as a kind of assimilation. Here are some examples involving my six scales; the symbol '>' this time means 'develops into':

1. Latin *cuppa* 'cup' > Spanish *copa* 'wine glass'
   Latin *gutta* 'drop' > Spanish *gota*
   Latin *siccu* 'dry' > Spanish *seco*
   Latin *flamma* 'flame' > Spanish *llama*

   This type of lenition is, for obvious reasons, called **degemination**.

2. Latin *habebat* 'he had' > Italian *aveva*
   Latin *faba* 'bean' > Italian *fava*

   The Italian examples illustrate a type of lenition called **spirantization** (conversion to a fricative; *spirant* is an old synonym for *fricative*, and *fricativization*, while used occasionally, is regarded by most linguists as clumsy and ugly).

3. English *wa*[t]*er* > General American *wa*[ɾ]*er*

   This is the well-known '*t*-tapping' of American English, in which /t/ and /d/ between vowels develop into the tap [ɾ], and hence the distinctive American pronunciation of words like *city*, *Betty*, *metal*, *Italy*, *writer*, *rider*, *medal*, and *body*. Some accents in Canada, England,

Northern Ireland, Australia, and New Zealand show the same phenomenon.

4. English *wa*[t]*er* > London, Glasgow, *etc. wa*[ʔ]*er*

And this is the equally well-known 'glottalization' of intervocalic /t/ in certain urban accents of Britain, and hence the distinctive Cockney and Glaswegian pronunciation of words like *little, bottle, better, city,* and *bottom.*

The development of an oral stop into a glottal stop is called **debuccalization**, a fancy Latinate word which just means 'removal of activity from the mouth'. You can see why.

5. Latin *sabanu* 'covering' > pre-Basque **zabanu* > Basque *zamau* 'tablecloth'

(The Basque word is borrowed from Latin.) This is the rarest of my six types in intervocalic position, and the example cited can readily be interpreted as an instance of assimilation of the plosive to the following nasal.

This is one type of **nasalization**, a change in which the velum, formerly raised (closed) during a certain segment, comes to be lowered (opened). Later we will be seeing other examples of nasalization.

6. Latin *strata* 'road' > Italian *strada*
   Latin *lacu* 'lake' > Italian *lago*

This type of lenition is called **voicing**, for obvious reasons.

It is possible for lenition to travel more than one notch to the right and to involve more than one of my six scales. Consider some examples of the development of Spanish from its Latin ancestor:

- Latin *cūpa* 'barrel' > Spanish *cuba* [kuβa] 'wine vat'
- Latin *catēna* 'chain' > Spanish *cadena* [kaðena]
- Latin *sēcūru* 'sure' > Spanish *seguro* [seɣuro]

Between vowels, the voiceless plosives of Latin have both become voiced (scale 6) and lenited all the way to approximants (scale 2).

Of course, it is possible for a lenition to continue to the point at which the affected segment disappears entirely, and several of my scales, especially (2), might reasonably have 'zero' added at the right-hand end. Such disappearance is called **loss** or **deletion**; here are some examples:

- Old English *hēafod* > English *head*
- Latin *catēna* 'chain' > pre-Basque **katena* > Basque *katea*
- Latin *regāle* 'royal' > Spanish *real*
- Latin *sedēre* 'sit' > Spanish *ser* 'be'

Lenition and loss are by no means confined to intervocalic position, though they are particularly common there. Here are a few examples in other positions. (Proto-Indo-European (PIE) is the remote ancestor of most European languages.) Word-initially:

- pre-Japanese *pana* 'flower' > Japanese *hana*
- PIE *kel-* > English *hill*
- PIE *porko-* 'pig' > Irish *orc*
- PIE *sweks* 'six' > Ancient Greek *hex*

Word-finally:

- pre-Turkish *dag* 'mountain' > *daɣ* > Turkish *dağ* [da:]
- Spanish *mismos* 'same' (plural) > dialectal Spanish *mi*[h]*mo*[h]
- Latin *nos* 'we', *vos* 'you' > Italian *noi*, *voi*

Note in particular the frequency with which other voiceless consonants develop into [h]. The sound [h] may be regarded as a kind of 'minimal' consonant, the last faint trace of anything that can be regarded as a consonant at all. Phonetically, of course, [h] is nothing but a voiceless vowel, involving an absolute minimum of articulatory effort. Even a very slight further reduction in that effort will cause the articulation to disappear altogether, and hence [h] is typically a weak and unstable consonant, and very frequently it does disappear.

Latin had an [h] in very many words, such as *habēre* 'have', *homō* 'human being', *honor* 'honour', *hōra* 'hour', *hortus* 'garden', *nihil* 'nothing', and *mihi* 'to me', but the consonant was completely lost at an early stage, and not one of these [h]s survives in any of the modern forms of Latin (it is true that <h> is sometimes still written today, as in Spanish *honor* and *hora* and French *homme* 'man', but this is purely for old times' sake: these [h]s have been pronounced by no one for 2000 years). Long after this loss of [h], both French and Spanish acquired a new [h]. Between the fifth and eighth centuries, French borrowed a number of Germanic words with [h], such as *hache* 'axe', *houx* 'holly', *hibou* 'owl', and *haie* 'hedge', and [h] thus rejoined the French phonological system, but by the sixteenth century these new instances of [h] were already disappearing, and, in spite of the bitter complaints of purists about '*h*-dropping', the new [h]s had disappeared by the eighteenth century. Spanish acquired some new instances of [h] from the lenition of [f]: hence Latin *fīcu* 'fig' became *higo*, *fīliu* ' son' became *hijo*, *farīna* 'flour' became *harina*, and *facere* 'do' became *hacer*, and all these words were then pronounced with [h]. As in French, these new [h]s have more recently been lost, and modern Spanish again generally lacks [h], except in a few regional varieties which have retained [h] in this last group of words. However, in many varieties of Spanish spoken in the south of Spain and in Latin America, the Spanish velar fricative [x], as in *general* 'general' [x]*eneral*, *juego* 'play, game' [x]*uego*, and *hijo* 'son' *hi*[x]*o*, has been lenited to [h], thus producing yet a third generation of [h]s in the language; it remains to be seen whether these new [h]s will also in turn disappear.

English, of course, has been losing [h]s for centuries. The Old English [h]s in words like *hnutu* 'nut' and *hlūd* 'loud' were lost centuries ago, and the [h] of *hit* 'it' has disappeared more recently. The [h]s in words like *whine* ([hw]*ine*) and *where* ([hw]*ere*) have totally disappeared from England and are now rapidly disappearing from American speech, and *whine* and *where* are thus becoming homophonous with *wine* and *wear*. Indeed, the vast majority of speakers in England have now lost *all* their [h]s, and hence make no difference between *hair* and *air*, or between *harm* and *arm*. Just as in sixteenth-century France, purists in England constantly decry this 'sloppy' *h*-dropping, but there is every reason to suppose that [h] is now on the way out of English, at least in England, and perhaps eventually in the rest of the English-speaking world.

Instances of [h] in native English words generally derive from the lenition of an earlier *[k]: such words as *head, heart, help, hill*, and *he* all began with [k] in a remote ancestral form of English, but this [k] was lenited first to [x] and then to [h], and the modern lenition of [h] to zero merely completes a process of lenition stretching over several thousand years. You would doubtless be startled to hear somebody pronounce words like *key, kill, like*, or *brick* with [h] or zero in place of [k], but lenition usually works more slowly than that, and there is no guarantee that the [k]s in modern English words will not also be ultimately lenited into oblivion. Indeed, the first faint signs of this have perhaps already appeared. In the English city of Liverpool, word-initial [k] has become an affricate [kx], and [k] in other positions has been lenited to the fricative [x]. Thus Liverpool speakers famously pronounce *key* as [kx]*ey*, *kill* as [kx]*ill*, *like* as *li*[x], and *brick* as *bri*[x]. We may here be witnessing the very first stages of a lenition process which, during the next thousand years or so, will once again remove the consonant [k] from the language.

Given that lenition is so natural and so frequent (and seemingly also so remorseless), you might begin to wonder why our languages have any consonants left at all. But, of course, lenition cannot be allowed to ravage our consonant systems unchecked: we have to communicate, and we would doubtless find it very difficult to communicate with nothing but vowels. Lenition must, therefore, be opposed by other processes which tend to maintain or restore consonants.

One of these is, obviously, borrowing. Centuries ago, Basque lost *all* instances of intervocalic [n], but since then it has borrowed hundreds of words from neighbouring languages with intervocalic [n], thus to some extent making good the loss. In Italian, intervocalic [b] was generally lenited to [v] centuries ago, but borrowing has likewise restored intervocalic [b] in this language. Almost all instances of ancestral [k] in English were long ago lenited to [x] and then to [h] or zero, but new instances of [k] were introduced by the devoicing of [g], and later also by the introduction of loan words like *sky, kilt*, and *skin* from Old Norse, *carry, carrot*, and *picture* from Norman French, *kinetic* from Greek, *actor* from Latin, and *kayak* from Eskimo; all this has helped to restore the frequency of [k] in English.

In the Basque case, intervocalic [n] was also restored to some extent by a further lenition. Pre-Basque had words with geminate [nn] between vowels;

after intervocalic [n] had been lost, these instances of [nn] were then lenited to [n] (scale 1), as in the case of *gonna* > *gona* 'skirt'.

There are various other processes, both phonological and morphological, which tend to oppose the effects of lenition, and we will be looking at some of them in this chapter and the next two. The most obvious one, however, is **fortition**, or **strengthening**: the evolution of a consonant from right to left on one of my scales.

Fortition is much less frequent than lenition, for the phonetic reasons described above, but it is by no means rare. Here are a few examples illustrating fortition on my six scales:

1. Latin *aqua* 'water' [akwa] > Italian *acqua* [akkwa]
   Latin *sapiat* 'he knows' > Italian *sappia*

   This type of fortition is **gemination.**

2. Latin *Maiu* 'May' [maju] > Italian *maggio* [maddʒo]
   Old Norse *þar* 'there' [θar] > Swedish *där*

3. pre-Basque *erur* 'snow' > western Basque *edur*

4. No examples found. The development of glottal stop into an oral stop is, at best, extremely rare.

5. Basque *musti* 'moist' (borrowed from Occitan, a language of southern France) > *busti* (in most dialects)

   This is **denasalization**.

6. Russian *xl'eb* 'bread' > *xl'e*[p]
   Russian *sad* 'garden' > *sa*[t]
   Russian *drug* 'friend' > *dru*[k]

   Such **devoicing** of consonants at the end of a word is extremely common in the languages of the world; it may perhaps be regarded as a kind of assimilation to the following silence.

3.4 *Addition and removal of phonetic features*

As we have seen, most types of phonological change involve the redistribution of phonetic features on segments: a feature is added to a segment or removed from a segment, or it spreads from one segment to another. Certain particular types of such feature rearrangement are so common that they are given individual names; the majority of these can be regarded as varieties either of assimilation or of lenition.

If you have done some phonetics, you will know that the /k/ of English *key* is articulated much farther forward in the mouth than the /k/ of *car*: because of the following palatal vowel /i/ in *key*, the closure for the /k/ is made closer to the palate, in order to ease the transition, as I explained at the beginning of this chapter. In this case, the **palatalization** of /k/ involves only a minor articulatory adjustment, but palatalization can, and often does, go much further than this.

In an ancestral form of English, the words *cheese, child,* and *chin* were all pronounced with an initial [k] (compare the German words *Käse* 'cheese', *Kind* 'child', and *Kinn* 'chin', which preserve this ancestral sound), and the word *church* was pronounced with two [k]-sounds (compare Scottish *kirk,* borrowed from Old Norse). In these cases, however, the palatalization of the [k] before a following front vowel (the word for 'church' anciently had an [e] on the end: Old English *cyrice*) went so far that the closure moved all the way to the front of the palate, resulting in the palato-alveolar [tʃ] which we now use in these words.

Less obvious is the phonetic motivation for **velarization**, in which the back of the tongue comes to be raised towards the velum during an articulation. In English, there has for centuries been a tendency to velarize the lateral [l] in syllable-final position. Unless you come from Wales, Ireland, or the Caribbean, you should be able to notice that the lateral in words like *ball, feel, field,* and *milk* is conspicuously 'dark' (velarized). (In fact, if you come from the Scottish lowlands or North America, you will probably find that *all* your laterals are velarized.) Centuries ago, this velarization of [l], in certain positions, went so far that the consonant lost its alveolar articulation altogether and became a velar glide, more or less a [w]. This is the reason for spellings like *walk, talk, yolk,* and *folk*: the earlier [l] was velarized all the way to [w], and since then the [w] has more or less merged into the preceding vowel. (The same thing happened in *calm* and *palm,* but here many speakers have restored the [l] under the influence of the spelling.) More recently, this process has been continuing: in the south-east of England *all* syllable-final [l]s have been reduced to [w], and a speaker from this area pronounces *ball* as *ba*[w], *feel* as *fee*[w], *field* as *fie*[w]*d,* and *milk* as *mi*[w]*k.* Standard Polish has done the same thing to dark [l]s in all positions. The Polish consonant spelled <ł> was formerly a dark [l] but is now pronounced [w], so that *długo* 'for a long time' is [dwugo], and the city-name *Łódź* sounds something like English *woods.*

Lowering of the velum during an articulation is **nasalization**, and this process chiefly affects vowels. Nasalization is most often induced by the presence of a neighbouring nasal consonant, especially a following one: the velum is lowered a little too 'early', and the preceding vowel acquires a nasal character. Many English-speakers, particularly in North America, have conspicuous nasalization of vowels before a nasal consonant, in words like *can't, don't,* and *punt,* and it takes only a slight delay in making the alveolar closure for the [n] to disappear altogether. Hence many Americans pronounce these words as [kæ̃t], [dõũt], and [pʌ̃t], with the nasalization of the vowel solely responsible for distinguishing these words from *cat* [kæt], *dote* [dout], and *putt* [pʌt].

Exactly the same process happened on a massive scale in the history of French: vowels were nasalized before syllable-final [n] or [m], and then the nasal consonant was simply lost. This is the origin of the modern French pronunciations like *pain* 'bread' [pɛ̃], *faim* 'hunger' [fɛ̃], *langue* 'tongue' [lɑ̃:g], and *bon* 'good' [bɔ̃].

In this last case, the end result was that two segments, an oral vowel and a nasal consonant, combined into a single segment, a nasal vowel. Effectively, the redistribution of features was so great as to change the number of segments in a word, leading to results which almost belong to the next section. Such a combination of two segments into one is called **fusion**. Fusion is very common in English with sequences like /tj/, /dj/ and /sj/. Do you pronounce *nature* as *na*[tj]*ure*, with a [t] followed by a yod, or as *na*[tʃ]*ure*, with a single segment, an affricate? Do you say *e*[dj]*ucation* or *e*[dʒ]*ucation*? And is *tissue* for you *ti*[sj]*ue* or *ti*[ʃ]*ue*? Does *can't you* come out as *can'*[tj]*ou* or *can*[tʃ]*ou*? The two-segment pronunciation was formerly usual for all of these, but fusion is now probably universal in *nature*, and it is normal for most (not all) speakers in *education* and *tissue*. With *can't you*, even a single speaker may sometimes use one and sometimes the other. In Czech, the former sequence [rj], with a trilled [r], has fused into the single consonant spelled <ř>, as in the name of the composer *Dvořák*: the famous fricative trill of Czech. In Swedish, the post-alveolar [r] has undergone fusion with a following dental or alveolar consonant, producing a single retroflex consonant, so that *fart* 'speed' is pronounced [fɑ:ʈ], *korn* 'grain' is pronounced [kʊ:ɳ], and *kors* 'cross' is pronounced [kʊʂ]. In western Basque, the word *joan* 'go', pronounced [xwan], has become in some regions [fan]: the voiceless fricative [x] has fused with the following labial [w] to produce the voiceless labial fricative [f].

The opposite of fusion is **unpacking**, also called **segmentalization**. Here the phonetic features formerly present in a single segment are split into a sequence of two segments. Unpacking is less common than fusion, but not rare. Basque *baño* 'than' and *ollo* 'hen', with a palatal nasal and a palatal lateral respectively, have become in eastern varieties *baino* [bajno] and *oilo* [ojlo], in which the palatal element has been removed from the nasal or lateral and converted into a distinct preceding segment, a palatal glide. Something similar is happening in contemporary French, but in the other direction. The French palatal nasal [ɲ], spelled <gn>, as in *gnon* '(a) blow' and *mignon* 'cute', has for many speakers been unpacked into the sequence [nj], producing [njɔ̃] and [minjɔ̃]. Unpacking is frequent when words are borrowed: for example, English-speakers, unable to reproduce the palatal nasal of Spanish *cañón*, have borrowed the word as *canyon*, with an alveolar nasal followed by a palatal glide; likewise unable to produce the front rounded vowel [y] of French *musique*, we have borrowed it as *music*, in which the front rounded vowel is unpacked into a front glide followed by a back rounded vowel. English-speakers learning Spanish or French often do the same things in trying to pronounce the unfamiliar words of those languages, producing a conspicuous English accent.

Finally, before leaving this section, I shall briefly note that there exist a few other labels for specific types of change which you may occasionally encounter, such as **affrication** (conversion of another sound into an affricate), **labialization** (addition of lip-rounding or lip-compression to a segment), **retroflexion** (conversion of another sound into a retroflex), **dentalization** (conversion of another sound into a dental), **glottalization** (addition of a glottal closure to a sound, or sometimes the conversion of another sound into a glottal stop), **rhotacism** (conversion of another sound into [r]), and **lambdacism** (conversion of another sound into [l]). The last two of these derive from the names of the Greek letters equivalent to R and L, and the others are generally self-evident if you know some phonetics. You will find examples of some of these in the exercises.

3.5 *Vowels and syllable structure*

Unlike consonants, vowels are produced without an obstruction of the airstream, and hence they have no precisely defined place of articulation. Understandably, then, vowels tend to be somewhat less stable over time than consonants in most languages – though it is reported that, in Pacific languages, vowels have historically been more stable than consonants.

The most frequent descriptive terms applied to changes in vowels are derived from phonetics in a very straightforward way. Here are these terms with examples:

- **raising**: Basque *astoa* 'the donkey' > *astua* in many varieties
- **lowering**: pre-French *[vī] 'wine' > French *vin* [vẽ]
- **fronting**: Basque *dut* 'I have it' > Zuberoan *düt* [dyt]
- **backing**: pre-Old English **dægas* 'days' > Old English *dagas*
- **rounding**: pre-Old Norse **allum* 'all' (dative pl.) > Old Norse *ollum*
- **unrounding**: Old English *bysig* [byzij] > English *busy* [bɪzi]
- **centralization**: Latin *campu* 'field' > Romanian *cîmp* [kɨmp]
- **lengthening** (also called **tensing**): Old English *c*[i]*ld* 'child' > Middle English *ch*[i:]*ld*
- **shortening** (also called **laxing**): Old English *fi:fta* 'fifth' > English *fifth*
- **diphthongization**: Latin *bonu* 'good', *bene* 'well' > Spanish *bueno*, *bien*
- **monophthongization**: Old French *eux* 'them' [ew], *aube* 'dawn' [awb] > French [ø], [o:b]

It is possible for more than one of these processes to affect the same vowel. Latin *demandare* 'ask' and *limaca* 'slug' give Italian *domandare* and *lumaca*, in which the first vowel has been both backed and rounded; Latin *ebriacu* 'drunk' yields Italian *ubriaco*, in which the first vowel has been backed, rounded, and raised; Latin *rota* 'wheel' gives Italian *ruota* [rwɔːta], in which the first vowel has been both diphthongized and lengthened.

In many cases it is very difficult to see any particular phonetic motivation for such changes: it just looks as though vowels like to move around. More mysteriously still, vowels are far more stable in some languages than in others. On the one hand, the vowels of Basque and of Italian appear not to have changed significantly for 1500 years at least. On the other hand, during that same period the vowels of English and of French have changed repeatedly and dramatically, and in many parts of the world the English vowels are changing rapidly at this very moment. A New York City pronunciation of *bad* can sound just like *beard*: a New Yorker's version of *Gee, that's too bad* often sounds to everybody else something like *Chee, des too beard*. In the prestigious accent of England called *Received Pronunciation*, or *RP*, the vowels of *cat* and *cut* have been moving so close together that they are now nearly indistinguishable. The linguist David Crystal has recently reported a striking instance of misunderstanding between two RP speakers resulting from this change. A High Court judge apologized to the lawyers in his court for a delay: it seemed he had left a crucial document at his weekend cottage, and would have to go back down there to fetch it. One of the barristers present suggested helpfully, 'Fax it up, m'lud.' The judge replied, 'Yes, I'm afraid it does, rather.'

In some cases, however, we can see a clear motivation for changes in vowels. One of these is the effect of **stress**. The additional energy involved in stressing a syllable may cause its vowel to become longer, tenser, more peripheral, sometimes even higher; stress may also tend to diphthongize a vowel. An unstressed vowel, in contrast, may become shorter and more central. In languages with strong stress, like English and Russian, these effects are very conspicuous. Compare the qualities of the stressed and unstressed vowels in a set of words like *photograph*, *photography*, and *photographic*. As is usual in English, most of the unstressed vowels lose the distinctive phonetic characteristics which they have when stressed and just appear as the indistinct central vowel schwa [ə]. Such conversion to schwa is a very common type of vowel **reduction**: reduction is the removal of some or all of the phonetic characteristics that distinguish one vowel from another. Reduction can even go as far as total loss of the vowel, as illustrated in the next section.

Another factor in vowel change is **syllable structure**. Languages seem universally to prefer certain types of syllables, with CV being the most frequent, or 'unmarked', syllable structure, followed by CVC. Very commonly also, we observe a tendency for a vowel in an open syllable (one with no final consonant) to be long and for one in a closed syllable (ending in a consonant) to be short: note the difference in the length of the vowel /iː/ in *see* and *seat*. There is a particular tendency for a vowel to be short if it is followed by a consonant cluster: note that the long vowel of Old English *fiːf* 'five' was shortened before the cluster in *fifth*, and that the short vowel of *cild* 'child' was lengthened in the singular but not in the plural *children* (the original long vowel [i:] has been further diphthongized to [ai], thereby exaggerating the earlier length distinction).

Particularly unstable are vowels in **hiatus**: two consecutive vowels with no intervening consonant. Such sequences are apparently uncomfortable, and languages employ a variety of strategies for eliminating the hiatus. Most of these strategies can be illustrated from Basque. The Basque definite article is *-a*, which is suffixed to a preceding noun. If that noun ends in a vowel, a hiatus is produced, and the various dialects of Basque have resolved the hiatus in several different ways.

Consider *asto* 'donkey' and *lore* 'flower'. The definite forms of these are *astoa* 'the donkey' and *lorea* 'the flower' in the standard orthography. Many eastern dialects have resolved the hiatus by converting these forms into *ast*[w]*a* and *lor*[j]*a*. We call this **glide-formation**: one of the vowels (usually the higher one) is converted into a non-syllabic glide. Western dialects, however, do something different: they have *ast*[u]*a* and *lor*[i]*a*, in which the first vowel has merely undergone raising, thereby making it as different as possible from the adjacent vowel.

Now consider *zaldi* 'horse' and *buru* 'head', with definite forms *zaldia* and *burua*. Eastern varieties have left these unchanged, but western varieties have this time eliminated the hiatus in a rather different manner: they have *zaldi*[j]*a* and *buru*[w]*a*, in which glides have simply been inserted between the adjacent vowels, thus producing a CV structure. This is **glide-insertion**, and you can see that the glide matches the preceding high vowel in quality. In the case of *zaldia*, many western varieties have gone further: they have *zaldi*[ɟ]*e*, *zaldi*[ʒ]*e* or even *zaldi*[ʃ]*a*, in which the glide has been converted to a plosive or a fricative; this is called **glide-strengthening**, and it is a kind of fortition (some of these have also raised the final vowel).

Finally, consider *neska* 'girl'. The expected definite form would be **neskaa*, but this is found nowhere. Most varieties have the definite form *neska*, in which the two identical vowels have simply combined into one, in a process called **coalescence**. Some western varieties, however, have instead either *nesk*[e]*a* or *nesk*[i]*a*, in which the first vowel has been raised.

A particularly striking process is **compensatory lengthening**, in which a vowel is lengthened at the same time that another segment is lost from the word, thereby roughly preserving the total time required to pronounce the word. It is thought that the ancestral form of English *five* was something like **finf*, with a short vowel (compare German *fünf*), but that the [n] was lost early, and the preceding vowel was lengthened to [i:] in compensation. Old French *beste* 'beast', *feste* 'festival', and *maistre* 'master' were all pronounced with [ɛs], but syllable-final [s] was lost, and the vowel underwent compensatory lengthening, producing modern French *bête* [bɛ:t], *fête* [fɛ:t], and *maître* [mɛ:tr]. The diacritic in the spelling marks the vowel as long, but there is a recent tendency to shorten these long vowels, making *maître*, for example, homophonous with *mettre* 'put', which has always had a short vowel, and the French Academy has recently proposed dropping the length mark from the French spelling system.

Other, rather different, cases of compensatory lengthening are represented by the change of pre-Hindi *satt* 'seven' into Hindi *sa:t* and by the change of Proto-Slavic *bogŭ* 'God' into early Serbo-Croatian *bo:g*.

Occasionally we find consonantal changes which also operate in such a way as to maintain a preferred syllable structure and avoid hiatus. A good example occurs in the *non-rhotic* accents of English, in which the historical /r/ has been lost everywhere except before a vowel, so that *far* and *dark* are pronounced /fɑ:/ and /dɑ:k/. The /r/ is retained before a vowel, and so *far away* is realized as /fɑ:rəweɪ/, thereby avoiding hiatus. Many speakers with non-rhotic accents have extended this **linking r** to cases in which no /r/ was historically present, producing the well-known **intrusive r** of much of England and New England: *Cuba*[r] *and China, the idea*[r] *is, I saw*[r] *it, this bra*[r] *is made of . . . , awe*[r]-*inspiring*, and sometimes also *draw*[r]*ing* and *withdraw*[r]*al*. I have even heard the name of the squash player *Lisa Opie* pronounced as *Lisa Ropie*.

3.6   *Whole-segment processes*

Certain phonological changes are somewhat unusual in that they involve, not just changes in the nature of segments, but a change in the number or ordering of segments, and these we call **whole-segment processes**.

We have already seen instances of deletion as the end result of lenition, but not all deletions are like that: it is possible for a segment simply to disappear at one go. For example, the words *knee*, *knot*, and *knife* were once pronounced, as the spelling still suggests, with an initial cluster /kn-/. Several centuries ago, however, people simply dropped the /k/, with no lenition via [x] and [h]. The same thing has happened to a whole range of final consonants in French. French words like *lit* 'bed' /li/, *gros* 'big' /gro/, *soûl* 'drunk' /su/, *murs* 'walls' /myr/, *part* 'leaves' (verb) /par/, and *aimer* 'love' /ɛme/ were all formerly pronounced with the final consonants that are still there in the spelling, but all these consonants were simply dropped. Loss of an initial segment, as in *knee*, is called **aphaeresis** (less commonly **aphesis**), while loss of a final segment, as in French *lit*, is **apocope**.

Aphaeresis and apocope may also apply to vowels, and in fact some linguists apply these two terms *only* to the loss of vowels, but there seems little point in such a restriction. The word *especial* is now usually reduced to *special*, and *opossum* is commonly reduced in many areas to *possum*, both showing aphaeresis, and the words *make* and *time*, as the spelling suggests, once had a final vowel which has undergone apocope.

Word-medially, consonants are rarely lost abruptly except in the simplification of clusters, as illustrated by the loss of the first /d/ in *Wednesday*. Much more frequent is **syncope**: the loss of a medial vowel. English words like *chocolate* and *camera* have now lost the vowel in the second syllable for nearly all speakers, and many speakers in England have further lost the first vowel in words like *police* and *correct*, the second vowel in words like *medicine* and *battery*, and the third vowel in words like *dictionary*. Such syncope was pervasive in late Latin: compare Latin *saeculu* and Spanish *siglo* 'century', Latin *littera* and Spanish *letra* 'letter', Latin *dominicu* and Spanish *domingo* 'Sunday', Latin *paupere* and Spanish *pobre* 'poor', Latin *asinu* and Spanish *asno* 'donkey'.

It is also possible for entire new segments to be added to words, and again we have a collection of specific terms for such addition (well, I did warn you about the terms). Adding a segment at the beginning of a word is **prothesis**, and only vowels are commonly added in this position. In late Latin, the vowel /e/ was added before any word-initial cluster beginning with /s/, and we can still see the result in Spanish: Latin *spatha* 'sword' > Spanish *espada*; *statu* > *estado* 'state'; *scala* > *escala* 'ladder'; *smeralda* > *esmeralda* 'emerald'. Such prothesis is still regularly applied to loan words in Spanish today, producing results like *esnob* 'snob', *eslálom* 'slalom', *estricnina* 'strychnine', and *Estrasburgo* 'Strasbourg'. In Basque, in which no word can begin with an /r/, loan words have for 2000 years been borrowed with a prothetic vowel, ranging from *arrosa* 'rose' and *Erroma* 'Rome', borrowed from Latin *rosa* and *Roma*, down to such recent loans as *erradio* 'radium', *errubi* 'ruby', and *Errusia* 'Russia'.

The addition of a segment to the end of a word is occasionally called **paragoge**, but only consonants are commonly added in this position, and usually only after another consonant, and most linguists prefer to call this **excrescence**. Middle English *amonges*, *amiddes*, and *betwix* have acquired an excrescent /t/, producing *amongst*, *amidst*, and *betwixt*. A very odd example is the development of *no* into colloquial *nope*, presumably from our habit of closing our mouths after uttering this word. Final excrescence is not common.

When it comes to adding segments to the middle of a word, our terminology is in something of a muddle. This is widely called **epenthesis**, but some people would apply this term only to the insertion of a vowel between consonants, and exactly such vowel addition is also called both **anaptyxis** and **svarabhakti** (this last from Sanskrit, the classical language of India). (Moreover, some people use 'epenthesis' more broadly for *any* addition of a segment in any position.) The insertion of a consonant between consonants is once again called **excrescence**. Anaptyxis happens sporadically in English: you may have heard *athlete* pronounced as *athalete*, or *film* pronounced as *fillum* – not to mention the distinctive Cockney pronunciation of *Henry* as *Ennery*. These have not so far become standard English. In contrast, the early Latin words *faclis* 'easy' and *poclum* 'goblet' appear in standard classical Latin as *facilis* and *poculum*, with anaptyctic vowels matching the following vowels in quality. Anaptyxis may also affect loan words: Arabic *waqt* 'time' and *ism* 'name', with final clusters not permitted in Turkish, were borrowed into Turkish as *vakit* and *isim*. All these examples have the effect of reducing consonant clusters and of adjusting the forms of words towards the seemingly universally preferred CV structure.

Consonantal epenthesis is not rare in the history of English. Most of us pronounce *prince* just like *prints*, with a /t/ between the /n/ and the /s/. Once again, this is phonetically understandable: moving from [n] to [s] requires changes in the position of the vocal folds, the velum and the tongue, and it's difficult to do all these simultaneously, so we leave the tongue movement for last, producing an automatic [t] as a result. Earlier examples in the same vein include the change of Old English *æmtig* and *thymel* to modern *empty* and *thimble*, and of Middle English *nemel* and *thuner* to *nimble* and *thunder*.

Table 3.1 sums up this terminology. A rather unusual type of whole-segment process is **metathesis**: changing the order of segments in a word. This is not common in English, but a good example is Old English *wæps*, which has become *wasp* in modern English, with metathesis of the last two consonants (in fact, some regional varieties have *wops* today). Since the Old English period, speakers have been vacillating between *ask* and *aks*; the first has finally won out, but again some regional varieties have *aks* (often spelled *ax*, as in *He axed me a question*). Metathesis is rather frequent in the history of Spanish. The Latin words *crepare*, *parabola*, *miraculu*, *periculu*, and *crocodilu* should, by the regular developments, have yielded Spanish **crebar* 'break', **parabla* 'word', **miraglo* 'miracle', **periglo* 'danger', and **crocodilo* 'crocodile', but the actual forms are *quebrar*, *palabra*, *milagro*, *peligro*, and *cocodrilo*, all showing metathesis. (In some cases two consonants have exchanged places; in others, one consonant has just moved to a different position.)

More dramatic still is **haplology**, in which one of two consecutive identical or similar syllables is lost. The combination of the Latin stem *nutri-* 'give milk to' with the female agent suffix *-trix* should have yielded **nutritrix*, but the actual form is *nutrix* 'wet-nurse', in which one of the two *-tri* sequences is dropped. Similarly, the combination of Basque *sagar* 'apple' with *ardo* 'wine' should give **sagar-ardo*, but the word is *sagardo* 'cider', also with haplology,

Table 3.1 Summary of whole-segment processes

	Initially	Medially	Finally
Addition	prothesis	epenthesis [anaptyxis, svarabhakti, excrescence]	paragoge [excrescence]
Removal	aphaeresis	syncope	apocope

and Basque *maite* 'beloved' plus *-tasun* '-ness' should give **maitatasun*, but the result is *maitasun* 'love'. In English, the regular adverbs **gentle-ly* and **simple-ly* are reduced by haplology to *gently* and *simply*.

The opposite of haplology, the repetition of a syllable, does occur and is called *reduplication*, but this is strictly a morphological process, and not a phonological one, and hence is not treated here.

3.7 *The regularity issue: a first look*

Here I shall introduce for the first time an issue which will be a recurrent theme in this book: is phonological change *regular* or not? That is, when a change in pronunciation is introduced into a language, does it apply to all words of a relevant form, or only to some of them? This question has been a central issue in historical linguistics for well over a hundred years, and the answer is neither obvious nor simple.

Certain changes are conspicuously not regular at all, such as metathesis. Latin *miraculu* 'miracle' has undergone metathesis in producing Spanish *milagro*, but most Latin words underwent no metathesis. Metathesis is almost always a **sporadic change**: a change that happens once in a while to this word or that, in a seemingly arbitrary manner, and no more.

But most changes do not appear to be like this. If you have some experience of the vernacular speech of London, you will have noticed that the consonant /t/, at the beginning of a word, is pronounced as an affricate [t^s]. And this happens with every single word beginning with /t/ followed by a vowel: *time*, *take*, *two*, *tell*, *tooth*, and so on are all pronounced with [t^s]. In this case, it appears that the change of the historical [t^h] to [t^s] has been completely regular: it has applied to every relevant word.

Many of the other changes mentioned in the chapter appear to have been equally regular. The Latin geminates were invariably reduced to single consonants in the development of Spanish, as in *cuppa* > *copa* 'cup'; not a single geminate survived. American speakers who use a tapped /t/ between vowels do so in every single case (providing the second vowel is not stressed; such stress blocks the change, as in *attack*). Old Japanese /p/ has developed into modern /h/ in every single word containing it (except when it was geminated; this also blocked the change). The former Turkish /g/ has been lenited after a vowel in every relevant word in the language. All word-final obstruents in Russian have been devoiced, without exception. And so it goes: thousands and thousands of pronunciation changes have been identified in the histories of many hundreds of languages, and they almost always appear to be highly regular: they have applied to every relevant word.

But there are exceptions. Latin *strata* 'street' and *lacu* 'lake' have yielded Italian *strada* and *lago*, with voicing of the intervocalic consonant, and dozens of other words show the same voicing, but the majority of Italian words have not undergone such voicing: Latin *rota* 'wheel' and *ficu* 'fig' give Italian *ruota* and *fico*, and not **ruoda* and **figo*. This is a puzzle which has long vexed italianists, especially since in Spanish, another modern form of Latin, every single word has undergone this voicing: Spanish has *rueda* and *higo* for the last two words, and so on throughout the vocabulary.

It is, therefore, too much to claim that 'ordinary' sound changes (that is, those other than the purely sporadic ones like metathesis) are invariably regular, and that's all there is to it. It is only very recently that linguists have managed to learn enough about the mechanisms of language change to provide plausible explanations for why many changes are regular but others not, and these explanations will have to wait until much later in the book. For now, I shall merely adopt a policy as a basis for further discussion: sound change is normally regular, and the cases that are not regular are puzzles calling for an explanation. This policy has proved to be of great benefit in historical linguistics, and it will provide a firm foundation for our discussion in this book, in spite of the fact that it is not strictly true. By the time you have finished this book, you will understand both why it is not true and why it is none the less an excellent working hypothesis.

3.8 *Summary*

In this chapter we have surveyed phonological change from a syntagmatic point of view: that is, from the point of view of changes in the sequence of speech sounds making up the pronunciations of particular words, or occasionally sequences of words. We have seen that the majority of such changes can be understood in terms of the movements of the vocal organs during speech, and sometimes more particularly in terms of a tendency to reduce articulatory effort. We have learned a no doubt depressing number of technical terms which will allow us to label economically almost any sound change we are likely to encounter. Finally, we have had our first brush with the idea that a phonological change may be regular – that is, that it may apply without exception to every single word in the language of a relevant form. This idea you should keep at the back of your mind while reading the following chapters; I shall return to it at intervals.

Further reading

J. C. Wells (1982) is a comprehensive survey of the various accents of English, including an account of the changes which have occurred in the different regional varieties of English around the world and those which are happening now. A wealth of data on the changes occurring in English pronunciation today can be found in Labov (1994). The standard histories of English, French, German, Spanish, Italian, and Portuguese listed in the Further Reading in Chapter 1 all include detailed descriptions of the major changes in pronunciation which have occurred in those languages during the last 1500 or 2000 years. Some other textbooks of historical linguistics devote considerably more space to phonological change than I am doing here, notably Hock (1986) – though note that almost all of Hock's examples are taken from very ancient languages indeed, and you might prefer to read his several chapters in small chunks. Bloomfield (1933) is a classic textbook of general linguistics whose chapter on phonological change is still eminently readable.

Exercises

Note: If you are familiar with the standard notation for writing phonological rules, you may find it convenient in attempting these exercises to write out rules for the phonological changes you identify. Some of these exercises introduce topics which will be discussed in the next chapter.

Exercise 3.1

This exercise is designed merely to let you test your command of the technical terms introduced in the chapter. How would you label each of the following changes?

(a) pre-Icelandic *$bro[\theta]er$ > Old Icelandic $bro[\eth]er$ 'brother'

(b) pre-Greek *$g^w ous$ > Greek *bous* 'cow'

(c) Basque *bake* 'peace' > western Basque *pake*

(d) pre-Latin *$flo{:}ses$ > Latin $flo{:}res$ 'flowers'

(e) English *Deborah* (three syllables) > *Debra* (two syllables)

(f) pre-Finnish *$k\ddot{a}ti$ > Finnish $k\ddot{a}si$ 'hand'

(g) English *furore* (three syllables) > American English *furor* (two syllables)

(h) Latin *lege* 'law' [lege] > Italian *legge* [leddʒe]

(i) This is thought to be the history of the French word *cent* [sɑ̃] 'hundred' over the last 6000 years or so; if you don't find a suitable label for a particular step, try to coin one from your knowledge of phonetics:

[km̩tom] > [kemtom] > [kentom] > [kentum] > [kentũ] > [kentu] > [kento] > [kʲento] > [tsento] > [tsent] > [sent] > [sen] > [sẽ] > [sɑ̃]

Exercise 3.2

Certain English words which were formerly pronounced with a /t/ have lost that /t/, though we retain a <t> in the spelling. Among these are *soften*, *listen*, *fasten, hasten, castle, bustle, bristle*, and *mistletoe*. On the other hand, the /t/ has not been lost in words like *muster, blister, foster*, and *custom*, nor has it been lost in cases like *astound* and *extend*. Describe as accurately as you can the circumstances in which the /t/ was lost.

Now note the peculiar case of *often*. Some people pronounce a /t/ in this word while others do not. What do you suppose might have happened in this case?

Exercise 3.3

Old English had both long and short vowels, and the long vowels have changed in systematic ways during the development of modern English. Table 3.2 shows some typical examples; the Old English vowel letters have approximately their IPA values. Explain what has happened to the long vowels.

Exercise 3.4

Historically, intervocalic /n/ was categorically lost in medieval Basque, so that, for example, **ardano* 'wine' became *ardao*, **ini* 'reed' became *ihi*, and

Table 3.2

Old English	Modern English
1. *bruːn*	*brown*
2. *deːman*	*deem*
3. *doːm*	*doom*
4. *duːn*	*down*
5. *æːl*	*eel*
6. *æːfen*	*even(ing)*
7. *fiːf*	*five*
8. *heː*	*he*
9. *hæːþ*	*heath*
10. *haːm*	*home*
11. *huːs*	*house*
12. *iːs*	*ice*
13. *læːce*	*leech*
14. *meːd*	*meed*
15. *muːþ*	*mouth*
16. *miːn*	*my, mine*
17. *aːc*	*oak*
18. *raːd*	*rode*
19. *roːst*	*roost*
20. *roːt*	*root*
21. *soːþ*	*sooth*
22. *staːn*	*stone*
23. *teːþ*	*teeth*
24. *tiːd* 'time'	*tide*
25. *toːþ*	*tooth*
26. *hwiːt*	*white*

katena 'chain' became *katea* (the [h] in the second serves only to prevent hiatus). In some cases, however, the result was different:

(a) *zani* > *zain* 'watchful'
(b) *garanu* > *garaun* 'grain'
(c) *seni* > *sein* 'boy'
(d) *zunai* > *zuhain* 'hay'
(e) *usani* > *usain* 'odour'
(f) *azkone* > *azkoin* 'badger'
(g) *initz* > *ihintz* 'dew'
(h) *bedenikatu* > *bedeinkatu* 'bless'
(i) *zizani* > *zizain* 'worm'
(j) *arrani* > *arrain* 'fish'
(k) *lehone* > *lehoin* 'lion'
(l) *arrazone* > *arrazoin* 'reason'

Explain as clearly as you can what has happened in these cases. Note that this is *not* a metathesis: the development involved more than one step, and each step was a process discussed in the chapter.

Exercise 3.5

The Latin consonant /k/ was spelled <q> before <u> and <c> in all other cases. In the development of Latin into Spanish, this [k] has developed in an interesting way. In some cases, it remains [k] today. In other cases, it has changed into a voiceless fricative. That fricative is [θ] in standard European Spanish (Castilian) but [s] in most other varieties of Spanish, including all types of American Spanish. In still other cases, [k] has developed into a voiced velar fricative or approximant [ɣ]. Table 3.3 lists some Spanish words

Table 3.3

	Latin	Castilian	American	Orthography	Gloss
1.	*saccu*	[sako]	[sako]	*saco*	'bag'
2.	*caecu*	[θjeɣo]	[sjeɣo]	*ciego*	'blind'
3.	*caule*	[kol]	[kol]	*col*	'cabbage'
4.	*certu*	[θjerto]	[sjerto]	*cierto*	'certain'
5.	*cuna*	[kuna]	[kuna]	*cuna*	'cradle'
6.	*corona*	[korona]	[korona]	*corona*	'crown'
7.	*aquila*	[aɣila]	[aɣila]	*águila*	'eagle'
8.	*facile*	[faθil]	[fasil]	*fácil*	'easy'
9.	*pisce*	[peθ]	[pes]	*pez*	'fish'
10.	*iocu*	[xweɣo]	[hweɣo]	*juego*	'game'
11.	*capra*	[kaβra]	[kaβra]	*cabra*	'goat'
12.	*centu*	[θjento]	[sjento]	*ciento*	'hundred'
13.	*lacu*	[laɣo]	[laɣo]	*lago*	'lake'
14.	*facere*	[aθer]	[aser]	*hacer*	'make'
15.	*circa*	[θerka]	[serka]	*cerca*	'near'
16.	*vicinu*	[beθino]	[besino]	*vecino*	'neighbour'
17.	*dicit*	[diθe]	[dise]	*dice*	'says'
18.	*caelu*	[θjelo]	[sjelo]	*cielo*	'sky'
19.	*calcea*	[kalθa]	[kalsa]	*calza* [obs.]	'stocking'
20.	*flaccidu*	[laθjo]	[lasjo]	*lacio*	'withered'
21.	*quid*	[ke]	[ke]	*qué*	'what?'

illustrating these developments. Identify the circumstances in which each development occurs, and try to propose plausible phonetic reasons for the changes, in terms of what you have learned in the chapter. Is it possible to decide the order in which the various changes must have occurred? How satisfactory do you find your account?

Exercise 3.6

Like some other Australian languages, Yinwum has historically undergone some highly unusual phonological changes which are neither easy to classify nor easy to understand in phonetic terms. However, the changes were extremely regular, and all words were apparently affected in the same way. Table 3.4 shows some typical data. The first column gives the (asterisked) form each word is thought to have had in the ancestor of Yinwum, and the second the modern form. Describe the changes in as much detail as you can. If you are writing phonological rules, you may find the formalism somewhat stretched by these data. (Data from Hale 1976 and Dixon 1980.)

Table 3.4

	Ancestral	Modern	Gloss
1.	$*kalma-$	$ima-$	'arrive'
2.	$*wuna-$	$nwa-$	'be lying down'
3.	$*t^j u\eta ku$	ηke	'black'
4.	$*\eta ula$	lwa	'by-and-by'
5.	$*ru\eta ka-$	$\eta kwa-$	'cry'
6.	$*wari-$	$te-$	'dig'
7.	$*kuta$	twa	'dog'
8.	$*kuna$	nwa	'excrement'
9.	$*kaalka-$	$aki-$	'fall, die'
10.	$*puula$	$ulwa-$	'father's father'
11.	$*piin^j a$	$in^j a-$	'father's older sibling'
12.	$*piimu$	$imu-$	'father's sister'
13.	$*t^j aru$	tju	'foot'
14.	$*t^j ampa-$	$mpi-$	'give'
15.	$*jana-$	$ni-$	'go'
16.	$*n^j ilu$	lju	'he'
17.	$*n^j u\eta u-$	$\eta ju-$	'(to) him/her'
18.	$*\eta aju$	$aju-$	'I'
19.	$*t^j ipa$	pja	'liver'
20.	$*\eta an^j i$	$n^j i$	'me'
21.	$*min^j a$	$n^j a$	'meat, animal'
22.	$*papi$	pe	'mother's father'
23.	$*\eta at^j i$	$^n t^j i-$	'mother's father'
24.	$*kami$	me	'mother's mother'
25.	$*mukur$	$^n kur$	'mother's older brother'
26.	$*t^j alan$	lin	'mouth'
27.	$*ku\eta ka$	ηkwa	'north'

28. *$n^j ipi$	$^n pi$	'one'
29. *$pama$	ma	'person'
30. *$n^j at^j i-$	$^n t^j i-$	'see'
31. *$n^j iina-$	$ina-$	'sit'
32. *$n^j uuŋka-$	$i^n kwe-$	'smell'
33. *$jiipa$	$ipja-$	'south'
34. *$kalka$	ika	'spear'
35. *$jinta-$	$nti-$	'spear' (verb)
36. *$t^j uku$	ke	'tree'
37. *$kuut^j i-$	$ut^j i-$	'two'
38. *$kumpu$	mpu	'urine'
39. *$maji$	aji	'vegetable food'
40. *$ŋan^j i$	$n^j i$	'we'
41. *$ŋana$	na	'we all'
42. *$ŋali$	le	'we two'
43. *$ŋaani$	ani	'what'
44. *$waari$	$ate-$	'who'
45. *$n^j ipul$	$^n pjul$	'you' (pl.)
46. *$n^j untu$	$^n ti$	'you' (sing.)
47. *$ŋali$	li	'you and I'
48. *$japu$	pju	'younger brother'

4

Phonological change II: Change in phonological systems

As I pointed out in Chapter 3, changes in the sequence of speech sounds making up the pronunciation of particular words are called 'syntagmatic change'. Change in the phonological system of a language, in contrast, is called **paradigmatic change**. Recall from Chapter 2 that both French and English have undergone paradigmatic change – they have acquired new consonant phonemes – by borrowing words from each other: that is, the phonological system of each language has changed as a result of borrowing. Much more commonly, however, phonological systems change as a result of changes in pronunciation of the sort discussed in Chapter 3. In this chapter, we'll be looking at the various ways in which this can happen, and we'll also be asking whether we can understand such system changes in terms of linguistic theory.

4.1 Conditioning and rephonologization

Recall from the previous chapter that I am going to assume that a phonological change is normally regular, that it normally applies to every single relevant word. But what is a 'relevant word'? To answer this, I must introduce a fundamental distinction between two kinds of phonological change: **conditioned** and **unconditioned** changes.

An unconditioned change is one which applies to every single occurrence of a particular segment in the language, regardless of its position in a word and regardless of the nature of any neighbouring segments. For example, every single instance of the vowel /i:/ in Middle English has changed into the diphthong /ai/ in modern English. And, in the Gipuzkoan dialect of Basque, every single instance of earlier /j/ has somewhat remarkably developed into /x/. Unconditioned changes are fairly common with vowels but much less common with consonants.

A conditioned change, in contrast, is one which applies to a particular segment only in certain positions in a word – for example, only intervocalically or only word-finally or only in a stressed syllable or everywhere except after /s/. Thus, Latin /p t k/ became voiced in Spanish between vowels but remained voiceless in all other positions, and English /l/ was delateralized several centuries ago only when followed by a consonant and preceded by one of certain vowels, as in *folk* and *talk*, but not as in *milk* or *fall*. Conditioned changes are much more frequent than unconditioned ones.

In the majority of cases, an unconditioned change generally has only modest consequences for the phoneme system of the language undergoing it. The number of phonemes remains the same, and their distribution in words remains the same; all that changes is the phonetic character of one or more phonemes. So, in my Gipuzkoan Basque example, the former /j/ has simply been replaced by /x/, which didn't exist before, and every word that was formerly pronounced with [j] is now pronounced with [x]: hence *jan* 'eat' and *jaun* 'lord', formerly [j]*an* and [j]*aun*, are now [x]*an* and [x]*aun* in Gipuzkoan. But that's all: there have been no other consequences. Still, this kind of unconditioned change can be viewed as a very simple type of **rephonologization** (or **rephonemicization**): the reorganization of the phonological system of a language.

There are just two cases in which an unconditioned change can affect the number of phonemes in the system. First, one phoneme may undergo unconditional merger with another one, so that what were formerly two different phonemes are combined into a single phoneme. For example, an ancestral form of Spanish had the two phonemes /b/ and /v/, but these two have merged into a single phoneme in almost all modern varieties of Spanish. The ancient spelling distinction is still retained, so that Spaniards write *boto*, meaning 'dull', but *voto*, meaning 'vote', but these words are pronounced identically (in isolation, as [boto]), and Spanish-speakers simply have to learn, one by one, which words are conventionally spelled with *b* and which with *v*. This merger has reduced by one the number of phonemes in the language. (Merger is a particularly interesting sort of change, and it will be discussed further in Chapter 10.)

Second, the unconditioned loss of a segment naturally reduces the number of phonemes by one. As we saw in the previous chapter, both French and Spanish have lost the /h/ which they formerly had, thereby reducing the number of phonemes. Some linguists would interpret such loss as a kind of merger, a 'merger with zero', but I will distinguish loss from merger.

Conditioned changes, in most cases, have more complex effects upon the phonological system of a language. Let's begin with the simplest type of conditioned change, illustrated once again from Basque. Basque has two voiceless sibilants, a laminal sibilant notated <z> and an apical sibilant notated <s>. The language has no voiced sibilants. Now, in certain circumstances, notably before a nasal, the two Basque sibilants have become voiced. Thus, while *sasi* 'bramble' and *zezen* 'bull' have voiceless sibilants, *esne* 'milk' and *ozmin* 'biting cold' are pronounced with voiced sibilants. But this development has had no consequences at all for the phonological system: all that has happened is that the two sibilants have acquired voiced allophones before nasals.

But let's now turn to a similar case which has gone further. Pre-Old English had a velar plosive /k/, which was pronounced [k] in all positions, though doubtless with a more fronted allophone before a front vowel, just as in modern English *key* and *car*. At some time this slight palatalization was exaggerated, until /k/ was pronounced as an affricate [tʃ] before /i/ or /e/ or before a diphthong /ea/ or /eo/. Since there was no other [tʃ] in the language, this change again had no phonological consequences: the phoneme /k/ simply had two allophones, [tʃ] before a front vowel and [k] elsewhere. But then something else happened: the first element of the diphthongs /ea/ and /eo/ was lost after [tʃ]. As a result, the affricate [tʃ], which had formerly occurred only before front vowels, now found itself in some cases followed by a back vowel. In this position it therefore now contrasted with [k]. As a result, [tʃ] was no longer a predictable allophone of /k/: instead, it was itself a phoneme /tʃ/ contrasting with /k/. These developments are summarized in Table 4.1.

Such a development is called **loss of the conditioning environment**. In this case, the front vowel that had formerly conditioned the allophone [tʃ] was lost, and hence the distribution of [k] and [tʃ] was no longer predictable; thus the former phoneme /k/ split into two phonemes /k/ and /tʃ/. We call this **phonemic split**, or **split** for short, and you can see that split is the opposite process to merger. This kind of split, in which one phoneme simply divides into two phonemes, is sometimes given the rather curious name **secondary split**.

There is another, more complex, type of split which does not increase the number of phonemes in the language. Consider Latin rhotacism. Pre-Latin had the phonemes /s/ (a voiceless sibilant) and /r/ (a voiced liquid). At some stage, /s/ became voiced to [z] between vowels (a common assimilation). Since Latin had no phoneme /z/, this was a purely allophonic change with no phonological consequences at all. But then this new [z] was lenited to a liquid [r]. In doing so, it became identical to the existing /r/, and hence all

Table 4.1 The split of Old English /k/

	'cat'	'chaff'	'chin'
Stage I	[katt]	[keaff]	[kinn]
	/katt/	/keaff/	/kinn/
Stage II	[katt]	[tʃeaff]	[tʃinn]
	/katt/	/keaff/	/kinn/
Stage III	[katt]	[tʃaff]	[tʃinn]
	/katt/	/tʃaff/	/tʃinn/

words formerly containing intervocalic /s/ now had intervocalic /r/ instead. These developments are summarized in Table 4.2.

As a result, some instances of /s/ turned into instances of /r/. The number of phonemes did not change, but the distribution of /s/ and /r/ did change: the number of words containing /r/ increased, the number of words containing /s/ decreased, and all occurrences of intervocalic /s/ disappeared, so that /s/ could no longer occur between vowels in Latin. Overall, the original phoneme /s/ split; one member of the split simply continued /s/, while the other underwent merger with the existing /r/. This scenario of split plus merger is called **primary split**. Fig. 4.1 shows this graphically. In primary split, then, one result of the split merges with a second pre-existing phoneme; in secondary split, it finds nothing to merge with, and hence simply becomes a new phoneme by itself.

This rhotacism had important consequences for the structure of Latin: it introduced **alternations** in the forms of certain words. For example, as we have just seen, the noun *flōs* 'flower', which had formerly had the perfectly regular plural *flōses*, now came to have the irregular plural *flōres*, and the stem meaning 'flower' acquired an alternation between the forms *flōs-* and *flōr-*, with the second occurring before a vowel and the first elsewhere. This kind of outcome is very typical of conditioned phonological changes: though the change itself is regular, it introduces irregularities into the morphology. In Chapter 5 we shall examine the consequences of such changes for the morphology.

There is a further point, very important. If you have studied Latin, you will know that classical Latin has a number of words with intervocalic /s/, such as

Table 4.2 The split of Latin /s/

	'dear' (fem.)	'flower'	'flowers'
Stage I	[ka:ra] /ka:ra/	[flo:s] /flo:s/	[flo:ses] /flo:ses/
Stage II	[ka:ra] /ka:ra/	[flo:s] /flo:s/	[flo:zes] /flo:ses/
Stage III	[ka:ra] /ka:ra/	[flo:s] /flo:s/	[flo:res] /flo:res/

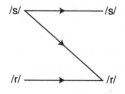

Fig. 4.1 Primary split

casa 'house', *rosa* 'rose', *causa* 'cause', *caseus* 'cheese', *esox* 'salmon', *ecclēsia* 'assembly, congregation', later 'church', *quasi* 'as if', *vīsum* 'seen', *vīsiō* 'vision', and, of course, the name *Caesar*. But how can those words be there, when I've just told you that sound change is normally regular, and that Latin intervocalic /s/ changed to /r/ without exception? Am I already in such trouble that I must abandon any claims that sound change is regular, and just confess that a change occurs sometimes but not other times?

No; far from it, as I'll explain in a moment. But first suppose that I did give up my claim that phonological change is regular. Suppose I just shrugged and said 'Ah, well, sometimes Latin intervocalic /s/ changed to /r/ and sometimes it didn't.' If I did that, then there would be nothing left to explain, no puzzles to solve, no further work to be done. This wouldn't be very interesting.

But I am in fact going to insist that the change of intervocalic /s/ to /r/ in Latin was absolutely regular. I therefore have a problem: how am I going to explain all those Latin words that have intervocalic /s/? How did those words come to be there?

There are at least two obvious explanations for them. Maybe, before reading further, you'd like to pause a moment and see if you can think what might have happened. Try it.

OK. The first possible explanation is easy: the words were not in the language when the change occurred. We know that the Latin rhotacism of /s/ was completed by the fourth century BC; after that, all the instances of intervocalic /s/ had vanished from the language. This was several centuries before the time of classical Latin, and Latin-speakers therefore had plenty of time to coin or borrow some new words containing intervocalic /s/. And that's what they did. The word *ecclēsia* 'assembly' was borrowed from Greek in the first century BC, and *esox* 'salmon' was borrowed from some other language, probably a Celtic language, at around the same time. The words *caseus* 'cheese' and *Caesar* appear to have been borrowed from a neighbouring Italian language, probably Sabine. By the time these words were borrowed, the change of /s/ to /r/ was history, and the new words were not affected by it.

The second possible explanation is slightly less obvious: the words were already in the language when the change occurred, but they didn't contain intervocalic /s/ at the time, and hence could not undergo the change to /r/. The simplest case is *causa* 'thing'. In Old Latin, this word is well attested in the form *caussa*, with a geminate /ss/. Unlike single /s/, geminate /ss/ did not undergo lenition to /r/: it remained unaffected by the change – unsurprisingly, since neither /s/ in *caussa* was intervocalic. Later, after the change to /r/ was completed, the geminate /ss/ in *caussa* underwent another, quite different, change: it was lenited to /s/, producing the classical form *causa*.

Slightly more complex is the case of *quasi* 'as if'. This is thought to have originated as a compound of *quam* 'how, as' and *sī* 'if' – just like its English equivalent. The original **quamsī* had probably been assimilated to something like **quansī* by the time of the rhotacism, but this form, too, did not contain intervocalic /s/ and hence was not rhotacized. Later, after rhotacism was finished, the cluster was simplified, and the classical form *quasi* was the result.

Most complex of all is the case of *vīsum* 'seen'. Now, apart from its intervocalic /s/, this form is strange in other respects. It derives from the verb *vidēre* 'see', whose stem is *vid-*, not **vīs-*. Moreover, the participial suffix in Latin is normally *-tum*: compare *amātum* 'loved', the participle of *amā-* 'love'. Therefore, we might have expected the participle of 'see' to be something like **vid-tum*. But the awkward cluster /dt/ is never found in classical Latin, and it seems that this cluster was simplified to something more pronounceable, probably /ss/. Hence, at the time of rhotacism, this word too contained /ss/, or at least something different from /s/, and this was again reduced to /s/ *after* the rhotacism was finished.

The word *vīsiō* 'vision' illustrates both of my explanations. This word did not exist at the time of rhotacism; it was coined by Roman scholars at a late date from the participle *vīsum* just described, at a time when educated Romans were trying to expand the vocabulary of their language to match that of the intellectually more advanced Greeks.

That leaves *rosa* 'rose', and this one is a puzzle. The word is widely attested in other languages with /d/ instead of /s/, as in Greek *rhodos* (the source of our word *rhododendron*, literally 'rose-tree'). So maybe this word too had something other than /s/ when rhotacism occurred. On the other hand, the change of intervocalic /d/ to a sibilant is well attested in Oscan and in Etruscan, two other neighbours of Latin. So maybe the Latin word was simply borrowed from one of these languages. Scholars are still not sure which explanation is correct in this case, but they're certain that one of them must be right.

There are two important lessons here. First, a sound change normally happens at some particular time in the history of a language, and then stops. Consequently, the phonological history of a language consists of a series of changes, each acting on what's left over from the last change. As a result of these accumulating layers of changes, the effects of earlier changes may be increasingly obscured by the effects of later ones. In our Latin example, various later changes reintroduced intervocalic /s/ into the language after the rhotacism had eliminated it; as a result, we can't immediately tell by looking at classical Latin that the language had, centuries earlier, lost every single intervocalic /s/. We know this only because of patient and careful investigation by historical linguists.

Second, our policy of insisting that sound change must be regular is *fruitful*. If scholars had thrown their hands in the air and declared the troublesome words to be mere exceptions to rhotacism, there would have been no reason to worry about them. By insisting on regularity, however, they were forced to find explanations for the odd cases, and, as you can see, they have been very successful in finding those explanations – and, as a result, they have wound up knowing rather more about the history of Latin than might otherwise have been the case. Even the few really nasty cases like *rosa* remain as puzzles to be investigated, and perhaps a future scholar will manage to find definitive solutions to these, too. But, without the regularity hypothesis as a guiding principle, there would be no reason for anybody even to look for such solutions.

4.2   *Phonological space*

If you have done some phonology, you will perhaps be acquainted with the conventional manner of laying out the phoneme system of a language. For example, Fig. 4.2 illustrates the consonant system and the vowel system of standard Modern Greek. Modern Greek has a fairly typical phoneme system. Note in particular the high degree of symmetry in the system: all obstruents occur in voiced–voiceless pairs, most vowels come in front–back pairs, and so on. Of course, the symmetry is by no means perfect: there is no velar nasal, affricates and liquids occur only in coronal position, the fricatives distinguish an extra place of articulation, there is only a single low vowel, and the glide /j/ is isolated. The departures from symmetry are easy to understand: the vocal organs themselves are far from symmetric, and some of the missing segments that would fill the gaps are difficult or even impossible to produce.

In fact, when you think about it, it is the *presence* of so much symmetry that

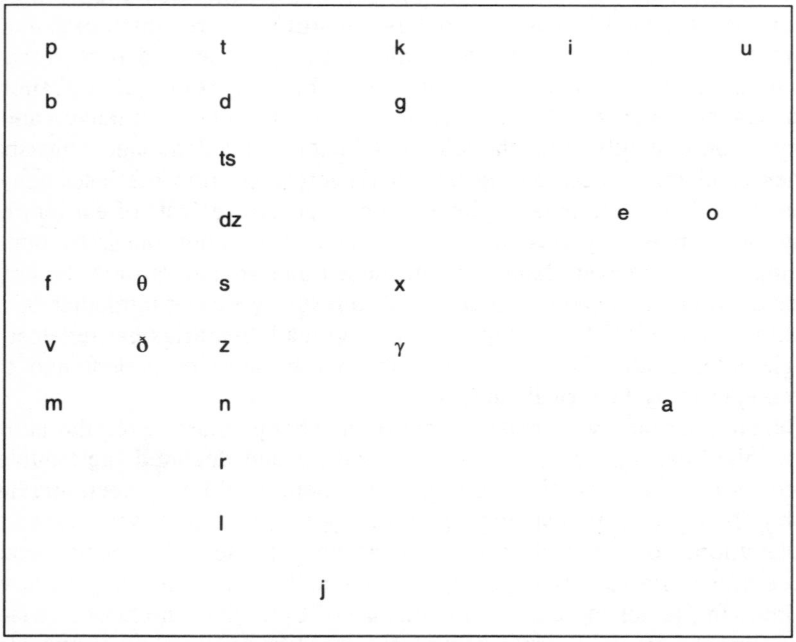

Fig. 4.2 The phoneme system of Modern Greek

really calls for an explanation. Why should Greek, or any language, have so much symmetry in its phoneme system? Why do we find so much symmetry in phoneme systems generally? Why don't we find many languages with very unsymmetric phoneme systems like, say, /p d ts v s x m w i y u e/?

This is a question for a phonologist, not for a historical linguist (your phonology teacher should be able to say something interesting about it). For our purposes, we need to know only that languages show a strong preference for symmetry in their phoneme systems, since this preference appears to play a part in phonological change.

Diagrams like Fig. 4.2 are laid out in a two-dimensional representation of **phonological space**. Phonological space is the sum of all the different parameters that are available in constructing speech sounds. Especially in the vowel diagram, our figure takes obvious advantage of the front–back dimension and the top–bottom dimension in the mouth, but there are many other dimensions that we can represent on paper only by using extra lines: the sideways dimension that distinguishes /r/ from /l/, the activity of the vocal folds, the position of the velum, the presence or absence of aspiration, affrication, or lip-rounding, the duration of segments, and others. Even so, phonologists have found such diagrams useful for certain purposes, and the same is true of historical linguists. For one thing, these diagrams can be convenient in representing graphically the effect of any phonological change which involves some degree of rephonologization, change in the phoneme system. But, as we shall see later, these diagrams may at times actually help us to *explain* why certain changes have occurred.

Let's consider some changes in English. Old English had a set of contrasting voiceless and voiced plosives and affricates: /p t k b d g tʃ dʒ/. But it had only voiceless fricatives: /f θ s ʃ h/ (you might prefer to write /x/ instead of /h/ for the last one, but this decision is immaterial here). Most of them had voiced allophones between vowels, but there were no contrasting voiced fricatives. Now recall from Chapter 2 that, during the Middle English period, we acquired a new voiced fricative /v/ as a result of borrowings from French. This new fricative disrupted the symmetry of the system: now there was a voicing contrast in just one position, and the new set of voiced fricatives consisted of /v/ plus a lot of blank spaces.

But things didn't remain like that. During the next couple of centuries, there were several further changes. English also acquired a second voiced fricative /ʒ/ in loans from French, and, very interestingly, the two fricatives /θ/ and /s/ split into contrasting voiceless and voiced phonemes: /θ/ and /ð/, and /s/ and /z/, respectively. As a result, the fricative system of modern English now looks like this:

$$\text{/f } \theta \text{ s } \int \text{ h/}$$
$$\text{/v ð z ʒ/}$$

Observe that symmetry has been restored by the introduction of a complete set of voiced fricatives matching the voiceless ones, except for /h/. Particularly interesting is the introduction of /ð/. The contrast between /θ/ and /ð/ carries a very low **functional load** – that is, we hardly ever make use of it to distinguish one word from another. It takes a bit of work to come up with rare and marginal minimal pairs like *thigh* and *thy*, *ether* and *either* (some pronunciations only), *wreath* and *wreathe*. Why do English-speakers bother to pronounce these two fricatives differently? It would scarcely make the slightest difference to comprehension if we just pronounced all of them with /θ/.

The answer appears to lie in that drive for symmetry. Old English already had the distinctive feature [± voice] for plosives and affricates, and we might reasonably conclude, therefore, that this feature was potentially available also for the fricatives. Once this feature was extended to one pair of fricatives, then not only was there no reason for it not to be extended to the others, but there was perhaps even a tendency to favour such a development, in order to get the maximum phonological work out of the feature. Indeed, some linguists would argue that it is precisely such a tendency to maximize the use of features that is responsible for the observed degree of symmetry in phoneme systems generally. In the English case, then, we might reasonably conclude that such pressures on the system strongly favour the maintenance of the /θ/–/ð/ contrast, even though this contrast does practically no work.

I can put this another way. If English had not acquired /ð/, our fricative system would look like this:

$$/f\ \theta\ s\ \int\ h/$$
$$/v\ z\ 3/$$

There would therefore be a **hole in the pattern**. And there is clear evidence that languages dislike having holes in their phoneme systems and tend to fill those holes. (Forgive my anthropomorphic language, but it's convenient.)

Examples comparable to the English case are easy to find. Most dialects of Basque, like Old English, have only a set of voiceless fricatives: /f/, /s/ (laminal), /ś/ (apical), and /ʃ/ (though some of these, as we saw above, have voiced allophones in certain positions). Loan words from French containing voiced fricatives are borrowed either with voiced plosives or with voiceless fricatives. In the Zuberoan dialect, however, the former glide /j/ some centuries ago underwent fortition into a voiced fricative /3/, thereby providing a voiced partner for /ʃ/. Since that time, the two fricatives /s/ and /ś/, just as in English, have split into pairs of voiceless and voiced fricatives, and French words are now borrowed into Zuberoan with voiced fricatives. Consequently, Zuberoan, like English, has acquired a complete set of voiced fricatives to match the voiceless ones (except for /f/); just as in English, the functional load of some of the new voicing contrasts is extremely low, but is apparently maintained by the pressure for symmetry. Dialects of Basque in which /j/ has not changed to a voiced fricative, in contrast, have shown no sign of acquiring any other voiced fricatives. (And we might wonder whether

Zuberoan will one day soon fill the remaining hole in its pattern by acquiring a /v/.)

While we're here, we might note something interesting: the conflict between various kinds of phonological pressures. The glide /j/ is a weak sort of consonant, not very consonant-like at all, and in most dialects of Basque it has undergone strengthening to some kind of obstruent. From a syntagmatic point of view, this strengthening has the agreeable effect of making syllables containing this consonant conform better to the preferred CV-type of syllable. In the Zuberoan case, however, the strengthening of /j/ to /ʒ/ produced an asymmetry in the consonant system, and the further changes in that system have served to restore symmetry. In other words, the resolution of a syntagmatic pressure (towards preferred syllable structure) at the same time introduced a paradigmatic problem (an asymmetric system), which then had itself to be resolved by further changes. Things like this are always happening in languages: it's impossible to optimize everything at the same time, and any change that optimizes one thing is likely to disrupt something else, leading to the possibility of further changes to repair the damage, which in turn introduce yet further strains on the system. It can be very illuminating to view phonological change as a ceaseless effort to keep responding to conflicting pressures, to keep fixing things that are not quite as neat as they might be. But perhaps now I really am becoming too anthropomorphic.

4.3 *Chain shifts*

That part of phonological space containing vowels is called the **vowel space**, and changes in vowel space often exhibit some remarkable behaviour. Let's consider the dramatic set of changes which affected the English system of long (tense) vowels at about the end of the Middle English period: the so-called *Great Vowel Shift* (GVS) of English.

Middle English had a symmetric system of seven long vowels: /i: e: ɛ: a: ɔ: o: u:/. These vowels occurred, for example, in the seven words *pine* /pi:n/, *gees* 'geese' /ge:s/, *bead* /bɛ:d/, *name* /na:mə/, *gote* 'goat' /gɔ:tə/, *goos* 'goose' /go:s/ and *doun* 'down' /du:n/, respectively. As you can see, all these words have changed their pronunciation drastically. What happened was this. The two high vowels /i:/ and /u:/ were diphthongized to /əi/ and /əu/, respectively. The two high-mid vowels /e:/ and /o:/ were raised into the /i:/ and /u:/ slots. The two low-mid vowels /ɛ:/ and /ɔ:/ were raised into the /e:/ and /o:/ slots. And the low vowel /a:/ was raised into the /ɛ:/ slot. All this is shown schematically in Fig. 4.3.

As you can see, there have been some further changes in most of these vowels, most obviously in the vowels of *bead* and *name*, but those additional changes happened later and need not concern us for the moment. What we're interested in just now is the fascinating little dance illustrated in Fig. 4.3. As

Fig. 4.3 The English Great Vowel Shift

you can see, during the GVS all the long vowels moved around the vowel space in a very orderly manner, with each non-high vowel occupying the place vacated by its neighbour, while the two high vowels moved out of the set of long vowels altogether by becoming diphthongs. This elaborate set of movements seems almost to have been orchestrated, but of course it wasn't: it was just a response to some kind of pressure on the vowel system.

A set of related changes like this one is called a **chain shift**, and you can see why we call it that. Chain shifts are by no means rare in vowel systems, and they occasionally even happen in consonant systems. But why should such an amazing rearrangement occur at all? What started the GVS, and why did it keep going until all seven vowels had moved to different places in the vowel space?

There are at least three possible ways in which the GVS might have proceeded. First, it could have started with the diphthongization of the two high vowels (we know that tense high vowels tend to diphthongize fairly readily). This diphthongization would have left two holes in the pattern where the high vowels had formerly been, and the two high-mid vowels could have been attracted upwards to fill those holes. This, in turn, would have left holes behind in the high-mid positions, inducing the low-mid vowels upwards to fill these new holes, leaving two more holes behind again, with the low vowel then rounding things off by moving up into one of those holes, leaving a final unfilled hole behind it. This kind of chain shift is a **drag chain**: a chain that starts with the introduction of some holes which 'drag' other segments into them, thereby creating more holes which in turn drag other segments into them, and so on.

But there's another possibility. The GVS could have started with the raising of /a:/ toward /ɛ:/, thereby threatening a merger of these two vowels. The vowel /ɛ:/ might have reacted to this threat by moving upwards, away from the incoming /a:/, but thereby threatening /e:/ in the same way. And /e:/ could have reacted similarly by moving up toward /i:/, which, unable to move any higher, got out of the way by diphthongizing. In this view, the back vowels, though not directly threatened, would simply have moved upwards in the same manner in order to maintain symmetry in the system. This sort of chain shift is a **push chain**: a chain that starts with a movement of one segment dangerously close to a second one, causing that second one to move out of the way and do the same thing to a third segment.

Finally, it's also possible, of course, that both these things happened. The shift might have started with the raising of /e:/ and /o:/, pushing /i:/ and /u:/ out of the way and dragging the other vowels upwards behind them.

Since the available data are rather sparse, it's not easy to decide just what did happen in this case. Some scholars have preferred to see the GVS as a drag chain, while others have argued for just the sort of push–drag combination I've just described. The issue is still being debated. The investigation of other chain shifts suggests that both pure drag chains and mixed push–drag chains are fairly common, while pure push chains are comparatively rare. All chain shifts, though, however they start, can be plausibly interpreted as continuing in order to maximize the use of the available phonological space: the farther apart the contrasting segments are in phonological space, the easier it is to tell them apart when listening to speech, and the less likely are misunderstandings.

Now note that the GVS produced a very odd and unbalanced system of long vowels: three front vowels, but only two back vowels, and no low vowel at all. This last is very strange: low vowels are the most vowel-like of all vowels and are virtually universal in languages. You might therefore expect that such an embarrassing gap in the system would have been quickly filled, and you'd be right. To start with, the short /a/ which had remained unaffected by all this activity was lengthened in a few words, as in *father*, thereby providing some new instances of /a:/ – but not very many. More recently other things have happened, but, interestingly, different things have happened in different varieties of English.

To begin with, /l/ was lost in certain circumstances, in words like *calm*, *palm*, *half*, and *calf*. These words have since undergone complex and variable developments (including the restoration of /l/ by some speakers in some of them, under the influence of the spelling), but most speakers have wound up with a long low /a:/ in some of these words, and some speakers have this vowel in all of them.

Next, the short vowel /ɒ/, as in *not* and *pot*, was unrounded and lowered in some (not all) accents, and the resulting /a/ was then lengthened to /a:/. This kind of pronunciation is now typical of North America: most Americans and Canadians pronounce *not* and *pot* with the long low vowel of *father*. This change has not affected most of the rest of the English-speaking world.

More recently still, the consonant /r/ has been lost everywhere except before a vowel in parts of England, in Wales, and in the eastern and southern

USA, and this new pronunciation has been carried to the southern hemisphere countries. A preceding short /a/ has undergone compensatory lengthening, and hence words like *far* and *dark* now have /a:/ for these speakers, and *farther* is pronounced just like *father*.

One way or another, then, that vanished /a:/ has been replaced in the English vowel system, providing yet another example of the way in which a change that resolves one problem introduces new problems which must then be resolved by yet further changes.

As for the imbalance between the three front and two back vowels resulting from the GVS, that too was eventually resolved, but the story of how this was done is so extraordinary that I reserve it for a later chapter (Chapter 10).

Not all chain shifts are as spectacular as the English GVS, and not all complex vowel changes are chain shifts, but it is none the less often useful to track vowel changes on a diagram of the vowel space to get an overall picture of what has happened.

Consider the history of the vowel system in Greek, a language whose vowels have undergone very substantial changes during the last three millennia. Recall from Fig. 4.2 that modern Greek has only the very simple vowel system /i ɛ a ɔ u/. Around 2800 years or so ago, the Greek of Athens (the ancestor of the modern language) had a much more elaborate system, with seven long vowels /i: e: ɛ: a: ɔ: o: u:/, five short vowels /i ɛ a ɔ u/, and four diphthongs /ɔi ai ɛu au/. (I omit the so-called 'long diphthongs' here.) The development of these twelve vowels and four diphthongs into the five vowels of modern Greek is mostly well understood. It is possible to display all of the changes simultaneously in a diagram like Fig. 4.4, but I'm sure you'll agree that such a display is not terribly enlightening, though it does at least show that no fewer than seven different vowels and diphthongs have merged into the single vowel /i/, a development called **iotacism**, from the name of the

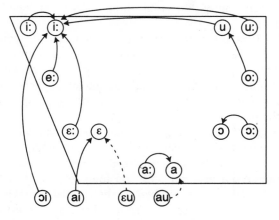

Fig. 4.4. The history of the Greek vowel system

Greek letter equivalent to I. (The dotted lines represent some rather peculiar developments explained below.)

We can get a better idea of the history of the Greek vowel system if we work through it step by step. Since I lack the space here to display every single step, I suggest you get a large sheet of paper and a pencil and draw the vowel system at each step, in the conventional manner, to keep track of what's happening. (There is some minor disagreement among specialists as to the details; here I follow Allen (1968).)

Step 1: We have the seven long vowels, five short vowels, and four diphthongs of the archaic period. The system is highly symmetric.

Step 2: The two high back vowels /u: u/ are fronted to /y: y/. (The motivation for such fronting is not obvious, but it's a fairly common change.) Symmetry is destroyed, as there are now holes in the high back position.

Step 3: The vowel /o:/ is raised to /u:/. This fills one of the two new holes, but leaves a new hole behind: /e:/ no longer has a back counterpart.

Step 4: The vowel /e:/ is raised to /i:/, merging with the existing /i:/. This restores symmetry, and the new system is once again perfectly symmetric apart from the absence of /u/.

Step 5: The vowel /ɛ:/ is raised to /e:/, wrecking the symmetry once again.

Step 6: The diphthong /ai/ is levelled to /ɛ:/, replacing the vanished /ɛ:/ and restoring a measure of symmetry.

Step 7: The diphthong /ɔi/ is levelled to /y:/, merging with the existing /y:/. There are no consequences for the system except the loss of a diphthong.

Step 8: Like its predecessor, the new /e:/ is raised to /i:/ and merges with the existing /i:/. Apart from the loss of two diphthongs, the system has returned to exactly the form it had at step 4, perfectly symmetric apart from the lack of /u/.

Step 9: The front rounded vowels /y: y/ are unrounded and merge with /i: i/, respectively. Greek now has a nearly symmetric system of five long vowels and four short vowels, plus the diphthongs /ɛu/ and /au/.

Step 10: Vowel length is lost: all vowels become short, and every long vowel merges with its short counterpart, except for /u:/, which has no short counterpart. Greek now has a perfectly symmetric five-vowel system, plus those two diphthongs.

Step 11: The diphthongs /ɛu/ and /au/ are converted to the sequences /ɛv/ and /av/. Since Greek already has a phoneme /v/, the diphthongs are effectively reduced to /ɛ/ and /a/, respectively, thus merging with the existing /ɛ/ and /a/. The sixteen nuclei of archaic Greek have been reduced to just five.

Only a few of these steps can plausibly be viewed as chain shifts: the fronting of /y:/ followed by the raising of /o:/ (steps 2 and 3), and perhaps the raising of /ɛ:/ followed by the levelling of /ai/ (steps 5 and 6). But there are other points of interest. First, observe the enduring tendency for tense vowels to be raised. We saw the same raising in the English GVS, and it appears to be a universal tendency in languages. In English, the vowels that were maximally high to start with diphthongized out of the system; in Greek, the high back vowels were fronted, but the high front vowels didn't go anywhere: instead, the high front position has historically acted as a sink, collecting and keeping vowels from other positions.

In most cases, these repeated raisings of tense vowels have helped to restore symmetry lost by earlier changes, but the exception is step 5, in which the raising wrecked the existing symmetry. Again we can see the tension between competing pressures: the pressure to raise tense vowels and the pressure to maintain a symmetric system.

Finally, note the interesting case of step 10. When contrastive vowel length was lost in Greek, as far as we can tell, it was lost simultaneously in all five vowels. This is an important observation, and it makes step 10 quite different from the earlier changes. In all the earlier changes, except perhaps step 2, each individual segment apparently behaved independently, and any given change generally affected only one segment. That's why I've described the history of Greek vowels in steps and advised you to draw a series of pictures. But step 10 is different. This time, the five long vowels did not behave independently: they all shortened at once. This suggests that, in step 10, what was being affected by the change was not individual segments but rather the distinctive feature [± long]. All the preceding changes can be illuminatingly expressed by statements about segments, like $o: \rightarrow u:$ or $ai \rightarrow \varepsilon:$. But step 10 cannot be so expressed, not if we want to make it clear what's happening. Instead, step 10 looks like this: [+ syllabic] $\rightarrow$ [− long]. This statement simply says 'All vowels become short.'

On the whole, historical phonologists have preferred to examine phonological change in terms of phonemes and phoneme systems; as my examples in this chapter suggest, this approach has proved to be illuminating and fruitful, and it is still the norm today. But cases like step 10 above suggest that it might also be profitable to look at things from a different point of view, from the point of view of distinctive features and phonological rules. The rise of generative approaches to phonology in the 1960s provided a framework for doing this, and generative phonologists have often been interested in demonstrating that their approach can shed light on some kinds of phonological change. To this approach we now turn.

4.4   *Phonological change as rule change*

Generative approaches to phonology are now quite diverse, and many of the more recent versions scarcely recognize the existence of segments at all. Here I shall consider only the version current in the 1970s and early 1980s, since this is the version which has been most extensively applied to studying phonological change. In this view, the phonology of a language consists of a set of distinctive features, certain permitted combinations of which make up a group of segments which are the (underlying) phonemes of a language, plus a set of phonological rules which apply in some order to the underlying forms of particular words in order to produce the surface phonetic forms. In this view, most phonological changes are seen essentially as changes in the phonological rules.

As I've already suggested, this approach is most obviously helpful in considering cases in which entire natural classes of segments are affected by a change, and not merely a single segment. Here's a simple example. As I remarked earlier, at some point in the history of Spanish, all three of the voiceless plosives /p t k/ became voiced to /b d g/ between vowels. A description of this in terms of individual segments would be cumbersome and would completely fail to express the obvious generalization. In a rule-based approach, however, we can express the change with a single rule:

Rule 4.1: $[-$ continuant, $-$ friction$] \rightarrow [+$ voice$] / V \underline{\quad} V$

The feature specification $[-$ friction$]$ is required to exclude affricates, which were not affected by the change, and this rule therefore simply states that all segments (except affricates) involving a complete oral closure become voiced between vowels. In the usual manner, this rule also applies to voiced plosives and to nasals, which are also $[-$ continuant$]$, but these were voiced to begin with, so the rule just applies to them harmlessly and vacuously. The only effect of the rule is to voice voiceless plosives in this position, which is what we require.

In the generative approach, then, the voicing of intervocalic plosives in Spanish is viewed as the addition of Rule 4.1 to the phonology of Spanish. Such **rule addition** is seen as a major pathway of phonological change, but other types of rule change are also attested.

If we can have rule addition, than perhaps we can also have **rule loss**: the disappearance of a rule from a language. Something like this must indeed have happened with Rule 4.1 in Spanish. At some stage, it stopped applying, and new instances of intervocalic /p t k/ entering the language, from whatever source, no longer underwent it. Hence modern Spanish is full of words with intervocalic /p t k/, like *copa* 'wine glass', *mito* 'myth', and *boca* 'mouth'. Rule 4.1 is now only a historical event in Spanish; it is no longer part of the language. The majority of sound changes are like this: they apply only for a while, and then disappear. But there are perhaps more interesting cases of rule loss.

Consider Yiddish. Yiddish is a distinctive offshoot of Middle High German (MHG), which is also the ancestor of modern standard German. MHG is itself descended from the earlier Old High German (OHG). Now in OHG, words could end in a voiced obstruent, for example, OHG *tag* 'day'. But, on the way to MHG, a change was introduced: all word-final obstruents were devoiced. We can represent this as Rule 4.2:

Rule 4.2: $[+$ obstruent$] \rightarrow [-$ voice$] / \underline{\quad} \#$

Hence, the earlier *tag* changed to *tac* /tak/, and so on for all other relevant words in the language: *weg* 'way' became *wec*, *aveg* 'away' became *avec*, *ab* 'off' became *ap*, *lied* 'song' became *liet*, and so on. A voiced plosive which was not word-final did not devoice: hence the plural forms like *tage* 'days', *wege* 'ways', and *lieder* 'songs' retained voiced plosives, producing as a result of set of alternations like /tag-/ 'day' (non-finally) ~ /tak/ (finally). Unlike the Spanish rule, Rule 4.2 has never been lost from standard German: though modern German orthography chooses to use spellings like *Tag* 'day', *Weg* 'way', *weg* 'away', *ab* 'off', and *Lied* 'song', all these words are in fact pronounced with final voiceless plosives.

Now Yiddish is descended from MHG, which already had Rule 4.2, but the modern Yiddish forms of the nouns are in fact *tog* 'day', *veg* 'way', and *lid* 'song', with final *voiced* plosives. On the other hand, grammatical words like *avek*, in which there are no alternations, have voiceless plosives in Yiddish. So what has happened?

We might suggest that Yiddish has added another new rule *voicing* final plosives and reversing the effect of Rule 4.1, but that would not explain why the final voiced plosives are found only in words that formerly had alternations: MHG *tac* 'day', *tage* 'days', but *avec* 'away'; Yiddish *tog*, *toge*, but *avek*. A more plausible scenario is this: non-alternating words like *avek* were first reanalysed as containing underlying final voiceless plosives, since there was no evidence from alternations to suggest otherwise. Alternating words like **tok* ~ **toge*, in contrast, continued to be regarded as having underlying voiced plosives and continued to undergo Rule 4.2. But then Rule 4.2 was simply *lost* from the phonology of Yiddish, thus restoring the final voiced plosives in all cases except those, like *avek*, which had already been reanalysed.

Such striking instances of rule loss are far less frequent than instances of rule addition, but cases like the Yiddish one suggest that rule loss is none the less a possible type of rule change.

A further, and very striking, type of rule change is **rule reordering**. Here is an instance from the Bizkaian dialect of Basque. All varieties of Bizkaian possess the dissimilation Rule 4.3, which raises a mid vowel before a non-high vowel:

Rule 4.3: V [− low] → [+ high] / ___ V [− high]

This rule is responsible for the typical Bizkaian alternations induced by the addition of the article *-a*: *asto* 'donkey' but *astua* 'the donkey', *lore* 'flower' but *loria* 'the flower'.

All varieties of Bizkaian also raise the vowel /a/ before /a/, but the details are not everywhere the same. Many varieties have Rule 4.4:

Rule 4.4: V [+ low] → [− low, − back] / ___ V [+ low]

Rule 4.4 raises /a/ to /e/ before /a/, and hence these varieties have alternations like *neska* 'girl' but *neskea* 'the girl'.

Observe that, in order to get the right result with underlying forms like *neska-a*, Rule 4.3 must precede 4.4, since, with the opposite ordering, Rule 4.4 would create new cases of /ea/ for Rule 4.3 to apply to. We might surmise, therefore, that Rule 4.3 entered the phonology of Bizkaian earlier than Rule 4.4.

In some other varieties of Bizkaian, however, while everything else is the same, the result is different with cases of underlying /aa/. In these varieties, *neska* has the definite form *neskia*. What has happened in these varieties?

We might, of course, argue that Rule 4.4 has simply been changed, so that its output, instead of bearing the feature specification [− low], bears the specification [+ high]. This would give the right result (check it), but such an analysis would be rather puzzling: why should this rule undergo such a seemingly arbitrary modification?

There is, however, another way of interpreting the Bizkaian case, one which does not require any changes at all in either rule: we can posit that Rules 4.3 and 4.4, in the second group of varieties, have simply *changed their order*, so that 4.4 now applies before 4.3. Table 4.3 shows the result in the (conservative) first group of varieties, and in the (innovating) second group, in which the rules have changed their ordering. Such **rule reordering** is now widely recognized as another important type of rule change. Now note something important: the rule reordering in Bizkaian has had the effect of creating new instances of /ea/ for Rule 4.3 to apply to. That is, 4.4, when it comes first, **feeds** 4.3, and the order '4.4 precedes 4.3' is therefore called **feeding order** for these rules. In a series of publications, the linguist Paul Kiparsky has argued that there is a universal tendency for rule reordering to take place so as to produce exactly this result: the maximization of feeding order. The Bizkaian case conforms entirely to Kiparsky's prediction: the **counterfeeding order** of the conservative varieties has been replaced, in the innovating varieties, by feeding order.

Yet another type of rule change is **rule simplification**, also called **rule generalization**. Here a rule simply loses one or more feature specifications, so that the new version looks simpler, and applies more generally, to a wider range of cases. Here is an example.

Table 4.3 Rule reordering in Bizkaian Basque

	'the flower'	'the girl'
Conservative		
underlying	lore+a	neska+a
Rule 4.3	loria	neskaa
Rule 4.4	loria	neskea
Innovating		
underlying	lore+a	neska+a
Rule 4.4	lorea	neskea
Rule 4.3	loria	neskia

All varieties of English have undergone a historical change by which a morpheme-final voiced plosive /b/ or /g/ is lost after a nasal. Hence words like *lamb*, *climb*, and *comb* have lost the final /b/ which they formerly had, and words like *long*, *sing*, and *fang* have likewise lost the final /g/ which they once had. In fact, this rule is still in the language today: no English morpheme can end in /mb/ or /ŋg/. On the other hand, the morpheme-final cluster /nd/ has been unaffected: words like *land*, *hand*, and *find* retain their final plosive. For most varieties of English, then, we can write Rule 4.5:

Rule 4.5: [− continuant, − friction, + voice] → Ø / [+ nasal, − coronal] ___ +

(The symbol Ø means zero − that is, no consonant at all; the specification [− friction] is necessary because affricates are not lost in words like *singe*, *lounge*, and *range*.) In some American accents, however, particularly in the south, final /d/ has been lost after /n/, so that *find* is pronounced like *fine*, *stand* is pronounced like *Stan*, and so on. For these varieties, the appropriate rule is 4.6:

Rule 4.6: [− continuant, − friction, + voice] → Ø / [+ nasal] ___ +

Rule 4.6 represents a simplification, or generalization, of Rule 4.5: the feature specification [− coronal] has been lost, so that the rule is simpler to write and applies to a wider range of cases.

Finally, there is one more type of rule change, rather more complex than the other types. This is **rule inversion**. This concept needs a little explaining.

In a rule-based approach to phonology, recall, we assume that each morpheme or word has an underlying form, and that this underlying form may be altered by the application of rules to produce the surface phonetic form. This surface form may be significantly different from the underlying form, and we say that the surface form is a **derived form**. If we confine our attention to just one rule at a time, we may represent all this schematically, as follows: underlying form → [rule] → derived form.

What happens in rule inversion is that speakers reanalyse this whole business, taking the original derived form as underlying and the original underlying form as derived from it. The original rule, therefore, must be 'turned around', or **inverted**, so that it now applies in the opposite direction. Here is an example from Basque.

Centuries ago, Basque underwent a change by which intervocalic /l/ was changed to /r/. We can represent this change by Rule 4.7:

Rule 4.7: l → r / V ___ V

For example, original **gali* 'wheat' became *gari*, and **haizkola* 'axe', a loan from Latin *asciola*, became *haizkora*. In word-formation, however, the final vowel of a first element has since ancient times been lost in Basque in most circumstances. Consequently, in word-formation, these nouns anciently appeared as *gal-* and as *haizkol-*, respectively. As a result, they form compounds and derivatives like *galbahe* 'wheat sieve' (*bahe* 'sieve'), *galgorri* 'a species of wheat' (*gorri* 'red'), and *haizkolbegi* 'hole in the axe-head for inserting the handle' (*begi* 'eye'). Since the /l/ in these formations was not intervocalic, it did not change to /r/, and these are the modern forms. Historically speaking, then, the underlying forms of these words are *gali* and *haizkola*, and *gari* and *haizkora* are the derived forms, obtained by the action of Rule 4.7. So far this is all perfectly straightforward.

But now comes the complication. Basque also has words in which intervocalic /r/ was historically present, such as *zamari* 'horse', a loan from Latin *sagmariu* 'pack-horse'. And this word, when it enters into word-formation, not only loses its final vowel as usual but further shows a combining form in /l/, as in *zamaldun* 'horseman' (*-dun* 'who has'). Forms like *zamaldun* cannot possibly result from the application of Rule 4.7, and neither can forms like *zamari*, which we know had /r/ to begin with. The only possible conclusion, then, is that Basque-speakers have inverted Rule 4.7. That is, forms like *gari*, with an /r/ originally derived by 4.7, have been reinterpreted as underlying, while forms like *galbahe*, originally representing the underlying form **gali* rather directly, have come to be reinterpreted as derived by rule. The rule that relates forms in /l/ and forms in /r/ can no longer be 4.7; instead, this has been replaced by an inverted rule something like 4.8:

Rule 4.8: $r \rightarrow l / V$ ___ $+ C$

Observe that, whereas the original Rule 4.7 was a purely phonological rule, applying in a purely phonological environment, the new Rule 4.8 is at least partly a morphological rule: its environment contains a morpheme boundary, and hence it only applies in word-formation, and not otherwise. The conversion of phonological rules to morphological rules is, in fact, a common phenomenon, and we shall be examining this phenomenon in the next chapter.

4.5 *Summary*

In the previous chapter we saw that phonological changes can often be understood as syntagmatic phenomena affecting the sequences of speech sounds within words and phrases. In this chapter we have seen further that many phonological changes have significant consequences for the phonological system of a language, and that these can often be illuminatingly investigated by examining the system of consonant and vowel phonemes arranged in phonological space. The maintenance or restoration of symmetry appears to be a powerful force in sound change, and chain shifts in particular can be more readily understood in terms of movement within phonological space. A crucial observation has been that there are always competing phonological pressures, both syntagmatic and paradigmatic; these can never all be satisfied at once, and a great deal of phonological change can be understood as endless attempts at satisfying these competing pressures, with each resulting change typically introducing new strains into the system. We have further seen evidence that the principle that sound change is regular is a very fruitful basis for examining the phonological history of a language, since clinging to this principle allows us to identify problematic data with great precision and often to find explanations for them, explanations which increase our understanding of the history of the language in question. Finally, while some changes apply only to particular segments, others apply instead to entire natural classes of segments, and these changes can often be considered most profitably within a rule-based framework like generative phonology, with each such change being interpreted as some kind of rule change.

Further reading

The study of phoneme systems and of phonological space was pioneered by the Prague School linguists more than half a century ago, notably in Trubetzkoy (1939). Useful surveys of phoneme systems can be found in Hockett (1955), Sedlak (1969), O'Connor (1973: ch. 7), Crothers (1978), Nartey (1979), Maddieson (1980a, 1980b, and especially 1984), Lass (1984: ch. 7), and Lindblom (1986). The use of these ideas in exploring phonological change, and the notions of holes in the pattern and chain shifts, were chiefly developed by the French linguist André Martinet, especially in Martinet (1955); more recently the American William Labov has been pursuing the investigation of chain shifts, especially in Labov (1994). The classic work on the application of generative phonology to phonological change is King (1969). The leading figure in the field has long been Paul Kiparsky, who has developed his ideas in a series of publications, among the more important of which are Kiparsky (1968a, 1968b [1974], 1971, and 1973 [1974]). Kiparsky (1988) is an overview of phonological change including some topics discussed later in this textbook.

Exercises

Wherever possible (it may not always be possible or helpful), you may like to write phonological rules for the changes you identify in each of the following problems and to put those rules into an appropriate historical order.

Exercise 4.1

Most varieties of Basque have the five oral vowels /i e a o u/. The Zuberoan (Souletin) dialect has six, the extra vowel being a front rounded vowel /ü/. Table 4.4 shows some Basque words, given both in their standard form, which represents the vocalism of most other dialects, and in Zuberoan. Try to explain what has happened in Zuberoan. Ignore any differences in the con-

Table 4.4

	Standard	Zuberoan
1. 'cuckoo'	*kuku*	*kükü*
2. 'debtor'	*zordun*	*zordün*
3. 'foot'	*oin*	*huñ*
4. 'gold'	*urre*	*ürhe*
5. 'good'	*on*	*hun*
6. 'head'	*buru*	*bürü*
7. 'he has me'	*nau*	*nai*
8. 'help'	*lagundu*	*lagüntü*
9. 'hold'	*eduki*	*edüki*
10. 'hundred'	*ehun*	*ehün*
11. 'hut'	*ola*	*olha*
12. 'I have it'	*dut*	*düt*
13. 'island'	*uharte*	*üharte*
14. 'long'	*luze*	*lüze*
15. 'man'	*gizon*	*gizun*
16. 'night'	*gau*	*gai*
17. 'red'	*gorri*	*gorri*
18. 'short'	*motz*	*mutz*
19. 'sole'	*zola*	*zola*
20. 'take'	*hartu*	*hartü*
21. 'we'	*gu*	*gü*
22. 'when?'	*noiz*	*nuiz*
23. 'who?'	*nor*	*nur*
24. 'you have it'	*duzu*	*düzü*

sonants; they are not relevant here. The data have been selected to avoid one or two complications.

Exercise 4.2

Hawaiian has undergone a number of unconditioned changes in the consonant system of its Proto-Polynesian ancestor. Table 4.5 lists some examples of these changes illustrating all the Proto-Polynesian consonants and their Hawaiian descendants. Identify the changes, and comment where possible on the order in which they occurred. Compare the resulting consonant system of Hawaiian with that of its ancestor, and comment on the degree of naturalness of the changes and on the degree of symmetry of the original phoneme system and of the resulting Hawaiian system. (Data from Crowley 1992).

Exercise 4.3

Spanish has the five vowels /i e a o u/. In some stems containing /e/ or /o/, these vowels alternate with the diphthongs /ie/ and /ue/ when stressed (the position of the stress is marked by an acute accent):

Table 4.5

		Proto-Polynesian	Hawaiian
1.	'back of canoe'	*takele	kaʔele
2.	'blow'	*pusi	puhi
3.	'branch'	*maŋa	mana
4.	'canoe'	*vaka	waʔa
5.	'constant'	*maʔu	mau
6.	'cry'	*taŋi	kani
7.	'dew'	*sau	hau
8.	'dodge'	*kalo	ʔalo
9.	'faeces'	*taʔe	kae
10.	'fermented'	*mara	mala
11.	'fire'	*afi	ahi
12.	'firemaking'	*sika	hiʔa
13.	'fish'	*ika	iʔa
14.	'forbidden'	*tapu	kapu
15.	'four'	*faa	haa
16.	'fruit-picking pole'	*lohu	lou
17.	'gall'	*ʔahu	au
18.	'hear'	*roŋo	lono
19.	'leg'	*vaʔe	wae
20.	'man'	*taŋata	kanaka
21.	'mouth'	*ŋutu	nuku
22.	'navel'	*pito	piko
23.	'nose'	*isu	ihu
24.	'octopus'	*feke	heʔe
25.	'quieten'	*naʔa	naa
26.	'root'	*aka	aʔa
27.	'scrotum'	*laso	laho
28.	'sea'	*tahi	kai
29.	'side'	*tafa	kaha
30.	'sit'	*nofo	noho
31.	'slap'	*paki	paʔi
32.	'tail'	*siku	hiʔu
33.	'thatch'	*kaso	ʔaho
34.	'two'	*rua	lua
35.	'up'	*hake	aʔe
36.	'wave'	*ŋalu	nalu
37.	'yam'	*ʔufi	uhi

tenér 'have'		*tiéne* 'has'
cerrár 'close'		*ciérre* 'fastener'
certitúd 'certainty'		*ciérto* 'certain'
contár 'count up'		*cuénta* 'account, bill'
podér 'be able to'		*puédo* 'I can'
venezoláno 'Venezuelan'		*Venezuéla* 'Venezuela'

In other words containing /e/ or /o/, however, there is no such alternation:

crecér 'grow'	*créce* 'grows'
meritório 'worthy'	*mérito* 'merit'
pelár 'cut the hair of'	*pélo* 'hair'
ponér 'put'	*póne* 'puts'
soledád 'solitude'	*sólo* 'alone'
costéño 'coastal'	*cósta* 'coast'

Propose a possible explanation for this difference in behaviour in terms of the phonological history of Spanish. You might like to compare your idea with the explanation given in a standard history of Spanish.

Exercise 4.4

Hungarian has the front vowels /i e ü ö/ and their long counterparts /í é ű ő/; it also has the back vowels /u o a/ and their long counterparts /ú ó á/. Hungarian has front-back **vowel harmony**: normally a word contains only front vowels or only back vowels, and the vowel of any suffix must harmonize in backness with the stem. Here are some examples:

kettő 'two'	*tanuló* 'pupil'
fehér 'white'	*sárga* 'yellow'
ügyes 'skilful'	*súlyos* 'heavy'
kert 'garden'	*kertben* 'in the garden'
ház 'house'	*házban* 'in the house'
hozunk 'we bring'	*ülünk* 'we sit'
varrunk 'we sew'	*verünk* 'we beat'

But the vowels /i í e é/ behave strangely. First, they can occur in words which otherwise contain only back vowels:

virág 'flower'	*kocsi* 'coach, car'
gyertya 'candle'	*vékony* 'thin'

Second, when they occur in back-vowel words, they are ignored in determining the backness of a suffix:

kocsiban 'in the car' (**not** **kocsiben*)

Third, some words containing *only* these four vowels take front-vowel suffixes, while others take back-vowel suffixes:

víz 'water'	*vízben* 'in the water'
kés 'knife'	*késben* 'in the knife'
kín 'torture'	*kínban* 'in the torture'
cél 'target'	*célban* 'in the target'

Propose a possible explanation for this curious behaviour in terms of the phonological history of Hungarian.

Table 4.6

Vowel	Typical word	Conservative	Advanced
1. /æ:/	*hand*	[æ:]	[i:(ə)]
2. /a:/	*got*	[a:]	[æ:]
3. /ɔ:/	*talk*	[ɔ:]	[a:]
4. /e/	*head*	[ɛ]	[ʌ]
5. /ɪ/	*sing*	[ɪ]	[ɛ]
6. /ʌ/	*bus*	[ʌ]	[ɔ]

Exercise 4.5

Many urban accents of the northern USA exhibit a set of clearly related changes in the qualities of certain vowels; these changes have been collectively dubbed the *Northern Cities Shift*. Table 4.6 lists the six different changes involved, in the order in which they appear to have occurred, from earliest to most recent. For each of the six vowels, I provide a representative word containing it, a conservative pronunciation from an American accent in which the shift has not occurred, and an advanced pronunciation from an accent in which the shift is maximally prominent. Note that /æ:/ is a tense (long) vowel in most American accents. (Data from Labov 1994.) These shifts are quite dramatic. Speakers who have not undergone the shifts, when listening to speakers who have undergone them, often mishear *Ann* as *Ian*, *socks* as *sax*, *chalk* as *chock*, *steady* as *study*, *sing* as *sang*, *bus* as *boss*, and so on.

Plot the movements of these six vowels on a diagram of the vowel space, and comment on what seems to have happened in these accents, in terms of the ideas introduced in the chapter.

Exercise 4.6

The Swiss German dialect of Schaffhausen has a back vowel /o/. Historically, this /o/ has been lowered to [ɔ] when followed by any non-lateral coronal, but not otherwise. Thus Schaffhausen has *holts* 'wood', *xopf* 'head', *bogə* 'bow', and so on, with a following labial, velar, or /l/, but *hɔrn* 'horn', *bɔdə* 'floor', *pɔʃt* 'post', and so on, with a following coronal other than /l/. Write a rule that accounts for this lowering.

In certain circumstances, most notably in the plural, the vowel /o/ is fronted to [ø], in the familiar Germanic process of *umlaut*. Thus, for example, the plural of *bogə* is *bøgə*, and the plural of *bɔdə* is *bødə*. Write a rule that accounts for this, citing the environment merely as [Plural].

In the neighbouring dialect of Kesswil, both the lowering of /ø/ and umlaut are also present, but the results are slightly different. Nouns which have [ɔ] in the singular have in the plural not [ø] but its lowered counterpart [œ], and hence *bɔdə* has the plural *bœdə*.

Now, both Schaffhausen and Kesswil possess a small number of forms containing front rounded [ø] in their stems followed by a coronal, such as *pløtsli* 'biscuit(s)' and *frøʃʃ* 'frog'. All such words, in both dialects, have only [ø] and never [œ].

Given these facts, propose an explanation of the phonological histories of Schaffhausen and Kesswil. (Data from Kiparsky 1968a.)

5

Morphological change

In this chapter we shall be examining **morphological change**, changes in the morphological structure of lexical items and of inflected forms, and changes in morphological systems. Morphological change has been extensively studied, and we now know a good deal about how it occurs. It is by no means simple, however, to draw sharp lines between the various types of morphological change which occur, since many individual changes exhibit features of two or three of the different types we would like to recognize; nor is it always easy to separate morphological change from syntactic change, the topic of the next chapter. Nevertheless, the central ideas in the study of morphological change are generally easy to understand.

5.1 *Reanalysis*

The simplest possible type of morphological change is **reanalysis**. In reanalysis, a word which historically has one particular morphological structure comes to be perceived by speakers as having a second, quite different, structure.

Some of the examples of the coining of new words which we considered in Chapter 2 illustrate reanalysis very well. The word *bikini* was originally a single morpheme, but it was reanalysed by somebody as having a structure along the lines of *bi-* 'two' plus *-kini* 'swimming costume'; as a result, the 'prefix' *bi-* could be replaced by a different prefix *mono-* 'one' to derive the new word *monokini* 'bikini with no top'. The Latin word *minimum* consisted in Latin of the morphemes *min-* 'little' (also found in *minor* and *minus*) and *-im-* 'most', plus an inflectional ending; however, thanks to the influence of the unrelated *miniature*, English-speakers have apparently reanalysed both words as consisting of a prefix *mini-* 'very small' plus something incomprehensible, leading to the creation of *miniskirt* and all the newer words which have followed it.

Observe something important. In each of these cases, there was no way that an observer could tell that a reanalysis had taken place until speakers began producing new forms which had not previously existed. This is commonly the case with reanalysis. Take the colloquial British word *grotty* 'dirty, nasty, shabby'. In origin, this is merely a clipped form of *grotesque*, but it now has a rather different meaning from *grotesque*, and it is unlikely that many speakers feel the two words to be closely related. Now *grotty* is an adjective, and it happens to end in what *looks* like the familiar suffix *-y*, which forms adjectives from nouns: *dirt/dirty*, *filth/filthy*, and so on. It is therefore possible that some speakers might reanalyse *grotty* as having the same kind of structure: *grot* + *-y*, with the meaning 'full of grot'. It is even possible that some speakers have already done this – perhaps even you yourself. But, short of going around interrogating people, we have no way of knowing whether this reanalysis has occurred or not – until we hear somebody say something like *This place is full of grot*, which was not previously possible. Once we hear such an innovating utterance, we know that reanalysis has taken place. (How do you feel about *This place is full of grot*? If you find this normal, or even possible, then you personally have carried out the reanalysis. If you don't, you haven't.)

The history of English provides some nice examples of reanalysis involving nothing more than the movement of a morpheme boundary, a type of change impressively called **metanalysis**. On the one hand, the former English words *naddre*, *napron*, and *noumpere* have become *adder* (a type of snake), *apron*, and *umpire*; on the other hand, the former *ewt* and *ekename* have become *newt* and *nickname*. What caused these odd changes? It was the English article *a(n)*. Forms like *a napron* and *an ewt* were apparently misheard as *an apron* and *a newt*, producing the modern forms. The same thing has happened to Arabic *nāranj*, which has come into English as *orange*, though in this case the *n* was lost in French, or rather in Occitan, in a rather similar way before the word was borrowed into English.

French provides a very striking case of multiple metanalysis. Our word *unicorn* derives from Latin, in which it is composed of *uni-* 'one' and *cornu* 'horn'. In English, nothing much has happened to this word, except that most speakers, knowing nothing of Latin, probably don't assign any internal structure to it: they just regard it as a single morpheme, on a par with *horse* or *giraffe*. Most European languages have the identical word, but the French word is the curious *licorne*. Where did this come from?

The original word, of course, was *unicorne*, a grammatically feminine noun. But the French word for 'a' with a feminine noun is *une* – and hence *unicorne* was misinterpreted as *une icorne*, and *icorne* therefore became the French name of the beast. But the French word for 'the' before a noun beginning with a vowel is *l'*. Hence 'the unicorne' was expressed as *l'icorne* – and this form in turn was reanalysed as a single noun *licorne*, producing the modern form.

By using the techniques to be described later in the book, linguists can often work out that a reanalysis must have occurred in some language long ago.

Here is an example from Basque, one which was unravelled only very recently by the Dutch linguist Rudolf P. G. de Rijk (de Rijk 1995).

Basque anciently had a word *dan* 'now'. At some stage, however, Basque acquired a second word for 'now', *orain*. This consists of the Latin loan *hora* 'hour' plus a Basque case-suffix meaning 'at'; its original literal meaning was 'at the hour', entirely parallel to modern English 'at the moment'. Now Basque readily forms *dvandva compounds* (copulative compounds) like *zuri-beltz* 'black-and-white', literally 'white-black', and *aitamak* 'parents', literally 'father-mothers'. It appears that the synonymous *orain* and *dan* were combined into just such a dvandva: *oraindan*, literally 'now-now', but probably comparable in sense to English 'right now'. Like any adverb of time, this could take the ablative case-suffix *-dik* 'from', producing *oraindandik*, which underwent phonological simplification to *oraindanik* 'from now on', a word which still exists in modern Basque.

This formation was perfectly regular and transparent. With time, however, the old word *dan* simply dropped out of the language in favour of the newer form *orain*, and the structure of *oraindanik* therefore became opaque to native speakers. Consequently, the original structure *orain-dan-ik* 'now–now–from' was reanalysed to *orain-danik* 'now–from', with the opaque sequence *-danik* being reinterpreted as meaning 'from, since'. At first this reanalysis would not have been visible. But then speakers began attaching the new morpheme *-danik* to other adverbs of time, like *orduan* 'then' and *iaz* 'last year', producing as a result things like *orduandanik* 'since then' and *iazdanik* 'since last year', which had not previously been possible. As a result of this reanalysis, Basque has acquired a new suffix, *-danik* 'since', whose origin in the ancient *dan* 'now' has been completely lost.

In the Basque case, it was the loss of *dan* as an independent word which triggered the reanalysis of the phrase containing it, and this is a common phenomenon. Recall from Chapter 2 the case of English *bryd-guma* 'brideman': it was the loss of *guma* 'man' as an independent word that led to the folk etymology in which the now opaque *bryd-guma* was re-formed into *bridegroom*.

Reanalysis can, however, take place without the loss of any elements. The American linguist Ronald Langacker has presented some interesting cases from the Uto-Aztecan languages of southwestern North America (Langacker 1977). Let us consider Uto-Aztecan reflexives.

At some ancient stage of the Uto-Aztecan family, there was apparently a reflexive element *na. This, however, did not occur in isolation, but only in longer phrases of certain kinds. In particular, to express a meaning like 'He is working by himself', the ancestral language used two complete clauses: 'He is working; he is by himself.' It is the second clause which interests us here. This was expressed as follows: $*pi\text{-}na\text{-}k^{w}a\text{-}yi$ 'he-self-by-be', with the usual Uto-Aztecan word order. Now, even though none of these four elements was lost from the language, Langacker demonstrates that this probably common sequence was reanalysed as consisting of only two elements: *pi-* and *-$nak^way\dot{i}$*. Since the Uto-Aztecan languages are post-positional, the meaning 'self' was transferred to *pi-*, while *-$nak^way\dot{i}$* was reinterpreted as a single postposition 'with, by'. That such a reanalysis must have occurred is shown by the fact that, in the Numic branch of the family, we find *pi* being used as the ordinary reflexive pronoun, while the new postposition *-$nak^way\dot{i}$* has simply been lost in that branch. Other languages underwent different reanalyses; for example, in Tarahumara the whole sequence *$pinak^way\dot{i}$* was reanalysed as a single intensive pronoun 'himself', which in turn has lost its intensive status and become the ordinary third-person pronoun 'he', though the form is now *binoy* by regular phonological change.

Cases like *an ewt > a newt* show that morpheme boundaries can be moved so as to shift a segment from one morpheme to another. But reanalysis can be more drastic: it can move entire morphemes from one word to another. Here's an example from Basque.

Basque anciently did not distinguish interrogative pronouns from indefinite pronouns, and hence *nor* meant both 'who?' and 'somebody', while *zer* meant both 'what?' and 'something'. (This is in fact very common in languages.) When one of these was used as the subject of a verb, however, the verb took the prefix *bait-* to indicate that the indefinite meaning was intended (this prefix also had other functions). Thus, 'Who is coming?' was *nor dator*, while 'Somebody is coming' was *nor bait-dator*. These pronouns took the ordinary case-suffixes, including the ergative case-marker *-k* to mark the subject of a transitive verb: hence *nork dakar* 'Who is bringing it?' but *Nork bait-dakar* 'Somebody is bringing it'.

What happened is that forms like *nor bait-dator* were reanalysed so that the morph *bait-*, instead of being a prefix on the verb, was taken instead as a suffix on the pronoun, and hence new indefinite pronouns *norbait* 'somebody' and *zerbait* 'something' were created. It is possible that such pronouns at first had the very odd case-inflected forms like ergative *norkbait* as a result, but such forms, if they did exist, were quickly replaced by more normal forms with the case-marking on the end. Hence today, 'Somebody is bringing it' is not *Norkbait dakar* but rather *Norbaitek dakar*; reshaped forms like these confirm that the reanalysis has taken place.

Reanalysis is not confined to morphology. In the next chapter we shall see that it is also a common process in syntactic change. For now, though, let us turn to a different kind of morphological change, the one which has attracted the most attention of all.

5.2 *Analogy and levelling*

Suppose I tell you (truthfully) that *ziff*, *zo*, and *zax* are all obscure English nouns denoting things that can be counted. What do you suppose their plurals are? Easy, I'm sure you'll agree: *ziffs*, *zos*, and *zaxes* – though notice that the plural ending is pronounced differently in each case. In such cases, you can effortlessly produce the correct plural form without thinking about it. How can you do that? You do it by invoking **analogy** – that is, you assume that the required plurals are formed according to a pattern which is already familiar to you from large numbers of other English nouns.

In this case, the pattern for forming plurals is so widespread and regular that it actually constitutes a *rule* of English grammar, just one of the many rules you acquired when you were learning English many years ago. But analogy does not always operate on such a large scale. Very often, speakers create forms by invoking an analogy with a much smaller number of existing forms, perhaps only a dozen or two, perhaps even only a single form. And such use of analogy is a very common and powerful pathway of language change generally, but most particularly of morphological change.

Let's begin with a simple example. English has a small class of nouns derived from Latin and commonly used with irregular plurals derived from Latin: *cactus/cacti*, *radius/radii*, *succubus/succubi*, and some others. All of these have singulars ending in *-us*. Now English also has a noun *octopus*, but this word is not derived from Latin: it's of Greek origin, and its Greek plural, if we used it in English, would be *octopodes*. In fact, however, the plural form which is used by many speakers is *octopi*, and perhaps you even use this form yourself. But where did it come from?

It came from analogy with the Latin nouns. Noticing the *-us/-i* pattern in the Latin nouns, many speakers have created an analogical plural for the Greek word. We can represent the process by a proportion:

   cactus:*cacti* :: *octopus*:?

The missing term required to complete the proportion is, of course, *octopi*, and that form, which formerly did not exist, has therefore been brought into the language.

This is the simplest type of analogy; for obvious reasons, it is sometimes called **proportional analogy** or **four-part analogy**. Examples of proportional analogy are very easy to find. English verbs provide a wealth of examples. Here's one:

   drive:*drove* :: *dive*:?

As a result of this analogy, the past tense of *dive*, which is historically *dived*, and still so for most speakers, has become *dove* for many eastern American speakers. This new form has not become standard, but here's another example:

   teach:*taught* :: *catch*:?

Apparently as a result of this analogy, the past tense of *catch*, which was formerly *catched* for all speakers, has become *caught*. This time, the innovating form *caught* has become standard and nearly universal, and the few speakers who still say *catched* are regarded as rustic or ignorant.

(Incidentally, you may occasionally come across the term *false analogy* applied to some of these cases, such as that of *dive/dove*, but this term is never used in linguistics, since it means nothing more than an instance of analogy that somebody dislikes. No doubt *caught* was once regarded as a 'false analogy' too.)

Proportional analogy is perhaps particularly conspicuous in inflected forms, but it also turns up in other circumstances in which it is perhaps a little less conspicuous, such as word-formation. On the analogy of *land* and *landscape*, we have recently created such forms as *seascape* and *moonscape*. By analogy with cases like *Japan* and *Japanese*, we have recently begun coining a large number of words with the general sense 'language typical of', such as *journalese, motherese, Americanese, headlinese*, and *officialese*. Simple analogy of this kind is a common factor in word-formation.

Cases like *moonscape* and *motherese* are sufficiently striking that you might notice one of these the first time you come across it. Some other cases, however, are much harder to spot, simply because the analogy in question has already become highly productive. A good example is the suffix *-able*. The Latin suffix *-bilis* occurs in a large number of words which have found their way into English: *imaginable, edible, invincible, portable, credible, tolerable*, and hundreds of others. In some cases, we have also borrowed the related Latin verb, as with *imagine* and *tolerate*. The existence of pairs like *imagine/imaginable* has induced English-speakers to extend the suffix *-able* to all sorts of other verbs not of Latin origin, including native English verbs, and so we now readily coin adjectives like *washable, likeable, lovable, burnable, unkillable*, and even *kissable*, as well as more elaborate forms like *machine-washable* and *biodegradable*. It is most unlikely that you would notice the first time you came across *unscratchable* or *varnishable*: this particular analogy has now become so widespread that it is effectively a rule of English word-formation.

The construction of new words by any of these analogical processes is sometimes called **analogical creation**, though this term is equally applied to instances of the construction by analogy of new inflected forms, like *octopi* and like some other cases we shall consider below.

A key fact about analogy is that it can sometimes block or reverse the effect of a regular phonological change. For example, there was a change in English by which /w/ was lost after /s/ and before /o/: hence *sword* has lost its /w/ in speech, though we still retain the traditional spelling. The same thing should have happened in forms like *swore* and *swollen*, but these are none the less pronounced with /w/ today. We are not sure quite what happened, but we know the reason is the existence of the related forms *swear* and *swell*. Either the analogy of these forms, which always retained their /w/, prevented the regular sound change from affecting *swore* and *swollen*, or the change did apply but the /w/ was later restored by the analogy with *swear* and *swell*. In the first case we speak of **analogical maintenance**; in the second, of **analogical restoration**.

Something similar occurs in Basque, in which intervocalic /n/ was categorically lost some centuries ago. But modern Basque has plenty of ancient nouns ending in /n/, like *gizon* 'man' and *lan* 'work', and these never lose their /n/ in inflections: *gizona* 'the man', *gizonak* 'the men', *lanean* 'at work', and so on. Since there is no evidence that /n/ was ever lost in such inflected forms, we are inclined to think that this is a case of analogical maintenance, but we can't be sure, especially since there is a third possibility in this case: that the presence of a morpheme boundary after the /n/ simply blocked the sound change. (But verb-forms *do* lose intervocalic /n/ before a morpheme boundary, making this last possibility unlikely here.)

These last examples bring us to an important point. Regular phonological changes very often disrupt regular inflectional paradigms, but at the same time the pressure of analogy tends to maintain or restore those regular paradigms. There is thus a fundamental conflict between sound change and analogy. This conflict is neatly summed up by a dictum often called **Sturtevant's paradox**, after Edgar Sturtevant, the American linguist who first stated it nearly a century ago: sound change is regular, but produces irregularity; analogy is irregular, but produces regularity.

Here is a splendid example of Sturtevant's parado. The majority of Latin verbs had perfectly regular inflectional paradigms, with each verb exhibiting a single constant stem taking a regular set of endings. However, Latin had a stress rule which assigned stress by counting syllables from right to left, so that the stem of a Latin verb was stressed in some forms but unstressed in others, depending on the length of the ending. During the development of spoken Latin into Old French, stressed vowels developed differently from unstressed vowels; in particular, stressed /a/ was diphthongized to /ai/, while unstressed /a/ was unaffected. This produced Old French verbal paradigms in which formerly regular verbs showed stem alternations. At a later stage, however, analogy intervened: the numerically fewer forms with /a/ were analogically replaced by forms in /ai/. This once again made the paradigms perfectly regular, as they are in modern French. All these developments are summarized in Table 5.1, in which the stressed vowels of Latin are marked with an acute accent and the forms undergoing analogical change are marked in boldface. This kind of analogical development illustrates Sturtevant's paradox exceedingly well. It is called **analogical levelling**, or **levelling** for short. Such levelling is extremely frequent in languages. Here is another example.

Recall from Chapter 3 that early Latin underwent a change in which intervocalic /s/ developed to /r/, and recall also that this change introduced alternations into previously regular paradigms, so that, for example, earlier *flōs* 'flower', plural **flōses*, became classical *flōs*, plural *flōres*, with an /s/ ~ /r/ alternation in the paradigm. This same change affected a number of other nouns, such as *honōs* 'honour', plural **honōses*, which became *honōs*, *honōres*. These are the forms found in our pre-classical Latin texts, but in the classical texts the forms of this noun are *honōr*, *honōres*. What happened? In this case,

Table 5.1 Analogical levelling in French

	Latin	Old French	Mod. French
1Sg	*ámo*	*aim*	*aime*
2Sg	*ámas*	*aimes*	*aimes*
3Sg	*ámat*	*aimet*	*aime*
1Pl	*amámus*	**amons**	**aimons**
2Pl	*amátis*	**amez**	**aimez**
3Pl	*ámant*	*aiment*	*aiment*

the /r/ found between vowels was generalized by analogy to all forms of the noun, thereby eliminating the alternation and once again producing a fully regular paradigm. In this case too, a regular sound change disrupted a perfectly regular paradigm; an irregular analogical levelling then restored a regular paradigm.

Observe that the levelling applied to only some nouns, like *honōs*; others, like *flōs*, were never affected by it and continued to have paradigms with alternations. This may seem odd, but the occurrence of analogy is generally quite unpredictable.

A somewhat more elaborate example occurs in English and German. These two languages share a remote common ancestor, and that ancestor underwent two regular sound changes: first, intervocalic /s/ changed to /r/ in certain circumstances only (before a stressed vowel), and then later all remaining instances of intervocalic /s/ changed to [z]. These changes left Old English with a number of verbs exhibiting rather complex alternations in their stems. Here, for example, are some forms of *cēosan* 'choose' in Old English; the fourth form is the Past Part(iciple):

Present	*cēosan*	[z]
Past Sg	*cēas*	[s]
Past Pl	*curon*	[r]
Past Part	*gecoren*	[r]

The modern English forms of these are *choose*, *chose*, *chose*, and *chosen*, respectively, with [z] in every case; the two past-tense forms are no longer distinguished. Analogical levelling has applied and generalized the [z] alternant right throughout the paradigm. Much the same thing has happened to other Old English verbs showing the same alternations, such as *frēosan* 'freeze' and *(for)lēosan* 'lose': modern English has *freeze*, *froze*, *frozen* but *lose*, *lost*, *lost*, the last having been only partially levelled. The ancient forms in /r/ survive only in a few instances which have become divorced from their original paradigms, such as *lorn* (the original participle of 'lose'), found in phrases like *a lone lorn figure* and *lovelorn* (originally 'love-lost'), and *forlorn*, the original participle of the now-lost prefixed verb *forlose*. Most English-speakers no longer connect these isolated forms with *lose*. The original alternations have vanished, save only in the verb *be*, whose past singular *was* and past plural *were* still retain the ancient alternation.

Old High German had exactly the same alternations as Old English. Here, for example, is part of the Old High German paradigm of *kiusan* 'choose':

Present	*kiusan*	[z]
Past Sg	*kōs*	[s]
Past Pl	*kurun*	[r]
Past Part	*gikoran*	[r]

Modern German too has levelled all such paradigms, but in a different way from English. The modern German forms of this verb (which is now rare and old-fashioned in German) are present *küren*, past singular *kor*, past plural *koren*, and past participle *gekoren*. That is, German has generalized the /r/ variant instead of the [z] one. The same occurs in German with the other verbs in this group, such as *frieren* 'freeze' and *verlieren* 'lose' (with the same prefix as English *forlose*).

Let's look at just one more example of levelling in English, a particularly interesting one which has not so far been extended to every possible case. Old English had the voiceless fricatives /f s θ/, which had voiced allophones [v z ð] between vowels or between a liquid and a vowel. As we saw in Chapter 4, English later acquired a set of contrasting voiced fricative phonemes /v z ð/, but the alternations remained. In the case of /f/ ~ /v/, the alternation still survives today in a number of cases, such as *leaf/leaves*, *knife/knives*, *wife/wives*, *life/lives*, *shelf/shelves*, *elf/elves*, and *wolf/wolves*. On occasion, it has even been extended to loan words, as in *scarf/scarves* (*scarf* is a loan from Old French), though most loan words, like *chief* and *mischief*, do not show it (though note *mischievous*). No doubt the spelling difference has helped to maintain the alternation in these cases. But even some of these cases have been lost, or partly lost. For you, what is the plural of *hoof*? *Hooves* or *hoofs*? Of *roof*? *Rooves* or *roofs*? Almost everyone now has *roofs*, and *hoofs* is probably now more frequent than *hooves*. English *dwarf*, which derives from Old English *dwerg*, should not show the alternation, and the standard modern plural is indeed *dwarfs*, though the celebrated fantasy writer J. R. R. Tolkien writes *dwarves* throughout his books; presumably he invokes the analogy with *leaves* and *elves* to make the word look more like native English.

In the case of /s/ ~ /z/, however, where the conventional spelling fails to represent the alternation, it has been levelled out to /s/ in all nouns except one: *house*, whose plural *houses* is still *hou*[z]*es* for most speakers – though even here a few speakers have levelled the plural to *hou*[s]*es*. Almost everyone, however, retains /z/ in the related verb *(to) house* and the derivative *housing*.

With the /θ/ ~ /ð/ alternation things are complicated. Formerly, English-speakers used /θ/ in the singular, but /ð/ in the plural, of all such pairs as *truth/truths*, *path/paths*, *mouth/mouths*, *moth/moths*, *wreath/wreaths*, and *death/*

deaths. (There was formerly a vowel before the plural *-s*.) But there has been a steady tendency for centuries to level these in favour of /θ/. The voiceless fricative is now the only possibility in *deaths*, but the others show considerable variation. You may find that you have /θ/ in some of the plurals but /ð/ in others, and your friends may differ from you on one or two of them, especially if they don't come from the same place as you. On the whole, Americans are perhaps more likely to retain /ð/ than are British speakers. I myself (I'm American) pronounce *moths* as *mo*[ðz], which my British friends find hysterically funny, since *mo*[θs] appears to be virtually universal today in Britain.

In some cases, the result of levelling is to split a single paradigm into two new paradigms, both of them regular. Pre-Latin **deiwos* 'heavenly, god' had a regular plural **deiwi*, but these forms underwent several quite regular phonological changes, crucially including the loss of *w* before *o*, and the result in classical Latin was singular *deus* but plural *divi*. The second of these no longer looked like a plural of the first, and levelling took place, but what happened is that *deus* acquired a complete new regular paradigm, including a new plural *dei*, while *divi* also acquired a complete new regular paradigm, with a new singular *divus*, and the result was two different words deriving from a single ancestor. Something similar has happened with English *staff*, whose plural was formerly *staves* (compare the cases like *knife/knives* above), but this word too has split, and we now have two words, *staff/staffs* and *stave/staves*. The English pairs *shade/shadow*, *mead/meadow*, and *cloth/clothes* also represent the splitting of what were originally single words.

The processes of word-formation discussed in Chapter 2 illustrate various types of analogy. Here I shall mention just two more, beginning with **contamination**. Contamination is an irregular change in the form of a word under the influence of another word with which it is associated in some way. For example, the opposite of *male* was formerly *femelle*, but the constant pairing of these two words has induced speakers to alter the second to *female*, in order to make it more like its opposite. Similarly, the word *overt* is borrowed from French *ouvert* 'open', and has final stress. The word *covert*, though, is in origin merely a variant of *covered*, and was formerly pronounced accordingly. But the frequent use of these two words as opposites has resulted in an alteration of the second: most people now pronounce *covert* to rhyme with *overt*.

A slightly different case is represented by *regardless*. This word, with its negative suffix *-less*, is very similar in meaning to *irrespective*, and many speakers have consequently altered the first to *irregardless*, a form which is now frequent, though not at present considered standard English.

Numerals appear to be particularly prone to contamination, probably because they are very often used in sequence while counting. The Latin numeral for 'nine' would have been **noven* if the word had developed regularly, but the classical form is *novem*, influenced by the following *decem* 'ten'. The Russian and Lithuanian numerals for 'nine' should have been *nevyni* and *nevjat'*, respectively, but the forms are *devyni* and *devjat'*, again influenced by the following *dešimt* and *desjat'* 'ten'. The original Basque *bederatzu* 'nine', preserved in the east, has become *bederatzi* in most dialects under the influence of the preceding *zortzi* 'eight'.

It is possible for contamination to apply in both directions. Old French had two words meaning 'native inhabitant', *citeien* and *denzein*; in Norman French, the first acquired a *z* from the second, and the second acquired an *i* from the first, leading to *citesein* and *denisein*, whence English *citizen* and *denizen*.

The other special type of analogy is **hypercorrection**. This occurs when a speaker deliberately tries to adjust his or her own speech in the direction of another variety perceived as more prestigious but 'overshoots the mark' by applying an adjustment too broadly. Sporadic hypercorrection is very common. A British speaker trying to acquire an American accent will carefully insert non-native /r/s into words like *dark* and *court*, but may overdo it and produce things like *avocardo*. I myself, being American, lack the British contrast between *do* and *dew*; attempting to acquire the British diphthong in *dew* and *new*, I occasionally overdo it and produce things like *What shall we dew?* Such hypercorrections are easily visualizable as instances of four-part analogy: in my case, *new* /nu:/ : /nju:/ :: *do* /du:/ : /dju:/.

On occasion such hypercorrections may establish themselves in the language. In Middle English, the word for 'throne' was *trone*, borrowed from French. But this word derives ultimately from Greek *thronos*, and English-speakers apparently re-formed their word to *throne* in order to show the Greek connection, or perhaps just to sound more erudite. But then they did the same thing to *autour*, which is not of Greek origin at all, producing as a result the modern form *author*, in which the dental fricative derives purely from hypercorrection.

5.3　*Universal principles of analogy*

Analogical change is irregular and seemingly unpredictable, but there have none the less been some serious attempts at identifying general principles of analogy. The most famous of these is the 'laws' of analogy proposed by the Polish linguist Jerzy Kurłyowicz in 1947. He proposes six such laws, as follows; here I have reworded his statements for the sake of clarity, at the expense of a certain measure of precision.

The first law: a complex marking replaces a simple marking. A standard example of this is provided by German. Old High German, the ancestor of modern German, had a variety of patterns for constructing plurals. One of these was exhibited by nouns like *gast* 'guest', plural *gesti*, in which the stem-vowel undergoes the change called **umlaut** under the influence of the vowel in the plural suffix. This noun comes into modern German as *Gast*, *Gäste*, with a double plural marking (umlaut plus suffix). Now the Old High German noun *boum* 'tree' had a plural *bouma*, with no umlaut, and this should have come into the modern language as *Baum*, **Baume*. Instead, German has *Baum*, *Bäume*. The double plural-marking has been extended from cases in which it is historically normal (like *Gast*) to others in which it is not regular.

The second law: a derived form is reshaped to make it more transparent and especially more similar to the simple forms from which it is derived. Basque provides a number of examples of this. The two nouns *ardi* 'sheep' and *ile* 'hair' formed an ancient compound **ardi-ile* 'wool'; this underwent the normal phonological processes of the language to yield *artile*, the most usual form today. But some speakers have replaced this by a new and more transparent formation *ardi-ile*. In effect, the regular but somewhat opaque formation *artile* has been re-formed to make it more transparent.

The third law: a form transparently consisting of a stem plus an affix serves as a model for reshaping related forms in which the stem-affix structure is opaque. Here is an example from Basque. The Basque question word *non ~ nun* consists of the interrogative stem *no-* plus the ordinary locative case-ending *-n*. By the process described in Section 5.1, this word has acquired a corresponding indefinite *nonbait ~ nunbait* 'somewhere'. But this form is now unusual among locative forms in that it does not end in the normal *-n*. (Compare *hemen* 'here', *orduan* 'then', *etxean* 'in the house', and so on.) In some western varieties of Basque, therefore, *nunbait* has been replaced by an innovating form *nunbaiten*, in which the locative case-ending has been reattached to the end of the word, on the model of all the other locative forms.

The fourth law: when a form undergoes analogical reshaping, the new form takes over its primary function, and the old form remains only in secondary functions. A simple example of this is English *brother*. This used to have a plural *brethren*, but a new regular plural *brothers* has been constructed by analogy and now serves as the ordinary plural, while the older *brethren* is now confined to special contexts, especially religious ones: nobody now says **I have two brethren*. Similarly, the compound of Old English *hus* 'house' and *wif* 'woman' developed by regular phonological change into *hussy*; now that the original compound has been renewed by the analogical formation *housewife*, *hussy* has lost its central meaning and become confined to a pejorative sense.

The fifth law: in order to re-establish a distinction of central significance, the language gives up a distinction of more marginal significance. Old French provides a good example. Latin had a large class of nouns inflected like *murus* 'wall'; in Latin, such nouns inflected as follows in the nominative and the accusative (the only cases surviving into Old French):

	Sg	Pl
Nom	murus	muri
Acc	murum	muros

By regular phonological changes, these forms gave rise to the following forms in Old French:

	Sg	Pl
Nom	murs	mur
Acc	mur	murs

For this class of nouns, then, Old French no longer had a systematic distinction either between singular and plural or between nominative and accusative. In order to maintain the more central distinction of number, the language therefore abandoned the less central one of case; the accusative forms were generalized, and French wound up with singular *mur* and plural *murs*, with no remaining distinctions of case.

The sixth law: a native form may be analogically reshaped under the influence of a non-native form, especially if the non-native variety is more prestigious. For example, Basque has a highly productive suffix *-tasun* for deriving abstract nouns: *bakartasun* 'solitude' (*bakar* 'alone'), *edertasun* 'beauty' (*eder* 'beautiful'). But the language has borrowed a number of abstract nouns from the neighbouring and more prestigious Spanish with the Spanish suffixes *-dad* and *-dura*. As a result, these suffixes have, for some speakers in some cases, replaced the native *-tasun*, and many Basques say *bakardade* for 'solitude' and *ederdura* for 'beauty'.

Building on Kuryłowicz's ideas, the Polish linguist Witold Mańczak (1958) has proposed nine rather more specific principles of analogy which he calls 'tendencies'. These are as follows; I provide an example for each one of them.

The first tendency: longer words are more often reshaped on the model of shorter words, rather than vice versa, except in inflectional paradigms. For example, Old English *huswif* 'housewife' underwent regular phonological change to *hussy*, but the word has been re-formed in modern English as *housewife*, on the model of its components *house* and *wife*, while *hussy* is now confined to a different sense, in line with Kuryłowicz's fourth law.

The second tendency: root alternation is more often abolished than introduced. This, of course, is precisely what is shown by most of the examples of levelling cited in Section 5.2, such as the French case shown in Figure 5.1. Obviously, however, this tendency is in direct conflict with Kuryłowicz's first law.

The third tendency: longer inflectional forms are more often reshaped on the model of shorter ones than vice versa, except in cases in which one form has a zero affix and another an overt affix. The Latin compound verb *calefacere* 'heat' (literally 'make hot') was remodelled on the basis of the common infinitive ending *-āre* (as in *amāre*) 'love') to produce the innovating *calefāre*, the source of modern French *chauffer*.

The fourth tendency: zero-endings are more frequently replaced by overt ones than vice versa. Earlier English had zero-plurals for some nouns; a few of these have survived, like *deer/deer*, but many others have gained a new overt plural ending, so that, for example, earlier *word/word* has been replaced by *word/words*.

The fifth tendency: monosyllabic endings are more frequently replaced by polysyllabic ones than vice versa. The traditional allative case-ending with place names in Basque is *-a*, and hence the town name *Zarautz* has allative *Zarautza* 'to Zarautz'. But some speakers have replaced this with the two-syllable variant *-era*, and hence they have *Zarautzera* 'to Zarautz'.

The sixth tendency: the forms of the indicative more often bring about the reshaping of other moods than vice versa. Portuguese is a language in which the historical subjunctive forms have been partly remodelled on the basis of the indicative.

The seventh tendency: the forms of the present more often bring about the reshaping of other tenses than vice versa. In early Latin, the third-singular ending was *-t* in the present but *-d* in the perfect, but classical Latin has *-t* in both tenses.

The eighth tendency: place names preserve archaisms in their local case-forms better than do related common nouns. In Basque, place names preserve the ancient locative ending *-n* and the ancient allative ending *-a*; most other noun phrases (NPs) have acquired a new locative *-gan > -an* and a new allative *-ra*.

The ninth tendency: when a place name undergoes analogy, its local case-forms affect the non-local ones more often than the other way round. A number of German place names contain an old locative ending, such as *Baden*, a spa town whose name is derived from *Bad* 'bath'.

5.4 *Morphologization*

Sometimes what was formerly an independent word becomes reduced to a bound morpheme, in the process typically losing its former lexical meaning and acquiring instead a mere grammatical function. We call this process **morphologization**, and it is exceedingly common. Indeed, there are linguists who would maintain that *all* bound morphemes originate in just this way.

Here is a simple example from Basque. It appears that Basque once had a noun **kide* meaning something like 'company' or 'association'. (The word still exists today, but it means 'colleague, associate, fellow'.) This came to be used rather frequently with genitive noun phrases to express the notion 'in the company of'. So, for example, the pronoun *gu* 'we, us', whose genitive case-form is *gure* 'our', could appear with **kide* together with the article *-a* and the locative case-ending *-n* 'in, at' to produce something like **gure kidean*, literally, 'in our company' (compare modern Basque *gure etxean* 'in our house', from *etxe* 'house'). Such phrases apparently became the most usual way of expressing accompaniment, and, as a consequence, the whole sequence of genitive *-(r)e* plus **kidean* was collapsed into a single grammatical ending, which, after some phonological reduction, appears in modern Basque as *-(r)ekin*. And this is now the ordinary Basque way of saying 'with': *gurekin* 'with us', *nirekin* 'with me', *neskarekin* 'with the girl', and so on. The independent noun **kide* has vanished from the language (in the relevant sense), leaving behind only a new case-ending, called the 'comitative' case. This example illustrates a very common pathway for the formation of new case-endings: the heavy phonological reduction of complete postpositional phrases together with grammatical reduction to bound forms.

Another, much more famous, instance of morphologization has occurred in the Romance languages (the modern descendants of Latin). Latin had a noun *mens* 'mind', whose stem was *ment-* and whose ablative case-form was *mente* (the Latin ablative was a case-form with miscellaneous, but largely prepositional, uses). Quite early, it became usual in Latin to use the ablative *mente* with an accompanying adjective to express the state of mind in which an action was performed; as was usual in Latin, the adjective had to agree with its noun *mente* as feminine singular ablative. We thus find phrases like *devota mente* 'with a devout mind' (i.e. 'devoutly') and *clara mente* 'with a clear mind' (i.e. 'clear-headedly'). At this stage, though, the construction was possible only with adjectives denoting possible states of mind; other adjectives, like those meaning 'new' or 'equal' or 'obvious', could not appear with *mente*, because the result would have made no sense: something like 'with an equal mind' could hardly mean anything.

But then speakers began to reinterpret the *mente* construction as describing, not the state of mind of somebody doing something, but the manner in which it was done. Consequently, the construction was extended to a much larger range of adjectives, and new instances appeared, like *lenta mente* (*lenta* 'slow') and *dulce mente* (*dulce* 'soft'), with the adjectives still in the correct grammatical form for agreement with the noun. As a result, the form *mente* was no longer regarded as a form of *mens* 'mind'; it was taken instead as a purely grammatical marker expressing an adverbial function, and it was therefore reduced from a separate word to a suffix.

Today this new suffix is the ordinary way of obtaining adverbs of manner in the Romance languages, entirely parallel to English *-ly* in *slowly* or *carefully*, and it can be added to almost any suitable adjective. Thus Spanish, for example, has *igualmente* 'equally' (*igual* 'equal') and *absolutamente* 'absolutely' (*absoluta* 'absolute'). Spanish still retains a trace of the ancient pattern: when two such adverbs are conjoined, only the last takes the suffix, and hence Spaniards say *lenta y seguramente* 'slowly and surely', and not *lentamente y seguramente*. In French, this is not possible, and a French-speaker must say *lentement et sûrement*.

The English adverbial suffix *-ly* has also been obtained by morphologization. Old English had a noun *lic* 'body', which has developed in various ways. As *lich*, it survives in *lich-gate*, a roofed gateway to a church where coffins were formerly placed to await the arrival of a clergyman (and players of certain fantasy games may also recognize *lich* in another context). The derivative *gelic* 'having a common body' is the source of our word *like*, as in 'She's just like you'. But, early on, the word *lic* also came to be compounded with nouns to express the sense of 'resembling' and then 'having the characteristics of': hence Old English *fæderlic* 'father-like', 'fatherly' and *manlic* 'man-like', 'manly'; here the original noun has since been reduced to a mere suffix. Finally, much the same thing happened with adjectives: a case-inflected form *lice* was added to an adjective to express the meaning 'in the manner of': hence Old English *slawlice* 'slowly' and *cwiculice* 'quickly', and here again the original noun has been reduced to a purely grammatical affix: our suffix *-ly* for making adverbs out of adjectives.

A particularly common type of morphologization is the conversion of free pronouns into affixes, either for verbal agreement or for marking possession in noun phrases. Consider Basque again. The agreement markers in Basque finite verbs are mostly very similar to the corresponding free pronouns. Thus, with the verb *joan* 'go', we have forms like these, in which the agreement marker is a prefix:

> *noa* 'I'm going'   (*ni* 'I')
> *hoa* 'you're going'   (*hi* 'you', intimate)
> *doa* 's/he's going'   (no pronoun)
> *goaz* 'we're going'   (*gu* 'we')
> *zoaz* 'you're going'   (*zu* 'you', unmarked)
> *doaz* 'they're going'   (no pronoun)

And when the agreement marker is a suffix:

> *dut* 'I have it'   (*ni* 'I')
> *duk* 'you have it'   (*hi* 'you', intimate)
> *du* 's/he has it'   (no pronoun)
> *dugu* 'we have it'   (*gu* 'we')
> *duzu* 'you have it'   (*zu* 'you', unmarked)
> *dute* 'they have it'   (no pronoun)

Most (but not all) of these affixes are so similar to the corresponding pronouns that they must derive from incorporation of free pronouns into the finite verb. The remaining cases are puzzling, but may reflect an ancient stem-alternation in the pronouns which has been levelled out of existence there.

In the Basque case, we have no historical records allowing us to see an earlier stage of development directly. With some other languages, we are more fortunate. Classical Mongolian, the language of Genghis Khan, is abundantly recorded, and this language had free possessive pronouns like *minü* 'my', which could either precede or follow a possessed noun. Hence, for example, with *morin* 'horse', Classical Mongolian could render 'my horse' either as *minü morin* or as *morin minü*. In modern forms of Mongolian, the free possessive pronouns still exist, but they have also been reduced to suffixes when following the noun. Hence Kalmyk Mongolian, in which 'horse' is now *möre*, has, for 'my horse', both *möre-m*, with a possessive suffix only, and *mini möre-m*, with the free possessive form *mini* 'my' preceding to provide a double marking of possession.

The developments illustrated here by Basque and Mongolian are exceedingly common in languages generally, and it is interesting to inquire how such morphologizations come about. In the majority of cases, it appears, the first step is **cliticization**: the reduction of a free form to a clitic. (A **clitic**, if this is not a familiar term, is an item which is less than an independent word but still something more than a bound affix.) Exactly such cliticization is typical of pronouns in the Romance languages. Consider French. In French, 'John will give the book to Mary' is *Jean donnera le livre à Marie*, with very similar word order to English. But 'He'll give it to you' is *Il te le donnera*, literally 'He you it will give', in which all three pronouns are clitics which are obliged to appear as a cluster just before the verb: there is no possibility of saying anything like **Il donnera le te*. These clitics still have some degree of independent existence, but they are none the less rigidly fixed to the preverbal position, unlike independent words. It is perfectly possible that these clitics will in the future lose their remaining traces of independent status and become fused into the verb, and indeed several linguists have argued that exactly this has already happened: whereas written French has, for 'John will give you the book', *Jean te donnera le livre*, spoken French very commonly has *Jean, il te le donnera, le livre*, in which the clitics seem to be acting very much like agreement markers in the verb. It is possible that French is becoming a language with extensive verbal agreement for subjects and objects, much like Basque or Swahili or some of the Caucasian languages. And, in all likelihood, the Basque and Mongolian constructions illustrated above proceeded by means of just such cliticization of what were originally independent words.

5.5   *Morphologization of phonological rules*

The term 'morphologization' is also applied to a kind of historical process very different from the phenomena we have just been discussing. This is the case in which a formerly regular phonological rule ceases to be productive, so that its effects come to be confined only to certain words and forms which were already in the language when the rule was active.

Middle English had contrasting sets of long and short vowels, and each long vowel was very similar in quality to its corresponding short vowel: the long vowel simply had greater duration. In certain phonological circumstances, however, the long vowels were regularly shortened. In particular, this happened to a long vowel which found itself followed by two or more further syllables, in a process known as **Trisyllabic Laxing**. At one time, this rule applied to all relevant cases; it was therefore purely a phonological rule, a constraint upon what was pronounceable in English.

Later, though, two things happened. First, all the long vowels changed their phonetic quality rather dramatically, in the Great Vowel Shift. As a result, each long vowel became very dissimilar in quality to its corresponding short vowel. (And short /u/ also changed its quality substantially.) Second, and most crucially, the rule of Trisyllabic Laxing ceased to be a part of the phonology of English: it no longer applied systematically to new instances of long vowels finding themselves three or more syllables from the end of a word. It is this second development which constitutes morphologization of the rule: the rule stopped being a general constraint upon the possible form of an English word, and became instead a morphological process which applied only to some words.

The remnants of the old rule are still highly visible in English today, in the form of alternations between vowels continuing the old long and short pairs of vowels. Here are some examples:

sane	sanity	saline	salinity
profane	profanity	crime	criminal
humane	humanity	sign	signify
vain	vanity	divine	divinity
grain	granular	type	typical
grave	gravity	conspire	conspiracy
serene	serenity	verbose	verbosity
clean	cleanliness	cone	conical
		mode	modify
		profound	profundity
		pronounce	pronunciation

But this process is no longer generally productive, and moreover the alternation has sometimes been lost from words which formerly showed it. Do you have the alternations or not in the following cases?

obese	obesity
pirate	piracy
private	privacy
grain	granary
code	codify

Probably no English-speaker has the alternation in *obesity*. It used to be present in *piracy*, which worked like *conspiracy*, but this pronunciation is now obsolete, except reportedly in English law courts. With *privacy*, both pronunciations are now common in Britain, but probably no American has the alternation. Most Britons pronounce *granary* with the vowel of *grand*, while most Americans use the vowel of *grain*. On the other hand, most Americans pronounce *codify* like *modify*, while Britons pronounce *codify* with the vowel of *code*. Even *pronunciation* has come to be pronounced by many speakers as though it were *pronounciation*, though this form is nowhere standard as yet.

In short, the rule of Trisyllabic Laxing has become morphologized: it is no longer automatic, and we just have to learn to which words it applies and to which it doesn't.

It is possible for a purely phonological rule to become morphologized in another way: by the effect of a phonological change. The ancestor of Spanish had two contrasting front mid vowels, /e/ and /ɛ/. The second of these underwent a phonological change by which it was diphthongized to [jɛ] when stressed, but not when unstressed; the first vowel underwent no such diphthongization. Consequently, the language acquired an absolutely regular alternation [ɛ] ~ [jɛ] depending upon the position of the stress. This alternation is still visible in modern Spanish, in which the diphthong is spelled <ie>: *perder* 'lose' (final stress) but *pierdo* 'I lose' (initial stress); *sentir* 'feel' (final stress) but *siento* 'I feel' (initial stress); *piedra* 'stone' (initial stress) but *pedrera* 'stone quarry' (stress on second syllable). But then a second phonological change intervened: the vowel /e/ merged with /ɛ/ to yield a single vowel phoneme /e/. Since original /e/ never diphthongizes, this merger produced a state of affairs in which some instances of /e/ diphthongize under stress while others do not: alongside the examples just cited, Spanish has cases like *vencer* 'conquer' (final stress) but *venzo* 'I conquer' (initial stress) and *pesca* 'fishing' (initial stress) but *pescado* 'fish' (stress on second syllable). As a result, diphthongization is no longer predictable, and Spanish-speakers simply have to learn which words alternate and which don't: the diphthongization has become morphologized.

The morphologization of phonological rules is clearly a phenomenon of some considerable theoretical interest, and there have been various attempts over the years at classifying phonological and morphological alternations in a principled manner and in trying to provide some kind of explanation for the differences. Here I shall briefly consider one such approach, one developed in the 1980s. This is **Natural Morphology**, an approach developed chiefly in Germany. The central claim of Natural Morphology (NM) is that certain types of forms and constructions are more natural than others, and that morphological changes usually proceed so as to increase the degree of naturalness. The Natural Morphologists are hardly the first linguists to make such claims; what sets the framework apart is its vigorous attempt at identifying natural forms explicitly. Natural forms, we are told, are really just *unmarked* forms, and these are identified on the facing page.

Natural (unmarked) forms

- occur very frequently in languages generally;
- occur frequently and in a variety of contexts in languages containing them;
- occur in pidgins or are introduced early in creoles (see Chapter 11);
- are acquired early by children;
- are comparatively resistant to loss in aphasia (disordered speech caused by brain damage);
- are relatively resistant to change;
- frequently result from changes;
- are exhibited by loan words and neologisms;
- are little affected by speech errors.

Some, though by no means all, of these putatively natural forms are those which are **iconic**: that is, they correspond to the principle of 'one-meaning-one-form'. For example, it may reasonably be maintained that a plural form like *dogs* carries 'more meaning' than a singular form like *dog*. Therefore, the plural form ought to contain more morphological material, and of course it does. Moreover, the plural marker *-s* is clearly visible tacked onto the end of the lexical morpheme *dog*: a seemingly ideal state of affairs. English plural patterns like *goose/geese*, *sheep/sheep*, and *radius/radii* are less natural, because they fall short of this ideally iconic arrangement in one way or another.

Consequently, we might expect iconic plurals like *dogs* to be 'natural' in the relevant sense, and to exhibit the requisite properties. Let's check. Iconic plurals comparable to *dogs* are certainly fairly common in the world's languages, but nowhere near universal. Plurals like *dogs* are certainly frequent in English in almost every conceivable context. Pidgins, however, rarely have overt plurals at all, and they are not necessarily introduced early into creoles. Regular plurals like *dogs* are certainly acquired early by children, earlier than the more complex and irregular plurals of some other languages. But regular plurals *are* easily lost in certain types of aphasia, like Broca's aphasia, which has catastrophic effects on regular grammatical forms (though irregular plurals are *less* affected). We can see no tendency for the iconic plurals to undergo change in English, but they certainly do result from change: the vastly complex patterns of plural formation in Old English have been replaced almost entirely by the iconic *-s* plural, which has spread to many hundreds of words which formerly didn't have it. Loan words and neologisms always acquire the iconic plural: *pizzas*, *modems*. And there is indeed little evidence that speech errors ever do anything much to iconic plurals: certainly nobody ever seems to replace an iconic plural like *houses* with something like *hice*, merely because of *mouse/mice*.

These are generally satisfactory findings, if not absolutely perfect. But what we're interested in here are the implications of all this for morphological change. Overlooking some subtleties, what NM now claims is that morphological change will tend to produce natural, unmarked, iconic morphology, of the type illustrated by *dog/dogs*, and not the opposite. As we have seen, this is true for the English plural: the iconic pattern has been spreading remorselessly for centuries at the expense of originally competing patterns which were not so natural, and now only a handful of items still retain any of the older patterns, like *goose/geese* and *sheep/sheep*. But what about past tenses?

The regular English past-tense pattern is represented by *love/loved*, which is just as iconic and natural as *dog/dogs*. And, once again, it is certainly true that the overall tendency in the language has for centuries been the growth of the iconic pattern at the expense of other, less natural, patterns, such as those found in *write/wrote* and *see/saw*, which were formerly far more frequent than they are now. But there are a few exceptions. The earlier, and fully natural, *catch/catched* has now been ousted by the decidedly less natural *catch/caught*, and, in American English, we also have the replacement of *dive/dived* by *dive/ dove*. Still, no proponent of NM is claiming that no morphological change can ever go the 'wrong' way, but only that such developments are likely to be far less frequent than the opposite changes, and that appears to be true.

Of course, we might wonder why there remain some exceptional forms like *geese* and *saw* which have so far resisted the putative historical trend towards 'natural' morphology. For some of these, the answer is obvious: forms like *saw* and *men*, being so exceedingly frequent, are typically learned so early by children that they are acquired even before the regular pattern is learned. For others, a different explanation is available: forms like *radii* and *forsook* are hardly likely to be learned at all except through reading and/or formal education, in which they are institutionalized. But that still leaves a few cases like *geese* and *clung*, for which neither explanation seems obviously adequate – though perhaps *geese*, at least, genuinely *was* an everyday word for most English-speakers until very recently.

Still, it can hardly be denied that the history of English morphology during the last thousand years has been one of a steady increase in naturalness. Consider the Old English inflections in Table 5.2. As you can see, this is anything but iconic: there is no identifiable genitive marker, no identifiable plural marker, and so on; moreover, the language had many other classes of nouns exhibiting different sets of endings from the ones appearing here.

But in modern English all we have left is *long day*, which can be used with a determiner like *the* or *a* and which can have the highly iconic plural marker -*s* attached to it, or the equally iconic possessive marker -*'s*. There is no other morphology, and we have to use prepositions like *of* or *to* to express relations handled in Old English by the morphology. The changes in English morphology have been of exactly the type predicted.

Now, if, as the proponents of NM maintain, morphological change tends strongly to proceed in such a way as to make morphology more natural, we might reasonably wonder why languages have unnatural morphology at all. But they do. Old English, like modern German or Russian, had an exceedingly complex and messy morphology that would hardly pass muster as 'natural' in even the most generous view – and there are plenty of languages, such as the

Table 5.2 Some Old English inflections

	'the long day'	'a long day'
Nom	*se lange dæg*	*lang dǣg*
Gen	*þǣs langa dæges*	*langes dǣges*
Dat	*þǣm langan dæge*	*langum dǣge*
Acc	*þone langan dæg*	*langne dǣg*
	'the long days'	**'long days'**
Nom	*þā langan dagas*	*lange dagas*
Gen	*þāra langena daga*	*langra daga*
Dat	*þǣm langum dagum*	*langum dagum*
Acc	*þā langan dagas*	*lange dagas*

Iroquoian and Athabaskan languages of North America, in which the morphology can reasonably be described as almost terrifyingly complex. How do languages acquire such unnatural morphology in the first place?

We can make a few suggestions. For one thing, it is clear that unnatural morphology often results from nothing more than the operation of regular phonological change upon what was originally a highly natural morphology. (The English 'umlauting' plurals like *geese* and *mice* derive from precisely such a source: they were once completely regular and iconic, but were disturbed by regular phonological changes.) For another, as we shall see in the next chapter, some morphology results from the reduction of syntactic constructions to bound forms, and this sort of change is not necessarily subject to the same principles as purely morphological change. But there are other factors to consider. As we shall see in the next section, languages which approach the iconic ideal of having a visibly distinct morpheme to carry each separate piece of grammatical information tend to have rather long words – and long words may themselves be regarded as unnatural from a different point of view.

But there must be more to it. Recall the case of the introduction of double plural-marking into German nouns discussed under Kuryłowicz's first law. This change seemingly went the 'wrong' way, in that it introduced stem-alternations (compare the English case just discussed, in which stem-alternations have been eliminated from nouns). Developments of this sort pose an awkward problem for NM, but the response of its proponents is very interesting, and sets NM apart from earlier and perhaps less sophisticated attempts at interpreting morphological change in terms of increasing iconicity.

The idea is that there are different, and sometimes competing, versions of naturalness, and that some of them may be language-specific. Both German and English have historically been languages in which stem-modification for grammatical purposes is an important feature of the morphology. English has generally gone down the road of eliminating these stem-alternations, but there is another possibility: stem-alternations can themselves be seen as natural for certain languages, and may therefore tend to be extended over time. We can, therefore, perhaps interpret the German developments as resulting from a conflict between two conceptions of naturalness: a universal one, which disfavours stem-alternations as non-iconic, and a language-specific one, which favours stem-alternations as a natural pattern in the language. Of course, this striking idea can be made to work only if the proponents of NM can find some principled way of explaining why particular resolutions of such conflicts are preferred in particular cases: it is hardly adequate merely to invoke a different set of principles for each change we encounter. It remains to be seen whether NM will be successful in achieving this.

One of the leading proponents of NM, Wolfgang Dressler, has tried to interpret cases of the morphologization of rules in terms of the framework.

Dressler (1985b) considers that rules introducing alternations can be classified into just three types. The first type consists of *Phonological Rules* (PRs). These rules are purely phonological; they apply without exception to all relevant forms, and their effect is merely to create forms which are pronounceable in the language. For example, Dressler argues that the three alternants of the English plural morpheme are derived by PRs: if /z/ is the underlying form of the plural suffix, then PRs convert this to /ɪz/ after a sibilant and otherwise to /s/ after a voiceless segment: hence *dogs*, *hills*, *days* (with /z/), but *matches*, *bushes*, *foxes* (with /ɪz/), and *cats*, *books*, *serfs* (with /s/).

The second type is *Mor(pho)phonological Rules* (MPRs). These are similar to PRs in that they can be written in the ordinary formalism used for writing phonological rules, and typically have some identifiable phonetic motivation, but differ in that they are lexically governed (that is, only certain words undergo them). Dressler's example is the English rule of **Velar Softening**, by which a velar plosive /k/ or /g/ is converted to /s/ (or /ʃ/) or /dʒ/ before a front vowel when a morpheme boundary intervenes. This is the rule that accounts for alternations like *electri*[k] - *electri*[s]*ity* and *analo*[g]*ue* but *analo*[dʒ]*y*. This rule commonly applies to words of French, Latin, or Greek origin, but it fails to apply in certain cases, like *monar*[k] - *monar*[k]*y*, and it never applies to native words: *do*[g] - *do*[g]*ie*. That is, this rule is lexically governed, and not automatic.

Dressler's third type is *Allomorphy Rules* (ARs). These are similar to MPRs in being lexically governed, but differ in that they cannot be formulated as ordinary phonological rules, at least not without invoking absurdly abstract underlying forms. An English example is the rule of Trisyllabic Laxing discussed above, in which, in Dressler's view, alternations like *sane* - *sanity* represent essentially arbitrary phenomena with no identifiable phonetic basis; he regards them as similar to cases of **suppletion** like *go* - *went* and *person* - *people*.

These three types differ in their behaviour. PRs are *always* applied, even to neologisms and to nonsense words coined in psycholinguistic experiments;

the other two types are typically not applied in such circumstances. So, a subject asked to pluralize the nonsense word *flaig* will produce *flaig*[z], with the normal plural form after /g/; asked to add the suffix *-ity*, however, the subject will usually produce *flai*[g]*ity*, with no softening of the velar and no change in the vowel. On the other hand, MPRs, like PRs but unlike ARs, may be invoked in word games and in jocular formations, such as in the formation from *Association football* of *soccer*, in which the Velar Softening is reversed. MPRs, then, represent a kind of intermediate stage in the morphologization of rules: a rule may begin as a PR, then become partly morphologized to an MPR, at which point it retains a degree of generality in spite of being now lexically governed, and finally become completely fossilized as an AR, an arbitrary process lacking any visible motivation. This general view is not particularly controversial, but the difficult part, of course, is to provide criteria for distinguishing the supposed three types of rule unambiguously, and Dressler in fact admits that the dividing lines are not sharp.

But Dressler then goes on to make an interesting claim about historical change: he claims that both the fully phonological PRs and the fully morphological ARs can be generalized in various ways so as to extend their domains, but that the intermediate MPRs, being neither properly phonological nor properly morphological, cannot undergo any kind of generalization. This claim, if correct, would represent a significant advance in our understanding of morphological change. However, not everyone is convinced that it is correct. For example, if you were so rash as to add the suffix *-ity* or *-ian* to a word like *metric* or *mythic*, how do you suppose you would pronounce the result? I suspect that most people would apply Velar Softening as usual, producing things like *metri*[s]*ity*, even though Velar Softening, as an MPR, should not be capable of extension to new cases.

5.6 *Change in morphological type*

Undoubtedly the most dramatic kind of morphological change is the replacement of the entire morphological system of a language by something completely different, what we call a change in morphological type. To describe this, I need first to say something about the concept of a morphological type.

It was noticed very early by European linguists that languages can differ very substantially in the nature of their morphological systems. The most famous early attempt at a classification is that of the German linguist Wilhelm von Humboldt in the early nineteenth century. Humboldt recognized three types of morphology. In an **isolating** language, there is no morphology at all, and every word consists of a single morpheme. Good examples of isolating languages are Vietnamese and many west African languages. Here is an example sentence from Vietnamese:

- Khi tôi dến nhà bạn tôi, chúng tôi bắt dầu làm bài.
- when I come house friend I, Plural I begin do lesson
- 'When I arrived at my friend's house, we began to do lessons.'

As you can see, each word consists of a single morpheme, with no prefixes or suffixes and no grammatical modification of any kind, except that the two words *bắt dầu* translate the English 'begin'. Even 'we' is expressed by combining 'I' with a plural word.

In an **agglutinating** language, a single word may consist of several morphemes, but each morpheme is a clearly distinct form, and the morphemes in a word are strung together one after another, rather like beads on a string. Among the agglutinating languages are Basque, Swahili, Turkish, and many Australian languages. Here is an example from Turkish; the abbreviations are Part(iciple), Obj(ect), Ger(und):

- Yap-tığ-ım hata-yı memleket-i tanı-ma-ma-m-a ver-ebil-ir-siniz.
- make-Part-my mistake-Obj country-Obj know-not-Ger-my-to give-can-Tense-you
- 'You can ascribe the mistake I made to my not knowing the country.'

In Turkish, a word typically consists of a string of morphemes; each morpheme has a single function and generally a single consistent form, apart from minor variations for purely phonological reasons. Consider some further examples: *ev* 'house', *evim* 'my house', *evler* 'houses', *evlerim* 'my houses', *evde* 'in the house', *evimde* 'in my house', *evlerde* 'in the houses', *evlerimde* 'in my houses'. Turkish-speakers (and linguists) sometimes amuse themselves by seeing how far they can go in stringing morphemes together. A classic example is *Avrupalılaştırılamıyanlardansınız*. Here *Avrupa* is 'Europe', *-lı* is 'from', *-laş* is 'become', *-tır* is 'cause', *-ıl* is Passive, *-amı* is 'unable', *-yan* is 'one who', *-lar* is Plural, *-dan* is 'from, of', and *sınız* is 'you', and the whole thing is 'You are of those who are unable to be caused to become European', or, in plain English, 'You're one of those we can't make a European out of'.

In an **inflecting** language, a word typically consists of several morphemes, but the morpheme boundaries are difficult or impossible to identify: instead, the several morphemes are wrapped up into a tight package. Among the inflecting languages are Latin, Russian, Old English, and many North American languages. Here is an example from Latin; the abbreviations are Neut(er), Plur(al), Obj(ect), Masc(uline), Sing(ular), 1st (Person), Pres(ent), Indic(ative), Act(ive):

- Arm-a vir-um-que can-ō.
- weapon-Neut-Plur-Obj man-MascSingObj-and sing-1stSingPresIndicAct
- 'Arms and the man I sing.'

In Latin, though the stems of words can often be isolated, the endings generally cannot be: each ending effectively consists of several morphemes, and endings cannot be decomposed into separate elements with meanings like 'plural' or 'masculine'. Moreover, the endings are not of consistent form: while the masculine noun *vir* 'man' has the singular object form *virum*, the masculine noun *dens* 'tooth' has the singular object form *dentem*. In short, then, an inflecting language has a very messy morphology which is difficult to analyse, in great contrast to agglutinating languages like Turkish, which are morphologically transparent.

Isolating languages are sometimes called *analytic* languages; inflecting languages are also called *fusional* languages; and agglutinating and inflecting languages together are called *synthetic* languages. Naturally, not all languages fit neatly into one of these three pigeonholes: for example, how would you classify English in this system? Nevertheless, the distinctions are convenient for labelling languages briefly. As you can see, isolating and agglutinating languages have a high degree of iconicity, while inflecting languages generally have a much lower degree.

Now it is quite clear that a language, given sufficient time, can change from one of these types to another. Nineteenth-century linguists were often inclined to assume a natural direction for such changes: isolating languages develop into agglutinating languages by compounding, and agglutinating languages develop into inflecting languages by complex phonological changes. And such developments are certainly attested. For example, classical Chinese was a paradigm case of an isolating language, but modern Chinese is different. It has acquired a number of suffixes, such as the plural suffix *-men* (*wǒ* 'I', *wǒmen* 'we'; *tā* 'he, she', *tāmen* 'they'), the completed-action suffix *-le* (*qù* 'go', *qùle* 'went'), and a number of word-forming suffixes like *-li* 'power' (*yǎnli* 'vision', from *yǎn* 'eye'; *mǎli* 'horsepower', from *mǎ* 'horse') and *-du* 'degree' (*chángdu* 'length', from *cháng* 'long'; *rèdu* 'temperature' from *rè* 'hot'). It has also acquired a very large number of compounds: *huǒchē* 'train', from *huǒ* 'fire' and *chē* 'vehicle'; *báicài* 'cabbage', from *bái* 'white' and *cài* 'vegetable'; *gémìng* 'revolt, make revolution', from *gé* 'remove' and *mìng* 'Heavenly Mandate'; *zúzú* 'completely', a reduplication of *zú* 'suffice'. Modern Chinese is beginning to look a bit like an agglutinating language, though it still has a long way to go before it resembles Turkish or Swahili.

But we now know that there is no reason to suppose that changes in morphology can proceed only in one direction. There is very good reason to suppose that a remote ancestor of Chinese was highly inflected, but the language apparently lost every trace of its ancient inflections and became exclusively isolating, and the isolating languages of West Africa appear to descend from an ancestor which was agglutinating. Old English was a highly inflected language somewhat resembling Latin, but English has lost all but a few traces of its earlier inflections: *goose/geese*, *take/took*, *hot/heat*, and some others. At the same time, the agglutinating character of the language has become more prominent: *love/loves/loved/loving*; *dog/dogs*; *write/rewrite/writer*; *happy/unhappy/happiness*. But modern English has a very high degree of isolating character: *You must have been sitting in front of the TV for hours*; *I have not been able to find a more interesting book than this one.*

How does a language change its morphology so dramatically? One way is contact with other languages. Earlier Armenian, for example, was strongly inflecting, but modern Armenian has become largely agglutinating, rather like Turkish, and seemingly because of centuries of contact with Turkish and its agglutinating relatives, and Vietnamese is thought by many specialists to have lost all of its ancestral morphology as a result of many centuries of contact with the isolating Chinese. More often, though, change of morphological type comes about for purely internal reasons. The elaborate case-systems of Latin and Old English depended crucially upon distinctions in the final syllables of inflected nouns; as phonological changes began to reduce and to obliterate those final syllables, prepositions came to be used more frequently to reinforce the case distinctions which were beginning to be lost; the increased use of prepositions made the case-endings less significant than previously, and so there was less reason to hang onto the remaining case-endings. Consequently, English, and the modern descendants of Latin like Spanish, French, and Italian, have lost their earlier case-systems completely (except in a few pronouns), and replaced them with analytical (isolating) constructions involving prepositions.

Like any kind of linguistic change, change in morphological type is under no obligation to occur. All the Athabaskan languages of western North America, like Apache and Navaho, exhibit an astoundingly complex and elaborate morphology of the inflecting type; the actual shapes of the morphs have changed substantially in the various Athabaskan languages, but the overall system has remained stable for thousands of years. In morphology, as elsewhere, it is not generally possible to predict what changes will occur, or even whether any changes will occur at all. As always, the best that we can do is to determine that certain types of change are more likely to occur than others.

Further reading

Chapter 23 of Bloomfield (1933), on morphological change, is still well worth reading today. Chapters 9 and 10 of Hock (1986) discuss morphological change, and particularly analogy, in some considerable detail, including Kuryłowicz's laws and Mańczak's tendencies. Anttila (1977) is an entire book on analogy, not easy going but well worth the effort. Morphologization is discussed, with numerous examples, in several chapters of Hopper and Traugott (1993). Natural Morphology is presented in Dressler (1985a, 1985b) and Wurzel (1989); brief surveys can be found in chapter 12 of L. Bauer (1988) and in chapter 4 of McMahon (1994). Morphological typology has been considerably developed since Humboldt; you can find further discussion in Horne (1966), Anttila (1988: ch. 16), Comrie (1989: ch. 2), and Lehmann (1992: 100–2).

Exercises

Exercise 5.1

The system of personal pronouns was considerably more elaborate in Old English than it is in modern English. Table 5.3 lists the Old English forms. Describe what has happened to these pronouns since Old English.

Exercise 5.2

Old English normally formed superlatives by means of a suffix *-ost* or *-est*, as in *heard* 'hard', *heardost* 'hardest', and *eald* 'old', *ealdest* 'oldest'. A few words, however, took a different suffix *-(u)m(a)*, as in *fore* 'before', *forma* 'most before', and *ūt(e)* 'out', *ūtem* 'most outer'. These irregular forms underwent two changes. First, they acquired an additional suffix, yielding *formest* and *ūtemest*. Then, the ending was altered in a phonologically irregular way, yielding the modern forms *foremost* and *utmost*. Explain why these two changes should have happened.

Exercise 5.3

Each of the following words has an interesting morphological history for one reason or another. Consulting a good etymological dictionary of English, find out what has happened in each case and explain it as clearly as you can, invoking wherever possible the ideas discussed in the chapter.

Table 5.3

	Nom	Acc	Dat	Gen
1Sg	*ic*	*mē*	*mē*	*min*
1Dual	*wit*	*unc*	*unc*	*uncer*
1Pl	*wē*	*ūs*	*ūs*	*ūre*
2Sg	*þū*	*þē*	*þē*	*þin*
2Dual	*git*	*inc*	*inc*	*incer*
2Pl	*gē*	*ēow*	*ēow*	*ēower*
3SgMasc	*hē*	*hine*	*him*	*his*
3SgFem	*hēo*	*hi(e)*	*hi(e)re*	*hi(e)re*
3SgNeut	*hit*	*hit*	*him*	*his*
3Pl	*hi(e)*	*hi(e)*	*him*	*hira*

(a) sand-blind   (h) darling
(b) cherry   (i) outrage
(c) universe   (j) flammable
(d) sodden   (k) bugbear
(e) unkempt   (l) workaholic
(f) ecdysiast   (m) penthouse
(g) software   (n) toward

Exercise 5.4

Table 5.4 lists some examples of change in verbal morphology. In each case, the language on the left is the direct ancestor of the language on the right. Note that the phonological change of */rst/ to /rt/ is regular in Pre-Celtic; the other changes illustrated are not phonological, but morphological. Identify the common feature of all these developments, and propose a principle of morphological change which is in evidence here. This principle is sometimes called **Watkins's Law**.

Exercise 5.5

There is clear evidence that the verb *phérō* 'carry' had the following forms in pre-Greek:

Table 5.4

Avestan	Modern Persian	
ah-mi	*hast-am*	'I am'
ah-ti	*hast-i*	'you are'
as-ti	*hast*	'he is'

Common Slavic	Polish	
*es-mi	*jest-em*	'I am'
*es-i	*jest-eś*	'you are'
*es-ti	*jest*	'he is'

PIE	Pre-Celtic	Common Celtic	
*bher-s-m	**ber-s-ū*	**ber-t-ū*	'I carried'
*bher-s-s	**ber-s-i*	**ber-t-i*	'you carried'
*bher-s-t	**ber-t*	**ber-t*	'he carried'

	Present			Imperfect	
1Sg	*phérō*	'I carry'		*épheron*	'I was carrying'
2Sg	**phéresi*	'you carry'		*épheres*	'you were carrying'
3Sg	**phéreti*	's/he carries'		*éphere*	's/he was carrying'

The forms without asterisks in fact survived into classical Attic Greek, but the remaining two did not. First, intervocalic /s/ was categorically lost in Greek. Much later, in Attic Greek, intervocalic /t/ changed to /s/ before /i/. These changes should have produced the following paradigm:

	Present			Imperfect	
1Sg	*phérō*	'I carry'		*épheron*	'I was carrying'
2Sg	**phérei*	'you carry'		*épheres*	'you were carrying'
3Sg	**phéresi*	's/he carries'		*éphere*	's/he was carrying'

But these are still not the classical Attic forms. Instead, we find the following forms in Attic Greek:

	Present			Imperfect	
1Sg	*phérō*	'I carry'		*épheron*	'I was carrying'
2Sg	*phéreis*	'you carry'		*épheres*	'you were carrying'
3Sg	*phérei*	's/he carries'		*éphere*	's/he was carrying'

Propose an explanation for the origin of the two unexpected forms, and comment on your account in the light of Mańczak's tendencies. (Data from Lehmann 1992: 219–20.)

Exercise 5.6

Consider the following facts about Basque.

(a) The ordinary allative case-ending is *-ra* 'to' (in the sense of 'motion to'): *etxera noa* 'I'm going to the house, I'm going home' (*etxe* 'house').

(b) This has an extended form *-raino ~ -raiño* 'up to, as far as, until', as in *etxeraino* 'up to the house, as far as the house'; this form is called the *terminative*.

(c) The Bizkaian dialect, which preserves a number of archaisms lost elsewhere, has a unique suffix *-giño* 'until', as in *oraingiño* 'until now'.

(d) Bizkaian and other dialects further exhibit a curious and seemingly ancient suffix *-do* in a few words, such as *egundo* 'until today, still, yet' (*egun* 'today') and *oraindo* 'until now, still, yet' (*orain* 'now').

(e) All dialects have a word *gain* 'top', which is very frequently used in postpositional phrases, as in *mahai gainean* 'on top of the table' (*mahai* 'table', *-ean* 'in, on, at').

Propose an explanation for the source of the terminative suffix *-raino*. (Data from de Rijk 1995.)

Table 5.5

	Prefix	Suffix	Pronoun
1Sg	*n-*	*-t*	*ni*
2Sg	*h-*	*-k*	*hi*
1Pl	*g-*	*-gu*	*gu*
2Pl	*z-*	*-zu*	*zu*

Exercise 5.7

In Section 5.4 above I presented some typical verb forms from Basque, illustrating some of the extensive agreement found in that language. Table 5.5 gives a summary of the agreement morphs and the corresponding free pronouns for the first two persons. It is certain that the two singular suffixes were originally *-da* and *-ga*. Have you any idea why these two suffixes should be out of line with the rest of the pattern?

The third person is much more complex. Basque has no third-person pronouns, and the third-person agreement suffix is zero. When the third person is due to be marked by a prefix, however, we find a startling range of morphs occupying the prefix slot: *d-* in the present tense, *z-* in the past tense, *l-* in 'irrealis' forms, zero in the ordinary imperative, and *b-* in the 'jussive' (the third-person imperative). For generations, specialists in Basque have agonized over these prefixes, proposing all sorts of lost pronouns and whatnot as sources, without success. Propose a better explanation.

6

Syntactic change

Until very recently, the study of syntactic change could be fairly described as being still in its infancy. The last few years, however, have seen an extraordinary burst of activity in this area; we now know a good deal about syntactic change, and a few general principles have begun to emerge. Some of the ideas we encountered in the last chapter will turn up again here, and indeed it can be difficult to draw a sharp line between morphological change and syntactic change.

6.1 Reanalysis of surface structure

Beyond any doubt, the single most important pathway of syntactic change is reanalysis. In the last chapter, we saw a number of examples of the reanalysis of morphological structure, but the reanalysis of sentence structure is no less important.

Let us begin with some simple examples. Many languages have a special grammatical item called a **copula**, which serves to link two elements of a sentence, especially two noun phrases. The English copula is the verb *be*, and its use is illustrated by examples like *Esther is a businesswoman* and *Paris is the capital of France*. But lots of languages have no copula: in Turkish, for example, the sentence *Ali büyük* means 'Ali is big', but it consists merely of the name *Ali* and the adjective *büyük* 'big', so the sentence structure is literally 'Ali big'. We may reasonably ask, then, how it is that some languages have acquired copulas in the first place.

Consider Mandarin Chinese. Modern Chinese has a copula *shì*, illustrated by examples like the following:

(6.1) *hūa shì hóng*
flower be red
'The flower is red.'

(6.2) *nà shì cāochǎng*
that be playground
'That is the playground.'

However, Archaic Chinese, the form of Chinese used until about the third century BC, did not have a copula, as shown by the next example; the item *yě* is a declarative (Decl) particle, used to indicate that a statement is being made, and not a copula:

(6.3) *Wáng-Tái wù zhě yě*
Wang-Tai outstanding person Decl
'Wang-Tai is an outstanding person.'

Now the item *shì* did exist in Archaic Chinese, but it wasn't a copula. Instead, it was a demonstrative meaning 'this':

(6.4) *zi yù shì rì kū*
Confucius at this day cry
'Confucius cried on this day.'

This demonstrative was frequently used in sentences like the following; here *suǒ* is a particle which nominalizes its clause:

(6.5) *qīan lǐ ér jiàn wáng shì wǒ suǒ yù yě*
thousand mile then see king, this I Nom desire Decl
'(To travel) a thousand miles to see the king, this is what I desire.'

And it is precisely this construction that led to the reanalysis of *shì* as a copula: the original X *shì* Y originally was literally 'X, this [is] Y', but it was reanalysed as meaning 'X is Y', and so *shì* became a copula. The reanalysis was assisted by the fact that, by the sixth century AD, *shì* had completely ceased to be used as a demonstrative in any other circumstances, and so from then on it occurred only in sentences like the last example.

A more recent example showing a similar development is Hebrew. Hebrew formerly had no copula in the present tense, but today it has a copula *hu*, which is obligatory in some contexts, optional in others, and prohibited in still others, according to complicated rules. Here are some examples in which it is obligatory, or nearly so:

(6.6) *David hu ha-ganav*
David be the-thief
'David is the thief.'

(6.7) *Moše hu student*
Moshe be student
'Moshe is a student.'

In Hebrew, the source of the copula *hu* is perfectly clear: it is the pronoun *hu* 'he', which is still also a pronoun:

(6.8) *hu ohev et-Rivka*
he loves Acc-Rivka
'He loves Rivka.'

It is clear what has happened. A construction with *hu*, originally meaning literally 'Moshe, he (is) a student' has been reanalysed as meaning 'Moshe is a student'. You will doubtless be familiar with the non-standard but exceedingly common English construction *John, he's a nice guy*.

That Hebrew *hu* is now a genuine copula is shown by cases like the next example:

(6.9) *ani hu ha-student še-Moše diber itxa alav*
I be the-student that-Moshe spoke with-you about-him
'I am the student that Moshe told you about.'

Here the subject is first person, and *hu* cannot possibly be interpreted as meaning 'he'.

These examples, and some additional ones, all discussed in Li and Thompson (1977), show that one possible source of a copula is a demonstrative or a pronoun used in a linking function. Such instances represent a very straightforward type of syntactic reanalysis, involving no more than a single word.

My next example, taken from Munro (1977), while it also describes the origin of a copula, illustrates a much more complex type of syntactic reanalysis. The Yuman language Mojave of North America has a copula *ido-*, as shown in the next example (the suffix *-č* is discussed below):

(6.10) *John $k^w a\theta ?ide:-č$ ido-pč*
John doctor-č be-Tense
'John is a doctor.'

Here the copula takes a tense-marker just like any other verb, and the sentence looks unremarkable enough. In fact, however, copular sentences in Mojave have one very strange characteristic. To see what this is, look at an example of a sentence without a copula:

(6.11) *John-č Mary iyu:-pč*
John-Subj Mary see-Tense
'John saw Mary.'

What this example shows is that the suffix *-č* normally marks subjects, and only subjects. Yet in copular sentences like (6.10), this suffix appears, not on the subject, but on the complement. This is very strange. How could this have come about?

The key point, Munro argues, is that the subject suffix *-č* appears only on the subjects of main clauses, and does not appear on the subjects of most types of subordinate clauses:

(6.12) *?-nakut ?ava u:čo:-l^y ?-navay-k*
my-father house make-in I-live-Tense
'I live in the house my father built.'

Here *?nakut* 'my father' does not take the subject suffix because it is the subject of a subordinate clause – in this case, a relative clause. We may therefore surmise that, in Example (6.10), *John* was originally not the subject of a main clause, but we still have to account for the presence of the subject suffix on the complement NP meaning 'doctor'. And here we promptly encounter an important lesson.

An earlier generation of linguists, noting the presence of the subject suffix on the word for 'doctor', might well have expended dozens or hundreds of hours in work trying to figure out how 'doctor' could originally have been the subject of (6.10). This may seem the obvious line to take, but it happens to be quite wrong: the complement meaning 'doctor' was *never* the subject of anything, at any point in the history of Mojave. So how can it bear the subject suffix?

The key to understanding the history of this Mojave construction is the recognition that Mojave sentences, like all sentences in all languages, have syntactic structure. That is, they are not just linear strings of words strung together one after another. In particular, sentences have *constituent structure*: they are built up from syntactic units having their own internal syntactic structure. And it was precisely this appreciation of constituent structure that enabled Munro to figure out what had happened in Mojave.

Her solution is as follows. Originally, Mojave had no copula, but it did have a full verb *ido-* meaning 'exist, be so, be the case'. And the original structure of Example (6.10) was as shown in Fig. 6.1 – that is, this sentence was originally complex in structure, with two clauses. The subordinate clause was *John kʷaθʔide:* 'John [be] doctor', and the subject *John* of this subordinate clause naturally took no subject suffix. This subordinate clause was in turn the subject of the main clause, whose verb was *idopč*, and this subject consequently took the subject suffix. This suffix was, of course, attached to the end of the subject, which meant that it had to go onto the last word of the subject clause, *kʷaθʔide:* 'doctor', which was not itself the subject of anything. The

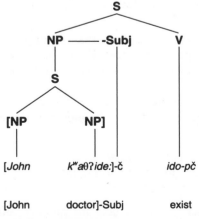

Fig. 6.1 A Mojave copular sentence

whole construction was therefore, more or less literally, '[John doctor]-č exists', that is, '[That John is a doctor] is the case'.

In fact, this might *still* be the structure of such copular sentences in Mojave: nothing I have said so far suggests that any reanalysis has taken place to make *John* the subject. However, Munro notes that some younger speakers of Mojave do not say things like (6.10); instead, they say things like (6.13):

(6.13) *John-č kᵂaθʔide: ido-pč*
John-Subj doctor be-Tense
'John is a doctor.'

This can only be so because the younger speakers, at least, have reanalysed copular sentences as consisting of single clauses, with the first NP being the subject of the whole sentence, and so they have removed the anomalous subject-suffix from the complement and attached it, as usual, to the first NP, now perceived as the subject. This reanalysis of copular sentences as consisting of single clauses may in fact have been carried out by Mojave-speakers generations ago, but, as is usual with reanalysis, we cannot tell that any reanalysis has occurred until we hear some speakers saying things that were not possible before.

Reanalysis, of course, is not confined to the creation of copulas: it is a pervasive phenomenon in syntactic change. Let us consider the origin of the English verb form called the **perfect**. This is the form constructed with the auxiliary *have*, as in *I have finished my dinner* and *She had studied in Paris*, in which *have* always combines with the verb form called the *perfective participle*. Now *have* is in other respects a fairly ordinary transitive verb meaning 'possess': *I have a copy of her new book*, *She has blue eyes*. So how did it come to be an auxiliary, and why a perfect auxiliary in particular?

Observe first that English has another, quite different, construction also involving *have* and a perfective participle, but with a different word order. This is a **stative** construction, illustrated by examples like *I have a couple of ribs broken* and *She has a daughter trapped in the war zone*. In great contrast to the perfect construction, there is no suggestion here that I did the breaking or that she did the trapping. (The identical construction in fact has several other, non-stative, uses, as in *I had my car stolen*, *She had her face lifted*, and *She has us convinced of her innocence*, but these other cases are not particularly relevant here.)

Now early Old English had a construction identical to the modern stative; this is illustrated in the next two examples:

(6.14) *Ic hæbbe þone fisc gefangenne*
I have the fish caught
'I have the fish caught' (= 'I have the fish in a state of being caught').

(6.15) *Ic hæfde hine gebundenne*
I had him bound
'I had him bound' (= 'I had him in a state of being bound').

Now, it is clear that, in such examples, the verb is *habban* 'have' alone, because the participles *gefangenne* 'caught' and *gebundenne* 'bound' agree in gender, number, and case with the object NPs *þone fisc* 'the fisc' and *hine* 'him', and hence the participles are modifiers of the object NPs. These constructions are therefore statives comparable to *I have a couple of ribs broken*.

Very early on, however, the agreement begins to disappear, and the participle stands instead in an invariant form. We therefore find numerous examples like (6.16):

> (6.16) *Ic hæfde hit gebunden*
>   I had it bound
>   'I had it bound' (= 'I had it in a state of being bound').

Here the participle *gebunden* shows no agreement. Crucially, we also find examples in which the stative meaning is impossible:

> (6.17) *þin geleafa hæfð ðe gehæled*
>   your faith has you healed
>   'Your faith has healed you.'

> (6.18) *Ac hie hæfdon þa . . . hiora mete genotudne*
>   but they had then . . . their food used-up
>   'But they had then used up their food.'

In (6.17), faith, being inanimate, cannot conceivably have a person, and in (6.18), the food, being all gone, cannot be had. These examples, therefore, cannot be statives: instead, they must be perfects, as shown by the English translations, even though the second one still shows agreement. And this is the origin of the English perfect, which has, of course, more recently undergone a change of word order in order to place the participle next to the auxiliary *have*, since the two are now considered to constitute a single verb form.

The English perfect therefore results from the reanalysis of an original stative construction, in this case accompanied by a shift in meaning. A sentence of the form 'I have him bound' originally meant 'I have him in my possession, in a tied-up state', but this could readily be, and was, reinterpreted as meaning 'I have tied him up'. The participle, formerly a modifier of the object NP, with which it necessarily agreed, was reanalysed as part of the verb form and lost its agreement; as part of the same process, the verb *have*, originally the main verb in the sentence and bearing its usual meaning of 'possess', was reanalysed as a mere auxiliary expressing perfect aspect, the function it still has today.

As some of the above examples suggest, reanalysis may be favoured by the absence or loss of overt morphology which is inconsistent with the reanalysis. A fine example of this is provided by the Old English verb *lician* 'be pleasing to'. This verb took as its subject an NP representing the thing which was pleasing, and it took a dative object representing the person who was pleased.

Given the usual subject–verb–object (SVO) order of Old English, we might therefore have expected sentences like (6.19):

(6.19) **Peran licoden þam cynge.*
pears were-pleasing the-Dat king-Dat

But, as the asterisk shows, this was not the normal construction in Old English. Instead, we find (6.20):

(6.20) *þam cynge licoden peran.*
the-Dat king-Dat were-pleasing pears
'Pears were pleasing to the king'; i.e. 'The king liked pears.'

Sentences involving this verb thus had an unusual word order, perhaps resulting from the nearly universal tendency in languages to put animate NPs first in the sentence. But the syntactic structure is still very clear: the NP 'the king' stands in the dative case, showing that it cannot be the subject, while the verb shows plural agreement with its plural subject, *peran*. As time passed, however, English lost many of its grammatical endings, including the dative endings, and by early Middle English the form was this:

(6.21) *The king liceden peares.*
the king were-pleasing pears
(same gloss)

Here the plural agreement on the verb is now the sole indication that the subject is *peares*, and not *the king*. But then the plural agreement suffix was lost too, and the form became the modern one:

(6.22) *The king liked pears.*

At this point, there was no longer any morphology left to indicate that the subject of the sentence was *pears*, rather then *the king*. Since English sentences are normally SVO, sentences with the verb *like* were therefore reanalysed to conform to the normal pattern: *the king* was now taken as the subject, *pears* was interpreted as a direct object, and *like*, formerly an intransitive verb taking a dative complement, was reanalysed as a simple transitive verb. As usual, we can tell that the reanalysis has occurred by looking at other utterances: we no longer say **Him liked pears* or **The king like pears*, which would have been the regular descendants of the Old English construction; instead, we say *He liked pears* and *The king likes pears*, with a subject form of the pronoun and verbal agreement with the new subject.

6.2 *Shift of markedness*

There is another important pathway of syntactic change, called **shift of markedness**. Languages typically have alternative constructions available for expressing ordinary and not-so-ordinary meanings. In English, for example, the ordinary (unmarked) word order is SVO, and we would therefore normally say *I can't recommend this book*, with SVO word order; this is the *unmarked form*. For special purposes, however, we can say instead *This book I can't recommend* – for example, when comparing the present book with other books. This construction, with its abnormal object–subject–verb (OSV) word order, constitutes a *marked form*: an unusual form used only in certain special circumstances.

Now, suppose English-speakers were to begin using this marked form more frequently than at present. Suppose, in fact, that we began using it so often that we were using it most of the time, and using the other construction, *I can't recommend this book*, only occasionally. What would be the result? First, the OSV construction, being used most of the time, would become the unmarked form, while the earlier SVO construction, being used only occasionally, would become the marked form. We would therefore have a *shift of markedness* between the two forms. Moreover, since the two forms involve different word orders, the originally unmarked SVO order would become marked, while the originally marked OSV order would become unmarked – and English would therefore have undergone a change of basic word order from SVO to OSV.

This has not happened in English, of course, but precisely this sort of development has occurred in the histories of a number of other languages. Consider Hebrew. Early biblical Hebrew had two distinct sets of verb forms, called the *imperfect* and the *perfect*. The imperfect forms were used most of the time for most purposes, while the perfect forms were used only occasionally for a few purposes. Importantly, the imperfect forms normally required verb–subject–object (VSO) word order, the ordinary word order of the language, while the perfect, a marked form, usually required a marked word order, SVO. Here are two examples from the book of Genesis:

(6.23) *va-yiqra? ?elohim la-yabaša ?erec*
        and-called[Imperf] God to-the-dry land
        'And God called the dry portion "land".'

(6.24) *ve-ha-?adam yada' ?et hava ?išto*
        and-the-man knew[Perf] Acc Eve wife-his
        'And Adam knew his wife Eve.'

With the passage of time, however, the perfect, the marked form with SVO word order, began to be used increasingly frequently in an ever larger set of functions, while the imperfect, with its unmarked VSO order, began to lose its functions to the perfect. This trend continued over centuries, and it can be plainly traced through the later books of the Bible. Table 6.1, taken from Givón (1977), the source of this study, shows this development graphically, for main clauses only, in six books of the Bible. When Genesis was written, Hebrew was clearly a VSO language; by the time of the Song of Solomon, many centuries later, it had become very largely an SVO language. This

Table 6.1 Shift in main-clause syntax in biblical Hebrew

Book	VS	SV	Total	% SV
Gen.	169	25	194	12.9
2 Kgs	174	53	227	23.2
Esther	99	36	135	26.7
Lam.	36	36	72	50.0
Eccles.	11	41	52	79.0
S. of S.	2	26	28	92.0

change occurred, not because Hebrew-speakers suddenly decided to move some phrases from one location to another, but merely because of a long-term tendency to shift various discourse functions from the VSO imperfect to the SVO perfect. In biblical Hebrew, then, a shift in the markedness of two competing constructions led eventually to a major syntactic change in the language: a change in its basic word order.

A shift in markedness need not produce such a dramatic result as a change in basic word order. Not so long ago, English had the two prepositions *before* and *behind* for expressing position in space, and these were the unmarked forms for expressing position. But a new marked form *in front of* was then introduced with the same meaning as *before*. This marked form came to be used with increasing frequency, until today it has all but driven *before* out of the language in its spatial sense: we can still use *before* in a few marked contexts, like *to be brought before a judge*, but we can no longer say things like **There is an apple tree before my house*. The only possible form for us is *There is an apple tree in front of my house*. The word *before* still exists, but it is now generally confined to temporal senses, as in *before the war*. Moreover, American English has taken things a step further, by introducing *in back of* as a frequent alternative to *behind*: Americans are now probably more likely to say *in back of the house*, rather than *behind the house*, though this last form has not yet dropped out of use entirely. Here we have two examples of the replacement of originally unmarked prepositions by originally marked complex constructions.

In a markedness shift, it is not always the case that a formerly marked form becomes unmarked and vice versa. The opposite may happen: the marked form may become even more highly marked, possibly to the point at which it disappears from the language, or nearly so. For a thousand years English has had two competing forms for constructing sentences involving prepositions and WH-words. The first is represented by examples like *To whom did you give it?* and *I married a woman with whom I went to school*; the second is illustrated by *Who did you give it to?* and *I married a woman I went to school with*. The first form has been the marked form for centuries, but there is no sign that it might take over from the second. Quite the contrary: the first, marked, form has been steadily declining in frequency for generations. Today it is probably entirely confined to the formal writing of a minority of speakers and to the careful speech of an even smaller minority: most English-speakers probably never use it at all. The marked form has become steadily more marked, and it may eventually disappear completely. (Engagingly, I have very often heard self-conscious speakers, in contexts that appear to call for a degree of formality, produce utterances like *From which language does the word ' geyser' come from?* Such speakers are clearly aware that the marked form exists, but they no longer have any real control over it: for them, the marked form is effectively dead.)

It is by no means easy to find good examples of syntactic change deriving from shift of markedness alone. Far more frequently, what we find is a more complex scenario involving both markedness shift and reanalysis. Some excellent examples are provided by changes involving **serial verb constructions**, a term whose meaning will shortly become clear. Here is a celebrated example from Mandarin Chinese, discussed by Li and Thompson (1974).

Chinese is primarily an SVO language, as illustrated by the typical sentence (6.25); *le* is a particle marking completed aspect:

(6.25) *Wǒ dǎ Zhāng-sān le*
I hit Zhang-san Asp
'I hit Zhang-san.'

However, alongside such sentences, Chinese has another construction with SOV word order and a preposition *bǎ* marking the object:

(6.26) *Wǒ bǎ Zhāng-sān dǎ le*
I Obj Zhang-san hit Asp
'I hit Zhang-san.'

The second construction is obligatory or preferred in a variety of circumstances, though the first construction is none the less very common in other circumstances. The SOV construction, with its case-marking preposition, seems a very surprising one to find in a predominantly SVO language. We might expend considerable ingenuity in trying to identify a source for the SOV construction; in fact, our abundant historical records for Chinese show rather clearly how it arose. Old Chinese did not have the SOV construction, but it did have a verb *bǎ* meaning 'take hold of, take'. Here is an instance from a ninth-century poem:

(6.27) *Shī jù wú rén shì yīn bǎ jiàn kàn*
poem sentence no man appreciate, should take sword see
'Since no one appreciates poetry, I should take hold of the sword to contemplate it.'

The origin of sentences like (6.26) is therefore clear: originally, *bǎ* was the verb 'take hold of', and such sentences contained *two* verbs, in what we call a serial verb construction. That is, the original force of (6.26) was 'I took Zhang-san [and] hit [him]'. This would have been a marked construction at first, but it came to be used increasingly in some circumstances, until today it is the unmarked form, or even the only possible form, in many circumstances. Alongside the markedness shift, there was a reanalysis: the first verb, 'take', was bleached of its sense and reinterpreted as a mere grammatical marker of a following object, and the second verb 'hit' was reinterpreted as the main (and only) verb in the sentence. Since *bǎ* is no longer felt as meaning 'take', the SOV construction has been extended to cases in which this older meaning would be quite inappropriate:

(6.28) *Zhāng-sān bǎ Lī-si pīping le*
Zhang-san Obj Li-si criticize Asp
'Zhang-san criticized Li-si.'

Here there is no suggestion that Zhang-san has taken hold of Li-si, or even that Li-si is necessarily present at all: *bǎ* is a grammatical marker, no more.

The linguistic literature now contains a large number of instances in which serial verb constructions have been reanalysed in one way or another, with a variety of syntactic consequences.

6.3 *Grammaticalization*

This last example, apart from illustrating both markedness shift and reanalysis, also illustrates yet a third pathway of syntactic change: **grammaticalization**. In the preceding chapter, we saw that lexical items can be reduced to bound morphemes, but they can also be reduced to grammatical items without entirely losing their status as words. Here is an example from English.

The progressive form of the verb *go* has been available for centuries in constructions like *I am going home*, in which *go* clearly retains its ordinary verbal sense. This same construction could also be used with a complement of purpose, in cases like *I am going to visit Mrs Pumphrey*, in which the verb *go* still had its ordinary meaning: the structure of such a sentence was [*I*] [*am going*] [*to visit Mrs Pumphrey*], broadly parallel to [*I*] [*am going*] [*home*]. Such a sentence could be uttered by a speaker who was actually on her way to Mrs Pumphrey's house, but equally, and crucially, it could be uttered by someone just about to set out, just like *I'm going home*. As a consequence, speakers began to reanalyse such utterances as expressing, not actual motion, but rather an intention for the near future. Accordingly, it became possible for something like *I am going to buy a new carriage* to be said by someone curled up comfortably at home with no immediate intention of moving.

This largely happened in the early nineteenth century, but the new usage has extended its domain very rapidly, and today we routinely say things like *You're going to like this book*, in which no relevant motion is even conceivable: the *be going to* construction has entirely lost its original connection with movement and become a mere grammatical marker of the (near) future. Together with this grammaticalization, the structure has been reanalysed: we no longer have the old structure [*I*] [*am going*] [*to buy a new car*]; instead, we have [*I*] [*am*] [*going to*] [*buy a new car*], in which *going to* forms part of a single grammatical marker. To see this, observe that this new *going to* can now be reduced to *gonna*, as in *I'm gonna buy a new car*. The same is not possible with the ordinary progressive of the verb *go*, as in **I'm gonna the beach*, in which *going* and *to* do not constitute parts of a single grammatical form.

Grammaticalization of this type has been called **bleaching**, and such bleaching of lexical meaning is a very common source of grammatical items; compare the case of Chinese *bǎ*, discussed above. Bleaching of verbs, as in the *going to* case, is probably the most frequent source of tense and aspect markers in languages. Another example from English is the verb *will*. This used to be a lexical verb meaning 'want', as in the Shakespearian form *What wilt thou?* 'What do you want?' Today, however, it has been reduced entirely to a grammatical marker, also a kind of future marker, as in *She will be home soon*. (But note the interesting difference of meaning between *I'll wash the dishes* (an offer) and *I'm going to wash the dishes* (a statement).) Cross-linguistically, verbs meaning 'go', 'come', 'want', and 'must' very often develop into grammatical markers of futurity.

A celebrated example of this occurs in the Romance languages like Spanish, French, and Italian, all of which are modern forms of spoken Latin. Classical Latin had a distinct future tense, illustrated by *cantabo* 'I'll sing', but this fell into disuse very early and disappeared from the language. It was replaced by several other constructions, such as (using the verb *cantare* 'sing' for illustration) *cantare volo* 'I want to sing', *cantare debeo* 'I must sing', and *cantare habeo* 'I have to sing'. This last form, involving the ordinary Latin verb *habere* 'have', is exactly parallel to the English *I have to sing*, and the Latin form once had the same meaning. With time, however, the last form won out over its competitors and became the ordinary way of expressing futurity. In this case, the verb *habere* was not merely bleached of its lexical meaning and reduced to a grammatical auxiliary; it also underwent heavy phonological reduction. Table 6.2 lists the forms in Latin and in modern Spanish. The old verb *habere* has been reduced to little more than a suffix marking the subject, while the *-ar(e)* that formerly marked the infinitive is now interpreted as the marker of future tense. Exactly the same thing has happened in most other Western descendants of Latin: 'I'll sing' is *je chanterai* in French, *cantarai* in Occitan ('Provençal'), *canterò* in Italian, and *cantarei* in Portuguese. All these forms provide a fine example of the reduction of syntax to morphology – that is, of the reduction of a construction to a morphological form. (In contrast, Romanian *voi cînta* continues the *volo* construction, while Sardinian *deppo kantare* continues the *debeo* construction, though with a change of word order in each case.)

This is not the end of the story, however. Just like its Latin predecessor, the Spanish future is now little used in speech. Instead of *cantaré*, Spanish-

Table 6.2 The Spanish future

Latin	Spanish	
cantare habeo	*cantaré*	'I'll sing'
cantare habes	*cantarás*	'you'll sing'
cantare habet	*cantará*	's/he'll sing'
cantare habemus	*cantaremos*	'we'll sing'
cantare habetis	*cantareís*	'you'll sing'
cantare habent	*cantarán*	'they'll sing'

speakers usually prefer to say *voy a cantar*, which is an almost exact translation of English 'I'm going to sing'. The equivalent French *je vais chanter* is also now very frequent, though perhaps not as frequent as its Spanish counterpart. It appears that these languages are now undergoing yet another round of grammaticalization, this time with the verb 'go' being reduced to a future marker.

Both the replacement of the original Latin future with the new Romance construction and the current replacement of the new Romance future with yet another construction are instances of what linguists call **renewal**: the replacement of an older set of forms by a newer set with approximately the same function. Such renewal is a pervasive process in languages: for a number of reasons, including the phonological erosion of grammatical affixes by phonological change, older grammatical systems fall into disuse and are replaced by new systems, which eventually undergo the same fate.

Grammaticalization is not confined to operating within single sentences; it is quite possible for grammaticalization to apply in such a way as to join two consecutive sentences into one. Observe the usual manner of constructing complement clauses in the Germanic languages:

- English: *I believe that she will take the job.*
- German: *Ich verstehe, daß Sie nicht kommen.* ('I understand that you're not coming.')
- Dutch: *Ik weet dat hij veel vrienden heeft.* ('I know that he has a lot of friends.')
- Swedish: *Jag trodde, att hans sista stund var kommen.* ('I thought that his last hour had come.')

In all these languages, the complement clause is introduced by a grammatical particle, a complementizer: *that, daß, dat, att.* In all but Swedish, this particle is more or less identical to the ordinary demonstrative *that*, as in *I know that*, and indeed this demonstrative is the historical source of the complementizer. But why should a demonstrative be used for this purpose?

It is clear what must have happened. In some ancient Germanic language, ancestral to all of the modern Germanic languages, the modern complement construction did not exist. Instead of using a single sentence with a subordinate clause, speakers used *two* separate sentences. So, instead of saying *I believe that she will marry him*, they said, literally, the following: *I believe that. She will marry him.* Here the demonstrative *that* is referring to the following sentence, which is syntactically entirely independent of the first sentence. Over time, however, this very frequent sequence underwent grammaticalization: the two sentences were combined into one, and the demonstrative was reduced to a mere grammatical particle and, in English at least, underwent phonological reduction. As a consequence, all these languages acquired a new construction for complement clauses, one which has been retained from prehistoric times down to the present day. For lack of evidence, we simply don't know whether this new construction replaced an older one or whether complement clauses had previously been non-existent in these languages.

On the whole, patterns for constructing subordinate clauses tend to be remarkably stable over long periods, and innovations are rare. Interestingly, however, a new construction has very recently appeared in American English, at least among some younger speakers. Direct quotations in English have for centuries been formed as follows: *I asked 'What's going on?'* But many younger Americans now use a completely new construction for this purpose; they say instead *I'm like 'What's going on?'* It's too early to tell if this new construction will establish itself in the language; if it does, you will be able to tell your grandchildren that a completely new syntactic structure appeared in English during your lifetime.

The examples discussed above and in the preceding chapter all illustrate the ordinary course of grammaticalization: an ordinary lexical item with an ordinary meaning comes to be used in some particular context; it is then bleached of its original meaning and becomes a mere grammatical marker in a syntactic construction; finally it is reduced to a bound morpheme, an affix, a piece of morphology. Naturally, there is no requirement that every slight tendency toward grammaticalization will go all the way, but, as a general rule, if anything happens at all, it will conform to this schema. Some linguists have accordingly posited a principle of *unidirectionality*, which holds that movement in the opposite direction is impossible. And it certainly appears to be true that movement the other way is very rare – but maybe not quite impossible. It is not difficult to find cases in which bound grammatical morphemes have developed into independent lexical items. Here are some examples.

Turkish has a grammatical suffix *-miş* or *-muş* which is attached to a verb to indicate reported speech: hence *Ali geldi* 'Ali has arrived' [I've seen him myself] but *Ali gelmiş* 'Ali has arrived' [I haven't seen him, but somebody has told me so]. This suffix is occasionally removed and treated as a separate word, as in the expression *Mişlere muşlara kulak vermem* 'I don't listen to mishes and mushes', i.e. 'I don't listen to gossip'. Basque has a suffix *-tasun* '-ness' used to form abstract nouns, as in *eder* 'beautiful' and *edertasun* 'beauty'. This suffix has been extracted and turned into an independent word *tasun* 'quality', and it even forms derivatives like *tasunezko* 'qualitative'.

Even English provides a few examples of this type. For instance, the suffix *-ism*, as in *socialism* and *monotheism*, has recently become an independent word *ism*, meaning 'creed, doctrine, system of belief', and we can now say things like 'I'm not interested in all these isms.' One wag has even coined a nonce-form *wasm*, meaning 'an outdated doctrine'! Nevertheless, such 'backward' developments appear to be idiosyncratic: they do not represent the norm.

6.4 *Typological harmony*

Above I referred to the notion of the *basic word order* of a language. This notion was introduced in a celebrated paper by the American linguist Joseph Greenberg in 1963 (Greenberg 1963a). The majority of languages do appear to have a basic word order, a 'normal' or 'unmarked' order of elements in a sentence. In English, for example, a sentence like *The Turks love backgammon* represents the normal, basic order; other orders are either highly marked, like *Backgammon the Turks love*, or absolutely impossible, like **Love the Turks backgammon* or **Backgammon love the Turks* (here the asterisk marks an ungrammatical sequence). In other words, the basic word order of English is SVO.

If we assume, as is commonly done, that basic word order is best expressed in terms of the ordering of subject, verb, and object, then there are six possible basic word orders: VSO, SVO, SOV, VOS, OVS, and OSV. Of these, SOV is probably the most frequent among the world's languages; SOV languages include Japanese, Turkish, Basque, and Quechua. Next most frequent is the SVO of English and of the majority of other European languages; SVO is also found in many African languages, such as Swahili. Considerably less frequent is VSO order, found, for example, in Welsh and Irish, in a number of Pacific languages, and in classical Arabic and early biblical Hebrew. The other three basic word orders are vastly less common, and for a while linguists suspected that they might be impossible, but all are now attested: Malagasy (in Madagascar) is VOS, Hixkaryana (in the Amazon basin) is OVS, and Apurinã (also in the Amazon) is reported to be OSV. We may therefore classify the majority of languages into one of these six word-order types. Such a classification according to structural features is called a **typology**.

Now a typology is only worth setting up if it proves to be fruitful: that is, if the languages in each group turn out to have other characteristics in common apart from the one used to set up the classification in the first place. In this case, Greenberg was able to show that a word-order typology does indeed lead to just such an illuminating result. Confining his attention to the three most frequent basic word orders, he found that SOV languages in general consistently exhibit certain additional grammatical characteristics, while VSO languages, with equal consistency, exhibit precisely the opposite characteristics. SVO languages, while slightly messier, pattern on the whole with the VSO languages, and Greenberg therefore simplifies his typology into VO languages and OV languages. These two groups display a number of systematic differences, some of which are listed in Table 6.3.

Naturally, not all languages with basic word orders behave 'perfectly': English, for example, violates pattern 3 (*the big house*, not **the house big*), and partially violates pattern 4 (*John's book*, but *the capital of France*). Basque is a perfect OV language except that it violates pattern 3, and Persian is a perfect VO language except that it violates pattern 1. On the whole, though, the tendency of languages to conform to one type or the other is very striking, and a language which fits almost perfectly into one type or the other is said to exhibit a high degree of **typological harmony**. Japanese, for example, is a virtually perfect OV language, while standard French is a virtually perfect VO language.

The field of syntactic typology has been greatly developed since Greenberg's pioneering contribution, but pursuing these developments is beyond the scope of this book. What interests us here is the consequences of typological harmony for syntactic change, and particularly for word-order change. We have already seen that biblical Hebrew underwent a change of word order from VSO to SVO, but of course it remained a VO language throughout. Other languages, however, have undergone a change from OV to VO, or vice versa. This can happen through contact with a more prestigious language, or it can happen purely through internal changes (recall the case of the Chinese *bǎ* construction). What is interesting, though, is that we rarely find just one

Table 6.3 Greenberg's word-order types.

VO languages	OV languages
1. Verb precedes object	1. Verb follows object
2. Auxiliary precedes main verb	2. Auxiliary follows main verb
3. Adjective follows noun	3. Adjective precedes noun
4. Genitive follows noun	4. Genitive precedes noun
5. Relative clause follows head	5. Relative clause precedes head
6. Prepositions	6. Postpositions
7. Case-marking absent	7. Case-marking present
8. Comparative adjective precedes standard	8. Comparative adjective follows standard

aspect of typology changing: if a language undergoes change in one or two respects among those listed in Table 6.3, then it usually undergoes corresponding changes in all or most of those respects.

English provides an interesting case in point. There is very good reason to believe that an exceedingly remote ancestor of English was very consistently SOV in its word order, though we have no records from this period (around 6000 years ago). In the early centuries AD, a much later ancestral form of English was spoken in the north-west of the European continent. And this time we do have records, in the form of what specialists call the North-west Germanic runic corpus, a modest collection of inscriptions in the ancient runic alphabet dating from the third to the seventh century AD. Here are a few examples (data from Lass 1994: 219–220):

(6.29) ek Hlewagastiz Holtijaz horna tawido
I H. H. horn did
'I, H. H., made [this] horn.'

(6.30) [me]z Woduride staina þrijoz dohtriz dalidun
me-Dat Woduridaz-Dat stone three daughters made
'For me, Woduridaz, three daughters made [this] stone.'

(6.31) ek Wiwaz after Woduride witada-hlaiban worahto
I Wiwaz after Woduridaz-Dat guard-loaf wrought
'I Wiwaz wrought [this] for Woduridaz [the] loaf-ward.'

As these examples suggest, Northwest Germanic was still primarily an OV language. But it was not completely harmonic: it had prepositions rather than postpositions, adjectives generally followed their nouns, and genitives could either precede or follow their nouns, depending upon the type of noun. Moreover, a small proportion of sentences (less than 20 per cent) show SVO order. The impression we have is that of a formerly SOV language which is changing towards SVO order.

The very earliest texts in Old English from Britain, in the eighth century, are not very different in their syntax. The following example is carved upon a gold ring from Lancashire in a mixture of runes and Roman letters:

(6.32) Æðred me ah Eanred mec agrof
Æthred me owns Eanred me carved
'Æthred owns me; Eanred carved me.'

Soon after, however, we find such OV patterns becoming increasingly rarer in Old English texts, while VO patterns become correspondingly frequent. Within a few centuries the OV word order had virtually vanished, and English was left with the VO word order which it still has today. Interestingly, the system of case-endings, so typical of OV languages, disappeared as well: modern English has the typically VO feature of no case-endings, apart from a handful still found on some pronouns like *I/me*. Oddly, though, our adjectives, which had formerly followed their nouns, moved so that they now precede their nouns; the adjective placement was out of line in the earlier OV stage and is again out of line today.

Though we have documentary evidence only for the later stages of the transformation, it seems that English has developed over some thousands of years from a rather consistent OV language to a rather consistent VO language. Similar evidence is available for some other languages, but only very rarely do we have written texts of sufficient age that we can plot the course of typological change over the millennia typically required for such a major syntactic change. One such case is perhaps Chinese.

In their 1974 paper, Charles Li and Sandra Thompson argue that Chinese has been slowly changing from SVO to SOV order over thousands of years. Our earliest records of Chinese, Archaic Chinese from the first millennium BC, reveal a language which is solidly of the VO type, except in NPs: adjectives, genitives, and relative clauses all precede their head noun in Archaic Chinese, just as they still do today. Beginning in the early centuries AD, however, a number of changes have disturbed the VO patterns of the archaic language. First, the original V + PP pattern (prepositional phrase follows verb) was replaced by a new PP + V pattern (PP precedes verb); the older pattern is now entirely confined to certain special circumstances. Second, the *bǎ* construction discussed above established itself, so that the original VO construction in transitive sentences was increasingly replaced by the pattern *bǎ* O V, which now predominates. Third, the earlier passive construction, of the form Subject V *by* Agent, was replaced by a new construction, of the form Subject *by* Agent V. Fourth, certain nouns were reduced to postpositions, an innovation in a previously exclusively prepositional language, and some of these postpositions have been phonologically reduced to something resembling case-suffixes, previously absent from the language (the prepositions are still present, however). Fifth, compound nouns and compound verbs, formerly very rare, have become exceedingly common in modern Chinese (Li and Thompson take compounds to be typical of OV languages, and there is evidence to support this position). Sixth, the language has acquired a set of suffixes marking aspect on verbs (again, there is evidence that such verbal suffixes are typical of OV languages).

It is not yet possible to claim that modern Chinese is a consistent OV language, but it certainly has a vastly greater degree of OV character than its Archaic ancestor, in which OV characteristics were confined to NPs. What is noteworthy, though, is that a number of seemingly unrelated developments, involving a variety of forms and constructions, have all apparently been working together, with the overall effect of shifting the whole language from a VO harmonic type to an OV type. This is an instance of what historical linguists call **drift**: the curious tendency of a language to keep changing in the same direction. Drift can be observed in every area of linguistic change (recall, for example, the continuing tendency of tense vowels in Greek to move upwards and forwards), but some linguists would maintain that instances of word-order change represent something more: a powerful, if somewhat mysterious, tendency for a language to move into one or the other of the two main harmonic types.

6.5 *Case study: the rise of ergativity*

English, like a majority of the world's languages, is an **accusative** language. That is, the subjects of intransitive verbs and the subjects of transitive verbs are treated identically for grammatical purposes, while direct objects are treated differently. A simple example of this is the case-marking on pronouns:

(6.33) She smiled.

(6.34) She saw me.

(6.35) I saw her.

Here the female pronoun takes the case-form *she* when it is an intransitive subject (6.33) or a transitive subject (6.34), but the form *her* when it is a direct object (6.35).

A sizeable number of languages exhibit a quite different pattern: intransitive subjects and direct objects are treated identically, while transitive subjects are treated differently. Basque is a good example: NPs like *gizona* 'the man' and *neska* 'the girl' can take either the case-ending zero or the case-ending -*k*, as follows:

(6.36) Gizona heldu zen.
       'The man arrived.'

(6.37) Gizonak neska ikusi zuen.
       'The man saw the girl.'

(6.38) Neskak gizona ikusi zuen.
       'The girl saw the man.'

Languages like Basque are called **ergative** languages. You can see that only a transitive subject takes the case-ending -*k*; both intransitive subjects and direct objects take the ending zero. In Basque, ergative morphology is thoroughgoing: ergative case-marking applies in all circumstances, and verbal agreement is ergative as well.

When European linguists first encountered ergative languages like Basque, they were quite bewildered by them, and they put forward quite a number of confused misinterpretations, some of which may still be encountered in popular books written by non-linguists. Today we have information on hundreds of ergative languages, and we no longer regard them as particularly exotic. The study of such languages has turned up a number of interesting points. One of these is that many ergative languages exhibit a *split* in their grammar: that is, they are ergative only in certain circumstances. One of the commonest splits is this: ergative morphology appears only in the perfect aspect or in the past tense, accusative morphology being found elsewhere. Here is an example from Pashto, an Iranian language spoken in Afghanistan; the label Nom(inative) denotes the ordinary subject case, while Obl(ique) denotes the ordinary non-subject case. First, in the present tense:

(6.39) ze de winem
I-Nom he-Obl see-I
'I see him.'

(6.40) day maa wini
he-Nom I-Obl see-he
'He sees me.'

(6.41) te maa winee
you-Nom I-Obl see-you
'You see me.'

Now, in the past tense:

(6.42) maa day wulid
I-Obl he-Nom saw-he
'I saw him.'

(6.43) taa ze wulidem
you-Obl I-Nom saw-I
'You saw me.'

Observe the differences. In the present tense, the subject is in the subject case and the verb agrees with it, while the object stands in the oblique case. But, in the past tense, it is the *object* which stands in the subject case, and the verb agrees with it, while the subject is in the oblique case.

How does ergativity arise? There is one obvious possibility. Early linguists often mistakenly described ergative constructions as 'passives'. As it happens, they are demonstrably not passives, but of course they might be *derived* from earlier passives. Suppose, in the Pashto case, that a sentence like (6.42) once meant, not 'I saw him', but rather 'He was seen by me'. Its structure would then have been, literally, 'By-me he was-seen'. This would explain at once why *day* 'he' is in the subject case (it was the subject) and why the verb agrees with it (verbs agree with subjects in Pashto), and also why *maa* 'I' is in a non-subject case (it wasn't the subject, but an oblique noun phrase of agent). So possibly the Pashto ergative construction derives from what was formerly a passive.

This looks plausible, but, of course, it doesn't explain why the ergative should have arisen only in the past tense. We would therefore like to have some historical information. Now, for the majority of ergative languages, we unfortunately lack any significant historical documentation, but there are exceptions. One of the major exceptions is the Indo-Iranian family of languages, to which Pashto belongs. For this group of languages we are lucky enough to have texts going back several thousand years, and so we can see the ergative construction developing over many centuries.

Consider Sanskrit, the 'Latin of India', the ancient language which is the ancestor of most north Indian languages like Hindi and Bengali, most of which are also ergative today. In Sanskrit, we really do find what appears to be a passive construction, and it was indeed mostly used in the past tense. Here Nom(inative) is the ordinary subject case, Acc(usative) is the ordinary object case, and Obl(ique) is an oblique case; *Ram* is a male name, while *Sita* is a female name. In the present tense:

(6.44) rāmaḥ sītām pṛcchati
Ram-Nom Sita-Acc asks-3Sg
'Ram asks Sita.'

And in the past tense:

(6.45) rāmeṇa sītā pṛṣṭā
Ram-Obl Sita-Nom was-asked-Female
'By Ram Sita was asked', i.e. 'Ram asked Sita.'

Word order was rather free in Sanskrit, and the subject did not have to come first. Most linguists have concluded, therefore, that the ergative constructions of the modern Indo-Iranian languages derive from original passives. At least in the past tense, these passives apparently came to be used more and more frequently, until they finally became the normal (unmarked) form, while the original active construction became so rare that it dropped out of the languages altogether. Since the passive no longer contrasted with an active, it was then reinterpreted as being itself an active construction, as it is today, but it still kept its original morphology, producing the ergative constructions we see today.

If it is right, this account illustrates two of the general pathways of syntactic change discussed above. First, there was a *shift of markedness*, as the formerly marked passive became so frequent that it turned into the unmarked form, while the formerly unmarked active became first highly marked and then obsolete. Second, there was a *reanalysis*, as the former passive construction was reanalysed as an active.

But why should the passive have become so frequent in the first place? We don't know, but one possible answer is politeness. Passives, being indirect and often impersonal, may often seem more polite and less abrupt than actives: compare the English passive *John's arm has been broken* with its corresponding active *Fred has broken John's arm*. Such developments are attested: for example, in Malagasy, the chief language of Madagascar, in which blunt statements are generally regarded as socially inappropriate, passives are much more frequent than actives.

But passives are not the only possible source of ergatives. Since ergative constructions are so often confined to the perfect aspect, we might wonder whether ergatives can be directly derived from perfect constructions, and there is good evidence that this does happen.

Recall the English perfect discussed above, in which what was originally a stative construction of the form *I have a window broken* (= 'One of my windows is broken') was reinterpreted as a non-stative perfect with the meaning *I have broken a window* (= 'I broke a window, and it's not fixed yet'). Note carefully that the stative construction was originally a *possessive* construction, essentially identical to *I have a dog*. It is known that possessives are a common source of statives, and hence of perfects. In English, this development has not led to ergativity, because English uses the transitive verb *have* to express possession. But lots of languages have no such verb.

So how do they express possession? They do it like this (Welsh *y* is a grammatical particle):

(6.46) Welsh:
    Y mae gardd gennyf i
    Prt is garden with me
    'A garden is with me', i.e. 'I have a garden'.

(6.47) Russian:
    U menja kniga
    at me book
    'A book [is] at me', i.e. 'I have a book'.

(6.48) Early Latin:
    Est mihi liber
    is to-me book
    'A book is to me', i.e. 'I have a book'.

(6.49) Fijian:
    saa ti'o vei au e dua a pua'a
    Asp be-at to me 3Sg one Art pig
    'A pig is to me', i.e. 'I have a pig'.

Constructions like these are very widespread. Observe that the thing possessed stands in the subject case and takes any verbal agreement going, while the possessor stands in an oblique case. Now, suppose such a language were to use its possessive construction to create a stative, and consequently a perfect, just as in English. The result would be perfect constructions with meanings like 'I have broken a window', but with subject-case marking on the object, verb agreement with the object, and oblique marking on the subject. Just such an origin has therefore been proposed for ergatives in a number of languages, especially in those in which ergativity is confined to the perfect aspect. Indeed, some linguists prefer to derive the ergative constructions of the Indo-Iranian languages from an earlier perfect which was itself obtained from a possessive construction; this has the advantage of explaining why, in these languages, ergatives are usually confined to perfect aspect or to past tense (past tenses are themselves often derived from earlier perfects).

There is a final point of some importance. If an ergative construction is historically derived from either a passive or a possessive, as just described, then it must pass through a stage in which the thing which ends up as the direct object must actually be the subject of the sentence. We might therefore be able to find languages which exhibit not only **morphological ergativity**, like Basque, but also **syntactic ergativity**, in which NPs that appear to be direct objects pattern like subjects. Such languages indeed exist. A famous one is the Australian language Dyirbal. Consider the following Dyirbal sentences, the first two intransitive, the third transitive; the two cases are called Abs(olutive) and Erg(ative), the Roman numerals are gender-class identifiers, and there is no Dyirbal word for 'and':

(6.50) balan guda buṇa-n
        the-II-Abs dog-Abs descend-Past
        'The dog went downhill.'

(6.51) bayi yara buṇa-n
        the-I-Abs man-Abs descend-Past
        'The man went downhill.'

(6.52) balan guda baŋgul yara-ŋgu bura-n
        the-II-Abs dog-Abs the-I-Erg man-Erg see-Past
        'The man saw the dog.'

Now, in English, with its accusative syntax, it is the glosses in (6.51) and (6.52), with their intransitive and transitive subjects, which can easily be joined together: 'The man went downhill and saw the dog.' We cannot do the same with (6.50) and (6.52), however: *'The dog went downhill and the man saw.' To combine these two, we have to use a different construction, either '. . . and the man saw it' or '. . . and was seen by the man'. But Dyirbal is different: the two that can be straightforwardly combined are (6.50) and (6.52):

(6.53) balan guda buṇan baŋgul yaraŋgu buran
        'The dog went downhill and was seen by the man.'

But attempting to do the same with (6.51) and (6.52) produces an ungrammatical result:

(6.54) *bayi yara buṇan balan guda buran

The only way to combine these two is to use a different construction, just as happened in English with a different pairing.

It may, therefore, be the case that syntactically ergative languages like Dyirbal are languages in which the shift of markedness I referred to above has already taken place, but the subsequent reanalysis has not occurred, and it may further be the case that the more numerous morphologically ergative languages like Basque and Pashto have historically passed through just such a stage of syntactic ergativity. But information is sparse, and no one really knows: while we are now satisfied that we know a good deal about the origins of ergativity, there is clearly still a lot that we don't understand.

6.6   *Syntactic change as restructuring of grammars*

In the 1970s the Chomskyan linguist David Lightfoot began pursuing a novel view of syntactic change, one which he calls **restructuring** of grammars; see especially Lightfoot (1979). The idea works like this. A child acquiring a first language eventually puts together in her head a set of rules, her internal grammar, and she uses these rules to construct and interpret utterances. As a general rule, the grammars constructed by each new generation of children will most likely be very similar to the grammars constructed decades earlier by their parents. With the passage of time, however, the accumulated weight of phonological, morphological, and syntactic changes may introduce such a level of complexity into the surface forms of utterances that mental grammars which are broadly similar to those of earlier generations may become ever more complex, with more rules and messier rules and a greater number of exceptions. At some stage, Lightfoot proposes, the effort of constructing the traditional sort of grammar, in the face of data now very different from those encountered by earlier generations, will become simply too great, and, as a result, a new generation of children will instead construct for themselves a very different sort of mental grammar, one which corresponds more closely to the data. This sudden discontinuity in the kinds of mental grammars constructed by successive generations is what Lightfoot calls 'restructuring'. (In some of his works, he uses the alternative term 'radical reanalysis', which I shall avoid here.)

Now the idea that children actively construct grammars in the heads as they acquire their first language is generally held to be one of the great insights of modern linguistics, and few linguists would deny its validity. That being so, Lightfoot's idea has an obvious *a priori* plausibility. Moreover, this idea is in principle testable, because a sharp discontinuity in mental grammars between one generation and the next might, in many cases, produce a sharp discontinuity in the kinds of utterances which are possible. Lightfoot has in fact attempted to demonstrate the existence of precisely such discontinuities, particularly in the history of English. Here we shall briefly consider one of his favourite examples, the history of the English modal auxiliaries like *can*, *will*, and *might*, which have well-known peculiarities.

Old English had no modal auxiliaries. The ancestors of the modern modals were all in the language, but they were neither modals nor auxiliaries: they were just verbs. Already, however, they were somewhat unusual verbs, of a type specialists call 'preterite-present' verbs, which means that their present-tense forms looked like the past-tense forms of most other verbs. For example, these verbs failed to take the third-person singular ending in the present, a feature the modals retain today: *She smokes French cigarettes, She wants to buy a car*, but not **She cans speak Italian*. Let us refer to the Old English ancestors of the modals as 'pre-modals'.

Lightfoot sees the development of the pre-modals as follows. First, he argues that a number of independent changes in English left the pre-modals increasingly isolated and anomalous among the verbs (I omit one change which is too complex to describe here):

1. The pre-modals lost the ability to take direct objects, and so previously possible utterances parallel to modern English **I can music* became ungrammatical.
2. All the preterite-present verbs which showed no signs of becoming modals, such as *witan* 'know' and *þurfan* 'need', gradually disappeared from the language, leaving the pre-modals isolated.
3. The past-tense forms of the modals lost their past-time meaning, and became detached from their present tenses, so that, for example, *would* and *might* were no longer felt to be the past tenses of *will* and *may*, but were felt to be distinct items.
4. The infinitival *to*, illustrated above in *She wants to buy a car*, appeared in the language and came to be used for constructing the complements of most verbs (like *want*), but *to* failed to spread to the complements of pre-modals: **She can to speak Italian*.

As a result, Lightfoot concludes, the pre-modals had become so sharply distinct from other verbs that eventually a new generation of speakers found it too difficult to analyse them as verbs at all. Instead, this new generation abruptly began constructing grammars in which these anomalous items were assigned, not to the category of verbs, but instead to a totally new category invented for the purpose: the category of modals. (It should be noted that Lightfoot here follows the usual Chomskyan position that the English modals are not verbs, a view which is shared by few linguists not of a Chomskyan persuasion.) Lightfoot dates this development very precisely to the sixteenth century, and he supports this conclusion by arguing that, in the sixteenth century, a number of dramatic changes affected these items all at the same time:

1. They lost their infinitives, and things like **She appears to can speak Italian*, formerly normal, became impossible.
2. They lost the ability to take the verbal affix *-ing*, and things like **This is musting (to) be done*, formerly possible, became impossible.
3. Sequences of these items became impossible, and things like **I will can do it*, formerly normal, became impossible.
4. They lost the ability to appear in the *have* perfect, and things like **We had might come*, formerly possible, became impossible.
5. The old pattern for negating all English verbs, including the pre-modals, ceased to be possible with true verbs and became restricted to the

modals, and so things like *She wants not this apple*, formerly normal, became impossible, while things like *She will not go* remained normal.

6. The old pattern of inversion in questions, previously possible with all verbs, likewise became restricted to the modals, and so things like *Ate she the apple?*, previously normal, became impossible, while things like *Will she go?* remained normal.

The key point here is Lightfoot's insistence that all six of these last changes happened more or less suddenly and simultaneously: if he is right, it would indeed appear that there was some kind of important discontinuity in the grammar of English.

Lightfoot's idea of the sudden restructuring of mental grammars is an appealing one; if it proves able to withstand critical scrutiny, it will constitute an important addition to our understanding of syntactic change. But hostile criticism has not been wanting, and his critics make a number of worrying charges, only two of which we have space to consider here. First, take another look at Lightfoot's initial list of four changes which, he says, preceded the restructuring. Does anything strike you?

The obvious problem is that at least some of these changes appear to suggest that the pre-modals were *already* significantly different from other verbs long before the sixteenth century. In particular, his changes (1) and (4) seem to imply that the pre-modals were already both losing ordinary verbal properties and gaining non-verbal properties, thereby calling into question his view that these items remained nothing more than anomalous verbs until the sixteenth century. This in itself would not constitute a fatal objection, but there is more.

His critics argue vociferously that the changes which he imputes to the sixteenth century and describes as both sudden and simultaneous were nothing of the sort. They believe that the historical record shows something quite different: first, that the six changes in his second list in fact occurred gradually, over centuries, just like the first four changes, and, second, that they were not simultaneous at all, but rather that each occurred spread out over a noticeably different stretch of time. If the critics are right, then Lightfoot's restructuring scenario cannot be maintained, and we are forced to recognize nothing more than a large number of gradual and independent developments.

Lightfoot continues to develop his research programme, and he has recently modified his views on certain points, but it seems fair to conclude that the great majority of historical linguists remains to be convinced that the restructuring of grammars is indeed a real phenomenon.

Further reading

The major synthesis of syntactic change is Harris and Campbell (1995). The papers collected in Li (1977) are a particularly valuable source of information on syntactic change, while the papers in Li (1975) deal explicitly with issues of word-order change. Several of the chapters in Hopper and Traugott (1993) deal with various aspects of syntactic change, particularly with grammaticalization. The classic discussion of word-order typology is Greenberg (1963a); valuable extensions of Greenberg's work can be found in volume 4 of Greenberg *et al.* (1978), in Hawkins (1983), and in selected chapters of Comrie (1989) and of Croft (1990); the last two books include chapters on the diachronic dimension of typology. Chapter 6 of McMahon (1994) presents a survey of all these issues. Both Traugott (1972) and Denison (1993) are readable studies of the history of English syntax. Convenient introductions to ergativity are Comrie (1978), Dixon (1979), and Dixon (1994); collections of studies include Plank (1979) and Dixon (1987); Anderson (1977) is a survey of the historical origins of ergativity. Lightfoot's analysis of English modals is presented in Lightfoot (1974), while his theory is presented in detail in Lightfoot (1979). Criticism of Lightfoot's ideas can be found in the special number of the journal *Lingua* (vol. 55, 1981), and also in Bennett (1979), in Aitchison (1980), and in Warner (1983). Lightfoot revises his ideas in Lightfoot (1981), and presents a summary of his views in Lightfoot (1988). McMahon (1994: ch. 5) provides an overview of the whole issue.

Exercises

Exercise 6.1

Many Polynesian languages are ergative, while others are not. Most Polynesian languages exhibit a verbal suffix which is reconstructed as *-Cia*; its use varies among the several languages. Here are brief summaries of several Polynesian languages. (Data from Chung 1978.) Examine these data and propose a plausible account of the history of Polynesian syntax. 'Prop' is a determiner used before a proper name.

(a) *Tongan* is ergative, with ergative case-marker *'e*. The suffix *-Cia* appears on the verb only in very restricted and somewhat idiosyncratic circumstances – for example, to show that an agent is non-human, non-specific or absent:

> *Na'e fafangu kinautolu 'e Sione*   [*-Cia* not possible]
> Past awaken them Erg John
> 'John awakened them.'

> *Ne'e fangu-na au 'e he nanamu 'o e kakalá*
> Past awaken-Cia me Erg the smell of the flower.'
> 'The smell of the flower awakened me.'

(b) *Nieuan* is not ergative. The suffix *-Cia* is severely restricted. Most often, this suffix converts a transitive verb to an intransitive one; the subject of such a derived verb corresponds to the direct object of the original transitive verb:

Ka e ponoti-a e hala i a Manā
But Tense close-Cia the road because.of Prop Mana
'The road was closed because of (by) Mana.'

(c) *Samoan* is ergative, with ergative case-marker *e*. The suffix *-Cia* may optionally appear or fail to appear on any transitive verb, with little difference in meaning:

Sā su'e a'u e le fānau a Fo'isia
Past search me Erg the children of Fo'isia
'Fo'isia's children were looking for me.'

Sā su'e-ina a'u e le fānau a Fo'isia
Past search-Cia me Erg the children of Fo'isia
'Fo'isia's children were looking for me.'

Very often *-Cia* serves to mark the absence, or the remoteness, of an agent:

'Ua pa'i-a lona mata
Perf touch-Cia his eye
'His eye was touched (accidentally).'

(d) *Maori* is not ergative:

Ka whana te hōiho i a Hōne
Tense kick the horse Acc Prop John
'The horse kicked John.'

It has a fully productive passive, in which the verb is suffixed with *-Cia* and the passive agent is marked by *e*:

Ka whana-a a Hōne e te hōiho
Tense kick-Cia Prop John by the horse
'John was kicked by the horse.'

The passive is much more frequent than the active, and is obligatory in certain circumstances.

Exercise 6.2

Most languages belonging to the Oceanic subgroup of the Austronesian family possess a reflex ('development') of an ancestral item which I shall here represent as *PANI. Since the phonological history of these languages is well understood, we can recognize this *PANI in each language, regardless of its modern form. The functions of these reflexes are quite varied and differ from language to language. Here is a representative sample. (Data from Lichtenberk 1985.)

Sugu: *goko wani-au*
           speak PANI-me
           'Speak to me.'

Lau: *fale-a fua-na*
           give-it PANI-his
           'Give it to him.'

Baki: *ko-dri o vani kiniu*
           you-take him PANI me
           'Bring him to me.'

Fijian: *e tiko vei Jone*
           it stay PANI John
           'It is with John.'

Tigak: *ga aigot-i pok an-iri*
           she prepare-it food PANI-them
           'She prepared food for them.'

Gitua: *guap uzak lam pay-gau*
           you.do knife come PANI-me
           'Bring the knife to me.'

Inakona: *igia ga vani-go na uvi*
           he he.Fut PANI-you Art yam
           'He will give you a yam.'

Manam: *tamoata boro i-an-a*
           man pig he.Real-PANI-me
           'The man gave me a pig.'

Propose a historical source for *PANI, and briefly explain what seems to have happened in many of these languages.

Exercise 6.3

Chamus is a dialect of Maa, a Nilo-Saharan language spoken in Kenya and Tanzania. It is a VSO language in which the subject may never precede the first verb in the sentence. It has masculine and feminine gender classes, and it has a 'narrative' prefix *n-*, which can appear on a verb which is *not* the first verb in a sentence. The language has a certain morpheme *-yyéú-*, which invariably stands first in its sentence. This morpheme has a variety of functions, illustrated below. (Data from Heine 1992.)

(a) It can occur with agreement prefixes typical of verbs, with a human
    subject and with an object noun phrase:
    k-á-yyéú n-daâ   *k-á-yyéú m-partút*
    k-1Sg-yyéú Fem-food   k-1Sg-yyéú Fem-woman
    'I want food.'   'I want a wife.'

(b) It can occur with agreement markers, with a human subject and a complement clause whose verb is prefixed with *n-*; two orders are possible:

k-á-yyéú nanU n-a-ló n-ka
k-1Sg-yyéú I n-1Sg-go Fem-home
'I want to go home.'

k-á-yyéú n-a-ló nanU n-ka
k-1Sg-yyéú n-1Sg-go I Fem-home
'I want to go home.'

(c) It can occur with agreement markers and any kind of subject, with a complement clause whose verb is prefixed with *n-*:

k-é-yyéú l-pyan n-é-rriá
k-3Sg-yyéú Masc-elder n-3Sg-fall
'The old man nearly fell.'

k-é-yyéú l-cáni n-é-uróri
k-3Sg-yyéú Masc-tree n-3Sg-fall
'The tree almost fell.'

(d) It can occur in an invariable third-singular form *(k)eyyéú* with no agreement and with a following complement clause whose verb *cannot* bear the prefix *n-*; that complement verb must precede its subject:

(k)eyyéú a-ók nánU kUlɛ
keyyéú 1Sg-drink I milk
'I was about to drink milk.'

(k)eyyéú e-ók nInyɛ kUlɛ
keyyéú 3Sg-drink s/he milk
'S/he almost drank milk.'

*(k)eyyéú nInyɛ e-ók kUlɛ
keyyéú s/he 3Sg-drink milk

(e) Its invariable form can be used to answer a yes/no question:

i-túm-o m-partút? (k)éyyeu a-túm
2Sg-get-Perf Fem-woman keyyéú 1Sg-get
'Did you get a wife?' 'No [but I almost did].'

Propose an account of the historical development of the morpheme *-yyéú-* which explains these observations as completely as possible.

Exercise 6.4

The Carib language Panare is verb-initial and subject-final. (Data from Gildea 1993.) When the subject is first or second person, no copula is required in the present tense:

maestro yu
teacher I
'I am a teacher.'

maestro amën
teacher you
'You are a teacher.'

With a third-person subject, a copula is obligatory. With an inanimate subject, the copula is *mën*; with an animate subject, it is either *këj* or *nëj*, with a difference in meaning:

*maestro e'ñapa
teacher Panare

*e'chipen manko
fruit mango

maestro këj e'ñapa
teacher *këj* Panare
'This Panare here is a teacher.'

e'chipen mën manko
fruit *mën* mango
'Mango is a fruit.'

maestro nëj e'ñapa
teacher *nëj* Panare
'That Panare there is a teacher.'

The demonstratives *mëj* 'this person who I can see now' and *kën* 'that person who I can't see now' at first glance behave straightforwardly:

maestro këj mëj
teacher *këj* this-guy
'This guy is a teacher here.'

maestro nëj kën
teacher *nëj* that-guy
'That guy is a teacher there.'

But now consider some further Panare copular sentences; note that /y/ affricates to /ch/ after /j/:

maestro nëj mëj
teacher *nëj* this-guy
'This guy was a teacher.'

maestro nëj chu
teacher *nëj* I
'I was a teacher.'

maestro nëj amën
teacher *nëj* you
'You were a teacher.'

maestro këj kën
teacher *këj* that guy
'That guy is being a teacher right now.' [i.e. he's off somewhere performing his teaching duties at this very moment]

Moreover, the items *këj* and *nëj* can also occur with ordinary verbs; a question mark indicates a sentence which sounds very strange to native speakers:

ë' púmanëpëj këj Toman
be-falling *këj* Thomas
'Tom is falling.'

?ë' púmanëpëj nëj Toman
be-falling *nëj* Thomas
'Tom is falling'
[but I can't see him]

yiupúmën këj Toman　　　　　　*yiupúmën nëj Toman*
fall *këj* Thomas　　　　　　　　fall *nëj* Thomas
'Tom is going to fall!'　　　　　'Tom is going to fall one day' **or**
　　　　　　　　　　　　　　　'Tom fell.'

Describe the behaviour of *këj* and *nëj* as accurately as you can, and propose a plausible historical development of the use of these items. What further evidence might you look for to check your hypothesis?

7

Relatedness between languages

In the preceding chapters we have examined the many different ways in which languages can change and considered how and why such changes might take place. Later, in Chapter 10, we'll be looking at the 'how' and 'why' of language change from a very different point of view. For the moment, though, we turn our attention to a different issue: the consequences of language change. After generations, or centuries, or millennia, of language change, what is the result?

7.1 The origin of dialects

When the Anglo-Saxons first settled in Britain some 1500 years ago, the several tribes who settled in various parts of the country were already speaking slightly different varieties of their continental language (which would not begin to be called English until a little later), but the differences were rather minor. With the passage of time, the inevitable processes of language change of course began to affect their newly installed English language: new words, new meanings, new pronunciations, and new grammatical forms began to creep into their speech, and, at the same time, old ones began to drop out of use. Nothing surprising here. However – and this is the key point – a change appearing in one place did not necessarily spread to the whole of the country.

Before the nineteenth century, no man could travel faster than a horse could take him, and very few people could even afford to own horses, so that travel normally meant travel on foot, or very occasionally by boat. For many centuries after the settlement, then, most people were tied firmly to their place of birth, and they rarely travelled as much as fifty miles away from there. Consequently, most of their dealings were with people from their immediate area, or at best with people in the next town or the next valley.

Now consider what this means in linguistic terms. Suppose a few people in one valley began using a new word or a new pronunciation. Perhaps the new form would be picked up by others in the valley, and gradually become general there. People in the next valley would therefore start to hear the new forms, and maybe they too would take a liking to them and begin to use them, thereby giving the people in the next valley again a chance to hear them. Then again, maybe they wouldn't. Perhaps they would just accept their neighbours' odd forms as typical of those neighbours but go on themselves using the older forms, or perhaps they would come up with some different new forms of their own. In the case of every such innovation – and there were thousands and thousands of them – people might or might not choose to adopt the innovation from their neighbours, and, if they didn't adopt it, their neighbours on the other side would hardly ever get to hear it at all.

With the passage of centuries, then, the relatively homogeneous English of the settlers began to break up into regional varieties that were becoming steadily more different from one another. Every local group of people spoke the language a little differently from their next-door neighbours, and these differences accumulated as you moved across the country, so that people living far apart from one another were speaking very different kinds of English indeed. People in different parts of England had different words for things, and they used different grammatical endings and different constructions. In short, English had broken up into what we call **regional dialects**, or **dialects** for short. Moreover, people in different areas were pronouncing their words very differently, and we therefore say that they were using different **regional accents**.

(A note on usage. In Britain, *dialects* are speech varieties differing in vocabulary and grammar, while *accent*s are varieties differing in pronunciation. In the USA, the term *dialect* is commonly understood as including features of pronunciation. This difference reflects the fact that, in the USA, accents are usually closely related to other regional features of usage, while in Britain a regional accent may be largely independent of regional grammar and vocabulary. In this book, I generally follow British usage. Note in any case that every single speaker of any language necessarily speaks it with some accent or other: it is impossible to speak English 'without an accent'. The most that anyone can do is to use the sort of accent that some other speakers regard as the most familiar, or the most prestigious, kind of accent. We return to this in Chapter 10.)

By about 1500, it is clear, people were often finding it exceedingly difficult to understand English-speakers from other areas. In a famous passage published in 1490, the printer William Caxton reports that an English merchant walked into a tavern in London and asked for *eggys*, and was told by the tavern-keeper that she could not understand French. The exchange became quite heated before another man stepped in and explained that the merchant was asking for *eyren*. This little bit of interpretation did the trick, and the merchant got his eggs. Here the merchant was using a northern word with a northern plural ending, while the tavern-keeper only knew the southern forms typical of London.

Caxton offered this story to illustrate the problems that he faced as a printer. He wanted to print books that could be read throughout England, but what words and forms should he use when the regional varieties of English differed so greatly?

It was Caxton himself who was responsible for the first steps at grappling with this bewildering regional variation. The words and forms selected by him, and by the printers who followed him, in many cases gradually came to be accepted as the standard English ones, and today we have a fairly homogeneous standard version of English which is at least accessible to all English-speakers, regardless of the sort of English they have grown up speaking.

None the less, regional differences are still very much with us, and they have been extended by the spread of English to Ireland, Wales, North America, the Caribbean, South Africa, India, Australia, New Zealand, and parts of southeast Asia and the Pacific during the last several centuries. (The lowlands of Scotland, in contrast, were settled by English-speakers around the same time as England.) You can easily tell an English person from a Scot, a North American, a Jamaican, or a southern-hemisphere speaker; perhaps you can quickly spot someone from Birmingham, or Glasgow, or New York, or Mississippi; very likely you can guess the approximate origin of someone from a different part of your own country.

Not long ago there was a signal reminder of just how different the regional varieties of English still are. A television company put out a programme filmed in the English city of Newcastle, where the local variety of English is famously divergent and difficult, and the broadcast version was accompanied by *English subtitles*! The producers were afraid that other speakers would be quite unable to understand the 'Geordie' speech of the performers. This ruffled quite a few feathers in Newcastle, but the producers had a point: I well recall that, the first time I met a Geordie speaker, it was some days before I could understand a single word he was saying.

In fact, variation in English is considerably greater than you might realize from your own experience. What do you think of the following examples? Are they familiar? Are they comprehensible? Are they English?

1. I done shot me a squirrel.
2. That will make Peter and I's job easier.
3. The lass divn't gan to the pictures, pet.
4. As well, there are three other cases of this.
5. I am not knowing where to find a stepney.
6. They're a lousy team any more.
7. She's the student that's books I borrowed.
8. If Hitler had invaded earlier, he may have captured Moscow.
9. She mustn't be in: her car's not there.
10. You must finish today your work.
11. I might could do it.

In fact, every one of these examples is routinely used by speakers of English in certain parts of the world, but not in other parts; speakers who don't use them typically find them very strange and sometimes even incomprehensible, a fact which would astonish the speakers who use them.

Example (1) is typical of much of the southern USA and means 'I shot a squirrel'. Example (2) is typically Australian, though it is occasionally heard elsewhere. Example (3) is from the Geordie speech of Newcastle and means 'The girl didn't go to the movies'. Example (4) is Canadian; most other speakers (including Americans) cannot use *as well* in this way. Example (5) represents the English of India and means 'I don't know where to find a spare wheel'. Example (6) is typical of much of the northeastern USA, and means 'They didn't use to be a lousy team, but now they are' – that is, it means exactly the opposite of 'They're not a lousy team any more'. (This one is particularly baffling for other speakers.) Example (7) occurs in a number of regional varieties all over the world, including Australia; other speakers require 'whose books'. Example (8) is typical of the English of England, though it is beginning to appear in several other places; it means '. . . he might have captured . . .' Example (9) is normal in Ireland and in areas influenced by Irish English, including parts of the USA and Australia. Example (10) is usual in the English of Malaysia and Singapore; other speakers require '. . . finish your work today'. Finally, example (11) is normal in much of Scotland and can also be heard in the Appalachian Mountains and the American south; it means 'I might be able to do it'.

Such regional differences not only persist but multiply. Linguists who study contemporary English are constantly reporting that new words, new pronunciations, or new grammatical forms have turned up and become established in Auckland or Liverpool or Albuquerque. Sometimes these new forms quickly become widely known and used; in other cases they remain purely local.

Regional fragmentation of this kind is in no way peculiar to English: it happens to every language which is spoken over any significant area. French, Spanish, German, Russian, Hindi, Arabic – all show extensive regional variation, sometimes beyond anything we find in English. Even Basque, spoken in an area only about 160 kilometres by 50 kilometres, exhibits greater regional diversity than does English, which is spoken on almost every continent. The variation in German is such that German-speakers from, say, Berlin and Bonn cannot understand each other at all if they use their own regional varieties, nor can a Syrian and a Moroccan communicate using their own local varieties of Arabic, nor a Sicilian and a Genoese if they stick to their own local Italian.

In recent centuries, especially in Europe, the extent of regional diversity has been somewhat obscured by the development of standard forms for the principal languages of nation states. For example, a standard form of German has been created and is now learned by all educated speakers of German, and this is what Germans speak to other Germans from different places, though they continue to use their local dialects at home with family and friends. To some degree, the influence of these new standards has tended to reduce the amount of regional diversity: you will have noticed that the northern form *eggs* has become standard and driven the southern form *eyren* out of the language, even in the remotest corners of southern England. But regional dialects are still very prominent, even in Europe. Here is an example from French, a language in which the standard form has been particularly successful at displacing regional varieties.

In the southeastern half of Belgium, the first language is French, and all Belgians from this area, of course, learn to use standard French with other French-speakers. But the local variety, called *Walloon*, was until very recently the first language of most people, and it's noticeably different from the standard, so different that some specialists prefer to label it a distinct language, rather than a dialect of French. Look at this passage, written in the Walloon of the Belgian province of Luxembourg (not to be confused with the country of the same name); it was written by Georges Pasau, Président du Musée de la Parole au Pays de Bastogne:

> I-gn-è a pô près kinze ans du d' ci, dj' asto amon Albêrt Lèyonârd èt dj' rawârdo pace k' on m' avot dit k' ou profèsseûr do Séminêre vlot nos vèy po pârler do walon. Dju m' sovin co k' dj' ê dmandé a ç' momint la: «Kin-âdje k' il è, don ç' curé la?» Dj' ê vite avou compris k' i n' astot nin pus curé k' mi, surtout cand dj' l' ê vèyou avou oune bèle djon.ne bwêcèle ki n' compurdot wêre lu walon, mês k' astot bin dècidé a l' aprinde avou dès profèsseûrs come Pierrot, come Jeannot, come Roger, ou come mi, di-st-i l' fou.

Even if you know French, you will find this passage startling and even incomprehensible in places, and not merely because of the somewhat distinctive orthography.

Here is a standard French version of the passage:

> Il y a à peu près quinze ans d'ici, j'étais chez Albert Leonard et j'attendais parce qu'on m'avait dit qu'un professeur du Séminaire voulait nous voir pour parler du wallon. Je me souviens ce que j'ai demandé à ce moment-là: 'Quel âge a-t-il donc, ce curé-là?' J'avais vite compris qu'il n'étais pas plus curé que moi, surtout quand je l'ai vu avec une belle jeune demoiselle qui ne comprenait guère le wallon, mais qui était bien décidée à l'apprendre avec des professeurs comme Pierrot, comme Jeannot, comme Roger, ou comme moi, dit-il, le fou.

And here is an English version:

> It's fifteen years ago now; I was with Albert Leonard, and I was curious because I had been told that a teacher from the Seminary wanted to see us to talk about Walloon. I still remember what I was wondering at that moment: 'So how old is that priest?' I quickly understood that he was no more a priest than I was, particularly when I saw him with a beautiful young girl who scarcely knew any Walloon but who was determined to learn it from teachers like Pierrot, like Jannot, like Roger, or indeed like me, he says foolishly.

In the nineteenth century, such regional variation began to attract the attention of a number of European linguists, and to their efforts we now turn.

7.2   *Dialect geography*

Before the nineteenth century, linguists in Europe had largely confined their attention to dead languages like Latin and ancient Greek and to the standard forms of modern languages like English, French, and German. More than a few linguists shared the common perception that non-standard regional varieties were nothing but ignorant and debased versions of the standard forms, unworthy of serious attention. In that century, however, there occurred one of the great developments in the history of linguistics: a number of scholars began to realize that regional forms were just as worthy of study as standard forms, and they turned their attention to constructing good linguistic descriptions of regional variation.

One way of doing this, of course, is to write grammars and dictionaries of regional dialects, and this approach was initiated by Johannes Schmeller, who in 1821 published a grammar of his own Bavarian dialect of German. This kind of valuable work is still with us; for example, the Walloon passage above is taken from an article on a dictionary of Walloon published in 1994. Here, though, I want to concentrate on another approach, the one called **dialect geography**.

Dialect geography consists of the painstaking collection of the regional forms used at intervals across a large area. Naturally, since variation is virtually limitless, the investigators must decide in advance which particular items they will look at and collect information on. They may decide to ask for the local name of the building that cows are kept in at night, or of a sliver of wood caught in a finger. They may be interested in the particular vowel sounds used in particular words, or in the particular grammatical forms of verbs or nouns. Such data must be collected by interviewing local people, and this calls for carefully designed techniques of elicitation, since people tend to get nervous when questioned by outsiders, and may be inclined to give what they hope are the 'right' answers, rather than what they actually say.

Around the middle of the century, a number of people threw themselves into such work in various parts of Europe. For example, the French amateur linguist Prince L. L. Bonaparte (nephew of Napoleon) collected data on the regional dialects of Basque and published in 1869 a map showing his classification of the language into regional dialects. These early efforts, however, were somewhat unsophisticated, and it took several decades to work out reliable procedures.

The German Georg Wenker introduced the questionnaire approach: he sent out questionnaires to schoolteachers in nearly 50000 localities in Germany and asked for the local equivalents of standard German sentences. This had the advantage of producing a huge volume of data (so much, in fact, that Wenker's results have still not been fully published), but the disadvantage that the schoolteachers, having no training, were highly inconsistent in their reporting and perhaps not always reliable.

Observing the difficulties with Wenker's approach, the French linguist Jules Gilliéron tried another technique. He trained a single worker, Edmond Edmont, in the skills of collecting information by personal interview. Edmont, who proved to be a talented and reliable investigator, then spent the years between 1896 and 1900 cycling around France, stopping in a total of 639 localities to make friends with the local people and ask his questions. While this programme produced a much smaller corpus of data, it had the great advantage that the data were completely consistent and very reliable. Gilliéron managed to collate Edmont's findings and to publish them in full by 1910.

And how does one publish such data? They could be published merely as lists, but dialect geographers have always preferred another type of presentation, more laborious and expensive but far more illuminating: the preparation of **dialect maps**. A single dialect map shows the regional variants found for a single linguistic variable – the local words for 'dragonfly' or 'headache', the local pronunciations of the word *arm* or *girl*, or whatever. Each locality covered is marked on the map with a symbol which represents its particular form; localities using the same form get the same symbol. If the boundary between two neighbouring forms turns out to be rather sharp, a line called an **isogloss** may be drawn on the map to show that boundary. Most often, the results of such a study are presented in a volume of dialect maps, a **dialect atlas**. Such atlases now exist for France, for Germany (only in part), for England, for the eastern USA, and for some other areas. The production of dialect atlases revolutionized linguistics by revealing for the first time clear evidence of the long accumulation of regional changes which I have been discussing in this chapter: each map provides a kind of snapshot of the linguistic position at the moment the data were collected. Ideally, of course, we would like to have a series of such snapshots taken at intervals of a generation or so, in order to see how the maps change, as local forms expand or contract their territory, as some disappear altogether while new forms appear and begin to spread out. Such is the cost of this work, however, both in time and in money, that we can almost never do this.

Here are some examples of dialect maps. Fig. 7.1 shows the past tense of the verb *dive* in the eastern USA, with its regional variants *dived*, *dove* (rhymes with *drove*), *duv* (rhymes with *love*), and *div* (rhymes with *sieve*). In this case, as you can see, the boundaries between competing forms are somewhat blurred, and sharp isoglosses are hard to draw.

Fig. 7.2 likewise shows the past tense of *see* in England. This time the investigators have felt able to draw isoglosses between the neighbouring forms.

Dialect maps are unquestionably of great value in displaying real language data in a vivid graphical manner. However, if you leaf through the pages of a dialect atlas and try to compare some of the maps, you will quickly notice something striking: the isoglosses on one map typically bear no relation to the isoglosses on the next. (Check this for yourself if your library has a dialect

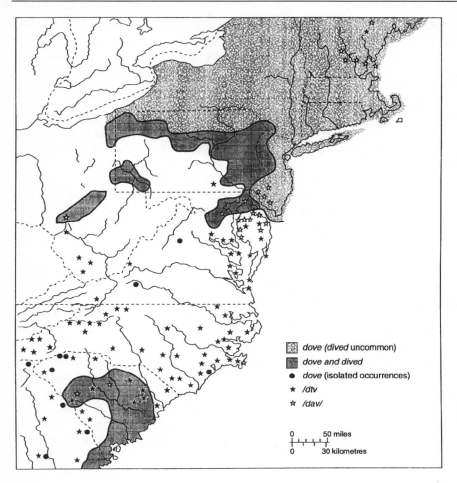

Fig. 7.1 The past tense of *dive* in the eastern USA
(Source: Atwood 1953: fig. 6)

atlas in it.) Rather, each particular linguistic form extends over its own particular area, and it doesn't seem to pay any attention to what other forms are doing. Nevertheless, if you lay dozens and dozens of dialect maps of the same region on top of one another, some structure will begin to emerge. In particular, you will sometimes find that a significant number of isoglosses lie very close together over much of their length. We call this state of affairs an isogloss bundle, and an isogloss bundle is the closest thing we normally find to a division between distinct dialects. For example, Fig. 7.3 shows the southern limit of six different words and forms in the French-speaking area. The six isoglosses correspond exactly only along the River Garonne in the

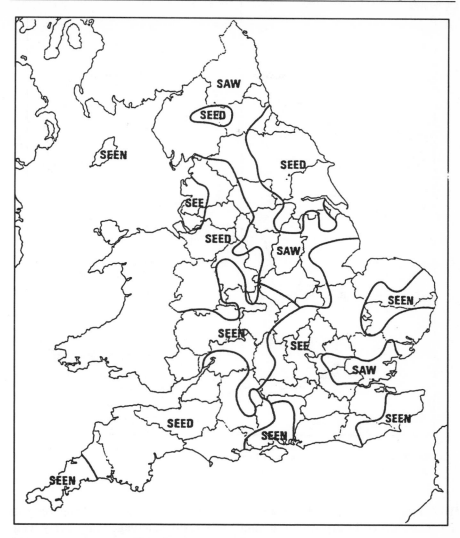

Fig. 7.2 The past tense of *see* in England
(Source: Upton *et al.* 1987: map 139)

west, which forms a natural boundary; elsewhere they follow somewhat different courses, but, as you can see, they all stay close enough together to constitute an isogloss bundle. Therefore we may provisionally conclude that this bundle represents a major boundary between the speech of the north and that of the south – and in fact we are looking at the most famous linguistic boundary in France: that between the *langue d'oil* in the north and the *langue d'oc* in the south, so called from their different words for 'yes'.

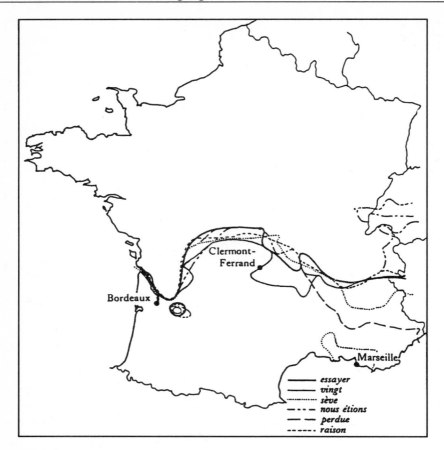

Fig. 7.3 An isogloss bundle in France
(Source: Chambers and Trudgill 1980: map 7.6)

By taking advantage of the presence of such isogloss bundles, dialectologists have succeeded in classifying a number of major languages into fairly well-defined dialects, each with a number of identifiable characteristics. For example, Figs 7.4 and 7.5 show the conventional division into dialects of English in England and in the eastern USA, respectively. (Wales and the Scottish highlands are excluded because English either has been introduced only very recently or is still a second language.)

In each case, the map broadly confirms the popular perception of the existence of 'northern', 'midland', and 'southern' dialects, though the boundaries that emerge from compiling isogloss bundles do not always match our preconceptions perfectly. In particular, the boundaries between the northern and midland dialects in both countries are perhaps somewhat farther north than we might have expected, suggesting that we are probably inclined to

Fig. 7.4 The major dialect areas of England
(Source: Trudgill 1990: map 9)

attach greater weight to certain features than to others in deciding for
ourselves whether we are hearing 'northern' or 'midland' speech.

In fact, specialists have further divided each of the three main dialect areas
into a number of smaller sub-dialects, only a few of which are shown on the
maps, though in the USA these further subdivisions are confined to the eastern
and southern coasts; elsewhere the very recent introduction of English and the

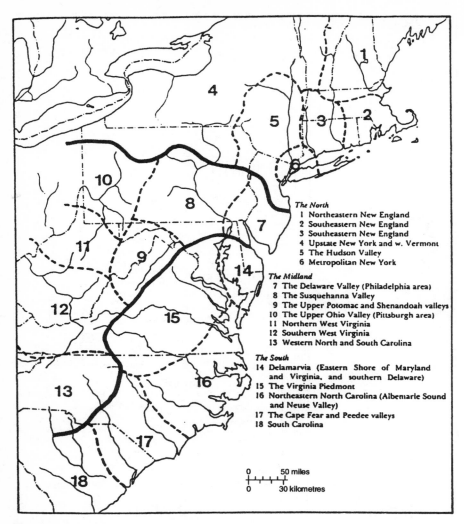

The North
1 Northeastern New England
2 Southeastern New England
3 Southeastern New England
4 Upstate New York and w. Vermont
5 The Hudson Valley
6 Metropolitan New York

The Midland
7 The Delaware Valley (Philadelphia area)
8 The Susquehanna Valley
9 The Upper Potomac and Shenandoah valleys
10 The Upper Ohio Valley (Pittsburgh area)
11 Northern West Virginia
12 Southern West Virginia
13 Western North and South Carolina

The South
14 Delamarvia (Eastern Shore of Maryland and Virginia, and southern Delaware)
15 The Virginia Piedmont
16 Northeastern North Carolina (Albemarle Sound and Neuse Valley)
17 The Cape Fear and Peedee valleys
18 South Carolina

0   50 miles
0   30 kilometres

Fig. 7.5 The dialect areas of the eastern USA
(Source: Kurath and McDavid 1961: map 2)

vast population movements have so far not allowed the formation of distinctive regional dialects.

7.3 *Genetic relationships*

So far we have seen that the remorseless processes of language change invariably produce ever-greater differences between the regional varieties of a language. And what would be the outcome if such regional changes were to accumulate without limit for centuries – for example, in English? Easy: the regional varieties of English would eventually become so different from one another that they would cease to be mutually comprehensible at all, and we would be forced to speak, not of different dialects, but of different languages. It is possible that English will not now break up into several distinct languages, thanks to the enormous advances in transport and communications which we have seen in recent dacades, but it would have happened otherwise.

And it is perfectly clear that such fragmentation of single languages into several different languages has happened countless times before. About 2500 years ago, Latin was an obscure little language spoken only in and around the small city of Rome. But the Romans proved to be ambitious, skilled in diplomacy, and powerful in war, and within a few centuries they had carved out an empire consisting of the entire area around the Mediterranean plus much of western Europe and the Balkans. Throughout the Roman Empire Latin was the language of administration, and in time it came to displace some dozens of earlier languages, as the subjects of the Empire gave up their own languages in favour of the more prestigious Latin. Hence Latin became the first language of several million people in southern and western Europe and in the Balkans.

Naturally, like any spoken language, Latin continued to change, but for a while the authority of Rome helped to maintain a degree of uniformity in the speech of vast areas, in spite of the changes which were taking place. The consonant [h] was lost everywhere, and so was word-final [m]. The vowel system was dramatically reorganized, as the five long and five short vowels and three diphthongs of earlier Latin were rearranged into a new system of seven vowels without length distinctions and at most one diphthong. Velar plosives came to be strongly palatalized before front vowels. The rich case-system began to collapse and to give way to the increasing use of prepositions, and new verbal inflections replaced some of the old ones. The preferred SOV word order of earlier Latin was replaced by SVO word order. New words were introduced: earlier *equus* 'horse' was replaced by *caballus*, originally a slang term meaning 'nag', and *pulcher* 'beautiful' was replaced by *formosus* (literally 'shapely') or *bellus*. Diminutives became increasingly popular and often replaced the words they were derived from.

By the early centuries of the Christian era spoken Latin was thus already very different from the *classical* language of several centuries earlier, which is the sort of Latin you will learn in school. Such **Vulgar Latin** (the term means only 'popular') was everywhere the first language, though educated people continued to use the more prestigious classical variety for scholarly writing. But popular speech was often recorded in writing as well – for example, in practical 'how-to-do-it' books on farming or cooking and, famously, in the graffiti preserved in the cities of Pompeii and Herculaneum, entombed in volcanic ash in AD 79. We even have a few prescriptive guides to the writing of proper classical Latin, such as the celebrated *Appendix Probi*, compiled in the sixth or seventh century, which contains advice like *auris non oricla* (for 'ear') and *tristis non tristus* (for 'sad'), showing directly the forms used by then in popular speech.

But such centralizing tendencies could not prevent the continued development of regional variation, and, when the Empire finally collapsed in the fifth century, there was no longer any significant resistance to the splintering of Latin into innumerable regional varieties. Within another couple of centuries, speakers of Latin in Spain, France, Italy, and the Balkans could no longer understand one another, nor could speakers from northern and southern France, or northern and southern Italy. By the eighth or ninth century it no longer made much sense to apply a single name to this babel of regional varieties, and people were therefore beginning to speak of 'Tuscan' or 'Provençal' or 'Leonese' in order to identify particular regional types of speech.

By this time Latin had effectively broken up into several quite distinct languages, but for a while there was no way of identifying a few well-defined languages with recognizable boundaries: there was just a vast dialect continuum. Eventually, though, some regional varieties began to acquire a measure of prestige. Around 1100 the speech of the Mediterranean coast of France became the vehicle of a brilliant literature, and for a while this so-called *Provençal* language seemed destined to become the basis of a major new standard, widely known and used, and there were similarly important literary developments based on the speech of the east coast of Spain and on that of Tuscany in Italy.

In most cases, though, it was not literature, but politics, that proved to be decisive. In France, the small and obscure region of Paris produced a series of shrewd and ambitious politicians and military men who gradually made their remote northern home the premier political force from the Channel to the Pyrenees; in Spain, the remote and dusty interior province of Castile produced a comparable series of effective kings and queens who likewise made themselves rulers of all Spain. Naturally, once Paris and Castile had become politically pre-eminent, the local speech varieties of those regions almost automatically acquired pre-eminence as well: if you wanted to get ahead, you learned to speak like the people who were in charge. As a result, Parisian French and Castilian Spanish, formerly no more than the local speech of cultural backwaters, regarded as laughably rustic and crude by the sophisticated intellectuals of Marseilles and Barcelona, gradually became the prestige forms of speech in their respective countries. In Italy, which was not politically unified until the nineteenth century, the cultural and literary importance of Tuscany was not displaced by political developments, and modern standard Italian is based upon the speech of Florence, and not on that of Rome, the capital city.

Eventually, then, first regional and then national standards came to be imposed upon the dialect continuum, and it became possible to speak, without doing too much violence to the complex linguistic facts, of just a few major languages, each representing a distinctive development of the spoken Latin of centuries earlier. We might, if we chose, give these modern descendants of Latin names like 'Parisian Latin' and 'Madrid Latin', but no one has seen any point in this, and we speak instead of *French*, *Spanish*, *Italian*, and so on. Unlike English, Latin really has broken up into a number of quite distinct regional languages, all of which started out centuries ago as nothing more than regional dialects of Latin.

We call these languages the **Romance languages** (the name means only 'Roman'), and there are more of them than you might have heard of. Apart from French, Spanish, and Italian, we have also *Portuguese* (in Portugal), *Galician* (in northwestern Spain), *Catalan* (in eastern Spain and one corner of France), *Occitan* (in the southern half of France, and commonly called 'Provençal'), *Romantsch* (in eastern Switzerland), *Sardinian* (in Sardinia), *Friulian* (in northeastern Italy), and *Romanian* (in Romania and in parts of several adjacent countries). (For political reasons, the Romanian spoken in the new republic of Moldova is officially regarded as a separate language, *Moldavian*.)

French, Spanish, and Portuguese are also widely spoken, of course, in the Americas, in Africa, in southeast Asia and in the Pacific, reflecting the former colonial empires of France, Spain, and Portugal. And two more Romance languages are spoken only in the Caribbean: these are *Haitian Creole*, a distinctive offshoot of French, now the mother tongue of the entire population of Haiti, and not mutually comprehensible with French, and *Papamiento*, a Spanish-based creole spoken in and around the island of Curaçao. (We discuss creoles in Chapter 11.) Finally, there was formerly at least one more Romance language, *Dalmatian*, spoken on the Adriatic coast of what is now Croatia, but the language died out in the eighteenth century. (Language death too we shall discuss in Chapter 11.)

We say that the Romance languages are **genetically related**, which means that they all started out as nothing more than regional dialects of a single ancestral language, and we speak of them as constituting a single **language family** – in this case, the **Romance family**. Whenever linguists find a group of languages which are clearly genetically related, we know immediately that the languages have developed from a common ancestor, a **proto-language**. In the case of the Romance family, their common ancestor is therefore called **Proto-Romance**. The Romance family is somewhat unusual in that we actually have records of something which can be more or less identified with Proto-Romance: Latin, and particularly Vulgar Latin. However, even if we didn't have any such records, we could still be sure that the proto-language must have existed once (and, using the techniques to be introduced in the next chapter, we could work backwards to discover important facts about that proto-language).

With most language families, we are not so fortunate as to have any records of the ancestral proto-language. Here is an example. Latin itself, of course, must have started off as a dialect of a still earlier language, and in fact several of its near relatives are attested. Around 500 BC, Italy was occupied by speakers of a startlingly large number of languages, and we have some modest written records of some of these (though not all). Three of them, Faliscan, Oscan, and Umbrian, were apparently fairly closely related to Latin, and Faliscan in particular was very close indeed. Latin is, therefore, a member of a wider family; we call it the **Italic family**, and the Italic languages, of course, must be descended from an ancestral language which we call **Proto-Italic**. This time, though, we find no trace of written records of this proto-language; it must have been spoken more than 3000 years ago, and its speakers were probably illiterate. Nevertheless, we can be confident that such a language was spoken by somebody somewhere, and that Latin originated as a regional dialect of it.

Historical linguists have been successful at identifying a sizeable number of such language families. English, for example, belongs to a group of languages chiefly spoken in northern Europe. Here are a few samples of some of those other languages; you can easily see the family resemblance.

- Dutch: De kat is in de keuken. 'The cat is in the kitchen.'
- German: Dies ist ein gutes Buch. 'This is a good book.'
- Swedish: Nils har en penna och en bok. 'Nick has a pen and a book.'
- Icelandic: Fólkið segir, að hún sé lík Anna. 'People say that she is like Anna.'

This family is called the **Germanic family**. The Germanic languages include *English*, *Frisian* (spoken in corners of the Netherlands and Germany and on several nearby islands), *Dutch*, *Afrikaans* (a distinctive offshoot of Dutch in South Africa), *German* (High and Low), *Yiddish* (a distinctive offshoot of medieval German), *Danish*, *Faeroese* (in the Faeroe Islands), *Norwegian*, *Swedish*, and *Icelandic*. We also know about some other Germanic languages which have died out, including *Gothic* (spoken by many of the invaders who overthrew the Roman Empire) and *Norn* (formerly spoken in the Shetland and Orkney Islands of Scotland). For several of these we have extensive records of earlier forms, including Old English, Old High German, and Old Norse (the language of the Vikings), among others.

Naturally, the Germanic languages are all descended from **Proto-Germanic**, but again the speakers of this ancestral language were illiterate and left us no records of their speech, but most specialists believe that Proto-Germanic was spoken in southern Scandinavia perhaps around 500 BC. And all these languages, from Icelandic to Gothic, started out more than 2000 years ago as regional dialects of Proto-Germanic.

The family resemblance among the Romance languages is almost blindingly obvious, and the same is true of the Germanic languages. Other equally obvious families can be identified in Europe and elsewhere, such as the **Celtic family** (including Irish, Scots Gaelic, and Welsh, among others), the **Slavic family** (including Russian, Polish, and Serbo-Croatian, among others), and the **Iranian family** (including Persian, Kurdish, and Pashto (the chief language of Afghanistan), among others).

Naturally, Proto-Italic, Proto-Germanic, Proto-Celtic, and all the rest must themselves have started out long, long ago as nothing but regional dialects of still more ancient ancestral languages. And one of the most stunning scholarly achievements of all time took place in the closing years of the eighteenth century and during the first few decades of the nineteenth, when linguists realized, to their own astonishment, that all the language families I have so far mentioned, and many others besides, could all be traced back to a *single* remote ancestor. Germanic, Italic, Celtic, Slavic, Iranian languages, and also Greek, Albanian, Armenian, the north Indian languages like Hindi, Bengali, and Gujarati, and some extinct languages of Anatolia and central Asia – all are derived from that one common ancestor by the slow accumulation of linguistic changes of the sort we examined in the first few chapters. This discovery was a great achievement, because the resemblances among English, Italian, and Russian, let alone Armenian, Kurdish, and Bengali, are very far from being obvious. In the next two chapters we'll be looking at how this discovery was made. For now I'll content myself with naming this gigantic family. Since the members of it have for millennia occupied territory ranging from India to western Europe, we call it the **Indo-European family**, and its remote ancestor, of course, is **Proto-Indo-European** (PIE).

Who spoke PIE, and where, and when? These are vexed questions, and there is no consensus about their answers; we shall be returning to these issues at intervals in the rest of the book. If you pressed me, though, I would confess that our best guess at the moment is that PIE was probably spoken about 6000 years ago, probably in eastern Europe, possibly in southern Russia or Ukraine, and conceivably by a people who have turned up in the archaeological record. But every one of these suggestions is highly controversial, even now the date, which is the one thing that most linguists used to feel fairly confident about, and the next three historical linguists you ask will very likely give you three different opinions. The one thing that is certain is that PIE was spoken by somebody, somewhere, at some time, and that its daughter languages now occupy a huge chunk of the globe.

Moreover, the Indo-European family is just one of a large number of language families which have been identified in all parts of the planet, though it happens to be the biggest one that we have so far managed to identify with confidence. The last section of this chapter will give you a brief rundown of some of these other families. For now, though, I turn to another question: the internal structure of a language family.

7.4 *Tree model and wave model*

Not all the Germanic languages are equally closely related. As you might have gathered from my brief illustrations above, English is fairly close to Dutch but much more distant from Icelandic. Frisian is often singled out as the closest living relative of English, while Gothic is the Germanic language that is most different from all the others. Like any language family, then, the Germanic family has an internal structure, with some languages being particularly closely related and perhaps forming subgroups within the family. It is desirable to have some way of representing such internal structure. The most widely used device is the **tree diagram**, introduced by the German linguist August Schleicher in the middle of the nineteenth century.

The idea behind the tree diagram is simple. Having identified a family of languages, we examine them to see which ones appear to be most closely related. In particular, we look for **shared innovations**, changes which have appeared in some members of the family but not in others. Here the thinking is that the languages which do not share a particular innovation probably split off early from the languages which do share it, and hence that the languages sharing the innovation probably had a single common ancestor at a later date. Not all innovations are equally useful in pursuing this question. Some changes, such as the loss of unstressed vowels or the palatalization of consonants before front vowels, are so phonetically natural and so frequent in the world's languages that they might easily appear independently in several related languages which have already diverged strongly. Other changes are less natural and hence more useful in grouping languages, such as the introduction of a new passive structure or the loss of word-final consonants.

Shared innovations must be distinguished from **shared archaisms**. If the ancestral language happened to have some interesting characteristic – say, a small class of nouns with irregular inflections – that characteristic might have happened to survive in some daughters while disappearing in others, and there is no reason to expect those daughters which retain it to be especially closely related. Shared archaisms are of little or no use in establishing groupings within families.

Once we have decided which languages are particularly closely related, we conclude that those languages must have had a common ancestor at a relatively late stage in history, while other languages, less closely related, must have split off earlier. The result of all our decisions can then be presented in graphic form as a tree. Fig. 7.6 shows the tree which is commonly drawn for the Germanic languages. This figure displays vividly some things we know to be true. For example, we can see at a glance that Dutch and Afrikaans are very closely related indeed, having diverged only about three centuries ago, when Dutch-speakers settled in South Africa, and that Gothic is very different from all the other languages, having already diverged from them 2000 years ago, which is when the Goths begin to appear in Greek and Roman records.

We can draw a similar tree for the Indo-European (IE) family. Fig. 7.7 shows the main branches of the IE family and some of the details of certain branches; unfortunately, the page isn't big enough to show every one of the

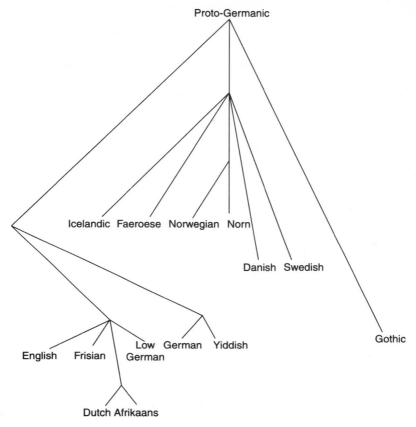

Fig. 7.6 The Germanic family tree

more than 600 known IE languages. In order to save space, I have omitted the prefix *Proto-* from the names of ancestral languages. Note that some main branches contain dozens of modern languages, while others contain only one. Note also that the large Indo-Aryan and Iranian branches are themselves fairly closely related; these two groups diverged from their common ancestor, Proto-Indo-Iranian, long after Indo-Iranian had separated from the rest of the family. The same is perhaps true of Baltic and Slavic, though in this case the historical facts are not yet agreed upon by all specialists, and a few specialists would also place Italic and Celtic into a single Italo-Celtic branch.

Tree diagrams like these are very convenient, and they are widely used in historical linguistics. They have the great advantage of displaying the connections between languages vividly and at a glance. But they also have one great drawback: they are not very realistic. In particular, the branching structure of a tree suggests that a single rather homogeneous ancestral language at some point split suddenly and decisively into two or more

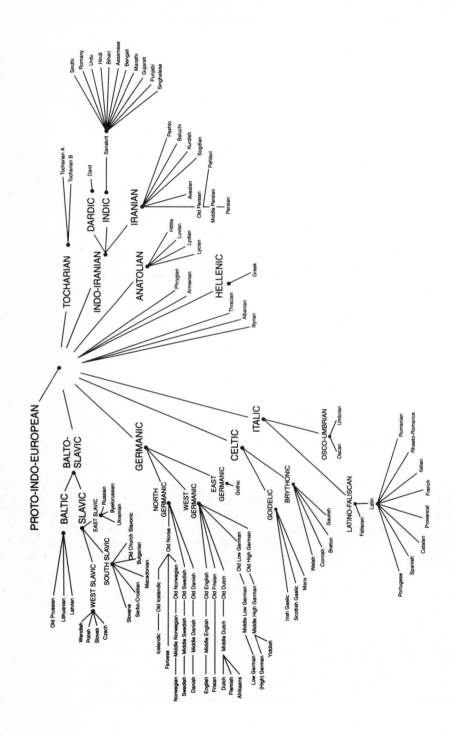

Fig. 7.7 The Indo-European family tree

separate daughter languages, which thereafter went their separate ways and had nothing further to do with one another. But we already know that this is not what really happens.

Recall from Section 7.3 that the Latin of the Roman Empire gradually dissolved into a vast dialect continuum, so that a traveller crossing the former Empire in the seventh or eighth century would have found the language changing only very gradually in any direction. Any speaker could communicate easily with people within a few dozen kilometres, with some difficulty with people 200 or 300 kilometres away, and not at all with people farther away than that. Nowhere were there any sharp boundaries separating one emerging new Romance language from another. It was only much later that particular regional varieties managed to impose themselves on large areas, and it therefore became possible to speak of clearly distinct languages like Spanish, French, and Italian.

There is nothing unusual about the Latin case: this is what always happens when languages break up over time. To take another case, the ancestral Indo-Aryan language of India has broken up into a vast dialect continuum occupying the larger part of the subcontinent. If you travel today across Pakistan, India, Nepal, and Bangladesh, you will find the same thing as my hypothetical Roman traveller: the language just changes gradually in all directions, and there are no sharp boundaries until you leave the Indo-Aryan language area altogether and bump into a non-Indo-Aryan language like Pashto, Tibetan, or Tamil. As in the European case, some regional varieties have acquired prestige and standard forms, and so we can speak of distinct languages like Urdu, Hindi, Gujarati, and Bengali, most of which are not mutually comprehensible (though Urdu and Hindi are virtually identical in ordinary speech; they differ chiefly in their writing systems and in their learnèd vocabularies). Apart from these regional standards, though, we find only continuity, and specialists are obliged to make arbitrary decisions about where to place boundaries between languages, which they need to do in order to get on with the business of describing the resulting languages; once we have decided what languages we are going to recognize, we can start drawing trees to show how these languages are related.

In short, it is the dialect maps of Section 7.2 which represent linguistic reality, and not the tree diagrams with their arbitrary and sudden splits. In 1856 the German linguist Johannes Schmidt therefore proposed a very different way of representing language families, the so-called **wave model**. A wave-model diagram looks something like a dialect map. The language names are spread about the page in some convenient arrangement, and each significant change which has occurred in some languages is represented by a closed curved line surrounding those languages. Fig. 7.8 shows the example of the Germanic languages, classified in terms of a number of changes which Germanic specialists consider to be particularly significant (taken from Robinson 1992). Study this diagram and compare it with the tree in Fig. 7.6 (this diagram does not include all the Germanic languages).

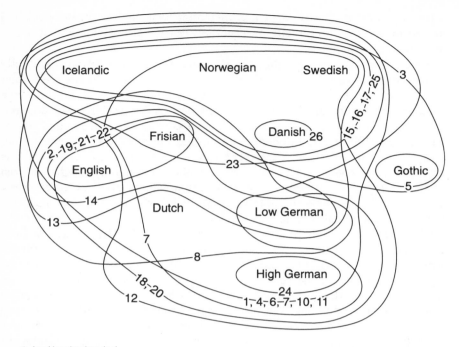

1 /æ:/ backed to /ɑ:/
2 /ɑ:/ from earlier /æ:/ restored
3 'sharpening'
4 /z/ > /r/
5 /fl-/ > /θl-/
6 masculine singular -s lost
7 masculine plural -s lost
8 reflexive pronoun lost
9 reduplicating verbs lost
10 inflected passive lost
11 umlaut introduced
12 dental fricatives lost
13 /n/ lost before /s/
14 /n/ lost before any voiceless fricative
15 extensive assimilation of consonant clusters
16 suffixed definite article introduced
17 mediopassive introduced
18 verbal infinitive becomes a noun
19 vowel 'breaking' introduced
20 consonant gemination in certain circumstances
21 palatalization and assibilation of /k,g/ before front vowels
22 metathesis of /r/
23 final /-n/ lost in inflections
24 High German consonant shift
25 pitch accent introduced
26 pitch accent converted to glottalization

Fig. 7.8 A wave diagram of the Germanic family

Note, by the way, that Fig. 7.8 includes some changes which occurred earlier in the histories of some languages but which have more recently disappeared: for example, the mediopassive which appeared earlier in the Scandinavian languages is now mostly vanished in the modern languages, except in Icelandic. As you might expect after looking at the earlier dialect maps, this wave diagram shows an altogether more complex picture than the corresponding tree diagram. 'Isoglosses' of one sort or another link languages which in the tree diagram are shown as having split apart very early, and as belonging to separate branches: Gothic and the Scandinavian languages, Frisian, and the Scandinavian languages, English, Frisian and Low German, and so on. A few of these, undoubtedly, are merely natural changes which have occurred independently in different branches of the family (note, for example, the loss of dental fricatives everywhere except in the distantly related Gothic, Icelandic, and English). Others, however, surely represent changes which spread across the Germanic-speaking area *after* the ancestors of the various Germanic languages had already begun to diverge quite strongly (note, for example, the loss of /n/ before /s/ in the Scandinavian languages and in some Western languages).

A wave diagram like this one therefore shows quite graphically the continuing contact between dialects and languages which have already begun to diverge, and thereby demonstrates the unreality of the sudden and decisive splits required by the tree model. None the less, the wave diagram still reveals the reality of the major splits posited in the tree diagram: you can see here that Gothic still comes out as the most divergent Germanic language, while both the Scandinavian languages and the west Germanic languages still appear to form coherent groupings, and even English and Frisian appear to form a valid subgroup.

In spite of its obvious advantages, however, the wave model also possesses a few shortcomings. Most obviously, it does not allow us to represent earlier and later stages of languages at the same time, something which the tree diagram does very easily. Wave diagrams are also tedious and cumbersome to prepare and to draw, and they are much harder on the eye. In practice, therefore, historical linguists generally use wave diagrams only when we want to draw attention to particular facts which cannot otherwise be easily presented; the rest of the time we use the simpler and more vivid trees.

7.5 *The language families of the world*

After some two centuries of comparative work, historical linguists have been rather successful at classifying the world's 6000 or so living languages, plus a number of recorded dead languages, into genetic families, often with a good deal of internal subgrouping. The majority of languages in the Old World have been assigned to scarcely more than a dozen families, some of them very large, though there remain some problem areas. The New World has so far proved much more difficult: even though it has far fewer languages than the Old World, specialists currently recognize 140 or more distinct American families. No doubt further research will reduce this number to some extent, but it really does appear that the Americas are linguistically far more diverse than most of the rest of the world (though see Chapter 13 for a contrary view).

Here I shall briefly review some of these families. I begin with the vast *Indo-European* family. This family is conventionally divided into ten branches, some of them much larger than others. The ten branches are as follows:

- *Germanic* (discussed above).
- *Italic* (discussed above, with all surviving Italic languages belonging to the *Romance* group).
- *Celtic*, divided into two branches: *Brythonic*, including Welsh, Breton, and the extinct Cornish, and *Goidelic*, including Irish, Scots Gaelic, and the extinct Manx. Almost nothing is known of the Celtic languages whch formerly occupied a vast area of Europe but which have long since disappeared.
- *Balto-Slavic*, divided into the *Baltic* and *Slavic* groups. Baltic consists of Latvian and Lithuanian and the extinct Old Prussian. Slavic consists of three groups: eastern (Russian, Byelorussian, and Ukrainian), western (Polish, Czech, Slovak, Wendish (in parts of Germany), and Kashubian (in northern Poland), and southern (Slovenian, Serbo-Croatian, Macedonian, and Bulgarian, plus the extinct Old Church Slavonic).
- *Albanian*, which some people think might be a descendant of the ancient Illyrian language once spoken in much of the Balkans.
- *Greek*, which has long constituted a single language.
- *Thraco-Phrygian*, including modern Armenian and at least two extinct languages, Thracian (in northern Greece) and Phrygian (in Anatolia).
- *Indo-Iranian*, divided into three branches. The *Iranian* languages include Persian (Farsi), Pashto (in Afghanistan and Pakistan), Kurdish (in much of the Middle East), Ossetic (in the Caucasus), and a large number of smaller languages. The Persian spoken in Tadjikistan is called Tadjik. Two very important ancient Iranian languages are well recorded, Avestan and Old Persian, the first being the language of the Zoroastrian religious texts and the second the language of the Persian Empire which fought the Greeks and Alexander. The huge *Indo-Aryan* branch includes Hindi, Urdu, Gujarati, Panjabi, Bengali, Nepali, and hundreds of other languages of the Indian subcontinent. The ancient ancestor of these is Sanskrit, the 'Latin of India', recorded in two forms: the earlier Vedic Sanskrit, the language of the Hindu scriptures, and the later Classical Sanskrit. Finally, the small *Dardic* branch includes Kashmiri and a few other languages.

- *Anatolian*, containing a number of languages, now all dead, formerly spoken in what is now Turkey. The most important of these is Hittite, the language of the Hittite Empire of the first millennium BC.
- *Tocharian*, consisting of just two languages, imaginatively called Tocharian A and Tocharian B, now dead but once spoken in central Asia in the Xinjiang–Uyghur province of China.

Adjoining Indo-European is the *Uralic* family. This is divided into the *Samoyed* languages of Siberia and the *Finno-Ugric* branch. This last includes the *Finnic* languages like Finnish, Lappish (Saami), and Estonian (among others), and the *Ugric* branch, containing Hungarian and a number of other languages. Most Uralic languages are spoken in the Russian Republic. Some scholars believe that the *Yukaghir* languages of Siberia are distantly related to Uralic in a larger *Uralic-Yukaghir* family.

Next door again is another large family, *Altaic*. This is divided into three branches. The *Turkic* branch includes Turkish, Azerbaijani, and a large number of central Asian languages. The *Mongolian* branch includes the several Mongolian languages, all descended from the speech of Genghis Khan's invaders. The *Tungusic* branch includes Evenki (Tungus), a major language of Siberia, and Manchu, the now nearly extinct language of the Manchu conquerors of China. The genetic unity of the Altaic family is very controversial, and some scholars reject the family altogether, but at present there seems to be widespread acceptance that the family is genuine.

Northeastern Siberia contains the *Chukchi-Kamchatkan* family (sometimes called *Luorawetlan*), whose main language is Chukchi.

Much of sub-Siberian Asia is occupied by the vast *Sino-Tibetan* family. This includes the several Chinese languages (called 'dialects' by the Chinese, but differing from one another as much as French and Romanian), plus Tibetan, Burmese, and many other less well-known languages. Thanks to the billion or so Chinese-speakers, this family has more speakers than any other family except Indo-European.

Southern India is occupied by the large *Dravidian* family, whose best-known member is Tamil. There is one Dravidian outlier in Pakistan, and linguists believe the family probably occupied most of the subcontinent before the spread of the Indo-Aryan languages several thousand years ago.

Southeast Asia is home to the *Austro-Asiatic* family, whose main branch is *Mon-Khmer*, including Khmer (Cambodian) and probably Vietnamese (this is controversial), among others. The *Munda* languages of eastern Asia constitute a second branch, and Nicobarese, spoken on some islands in the Indian Ocean, is the third branch.

Next door is the *Tai* family (also called *Daic*), which includes Thai, Lao, and dozens of other languages, many with millions of speakers. The small but engagingly named *Miao-Yao* family is scattered across much of southern China.

Beyond these three groupings lies the enormous expanse of the *Austrone-sian* family (once called 'Malayo-Polynesian'), stretching from Madagascar to Easter Island. This family includes Malagasy (in Madagascar), Malay, Indonesian, all the languages of Indonesia, all the languages of the Philippines, the indigenous languages of Taiwan, and all the languages of the Pacific. The *Polynesian* branch of the family includes such languages as Hawaiian, Tahitian, Samoan, and the Maori of New Zealand. Thanks chiefly to the phenomenal navigational skills of its speakers, this family occupied the greatest stretch of territory on the planet before the modern spread of the Indo-European languages into most corners of the world.

The large island of New Guinea is a major problem. A few Austronesian languages are spoken along the coast, but most of the island is occupied by about a thousand languages which have so far proved impossible to classify. These are collectively known as the *Papuan* languages, but this name is at present merely a convenient geographical label, and the Papuan languages have not been shown to constitute a single genetic family, or even a few large families.

Most of Australia is (or until recently was) occupied by a single large family, *Pama-Nyungan*. Only the northwestern corner contains a dense group of non-Pama-Nyungan languages, but specialists are inclined to think that these languages are more distantly related to the Pama-Nyungan group.

Africa and most of the Middle East are occupied by just four families, two of them very large. Most of northern and eastern Africa and part of western Africa, together with the Middle East, are occupied by the *Afro-Asiatic* family (formerly called 'Hamito-Semitic'). Six branches are recognized. Most familiar is the large *Semitic* branch, including Arabic, Hebrew, Maltese, several major languages of east Africa, and a number of dead but formerly important languages, including Akkadian (the language of the Assyrian and Babylonian empires) and Phoenician, with its African offshoot Punic. One more Semitic language is Aramaic, once spoken throughout much of the Middle East, but today confined to small areas in Iraq and Iran.

A second branch of Afro-Asiatic is ancient Egyptian, the language of the hieroglyphs, and its descendant Coptic, which died out only several centuries ago. A third is the *Berber* languages, formerly spoken right across North Africa but now largely displaced by Arabic. A fourth branch is *Chadic*, spoken in West Africa; the most important Chadic language is Hausa in northern Nigeria. A tiny fifth branch is *Omotic*, consisting of a few small languages in and near Ethiopia. The sixth branch is *Cushitic*, which extends along the Red Sea coast to the Indian Ocean; its best-known member is Somali. Specialists are not certain whether Cushitic is a valid grouping or not; it may just be that we are applying this label to the 'residue' of Afro-Asiatic languages which cannot be assigned to any recognized group.

South of the Sahara lies the *Nilo-Saharan* family, whose most famous member is Maasai in Kenya. The genetic unity of this family is in some doubt, and it may be that this label too is a purely geographical one.

The same question arises with the third African family, *Khoisan*, now confined to a small area in and near the Kalahari and Namib deserts of southern Africa, with two lonely outliers in Tanzania. These are the famous 'click languages', the ones with daunting names like !Kung. Their speakers, the Bushmen and the Nama (formerly Hottentots), clearly once occupied most of southern Africa, but they have been displaced by the spread of the Bantu (see below).

The fourth and largest family is the vast *Niger-Congo* (or *Niger-Kordofanian*) family, which occupies most of the African continent below the Sahara. Most of the prominent languages of West Africa belong to this family, including Igbo, Yoruba, Ewe, Twi, Temne, and Wolof, and it was very largely speakers of these languages who were carried as slaves to the Americas centuries ago. One formerly obscure branch of this family has, during the last 2000 years, spread out from a small area in Nigeria and Cameroon to occupy almost all of central, eastern, and southern Africa. This is the *Bantu* branch, which includes such languages as KiKongo in Zaire, LuGanda in Uganda, ChiChewa in Malaŵi, ChiBemba in Zambia, Shona and Ndebele in Zimbabwe, Zulu and Xhosa in South Africa (these two have exceptionally acquired click consonants from their Khoisan neighbours), and that most famous of all African languages, Swahili, formerly a trade language and now a major language throughout East Africa.

There remain in the Old World some small families and a few other problems. In the Caucasus, we find four small groups of typologically distinctive languages: *Northeast Caucasian*, *North-central Caucasian*, *Northwest Caucasian*, and *South Caucasian*, more commonly called *Kartvelian*). Most specialists now seem to agree that the northeastern and north-central groups can be united in a single family, but claims that the northwestern group can also be added have not so far won general acceptance. As for Kartvelian, which includes the best-known Caucasian language, Georgian, this does not appear to be remotely related to any of the northern groups.

The Tai family has proved to be a particular headache, since many linguists are convinced that the Tai group belongs to one of the major families of the area, but they can't agree what family that is, and everything from Sino-Tibetan to Austronesian has been put forward as a home for the Tai languages, so far with no sign of general consent.

Finally, there remain the **isolates**, single languages which do not appear to be related to anything else at all. Most famous of these is Basque, spoken at the western end of the Pyrenees in western Europe. We know that Basque is descended from a pre-Roman language called Aquitanian, and that it is the last surviving pre-Indo-European language in western Europe, but the most strenuous attempts at relating Basque to something else, in spite of invoking most of the languages on the planet, have been completely unsuccessful, and the frequent assertions to the contrary in the literature may be safely disregarded. Another famous isolate is Burushaski, spoken in two Himalayan valleys and also seemingly related to nothing else at all (not even to Basque, though people have tried that, too). Two more isolates are Gilyak and Ket, both spoken in Siberia, though Ket is in fact merely the last survivor of the *Yeniseian* family, some other members of which were recorded before they died out.

You may have noticed that I have not mentioned two of the major languages of Asia, Japanese and Korean. That is because these two languages constitute one of the biggest problems of all. For generations each of them has been regarded as an isolate. Even though the two of them are astoundingly similar in their grammatical structure, evidence of a common origin is almost impossible to find, and attempts to find a relative for Japanese have largely focused upon south Asia and the Pacific, so far without success. Recently, however, a number of linguists have begun to argue that there is clear evidence that Korean and Japanese are in fact related to each other, and that both of them are moreover related to the nearby Altaic family, perhaps most closely to its Tungusic branch. So far, however, the proponents of the Altaic link have not succeeded in convincing the majority of specialists that their evidence is good enough to support the hypothesis, and the issue continues to be debated.

As I remarked above, the Americas are linguistically far more diverse than the Old World, with at least 140 families being commonly recognized. Some of these families, however, are quite large. In the Arctic we find the *Eskimo-Aleut* family spanning the North American continent from Siberia to Greenland. There are two main Eskimo languages, Inuit (Inuktitut) and Yupik, while the more distantly related Aleut is spoken, naturally, in the Aleutian Islands of Alaska.

Farther south is the *Na-Déné* family. This consists of one large group, the *Athabaskan* (or *Athapaskan*) languages of western North America (such as Navaho and Apache), plus a few more distantly related languages in Alaska and British Columbia.

To the east of this is another large family, *Algonquian*, which covers (or covered) much of central and eastern North America and parts of the western plains. These were the languages first encountered by British and French settlers in North America, and all those colourful place names in eastern Canada, in New England, and along the east coast of the USA are of Algonquian origin, as are words like *skunk*, *woodchuck*, and *raccoon*. Among the better-known Algonquian languages are Cree, Ojibwa, Cheyenne, Blackfoot, Arapaho, and Mohican.

Tucked into the middle of the Algonquian territory, around the Great Lakes and the Finger Lakes of New York State and extending up the St Lawrence River, is the *Iroquoian* family. A number of these languages are recorded in place names: Huron, Erie, Oneida, Mohawk, and so on. One of these languages, Seneca, is the indigenous language of the area where I grew up. Iroquoian outliers are found as far south as North Carolina.

Most of the American Great Plains was formerly occupied by the large *Siouan* family, whose speakers provided the last desperate armed resistance to the US Army at Little Big Horn and Wounded Knee. Language names like

Lakota, Osage, Kansa, Hidatsa, and Crow are familiar to all English-speakers in one connection or another.

The American southeast is home to the sizeable *Muskogean* family, including Koasati, Creek, and Alabama. Much farther west we find the *Hokan* family, including Mohave and Havasupai, and the *Caddoan* family, including Wichita and Pawnee.

There are many other North American families: *Tunican, Salishan, Wakashan, Chimakuan*, and so on, plus the occasional isolate, like Yuchi in the southeast.

Much of Mexico and the southwestern USA is occupied by another large family, *Uto-Aztecan*. The chief member of this family, Nahuatl, was the language of the Aztec empire and is still widely spoken today, and the Hopi language is famed in the linguistic literature because of Benjamin Lee Whorf's celebrated articles about it which made the Sapir–Whorf hypothesis of linguistic relativity such a prominent feature of the linguistic landscape. In southern Mexico and Guatemala, we find the *Mayan* languages, still spoken by the descendants of the Mayan empire; knowledge of the modern Mayan languages assisted in the decipherment of the remarkable Mayan script, which was substantially achieved only in the late 1970s.

Much of northern South America and the Caribbean is (or was) occupied by the *Carib* family, which gives its name to the Caribbean Sea. A few years ago the Carib language Hixkaryana, with only 350 speakers, hit the headlines when it was found to be the first language ever discovered with OVS word order, thus providing a sobering reminder of the potentially devastating loss to linguistics when languages disappear.

In the Andes we find the *Quechuan* family, descended from the Quecha of the Incan empire. Farther east is the *Tupian* family, whose most important language, Guaraní, is remarkable for being the mother tongue of the majority of the population of Paraguay.

Again, many other families are recognized in South America, but this continent is still the least well investigated area on earth, and every now and again an entirely new language turns up, particularly in the Amazon rain forest.

It is clear that there is still a great deal of work to do in the Americas. From time to time someone proposes to group two or three existing families into one larger family, and some of these proposals have won widespread acceptance. For example, many specialists now agree that Siouan, Iroquoian, and Caddoan, plus a couple of isolates, can safely be grouped into a single larger family called *Macro-Siouan*. Partly because of the paucity of extensive and reliable descriptive work on most languages, however, and partly because American languages really do not appear to fall naturally into a handful of large families, most specialists are resigned to the necessity of several more generations of patient and careful work before the genetic picture of the New World can be declared even substantially complete – though in Chapter 13 I shall discuss a controversial attempt at taking a dramatic shortcut.

Further reading

There is a substantial literature on dialectology, both in general and dealing with the dialects of particular languages. Good general introductions include Petyt (1978), Chambers and Trudgill (1980), Francis (1983), and Trudgill (1994), which is very elementary. Trudgill (1986) is an introductory study of contact between dialects. Introductions to the dialects of English are, from simplest to most advanced, Hughes and Trudgill (1979), Trudgill (1990), Davis (1983), Trudgill and Chambers (1991), and Kirk *et al.* (1985). The dialect atlases are (for England) Orton *et al.* (1962–71) (data), Orton *et al.* (1978) (maps), Orton and Wright (1974) (atlas of words), and Upton *et al.* (1987) (a popular introduction with maps), and (for the eastern USA) Kurath (1949). Trudgill and Hannah (1994) looks at variation in English around the world. Robinson (1992) is a survey of the older Germanic languages, focusing on similarities and differences. Elementary introductions to the Indo-European family include Lockwood (1969), Lockwood (1972), and Baldi (1983).

There are innumerable popular books which provide information on the language families of the world; you might start with Crystal (1987; sect. IX). Two encyclopaedias, Bright (1992) and Asher (1994), provide good information on particular families. Voegelin and Voegelin (1977) is a comprehensive reference book on the languages and language families of the world, and Grimes (1992) is the latest edition of a regularly updated list of the world's languages. A classic but outdated summary is Meillet and Cohen (1952); a promised revision of this book has yet to appear. A recent comprehensive atlas of the languages of the entire world is Moseley and Asher (1994); if you are lucky, your library will have a copy of this magnificent but costly volume. The best history of the attempts at classifying languages into families is Ruhlen (1991); be warned, however, that the book contains a few errors, and that Ruhlen accepts as valid some recent very large-scale groupings which are rejected as unsubstantiated by the vast majority of historical linguists.

Exercises

Exercise 7.1

Each of the following paragraphs provides a few words and grammatical forms which are typical of some regional variety of English. How successfully can you identify each variety? (A good dictionary should give you some useful hints with the vocabulary.) If one of the varieties seems completely unremarkable, it's probably *your* variety. Many of the examples are taken from Trudgill and Hannah (1994).

Variety A

Coming home tomorrow he is.
You're going now, isn't it?

I can't do that, too.
It was high, high. (= It was very high.)
Is he ready? No, but he will in a minute.
I'll rise the drinks. (= I'll buy the drinks.)

del (a term of endearment)
llymru (a type of porridge)

Variety B

I'm seeing her in the weekend.
Will I close the window? (= Shall I close the window?)
The team is playing badly.
I have to uplift the children. (= I have to pick up the children.)
She's off to the varsity soon. (= to the university)

jack up 'arrange'
skite 'boast'
bach 'cabin, cottage'
pa 'village'

Variety C

I am going to cinema.
They like themselves. (= They like each other.)
The guests whom I invited them have arrived.
We should leave now, is it? (= shouldn't we?)
Hasn't he come home yet? Yes. (= No, he hasn't.)

balance 'change' (money returned to a customer)
carpet 'linoleum'
chop bar 'restaurant serving local food'
hot drink 'alcohol, spirits, liquor'
take in 'become pregnant'

Variety D

We did it already.
I've just gotten a letter from Sonya.
He snuck out of the house. (= sneaked)
I'm really buffaloed by this one. (= intimidated, defeated)
She drove right past me – she must not have seen me.
Have you got rye bread? Yes, I do.
The dog wants out.

homely 'unattractive, somewhat ugly'
school 'any educational establishment, including a university'
muffler 'silencer' (on a car)
rookie 'player in his first season'
zucchini 'courgette(s)'

Variety E

He'd a good time last night. (= He had a good time last night.)
Will I put out the light? (= Shall I put out the light?)
My hair needs washed. (= My hair needs washing.)
I doubt he's not coming. (= I expect he's not coming.)
I must go the messages. (= I must go shopping.)
I stay at Portobello. (= I live in Portobello.)

burn 'stream'
dreich 'dull'
outwith 'outside'
pinkie 'little finger'
shoogly 'wobbly, shaky'

Exercise 7.2

Below are three proverbs (A, B, and C) each rendered into the local speech of eight locations between Paris and Madrid. Which of the eight varieties appear to be most closely related? Is it possible to decide how many different languages are represented here?

Proverb A
1. *A chaque oiseau son nid est beau.*
2. *A chasqu' aucèu soun nis es bèu.*
3. *A cada ocell son niu es bell.*
4. *A cada ausèty lou nit qu'ey beròy.*
5. *A cada ausétch et so nit qu'éy bètch.*
6. *A cada paxarico li gusta lo suyo nido.*
7. *A cada pajarillo le gusta su nidillo.*
8. *Xori bakotxarendako bere kafira eder zako.*

Proverb B
1. *Comme est la chèvre, ainsi vient le chevreau.*
2. *Coum' es la cabra, ansin vèn lou cabrít.*
3. *Tal com és la cabra, aixi és el cabrit.*
4. *Tàu coum' èy la crabe, que bat lou crabòt.*
5. *Coum' éy era crapo, atàu que bat ec crabòt.*
6. *Como yé la craba, así será lo crabito.*
7. *Como es la cabra, así será el cabrito.*
8. *Nola ahuntza hala pitika.*

Proverb C
1. *Fille de chat prend les souris.*
2. *Filha de ca pren li gàri.*
3. *Filla de gat agafa ratolins.*
4. *Hilho de gat que gahe sourits.*
5. *Hilho de gat que gaho es souris.*

6. *Filla de gato pilla ratòns.*
7. *Hija de gato coge ratones.*
8. *Gatu umeak saguak hartzen.*

Exercise 7.3

The map in Fig. 7.9, taken from Upton *et al.* (1987), shows the regional words for 'young dog' in England. Look up the etymologies of *whelp* and of *pup(py)*, and comment on what seems to have happened with these words.

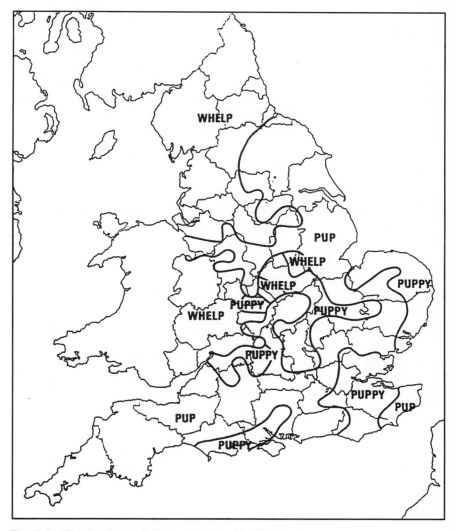

Fig. 7.9 The local words for 'young dog' in England

Exercise 7.4

In the north of Germany, the word for 'us' is *us*; in the south, it is *uns*. The map in Fig. 7.10 shows part of the boundary between these two forms in the early twentieth century, in the vicinity of the Rhine. Explain as fully as you can why the isogloss boundary has such a curious shape here.

Exercise 7.5

The map in Fig. 7.11, adapted from Dauzat (1922), shows the extent of the several regional words for 'mare' in French around 1900. Study the map and compare it with a map of the French-speaking region that shows features like mountains, rivers, and cities. Explain the form of the map as carefully as you can. Which words are older, which newer? Which have been spreading, which retreating? How are the discontinuities in the distribution of each form to be explained? Which form do you suppose is the standard French word? What geographical or political factors can you see at work? If you have access to an etymological dictionary of French or of Romance, look up the histories of the three words. Does your interpretation match those histories?

Exercise 7.6

Listed below are a number of significant changes which have affected some, but not all, of five major dialects of Basque: Bizkaian (B), Gipuzkoan (G),

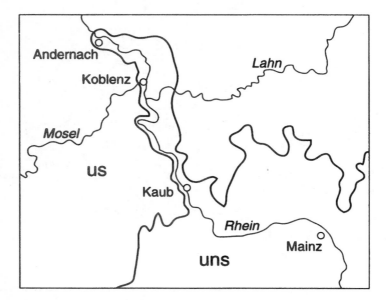

Fig. 7.10   Part of the *us/uns* isogloss boundary

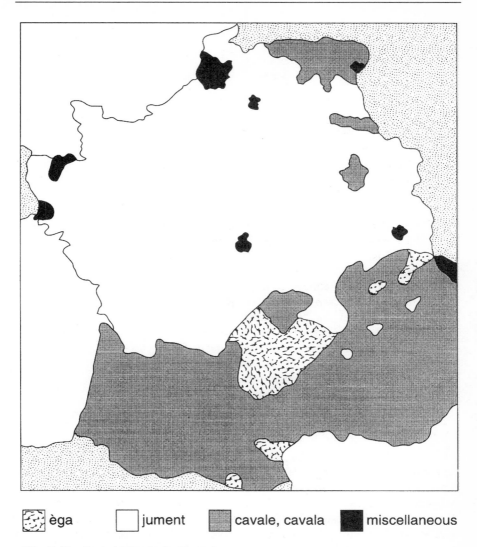

▨ èga   ☐ jument   ▨ cavale, cavala   ■ miscellaneous

Fig. 7.11 French words for 'mare'
(Source: Dauzat 1922)

High Navarrese (HN), Lapurdian (L), and Zuberoan (Z). Using these data, first construct a wave diagram for these dialects. Then try to draw a tree diagram for them, and discuss your degree of success.

1. Aspiration lost: B, G, HN
2. Nasal vowels lost: B, G, HN, L
3. Plosives voiced after /n/ or /l/: B, G, HN, L

4. $/u/ > /ü/$: Z
5. Contrastive voiced sibilants introduced: Z
6. Initial $/ʃ/ > /tʃ/$: B, G, Z
7. Intervocalic $/r/$ lost: Z
8. $/au/ > /ai/$: Z
9. Penultimate stress accent introduced: Z
10. $/j/ > /x/$: G
11. *$/ae/ > /e/$: HN, L, Z
12. *$/ae/ > /a/$: B, G
13. Allative *-la* introduced: Z
14. Dative plural *-er* introduced: Z
15. Comitative *-ekin* > *-eki*: Z
16. Comitative *-gaz* introduced: B
17. Verbal plural marker *-te* generalized: G, HN, L
18. Past-tense marker *e-* replaced by *ze-*: G, HN, L, Z
19. Gerunds like *joaite* 'going' altered to *joate*: B, G, HN, Z
20. Auxiliary **ezan* replaced by *egin*: B
21. Auxiliary *dau* reduced to *du*: G, HN, L, Z
22. Future marker *-ko* generalized: B, G
23. Future marker *-en* generalized: Z
24. *eduki* 'hold' generalized for 'have': B, G
25. Third-person pronoun *bera* introduced: B, G
26. Question particle *al* introduced: G
27. Present potential becomes future: Z
28. Genitive object of gerund lost: B, G, HN, Z

Exercise 7.7

As is sometimes shown by wave diagrams, a change can spread across boundaries between language varieties which have already diverged substantially. In fact, it is even possible for a change to spread across boundaries between languages which are only very remotely related, or not related at all. A famous case in western Europe is the spread of uvular $/r/$. Three centuries ago, all western European languages had some kind of coronal $/r/$, but today a uvular $/r/$ is found in many varieties of eight languages: Basque, French, Italian, German, Dutch, Danish, Norwegian, and Swedish. Fig. 7.12 shows the approximate distribution of uvular $/r/$ today (it is still spreading). Examine this figure and try to propose an explanation for the steady historical spread of uvular $/r/$ in Europe. You will need to remember what was said in Chapter 2 about borrowing between languages, and you may find it helpful to recall what you know about political power and about linguistic and cultural prestige in the eighteenth and nineteenth centuries. You may also find it helpful to consult a map of Europe showing the locations of major cities.

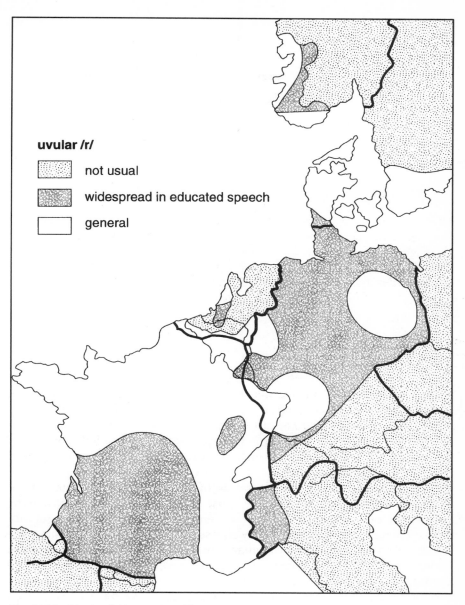

uvular /r/

not usual

widespread in educated speech

general

Fig. 7.12 Uvular /r/ in western Europe

8

The comparative method

Thus far, we have examined the various types of linguistic change, and considered the consequences of such changes in the form of dialects and language families. In this chapter and the next, we'll be turning our attention to the **historical methods**, the principal methods which linguists have developed in order to establish that certain languages are genetically related and to recover the histories of individual languages and of language families.

8.1 Systematic correspondences

Earlier in the book, I pointed out that there is good reason to believe that phonological changes are typically *regular* – that is, that they typically apply to all relevant words, and not just to some of them. I have still not demonstrated that this belief is necessarily true, but for the moment let's continue to assume that it probably is true; the reason for making this assumption will become clear in a little while.

Now, if we construct lists of words of similar meanings from several languages and put them side by side, most of the time we will notice nothing beyond the obvious fact that different languages have different words for things. Even if we somewhat astutely choose a set of words from one language which are phonologically very similar, most of the time we still get the same boring result. Table 8.1 shows an example involving English, Welsh, and Basque, all spoken in western Europe:

Nothing very interesting here. But sometimes, if we have made a good choice of languages, we get a different result, one that is not boring at all. Table 8.2 shows an example involving several languages of western and southern Europe. What do you see here? Of course, you will note some striking resemblances among these four words in the five languages, but the resemblances are not the point – in fact, they are almost irrelevant. What is significant is the *patterns* we can see, and one pattern in particular stands out: the word-initial consonants. Again and again, we notice that a word that starts

Table 8.1 A comparison of three languages

English	Welsh	Basque
make	*gwneud*	*egin*
moon	*lleuad*	*hilargi*
mare	*caseg*	*behor*
my	*fy*	*nere*
melt	*toddi*	*urtu*
moth	*gwyfyn*	*sits*

Table 8.2 A systematic correspondence

	Sardinian	Italian	Romansh	French	Spanish
'100'	kɛntu	tʃɛnto	tsjɛnt	sã	θjen
'sky'	kɛlu	tʃelo	tsil	sjɛl	θjelo
'stag'	kɛrbu	tʃɛrvo	tsɛrf	sɛʀ	θjerbo
'wax'	kɛra	tʃera	tsaira	siʀ	θera

with /k/ in Sardinian starts with /tʃ/ in Italian, with /ts/ in Romansh (spoken in eastern Switzerland), with /s/ in French, and with /θ/ in European Spanish (American Spanish has /s/ in every one of these words). We can sum up the pattern as follows (the hyphens indicate that we are talking only about word-initial position):

Sard *k-* : It *tʃ-* : Rom *ts-* : Fr *s-* : Sp θ-

This kind of pattern is called a systematic correspondence, and systematic correspondences are of crucial importance in identifying genetic links among languages. In the present case, there are two further points to be noted. First, the correspondence illustrated does not apply only to these four words; it also applies equally well to a number of other words. Second, this is not the only systematic correspondence connecting these five languages: there are dozens of others. One of these is the correspondence Sard *r* : It *r* : Rom *r* : Fr ʀ : Sp *r*, which shows up in the last two words and in dozens of other words (no hyphens this time, because this correspondence applies in all positions, without exception).

How can we explain the existence of systematic correspondences? With certain rather obvious reservations, discussed below, there is only one expla-nation which can possibly be considered: the languages must be genetically related. And how does that follow? Easy: in the common ancestor of these five languages, the words for '100', 'sky', 'stag', and 'wax' all began with the same sound, and that sound has changed *regularly*, but differently, in each language. The existence of systematic correspondences provides powerful support for the idea that sound change is generally regular, and hence systematic correspondences provide some of the strongest possible evidence that languages displaying them must be genetically related.

And what was that ancestral sound in our case? This kind of question is often more difficult to answer, even though we may be certain that there was such an ancestral sound. But the difficulty is not insuperable. The best way to approach the question is this: what sort of sound could have developed naturally into the sounds we find in the daughter languages? Recall from Chapter 3 that certain types of phonological change are far more natural and frequent than others, and we would therefore prefer a solution to our problem which invokes only such natural changes. Thus, in our case, we are hardly likely to consider something like [p] or [w] or [n] or [l] or [e] for the ancestral sound: the resulting sound changes in all the five daughters would be like nothing anybody has ever seen. If it were not for the Sardinian evidence, we might consider something like [ts], since Romansh has [ts] anyway and since a change from [ts] into [tʃ], [s], or [θ] looks reasonable enough. But that would require a change from [ts] to [k] in Sardinian, and this too would be a bizarre change of a sort not known to occur elsewhere.

In fact, of course, a satisfactory decision can be made only after we have considered the totality of evidence from all the languages involved. As it happens, specialists have long since concluded that the ancestral sound in question here must have been *k- (the asterisk marks a sound which is not directly recorded, but which linguists have concluded was probably the original sound). With *k- as the ancestral sound, Sardinian becomes easy: it has done nothing at all. But what about the other four languages? Why should a velar plosive develop into some kind of sibilant pronounced near the front of the mouth?

Well, in what circumstances might a [k] tend to move towards the front of the mouth? Think about this a minute before reading on, and have another look at the words in Table 8.1.

If you remember what you read in Chapter 3, the most obvious thing to consider is an assimilation: a [k] might move towards the front of the mouth if the sound next to it is pronounced in the front of the mouth. So, since there is no preceding sound in the words in question, look at the sound following the initial consonant in each one of the four words in all five languages. What do you see? That's right – a front vowel.

Even in English, the /k/ in, say, *key* is pronounced much farther forward in the mouth than the /k/ in *car*, because of the influence of the following front vowel. We may therefore surmise that the ancestral *k-, in all the daughter languages except Sardinian, when followed by a front vowel, moved so far forward that it developed into something like [ts] or [tʃ], with French and

Spanish then going further and losing the occlusion altogether (a lenition) and thus winding up with fricatives in place of the ancestral [k].

All this makes perfect sense, since all the phonological changes we now need to posit are ones familiar from the study of many other languages. Even English long ago underwent something rather similar: German *Kinn* 'chin', *Käse* 'cheese', and *Kind* 'child' represent the approximate forms which the English words had many centuries ago, but English underwent much the same development as Italian, turning its original *$*k$-* into [tʃ] before a front vowel.

Finally, returning to our five languages, I expect you've already realized that all five are Romance languages, and you perhaps recall from Chapter 7 that the Romance languages are all descended from a spoken form of Latin. Since Latin is recorded, we can check to see what the written forms of the Latin words were. In fact, they were *centum* '100', *caelum* 'sky', *cervus* 'stag', and *cera* 'wax'. We might therefore feel justified in concluding that Latin orthographic <c> represents the sound [k] in all these words, and that is exactly what latinists have decided on independent grounds.

These five languages (and all the other Romance languages) are thus genetically related: they are all descended from a common ancestor. The words for '100' in these five languages are **cognate**: that is, they are descended from the same single ancestral word in that common ancestor, and of course the other sets of words are also cognate. Given the abundant systematic correspondences linking these four words and hundreds of other words in the Romance languages, we could be sure of this conclusion even if we had no Latin data to confirm it.

Most of the time, of course, we are not so fortunate as to have such direct ancient confirmation that languages are genetically related, but, when we can find systematic correspondences, we may none the less be sure that they are so related. Look at the data in Table 8.3. (Hyphenated forms are stems; bracketed morphs are prefixes; the Greek represented is ancient Greek; the Irish word means 'tonight', not 'night', and it is archaic.) If you examine the word-initial consonants, you will see several systematic correspondences (the symbol Ø means 'zero', i.e. no consonant at all):

Eng *f-* : Lat *p-* : Gk *p-* : Ir Ø
Eng *s-* : Lat *s-* : Gk *h-* : Ir *s-*
Eng *n-* : Lat *n-* : Gk *n-* : Ir *n-*

Of course, some of the words don't match: the Greek word for 'fish' and the Irish words for 'foot', 'for', and 'sweet' don't show the expected correspondences. Why do you suppose that is?

The simple answer is that these words are not cognate with the words in the other languages: in these instances, the ancestral word has been lost and replaced by a different word. Recall from Chapter 2 that the loss and replacement of words is a common kind of change. Such lexical replacement can always be expected to disrupt the pattern of correspondences to some extent; moreover, the greater the time that has elapsed since the ancestral

Table 8.3 Further systematic correspondences

English	Latin	Greek	Irish
fish	*piscis*	*ikhthys*	*iasg*
father	*pater*	*pater*	*athair*
foot	*ped-*	*pod-*	*troigh*
for	*pro*	*para*	*do*
six	*sex*	*hexa*	*se*
seven	*septem*	*hepta*	*seacht*
sweet	*suavis*	*hedys*	*milis*
salt	*sal*	*hal*	*salann*
new	*novus*	*neos*	*nua*
night	*noct-*	*nykt-*	*(in)nocht* 'tonight'
nine	*novem*	*(en)nea*	*naoi*

language, the larger the number of ancestral words replaced in each daughter language, and hence the harder it is to find cognates and to spot systematic correspondences.

Since Latin is itself the ancestor of the Romance languages, it should be obvious that we are here looking at a set of languages which are genetically related at a point much further back in time than are the Romance languages. The Romance languages began to diverge from their Latin ancestor less than 2000 years ago, but English, Latin, Greek, and Irish must have split off from their common ancestor many thousands of years ago – after all, Greek itself is attested as early as the second millennium BC. That means that these four languages have had some thousands of years to change independently and to become ever more different from one another. Accordingly, it is much harder work to identify systematic correspondences and cognates among these languages than it is for Romance, but, as you see, this can still be done.

And what ancestral consonants should we posit here? For the first set, the consensus of scholars is **p-*, since lenitions of [p] to [f] or Ø are frequent and readily understandable, while fortitions of other consonants to [p] are comparatively rare. For the second set, we posit **s-*, which requires no change at all except a lenition to [h] in Greek – again, you'll recall from Chapter 3, a familiar sort of change. Finally, for the third set there appears to be nothing to discuss: the ancestral **n-* has remained unchanged in all the daughter languages.

By now you have doubtless realized that we are looking here at a few of the languages belonging to the vast Indo-European family sketched out in Chapter 7, and that the ancestral sounds **p-*, **s-*, and **n-* which we have posited must therefore be among the sounds of PIE, the remote ancestor of all these languages. Since we believe that PIE was spoken at least 6000 years ago, it follows that the ancient initial [s] of *six* and *salt*, and the ancient initial [n] of *new* and *night*, have remained unchanged for some 6000 years down into present-day English. The ancestral [p], in contrast, has changed into [f] in English, but it has done so with great regularity, and so the relationship is still clearly visible. Even six millennia of accumulated phonological change and lexical replacement have not been enough to obliterate all traces of the ancestral language.

In fact, in the case of Indo-European, 6000 years have not been enough to prevent historical linguists from establishing rather easily that the languages are related. With this family, though, we have something of an unfair advantage, since early forms of Latin, Greek, Indo-Iranian, and Anatolian are attested as early as the first millennium BC, and sometimes even the second millennium BC. There are very few other families for which we possess such early records. We might wonder, therefore, how far back we can go in establishing genetic links between languages.

Clearly there must be a limit to this. Only a handful of scholars (most of them archaeologists) would deny that we have been speaking languages since fully modern humans first appeared on the planet a little more than 100000 years ago, and more than a few would put the origins of language very much further back in time, perhaps one or two million years ago, at the time of our early hominid ancestors. Further, most linguists would probably be happy to concede that all human languages are ultimately descended from a single common ancestral language, perhaps one that arose along with our own species. But we just can't trace genetic links back in time forever: eventually, the accumulated weight of phonological change, lexical replacement, and grammatical re-formation becomes so great that the last faint traces of a common ancestry must be extinguished, or at least disappear into the background noise of chance resemblances. How long does it typically take for this to happen? That is, for how long can two or more languages diverge from their common ancestor until we can no longer see the slightest evidence of their common origin?

There can be no hard and fast answer to this question, since it's always possible that some languages will change more slowly than average and thus preserve remnants of their common ancestry longer than average. If you put this question to a group of historical linguists, though, most of them will probably give you an estimate of about 6000–8000 years, even in the most favourable cases, the families for which we have lots of languages and some substantial early texts. A few will go as high as 10000 years ago, which is a nice round number. Almost everyone, though, will be deeply pessimistic about the chances of ever tracing any genetic links further back in time than that. Almost everyone – but not quite everyone. In Chapter 13, we will encounter a few mavericks who believe that we can realistically push things back to perhaps 15000 years ago – and also, amazingly enough, a couple who think we can trace things back all the way to the ancestral human language itself. But don't get carried away: the overwhelming majority of historical linguists are deeply sceptical of 15000 years and would reject the last idea as absurd beyond comment. Let's say 6000–8000 years.

8.2 *Comparative reconstruction*

We have already seen that the existence of systematic correspondences allows us to make at least educated guesses about the sounds that must have been present in particular words in ancestral proto-languages. But we can often go much further than this, in several respects. First, we may be able to work out, not just individual ancestral sounds, but *all* the ancestral sounds in individual words. Second, as an immediate consequence, we may be able to work out roughly what whole words must have sounded like in the ancestral language. Third, as a further consequence, we may be able to work out what the entire phonological system of the ancestral language must have been like: what phonemes it had, and what the rules were for combining those phonemes. This process is **comparative reconstruction**, and the procedure we use for doing it is the **comparative method**. The comparative method is the single most important tool in the historical linguist's toolkit, and we have in many cases enjoyed great success in *reconstructing* important aspects of unrecorded proto-languages.

Informally, the comparative method works like this:

1. We first decide by inspection that certain languages are probably genetically related and hence descended from a common ancestor.
2. We place side by side a number of words with similar meanings from the languages we have decided to compare.
3. We examine these for what appear to be systematic correspondences.
4. We draw up tables of the systematic correspondences we find.
5. For each correspondence we find, we posit a plausible-looking sound in the ancestral language, one which could reasonably have developed into the sounds that are found in the several daughter languages, bearing in mind what we know about phonological change.
6. For each word surviving in the various daughters, we look at the results of (5) and thus determine what the form of that word must have been in the ancestral language.
7. Finally, we look at the results of (5) and (6) to find out what system of sounds the ancestral language apparently had and what the rules were for combining these sounds.

This, of course, is a vastly oversimplified picture of what happens in practice, but it gives you the general idea of what's going on. Let's look at a typical example, but first a warning. In practice, the successful use of the comparative method requires the use of large amounts of vocabulary from all the languages being compared. But, in a textbook, I just don't have the space to provide such huge numbers of data. I am therefore obliged to present, somewhat artificially, small sets of data by way of illustration: no more than fifty words, often no more than ten. This is not realistic, but it's the best that can be done in a textbook. But do not think that comparative reconstruction is normally done on tiny sets of data: it is not.

Table 8.4 lists, in phonemic transcription, a number of words from four western Romance languages: Portuguese, Spanish, Catalan, and French. Unless otherwise marked with an acute accent, stress falls upon the next-to-last syllable of a word of more than one syllable. We are interested in reconstructing Proto-Western-Romance as far as possible. We will therefore work through the data in an orderly way. I suggest you keep a copy of Table 8.4 handy to consult as we go; you might like to photocopy it. Read the next few pages *very* slowly and carefully, and check against the data in the table at every opportunity. This exercise will require a great deal of time and thought, but there is no other way to do comparative reconstruction.

We now begin setting up systematic correspondences. This may require some trial and error. Let's begin with the correspondences involving voiceless plosives, shown in Table 8.5.

For correspondences (1) and (3) we can clearly reconstruct *$*p$*. But (2) is a slight problem. We would also like to reconstruct *$*p$* here, but Portuguese is a problem, since it doesn't show the expected /p/. Before trying to reconstruct something different, though, let's look for a conditioning factor. Note that, in item [25], all the languages except Portuguese have an /l/ following the initial /p/, while Portuguese has no /l/ either. Hence the correspondence is more accurately stated as P /š-/ : S /pl-/ : C /pl-/ : F /pl-/, and we can therefore reconstruct initial *$*pl$* in this word, with *$*pl$* developing into /š-/ in Portuguese.

For sets (4) and (5), we reconstruct *$*t$*. Set (6) is a problem, but observe that Catalan and French regularly fail to show the final vowels visible in Portuguese and Spanish. Hence the expected /t/ in Catalan and French would have been word-final, and we may reasonably suppose that these two languages have simply lost word-final /t/. We therefore reconstruct *$*t$* for this case too. Sets (7) and (8) are even messier, but note that they look just like sets (5) and (6) apart from Portuguese. As a matter of economy, let us therefore reconstruct *$*t$* here too, and assume that there is some conditioning factor for the development of /t/ to /č/ in Portuguese – a rather natural change, after all, in some environments, and we do have a following /i/ here.

For sets (9) and (11) we reconstruct *$*k$*. Set (13) looks very much like set (6), and so we draw the same conclusion: we reconstruct *$*k$*, and assume that final /k/ has been lost in Catalan and French. Set (12) is awkward: it seems as though French has this time failed to lose final /k/, as expected. Let us provisionally reconstruct *$*k$* here too, and merely note the problem for later attention. That leaves set (10), in which French has /š/ in place of the expected /k/. Can we find a conditioning factor? Before reading further, compare the cases in set (10) carefully with those in set (9), and see if you can spot a conditioning factor.

Table 8.4 Western Romance

	Portuguese	Spanish	Catalan	French
1. 'against'	kõtra	kontra	kontrə	kɔ̃tr
2. 'bag'	saku	sako	sak	sak
3. 'bald'	kalvu	kalbo	kalp	šov
4. 'beard'	barba	barba	barbə	barb
5. 'believes'	kre	kree	krew	krwa
6. 'big'	grãdi	grande	gran	grã
7. 'blood'	sãgi	saŋgre	saŋ	sã
8. 'bright'	klaru	klaro	kla	klɛr
9. 'country'	pajíš	país	pəís	pei
10. 'court'	korti	korte	kor	kur
11. 'cup'	kopa	kopa	kop	kup
12. 'daughter'	fiʎa	ixa	fiʎə	fij
13. 'dear'	karu	karo	kar	šɛr
14. 'fire'	fɔgu	fwego	fɔk	fø
15. 'five'	sĩku	θinko	siŋ	sɛ̃k
16. 'foot'	pɛ	pje	pɛw	pjɛ
17. 'game'	žɔgu	xwego	žɔk	žø
18. 'green'	verdi	berde	bɛrt	vɛr
19. 'hard'	duru	duro	du	dyr
20. 'high'	altu	alto	al	o
21. 'honey'	mɛl	mjel	mɛl	mjɛl
22. 'iron'	fɛrru	jerro	fɛrru	fɛr
23. 'lady'	dama	dama	dam	dam
24. 'late'	—	tardo	tar	tar
25. 'lead' (metal)	šũbu	plomo	plom	plɔ̃
26. 'low'	bajšu	baxo	baš	ba
27. 'moon'	lua	luna	ʎunə	lyn
28. 'new'	nɔvu	nwebo	nɔw	nøf
29. 'says'	diš	diθe	diw	di
30. 'sea'	mar	mar	mar	mɛr
31. 'seal'	selu	seʎo	səžeʎ	so
32. 'seven'	sɛči	sjete	sɛt	sɛt
33. 'sky'	sɛu	θjelo	sɛl	sjɛl
34. 'so much'	tãtu	tanto	tən	tã
35. 'strong'	fɔrti	fwerte	fɔrt	fɔr
36. 'ten'	dež	djeθ	dɛw	dis
37. 'thousand'	mil	mil	mil	mil
38. 'tooth'	deči	djente	den	dã
39. 'tower'	torri	torre	torrə	tur
40. 'well' (adv)	bej	bjen	be	bjɛ̃
41. 'wine'	vĩñu	bino	bi	vɛ̃
42. 'weight'	pezu	peso	pɛs	pwa
43. 'what'	ke	ke	kɛ	kwa
44. 'white'	brãku	blanko	blaŋ	blã
45. 'you (sg)'	tu	tu	tu	ty

Table 8.5 Correspondences involving voiceless plosives

	Portuguese	Spanish	Catalan	French	
(1)	p-	p-	p-	p-	[9, 16, 42]
(2)	š-	p-	p-	p-	[25]
(3)	-p-	-p-	-p	-p	[11]
(4)	t-	t-	t-	t-	[24, 34, 39, 45]
(5)	-t-	-t-	-t-	-t-	[1]
(6)	-t-	-t-	Ø	Ø	[10, 20, 34, 35?]
(7)	-č-	-t-	Ø	Ø	[38]
(8)	-č-	-t-	-t	-t	[32]
(9)	k-	k-	k-	k-	[1, 5, 8, 10, 43]
(10)	k-	k-	k-	š-	[3, 13]
(11)	-k-	-k-	-k	-k	[2]
(12)	-k-	-k-	Ø	-k	[15]
(13)	-k-	-k-	Ø	Ø	[44]

There is one, but it's subtle. Items [3] and [13] are the only ones in which the /k-/ of the other three languages is followed by /a/. So let's assume that original /k-/ developed to /š-/ in French always and only before /a/. That works, but is it phonologically plausible? Well, we might expect a /k/ to be palatalized before a front vowel, so, if we can assume that /a/ in French has (or once had) a very front realization, it's just about plausible – and note that French now has /ɛ/ in these words. Let's therefore reconstruct *k here too, on grounds of economy. (The alternative would be to reconstruct an additional phoneme, say a palatalized velar *k', but, since we have a conditioning factor available, that hardly seems to be necessary.)

So far, then, we have reconstructed three voiceless plosives *p *t *k for our proto-language, with palatalization or loss in mostly identifiable circumstances in all the languages except Spanish. Now let's look at the correspondences involving voiced plosives, shown in Table 8.6.

These are altogether messier than the voiceless plosives, particularly the labials. In sets (14) and (16), all four languages have /b/, while in (15) and (17), only Spanish and Catalan have /b/ (or /p/), while Portuguese and French have /v/. Can we find a conditioning factor? Have a look and see if you can find one.

Not much leaps to the eye. If you make a list of the environments for all the cases in these four sets, they look pretty miscellaneous. With more data, perhaps we could spot something, but, as it stands, if we try to reconstruct *b for all four sets, we're going to have to posit a change to /v/ in some rather mysterious circumstances. This time, then, it looks as though we have to reconstruct two different segments. The obvious guesses are *b for sets (14) and (16) and *v for sets (15) and (17), with a merger of these two in Spanish and Catalan, and a devoicing of final [b] in Catalan. So let's do that.

Table 8.6 Correspondences involving voiced plosives

	Portuguese	Spanish	Catalan	French	
(14)	b-	b-	b-	b-	[4, 26, 40, 44]
(15)	v-	b-	b-	v-	[18, 41]
(16)	-b-	-b-	-b-	-b	[4]
(17)	-v-	-b-	-p	-v	[3]
(18)	-v-	-b-	-w	-f	[28]
(19)	-b-	-m-	-m	Ø	[25]
(20)	d-	d-	d-	d-	[19, 23, 29, 36, 38]
(21)	-d-	-d-	Ø	Ø	[6]
(22)	-d-	-d-	-t	Ø	[18]
(23)	?	-d-	Ø	Ø	[24]
(24)	g-	g-	g-	g-	[6]
(25)	-g-	-g-	Ø	Ø	[7]
(26)	-g-	-g-	-k	Ø	[14, 17]

While set (18) is seemingly more complicated, it should remind you of what we decided above. There, it appeared, final consonants were lost in Catalan and French – except for the labial /p/. This time we have another final labial, so let's reconstruct *v here, on the basis of the Portuguese and Spanish evidence, and assume that final /v/ develops as shown in Catalan and French. (Note that final /b/ is not lost in French in set (16).)

Finally, set (19) is so messy that it might be a good idea to leave it for later.

But we have a clear pattern emerging here. Catalan and French tend to lose final vowels, and the resulting final consonants are usually lost if they are coronal or velar – though once in a while they survive, in circumstances we haven't identified. This pattern is repeated in the next two groups, and we can therefore reconstruct *d and *g with some confidence.

Let us turn our attention to the nasals, shown in Table 8.7; here the notation $\tilde{V}$ means a nasalized vowel. For set (27) we at once reconstruct *n. For sets (28) to (32) we would like to do the same, but we have some work to do to explain the variable behaviour in all the languages but Spanish. We can see that nasal vowels generally result in Portuguese and French when the nasal is syllable-final in the other languages. Set (30) differs in that the nasal is not syllable-final, and this time we get Ø in Portuguese and -n in French. In set (29), Catalan shows an unexpected velar nasal, but here Portuguese and Spanish show a following velar plosive, so we can take this as a reasonable conditioning factor, even though the velar plosive has disappeared in Catalan itself (we already know that Catalan loses final consonants). In set (32), and perhaps also in set (33), Catalan has apparently also lost a final *n. That leaves only the Portuguese palatal nasal in set (32) to account for. Here we might have expected zero, by analogy with set (30), but note that in item [41], the only one in set (32), the nasal is preceded by the vowel /i/, so let's assume this is the conditioning factor.

Table 8.7 Correspondences involving nasals

	Portuguese	Spanish	Catalan	French	
(27)	n-	n-	n-	n(-)	[28]
(28)	-Ṽ-	-n-	-n-	-Ṽ-	[1, 6, 15, 34, 38]
(29)	-Ṽ-	-n-	-ŋ	-Ṽ	[7, 44]
(30)	-∅-	-n-	-n	-n	[27]
(31)	-Ṽ	-n	-∅	-Ṽ	[40]
(32)	-ñ-	-n-	-∅	-Ṽ	[41]
(33)	m-	m-	m-	m-	[21, 30, 37]
(34)	-m-	-m-	-m-	-m	[23]
(35)	-Ṽ-	-m-	-m	-Ṽ	[25]

For sets (33) and (34), of course, we reconstruct $*m$. Set (35) is a puzzle, but recall that Portuguese and French get nasal vowels from a syllable-final $*n$, so let's assume that the same happens with syllable-final $*m$.

Hence we reconstruct two nasals, $*n$ and $*m$. Of these, $*n$ remains in all positions in Spanish and initially in all four languages; French converts $*n$ to nasalization in syllable-final position but otherwise retains it; Portuguese also converts $*n$ to nasalization syllable-finally, but loses it intervocalically except after i, where it becomes $ñ$; Catalan loses $*n$ finally, converts it to a velar nasal before an original velar plosive, and otherwise retains it. With $*m$, Portuguese and French convert this to nasalization syllable-finally, but $*m$ is otherwise unchanged everywhere.

Next, the fricatives, shown in Table 8.8. For set (36), it seems we should reconstruct $*s$. But now what do we do with set (37)? Comparison of items [32] and [33] reveals no conditioning factor for the $s/θ$ contrast in Spanish. It really looks as if we need to reconstruct *two* sibilants. We might call them $*s$ and $*θ$, but here I will cautiously call them $*s_1$ and $*s_2$; these remain distinct in Spanish as /s/ and /θ/, respectively, but fall together in the other languages. Naturally, we would like to reconstruct $*s_2$ also for sets (38) and (39), but French and Portuguese are a problem. (Catalan /w/ is surprising, too, but let's assume that this has something to do with the usual Catalan loss of final consonants.) Rather than multiply sibilants, though, let's assume that there must be some conditioning factors at work: note that the segment in question is word-final in Spanish in set (39) but word-medial in set (38). Now it looks as if we need to reconstruct $*s_1$ for sets (40) and (41), with the familiar loss in final position in French (but not in Catalan this time), and different results in Portuguese depending on position. Finally, for sets (42) and (43), we can easily reconstruct a single segment, with different positions in the word accounting for the variable outcomes, but what should that segment be? If we choose $*ž$, we have a curious devoicing in intervocalic position in Portuguese. Let us therefore choose $*š$, which undergoes initial voicing in all but Spanish and becomes /x/ everywhere in Spanish.

Table 8.8 Correspondences involving fricatives

	Portuguese	Spanish	Catalan	French	
(36)	s-	s-	s-	s-	[2, 7, 31, 32]
(37)	s-	θ-	s-	s-	[15, 33]
(38)	-š	-θ-	-w	Ø	[29]
(39)	-ž	-θ	-w	-s	[36]
(40)	-z-	-s-	-s	Ø	[42]
(41)	-š	-s	-s	Ø	[9]
(42)	ž-	x-	ž-	ž-	[17]
(43)	-š-	-x-	-š	Ø	[26]
(44)	f-	Ø-	f-	f-	[12, 22]
(45)	f-	f-	f-	f-	[14, 35]

Hence we reconstruct three sibilants, $*s_1$, $*s_2$, and $*š$, with the developments outlined.

For set (45), we obviously reconstruct $*f$. Set (44) is at first puzzling, but observe that, in set (45), Spanish /f-/ is always followed by /w/, but never so in set (44). We may therefore reconstruct $*f$ for both sets, with initial $*f$- retained in Spanish before /w/ but lost otherwise.

Next, we examine the liquids, shown in Table 8.9. For sets (46) and (47) we reconstruct $*r$. For sets (48) to (50), we'd like to do the same, but we need some conditioning factors to explain the losses. We already know that Catalan tends to lose final consonants, and for the unique set (49) we can appeal to the presence of the awkward cluster $*ngr$ to account for the additional losses in Portuguese and French. For set (51), however, we must apparently reconstruct $*rr$, which we might view either as a distinct consonant or as a gemination of $*r$; since we have reconstructed no other geminates, let's treat it as a separate consonant.

For sets (52) and (53) we reconstruct $*l$. Set (54) is more difficult, but note that the items in this set all have /alC/ in the other languages, where C is a consonant, while French has /o/. Let's therefore reconstruct $*l$ for this set too, and posit that $*al$ has developed to /o/ in French before a consonant – a very common type of change, as it happens. For set (55), only Portuguese is a problem, but note that we have already explained the loss of $*l$ in item [25], while item [33] is the only one in the data with an intervocalic l, so let's assume that $*l$, like $*n$, was simply lost intervocalicaly in Portuguese. Set (56) presents a different problem, but observe that this is the only set with word-initial l, so let's reconstruct $*l$ here, too, and posit a change of initial $*l$ to ʎ in Catalan. Set (57) is a much bigger puzzle. Since we have already decided that intervocalic $*l$ is lost in Portuguese, we can't reconstruct $*l$ here, because Portuguese shows intervocalic /l/ in this set. We must therefore reconstruct something different. We could try $*ʎ$, but then we have a problem with set (58), which is different from (57) but which also looks like a good bet for $*ʎ$.

Table 8.9 Correspondences involving liquids

	Port	Sp	Cat	Fr	
(46)	-r-	-r-	-r-	-r(-)	[1, 4, 5, 6, 10, 13, 18, 24, 35]
(47)	-r	-r	-r	-r	[30]
(48)	-r-	-r-	Ø	-r	[8]
(49)	Ø	-r-	Ø	Ø	[7]
(50)	-r-	-r-	Ø	-r	[19]
(51)	-rr-	-rr-	-rr-	-r	[22, 39]
(52)	-l-	-l-	-l-	-l-	[8]
(53)	-l	-l	-l	-l	[21, 37]
(54)	-l-	-l-	-l(-)	Ø	[3, 20]
(55)	Ø	-l-	-l(-)	-l(-)	[25, 33]
(56)	l-	l-	ʎ-	l-	[27]
(57)	-l-	-ʎ-	-ʎ	Ø	[31]
(58)	-ʎ-	-x-	-ʎ-	-j	[12]
(59)	-r-	-l-	-l-	-l-	[44]

Without further data, we appear to be at an impasse, and so I shall somewhat helplessly reconstruct $*\Lambda_1$ for (57) and $*\Lambda_2$ for (58), while recognizing that this is phonetically very implausible. Finally, set (59) is a mystery, since Portuguese differs here from every other set, and particularly from set (52), which is otherwise identical. We might decide to set up yet another liquid here, but we've already reconstructed five liquids, and not many languages have six contrasting liquids, so let's just reconstruct the obvious $*l$ and assume that there is an invisible conditioning factor for the odd Portuguese development.

So far, then, we have reconstructed the following phonemes for Proto-Western-Romance: $*p$, $*t$, $*k$, $*b$, $*d$, $*g$, $*v$, $*m$, $*n$, $*s_1$, $*s_2$, $*š$, $*f$, $*r$, $*rr$, $*l$, $*\Lambda_1$, and $*\Lambda_2$. These apparently suffice to account for all the data, apart from one or two puzzling forms which we have placed aside as problems.

We now need to reconstruct the vowels. For lack of space, I won't attempt that here; instead, I suggest that you continue the reconstruction by yourself, drawing up correspondence sets for the vowels and reconstructing an appropriate vowel system for the proto-language. It would be a *very* good idea to attempt this before reading further.

As it happens, these data require seven different proto-vowels, and only seven. (In fact, it is only in stressed syllables that we require seven vowels; elsewhere, five suffices.) These I shall represent as $*i$, $*e$, $*\varepsilon$, $*a$, $*\mathfrak{o}$, $*o$, and $*u$. When we have finished, we can then display the reconstructed PWR forms of all forty-five items; this is done in Table 8.10. With just a couple of outstanding puzzles, the forms in this table appear to represent the best available reconstructions. You can see that Spanish appears to be the most conservative of the four languages and French the least conservative.

Table 8.10 Proto-Western-Romance

Gloss	Reconstruction	Gloss	Reconstruction
1. 'against'	*kontra	24. late	*tardo
2. 'bag'	*$s_1$ako	25. lead	*plombo
3. 'bald'	*kalvo	26. low	*bašo
4. 'beard'	*barba	27. moon	*luna
5. 'believes'	*kree	28. new	*nɔvo
6. 'big'	*grande	29. says	*dis₂e
7. 'blood'	*$s_1$angre	30. sea	*mar
8. 'bright'	*klaro	31. seal	*s_1eʎ₁o
9. 'country'	*país₁	32. seven	*s_1ɛte
10. 'court'	*korte	33. sky	*s₂ɛlo
11. 'cup'	*kopa	34. so much	*tanto
12. 'daughter'	*fiʎ₂a	35. strong	*fɔrte
13. 'dear'	*karo	36. ten	*dɛs₂
14. 'fire'	*fɔgo	37. thousand	*mil
15. 'five'	*s₂inko	38. tooth	*dɛnte
16. 'foot'	*pɛ	39. tower	*torre
17. 'game'	*šɔgo	40. well	*bɛn
18. 'green'	*verde	41. wine	*vino
19. 'hard'	*duro	42. weight	*peso
20. 'high'	*alto	43. what	*ke
21. 'honey'	*mɛl	44. white	*blanko
22. 'iron'	*fɛrro	45. you	*tu
23. 'lady'	*dama		

And is this reconstruction the definitive last word on Proto-Western-Romance? No, it is not. Examination of a much wider set of data has shown that we have oversimplified in a few places, and specialists in fact reconstruct a couple more consonants in addition to the ones we have identified here, and they make different reconstructions in several cases.

8.3   *Pitfalls and limitations*

The comparative method is not a form of magic. We cannot just pick some arbitrary languages, compare them, and expect to see systematic correspondences pop up in front of our eyes – even if the languages selected truly are genetically related, which is unlikely to be so with languages chosen arbitrarily. The method has to be applied thoughtfully and carefully, and we have to take advantage of every available piece of information we have which might possibly be relevant. Further, we have to be aware of a number of pitfalls, of potential difficulties which might lead us into error. Here I will discuss some of these difficulties.

Perhaps the most obvious point is that the comparative method cannot recover any feature of the ancestral language which has disappeared without trace in all the attested daughters. For example, not one of the Romance languages shows the slightest evidence for an ancestral consonant /h/, and we therefore reconstruct Proto-Romance without an /h/ – and yet we happen to know, on independent grounds, that the Latin ancestor of the Romance languages *did* have an /h/. It's just that this consonant vanished completely everywhere, and so we have no reason to reconstruct it.

A more interesting point is the following question: how do we know which languages to compare at all? In some cases, this is easy. The Polynesian languages, or the Bantu languages, or the Algonquian languages, are all so strikingly similar to one another, in phonology, grammar, and vocabulary, that no one examining several of these languages could fail to realize that they must be related. The same is true of the Indo-European languages, or rather of some of them. Some of the earliest-attested languages, like Latin, Greek, Avestan (the earliest known Iranian language), and Sanskrit (the ancient language of northern India) are likewise so similar that, almost as soon as European linguists began to acquire a knowledge of the eastern languages in the late eighteenth century, they realized that all these languages simply must be related. After that, it didn't take long to realize that Germanic, Baltic, and Slavic were also part of the same family. Celtic and Armenian took a little longer, because these languages have changed more dramatically than most other Indo-European languages. Most difficult of all was Albanian, which has no particularly close relatives and which has undergone a simply stupendous amount of lexical borrowing, leaving its inherited Indo-European vocabulary perhaps no greater than 200 words. Still, the Indo-European languages are sufficiently closely related that their affinity is impossible to deny.

However, in virtually all of the Old World, and in much of the New, the languages whose genetic affinity is obvious upon inspection have already been identified: this is why I was able to list language families so confidently in Chapter 7. Even in such comparatively ill-studied regions as New Guinea and the Amazon rainforest, linguists have already picked up most of the obvious genetic links. In historical linguistics, as in geography, the age of the great discoveries is over. There is now perhaps no possibility that you will be able to glance at descriptions of two or three Brazilian languages and spot a genetic relationship which has not previously been noticed.

That doesn't mean, however, that there is nothing more to be done – far from it. It is hardly likely that we have already identified all of the genetic links which can ever be discovered. It's merely that we have reached the limits of what we can hope to achieve by mere inspection of attested languages, and we now have to turn to other approaches.

Chief among these is the comparison of proto-languages. Once we have good reconstructions of a number of proto-languages, we can then inspect these in the same way earlier linguists did with attested languages, to see if we can spot any evidence of remote genetic links. For example, linguists have been rather successful in reconstructing Proto-Siouan and Proto-Iroquoian, and it was very largely the comparison of these proto-languages which allowed specialists to conclude that the Siouan and Iroquoian languages (and some others) must be linked in a larger Macro-Siouan family.

Of course, we can only do this after we have succeeded in assembling moderately complete pictures of our proto-languages. In some cases, as with Proto-Indo-European and Proto-Algonquian, this has already been done in considerable detail, and we are well placed to compare these proto-languages with others. For example, it was noticed decades ago that Yurok and Wiyot, two seemingly isolated languages of California, show striking affinities with Proto-Algonquian. Table 8.11, for instance, shows the personal agreement markers in verbs in all three languages. Such systematic grammatical matches can scarcely result from anything other than a genetic link, and hence specialists are now satisfied that these two languages, spoken many hundreds of miles away from the nearest Algonquian language, must nevertheless be related to them in a larger family sometimes called *Algic* – a conclusion which might have been much harder to reach if we had compared Yurok and Wiyot only with particular Algonquian languages of the present day.

In the majority of cases, though, reconstruction of proto-languages has not proceeded far enough for us to appeal to them readily in seeking out distant comparisons. Even Proto-Afro-Asiatic and Proto-Niger-Congo, the ancestors of huge families containing large numbers of attested languages, have not as yet been reconstructed in any great detail. In the Niger-Congo case, this is chiefly due to the huge size of the family, which contains dozens of groups and subgroups and perhaps 1000 languages in total. Ideally, we need to work from the bottom up, reconstructing recent proto-languages and comparing those to obtain more distant proto-languages, until we finally work back all the way to Proto-Niger-Congo – a procedure which is, naturally, enormously time-consuming. In the Afro-Asiatic case, the problem appears to be the time depth: the ancestral language is thought to have been spoken at least 8000 years ago, and the mass of accumulated changes in all the daughters is so great that systematic correspondences and grammatical parallels are just at the very edge of our ability to reconstruct, or perhaps even beyond, and so we may never have a satisfactory picture of Proto-Afro-Asiatic.

Most historical linguists are therefore resigned to the necessity of further generations of patient reconstruction before we will be in a position to place

Table 8.11 Algonquian, Yurok, and Wiyot

	Proto-Algonquian	Yurok	Wiyot
1st person	*ne-	*ne(t)-	ʔne-	d-
2nd person	*ke-	*ke(t)-	k'e-	kh-
3rd person	*we-	*we(t)-	ʔwe-	w-

the resulting proto-languages side by side to see if anything then leaps out at us – though in Chapter 12 we will consider whether statistical methods might be invoked to make the job easier, and in Chapter 13 we will look at some highly controversial attempts at finding truly dramatic short cuts.

But even painstaking reconstruction can go astray if it is not applied with sufficient care. Consider the data in Table 8.12. These are very striking matches, and you can quickly see what look like convincing systematic correspondences. For example, we have multiple instances of Arabic x : Urdu x : Turkish h : Swahili h : Malay kh, and also of Arabic q : Urdu q : Turkish k : Swahili k : Malay k, among others. At first glance, therefore, you might think that we were looking at prima-facie evidence of a genetic link. But we are not. In fact, there is no reason to believe that any two of these five languages are genetically related: they all belong to different major families. So what is the explanation for these striking matches, apparently complete with systematic correspondences? Think about this for a minute. What could account for such data, if not a genetic relationship?

The solution lies in something we discussed in Chapter 2: borrowing. All these words, and hundreds of others, have been borrowed into a large number of Asian and African languages from a single source. That source is Arabic. In the eighth century, the Arabs burst out of their desert homeland, and, for the next few centuries, Arab soldiers, traders, and scholars made their presence felt across much of the Old World. Wherever the Arabs went, their Arabic language went with them, and such was the brilliance of Arab civilization that Arabic words were borrowed in their hundreds into local languages everywhere. And, just like English-speakers borrowing words from Norman French, the speakers of Urdu, Turkish, Swahili, and Malay adjusted the pronunciations of the borrowed words to match the phonologies of their own languages – and so the Turks, for example, lacking the Arabic sounds [q], [x], and [w], systematically replaced these unfamiliar sounds with the nearest Turkish equivalents, [k], [h], and [v]. This is why we appear to see 'systematic correspondences' which are totally spurious.

In this case, the borrowing took place in historical times, and it is a trivial matter to identify these numerous loan words and to exclude them from

Table 8.12 A pitfall

	Arabic	Urdu	Turkish	Swahili	Malay
'news'	*xabar*	*xabar*	*haber*	*habari*	*khabar*
'time'	*waqt*	*vaqt*	*vakit*	*wakati*	*waktu*
'book'	*kitāb*	*kitāb*	*kitap*	*kitabu*	*kitab*
'service'	*xidmat*	*xidmatgari*	*hizmet*	*huduma*	*khidmat*
'beggar'	*faqir*	*faqir*	*fakir*	*fakiri*	*fakir*

consideration. But loan words are not always so easy to identify. There is no reason to doubt that the borrowing of words has been going on for as long as human beings have had at least two different languages to speak. Hence, some loan words have been present in the borrowing languages for so long that they are almost indistinguishable from native words. Identifying such ancient loans is thus a crucial issue: if we inadvertently accept several dozen ancient loans as native words, we may be fatally misled into seeing a genetic link where none exists.

The best way of coping with this problem, when searching for possible genetic links, is to confine ourselves to what I called *basic vocabulary* in Chapter 2: pronouns, grammatical words, body-part names, the lower numerals, and other high-frequency items which are not often borrowed. Words for 'me', 'two', or 'head' are very rarely borrowed, while words like 'news', 'book', and 'service' are far more likely to be borrowed. Hence, if we can't find any evidence for a genetic link when comparing the basic vocabularies of two candidate languages, we should be rather suspicious if we then stumble across apparent 'cognates' with meanings like 'chariot', 'caterpillar', 'stocking', or 'bronze': they might very well be ancient loans.

There is another potential pitfall, one which looks innocuous at first glance but which has in practice often produced monumental confusion among linguists who were not sufficiently aware of it. Take a look at Table 8.13, which compares some words from Hawaiian and ancient Greek. Very striking, right? What do you suppose is going on this time? How can we explain these data? Could Hawaiian and Greek be genetically related? Could the Greeks and the Hawaiians somehow have contrived to borrow words from each other, or both from some third language? Did a Greek ship manage to reach Hawaii a couple of thousand years ago?

No. The true explanation is far less interesting than any of these exciting suggestions. Have you figured out what it is? If not, give yourself another minute to think about it before reading on.

Table 8.13 Another pitfall

Hawaiian		Ancient Greek	
aeto	'eagle'	*aetos*	'eagle'
noonoo	'thought'	*nous*	'thought'
manao	'think'	*manthano*	'learn'
mele	'sing'	*melos*	'melody'
lahui	'people'	*laos*	'people'
meli	'honey'	*meli*	'honey'
kau	'summer'	*kauma*	'heat'
mahina	'month'	*men*	'moon'
kia	'pillar'	*kion*	'pillar'
hiki	'come'	*hikano*	'arrive'

The explanation is this: we are looking at a bunch of pure coincidences. Entirely by chance, Hawaiian and Greek happen to have settled on some words which are very similar in form and meaning. That's all there is to it: no Greeks in the Pacific, no Hawaiian migrations from Greece, nothing interesting at all – just pure chance.

It is possible that you find this very hard to believe. Many people with little experience of comparative linguistics are incredulous when they are told that such impressive-looking lists are the result of sheer coincidence; they protest indignantly, 'But this just *can't* be coincidence. Look at the words for "honey" – they're absolutely identical! There *must* be another explanation.' As we shall see later in the book, even a number of professional linguists have taken this line, and insisted hotly in the literature that data-sets like Table 8.13 just *have* to be considered evidence for some kind of connection.

Well, sorry, but they're wrong. Every language has thousands of meanings to provide forms for, and only a small number of speech-sounds to construct those forms, and hence, by the ordinary laws of probability, any arbitrary languages will always exhibit a number of such coincidences – maybe only eight or ten, maybe dozens, depending chiefly on how similar their phonologies are and on how willing you are to accept some pair of words as similar. Failure to appreciate this truth is merely one more manifestation of that very widespread human failure to understand the laws of probability. For example, how many arbitrary people do you need to assemble in one room before there is a better than 50 per cent chance that at least two of them will celebrate their birthdays on the same date? Fifty? 100? 183? Any idea?

In fact, the answer is twenty-three. By the time you have forty people in the room, the probability of shared birthdays is around 90 per cent. You can win a few bets this way, since most people won't believe these figures. And languages are no different: chance coincidences of form and meaning will always be present, and we must, of course, be careful to exclude them from our comparisons. But how can we do that?

There are two things we can do. First, we can insist on systematic correspondences and deny the value of mere resemblances. This is what most historical linguists do: aware that mere resemblances can always be the result of chance, they assign full weight only to systematic correspondences, which (once loan words have been excluded) can result only from a genetic relationship. Second, we can apply statistical tests to our data, in a manner to be explained in Chapter 12, to see whether we have anything more than we would expect by chance alone. Both of these are good policies. But, whatever we do, we must not allow ourselves to be persuaded that a mere list of arbitrary and unsystematic resemblances, however long, by itself constitutes persuasive evidence for anything. It is sad to report that a number of linguists have failed to grasp this elementary point, and have as a result squandered their careers in collecting lists of resemblances among whichever languages have caught their eye (always with success, of course). They have proudly announced their 'findings' and declared them to be evidence of an ancient link between the languages they are looking at, and they are baffled and hurt when no one pays the slightest attention.

Yet another pitfall is presented by nursery words, imitative words, and phonaesthetic words generally (a phonaesthetic word is one which is coined more or less out of thin air because it has an appealing sound). Nursery words like *mama* and *tata* are found all over the planet with meanings like 'mother', 'father', 'breast', 'milk', and they cannot be cited as evidence for anything. The same is true of imitative words. For example, items of the general form *ber(ber)* are found everywhere as onomatopoeic words for 'boil', and they often acquire transferred senses like 'hot', 'fire', or 'cook'; such forms should not be adduced as comparative evidence, because they are so treacherous. A fine example of a phonaesthetic word is the Basque word *pinpirin* 'butterfly', which has often been compared with similar-looking names for insects in various other languages. However: (1) it has been established by vasconists (specialists in Basque) that no native Basque word of any antiquity ever begins with /p/; (2) this word has a large number of variant forms which are not at all typical of ordinary phonological variation in Basque; (3) it means not only 'butterfly' but also 'bud', 'garfish', 'undeveloped fruit', 'pretentious', 'elegant', and 'favourite'; (4) it is confined to one small corner of the Basque country, all other regions having quite different (and mostly also phonaesthetic) words for 'butterfly'; (5) this region shows a notable fondness for phonaesthetic words in *pin-* or *pan-*. It is therefore safe to conclude that this item is a recent and localized formation in Basque, one which cannot reasonably be projected into the distant past and adduced in comparisons.

Finally, there is one more potential pitfall in comparative work, perhaps the most surprising of all. This involves a type of mistake which is easy to avoid in principle, but apparently not always in practice. Take a look at Table 8.14, which presents a selection of proposed cognates between Basque and the North Caucasian languages. You will quickly note that this is another list of miscellaneous resemblances, but that is not the point here. There is something else which has gone wrong here, but it's probably impossible to spot, or perhaps even to guess. And what is that?

Well, to start with, the Basque words *akain, azeri, beko, gela, kaiku, kolko, kuma, matel, mulo,* and *tiña* are all loan words from neighbouring languages (Latin or Romance). Moreover, *kolko* 'space between one's chest and one's clothes' and *tiña* 'ringworm' do not have the meanings imputed to them, and *mulo* 'haystack' is glossed as 'small hill' only in one very doubtful source. (It is completely out of order to cite forms or meanings which are severely localized or attested only in sources of questionable reliability when such forms and meanings conflict with the bulk of the evidence available.) Basque *birika* is attested in our earliest texts as *biri*, showing that *-ka* is a late accretion to the word. Basque *d-* is not a third-singular prefix, but a present-tense prefix. Basque *maño* does not mean 'masculine'; it means '(little) mule', and the confusion has arisen because Spanish *macho*, used to gloss it in

Table 8.14 An unexpected problem

Basque		*Caucasian*	
abets	'voice'	abžə	'voice'
akain	'tick'	*q'(q')in?V	'louse'
azeri	'fox'	zeru, zaru	'fox'
beko	'face, beak'	*bĕk'wV	'mouth'
beri	'this same'	abri	'this'
(bi)rika	'lung'	*jerkʷi	'heart'
d-	3Sg prefix	d-	3Sg prefix
gela	'room'	*qəlV	'dwelling'
*ika	'one'	ak'ə	'one'
ilu	'move'	-la-ra	'go'
kaiku	'wooden bowl'	*qwaqwV	'vessel'
kala	'castle'	*qəlV	'house'
kolko	'female breast'	-k'ək'a-	'female breast'
kuma	'mane'	q'(q')amhā	'mane'
maño	'masculine'	*mVnXV	'male'
matel	'cheek'	*mət'V	'face'
mulo	'small hill'	*muʕalV	'mountain'
tiña	'tick'	*t'ānhV	'nit'
tu	'spit'	*tuk'	'spit'
(u)kab(il)	'fist'	*GwabV	'paw'
(u)kondo	'elbow'	*q'wVntV	'elbow'
zaro	'night'	*śʷVrV	'night'
ze	'small'	-sa	'small'
ziri	'sharp'	-ć'ar	'sharp'

a bilingual dictionary, means both 'mule' and 'masculine'. Basque *tu* is an imitative word, and many of the languages on the planet have similar imitative words for 'spit' (think about it). Basque *ukabil* and *ukondo* are both transparent and completely regular compounds of *uko* 'forearm', with *-bil* 'round' and *ondo* 'bottom'. Basque *ze* can be securely reconstructed as **zene*, destroying the match. Finally, the alleged Basque **abets* 'voice', **beri* 'this same', **ika* 'one', **ilu* 'move', **kala* 'castle', **zaro* 'night', and **ziri* 'sharp' do not exist at all: these are either blunders resulting from misunderstanding the secondary sources used or sheer fantasies on the part of the people drawing the comparisons.

The point of all this is that the people who drew these comparisons did not know anything about Basque. They contented themselves with extracting items incomprehendingly from bilingual dictionaries and other secondary sources, not all of them reliable sources of information, and as a result they made a spectacular series of blunders. So: you can't always trust data merely because you see them in print. If you see comparative work done by specialists in the relevant languages, then you can (probably) trust it. But, when you see work done by people on languages they don't know well, you should be very cautious about accepting any of it at face value. It's hard enough to do historical work on languages you know intimately; trying to work on languages you don't know is likely to lead to disaster.

8.4   *The Neogrammarian Hypothesis*

Throughout this book I have been assuming that phonological change is usually regular, that a sound change typically applies without exception to all words of relevant form in the language. In this chapter we have seen that we can find systematic correspondences between languages which are genetically related, even when these languages have spent many thousands of years diverging from their common ancestor. Such correspondences provide excellent confirmation of the overriding regularity of sound change. Still, there do appear to be cases in which regularity is not observed.

Recall from Chapter 3 the case of intervocalic plosives in Italian, which have sometimes undergone voicing but other times not, in a seemingly haphazard manner. Old English *hūs*, *mūs*, *lūs*, *dūn*, *tūn*, *mūþ*, all with /u:/, have developed into modern English *house*, *mouse*, *louse*, *down*, *town*, *mouth*, all with /aʊ/, because of the GVS, but Old English *rūm*, also with /u:/, has become *room*, still with /u:/. And other cases like these are not difficult to find.

Noting such troublesome data, the nineteenth-century founders of historical linguistics were mostly inclined to the view that sound change is *not* regular. They spoke of sound changes as 'tendencies', and were quite happy to accept that sound changes could apply to some words but not to others. An illustration that particularly engaged their attention is one of the most celebrated of all sound changes. This is the **First Germanic Consonant Shift**, which applied in prehistoric times in Proto-Germanic to a number of the consonants inherited from PIE. (This consonant shift is also familiarly known as **Grimm's Law**, because it received its fullest presentation in the work of the distinguished German linguist Jacob Grimm, one of the Brothers Grimm of fairy-tale fame, though Grimm was not the first to formulate it.)

The principal effects of the First Germanic Consonant Shift are illustrated in Table 8.15. Here Latin, Greek, Lithuanian, and Sanskrit, which did not undergo the shift, are used to illustrate the consonants of PIE, while Gothic, Old English, and Old Norse represent the shifted consonants of Proto-Germanic. This table shows clearly what happened to the Germanic consonants when Grimm's Law applied regularly. We may summarize these developments as follows:

$$*p > f \qquad *b > p \qquad *bh > b$$
$$*t > þ \; [\theta] \qquad *d > t \qquad *dh > d$$
$$*k > x \qquad *g > k \qquad *gh > g$$

Table 8.15 The First Germanic Consonant Shift

	Gothic	**Old English**	**Old Norse**	
Lat *piscis*	*fisks*	*fisc*	*fisk*	'fish'
Lat *tu*	*þu*	*þu*	*þu*	'thou'
Lat *canis*	*hunds*	*hund*	*hundr*	'dog'
Lat *quis*	*hwas*	*hwa*	*hverr*	'who'
Lith *trobà* 'house'	*þaúrp* 'field'	*þorp* 'village'	—	
Lat *decem*	*taíhun*	*tien*	*tio*	'ten'
Lat *ego*	*ik*	*ic*	*ek*	'I'
Lat *vivus* (< **gwiwos*)	*qius*	*cwicu*	*kvikr*	'alive'
Skr *bharami*	*baíran*	*beran*	*bera*	'bear'
Grk *thyra*	—	*duru*	—	'door'
Lat *longgus*	*laggs*	*lang*	*langr*	'long'

Table 8.16 An exception to Grimm's Law

	PIE	**Germanic**
'stand'	Latin *stāre*	English *stand*
'fish'	Latin *piscis*	Gothic *fisks*
'captive'	Latin *captivus*	Old English *hæft*
'spit'	Latin *spuere*	Old High German *spiwan*
'is'	Latin *est*	Gothic *ist*
'night'	Latin *noct-*	Gothic *nahts*

However, there are a number of words in which the expected result is not found. One group of such words is shown in Table 8.16. In each of these, the original voiceless plosive remains a plosive and fails to develop to the expected fricative. It was quickly realized, however, that there was a simple explanation for these exceptions. Can you see what it is? Take a look before reading further.

In every one of these exceptions, the plosive in question is immediately preceded by another voiceless consonant. Hence we may say that the consonant shift occurred *except* immediately after a voiceless consonant. That is, Grimm's Law was a *conditioned* change, of the sort we discussed in Chapter 3: it occurred in certain circumstances but not in other circumstances, and the difference between the two outcomes is predictable in terms of the neighbouring sounds.

This discovery was encouraging, but unfortunately there remained another group of exceptions for which no such simple explanation was available. These other exceptions are illustrated in Table 8.17. This time, as you can

Table 8.17 Further exceptions to Grimm's Law

	PIE	Germanic
'father'	Greek *patér*	Old English *fæder*
'over'	Greek *hypér*	Old High German *ubar*
'mother-in-law'	Greek *hekurá*	Old High German *swigur*

see, the PIE voiceless plosives */p t k/ fail to develop as usual into voiceless fricatives /f þ x/. Instead, they develop into *voiced* plosives /b d g/. No conditioning factor is visible in the Germanic words, and linguists therefore felt obliged to conclude that Grimm's Law was simply not a regular change, and that sound changes in general were not regular.

In the 1870s, however, the modest and retiring Danish linguist Karl Verner made a brilliant discovery. (By Verner's own account, his idea came to him while he was dozing under a tree, and it was only with great difficulty that his friends succeeded in persuading him to publish it.) Be that as it may, Verner's article has been described as '[perhaps] the single most influential publication in linguistics'. What Verner spotted may be illustrated very easily. Compare the forms of the Sanskrit verb *vártate* 'turn' and the cognate Old English verb *weorþan* 'become' (as you can see, the apparent exceptions to Grimm's Law often produced consonantal alternations in Germanic verb stems). Study these forms for a minute. Can you see what Verner saw? Can you see a possible conditioning factor for the two different outcomes?

Sanskrit	*vártate*	*vavárta*	*vavrtimá*	*vavrtāná*
Old English	*weorþan*	*wearþ*	*wurdon*	*worden*

The key point here is the position of the *accent* in Sanskrit. Sanskrit, along with Greek and Lithuanian, largely preserves the position of the PIE accent, while Latin does not and Germanic certainly does not: in Germanic, almost all words have initial stress, as a result of a change in Proto-Germanic. However, if you look back through the data in the preceding tables, you will see that Grimm's Law applies regularly to produce voiceless fricatives *whenever the consonant was immediately preceded by the PIE accent* (or whenever it was word-initial). But, whenever the consonant was not initial and was not immediately preceded by the accent, a different change occurred, producing voiced plosives. This change to voiced plosives has ever since, of course, been known as **Verner's Law**.

So, we can now interpret the data as follows. Early Proto-Germanic retained the PIE accent, and there were two different consonant shifts: Verner's Law in one set of circumstances and Grimm's Law in a different set of circumstances, both changes being completely conditioned by the phonological environment. In a third set of circumstances, immediately following a voiceless consonant, neither shift occurred, and nothing happened. After both shifts had applied, the word-accent in Proto-Germanic was moved to the initial syllable, destroying the conditioning environment which had earlier been responsible for the different outcomes.

There are several lessons here. First, these data show indisputably that sound changes can be, and often are, phonologically conditioned – that is, the historical development of a sound may depend upon its environment. Second, that environment need not consist only of neighbouring segments; suprasegmentals like word-accent may also be of crucial relevance.

But it is a third lesson for which Verner's contribution is chiefly remembered. The discovery of Verner's Law removed *all* of the outstanding exceptions to Grimm's Law. When we recognize both Grimm's Law and Verner's Law, *every single word* in Germanic can be seen to have developed perfectly regularly. This outcome at once suggested to a number of linguists that sound changes must *always* be regular, and that apparent exceptions must mean only that we have not yet succeeded in identifying the relevant conditioning factors. This position, the absolute regularity of sound change, was taken up with enthusiasm by a group of younger linguists, mostly at the University of Leipzig, who began loudly proclaiming their new doctrine. Older linguists, deeply sceptical of such a doctrine, jeered at the youngsters as *Junggrammatiker*, literally 'young grammarians', but this word is commonly rendered into English as *Neogrammarians*. The young linguists accepted the label with pride, and their doctrine became known as the **Neogrammarian Hypothesis**. Among the leading Neogrammarians were Karl Brugmann, Berthold Delbrück, August Leskien, and Hermann Osthoff. It is Brugmann's formulation of the Neogrammarian Hypothesis that is best known: 'Every sound change takes place according to laws that admit no exception.' For the Neogrammarians, sound changes were no longer just tendencies: instead, they were absolute laws.

As so often happens in scholarly disciplines, the older opponents of the new doctrine gradually retired or died, leaving the field to the younger generation who fervently espoused the doctrine. By the end of the nineteenth century, the Neogrammarian Hypothesis had become the established orthodoxy in historical linguistics: the writings of the Neogrammarians were now the standard textbooks, and each new generation of students was being firmly trained in the new approach.

Not that opposition vanished overnight. Chief among the opponents of the Neogrammarians was the German linguist Hugo Schuchardt, who, though born in the engagingly named German town of Batman, spent his whole career at Graz in Austria. Schuchardt, a hypochondriac who rarely travelled and who sometimes delivered his university lectures from his bed, was a formidable if eccentric figure. Among his other achievements, he virtually founded the study of creoles, and he was an outstanding vasconist: coming to Basque late in life, he took the study of that language, formerly little more than an amateur pastime, and turned it into a serious scholarly discipline. But

Schuchardt had a background in dialectology, and, like many dialectologists, he could not reconcile the bold new doctrine with the complex and messy facts he found in the examination of real language data, and he preferred to maintain the dialectologists' own particular creed: 'Every word has its own history.'

Schuchardt's fierce attacks upon the Neogrammarian ideas led to ostracism. By the end of his career, he had virtually been declared an unperson by the new linguistic establishment, and for decades after his death the standard textbooks noted him, if at all, as a figure of fun: a crotchety old stick-in-the-mud who had never been able to grasp the new scientific approach of the Neogrammarians. However, as we shall see in Chapter 10, it was Schuchardt who ultimately had the last laugh.

The Neogrammarian Hypothesis was warmly received because it seemed to many linguists to be a more rigorous and scientific approach than had previously been practised. For the Neogrammarians, the earlier linguists had pursued little more than butterfly-collecting, noting some changes here but some exceptions there, and taking no interest in explaining the exceptions. In the new doctrine, real exceptions could not exist. There could only be *apparent* exceptions, and the job of historical linguists was to find the explanations for those apparent exceptions, explanations which simply *had* to exist.

The new doctrine proved to be valuable, for an obvious reason. If you don't believe that problematic data need an explanation, then you're not going to look for one, and hence you're not likely to find an explanation even if one exists. If, however, you are convinced that there must be an explanation, then looking for it becomes a high priority, and, if there really is one, there is an excellent chance that you will find it. Like Verner before them, the Neogrammarians were often successful in finding explanations for troublesome data, and these successes reinforced their belief that they must be right. Exceptional data for which no explanation could be found were explicitly recognized as problems requiring further work, an approach which is in fact typical of scientific work in all disciplines. (For example, all existing theories of gravity utterly fail to account for the orbit of Neptune, but no astrophysicist is prepared to abandon our highly successful theories of gravity merely because of that planet's peculiar orbit: Neptune is merely seen as a problem requiring further work, a problem which will doubtless be solved one day.)

Today most historical linguists probably still take the Neogrammarian approach as their everyday working method, as the approach which is to be preferred unless they can find good reason to look at things differently. Nevertheless, as we shall see in Chapter 10, the Neogrammarian Hypothesis has run into some surprising difficulties from an unexpected direction.

8.5   *Semantic reconstruction*

Once we have established the systematic phonological correspondences linking the members of a family, on the basis of words with very similar meanings in all or most of the daughters, we are invariably faced with a residue of further words which, on the basis of their phonological forms, would appear to be cognates, but which have different meanings in the various daughters. A few of these may be chance resemblances, not cognate at all, but others will be true cognates which have undergone significant shifts in meaning. As we saw in Chapter 2, change in meaning is far from rare. Even if an ancestral word survives for millennia in several daughter languages, there is no guarantee that it won't change its meaning in some or all of those daughters, perhaps radically. Such shifts can make genuine cognates very difficult to detect. Our first problem, therefore, is to try to decide if the words are cognate.

A simple case is English *chin*, which, by the ordinary systematic correspondences, ought to be cognate with Latin *gena* 'cheek', Greek *genus* 'lower jaw', and Old Irish *gin* 'mouth', none of which means 'chin'. However, as I mentioned in Chapter 2, names of face-parts are notorious in the world's languages for changing their meanings, and hence scholars are satisfied that all of these words genuinely are cognate: this degree of semantic shift is familiar and permissible. In this case, our best guess is that the original meaning of the PIE word was 'jaw, chin'.

Much nastier is the case of English *clean* and German *klein*. English and German are fairly closely related, and, by the usual correspondences, these words ought to be cognate – and yet the German word means 'small'. Is it really possible that two such dissimilar meanings could arise from a single source? Could we just be looking at two unrelated words whose resemblance is the result of chance? As it happens, we have abundant textual evidence for earlier German, and the earliest attested sense of the German word is 'bright, shining'. With some assistance from the texts, therefore, scholars have concluded that the German word has undergone an extraordinary sequence of semantic shifts, roughly 'shining' > 'clean' > 'fine' > 'delicate' > 'small'. Everyone is therefore satisfied that the words really are cognate – but, if there had been no textual evidence to consult, possibly very few linguists would have been happy to accept such a seemingly bizarre shift in meaning, and we would remain uncertain whether the two words were actually cognate at all.

In the majority of cases, we have no texts to consult, and so it becomes an issue to decide how much leeway in meaning we can allow before we are forced to conclude that the words we are looking at, however persuasive the phonological match might be, are most likely not related at all. As I pointed out in Chapter 2, the search for universals of semantic change has not so far yielded many reliable principles, and so, in practice, we are forced to rely largely on experience. If certain types of semantic change are well attested in a number of languages, we may feel fairly confident about positing similar changes in other languages. But, if we seem to require a semantic shift not otherwise recorded, then, unless we have some pretty impressive supporting evidence from somewhere, we are probably wise to be suspicious, or at least to reserve judgement.

Even when we are quite certain that words are cognate, it may be a tricky problem to reconstruct the original meaning. PIE *agro-* is the source of Sanskrit *ajrás* 'uncultivated field, pasturage', of Greek *agrós* and Latin *ager* '(cultivated or uncultivated) field', and of Gothic *akrs* and its Germanic cognates 'cultivated field' (English *acre* is cognate). These senses conflict: did the word originally mean 'cultivated field' or 'uncultivated field' or perhaps something else?

Some significant evidence comes from derivatives of the word. Latin *agrārius* 'agrarian' is not much help. But Latin *agrestis* 'wild', Greek *agrios* and *agroteros*, both 'wild', and Greek *agraulós* 'spending the night in the open' all rather point to the conclusion that *agro-* might once have denoted specifically 'uncultivated land'. Moreover, Latin *peregrinus* 'foreign', literally 'beyond the *ager*', appears to imply that Latin *ager* had once meant something like 'known land around a settlement'. This weight of evidence suggests that 'uncultivated land' was probably the earliest sense of the word, and that 'cultivated field' was a later innovation.

Confirmation comes from the observation that *agro-* itself appears to be a derivative of PIE *ag-* 'drive (animals)': no doubt the *agro-* was the (uncultivated) land to which animals were driven for pasturage.

This example illustrates the necessity of considering words, not in isolation, but together with other words which are morphologically related. A further valuable practice is to consider together words which are related, not morphologically, but semantically.

We have seen that historical linguists have often been very successful in reconstructing sizeable vocabularies for their proto-languages. But no language has a vocabulary which is just a miscellaneous collection of individual words. Instead, certain areas (at least) of the vocabulary of any language are *structured*: that is, words within a certain area of meaning are related in important ways. For example, pronouns, numerals, and kinship terms typically show a good deal of organization, and the same may be true of colour terms, cooking terms, names of plants and animals, verbs of motion, and many other areas. Such a potentially structured part of the lexicon may be called a **lexical domain** or a **semantic domain**. A good description of a modern language will usually devote some attention to these domains, and historical linguists may also be interested in reconstructing such structured domains within their proto-languages.

Unfortunately, work in this area is largely still in its infancy, with the partial exception of Proto-Indo-European. Let us briefly consider some examples.

It is easy to reconstruct PIE *owi-* 'sheep'. This shows (apparently) that PIE-speakers were acquainted with sheep. But does it follow that they practised sheep-herding on a significant scale? We can examine this question by looking for other words in the same domain. We find that we can also reconstruct PIE words for 'lamb' and for 'wool', which is very encouraging. Moreover, there are good PIE reconstructions for 'goat' and 'he-goat', confirming that small cattle were a prominent feature in the life of the PIE-speakers. On top of that, the PIE root *peku-*, in all the languages in which its descendants appear, denotes 'sheep and goats' (at least). We may therefore be confident, on the basis of this network of related words, that PIE was spoken by people for whom sheep and goats were an important part of the economy.

More interesting is the case of the Indo-European (IE) numerals. PIE numerals for 'one' to 'ten' can be confidently reconstructed, and their reflexes appear in all IE languages. After 'ten', though, things get complicated: we find a variety of systems and formations in the daughter languages, involving addition, subtraction, and multiplication, and we find counting in both tens and twenties. For example, Germanic and Baltic render '11' and '12' as 'one left' and 'two left' (Old English *endleofan* and *twelf*), while Latin and Greek have 'one-ten' and 'two-ten'. The numerals '18' and '19' are 'eight-ten' and 'nine-ten' in Germanic, but 'two from 20' and 'one from 20' in Latin. For '20', Germanic has 'twice ten', while Latin, Greek, and Sanskrit all have the curious formation 'in-half ten'.

Earlier generations of European linguists, all of them speakers of IE languages, tended to assume without discussion that such a fine, upstanding proto-language as PIE, the speech of those splendid folk who carried their language into a huge area of the globe, must naturally have been equipped with a full set of numerals up to '100', at least, and therefore tried stoutly to reconstruct a PIE numeral system of this size, invoking in the process any number of 'replacements' and 'analogical formations' to account for the wide discrepancies in the formation of the attested numerals. More recently, however, some specialists have begun to question this assumption, and to put forward the awful suggestion that the speakers of PIE *could not count beyond ten*. Their idea is that the numbers beyond 'ten' were created independently in the various daughter languages after they had diverged from the ancestral tongue.

This makes a good deal of sense, and there is support for it. Most notably, the PIE word **kmtóm*, found in all daughters and meaning '100', did not necessarily have that precise sense in PIE. In Homeric Greek, the word seems to have meant simply 'a large number', while in Germanic it often means '120' or '112', as in the British *hundredweight* '112 pounds'. It therefore appears too rash to assume without discussion that PIE had numerals all the way up to 100 and even beyond.

There is a moral here: even if a feature is found in all the daughter languages, we cannot presume it must necessarily have been present in the ancestral language, unless no other reasonable explanation is available.

8.6 *The use of typology and universals*

Linguists have long been interested in **typology** (the classification of languages into structural types) and **universals** (statements which are true of all languages), but, as I pointed out in Chapter 6, it is chiefly since the pioneering work of Joseph Greenberg in the 1960s that these topics have often been seen as central concerns – and historical linguistics has not been immune.

The natural sciences have a *principle of uniformity*, which may be informally stated as follows: the same natural laws apply everywhere, all the time, whether we're looking or not. Historical linguistics has its own version of this: prehistoric languages were not different from modern languages. Human languages have been spoken, we believe, for at least many tens of thousands of years, and so the few thousands of years into the past that we can reach with our historical methods cannot take us appreciably closer to the remote origins of language. Consequently, we should not find ourselves reconstructing proto-languages that have properties different from anything we can see in modern languages.

This principle is not infrequently invoked in evaluating proposed reconstructions. A simple example is provided by the reconstructed vowel system of PIE. It seems quite clear to specialists that /e/ and /o/ alternated in PIE roots for purely grammatical reasons, as reflected in such cases as Greek *legō* 'say' and *logos* 'word', or in Latin *tegō* 'cover' and *toga* 'covering'. Further, the vowels /i/ and /u/ seem to occur only as positional variants of the glide consonants *y (= [j]) and *w. Finally, /a/ does not seem to occur at all except as a conditioned variant of /e/ in certain circumstances (see Chapter 9). Consequently, a number of linguists have reached the conclusion that PIE had only a single vowel, commonly represented as *e, with all other vowels deriving from *e, *y, or *w. But no language is known that has only a single vowel, and this reconstruction is therefore suspect. The smallest number of vowels that we ordinarily find is three, usually /i u a/, though the North Caucasian language Kabardian is sometimes described as having only two (this is controversial). Hence many specialists would prefer to posit for PIE a more normal vowel system, with at least three vowels and possibly four or five. The thinking is that, no matter how clever we might be in deriving all the later vowels from just one vowel, a one-vowel language is not reasonable: it conflicts with everything we know about attested languages.

Here is a morphological example. The linguist James Anderson, in attempting to make sense of the so far undeciphered inscriptions written in the ancient Iberian language of Spain, has posited an extraordinary process of sequential metatheses as operating regularly in that language, so that, for example, an underlying sequence *t + be + din* is successively metathesized from *tbedin* to *tebdin* to *tebidn* to *tebind*, in order to produce a phonologically acceptable result (J. Anderson 1973: 76–8). This may be ingenious, but no known language exhibits such sequential metatheses, and hence few linguists would consider this a plausible interpretation.

On the syntactic side, the American linguist Winfred Lehmann has noted, in a series of publications, that the earliest IE languages display a number of characteristics typical of SOV languages; many of his observations were made a century ago by Berthold Delbrück: verb-final sentences are frequent; there are postpositions instead of prepositions; modifiers usually precede nouns;

subordinate clauses often precede main clauses; there is an extensive case-system. Lehmann therefore proposes, on typological grounds, that PIE must have been an SOV language. He supports his case with further observations. For example, even though all the daughter languages have relative pronouns, they use different items for this purpose, and no relative pronoun can be securely reconstructed for PIE (absence of relative pronouns is another typical SOV characteristic).

The point of Lehmann's case, following Greenberg's observations, is that it is hardly normal for a VO language to have all these characteristics, and hence PIE must have been SOV in order to maintain typological harmony. Lehmann's conclusions are controversial, but his case is substantial, and he has succeeded in persuading a number of other specialists that PIE was indeed a typical SOV language. Since the great majority of modern IE languages are SVO or VSO, it follows that they have undergone a change of word order.

But undoubtedly the most famous and controversial instance of a typological criticism of a reconstructed is that involving the PIE plosive system. Since the early nineteenth century, specialists have generally agreed that PIE had at least the following plosives:

$$
\begin{array}{llll}
p & t & k & k^w \\
b & d & g & g^w \\
bh & dh & gh & gh^w
\end{array}
$$

(Some would add a fifth, palatal, order $/k^j\ g^j\ gh^j/$, but this is irrelevant here.) This reconstruction is very successful at accounting for the phonologies of the daughter languages. In particular, the /p/ series and the /b/ series appear to survive unchanged in most branches of Indo-European, apart from Germanic, Armenian, and Tocharian, which are assumed to have undergone changes, while the /bh/ series appears to survive unchanged in Sanskrit and to have undergone understandable changes elsewhere. So, for example, PIE *ped- 'foot' yields *ped-* in Latin, *pod-* in Greek, and *pad-* in Sanskrit; PIE *dekm 'ten' yields Latin *decem*, Greek *deka*, and Sanskrit *dáśa* (with palatalization of *k); and PIE *bher- 'carry, bear' yields Latin *fer-*, Greek *pher-*, and Sanskrit *bhar-*.

Many years ago, however, the great Russian linguist Roman Jakobson pointed out that this reconstructed system is typologically aberrant, in that it has a 'voiced aspirated' series $/bh\ dh\ gh\ gh^w/$ but no voiceless aspirated series $/ph\ th\ kh\ kh^w/$. No attested language has ever been found with such a system. Many languages have no aspirated plosives; some have only voiceless aspirates; others (like Sanskrit) have both voiceless and voiced aspirates. But no known language has voiced aspirates but no voiceless ones. Indeed, typologists have often proposed a phonological universal: if a language has voiced aspirates, it has voiceless aspirates. And the reconstructed PIE system violates this universal. So we have a problem.

One way out is to argue that PIE also had a fourth, voiceless aspirated, series $/ph\ th\ kh\ kh^w/$, and a number of linguists have attempted to find evidence for such an additional series of plosives. On the whole, though, such evidence is sparse and unconvincing, and most specialists are not persuaded by it.

Accordingly, a number of linguists have in recent years adopted a more robust line: they argue that the traditional reconstruction is wrong and should be replaced by a typologically more reasonable system. Most such proposals suggest the same solution, one which has become known as the **glottalic theory** of PIE. The glottalic theory of PIE was first suggested by the French linguist André Martinet as early as 1953, but it attracted no attention at the time. Then, in 1973, the American Paul Hopper, and, independently, the Georgian Thomas Gamkrelidze and the Russian Vjačeslav Ivanov put forward a more fully developed version of the idea. All of them begin with an interesting observation: in PIE, the segment commonly reconstructed as *b was extremely rare, perhaps even non-existent – a very odd state of affairs for a voiced labial plosive. They then ask this question: in what series of plosives is a labial member often missing?

The answer they suggest is a *glottalic* (that is, an ejective) series. Very many languages have a series of ejective consonants, which are pronounced with a simultaneous glottal stop and the larynx moving up like a piston to expel air from the mouth with an audible pop when the closure is released. Such plosives are notated [p' t' k' q'], and so on, in the IPA. And what is interesting is that ejectives are most frequent in the back of the mouth; they are less frequent towards the front, and some languages with ejective consonants lack a labial ejective altogether. This makes some phonetic sense, since it appears to require greater articulatory effort to produce an ejective at the front of the mouth.

The proposal, then, is that the PIE series traditionally reconstructed as voiced plosives /b d g g^w/ was actually an ejective series /p' t' k' $k^{w'}$/, which would at once explain why the segment /p'/ (the traditional /b/) was rare or absent. Of course, this proposal by itself does not solve the typological problem, since the voiced aspirated series is still there. But Hopper and Gamkrelidze and Ivanov go on further to reinterpret the former /p t k k^w/ series as a voiceless aspirated series /ph th kh kh^w/. Their resulting system now looks like this:

$$\begin{array}{llll} ph & th & kh & kh^w \\ bh & dh & gh & gh^w \\ p' & t' & k' & k^{w'} \end{array}$$

And this series is typologically natural.

This new analysis has certain additional advantages. For example, it is well known that PIE roots did not permit two occurrences of the /b/ series, and hence roots like *bed- were impossible. This makes little sense in the traditional reconstruction, since such sequences are perfectly normal in thousands of languages. But, in the new system, the impossible roots are reinterpreted as having the form *$p'et'$-, with two consecutive ejectives – and it is a fact that languages with ejective consonants, such as the Caucasian languages, do not permit such sequences of ejective consonants, for sound phonetic reasons: it is difficult to move the larynx up and down rapidly enough to produce ejectives one after another.

The glottalic theory of PIE has accordingly won a measure of support among specialists, since it simultaneously solves the typological problem and provides explanations for certain other puzzling facts. If it wins the day, it will be a paradigm case of the application of typological reasoning to a historical problem. But the theory is not without its critics, who argue that the supposed advantages are more apparent than real, and point out that it requires all the daughter languages *except* Germanic and Armenian to have undergone substantial phonological change. At present the glottalic theory is supported by perhaps no more than a sizeable minority of Indo-Europeanists. Only time will tell what the outcome will be.

Finally, lest you should get the impression that arguments from typology and universals must always be decisive, let's look at one more case. Michelena (1977) is a magisterial reconstruction of the phonology of an ancestral stage of Basque dating to around 2000 years ago. This reconstruction has been enormously successful, but it has one curious feature: it posits that pre-Basque entirely lacked a consonant /m/. In modern Basque, /m/ is very frequent indeed, though it mostly occurs in loan words and in phonaesthetic formations. For the small number of clearly ancient native words containing /m/ today, Michelena posits a source either from */b/ (as in *mihi* 'tongue' < *bini* and *mehe* 'thin' < *bene*) or from a cluster */nb/ (as in *seme* 'son' < *senbe*).

Several non-specialists in Basque have attacked this reconstruction on the universalist ground that languages without /m/ are virtually unheard-of. This may appear a worrying argument, but consider some facts:

- Most (possibly all) of the native words with /m/ today either contain, or formerly contained, an /n/ in the following syllable (like *mihi* and *mehe*), and so we can invoke a nasal assimilation of */b/, a process which is abundantly attested in loan words.
- In the dialects of Basque retaining the ancient aspiration /h/, that /h/ can readily follow *any* liquid or nasal *except* /m/: *senhar* 'husband', *alhaba* 'daughter', *erhi* 'finger', *urrhe* 'gold', and so on – but */mh/ is absolutely unattested, just as is */bh/.
- Virtually every ancient Basque consonant makes an appearance somewhere in the rich inflectional morphology of the language, and /n/ in particular is very frequent indeed – but /m/ is absolutely lacking in the inflectional morphology.
- Basque is very rich in word-forming suffixes, and almost all other consonants occur in some of these suffixes, but, with the single exception of the abstract-noun-forming suffix *-mendu*, borrowed from Latin *-mentu*, /m/ is totally absent from these suffixes.
- In grammatical words like pronouns, conjunctions, determiners, quantifiers, and postpositions, /m/ is absolutely lacking.

In this case, then, the evidence for the correctness of Michelena's reconstruction is overwhelming: pre-Basque had no /m/. We must therefore accept this conclusion, now matter how strange it may seem from a cross-linguistic point of view. This time the evidence is too substantial and monolithic to be overridden by universalist considerations.

In fact, the absence of /m/ may not be so unusual as the critics suggest. In the famous UPSID sample of the world's languages reported in Maddieson (1984), fully 5 per cent of languages either lack /m/ altogether or have it only very marginally. But, even if pre-Basque were the first language ever discovered without an /m/, we would still have to respect the internal evidence from Basque. Typological and universalist arguments cannot be taken as absolutely decisive.

8.7   *Reconstructing grammar*

Historical linguists have often enjoyed great success in reconstructing ancestral phonological systems and vocabularies. Naturally, we would also like to be able to reconstruct as much as possible of ancestral grammatical systems. How feasible is this goal?

With morphology, it is often highly feasible. Like a lexical item, a bound morpheme typically has a fixed phonological shape, it typically remains a part of the language from one generation to the next, and it undergoes the ordinary processes of phonological change. However, as we saw in Chapters 5 and 6, morphological patterns may often be severely disturbed by such processes as analogy, grammaticalization, renewal, and typological shift. The several daughters of an ancestral language may therefore diverge much more dramatically in their morphology than they do in their phonology, or even in their lexicons. Consequently, it is not very often that a group of daughter languages will exhibit morphological systems which are virtually identical apart from the effects of phonological change. Still, linguists have, in many cases, succeeded in reconstructing substantial portions of the morphology of a proto-language.

Consider the nominal morphology of PIE. All of the oldest IE languages have three grammatical genders, masculine, feminine, and neuter, and so we may reasonably assume that PIE had the same. All of these same daughters exhibit a large number of noun classes, with each class taking a somewhat different set of grammatical endings, and we may confidently project the same property back to PIE, even though the daughters do not always agree as to how many classes they have or which nouns belong to which classes. All IE languages distinguish singular and plural, and the oldest languages show at least traces of a dual, so that we may suppose that PIE distinguished all three numbers. All the oldest daughters exhibit extensive case-systems for nouns, and therefore so, in all likelihood, did PIE.

But the daughters do not distinguish the same number of cases: Greek has four cases, with fragmentary or archaic traces of two more; Latin has five, with a sixth case distinguished for only one class of nouns and fragmentary traces of a seventh; Gothic has five, but not quite the same five as Latin; Sanskrit has no fewer than seven. We might therefore surmise that PIE had seven or more cases, with some of them being lost in each of the daughter languages, but we must not be rash about this: it is always possible that (say) Sanskrit has acquired some new cases not present in PIE.

As it happens, many of the case-endings in the oldest IE languages are similar enough in form to show that they are cognate and have therefore been directly inherited from PIE. Table 8.18 illustrates these endings for the noun meaning 'foot' in Greek, Latin, and Sanskrit, and a possible PIE reconstruction. Scholars do not agree about all the details, and here I follow Lehmann (1993: 145) in most respects. Latin and Greek forms which are not inherited from PIE are excluded; bracketed forms are marginal or archaic. You will see that Sanskrit appears to be by far the most conservative language in its nominal morphology, though note the effect of the categorical pre-Sanskrit change $*e > a$. In spite of the complications, then, it is often possible to reconstruct prehistoric morphological systems in some detail.

There is one further point that needs to be stressed. In reconstructing morphology, some of the most valuable evidence of all, when we can find it, consists of **shared anomalies** – unusual morphological idiosyncrasies common to two or more languages. These, when they turn up, constitute very powerful evidence that the languages are related and that the anomalies must have been inherited from the parent language.

Table 8.18 The inflection of PIE *$p\bar{e}s$* 'foot'

	PIE	Sanskrit	Greek	Latin
Singular				
Nominative	*$p\bar{e}s$	pāt	poús	pēs
Accusative	*pédm	pādam	póda	pedem
Instrumental	*pedé	padā		
Dative	*pedéy	padé	[podí]	pedi
Ablative	*pedés	padás		
Genitive	*pedés	padás	podós	pedis
Locative	*pedí	padí		[pede]
Plural				
Nominative	*pédes	pādas	pódes	pedēs
Accusative	*pédns	padás	pódas	pedēs
Instrumental	*pedbhís	padbhís	[po-pi]	
Dative	*pedbh(y)ós	padbhyás		pedibus
Ablative	*pedbh(y)ós	padbhyás		pedibus
Genitive	*pedōm	padām	podôn	pedum
Locative	*petsú	patsú	[posí]	

Consider English and German, two Germanic languages known to be fairly closely related. These share a significant amount of their regular morphology: English *deep/deeper/deepest*, German *tief/tiefer/tiefste*; English *love/loved/ loved*, German *lieben/liebte/geliebt*. This, of course, is already good evidence for a genetic link (recall the case of Yurok, Wiyot, and Proto-Algonquian discussed above). But English and German also share a number of morphological anomalies: English *good/better/best*, German *gut/besser/beste*; English *sing/sang/sung*, German *singen/sang/gesungen*. It is almost unimaginable that such shared peculiarities could result from anything other than common inheritance – in this case, from Proto-Germanic. Therefore, not only do such forms confirm the relationship between English and German, but they also tell us something about the morphology of Proto-Germanic.

Something similar can be observed with the earliest attested Indo-European languages. Latin, Sanskrit, and Hittite all exhibit a class of nouns with rather peculiar behaviour, the so-called *heteroclitic nouns*. Such nouns present a highly unusual alternation in their inflection between stems in *-r* and stems in *-n*: Latin *iecur* 'liver', genitive *iecinoris*; Sanskrit *ūdhar* 'udder', genitive *ūdhnas*; Hittite *watar* 'water', genitive *wetenas*; Latin *iter* 'road', genitive *itineris*; Sanskrit *ásrg* 'blood', genitive *asnás*. Such stem-alternations are out of line with the more usual morphology of these languages, and it cannot be reasonably doubted that this odd pattern has been inherited in every case from the ancestral language, PIE. Already in Latin and Sanskrit the heteroclitic inflectional pattern is rare and unproductive; it is clearly no more than a fossilized residue of some ancient state of affairs. In Hittite, though, heteroclitic nouns are numerous, and it seems that the pattern was still highly productive in that language. We may, therefore, surmise that the heteroclitic declension was an important feature of PIE, or perhaps even of some ancestor of PIE, and that it had been steadily losing ground to other, more familiar, types of inflection during the period when PIE was breaking up into its several daughter languages.

Morphology, then, can often be reconstructed in some detail, and comparative work on morphology may shed considerable light on the nature of the proto-language we are working on. With syntax, however, things are far more difficult. Indeed, more than a few linguists would maintain that the reconstruction of syntax is impossible in principle. Consider, for example, the word order of PIE. Among the attested languages, we find VSO order in Celtic, SOV order in Indo-Iranian, and SVO order in most of the other languages (though Germanic is rather complicated). But does this information allow us to reconstruct a basic word order for PIE? Probably not, in fact surely not. The problem is that syntactic structures do not have quite the same kind of individual existence as lexical items or even grammatical morphemes. A lexical item may persist as a recognizable entity over many generations; for example, PIE **new-* still survives in English today as *new*, some 6000 years later. But syntactic patterns like word order do not behave like this: an ancient SOV order (say) does not develop gradually and continuously into an SVO order; instead, a large number of individual smaller changes in grammar are responsible for the cumulative effect of a word-order change (recall the Chinese case from Chapter 6).

On the other hand, we saw above that Winfred Lehmann, by concentrating on a large number of smaller grammatical details, has been able to construct at least a substantial case that PIE must have been an SOV language. Perhaps, therefore, it is going too far to claim that no syntactic reconstruction can ever be done at all, but it does appear that syntax must always be a less fertile field for reconstruction than phonology or lexicon, or even morphology.

8.8 *The reality of proto-languages*

It is accepted by everyone that genetically related languages must have had real ancestors, real languages spoken by real people. Comparative reconstruction allows us to recover substantial information about such long-vanished ancestral languages. Naturally, we can't hope to recover a proto-language down to the last detail. There must always be aspects of an ancestral language which have disappeared without trace in every recorded daughter, or which have undergone such complex developments that untangling them is beyond our powers. Nevertheless, in favourable cases like Proto-Algonquian, Proto-Romance, or even Proto-Indo-European, we are confident that our substantial reconstructions of phonology, lexicon, morphology, and even syntax represent a very good approximation to the ancient linguistic facts. But are we right to be so confident? Is it really possible to recover the speech of people long dead?

Consider a simple case like the reconstructed PIE word *kmtóm '100'. With no more than minor disagreements over small details, everyone accepts this reconstruction as valid. But what exactly does it represent?

Broadly speaking, there have been two kinds of answer proposed. A minority of linguists would take a very conservative, even pessimistic, view of such a reconstruction. They argue that this *kmtóm is nothing more than a piece of algebra, a kind of notational shorthand which summarizes in a convenient manner the correspondences we find among real language data like Latin *centum*, Greek *(he)katón*, Sanskrit *śatá*, Gothic *hunda*, and so on. In this view, we have no right to presume that *kmtóm represents any kind of phonetic reality, because ancient phonetic reality is unrecoverable. This sceptical view gains added force when we find, as we shall in the next chapter, that advances in the reconstruction of PIE have led to the (very successful!) reconstruction of PIE forms such as $*g^w rHtó$-, $*plHnó$-, and $*bhwHtó$-, which scarcely look like pronounceable words in a natural language.

The majority of historical linguists reject this gloomy point of view. They consider that such reconstructions, being based on real language data and on an understanding of real language changes, can be trusted in most respects.

These linguists are happy to believe that the speakers of PIE really did pronounce their word for '100' (or whatever it meant!) with a voiceless velar plosive, a syllabic bilabial nasal, and so on. Naturally, it is the proponents of this second view who are most inclined to attach importance to typological arguments and to linguistic universals. If you believe that the phonemes reconstructed for a proto-language are nothing but empty algebraic symbols, you are hardly likely to care what symbols those are, or to bother your head about whether the resulting system looks phonologically plausible. But, if you sincerely believe you are reconstructing something very close to an ancient phonetic reality, you are not going to be happy with a reconstructed system that looks like nothing ever encountered in a natural language.

On the whole, then, it would seem best, if only as a methodological principle, to cling to the second view. After all, it hardly seems likely that our successful reconstructions can be *totally* devoid of linguistic reality, and therefore it is surely better to attach some weight to arguments from typology and universals. In historical linguistics, as in any discipline, it is usually unwise to reject any possible evidence from any possible source. We do not have to believe that our reconstructions are perfect, down to the last phonetic detail, in order to believe that we have been substantially successful in reconstructing a vanished linguistic reality.

There is a further point to be considered. Our reconstructed proto-languages often come out looking very homogeneous. But we know that real languages are not like that. A real language always exhibits some degree of regional variation (it is spoken differently in different places) and also social variation (different people speak it differently even in the same place, and the same person speaks it differently on different occasions). In so far as our reconstructions fail to reveal such variation, then, we can be sure that they are, to some extent, oversimplifications of languages that were surely messier than our reconstructions make them appear.

Further reading

There is an abundant literature on the comparative method. Classic presentations include Bloomfield (1933: ch. 18), Hoenigswald (1950) (very brief), Hoenigswald (1960) (book-length), Thieme (1964), and Hoenigswald (1973). Recent brief introductions include Baldi (1991b) and the articles in Bright (1992) and Asher (1994). All other textbooks of historical linguistics devote some attention to the comparative method; particularly noteworthy is Anttila (1988), whose chapter on the topic is exceptionally detailed and highly recommended. Also highly recommended is Fox (1995), a book-length treatment of reconstruction and related issues. Among the many examples of the successful application of the comparative method, I would particularly draw attention to Bloomfield (1925, 1946) on Proto-Algonquian and Hall (1950, 1976) on Proto-Romance. A number of readable comparative studies can be found in Baldi (1990), some of them reprinted in Baldi (1991a). Campbell and Mithun (1979) contains a good deal of work on native American languages.

For a historical account of the development of the comparative method and of the Neogrammarian Hypothesis, see the article on historical linguistics in Asher (1994), which is brief, or Pedersen (1931), especially ch. 7. Vennemann and Wilbur (1972) examines the confrontation between Schuchardt and the Neogrammarians.

Benveniste (1954) is an illuminating study of semantic reconstruction, while chapter 12 of Harris and Campbell (1995) is a textbook examination of syntactic reconstruction.

Exercises

Exercise 8.1

Generally speaking, a finite Basque verb agrees in person and number with its subject, without exception. It may also agree with its direct object in person and number; there is, however, no overt agreement marker for a third-singular object:

> *Neska ikusi dut*   *Neskak ikusi ditut*
> girl-the saw Aux-I   girls-the saw Aux-them-I
> 'I saw the girl.'   'I saw the girls.'

When, as here, the direct object is definite, object agreement is obligatory in all dialects and has been so since our earliest texts. But, when the object is indefinite, there are two possibilities: agreement or no agreement:

> *Neska bat ikusi dut*
> girl a saw Aux-I
> 'I saw a girl.'

> *Neska batzuk ikusi dut*   *Neska batzuk ikusi ditut*
> girl some saw Aux-I   girl some saw Aux-them-I
> 'I saw some girls.'   'I saw some girls.'

The distribution of these last two forms is as follows. In the eastern dialects, absence of agreement is usually obligatory. In the central dialects, agreement is obligatory. In the westernmost (Bizkaian) dialect, agreement is obligatory today but was optional in the earliest texts in that dialect.

Explain what has been happening to object agreement in Basque, and describe the earliest reconstructible state of affairs. Comment on the geographical distribution of the two patterns.

Exercise 8.2

A number of Indo-European languages have a demonstrative pronoun meaning 'that' which is inflected in a similar, but decidedly irregular, manner in all of them (the Old English item is the source of modern *that* and *the*, and the Greek word too means 'the'). The similarities are great enough for linguists to have managed to reconstruct the paradigm of the PIE demonstrative. Table 8.19 lists the forms in several languages; bracketed forms are innovations not directly inherited from PIE. The languages are S(an)k(ri)t, Greek, Lith(uanian), Go(thic), and O(ld) E(nglish). (Data from Anttila 1988: 358.)

The reconstructed PIE forms are unusual in several respects. First, the *s-/t-* alternation in the stem is unique. Second, the nominative singular masculine lacks the usual PIE case-ending *$*-s$*. Third, the *-sm-* formative in the dative is unparallelled.

Now, propose answers to the following questions. In the nominative singular masculine:

(a) How did Sanskrit acquire the form *sás*?
(b) How did Old English acquire the form *þe*?
(c) How did Lithuanian acquire the form *tàs*?

Otherwise:

(d) How did some dialects of Greek acquire the nominative plural masculine form *hoi*?
(e) Where might you look for a source for the final *-a* in the Gothic accusative singular forms, and for the remaining innovations in Greek and Lithuanian?

Exercise 8.3

The word-forms in Table 8.20, taken from four Turkic languages, illustrate a number of monosyllabic nouns and numerals with inflectional and derivational suffixes. So far as is possible with these very scanty data, propose a reconstructed Proto-Turkic form for each of the sixteen items, and describe the changes which have occurred in each language. Point out and discuss any

Table 8.19

	PIE	Skt	Greek	Lith	Go	OE
NomSgMasc	*so	sá[s]	ho	[tàs]	sa	sē [þe]
AccSgMasc	*tom	tám	tón	tā	þan[a]	þone
GenSgMasc	*tosyo	tásya	toîo	[tõ]	þis	þæs
DatSgMasc	*tosmōi	tásmāi	[tôi]	tamui	þamma	þæm
NomAccSgNeut	*tod	tád	tó	ta[ī]	þat[a]	þæt
NomPlMasc	*toi	té	toí, [hoi]	tie	þai	þā

difficulties. Here <š č j> = IPA [ʃ tʃ dʒ], <y> = IPA [j], and <ü ö ɪ> IPA [y œ ɯ]. (Data from Hahn 1991.)

Exercise 8.4

Tabla and Sentani are two closely related Papuan languages of New Guinea. Consider the cognates listed in Table 8.21, identify the systematic correspondences, and reconstruct forms for Proto-Tabla-Sentani. Comment on your decisions and on any difficulties. Material in parentheses is not cognate. (Data from Gregerson and Hartzler 1987.)

Table 8.20

	Qazaq	Uzbek	Uyghur	Turkish
'my way'	*jolɪm*	*yolim*	*yolum*	*yolum*
'my lake'	*kölɪm*	*kolim*	*kölüm*	*gölüm*
'salty'	*tuzdɪ*	*tuzli*	*tuzluq*	*tuzlu*
'dairy'	*sütti*	*sutli*	*sütlük*	*sütlü*
'our way'	*jolɪmɪz*	*yolimiz*	*yolumiz*	*yolumuz*
'our lake'	*kölimiz*	*kolimiz*	*kölümiz*	*gölümüz*
'tenth'	*onɪnšɪ*	*oninči*	*ʔonunči*	*onunju*
'third'	*üšinši*	*učinči*	*ʔüčünči*	*üčünjü*
'the way's'	*joldɪ*	*yolni*	*yolni*	*yolun*
'the lake's'	*köldi*	*kolni*	*kölni*	*gölün*
'salt-free'	*tuzsɪz*	*tuzsiz*	*tuzsiz*	*tuzsuz*
'milk-free'	*sütsiz*	*sutsiz*	*sütsiz*	*sütsüz*
'its way'	*jolɪ*	*yoli*	*yoli*	*yolu*
'its lake'	*köli*	*koli*	*köli*	*gölü*
'the salt' (Acc)	*tuzdɪ*	*tuzni*	*tuzni*	*tuzu*
'the milk' (Acc)	*sütti*	*sutni*	*sütni*	*sütü*

Table 8.21

	Tabla	Sentani
1. 'arrow'	pəra	fəla
2. 'bad'	peko	peɣo
3. 'bedbug'	opi	obi
4. 'bitter'	pet	fær
5. 'blood'	saa	haa
6. 'casuarina'	jaru	jalu
7. 'cheek'	katu	kahu
8. 'coconut'	to	ho
9. 'daughter'	womi	omi
10. 'day'	dai(sjə)	rai
11. 'dead'	tətə	hərə

Table 8.21 Continued

	Tabla	Sentani
12. 'dirty'	niki	niki
13. 'dog'	joku	joɣu
14. 'drum'	waku	waɣu
15. 'eat'	anə-	anə-
16. 'egg'	doŋ	ro
17. 'excrement'	etə	əhə
18. 'fat'	ju	ju
19. 'fence'	erə	ələ
20. 'fish'	ka	ka
21. 'frog'	sika	hikæ
22. 'good'	poi	foi
23. 'hand'	mə	mə
24. 'hole'	buru	pulu
25. 'hut'	parə	falə
26. 'in front of'	bə(tu)	pə
27. 'leg'	oto	oro
28. 'life'	wari	wali
29. 'like' (v.)	kəna	kəna
30. 'louse'	miŋ	mi
31. 'mango'	(e)wei	wæi
32. 'matoa'	emə	əmə
33. 'middle'	noro	nolo
34. 'moon'	oko	oɣo
35. 'nest'	narə	nalə
36. 'path'	nipi	nibi
37. 'penis'	muŋ	mu
38. 'pig'	opo	obo
39. 'pus'	jəmə	jəmə
40. 'raw'	koru	kolu
41. 'road'	nipi	nibi
42. 'rope'	sa	ha
43. 'skirt'	maro	malo
44. 'soil'	kani	kani
45. 'sugar cane'	juŋ	ju
46. 'sun'	su	hu
47. 'tail'	dəmə	ramə
48. 'three'	namiŋ	name
49. 'tongue'	peu	fæu
50. 'tree trunk'	no	no
51. 'two'	be	pe
52. 'very'	təre	hələ
53. 'village'	jo	jo
54. 'vomit'	mike	mikæ
55. 'water'	bu	pu
56. 'west'	wai	wai
57. 'wind'	aru	alu

Exercise 8.5

Table 8.22 lists the forms of a number of Basque words in four dialects: B(izkaian), G(ipuzkoan), L(apurdian), and Z(uberoan). Identify the systematic correspondences, and reconstruct the forms of the words in an earlier stage of Basque. Comment on your decisions and on any difficulties. Note that <s> and <ś> represent laminal and apical sibilants, <ts> and <tś> are the corresponding affricates, <ñ> is a palatal nasal, <ʎ> is a palatal lateral, <r> is an apical trill, <ɾ> is an apical tap, <ʀ> is a voiced uvular fricative, and <ü> is a front rounded vowel.

Table 8.22

	B	G	L	Z
1. 'bird'	tʃoɾi	tʃoɾi	ʃoɾi	ʃoi
2. 'blind'	itsu	itśu	itśu	ütśü
3. 'bowel'	eśte	eśte	heʀtse	hertse
4. 'bring'	ekari	ekari	ekhaʀi	ekhari
5. 'crazy'	śoɾo	soɾo	soɾo	soo
6. 'daughter'	alaba	alaba	alhaba	alhaba
7. 'donkey'	aśto	aśto	aśto	aśto
8. 'eat'	dʒan	xan	ɟan	ʒan
9. 'eight'	śortsi	sortsi	soʀtsi	sortsi
10. 'fire'	śu	śu	śu	śü
11. 'five'	bośt	bośt	boʀts	borts
12. 'flute'	tʃiɾula	tʃiɾula	ʃiɾula	ʃiula
13. 'grapes'	maats	maatś	mahatś	mahatś
14. 'head'	buɾu	buɾu	buɾu	büü
15. 'hen'	oʎo	oʎo	oilo	oʎo
16. 'hit'	dʒo	xo	ɟo	ʒo
17. 'house'	etʃe	etʃe	etʃe	etʃe
18. 'long'	luśe	luse	luse	lüse
19. 'new'	beri	beri	beʀi	beri
20. 'old woman'	atso	atśo	atśo	atśo
21. 'proud'	aro	aro	haʀo	haro
22. 'salt'	gats	gatś	gats	gats
23. 'seeking'	biʎa	biʎa	bilha	bilha
24. 'sir'	dʒaun	xaun	ɟaun	ʒaün
25. 'six'	śei	śei	śei	śei
26. 'sound'	śoñu	śoñu	śoinu	śoñü
27. 'stone'	ari	ari	haʀi	hari
28. 'ten'	amar	amar	hamaʀ	hamar
29. 'than'	baño	baño	baino	baño
30. 'wheat'	gaɾi	gaɾi	gaɾi	gai
31. 'window'	leio	leio	leiho	leiho
32. 'word'	its	its	hits	hits
32. 'yellow'	oɾi	oɾi	hoɾi	hoi
33. 'yesterday'	atso	atso	atso	atso
34. 'you'	śu	su	su	sü

Exercise 8.6

Most of the examples of reconstruction we have seen so far involve isolated lexical items, but linguists are not always so fortunate. Not infrequently, we have to work with highly inflected forms of lexical stems or roots. Tables 8.23–8.25 list three forms of a number of verbs in three Slavic languages. Try to reconstruct a single invariant ancestral (Proto-Slavic) form for each verb stem, and reconstruct as much as you can of the Proto-Slavic morphology. Note that certain verbs in some languages exhibit aspectual prefixes or suffixes in some or all forms; these affixes you will need to identify and to remove from consideration. The diacritic ' marks a palatalized consonant; Czech $\check{r}$ is a palatalized rhotic; Russian $\ddot{e}$ denotes a former *e* which has developed to *o*.

Table 8.23 (Russian)

		Infinitive	1Sg Present	Past (masc.)
1.	'be able'	*moč*	*mogu*	*mog*
2.	'burst'	*pučit'*	*jpuču*	*pučil*
3.	'fall'	*pas't'*	*padnu*	*pal*
4.	'flash'	*m'ignut'*	*m'ignu*	*m'ig*
5.	'flow'	*prat'eč*	*prat'eku*	*pratek*
6.	'help'	*pamoč*	*pamagu*	*pamog*
7.	'lead'	*v'es't'i*	*v'edu*	*v'ël*
8.	'pierce'	*bodnut'*	*bodnu*	*bodnul*
9.	'say'	*atr'ečs'a*	*atr'ekus'*	*atr'eks'a*
10.	'shake'	*tr'as't'i*	*tr'asu*	*tr'as*
11.	'steal'	*kras't'*	*kradu*	*kral*
12.	'tighten'	*t'agat'*	*t'agaju*	*t'agal*

Table 8.24 (Czech)

		Infinitive	1Sg Present	Past (masc.)
1.	'be able'	*motsi*	*mohu*	*mohl*
2.	'burst'	*puknouti*	*puknu*	*pukl*
3.	'fall'	*padnout'i*	*padnu*	*padl*
4.	'flash'	*mihnouti*	*mihnu*	*mihl*
5.	'flow'	*prote:tsi*	*proteku*	*protekl*
6.	'help'	*pomotsi*	*pomohu*	*pomohl*
7.	'lead'	*ve:st'i*	*vedlu*	*vedl*
8.	'pierce'	*bodnout'i*	*bodnu*	*bodl*
9.	'say'	*ři:tsi*	*řeknu*	*řekl*
10.	'shake'	*třa:st'*	*třesu*	*třa:sl*
11.	'steal'	*kra:st'i*	*kradu*	*kradl*
12.	'tighten'	*sta:hnouti*	*sta:hnu*	*sta:hl*

Table 8.25 (Serbo-Croatian)

	Infinitive	1Sg Present	Past (masc.)
1. 'be able'	moči	mogu	mogao
2. 'burst'	jpuči	puknem	pukao
3. 'fall'	pasti	padnem	pao
4. 'flash'	mignuti	mignem	migao
5. 'flow'	proteči	protečem	protekao
6. 'help'	pomoči	pomognem	pomogao
7. 'lead'	povesti	pvedem	poveo
8. 'pierce'	bosti	bodem	bo
9. 'say'	reči	reknem	rekao
10. 'shake'	tresti	tresem	tresao
11. 'steal'	krasti	kradem	krao
12. 'tighten'	steči	stegnem	stegao

9

Internal reconstruction

The comparative method is the most important of the historical methods, but it can be used only when we have identified two or more languages sharing a common ancestor. It cannot be applied to a language with no known relatives, and it may be of minimal use with a language whose only identifiable relatives are very distantly related to it. In such circumstances, we must fall back on a second method, one which requires no data from related languages. This is the **internal method**, which can sometimes be applied to a single language so as to allow us to reconstruct important characteristics of earlier stages of that language; such reconstruction is **internal reconstruction**. In this chapter, we'll look at how internal reconstruction can be done.

9.1 *A first look at the internal method*

The term *internal reconstruction* is in fact applied to several slightly different procedures. In the simplest and most central of these, we proceed as follows:

1. We note that a certain pattern is visible in the language.
2. We note that some forms are exceptions to this pattern.
3. We hypothesize that the exceptional forms originally conformed to the pattern.
4. We posit an ancestral stage of the language with no exceptional forms.
5. We identify the changes that disrupted the original perfectly regular pattern and led to the introduction of exceptional cases.

As always, when carrying out step (5) we attempt to ensure that the changes we are positing are as natural and comprehensible as possible.

Here is a simple example. A certain class of Latin verbs forms its first-singular present by suffixing -*o* to the stem, its infinitive by suffixing -*ere*, its first-singular perfect by suffixing -*si*, and its supine by suffixing -*tum*. (Note that Latin *x* represents [ks] and is equivalent to *cs*.)

(1) *carpo*   *carpere*   *carpsi*   *carptum*   'pluck'
     dico   *dicere*   *dixi*   *dictum*   'say'
     duco   *ducere*   *duxi*   *ductum*   'lead'
     repo   *repere*   *repsi*   *reptum*   'creep'
     scalpo   *scalpere*   *scalpsi*   *scalptum*   'carve'
     serpo   *serpere*   *serpsi*   *serptum*   'crawl'

However, a number of verbs in this class show slightly anomalous behaviour. Here is one group:

(2) *cingo*   *cingere*   *cinxi*   *cinctum*   'gird'
     figo   *figere*   *fixi*   *fictum*   'fix'
     fingo   *fingere*   *finxi*   *finctum*   'form'
     infligo *infligere* *inflixi*   *inflictum* 'strike on'
     iungo   *iungere*   *iunxi*   *iunctum*   'join'
     nubo   *nubere*   *nupsi*   *nuptum*   'marry'
     pingo   *pingere*   *pinxi*   *pictum*   'paint'
     rego   *regere*   *rexi*   *rectum*   'rule'
     scribo   *scribere*   *scripsi*   *scriptum*   'write'
     stringo *stringere* *strinxi*   *strictum*   'strip'
     sugo   *sugere*   *suxi*   *suctum*   'suck'
     tego   *tegere*   *texi*   *tectum*   'cover'
     ungo   *ungere*   *unxi*   *unctum*   'anoint'

On the basis of the stem exhibited in the first two columns, we would have expected **figsi*, **figtum* for 'fix', **nubsi*, **nubtum* for 'marry', and so on throughout the list. Let us therefore posit that these *were* the forms in some ancestral variety of Latin. What changes do we now have to recognize on the way to classical Latin? Easy: a voiced plosive *b* or *g* is devoiced when it is followed by a voiceless consonant like *s* or *t*. This is a perfectly natural phonological change, one of voicing assimilation in clusters. Can we check that our scenario is plausible? Yes, we can. Is it obvious to you what additional evidence we should look for? Think about it a minute.

What we need to do is to look to see if there are any Latin words with clusters like *bs* and *gt*. As it happens, there are none, exactly as our account predicts. All such clusters, wherever they existed, must have undergone voicing assimilation. (There are a few *apparent* exceptions, like *urbs* 'city', but these are purely orthographic: this word was in fact pronounced [urps].)

Note, by the way, that we might in principle have tried the opposite reconstruction. We might have posited that the third and fourth columns represent the ancestral state of affairs, and that verb stems like **cinc-*, **fic-*, and **nup-* might have undergone voicing of plosives in intervocalic position or after a nasal, so that original **cinco*, **fico*, and **nupo*, for example, would have been voiced to the attested *cingo*, *figo*, and *nubo*. Voicing in such positions is also a perfectly natural process, so you might think at first glance that this second account was equally plausible. But it's not. Can you see why? If not, ponder the data for a minute.

If you still haven't spotted it, look again at the *first* set of forms, the ones I described as regular. Observe that forms like *carpo*, *dico*, and *duco* do *not* undergo any intervocalic voicing. So, if we tried to postulate originally voiceless plosives in the second group, we could give a good-looking account of that group, but we would then be unable to explain the first group. Positing original voiced plosives in the second group leads to no such difficulties, and so that is the solution we adopt.

This is a point you must always bear in mind in any historical work, not just in internal reconstruction. If you propose a particular change in order to explain some problematic data, you must then check to see if your proposed change messes up some other data that were not a problem before. Failure to do this will lead you quickly into serious trouble.

So: we reconstruct the verb for 'cover' as the originally entirely regular *tego*, *tegere*, **tegsi*, **tegtum*, by the process of internal reconstruction, and we posit a single phonological change, a voicing assimilation applying to obstruent clusters.

We are not done with this class of Latin verbs, because other verbs in this class exhibit different anomalies. Here are a few; note that *qu* and *gu* represent [kw] and [gw], respectively, while *v* represents [w]:

(3)	*como*	*comere*	*compsi*	*comptum*	'deck'
	demo	*demere*	*dempsi*	*demptum*	'take off'
	promo	*promere*	*prompsi*	*promptum*	'bring out'
	sumo	*sumere*	*sumpsi*	*sumptum*	'take up'
(4)	*coquo*	*coquere*	*coxi*	*coctum*	'cook'
	exstinguo	*exstinguere*	*exstinxi*	*exstinctum*	'extinguish'
(5)	*flecto*	*flectere*	*flexi*	*flectum*	'bend'
	necto	*nectere*	*nexi*	*nectum*	'bind'
(6)	*cedo*	*cedere*	*cessi*	*cessum*	'yield'
	claudo	*claudere*	*clausi*	*clausum*	'close'
	divido	*dividere*	*divisi*	*divisum*	'divide'
	explodo	*explodere*	*explosi*	*explosum*	'hiss off'
	laedo	*laedere*	*laesi*	*laesum*	'hurt'
	ludo	*ludere*	*lusi*	*lusum*	'play'
	rado	*radere*	*rasi*	*rasum*	'scrape'
	rodo	*rodere*	*rosi*	*rosum*	'gnaw'
(7)	*gero*	*gerere*	*gessi*	*gestum*	'carry'
	uro	*urere*	*ussi*	*ustum*	'burn'
(8)	*traho*	*trahere*	*traxi*	*tractum*	'draw'
	veho	*vehere*	*vexi*	*vectum*	'carry'
	vivo	*vivere*	*vixi*	*victum*	'live'

(9)				
edo	*edere*	*edi*	*esum*	'eat'
emo	*emere*	*emi*	*emptum*	'buy'
excudo	*excudere*	*excudi*	*excusum*	'hammer out'
premo	*premere*	*pressi*	*pressum*	'press'
rumpo	*rumpere*	*rupi*	*ruptum*	'break'

Try to reconstruct the ancestral forms of each of these subclasses of verbs. Take your time, and do your best before reading further. Each subgroup is perhaps a little more difficult than the one before it, and subgroup (9) is a mixed bag of difficult forms.

Subgroup (3) consists of stems ending in *m*, and we might have expected the last two columns to show forms like **comsi* and **comtum*. Instead, we find *compsi* and *comptum*, and so on. But this is easy to understand: it is difficult to coordinate all the speech organs perfectly enough to move from *m* to a voiceless coronal obstruent, and the slightest mistiming will immediately produce an epenthetic *p* in between. By way of confirmation, we never find Latin words with the clusters *ms* and *mt*; instead, we find only *mps* and *mpt*.

Subgroup (4) is not much harder. These verbs have stems in *kw* and *gw*, and we might have expected **co*[kw]*si* and **co*[kw]*tum* in the last two columns. But such clusters are almost impossible to pronounce (and are not found at all in Latin), and we may therefore conclude that the glide [w] was simply lost in these clusters, while remaining before a vowel.

Subgroup (5) shows stems in *ct*, and we might have expected forms like **flectsi* and **flecttum*. Again these are awkward clusters, and we may reasonably infer that **cts* was reduced to *cs* (= *x*), while **ctt* was reduced to *ct*, yielding the observed forms.

Subgroup (6) apparently shows stems in *d*, and so we could posit forms like **rodsi* and **rodtum* for the verb meaning 'gnaw', and so on. Now, by parallelism with subgroup (2), we might expect **ds* to be devoiced to **ts*, but that's not what we find – and in fact *ts* is absolutely unattested in Latin. It looks, then, as though the original cluster **ds* was reduced all the way to *s*, producing the observed result, and that the cluster **dt*, also unattested in Latin, was likewise reduced to *s*. This explains all the verbs in this subgroup except for the one meaning 'yield', where we find *cessi* and *cessum* in place of the now expected **cesi* and **cesum*. This is a puzzle: we might have expected the clusters **ds* and **dt* to be reduced first to **ss* and then to the observed *s*, but this verb does not appear to have developed like the others. Either it has developed irregularly, or its original form was something more complicated than we have assumed, such as perhaps **ceddo*, **ceddere*. We cannot tell, and here we have reached the limits of what we can achieve with internal reconstruction.

Subgroup (7) appears to show stems in *r*, and so our first guess is to posit for the last two columns forms like **gersi* and **gertum*. This means, of course, that we must also postulate the development of **rs* to *ss* and of **rt* to *st*. The first of these looks phonetically natural enough, but it is troubling to find, on looking, that Latin has words like *ursus* 'bear' and *cursus* 'course', which have apparently undergone no such change. The second change does not seem particularly natural, and again Latin has plenty of words like *certus* 'certain' and *fortis* 'strong', which have undergone no such change. We have a problem. But there is no rule in linguistics that says we have to take the leftmost column as representing the most conservative form of a stem, so let's make the opposite choice. Let's try positing stems *$*ges-$* and *$*us-$* for these verbs. That means that the last two columns are perfectly regular, but we are now postulating *$*geso$*, *$*gesere$* for 'carry' and *$*uso$*, *$*usere$* for 'burn'. Consequently, we are forced to posit a quite different sort of phonological change: the change of original *$*s$* to r between vowels. Ever seen that before? Yes, in Section 4.1 we observed that original *$*s$* did indeed develop into r in intervocalic position in early Latin, producing alternations like *flos* 'flower', plural *flores*. We have solved our problem: these verbs had stems ending in s.

Subgroup (8) is decidedly nastier. The last two columns suggest stems ending in c or g, but instead we find h or v in the first two columns. We could, of course, suggest that the first two columns represent the ancestral stems, and that original *$*h$* and *$*v$* both developed into c (= [k]) before s or t, but these are not obviously natural changes, and it is hard to feel confident about such a scenario. Again, we seem to have reached the limit of what we can achieve with internal reconstruction: there is something about the histories of these verbs which escapes us.

Finally, subgroup (9) is a whole collection of nasties. In each case, we can easily explain some of the observed forms by appealing to one of the subgroups we have just been considering, but for every verb there is at least one form which is so irregular that we appear to have no hope of explaining it by internal reconstruction: it really looks as though some of these forms were never regular to begin with, but were simply constructed in an irregular manner. Internal reconstruction can tell us nothing about this. Remember, our original assumption was that irregular forms were once regular; if that assumption does not hold, we are powerless.

To sum up this exercise, we began by noting that the Latin verbs in a certain class generally show a consistent type of behaviour which we can reasonably regard as regular. Some of these verbs, however, show irregularities of one sort or another. In each case, we have proceeded by assuming that the irregular forms were once regular, and that the irregular forms developed as a consequence of regular phonological changes in the language. (Recall the first half of Sturtevant's Paradox: phonological change is regular, but produces irregularities.) In this way, we have succeeded in reconstructing earlier regular forms for many of the verbs in question, and we have further succeeded in identifying a number of regular phonological changes which must have applied to ancestral forms of Latin. This is typically what happens in internal reconstruction.

Observe further that the irregularities in this case consisted of **alternations** in the forms of certain verb stems. Alternations are by no means the only grist for internal reconstruction, but they are very frequently the kind of data we deal with when reconstructing internally. In the next section, we explore this topic further.

9.2 *Alternations and internal reconstruction*

Alternations in the forms of particular stems or affixes are exceedingly frequent in the languages of the world, and in most cases such alternations result from the application of regular phonological changes to what were originally non-alternating morphemes. This makes alternations particularly profitable targets for internal reconstruction.

Consider the German alternations illustrated in Table 9.1 (the vowel alternations in some forms are irrelevant here and will be ignored). You can see from the table that there are two kinds of stems in German. One group, such as /ta:t/ 'deed' and /verk/ 'work', shows no alternations, while a second group, including /ra:t/ ~ /re:d-/ 'wheel' and /tsverk/ ~ /tsverg-/ 'dwarf', shows alternations in the voicing of stem-final plosives. Invoking the principle that alternations derive from non-alternating forms by phonological change, we may therefore reconstruct for the second group invariant stems with final voiced plosives, like */pfa:d/ 'path', */ra:d/ 'wheel', and */tsverg/ 'dwarf'. The phonological change required is nothing more than devoicing of word-final plosives, an extremely common and natural development. Thus, for /bunt/ 'mottled' and /bunt/ 'league', we reconstruct the histories shown in Table 9.2. Since modern German contains no word-final voiced plosives, this reconstruction looks very satisfactory, and it can be confirmed by comparison

Table 9.1 Voicing alternations in German

	Singular	**Plural**
'deed'	/ta:t/	/ta:tən/
'path'	/pfa:t/	/pfa:də/
'degree'	/gra:t/	/gra:də/
'edge'	/gra:t/	/gra:tə/
'councillor'	/ra:t/	/re:tə/
'wheel'	/ra:t/	/re:dər/
'hand'	/hant/	/hendə/
'mottled'	/bunt/	/buntə/
'league'	/bunt/	/bundə/
'healthy'	/gəzunt/	/gəzundə/
'work'	/verk/	/verkə/
'dwarf'	/tsverk/	/tsvergə/
'advised'	/ri:t/	/ri:tən/
'avoided'	/fərmi:t/	/fərmi:dən/

with related Germanic languages – for example, German /hant/ and English *hand*.

Observe, however, that grammatical words like /mit/ 'with', /ap/ 'off', and /vek/ 'away' never take suffixes and therefore can never exhibit any alternations. Consequently, we have no way of telling, from internal reconstruction alone, whether these words originally ended in a voiced plosive or a voiceless one. Internal reconstruction can be successfully applied only when there is material to work with, especially alternations.

Let us turn now to a slightly more complex example. Ancient Greek has a class of masculine nouns and adjectives in which the nominative singular form is marked by the case-ending *-s*, the genitive singular is marked by the case-ending *-os*, and the nominative plural is marked by the ending *-es*. Table 9.3 lists a few examples.

Here we shall ignore the position of the word-accent, which turns out not to be relevant (though it *might* have been relevant, of course). The first two words, those for 'guard' and 'vulture', appear to be perfectly regular: the endings are added to the same stem in every instance. But the words for 'serf' and 'hope' are a little more complicated. The second and third columns clearly show the stems /t^hɛ́:t-/ and /elpíd-/, and so we might have expected the nominative singular forms */t^hɛ́:ts/ and */elpíds/. But we find instead /t^hɛ:s/ and /elpís/. We may therefore surmise that the word-final clusters */-ts/ and */-ds/ have been reduced to /-s/ in Greek – a plausible

Table 9.2 Final devoicing in German

	'mottled'		'league'	
	Sg	**Pl**	**Sg**	**Pl**
pre-German	*bunt*	*buntə*	*bund*	*bundə*
Devoicing	*bunt*	*buntə*	*bunt*	*bundə*

Table 9.3 Nominative and genitive in ancient Greek

Nom Sg	**Gen Sg**	**Nom Pl**	
/p^hýlaks/	/p^hýlakos/	/p^hýlakes/	'guard'
/gýps/	/gypós/	/gýpes/	'vulture'
/t^hɛ:s/	/t^hɛ́:tos/	/t^hɛ́:tes/	'serf'
/elpís/	/elpídos/	/elpídes/	'hope'
/méla:s/	/mélanos/	/mélanes/	'black'
/stá:s/	/stántos/	/stántes/	'standing'

enough change, and one supported by the observation that we never find any Greek words ending in /ts/ or /ds/.

The words for 'black' and 'standing' are different again. The last two columns exhibit the stems /mélan-/ and /stánt-/, and so we might have expected nominative singulars */mélans/ and */stánts/. Instead, we find /méla:s/ and /stá:s/. Of course, we have already decided that word-final */-ts/ developed to /-s/, so that the second should have become */stáns/. But the attested forms, with no nasals but with long vowels, oblige us to posit a loss of */n/ before word-final /s/, with compensatory lengthening of the preceding vowel.

We have therefore reconstructed an earlier stage of Greek in which all of these words were perfectly regular, and we have identified several phonological changes which applied on the way to ancient Greek: reduction of */ts/ and of */ds/ to /s/, and loss of */n/ before /s/ with compensatory lengthening of a preceding vowel. The history of the nominative singular forms is shown in Table 9.4.

The internal method will not always be capable of producing an unambiguous reconstruction, even when the conditioning factors for an alternation are highly visible. Table 9.5 shows the paradigm of the Old English noun *dæg* 'day', in which æ is a front vowel and *a* a back vowel:

It's not difficult to see what the conditioning factors must be: we find the back vowel *a* in the stem when the following syllable contains a back vowel, but the front vowel æ when the following syllable contains a front vowel or when there is no following syllable. But we are still left with two plausible possibilities: (1) the stem was originally *dæg-*, and the vowel was backed

Table 9.4 The history of Greek nominatives

	'guard'	'vulture'	'serf'	'hope'	'black'	'standing'
Original	p^hylaks	$gyps$	$t^h\varepsilon{:}ts$	$elpids$	$melans$	$stants$
ts, ds > s	p^hylaks	$gyps$	$t^h\varepsilon{:}s$	$elpis$	$melans$	$stans$
Vn > V: before s	p^hylaks	$gyps$	$t^h\varepsilon{:}s$	$elpis$	$mela{:}s$	$sta{:}s$

Table 9.5 Vowel alternations in Old English

	Sg	Pl
Nom	*dæg*	*dagas*
Acc	*dæg*	*dagas*
Gen	*dæges*	*daga*
Dat	*dæge*	*dagum*

(assimilated) before a following back vowel; (2) the stem was originally *dag-*, and the vowel was fronted when there was a following front vowel, or at least when there was no following back vowel. The first hypothesis might look simpler, but of course we have to consider the possibility that the nominative and accusative singular once contained a second syllable with a front vowel, and that this syllable was lost after fronting of an original *dag-*. Here, therefore, we are helpless: we can see that there must have been a single form of the stem before the alternation was introduced, but internal reconstruction cannot help us to decide what that original form was. (As it happens, the comparative evidence from other Germanic languages allows us to conclude that *dag-* was the original form, and that *dæg-* results from a fronting process before a front vowel. The nominative and accusative singular did indeed once contain a second syllable with a front vowel, already lost by the time of Old English.)

9.3   *Case study: the laryngeal theory of PIE*

Linguists in the nineteenth century were very successful at reconstructing important characteristics of the structure of PIE by the comparative method. Among their successes was the reconstruction of many hundreds of PIE roots. Because of the extensive presence in PIE of **ablaut**, the use of vowel changes in roots for grammatical purposes (as in English *sing/sang/sung*), most of these roots could be reconstructed with the same underlying vowel, usually represented as *e*. Furthermore, the great majority of PIE roots proved to have the structure CVC-, or else this same structure with the addition of a resonant: *i, u, n, r,* or *l*, or with a prefixed *s*. Table 9.6 shows a few typical examples.

The pervasiveness of this root pattern is quite striking. Nevertheless, there are a number of exceptions. Quite a few roots fail to show the expected CVC-pattern, and show instead either CV- or VC-. Moreover, a number of such roots apparently cannot be reconstructed with the usual vowel *e; instead, they require *a or *o, and further, in the CV- roots, the vowel is usually long. Table 9.7 lists some of these exceptional roots.

The existence of these anomalous roots had long been recognized, but for a long time it seems not to have occurred to anyone that there was a problem worthy of investigation. In 1879, however, an obscure young Swiss student made a striking suggestion. Applying the technique of internal reconstruction, he suggested that these anomalous roots had once been perfectly regular roots of the usual CVC- type, but that certain consonants present in an ancestor of PIE had simply been lost, producing the observed CV- and VC- patterns. Further, he proposed that the loss of a root-final consonant had caused the process of compensatory lengthening (which you will recall from Chapter 3), thereby accounting for the long vowels found in most of the CV- roots. Finally, and most strikingly, he proposed that some of the lost consonants

Table 9.6 Some typical PIE roots

*bhel-	'shine'	*nebh-	'cloud'
*bher-	'carry'	*nem-	'allot'
*deik-	'show'	*ped-	'foot'
*deuk-	'lead'	*pel-	'thrust'
*dher-	'dark'	*pet-	'fly'
*dhwer-	'door'	*plek-	'plait'
*gel-	'form into a ball'	*reg-	'go straight'
*ger-	'curve'	*reudh-	'red'
*ghebh-	'give'	*reup-	'snatch'
*ghel-	'shine'	*sed-	'sit'
*gher-	'enclose'	*sek-	'cut'
*gwel-	'throw'	*sem-	'one'
*kel-	'strike'	*spek-	'observe'
*ker-	'horn'	*spen-	'stretch'
*kers-	'run'	*sreu-	'flow'
*kwel-	'revolve'	*stel-	'put'
*leg-	'collect'	*tel-	'lift'
*legwh-	'light (not heavy)'	*ter-	'rub'
*leip-	'stick'	*wed-	'water'
*leuk-	'light, bright'	*wegh-	'go'
*meg-	'great'	*weid-	'see'
*mel-	'soft'	*weik-	'clan'
*melg-	'milk'	*wel-	'turn'
*merg-	'boundary'	*wer-	'speak'
*meug-	'slimy'	*yeug-	'join'

Table 9.7 Some exceptional PIE roots

*ag-	'lead'	*kē-	'sharpen'
*ak-	'sharp'	*mā-	'good'
*ank-	'bend'	*mē-	'measure'
*ar-	'fit together'	*od-	'smell'
*aug-	'increase'	*op-	'work'
*bhā-	'speak'	*pā-	'feed, protect'
*dhē-	'put, set'	*sā-	'satisfy'
*dō-	'give'	*sāg-	'seek out'
*ed-	'eat'	*sal-	'salt'
*em-	'take'	*sē-	'sow'
*er-	'set in motion'	*smē-	'smear'
*es-	'be'	*snā-	'swim'
*ghrē-	'grow, green'	*stā-	'stand'
*gnō-	'know'	*wē-	'blow'

had, before disappearing, affected the quality of the root vowel, variously turning the original *e into *a* or *o*.

The student's name was Ferdinand de Saussure, and Saussure, of course, later went on to revolutionize the whole subject of linguistics and to become known as the founding father of theoretical linguistics. He called his hypothetical consonants 'sonant coefficients', but this name was later replaced by the term **laryngeals**, still in use today. Saussure's **laryngeal theory** originally posited only two lost consonants, but other workers later added a third, and it is the three-laryngeal version which is most widely cited today and which I shall therefore present here. (Incidentally, the term 'laryngeal' should not be taken too literally: the theory does not require that the lost consonants should have been laryngeal in the strict phonetic sense, but only that they should have existed and then been lost.)

The three-laryngeal version of Saussure's hypothesis recognizes three lost consonants, often represented rather arbitrarily as $*h_1$, $*h_2$, and $*h_3$. Of these, it is assumed that $*h_1$ had no effect on the quality of a neighbouring vowel, that $*h_2$ lowered original $*e$ to a, and that $*h_3$ rounded original $*e$ to o. All three are assumed to have caused compensatory lengthening when lost from root-final position. Here, then, is the explanation of the anomalous roots provided by the laryngeal theory:

$$*h_1es- > *es-\ \text{'be'} \qquad *dheh_1- > *dh\bar{e}-\ \text{'put'}$$
$$*h_2eg- > *ag-\ \text{'drive'} \qquad *steh_2- > *st\bar{a}-\ \text{'stand'}$$
$$*h_3ed- > *od-\ \text{'smell'} \qquad *deh_3- > *d\bar{o}-\ \text{'give'}$$

As you can see, the hypothetical laryngeal consonants, together with the phonological developments proposed by Saussure, perfectly explain the observed forms of the anomalous roots:

$$*h_1e > *e \qquad *eh_1 > *\bar{e}$$
$$*h_2e > *a \qquad *eh_2 > *\bar{a}$$
$$*h_3e > *o \qquad *eh_3 > *\bar{o}$$

In fact, Saussure's laryngeals do a great deal more than this: they help to explain a number of peculiarities and anomalies in the forms of words in several of the ancient Indo-European languages. Unfortunately, I cannot go into these matters here without delving too deep into the intricacies of PIE morphology; you can find more information in the Further Reading.

For some years the laryngeal theory attracted little attention from specialists: it was viewed as little more than a clever paper exercise, lacking any basis in hard evidence. But just such evidence eventually turned up, in a surprising fashion.

Just about the time that Saussure was proposing his hypothesis, a previously unknown language was discovered in a library of inscriptions excavated at Boğazköy in Turkey; for want of a better name, the language of these inscriptions was dubbed 'Hittite', after the Old Testament name of an important Anatolian empire. During the First World War, a young Czech scholar, Bedřich Hrozný, succeeded in deciphering the Hittite inscriptions and in demonstrating, in the face of considerable resistance, that Hittite was a very ancient and previously unknown IE language, though a rather divergent one.

(Engagingly, the Hittite word for 'water' turned out to be *watar*, cognate with the English word.)

The progress of Hittite studies was slow, and not just because of the war. The American linguist Winfred Lehmann reports that Hrozný's work was taken up by a brilliant young linguist called Carl Marstrander; Marstrander, asked by a friend to provide some business to an impecunious bookbinder, took all of his Hittite materials to the shop to be bound – and that night the bookbinder's shop burned to the ground. Still, the IE status of Hittite gradually came to be accepted, and steady progress was made in interpreting the texts.

Then in 1927 the young Polish linguist Jerzy Kuryłowicz (the same Kuryłowicz whom we met in Chapter 5) pointed out that some of the IE words recorded in the Hittite texts were written with a consonant in exactly the positions posited by Saussure nearly half a century earlier. The consonant symbol used is one regularly used in other languages of the area for representing sounds resembling [h], and it is therefore commonly transcribed as h. For example, the PIE root *plā- 'flat', reconstructed by Saussure as *$pleh_2$-, appears in Hittite *pal-ḫi-i-iš* 'broad', and PIE *os- 'bone', reconstructed as *h_3es-, appears in Hittite as *ḫastai*. In fact, further investigation has revealed that Saussure's *h_2 and *h_3 apparently survived regularly in Hittite as h, while *h_1 had apparently disappeared without trace.

This direct evidence from Hittite (which is the source of the term 'laryngeal') persuaded most specialists that Saussure's reconstruction was indeed correct, and that some ancestral form of PIE must actually have had a set of consonants which disappeared, with the phonological consequences that he envisaged. Today most Indo-Europeanists accept the laryngeal theory as correct, though there is naturally quibbling about the details, and a few specialists still reject the hypothesis entirely.

The laryngeal theory is without doubt the most famous instance of internal reconstruction in the whole linguistic literature. Observe that, unlike most applications of the method, this one was not primarily addressed to alternations. While it has in practice led to some understanding of a few troublesome alternations, it was originally directed at a purely phonotactic anomaly: the observation that a few roots did not exhibit the canonical structure for PIE roots. And none of it would have come about at all if Saussure, alone among generations of specialists, had not noticed that there was an anomaly, a puzzle to be investigated. The first step in solving any problem is always the recognition that there exists a problem to be solved.

Naturally, linguists have been unable to resist the temptation of trying to guess the phonetic nature of the 'laryngeal' consonants, even though this problem is probably impossible in principle. At present, the favourite guesses are that *h_1 was probably a glottal stop [?], that *h_2 was very likely some kind of voiceless fricative like [h] or [x], and that *h_3 might have been a voiced fricative like [ɣ], probably with lip-rounding, to account for its rounding effect on neighbouring vowels. Glottal stops and back fricatives are favoured because it is well known that such consonants are easily lost in languages generally, but, barring the discovery of another ancient IE language which preserves the laryngeals in some more explicit form even than Hittite, we will never know.

9.4 *Internal reconstruction of grammar and lexicon*

On occasion it is possible to use the internal method to reconstruct significant features of the grammar or the vocabulary of an earlier stage of a language. In fact, we have already seen some examples of this. Recall from Section 6.1 that Pamela Munro has succeeded in reconstructing the earlier form of copular sentences in Mojave by observing that such sentences in modern Mojave appear to be out of line with ordinary sentence structure. And recall too from Section 2.5 the case of Basque *urdin*: today this word means only 'blue', but the existence of compounds like *gibelurdin*, denoting a mushroom with a bright green underside, and *mutxurdin* 'old maid', in which *urdin* can only be interpreted as 'grey', demonstrates that *urdin* must formerly have covered all of green, blue, and grey, before the introduction of new colour terms like *berde* 'green' and *gris* 'grey', both loans from Romance.

Such applications of the internal method may be possible when we find that certain forms, functions, or senses of linguistic elements are seemingly out of line with more usual behaviour. Consider the case of English past participles. English regular verbs, or 'weak verbs', form their past participles with a suffix *-ed*: *love/loved, paint/painted*, and so on. However, a number of irregular verbs, mostly the 'strong verbs', use the suffix *-en* instead: *write/written, take/ taken*, and so on. This second pattern is now unproductive: all new verbs entering the language employ the first pattern: *access/accessed, commute/ commuted, escalate/escalated*. A few older verbs, however, show curious behaviour: they form their participles normally with *-ed*, but these participles have adjectival forms which exhibit *-en* instead. Examples: *He has shaved*, but *He is clean-shaven*; *The lead has melted*, but *This is molten lead*; *I have mowed the lawn*, but *This is new-mown hay*. We may therefore surmise that the forms *shaven, molten*, and *mown* represent the original forms of the participles, and that these original forms have been displaced in verbal use by new analogical forms in *-ed*, leaving the adjectival forms isolated. As it happens, our historical records confirm that this view is correct. In fact, our records allow us to identify a few more cases of this process which might otherwise have escaped our attention: it has probably never occurred to you that *sodden*, as in *Her clothes are sodden*, has anything to do with *seethe*, as in *This lamb has been seethed in milk*, but in fact *sodden* is the old participle of *seethe*, now virtually unrecognizable as such.

Something similar occurs with certain adjectives and adverbs. The adjective *good* has an irregular adverb *well*, which occurs in a number of adjectives formed with participles: *well built*, *well developed*, *well liked*, *well thought out*, and so on. Its opposite *bad*, however, forms a regular adverb *badly*. But the related adjectives are not formed with *badly*; instead they are formed with *ill*: *ill-considered*, *ill-disposed*, *ill-favoured*, *ill-mannered*, *ill-timed*, and so on. Again, therefore, we may suppose that *bad*, like *good*, formerly had an irregular adverb, in this case *ill*, and that this *ill* has been displaced in ordinary use by an analogical formation *badly*. And again our records confirm this reconstruction: we can no longer say things like **You have done ill*, but you may be familiar with such usages from reading older English literature.

These English cases, you may already have spotted, are illustrations of Kuryłowicz's fourth law: an analogical formation takes over in the primary function, leaving the older form confined to secondary functions. Instances of this kind are particularly fertile ground for the application of internal reconstruction.

The degree to which internal reconstruction can be reliably applied to syntax is much debated among linguists. Consider the case of French. In modern standard French, the word order in sentences with full NPs is SVO:

(9.1) *Jean a vu Pierre.*
   John has seen Peter
   'John saw Peter.'

(9.2) *Je donnerai le livre à toi.*
   I will-give the book to you
   'I'll give the book to you.'

But when the NP arguments are pronouns, the order is different; it's SOV:

(9.3) *Il l'a vu.*
   he him has seen
   'He saw him.'

(9.4) *Je te le donnerai.*
   I you it will-give
   'I'll give you it.'

Some linguists would argue that the alternation between SVO order with full NPs and SOV order with pronominal NPs represents just another instance of the kind of alternation to which the internal method may reasonably be applied. They further suggest that it is pronouns which tend to be conservative in their behaviour, and hence that in this case we can reconstruct an original SOV word order for French sentences generally, with pronominal NPs retaining the older order but other NPs showing the result of an innovation in French word order, a shift to SVO.

It is not easy to know what to make of such an argument. On the one hand, we have independent evidence that spoken Latin, the ancestor of French, was indeed an SOV language, as internal reconstruction would suggest in this case. On the other hand, it is far from clear that the order used with pronouns directly continues a Latin sentence structure: the French pronouns are *clitics*, unstressed items bound to certain positions in the sentence, and there is a universal tendency for clitics to appear in certain positions, of which one is immediately before the verb, as in French. The placement of pronominal NPs in French may therefore be an accident having nothing to do with the ancestral word order of the language.

The point of such arguments is that there are many other languages for which we have no historical information at all, and we would therefore like to know whether such grammatical alternations can serve as the basis for internal reconstruction or not. Consider Basque. Basque is an SOV language: 'John loves Ann' is expressed as *Jonek Ana maite du*, literally 'John Ann loves' (*du* is an auxiliary). But the pattern for agreement in the verb or auxiliary is different: 'I love you' is *maite zaitut*, in which the prefix *z-* on the auxiliary marks the object 'you', while the suffix *-t* marks the subject 'I', and the form is literally 'love you-Aux-I'. May we therefore conclude that some ancestral form of Basque had OVS word order? Nobody knows, but most linguists would probably be very cautious about leaping to such a conclusion, since it is not difficult to envisage other pathways by which the OVS order of agreement might have come about.

Further reading

Two classic treatments of internal reconstruction are Hoenigswald (1944) and Marchand (1956). Convenient brief introductions are the article in Miranda (1975), Asher (1994), which is *very* brief, and Ringe (forthcoming). Two textbooks which devote a good deal of space to discussing the method are Hock (1986: ch. 17), and Fox (1995: chs. 7–8). Some examples of internal reconstruction can be found in Borgström (1954) (pre-PIE), Chafe (1959) (Seneca), and Anttila (1973) (Finnish). A rather critical view of the internal method is taken in Lass (1975).

The laryngeal theory was first presented in Saussure (1879). There are very many surveys, some of them more critical than others. Among these are Lehmann (1952: ch. 3; 1993 *passim*), Polomé (1965), Winter (1965), Keiler (1970), Szemerényi (1973), Jonsson (1978), Beekes (1984, 1989), Hock (1986 *passim*), and Lindeman (1987).

Exercises

Exercise 9.1

In Maori (the indigenous language of New Zealand), the passive form of a verb is constructed by adding a suffix to the active form, but the form of that suffix appears quite variable. Table 9.8 lists some typical Maori verbs. Using

Table 9.8

	Active	Passive
'call'	*karaŋa*	*karaŋatia*
'drink'	*inu*	*inumia*
'enter'	*tomo*	*tomokia*
'seize'	*mau*	*mauria*
'sit'	*noho*	*nohoia*
'touch'	*paa*	*paaŋia*
'turn'	*huri*	*hurihia*

the internal method, reconstruct an ancestral version of the Maori verbal system which is perfectly regular. Identify any phonological changes required by your analysis to account for the attested forms; comment on the naturalness of those changes; and explain where you would look in Maori for evidence confirming that your analysis is correct.

Exercise 9.2

In English, as in many languages, the word *head* is commonly used both literally and metaphorically in word-formation: *headband, headache, head-rest, headwaters, head teacher* (British for 'school principal'), *head waiter, headquarters, headlight, headstone,* and so on. In German, however, things are little more complicated. The ordinary word for 'head' is *Kopf*. In word-formation, though, we usually find, not *Kopf*, but a different item *Haupt*: *Hauptakteur* 'leading light', *Hauptakzent* 'main stress' (in phonetics), *Hauptbahnhof* 'central (rail) station', *Hauptbetrieb* 'headquarters', *Hauptfach* 'major subject' (at university), *Hauptmann* 'captain', *Hauptschalter* 'master switch' (in electricity), *Hauptstraße* 'main street, high street', *Hauptstütze* 'mainstay', and dozens of others. In a few cases, though, we do find *Kopf* used: *Kopffüßer* 'cephalopod', *Kopfhörer* 'headphone', *Kopfseite* 'front page' (of a newspaper), *Kopfsprung* 'header, head-first dive', *Kopfstimme* 'falsetto', *Kopfstütze* 'headrest' (e.g., in a car), *Kopfwäsche* 'shampoo', and some others.

Explain what seems to have happened in German, and reconstruct an earlier stage of the German lexicon.

Exercise 9.3

In word-formation in Basque, a final vowel is regularly lost in the third or later syllable of the first element:

itsaso 'sea' + *gizon* 'man' → *itsasgizon* 'sailor'
burdina 'iron' + *bizi* 'living' → *burdinbizi* 'magnet'
uztarri 'yoke' + *-gile* 'maker' → *uztargile* 'yoke-maker'

Moreover, a final *i* is lost in the second or later syllable of the first element:

harri 'stone' + *-gin* 'who makes' → *hargin* 'stonecutter'
ogi 'bread' + *-gin* 'who makes' → **oggin* → *okin* 'baker'
herri 'country' + *-kide* 'fellow' → *herkide* 'compatriot'

Some words, however, exhibit unexpected behaviour when they occur as the first element:

gaztai 'cheese' + *bera* 'soft' → *gaztanbera* 'cottage cheese'
ardao 'wine' + *-du* (verb-forming suffix) → *ardandu* 'ferment'
artzai 'shepherd' + *-tza* 'profession' → *artzantza* 'sheepherding'
katea 'chain' + *begi* 'eye' → *katenbegi* 'link of chain'
balea 'whale' + *bizar* 'beard' → *balenbizar* 'whalebone'

euskara 'Basque language' + *-dun* 'who has' → *euskaldun* 'Basque-speaker'
haizkora 'axe' + *begi* 'eye' → *haizkolbegi* 'hole in axe-head for shaft'
merkatari 'merchant' + *-go* (collective) → *merkatalgo* 'commerce'
gari 'wheat' + *buru* 'head' → *galburu* 'head of wheat'

Propose internal reconstructions for these exceptional words, and identify the phonological developments required. Where would you look for further evidence to support your reconstructions?

Exercise 9.4

The earliest attested Germanic languages are Gothic, Old English, Old Norse and Old High German. All of these exhibit *ablaut* – change in vowel quality – in the stems of verbs. By applying comparative reconstruction to these four languages, we can reconstruct with considerable confidence the forms of the ancestral language, Proto-Germanic. Table 9.9 lists some typical verbs from Proto-Germanic. By applying the internal method, reconstruct an earlier set of forms which is perfectly regular, and identify any phonological changes which must have occurred between your reconstruction and the forms cited here. Comment on any difficulties.

Table 9.9

Present Infinitive	3Sg Preterite	3Pl Preterite	
*bi:tanã	*bait	*bitun	'bite'
*beudanã	*baud	*budun	'order'
*bindanã	*band	*bundun	'tie'
*werpanã	*warp	*wurpun	'throw'

Exercise 9.5

The definite article in Basque is a suffix, -*a* in the singular and -*ak* in the plural. Thus, for example, the noun *mendi* has the forms *mendia* 'the mountain' and *mendiak* 'the mountains' in the Absolutive case, the case that takes no case-suffix. But Basque also has an extensive case-system, in which every case (except the Absolutive) is marked by an invariable case-suffix. Table 9.10 lists some of the case forms for *mendi* 'mountain' and *gizon* 'man'. As you can see, the addition of a case-suffix often induces changes in the form of the noun phrase to which the suffix is added. Propose a reconstruction in which every morpheme has a single constant form, and identify any phonological changes required to produce the modern forms. It may help you to know that, in Basque, the vowel *e* is regularly inserted to break up a consonant cluster arising in inflection.

Exercise 9.6

Like other Celtic languages, Welsh exhibits a set of **mutations**, changes in the quality of word-initial consonants in certain grammatical environments. Welsh has three such mutations, the *soft mutation*, the *spirant mutation*, and the *nasal mutation*, each of which occurs in different circumstances. Here I cite just three of these: the possessive *də* 'your' causes soft mutation in a following noun, while *i* 'her' causes spirant mutation, and *və* 'my' causes nasal mutation. Table 9.11 shows the effects with three typical nouns; note that the nasal consonants in the last column are voiceless.

Now the data from the modern language are not sufficient to allow us to perform a complete internal reconstruction of these alternations. Nevertheless, you should be able to make some plausible suggestions as to what a good internal reconstruction might look like, one in which the alternations are

Table 9.10

	Sg	Pl
Absolutive	*mendia*	*mendiak*
Ergative	*mendiak*	*mendiek*
Dative	*mendiari*	*mendiei*
Genitive	*mendiaren*	*mendien*
Instrumental	*mendiaz*	*mendiez*
Absolutive	*gizona*	*gizonak*
Ergative	*gizonak*	*gizonek*
Dative	*gizonari*	*gizonei*
Genitive	*gizonaren*	*gizonen*
Instrumental	*gizonaz*	*gizonez*

Table 9.11

	Basic Form	'your N'	'her N'	'my N'
'head'	$p\varepsilon n$	$d\vartheta\ ben$	$i\ f\varepsilon n$	$v\vartheta\ \underset{\circ}{m}\varepsilon n$
'house'	$ti{:}$	$d\vartheta\ di{:}$	$i\ \theta i{:}$	$v\vartheta\ \underset{\circ}{n}i{:}$
'cat'	$ka\theta$	$d\vartheta\ ga\theta$	$i\ xa\theta$	$v\vartheta\ \underset{\circ}{\eta}a\theta$

phonologically regular. Suggest some possible reconstructions for the three possessives, and identify any required phonological changes leading to the modern state of affairs. The spirant mutation is much harder than the other two.

10

The origin and propagation of change

10.1 *The Saussurean paradox*

During the nineteenth century most linguists were inclined to see a language as a collection of individual elements: speech sounds, words, grammatical endings, and so forth. In this essentially atomistic point of view, language change could be interpreted as the replacement of one element by another: one speech sound replaces another, one word replaces another, one grammatical ending replaces another. Early in the twentieth century, however, the great Swiss linguist Ferdinand de Saussure proposed a radically different way of looking at a language, which has become known as **structuralism**. From the structuralist point of view, a language is best regarded rather as a system of relations, a system consisting of a number of interlocking subsystems, such as the phonological system, the verbal system, and the pronoun system. For a structuralist, an individual element is defined chiefly by the role it plays in the system, by the way it is related to other elements in the system.

This structuralist view has been enormously influential, and since the 1930s virtually all linguistic work has been carried out within the structuralist paradigm, with very considerable success. But the structuralist revolution brought with it a new puzzle: if a language is primarily an orderly system of relations, how is it that a language can change without disrupting that system? To put it another way, how can a language continue to be used effectively as a vehicle for expression and communication while it is in the middle of a change, or rather in the middle of a large number of changes? This puzzle is known as the **Saussurean paradox**, and it is not a trivial issue.

Consider some simple analogies. How can anyone play football or chess successfully if the rules of football or chess are being constantly changed during play? How can an orchestra play a symphony if the score of the symphony is changing during the performance? How can a case be tried in court if the law is constantly changing during the trial? Such analogies would appear to suggest that the constant changes in our language must of necessity have an adverse effect on our ability to use it successfully.

And yet this is not so. Apart from the handful of specialists who are deliberately looking for evidence of change in contemporary speech, people hardly ever even notice the existence of changes in their language; when we do notice a change, it is usually no more than a new word or two. When we recall how dramatically English has changed in the last forty generations or so, since the time of Alfred the Great, this issue becomes altogether mysterious. How on earth can a language be transformed so utterly, in such a seemingly short time as forty generations, while at the same time its speakers go on speaking it happily without being disturbed by the changes and usually without even noticing them?

Before about 1960, no one had any real idea what the answer might be to this question, and the Saussurean paradox was regarded as a great mystery. A few linguists tried to maintain that language change was typically so slow and gradual as to be imperceptible. Such gradual change may indeed be possible with certain kinds of sound change: for example, we can at least conceive that the Great Vowel Shift of English might have proceeded via a steady sequence of tiny changes in the qualities of the participating vowels. But the great majority of changes cannot possibly be gradual and imperceptible in this way. When one word is replaced by another, when one grammatical form or construction is replaced by another, the change simply cannot proceed by small steps: a speaker must use one form or the other, and that is the end of it. Language change cannot, in general, be gradual in the manner suggested. (It can, however, be gradual in at least two other, very different, ways, to be considered below. Can you think of two ways in which native English *anleth* could have been gradually replaced by the French loan *face?*)

The resolution of Saussure's paradox had to wait until the 1960s. In that decade there occurred one of the great breakthroughs in our understanding of the nature of language, a breakthrough which has allowed us at last to provide a reasonably satisfying answer to the question of how a language can continue to be used while it is changing. In an outstanding example of the enrichment of one branch of linguistics by another, the breakthrough was achieved not by the historical linguists, but instead by the practitioners of a fledgeling branch of the discipline which was then just beginning to establish itself: sociolinguistics. To that story we now turn.

10.2 *Variation and social stratification*

No language is totally homogeneous. We saw in Chapter 7 that a language normally exhibits a significant degree of regional variation. But this is not the only important kind of variation. Even in a single locality, we can often find a substantial degree of variation. For one thing, there is variation between social groups. Women do not speak like men; middle-class people do not speak like working-class people; television newsreaders do not speak like disc jockeys.

For another, even within a single group, there is variation between individuals: there are probably noticeable differences between your speech and the speech of your closest friends, even if you all have very similar backgrounds. For a third, even a single person doesn't always speak in the same way. It's hardly likely that you speak in exactly the same manner when you're relaxing with friends in a pub or a bar and when you're being interviewed for a job. And even in a single conversation you may exhibit a surprising amount of variation. Consider, for example, the sentence *Aren't you going home?* On one occasion, you might pronounce this with a /tj/ sequence in *aren't you*, but the next time you might use the affricate /tʃ/ instead; you might pronounce *you* with a full vowel once but with a schwa the next time; you might pronounce *going* as two syllables once but as one syllable the next time; you might pronounce *going* with a velar nasal /ŋ/ once but with a coronal nasal /n/ the next time; and so on. Similarly, you might say *compact disc* one moment and *CD* the next; you might say *telephone* one moment and *phone* the next; you might say *I got cheated* one moment but *I got ripped off* the next.

For generations, linguists had very little idea what to make of this kind of variation. On the whole, most linguists were inclined to consider the speech of educated people as the primary object of description and investigation, while the vernacular speech of uneducated people was usually dismissed as being of no consequence – except in dialectology, in which the speech of elderly, uneducated, rural speakers was commonly considered to be the most suitable for investigation. Since earlier linguists were overwhelmingly male, there was perhaps also a comparable tendency to treat men's speech as the norm, while women's speech, where it differed, was often disregarded as inconsequential. Otherwise, though, the very high degree of variation within a single community was, for the most part, simply ignored: at best it was considered to be a peripheral and insignificant aspect of language, no more than erratic and even random departures from the norms, while at worst it was regarded as a considerable nuisance, as a collection of tiresome details getting in the way of good descriptions.

This was more or less the mind-set which the sociolinguists encountered in the 1960s, and which they set about confronting in the most direct way possible: by making variation itself the object of their investigations. Sociolinguistics may be usefully defined as the study of variation in language, and, as I observed above, this study has transformed our understanding of how language works.

The earlier linguists had often referred to this exasperating variation as *free variation*, a label implying that such variation was essentially arbitrary and of no significance. One of the central findings of the sociolinguists has been that variation is typically not arbitrary at all, and that it is very far from being insignificant. This was not easy to discover, however, because, if you listen to people speaking, you will find that, just as I have suggested, the same speaker will sometimes use one form and sometimes another, in a seemingly aimless manner. It is simply not possible to conclude, in most cases, that speaker X uses form A while speaker Y uses form B. Mere observation, therefore, leads to no interesting results.

But mathematics has long provided a powerful tool for extracting significant information from what appears to be a noisy jumble of data. That tool is statistics, and it was the introduction of statistical approaches into sociolinguistics that led to the breakthrough that concerns us here.

In the early 1960s a young American chemical engineer decided to turn his back on engineering and to take up the study of language. His name was William Labov, and Labov set out to explore the speech of Martha's Vineyard. Martha's Vineyard is a small and somewhat isolated island lying off the coast of Massachusetts, and the speech of the islanders is characterized by the presence of a well-known idiosyncrasy: the centralization of the first element of the diphthongs /ai/ and /au/, as in *light* and *house*. Such centralization is a familiar characteristic of certain other varieties of English, notably of Canadian English, but it is not usual in New England, except in Martha's Vineyard.

Armed with a tape recorder and a knowledge of statistics, Labov therefore set out for the island, where he spent a considerable time making friends with the local people and recording their speech. He then sat down to examine his recordings. First, he collected all the instances of relevant words on his tapes and transcribed them in phonetic notation. Sure enough, he found that each individual speaker used a range of pronunciations for words like *light* and *house*: sometimes the diphthongs were strongly centralized, sometimes they were more weakly centralized, and sometimes they weren't centralized at all. This is exactly the kind of observation which had induced earlier linguists to conclude that there was nothing going on worthy of study.

But Labov was convinced his data were more interesting than a hasty dismissal would suggest, and he set out to show this by using a simple statistical technique which has since become known as the **quantitative approach** to language variation. He decided that he could distinguish, by ear, four different degrees of centralization: none, a little, quite a bit, and a maximal amount. To these four degrees he assigned the numerical values 0, 1, 2, and 3, respectively. He then patiently tabulated the number of occurrences of each type of pronunciation in the speech of each one of his subjects. For each subject, he then calculated the *average* degree of centralization of each diphthong in that subject's speech. As a result, each subject wound up being characterized by two numbers between 0.00 (no centralization at all) and 3.00 (maximal centralization in every case), one for /ai/ and one for /au/. Each of these numbers Labov called the *centralization index* (CI) for that diphthong for that subject. So, for example, a subject whose CI for /ai/ is 0.23 hardly ever uses any centralization, while a subject whose CI is 2.44 uses a great deal of centralization most of the time. As it happens, Labov's subjects showed CIs for /ai/ ranging from 0.00 to 2.11, and similar values for /au/.

So far, then, Labov had managed to demonstrate that individuals on Martha's Vineyard differed substantially from one another in the degree of centralization they used. Now this was already progress: while almost every single speaker fluctuates between more and less centralized pronunciations, the statistical approach shows that individuals none the less perform quite differently in their overall behaviour. But this doesn't yet tell us anything about language change.

Labov therefore took the crucial step of looking for *correlations* between CIs and other factors. Naturally, he looked first at age. Table 10.1 shows his results for five age groups. This table shows a very interesting pattern: centralization increases steadily with decreasing age, except for the youngest group, which exhibits a sharp drop in centralization. These young speakers are a puzzle, but let's ignore them for the moment. If we do, there appear to be two possible explanations.

- *Explanation 1*: There has been a steady increase in the extent of centralization over time, with each new generation centralizing more than the preceding generation. This phenomenon is called **generational change**: a change that continues to go further with each new generation.
- *Explanation 2*: It is characteristic of Martha's Vineyard that speakers steadily decrease the extent of their centralization as they grow older. This phenomenon is called **age-grading**: speakers continuously change their own speech over time.

Which explanation is correct? In most circumstances we could only find out by monitoring the people of the island for another generation or two and watching what happens. In this case, though, Labov was lucky, because Martha's Vineyard was included in the *Linguistic Atlas of New England* (*LANE*), a very detailed dialect atlas published in 1941 and based on data collected on the island in 1933. Four subjects from the island were included in the atlas; these were aged between 56 and 82 in 1933. The detail with which their speech was reported in *LANE* is sufficient for Labov to be able to estimate the probable CIs for these speakers. Before reading further, therefore, ask yourself this question: what would each of our two possible explanations predict for the CIs of these 1933 subjects?

What Labov found was this. The four earlier subjects had a combined average CI for /ai/ of 0.86, but for /au/ their combined CI was only 0.06 –

Table 10.1 CIs and age

Age	CI /ai/	CI /au/
75+	0.25	0.23
61–75	0.35	0.37
46–60	0.62	0.44
31–45	0.81	0.88
14–30	0.37	0.46

effectively zero. This is enough to disconfirm the age-grading hypothesis. Clearly the centralization of /au/ has been increasing steadily from zero in 1933, while /ai/ has been behaving in a more complex fashion: it used to be moderately centralized, but its degree of centralization has first decreased and then increased again. We therefore have a case of generational change, but one which is more complex than we might have anticipated. Something very interesting has been going on with centralization on Martha's Vineyard – but what, and why?

Seeking more information, Labov tried looking for other correlations with non-linguistic factors. The two main occupations on the island have traditionally been fishing and farming, and so Labov checked the CIs of these occupational groups. There is also a notable social division on the island between the town-dwellers ('down-islanders') and the inhabitants of the rural areas ('up-islanders'). The results are shown in Tables 10.2 and 10.3.

Again we find some striking results. The fishermen centralize far more than anybody else on the island, while the farmers show less centralization than most people. And the rural up-islanders centralize nearly twice as much as the down-islanders in the towns. This is all extremely interesting, but we still don't know what's going on.

Lest you think that Labov could find correlations between CIs and anything at all, including perhaps the length of speakers' surnames, take a look at Table 10.4. There are three main ethnic groups on the island: those of English descent, those of Portuguese descent, and those of native American descent ('Indians'). This time, as you can see, there are no particular correlations at all. Knowing speakers' ethnic backgrounds tells you nothing about their likely speech patterns.

At this point Labov decided that an explanation of the change in the speech

Table 10.2 CIs and occupation

Occupation	CI /ai/	CI /au/
Fishermen	1.00	0.79
Farmers	0.32	0.22
Others	0.41	0.57

Table 10.3 CIs and geography

	CI /ai/	CI /au/
Towns	0.35	0.33
Rural areas	0.61	0.66

Table 10.4 CIs and ethnic group

	CI /ai/	CI /au/
English	0.67	0.60
Portuguese	0.42	0.54
Indians	0.56	0.90

of Martha's Vineyard had to be sought in social factors. After his many conversations with the locals, he began to put together a picture of the social forces which had been shaping life on the island. Here is a brief summary.

For centuries Martha's Vineyard had been isolated and generally self-sufficient. Fishing and whaling were the backbone of the economy, and the islanders grew enough food to support themselves. There was very little contact between the island and the mainland: the islanders only rarely went to the mainland, and few people from the mainland visited the island.

From about 1940 onwards, however, things began to change. Two major wars meant that many young men had to leave the island to fight, gaining in the process considerable experience of life on the mainland. Moreover, many young people began travelling to the mainland to attend university, giving them too a large taste of mainland life for the first time. Meanwhile, the island's economy was declining precipitously. Fish stocks declined, and the fishing industry suffered grievously. New agricultural techniques and regulations meant that more and more material and equipment had to be ferried in from the mainland, very expensively; the same ferry charges made it difficult for islanders to sell their produce on the mainland at a profit.

The slack in the economy was taken up by a new phenomenon: tourism. Martha's Vineyard is a beautiful place, and every summer more and more visitors from the mainland flocked to the island for holidays. By the time of Labov's study, the 6000 inhabitants of the island were hosting about 42,000 summer visitors a year. Much more prosperous than the islanders, the visitors threw money around lavishly but also exposed the islanders, especially the younger ones, to the more obvious attractions of the mainland lifestyle: plenty of money, flashy cars, the ability to travel and take holidays. Insidiously, the wealthy visitors also bought up the local houses as summer homes: by the time of Labov's visit, every single house on the entire north coast of the island, with only one or two exceptions, had been sold to a mainlander, and their former inhabitants, the descendants of sea captains and whalers, had retreated into cottages in the interior.

The result of all this, concludes Labov, is a set of conflicting social pressures on the islanders. On the one hand, they are drawn to the traditional way of life on the island, where families are close, where people live in the same house for generations, where everybody knows everybody else. On the other hand, they are drawn to the exciting new way of life on the mainland, where people can choose from a wide range of careers, make lots of money, enjoy a much greater range of creature comforts, and see the world.

People react differently to these pressures, but sooner or later every islander has to make a choice: to stay on the island and try to eke out a decent living in the difficult economic circumstances (the island is the poorest county in Massachusetts, and by some way), or to leave the island and make a life on the mainland. And the response to these pressures, Labov suggests, is the key to understanding the linguistic facts.

He interviewed his sixty-nine subjects about their plans and their view of the island, and he then divided these people into three groups: *positive* (they were strongly committed to the island, and intended to stay there), *neutral* (they had no strong views either way), and *negative* (they wanted to leave the island, and intended to do so as soon as possible). The CIs of these three groups are shown in Table 10.5; the last group is naturally rather small, since most people who wanted to leave the island had already done so, and hence could not be included in Labov's sample. This table shows the greatest degree of stratification of all the factors Labov looked at, and here we find a large part of our explanation. In Labov's interpretation, *centralization has become a linguistic marker of a positive attitude to the island.* That is, people who are committed to the island exhibit a high degree of centralization, while those who want to leave hardly centralize at all. On Martha's Vineyard, then, a speaker with a high CI is, in effect, announcing to the world 'I am committed to the island.'

We can now understand the data in the earlier tables. Because of the disastrous decline in the fishing industry, the fishermen are the most beleaguered group on the island, and the handful of men who still cling defiantly to their traditional vocation are of necessity among those most strongly committed to the island – hence their very high CIs. Since the fishing industry is concentrated in the rural up-island, this region has higher CIs than the towns down-island. And we can now understand too why the age correlation goes wrong with the youngest group: this group includes a sizeable number of people who want to leave the island but haven't yet managed to do so, and their very low CIs are bringing the average down. By the age of 30, though, most people who want to leave have gone, and are not there to be counted.

Table 10.5 CIs and attitude to the island

Persons	Attitude	CI /ai/	CI /au/
40	Positive	0.63	0.62
19	Neutral	0.32	0.42
6	Negative	0.09	0.08

As confirmation, Labov interviewed four 15-year-old high-school students. Two of these had already decided to leave the island after finishing school; these had CIs of 0.00 and 0.40, and of 0.00 and 0.00. The other two had decided to stay on the island; they had CIs of 0.90 and 1.00, and of 1.13 and 1.19.

What we find on Martha's Vineyard, then, is a fine example of the **social stratification** of a linguistic variable. As we shall see later, linguistic variables more often correlate with social factors like sex and social class, but on Martha's Vineyard the relevant factor is attitude to the island. Here, the way you speak announces which group you belong to: pro-island or pro-mainland.

But how did all this get started? This is a more difficult question, but Labov has a reasonable suggestion to make. In the 1930s, centralization of /au/ was non-existent, while centralization of /ai/ was significant but declining overall. Labov suggests that a handful of speakers, unquestionably up-island and probably fishermen, just happened by chance to have a higher than average degree of centralization of /ai/, and that these were people who were well known for their unwavering commitment to the island way of life. Other speakers, beginning to feel the pressures from the mainland, and deciding to commit themselves to the island, took these people as models and began to imitate them. In particular, they began to imitate the older speakers' centralization, and, perhaps inevitably, they went too far: they began to centralize /ai/ *more* than their models did, and they also began to extend the centralization to /au/. As time passed, and the pressures increased, new generations making the same decision continued the process, introducing ever greater degrees of centralization.

Interestingly, the islanders do not, on the whole, appear to be consciously aware of what they're doing, though they are at least dimly aware that some people speak differently from others. Labov provides an interesting anecdote. One young man had earlier left the island to attend university and then worked for some time in a city on the mainland. Deciding he didn't like it after all, he returned to the island and started a business. This man had a CI of 2.11, the highest value recorded for any speaker, as though he were trying to compensate for his earlier mistake. One night at dinner, his mother remarked, 'You know, he didn't always speak that way. It's only since he came back from college. I guess he wanted to be more like the men on the docks.'

This anecdote represents a rare instance of a speaker's noticing a change in someone's speech. But the young man involved was probably rather atypical: most speakers on the island probably do not change their speech deliberately and significantly during adulthood. As the age data in Table 10.1 suggest, most speakers probably acquire their speech patterns early in life and then maintain them without further change.

Nevertheless, Labov's data show clearly that a change is in progress on Martha's Vineyard, and has been for some time. But that change only shows up when we examine the data in the right manner: simply by listening to people speak, we can observe no changes happening. All that we observe directly is *variation*. But that very variation conceals a change which is in progress: even if individuals don't change their own speech, the speech of the whole community is, and has been, changing steadily. For our purposes, this last conclusion is the most important of all.

There are thus three lessons to be learned from Martha's Vineyard.

1. The quantitative (statistical) approach to variation can reveal systematic differences between individuals and groups which are not otherwise evident.
2. A linguistic variable may exhibit social stratification, with members of different groups using different values of the variable.
3. A change in progress shows up as variation.

The importance of these conclusions has been reinforced by dozens of more recent studies, some of which we shall be examining below.

10.3   *Variation as the vehicle of change*

The quantitative method pioneered on Martha's Vineyard has been developed by Labov and others and applied to the study of a large number of linguistic variables in a large number of speech communities. By using this approach sociolinguists have again and again been able to find interesting correlations between the variables they are looking at and non-linguistic social factors. The particular social factor identified on Martha's Vineyard, attitude to the island, is a somewhat unusual case. Far more commonly, the relevant social factors turn out to be more obvious and familiar ones.

Naturally, one of the most obvious of these factors is social class. In most speech communities of any size, there is conspicuous social stratification, with some people belonging to more prestigious classes than others. Of course, the criteria for determining class membership are complex and variable, involving such factors as income, family background, vocation or profession, and skin colour, and the same factors are not equally important in every community. The important thing for our purposes here, though, is that, in a number of societies, sociologists have already, for their own purposes, worked out reasonable criteria for assigning individuals to particular social classes. Sociolinguists can therefore take advantage of these independently derived criteria in their own work.

While it is perfectly possible to investigate the possible relation between social classes and linguistic variables while excluding all other factors, it has become commonplace to use a slightly more elaborate approach, also invented by Labov, in which the investigator looks simultaneously at social class and at a second factor which we can call **context** or **degree of formality**. This two-dimensional approach is favoured because we find in practice that it often yields very illuminating results about the nature of variation in a community.

Let's look at a typical example of this approach. This one was carried out by the British sociolinguist Peter Trudgill in the English city of Norwich, as one part of a wide-ranging investigation of variation in the speech of Norwich. The variable Trudgill chose to look at is the variation between two types of pronunciation of verb forms ending in -*ing*, such as *going*. In Norwich, as elsewhere, there are two possible pronunciations for such forms: one with a final velar nasal, which corresponds quite well to the conventional spelling, and another with a final coronal nasal, often represented in writing as *goin'*. This variable Trudgill notates as (ng). (It has become conventional to represent a sociolinguistic variable by some convenient symbol placed in parentheses.)

As always in quantitative work, Trudgill tape-recorded the speech of his subjects and counted the instances of each type of pronunciation for each one of his subjects. But he did something more: he put each of his subjects into four different contexts and recorded their speech separately for all four contexts. The four contexts were *casual speech* (CS), in which the subject is engaging in ordinary, relaxed conversation, *formal speech* (FS), the self-conscious speech of a formal interview, *reading-passage speech* (RPS), in which the subject reads aloud from a written text, and *word-list speech* (WLS), in which the subject reads aloud a list of written words, one at a time. Then, using the independent criteria just referred to, he assigned each of his subjects to one of five social classes: the *middle middle class* (MMC), the *lower middle class* (LMC), the *upper working class* (UWC), the *middle working class* (MWC), and the *lower working class* (LWC). For the subjects in each class and in each context, he then calculated an average value of the variable (ng), expressed as the percentage of *goin'*-style pronunciations used. His results are shown in Table 10.6 and Figure 10.1. As you can see, every group of speakers uses both types of pronunciation, and it is generally impossible to predict which form a given speaker will use on the next individual occasion: naïve observation would once again yield nothing but variation. But the quantitative approach at once reveals a very striking pattern.

Table 10.6 The variable (ng) in Norwich (percentages of -*in'* forms)

	WLS	RPS	FS	CS
MMC	0	0	3	28
LMC	0	10	15	42
UWC	5	15	74	87
MWC	23	44	88	95
LWC	29	66	98	100

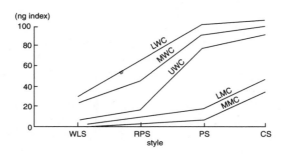

Fig. 10.1 The variable (ng) in Norwich

First, in any given context, a member of a lower-ranking class consistently uses a higher proportion of *goin'*-style pronunciations than a member of a higher-ranking class. Second, everybody uses a higher proportion of *goin'*-style pronunciations as the context becomes more informal and a lower proportion of *goin'*-style pronunciations as the context becomes more formal. The graph displays this behaviour very vividly.

From these results, we can also conclude that one of the two types of pronunciation has greater overt prestige in Norwich than the other. Which is it, and why?

Let's look at a second example in the same vein. This time it's Labov's work again. Here the setting is New York City and the variable (r) is the two types of pronunciation of words containing non-prevocalic /r/ – that is, words like *car*, *more*, *dark*, and *shirt*, in which /r/ is not followed by a vowel. Speakers in New York sometimes pronounce this /r/ (we call this a **rhotic** style) and sometimes not (we call this a **non-rhotic** style); in the non-rhotic style, *guard* may become identical to *god*, *dark* may become identical to *dock*, and so on. Again all individuals use both types of pronunciation, and again the quantitative approach uncovers a clear pattern, shown in Fig. 10.2. The social classes recognized are the upper middle class (UMC), the lower middle class (LMC), the upper working class (UWC), the middle working class (MWC), the lower working class (LWC), and the lower class.

Again, we see the same general pattern we saw in the Norwich case. In a given context, the members of each class use a higher percentage of rhotic (/r/-ful) pronunciations then the members of the next lower class, and everybody shifts towards a higher proportion of rhotic pronunciations as the context becomes more formal. (Question: which type of pronunciation is more overtly prestigious in New York?) But this time there is one striking difference: two of the lines cross. The second highest group, the lower middle class, actually uses more rhotic pronunciations in the most formal context than do the highest group, the upper middle class. This phenomenon has turned up in a number of

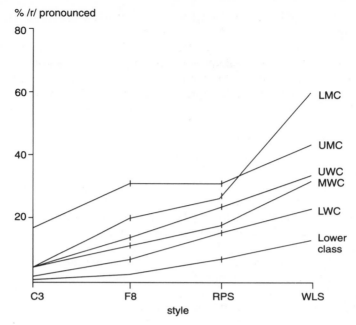

Fig. 10.2 The variable (r) in Norwich

other such studies, and always it appears to be the second highest class which jumps above the highest class in the most formal context. Labov calls this phenomenon **hypercorrection**, but the term is unfortunate, since 'hypercorrection' has long been used in linguistics in a slightly different sense, and here I shall use the label **overadjustment**. Very frequently, it seems, the members of the second highest class overadjust their speech in very formal contexts towards prestige forms, as though they were particularly insecure about their speech and perhaps also about their social position.

These two studies are in no way isolated or exceptional. Very similar patterns have turned up wherever sociolinguists have looked, in Europe, in North America, in Asia, in Africa. Such findings are of critical importance for understanding the processes of language change and for finding a resolution of Saussure's paradox.

As I remarked above, an earlier generation of linguists was inclined to see variation as peripheral, as insignificant, as inconvenient, perhaps even as pathological. What the sociolinguists have found is that the truth is precisely the opposite.

First, they have shown that variation is *normal* in language. Linguistic variation is characteristic of all speech communities; it is a central and inescapable feature of the speech of every community and of every individual. Indeed, it is the *absence* of variation which would be pathological: today we would be dumbfounded to stumble across a community of any size in which everyone spoke in an invariant manner in all circumstances, and we would suspect that something fishy was going on.

Observe that these findings do not contradict Saussure's conclusion that a language is a highly structured system of relations among linguistic elements: they merely demonstrate that the nature of that system is considerably richer and more complex than we had previously suspected. When you learn to speak a language fluently, not only do you master the phonology, the grammar, the vocabulary, and so on, but you also master the proper use of the innumerable linguistic variables characteristic of your community.

Second, the sociolinguists have demonstrated that linguistic variables very often have social significance, in that your use of the variable features carries important information about your place in the community. The striking graphs show that such social significance is well known to speakers, in some fashion at least, since they automatically adjust their speech in response to changing contexts, though it does not follow that speakers are necessarily highly conscious of the linguistic details.

Third, and most critically, variation has a time dimension. In the case of Norwich, there is no reason to doubt that the situation with respect to the (ng) variable has been stable for generations, perhaps even for centuries. So far as we can tell, the frequency of the two variants is not tending to change over time.

In New York, however, the situation is very different: we have clear evidence that the position *is* changing over time. The data collected from New York in the 1930s and published in a dialect atlas show almost no trace of rhotic speech at the time: non-rhotic pronunciations appear to be nearly universal. Data collected in the 1950s and the 1960s, however, show noticeably higher frequencies of rhotic speech. Further, it appears that rhotic pronunciations are becoming steadily more frequent in New York today. Unlike Norwich, then, New York is showing a steady change over time in the distribution of the two types of pronunciation. But that change is not proceeding simply: we do not merely find younger speakers using more /r/s than older speakers, as we might have expected. Instead, different social groups are responding differently, and the facts are complex. Lower-middle-class speakers are behaving differently from upper-middle-class speakers; in some classes, older speakers appear to be actually increasing the frequency of their rhotic pronunciations, while younger speakers in the same classes show little tendency to do the same; working-class speakers whose jobs bring them into regular contact with middle-class speakers are behaving differently from working-class speakers whose jobs don't; and so on. Among the many interesting details he came across in his lengthy study, Labov reports that many parents show a marked tendency to use a much higher than normal proportion of rhotic pronunciations when scolding their children, as if unconsciously to put across the message that rhotic pronunciations are desirable.

So, though the facts are complex, we have good evidence that New York City is slowly changing from an earlier state in which non-rhotic pronunciation was the norm, prestigious and practically universal, towards a state in which rhotic pronunciation represents the prestige norm. It is entirely possible that New York will eventually go all the way and shift to totally rhotic speech of the sort found throughout the American Midwest, but we can't be sure of that: only time will tell. In the meantime, though, a linguistic change is clearly applying to New York City English, and *the vehicle of that change is variation*. That is, the change is proceeding through the mechanism of a steady shift in the frequencies of competing forms, what I have been calling variants. And this, we now believe, is exactly the way that most language changes proceed: by a shift in the frequencies of competing variant forms.

And so we have a resolution of the Saussurean paradox. Changes can proceed without disrupting the system of a language because the vehicle of change is variation, and variation is always present – indeed, it is a central characteristic of speech.

We can thus gain an understanding of how the change is proceeding in New York, but that doesn't explain how the change got started in the first place. Very often it is far more difficult to explain how a change gets started than to explain how it propagates itself, but in this case the answer is not hard to find.

Like the southeast of England, the east coast of the USA has for generations been characterized by non-rhotic speech. West of the Appalachian Mountains, however, in the American Midwest, rhotic speech has been universal for at least as long. In the past, eastern Americans tended to look to prestigious east coast cities like Boston and Philadelphia for their linguistic models, or even to England, while Midwestern speech was considered rustic by comparison. In the last few decades, however, things have changed: radio, films, and above all television are now dominated by rhotic speakers from the Midwest and the West, and there is a steadily growing perception that such *General American* speech, as it is called, now represents the norm for American speakers, and not the non-rhotic speech of the coast. Like everyone else, New Yorkers have been constantly exposed to the once unfamiliar speech of the Midwest, and so it is hardly surprising that such a prominent Midwestern feature as rhoticity has crept into New York speech, where it is now steadily extending its presence.

These two questions, How does a change start? and How does a change propagate itself?, are often referred to respectively as the problems of **actuation** and **implementation**. As you can see, the work of the sociolinguists has primarily addressed the issue of implementation, and with considerable success. On the whole, our understanding of actuation is still, by comparison, in its infancy, and this is doubtless an area which will be receiving further scrutiny in the future.

A classic instance of a change which can only be understood in terms of variation and social stratification is provided by the history of certain English vowels. Middle English had seven long vowels, three of which are relevant to our story: the vowel of *mate* (Middle English /a:/), the vowel of *meat* (ME /ɛ:/), and the vowel of *meet* (ME /e:/). There is not the slightest doubt that these three vowels were distinct in Middle English and that they had the pronunciations I have just assigned to them; indeed, these Middle English pronunciations are precisely the reason for the spellings which we still use today: *mate, hate, late* versus *meat, seat, read* versus *meet, see, heel.* Like all the Middle English long vowels, these three underwent a change of quality (in all three cases, a raising) during the Great Vowel Shift, which mostly took place during the fifteenth and sixteenth centuries. That vowel shift is of no direct relevance to our story, but another change is.

We have abundant testimony to the pronunciation of English in London in the sixteenth century, in the form of descriptions by the phoneticians of the day and of the rhymes used by poets, and it is clear that, early in that century, a merger had occurred between the vowel of *mate* and the vowel of *meat.* That is, these two words had become homophones, and the same was true for other relevant pairs such as *hate* and *heat* and *mane* and *mean.* This, of course, is not the sort of pronunciation we are familiar with today, not even in London, but in fact it still survives in parts of Ireland, where the local pronunciations of *meat* and *tea,* for example, sound to the rest of us like *mate* and *tay.* Let us call this type of pronunciation *System I.*

However, we have equally abundant testimony to the pronunciation used in London in the seventeenth century, and this does not conform to System I. Instead, we find a merger between the vowels of *meat* and *meet,* with the vowel of *mate* remaining distinct. In the seventeenth century, then, *meat* sounded just like *meet,* both of which sounded different from *mate, bean* rhymed with *seen* and not with *mane, seas* rhymed with *freeze* and not with *maze,* and so on. Let's call this type of pronunciation *System II.*

System II is, of course, the type of pronunciation that virtually all English-speakers use today. But the change from System I to System II constitutes a huge puzzle. Why? Because, on the face of it, the change involved a reversal of a merger – and the **reversal of merger** is theoretically impossible.

Of course, the development of System II from Middle English also involved a merger, but *this* merger is of no significance here. The problem is this. In the sixteenth century, speakers had completely merged the vowels of *mate* and *meat,* and no longer made any distinction between them at all. Therefore, it would seem, in order for their descendants to change to System II, in which the *mate/meat* merger had not occurred, those descendants had to reverse the merger. That is, they had to figure out which of the *mate/meat* words had, generations earlier, contained the lower *mate* vowel, so that they could separate those words out, and which had earlier contained the higher *meat* vowel, so that they could separate out those words too (and then merge them with the *meet* words). But how could they do this?

Speakers do not have access to the history of their language. Consider a parallel. Unless you come from certain parts of East Anglia or south Wales, you certainly pronounce *nose* and *knows* identically. But, in Middle English, these words contained different vowels, vowels which, as it happens, have also undergone merger everywhere except in East Anglia and south Wales.

Can you tell which words formerly contained the *nose* vowel and which the *knows* vowel? I am quite sure you cannot. I can't do it myself without checking the historical records. Indeed, you were probably not even aware until this moment that there ever were two different vowels in the *nose* and *knows* words.

Those early modern Londoners, with their System I pronunciation, must have been in the same position. How could they possibly know which words had once had the lower vowel and which the higher, since they didn't make any distinction themselves? How could they even know that there had ever been a difference at all?

For many years linguists agonized over this problem, without resolving it. In 1962, the distinguished Chomskyan linguist Morris Halle, in apparent desperation, put forward an astounding explanation: taking advantage of the abstract underlying forms permitted by Chomskyan linguistics, he suggested that several generations of speakers must have managed to keep the *mate* and *meat* vowels distinct in their heads, even though they always pronounced these vowels identically, and even though they never heard anybody else making the distinction. To most linguists, this account is nothing less than mysticism, and it can't possibly be taken seriously. But that still leaves us with the problem.

In 1968, however, in the very paper that is now considered to have revolutionized the study of language change, three sociolinguists, Uriel Weinreich, William Labov, and Marvin Herzog, pointed out that a simple and decidedly non-mystical explanation was available, and that that explanation had moreover been found decades before by specialists in sixteenth- and seventeenth-century English, but that it had been lying unnoticed in the specialist tomes ever since.

If we examine the representations of contemporary speech in the writings of the period, such as the plays of Shakespeare, who wrote in the late sixteenth and early seventeenth centuries, we find that *both* types of pronunciation are present – but with a difference. System I is found in the speech of refined, upper-class characters (who of course constitute the majority of the leading characters in Shakespeare), while System II is typical of lower-class speakers – servants, clowns, and the like. Therefore, both types of pronunciation were in use, and both types were undoubtedly well known to most people, but once again there was significant social stratification: upper-class speakers used one set of vowels, while lower-class speakers used the other.

So what happened? Easy: there was a change in the *social significance* of the two types of pronunciation. Earlier, it was System I which was regarded as being the more prestigious, and so educated upper-class speakers used that, while avoiding the much less prestigious, and probably vulgar, System II. At some point, though, perceptions changed: System II came to be regarded as more prestigious, and so later generations of upper-class speakers used that, and System I came in turn to be regarded as non-prestigious and possibly as vulgar. (Observe that this change in perceived prestige is reminiscent of what is going on in New York, and we might surmise, therefore, that the change was accompanied by a good deal of variation for a while, before System II finally won out.)

Now in those days there were no sound recordings of any kind, and our only records are written ones. People who could write were by definition educated, and therefore they used the type of pronunciation regarded at the time as most prestigious. Poets based their rhymes on prestige speech; phoneticians described the type of pronunciation they regarded as most prestigious and desirable; distinguished characters in literature had prestige speech put into their mouths. But there were always large numbers of people using the low-prestige variety; it's merely that their speech didn't get recorded very often – practically never, in fact, except in the mouths of lower-class characters in literature, who were given non-prestige speech specifically to show their low social status. And, in all likelihood, there were plenty of people, perhaps almost everybody, who used both types of pronunciation in a variable manner, but we have no data.

It is therefore a grave oversimplification to declare, as we formerly did, that Londoners used System I in the sixteenth century but System II in the seventeenth century. Both types of pronunciation were always in use, but only one of them tended to be recorded at any given time.

And why did the shift in prestige take place? We don't have the information to answer this, but in all likelihood what happened was merely an instance of the exceedingly common process we call **change from below**: a stigmatized feature which is not present in prestige speech but which is widespread in non-prestige speech begins to creep up the social ladder into the mouths of prestige speakers, gaining ground steadily until it becomes accepted as the prestige norm, with the older prestige form becoming stigmatized in turn.

This sort of thing happens all the time. In England, the loss of /r/ in words like *far* and *dark*, and the loss of /h/ in words like *why* and *whale*, were once stigmatized as 'vulgar'; none the less they have crept into educated speech to the point at which they are now regarded as the norm, and speakers who still pronounce the /r/s in *far* and *dark* are regarded as laughably quaint and rustic, while the pronunciation of the /h/s in *why* and *whale* is now no more than a pedantic affectation in England. Comparable developments are occurring today. For example, the 'glottalization' of popular London speech has for generations been regarded by educated speakers as vulgar; it is nevertheless invading middle-class speech at a surprising rate, and it has recently even been heard in the speech of some of the younger members of the Royal Family. The motivation for changes from below remains somewhat obscure, but there is no doubting their frequency.

The solution to the problem of the apparent reversal of merger, then, is simple, almost banal. Indeed, it was hardly a linguistic change at all, but rather a social one. Comparable social changes can be observed in every domain. Not so many years ago, it was unheard of in most social circles for a man to wear earrings or a ponytail; these were among the exclusive prerogatives of women. Today, though, ponytails and earrings are commonplace among both working-class and middle-class men; they are even sported by prosperous yuppies working for august banks and investment firms. True, I have yet to see a British MP or an American congressman decked out in this fashion, but give it another ten years . . .

There is an important reminder here. Earlier in the book, I pointed out the importance of the historical linguists' version of the *principle of uniformity*: ancient languages were not different from modern ones. That principle applies equally to social factors. There is no good reason to suppose that, centuries or millennia ago, social factors were less important than now. Like us, our ancestors had their social distinctions, and undoubtedly these distinctions were well represented in speech. In Shakespeare's London, in King Alfred's England, in Caesar's Rome, in ancient Egypt or Babylon, there were doubtless more and less prestigious ways of speaking, and there must have been countless occasions on which some stigmatized feature of vulgar speech eventually passed into the prestige speech of the upper classes.

I shall close this section with an amusing little example of this ceaseless change from below. Old French had a diphthong [ɔj], spelled *oi* in the conventional orthography, as in *moi* 'me', *loi* 'law', *soil* 'soil', *point* 'dot', *voix* 'voice', and *chois* 'choice' (modern *choix*). You can see that some of these were borrowed into English, where nothing much has happened to the diphthong. In medieval French, though, the nucleus of the diphthong was shifted from the first to the second element, producing the pronunciation [wɛ]. This remained the norm in polite speech for centuries; however, in popular speech, it was eventually shifted to [wa]. By the time of the French Revolution, [wa] was virtually universal among the mass of French-speakers, but the French court and the aristocracy continued to use the more prestigious [wɛ]. In 1793, after the Revolution, the court was dispersed, and many aristocrats and members of the royal family fled in fear of their lives. After things had settled down a few years later, these high-ranking refugees returned to Paris with their prestige speech, only to be told that, in their absence, the popular [wa] had become the prestige form, and hence that they were now speaking a non-prestigious form of French. I don't know how many of them gritted their teeth and deliberately changed to [wa], but certainly the old [wɛ] did not outlive them, and [wa] is universal in France today.

10.4 *Lexical diffusion*

Because of their refusal to pay any attention to variation, earlier linguists were not generally aware of the existence of changes underway in their own languages or in the languages they were studying. Today's linguists, in contrast, are keenly aware that changes are everywhere in progress at this very moment, and naturally we are often interested in studying the course of those changes. But how can this be done?

As we saw above, we are occasionally lucky enough to have good descriptions of some speech community compiled a generation or two ago, and hence we can compare those descriptions with our own observations of the same communities today, in order to find out what has changed. Studies of this sort are called **real-time** studies: we simply compare earlier and later stages in the development of the same community.

Most of the time, though, we are not so fortunate as to have good descriptions dating back thirty or forty years. So what can we do? Obviously, we could in principle simply watch a community for the next thirty or forty years to see what happens, but most linguists would prefer to get some results they can publish before they reach retirement age, and so we would like to have some other approach at our disposal.

There is such an approach, and it makes use of what we call **apparent time**. The idea is simple: we assume that most people learn their language in childhood, and that, after adolescence, they do not normally introduce any further significant changes into their speech. Thus, we can merely compare the speech of people of different ages within a single community to see what differences exist, and then we conclude that those differences result from changes which have affected the speech of younger speakers only. This approach is not without its pitfalls, but we have nevertheless managed to make some illuminating discoveries by using it.

Here I want to discuss a particularly striking and important discovery which has chiefly resulted from the study of apparent time, though real-time studies have also occasionally been invoked. This work pertains to phonological change, and in particular it focuses on the way in which a sound change applies to relevant words.

Recall the Neogrammarian Hypothesis, which maintains that a sound change applies exceptionlessly to all relevant words. For reasons explained earlier in the book, I am still assuming that this hypothesis is essentially correct, but very shortly now I am going to call this assumption strongly into question. Now the proponents of the Neogrammarian Hypothesis in the past were mostly inclined to assume that sound changes were in general *phonetically gradual* – that is, that a sound change typically proceeds via tiny changes in the phonetic quality of segments. But is this so?

Certainly phonetic gradualness seems plausible enough for some types of changes, and we sometimes do find examples of phonetically gradual changes. For instance, the centralization of /ai/ and /au/ on Martha's Vineyard is apparently proceeding by small and steady increases in the degree of centralization over time, even though individuals fluctuate very considerably in the pronunciations they use. But many other sound changes cannot possibly be phonetically gradual. Whole-segment processes like insertion, loss, and metathesis cannot conceivably be phonetically gradual: no one can insert 5 per cent of a segment, or move 10 per cent of a segment to a different position in the word. Whole-segment processes are of necessity *phonetically abrupt*. But other types of phonological change are usually also phonetically abrupt. To take one example, the devoicing of voiced consonants, a very common type of change in certain environments, is hardly likely to proceed by a gradual reduction in the degree of voicing: 100%, 75%, 40%, 15%, 5%, zero. Instead, voicing is usually lost abruptly: a speaker uses either a voiced segment or a voiced one, with nothing in between. To take another example, the curious change of [ʃ] to [x], which occurred in Early Modern Spanish, is most unlikely to have involved a gradual movement of the consonant from the prepalatal region to the velum: instead, the pronunciation just 'jumped' from one place to the other.

Even so, it was until recently still widely assumed that changes in vowel quality, at least, were usually phonetically gradual, and of course almost everyone continued to believe that a sound change necessarily affected all relevant words in the language simultaneously. But these beliefs too have now been shattered by the discovery of a phenomenon called **lexical diffusion**.

Though the possibility of lexical diffusion had occasionally been suggested by earlier linguists, its indisputable existence was first demonstrated around 1970 by the Chinese–American linguists Matthew Chen and William Wang and their colleagues in connection with Chinese dialects. Since then, lexical diffusion has been uncovered so frequently that it has begun to be recognized in some quarters as constituting virtually the paradigm mechanism of phono-logical change.

Rather than consider the Chinese data, I shall here look at what is perhaps the most celebrated case of lexical diffusion yet uncovered: the so-called 'short-*a* tensing' in urban American varieties, and especially in Philadelphia.

Modern English inherited from Middle English the vowel /æ/, as in *cat*. Historically, this is a lax vowel: it is phonetically short, it is a pure vowel and not a diphthong, and it cannot end a syllable. Now this vowel has been undergoing tensing in a number of varieties of English; for example, some well-educated speakers in England pronounce *bad* with a conspicuous cen-tring diphthong. Tensing occurs also in my own Midwestern American accent, in which the vowel of *bad* is phonetically just as long as the historically tense vowel in *bead*. Tensing is also found in New York City, where its presence is phonologically conditioned: it occurs before a voiceless fricative, before a voiced plosive, and before /m/ or /n/, but not elsewhere. This last case, of course, is precisely the sort of sound change which the Neogrammarian Hypothesis maintains as the normal and only type of sound change. But it is the nature of the tensing process in Philadelphia which has proved to be most illuminating.

In this city, the vowel /æ/ has been undergoing a tensing process which both lengthens and raises it and usually also converts it to a diphthong. Thus, for example, *mad* is commonly pronounced [me:əd] in Philadelphia (and it may go as high as [mɪ:əd] in New York). So far there is nothing remarkable going on. But detailed studies of Philadelphia speech have revealed something totally unexpected: only *some* words undergo tensing, while others do not.

For a typical Philadelphia speaker, the tense vowel occurs in *mad*, *bad*, and *glad*, but not in *sad*, *dad*, or *Brad*, and also not in *cab* or *brag*; it occurs in *can't*, *aunt*, and *man*, but not in *ran*, *swam*, or *began*; it occurs in *last*, *pass*, *half*, *ass* and *ask*, but not in *ash* or *cash* or *after* or *Afghan*; it occurs in *answer*, *ancestor*, and *anchovy*, but not in *aspirin* or *astronaut*; it occurs in *ham* but not in *hammock*; and so on. Speakers may vary as to which particular words show tensing; they may vary in their degree of tensing of different words or occasionally even of the same words. But the key point is this: *it is impossible to predict which words will show tensing and which not.* The best we can do is to note that particular phonological environments or membership in particular word-classes either favours or disfavours tensing, but that's all.

What we are looking at, then, is a **lexical split**. Some of the words with lax /æ/ still have a lax vowel, while others have undergone tensing and now have a different, tense, vowel. This split appears to be unconditioned: some words have gone one way, some the other, in an unpredictable manner, and that's all there is to it. This conclusion is surprising, even puzzling, since such unconditioned splits are apparently incompatible with the hypothesis of regular sound change.

How did this happen? The interpretation which has come to be placed on this curious state of affairs is that, at some earlier stage, the words containing /æ/ underwent, in Philadelphia, the process we now call *lexical diffusion*: that is, some of them moved out of the class of words with lax /æ/ and into the class of words with tense /æː/, which had originally been empty. But did they all move at once, or did they cross over one or two at a time? Without historical information, we can't tell. But there is one thing we can usefully do: we can look to see if any more words are currently being transferred from one class to the other.

In the centre of Philadelphia, the position at present appears to be remarkably stable: we can see no evidence that more words are diffusing. In the suburbs, however, things are different. For example, the word *planet*, which normally has a lax vowel in Philadelphia, usually has a tense vowel in several of the suburbs, and in South Philadelphia this tense pronunciation is now categorical among young children. This word, at least, is therefore in the process of diffusing from the lax class to the tense class. There is also evidence that several other words are doing the same, including *Sally*, *alligator*, and possibly even *sad*, though the evidence is so far less compelling than for *planet*.

It is therefore possible that lexical diffusion is continuing in Philadelphia, and it is conceivable that this diffusion may one day go all the way, that every word with lax /æ/ will be transferred into the tense class, leaving the lax class empty. If that happens, the result of the whole lengthy process will be something indistinguishable from a regular sound change. A historical linguist looking at Philadelphia generations from now might therefore very well conclude that lax /æ/ had undergone a perfectly regular tensing there. But we, with the advantage of catching the change in progress, can see that no such thing is going on: instead, the sound change is applying to a few words at a time, moving them from one class to the other, while temporarily (at least) leaving other relevant words completely unaffected.

Such lexical diffusion provides the most direct refutation possible of the Neogrammarian Hypothesis. That hypothesis requires all relevant words to be affected equally when a change occurs, but lexical diffusion affects only a few words at a time. Since we now have a number of indisputable cases of lexical diffusion on record, the Neogrammarian Hypothesis can now be seen to be falsified: even if some sound changes do proceed absolutely regularly, others do not. Wherever he is now, Hugo Schuchardt, that crusty old opponent of the Neogrammarians, must be breaking out a celebratory bottle at the news.

Indeed, some linguists have now gone so far as to declare that *all* sound changes proceed by lexical diffusion, and that the frequent cases of apparently regular change which we find in our historical data merely represent those cases in which lexical diffusion finally did succeed in transferring every single word from one class to the other, before running out of steam. This may perhaps be so, but it is too early to be making such rash declarations. We are not yet in a position to conclude that regular change, of the sort envisaged by the Neogrammarians, never occurs at all, and in fact the overwhelming frequency of apparently regular changes must make us suspicious of any claims that such regular changes can result only from lexical diffusion. There is clearly a lot of work to be done here.

None the less, the discovery of lexical diffusion is a significant advance in our understanding of historical change, and it at once offers a solution to a number of long-outstanding puzzles. Consider the *meat/meet* merger discussed above. Most of the words which historically had the vowel of *meat* have indeed merged with the *meet* words, but not quite all of them. The words *steak*, *great*, and *break*, as their traditional spelling suggests, originally had the same vowel as *meat*, *read*, and *beak* – and yet these words have not undergone the merger with the *meet* words. Previously, linguists were inclined to mutter the words 'dialect mixing' upon encountering exceptional cases like these, but this label is not so much an explanation as an admission of defeat.

Now, however, we can put forward an interesting explanation. The *meat* words were moved into the *meet* class by lexical diffusion; after this change had transferred most of the relevant words, it ran out of steam, and the last few words in the *meat* class, like *great*, never got transferred. Such words are referred to as the **residue** of the change: in the diffusionist view, they just got left behind.

As you can see, though, the words in the residue, like *steak*, *great*, and *break*, have undergone the other merger, this time with the *mate* words. These words, then, have undergone the merger that led to my System I pronunciation above, while most other words have undergone the different merger leading to System II pronunciation. We can therefore imagine a slightly more complex scenario: *both mergers were operating at the same time and competing for the* meat *words*. This kind of situation has turned up in other cases, and we call it **competing changes**.

When we think about it, there is no reason at all why the innovations that appear in a language at around the same time should all be mutually compatible: why shouldn't some of them be in conflict with others? If two conflicting changes appear together, it does not seem unreasonable that they should 'compete' for the same words, with some words eventually going one way and some the other, as has perhaps happened with *meat* and *break*. Such a scenario would have been inconceivable to the Neogrammarians, but, if lexical diffusion is as common as we now suspect it is, this scenario is not only conceivable but perhaps even likely. A century ago, historical linguists were convinced that the pathway of phonological change was thoroughly understood; today, we have begun to realize that there is a great deal we have yet to learn.

In the next section, I turn to yet another startling recent discovery about phonological change.

10.5 *Near-mergers*

As we saw in Chapter 4, a common type of phonological change is merger: two phonemes which formerly contrasted cease to contrast, and the number of phonemes in the system is reduced. Ordinarily, a merger produces a number of new homophones. For example, the *meat/meet* merger discussed above turned into homophones such pairs as *meat* and *meet*, *sea* and *see*, *team* and *teem*, all of which had been completely distinct in pronunciation before.

We have a simple way of testing to see whether particular pairs of words are homophones for a particular speaker or not: the **minimal-pair test**. This test can be carried out in several ways. A simple way is the following: the speaker is asked to pronounce each of the two words several times while being recorded, and his pronunciations are then played back to him in a different order. If he can consistently tell which word is which, the words contrast, and he has not undergone a merger; if he cannot tell them apart, they are homophones for him, and he has undergone the merger.

This beautifully simple technique has been used countless times by linguists constructing descriptions of particular languages or varieties, and. on the face of it, the method looks so reliable as to be foolproof.

In one respect it probably is foolproof. If the subject can consistently hear a difference in his own speech, then his pronunciations must be truly different. In the same way, we might reasonably assume that a speaker who consistently fails to hear any difference in his own speech does not make any difference in speaking. But this second presumption, obvious though it may seem, has recently been shown to be false.

For some years now, Labov and his colleagues have been uncovering a series of cases of what they call **near-mergers**. In a near-merger, a speaker produces a consistent, but rather small, difference between two sets of words, but, at the same time, that speaker simply cannot hear the difference in recordings of his own speech (or in the speech of his neighbours who share the near-merger), and typically insists that there is no difference. All reported cases of near-mergers involve vowels.

Here is a typical example, from Albuquerque, New Mexico. A high-school student called Dan was found to have a near-merger between the vowel of *pool* and the vowel of *pull*, both in his spontaneous speech and in the minimal-pair test. Instrumental analysis showed that he made a small but rather consistent difference between these two vowels, though with a certain degree of overlap. Dan himself, on listening to recordings of his own speech, could not distinguish the two vowels: he could not tell if he was pronouncing *pool* or *pull*, *fool* or *full*, *who'd* or *hood*. His girlfriend Didi and Didi's brother Hal did not have the near-merger and had no trouble in distinguishing such pairs of words in their own speech. When listening to Dan's speech, however, they found it very difficult to decide which word he was pronouncing, yet they were still able to guess correctly in 83 per cent of cases.

Now 83 per cent success is a very odd result to get in a minimal-pair test. Normally, we would expect to get one of only two results: either the listener cannot tell the words apart at all, and hence gets only the chance score of 50 per cent right, or the listener can tell the words apart easily, and hence scores 100 per cent success. The result obtained here shows that Dan usually distinguishes the words clearly enough for listeners who make a distinction to tell which word he is pronouncing, but not always. Such behaviour was previously entirely unknown in linguistics, but there is a rapidly growing body of evidence suggesting that near-mergers are very common indeed.

Near-mergers have been reported for classes of words represented by *pool* and *pull* in Albuquerque and also in Salt Lake City and in parts of Texas (this one appears to be widespread in the southwestern USA), for *cot* and *caught* in Pennsylvania, for *too* and *toe*, and also for *beer* and *bear*, in Norwich, for *source* and *sauce* in New York City, for *line* and *loin* in Essex, for *furry* and *ferry* in Philadelphia, and quite a few others. Near-mergers were at first regarded as an exotic rarity, and some critics even refused to believe that they existed at all, but now we begin to suspect that near-mergers are positively commonplace.

The reality of near-mergers can no longer be doubted, but their existence causes problems for historical linguists. Most obviously, when we find the commentators of the past insisting that they make no distinction between two sets of words which had earlier been distinct, we can no longer be sure whether those commentators are reporting a genuine merger or only a near-merger. Indeed, Labov has suggested that a number of historically reported mergers may in fact have been only near-mergers, possibly including the *mate/meat* merger in London discussed earlier in the chapter. The point is important because a true merger, once it has occurred, cannot be reversed, at least not without the influence of speakers who have not undergone it, while a near-merger has no such irreversible consequences.

Moreover, recent work has shown that there may be interesting and complex relationships between mergers and near-mergers. Here we shall look at one of these in connection with the *cot/caught* merger.

Modern English inherited from Middle English two vowels which were rather similar in phonetic quality: the vowel of *cot* and the vowel of *caught*. Both vowels were low, both were back, and both were rounded; the difference between them was chiefly a matter of length, since the *caught* vowel was somewhat longer than the *cot* vowel. But one of the consequences of the GVS and its aftermath was that the very clear length distinctions of the Middle English vowels were generally obliterated in favour of distinctions between pure vowels and diphthongs – and both of the vowels in question entered Modern English as pure vowels, as they still are today. Hence, in terms of the vowel space, as discussed in Chapter 4, it was a rather uncomfortable state of affairs having two contrasting vowels squeezed so closely together in the mouth.

As one might expect, this apparently unstable situation has been resolved in almost all varieties of English in such a way as to relieve the pressure, but not all varieties have adopted the same solution. In England, the pressure was relieved by raising the *caught* vowel away from the *cot* vowel. As a result, an Englishman's pronunciation of *caught* sounds to an American rather like *coat*. (There is no new conflict for the Englishman, because the *coat* vowel has likewise moved to make room, in a classic instance of a chain shift, and the Englishman's *coat* sounds to American ears something like *Kate*.)

Some American varieties, notably that of New York, have undergone a shift similar to that of England, but most American varieties have done something else: they have fronted and unrounded the *cot* vowel, thereby moving it away from *caught* and merging it with the historically distinct vowel of *father*. Consequently, an American's pronunciation of *cot* sounds to an Englishman something like his own pronunciation of *cart*: roughly, *kaht*.

Still other varieties have adopted a very different solution: they have simply merged the vowels of *cot* and *caught*. This has happened in Scotland, and also in Canada: Scottish and Canadian speakers normally do not distinguish *cot* and *caught* at all.

All these solutions have the effect of relieving the pressure in the vowel space, and we might therefore expect all of the resulting vowel systems to be stable. But this is not so: something unexpected is happening in the USA.

In recent years, linguists have noticed that the *cot/caught* merger, typical of Canada but once apparently unknown in American English, has appeared in several widely separated areas of the USA and is moreover spreading out rather rapidly from these **focal areas**, as they are called. This is surprising, because the typical American realizations of the *cot* and *caught* vowels are not very similar at all, and so it is not obvious what factors might have favoured their merger.

We might suspect that the Canadian pattern was simply spreading southwards, but the data do not bear out such a suggestion: the areas where the merger is occurring are not close to Canada, and the areas close to Canada are not undergoing the merger. For example, in western New York State, where I come from, there is as yet no trace of the merger: the vowels of *cot* and *caught* remain distinct for all speakers, even though we are close to the Canadian border, and the same appears to be true of Detroit, just to the west of us, or at least this was so a few years ago. In contrast, to the south of us, in Pittsburgh and in western Pennsylvania generally, an area which is much farther away from Canada, the merger appears to be categorical: no speakers in this area still have the contrast, not even variably. And the merger is clearly spreading out eastwards across Pennsylvania: in central Pennsylvania, younger speakers show the merger, while older speakers do not.

Or do they? While looking at the spread of the merger across Pennsylvania, Labov stumbled across something rather surprising. As I have just said, younger speakers in central Pennsylvania simply show the merger, which has been spreading towards them from Pittsburgh. It is the older speakers who do something unexpected. In their ordinary, informal speech, they show, as expected, no trace of the merger: they distinguish the vowels of *cot* and *caught* just as clearly as I do, and as most Americans do. However, when they are asked to perform the minimal-pair test described above, they use a very different type of pronunciation: they exhibit a near-merger between the two vowels. Like other speakers with near-mergers, they make a very small but consistent distinction between the two vowels, but they have difficulty in hearing the difference, and they often claim that there is no difference.

In other words, the incoming change has affected their self-conscious speech very strongly, producing, though, not the full merger typical of younger speakers in the area, but a near-merger; at the same time, their ordinary spontaneous speech, which represents the pronunciation they learned in childhood and have used all their lives, has been completely unaffected. Labov has dubbed this surprising phenomenon the **Bill Peters effect**, after the first individual he encountered who exhibited it.

The existence of the Bill Peters effect shows us some very interesting things. First, contrary to what most linguists had previously believed, it is entirely possible for older speakers to acquire incoming changes. (Some of the examples discussed earlier in this chapter make the same point, but not so vividly as the Bill Peters effect.) Second, it is possible for self-conscious speech to be substantially affected by incoming changes while spontaneous speech remains unaffected. This is probably not so surprising, since we know that lots of people deliberately try to change their speech in adulthood to conform to perceived prestige norms – though note that we have at present no evidence that the Bill Peters effect involves conscious and deliberate modifications. Third, and most surprisingly, the effect of such incoming changes late in life can apparently suppress, very effectively, speakers' knowledge of their own ordinary speech, to the point at which they are quite unaware of the very large distinctions which they ordinarily make and which are blatantly obvious to outsiders.

Results like these are fascinating and worrying. They appear to call into question such fundamental notions as the idea that a speaker 'has' a phoneme system, as well as the idea that speakers can perform such seemingly simple tasks as deciding, with reasonable accuracy, whether they pronounce two words identically or differently. Such results are clearly telling us important things about language change, but at present these phenomena are still so new to us that we have little idea how we should try to take them into account. The deeper we look, the messier the facts of language behaviour appear to be, and the messier the facts of language change appear to be. It seems almost a wonder now that our venerable assumptions of the homogeneity of language and of the regularity of language change have proved to be as successful as they have.

10.6   *A closing note*

A long-running theme in the study of language change has been the issue of gradualness versus abruptness. Are changes typically gradual or typically abrupt? We cannot even begin to answer this question until we phrase it more precisely, for in fact there are several entirely different kinds of gradualness and abruptness that need to be distinguished. The first two apply only to phonological change, while the last two apply to all types of change.

First, we can distinguish *phonetic gradualness* from *phonetic abruptness*. A phonetically gradual change is one in which the pronunciation of a word, or of a class of words, changes by imperceptible small steps from an earlier form to a later form, possibly over many generations. A phonetically abrupt change is one in which the earlier pronunciation is replaced at once by the later one, with no intervening stages.

Second, we can distinguish *lexical gradualness* from *lexical abruptness*. A lexically gradual change is one which applies only to a few words, but which, over time, comes to apply to more and more words, until it has (possibly) applied to all relevant words, again possibly over many generations. A lexically abrupt change is one which applies simultaneously to all relevant words.

Third, we can distinguish *individual gradualness* from *individual abruptness*. In an individually gradual change, an innovating form at first appears only occasionally in the speech of a particular individual; over time, the innovating form becomes steadily more frequent in that person's speech, while the conservative form becomes correspondingly less frequent, until the innovating form is (perhaps) the only one used by that individual.

Finally, we can distinguish *social gradualness* from *social abruptness*. In a socially gradual change, an innovating form is at first used by only a few individuals; over time, the innovating form comes to be used by ever more individuals, while the conservative form is used by correspondingly fewer people, until the innovating form is (perhaps) the only one used in the community.

(For this last category I could in principle make a further distinction between the propagation of change among speakers in a single community, such as a single city or town, and the propagation of change across a large geographical expanse, such as the USA. But no one has ever proposed that a change instantaneously affects all speakers over a vast area, and everyone accepts that changes typically spread gradually across large areas. I shall therefore confine my attention to single communities.)

For the first type, it makes little sense to speak of a change's *going to completion*. Except in the case of total loss of a segment, there is no way of knowing that a phonetic development has gone to completion, except perhaps by observing that nothing more appears to be happening. For the other three types, however, we can readily consider the issue of whether the change has gone to completion. A lexically gradual change has gone to completion when there are no relevant words left for it to apply to; an individually gradual change has gone to completion when the individual no longer uses the conservative form at all; a socially gradual change has gone to completion when there are no people left using the conservative form.

So: how does language change? The Neogrammarians, of course, maintained that sound change was normally phonetically gradual but, crucially, always lexically abrupt. They did not normally consider the third issue, but quite probably they would have expected sound change to be individually abrupt, since they didn't have any time for variation. The social issue, too, they seem rarely to have considered.

Lexical diffusion, of course, is very different. The view of the linguists developing this idea is that sound changes are typically phonetically abrupt but lexically gradual – precisely the opposite of the Neogrammarian view. Lexical diffusion tolerates a degree of individual gradualness, but on the whole it is more consistent with a claim of individual abruptness. It has no particular claims to make on the social issue, but it is very compatible with social gradualness.

The theoretical battle lines are well drawn, then, but what do we actually see when we look at a change in progress? What about Martha's Vineyard? Well, the centralization taking place there appears to be phonetically gradual (the degree of centralization has been increasing steadily for decades), lexically abrupt (all relevant words are affected simultaneously, though there are phonological factors favouring centralization in some particular words), individually abrupt (most people acquire their degree of centralization early in life and then don't change it), and socially abrupt (for the same reason). At first glance, then, centralization on Martha's Vineyard looks rather like the

Neogrammarian type of change, though with the big provisos that many people in the community never participate in the change at all, and that individuals do not use the same pronunciation of a given word every time, things which probably shouldn't happen in the Neogrammarian model. In contrast, lexical diffusion does not appear to be a factor.

How about /æ/-tensing in Philadelphia? Here we suffer from the fact that most of the changes happened before we could watch them, but I can at least comment upon what's visible now. Tensing is phonetically abrupt (no intermediate forms), lexically gradual (of course), individually abrupt (on the whole, people do not change their behaviour much over time), and (probably) socially gradual (we can anticipate that the innovating forms now heard in the suburbs will spread into the city). Here we have a case of lexical diffusion, and the Neogrammarian account gets nothing right.

The clearest lesson we can take away from examining many different cases of change is that there is no single model of language change, no single version of the truth. Some changes proceed in a very different way from others, and thus our various models can never be better than reasonable approximations to reality in some particular cases. And we continue to find startling new phenomena whose existence was previously unsuspected and which cannot easily be handled by any of our theoretical frameworks – recall Bill Peters, who has undergone a change to his self-conscious speech but not to his spontaneous speech, or Dan in Albuquerque, who is convinced he has undergone a merger that hasn't happened. It may well be that the study of how language change proceeds still has quite a few surprises in store for us.

Further reading

The classic statement of the sociolinguistic approach to language change is Weinreich, Labov and Herzog (1968); this is essential reading. Most of Labov's classic early papers, including the Martha's Vineyard paper, are collected in Labov (1972). Labov's major study of social stratification in New York is Labov (1966). Peter Trudgill's work in Norwich is presented in Trudgill (1974). Chambers (1995) is a useful survey of sociolinguistic factors; chapter 4 pays particular attention to social factors in language change. Many textbooks of sociolinguistics have useful things to say about variation and social stratification, and often too about variation as the vehicle of change; among these are Hudson (1980), Trudgill (1995), and especially Holmes (1992) and Romaine (1994). Some of the essays collected in Quirk (1995) deal with variation and change at various times in English, ranging from Chaucer to the present day. A major synthesis of Labov's thinking is to be presented in a series of three volumes, of which volume i has already appeared as Labov (1994); it appears that volume ii will deal most directly with the issues addressed in this chapter. McMahon (1994) is a major textbook of language change in which chapters 3 and 9 deal specifically with variation and change. A textbook devoted wholly to variation and change is Milroy (1992); section 3.7 of this book provides a reasoned defence of the quantitative approach in response to several criticisms of it, with references. The classic presentations of lexical diffusion are Wang (1969) and especially Chen and Wang (1975); McMahon (1994) provides a survey with references in chapter 3.

Exercises

Exercise 10.1

In the vernacular (uneducated) speech of many parts of Ireland, the vowels in words like *mate* and *meat* are commonly described as having undergone merger. In the Irish city of Belfast, vernacular speakers use four distinguishable pronunciations of the vowels in these words: a high mid diphthong [ɪe], a high mid pure vowel [e(:)], a mid pure vowel [ẹ(:)], and a low mid pure vowel [ɛ]. Table 10.7 shows the number of tokens (individual occurrences) of each of these four pronunciations in more than 150 occurrences of the two words *mate* and *meat*. Do you agree that the vowels of *mate* and *meat* have merged in Belfast? If not, how would you characterize the position in Belfast? Does your conclusion necessarily hold for other parts of Ireland where the merger has been reported? (Data from Milroy and Harris 1980.)

Exercise 10.2

Most varieties of Basque have two contrasting rhotic phonemes, an alveolar tap notated *r* and an alveolar trill notated *rr*. These contrast freely between vowels, and there are many minimal pairs: *hurra* 'the hazelnut' but *hura* 'that one', *gorri* 'red' but *gori* 'fiery', *gorra* 'deaf' (definite) but *gora* 'up', *erre* 'burn' but *ere* 'also', and so on. In about two-thirds of the French Basque Country, however, the former trill *rr* has changed to a voiced uvular fricative, somewhat as in French. The change is categorical: all words like *hurra*, *gorri*, and *gorra* are invariably pronounced with uvulars. (In the remaining third of the French Basque Country, though, there is no trace of the uvular, and *rr* remains an alveolar trill.) With the tap *r*, however, things are more complex.

Table 10.7

	mate	*meat*
[ɪe]	33	0
[e(:)]	60	20
[ẹ(:)]	6	38
[ɛ]	0	2

Some words with *r* now also have a uvular pronunciation, while others retain the alveolar tap. So, for example, *hura* 'that one' has a uvular, but *ura* 'the water' does not; *gari* 'wheat' has a uvular, but *ari* 'busy' does not; *bero* 'hot' has a uvular, but *bere* 'his/her own' does not. What would you conclude is going on in the French Basque Country?

Visits to the region some years apart have revealed that the situation with respect to these words is not stable, but is changing fairly rapidly over time. What do you suppose is the nature of the change?

Can you make any suggestions about the likely course of the change from an alveolar trill to a uvular fricative for *rr*? Could it have been gradual in any sense?

Exercise 10.3

In Philadelphia, as in most American cities, there are noticeable differences in vernacular (uneducated) speech between blacks and whites. Table 10.8 provides data for four variables of interest: standard *He likes it* vs. non-standard *He like it* (notated *3Sg* in the table below), standard *He's a teacher* vs. *He a teacher* (notated *Cop*), standard *John's book* vs. non-standard *John book* (notated *Poss*), and standard *I didn't do it* vs. non-standard *I ain't do it* (notated *Aux*). (Here I use the label 'standard forms' for what might more neutrally be called 'white norms'.) Four groups of speakers are distinguished: blacks who have little contact with whites (notated *B*), blacks who have considerable contact with whites (notated *B(W)*), whites who have considerable contact with blacks (notated *W(B)*), and whites who have little contact with blacks (notated *W*). The table shows the percentage of non-standard forms used by each of the four groups for each of the four variables. Now these data are not adequate for drawing any firm conclusions about language change, since they include no dimension of time or even of age. Still, they are very suggestive. Consider the data, and answer the following questions as best you can. (Data from Ash and Myhill 1986.)

a) Why do three of the four groups show variation in respect of all four variables, and why does the fourth group show no variation at all?
b) Among the two groups of people who have considerable contact with

Table 10.8 (% use of non-standard variant)

Group	3Sg	Cop	Poss	Aux
B	73	52	79	43
B(W)	16	04	15	08
W(B)	12	08	02	20
W	00	00	00	00

people of the other colour, why do blacks assimilate more strongly to white norms than the other way round? (Be careful – this question is not as simple as it looks!)

c) Why do whites who have considerable contact with blacks have larger percentages of non-standard forms for two of the four variables than do blacks who have considerable contact with whites?

d) Why do blacks who have considerable contact with whites come closer to white norms for some variables than for others?

e) The investigators who collected these data also report that the two groups who have little contact with people of the other colour both show no tendency at all to adjust toward the norms of the other group, and that changes observable in the speech of one group are not observed in the speech of the other. If this state of affairs should continue for several generations, what will be the likely linguistic consequences?

Exercise 10.4

Fig. 10.3 shows the range of realizations of the nuclei of four vowels in the vowel space for four New Yorkers of varying age. The symbols have the following significance: /o/ is the vowel of *not*, /ah/ is the vowel of *father*, /oh/ is the vowel of *law*, and /uw/ is the vowel of *boot*. Assuming that these sparse data are typical, what appears to be happening to the vowel system of New York City? (Data from Labov 1994: 203.)

Exercise 10.5

In the Spanish of Panama City, the consonant spelled *ch* (as in *muchacho* 'boy') has two realizations: an affricate [tʃ] and a fricative [ʃ]. In 1969, and again in 1983, the usage of a number of speakers was investigated. Fig. 10.4 shows the percentage of fricative realizations used by speakers in various age groups in the two investigations; the age groups used in the two studies were not quite identical. Examine the graph, and explain as best you can what appears to be happening in Panama City. Can you see any evidence of generational change, of age grading, or of any other kind of change? Is it possible to predict what a similar study might find today? (Data from Cedergren 1973, Cedergren 1984, and Labov 1994.)

Exercise 10.6

Skikun is an Atayalic language of Taiwan. A large number of words in Skikun have two very different pronunciations; in most cases a particular speaker uses only one or the other, though a few speakers vary between both pronunciations for certain words. Table 10.9 shows the pronunciations of thirty-two representative words used by ten representative speakers of both sexes and of varying ages. Identify any changes that appear to be underway in Skikun, and

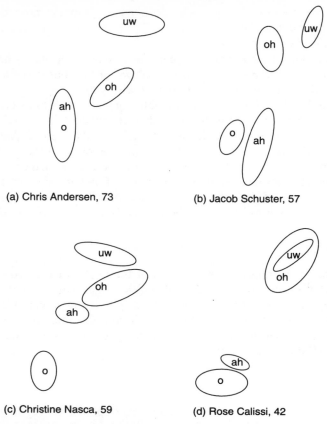

(a) Chris Andersen, 73

(b) Jacob Schuster, 57

(c) Christine Nasca, 59

(d) Rose Calissi, 42

Fig. 10.3 Four New York vowel systems

explain the nature of those changes as fully and explicitly as you can. (Data from Paul Li 1982.)

Exercise 10.7

Old English /h/ has been universally lost word-finally and before a consonant, and generally also before an unstressed vowel. Before a stressed vowel, however, its history has been more complex. As a general rule, it has been lost from vernacular speech in England in all but three small areas: one in the far north, one in the west and one in East Anglia (including the city of Norwich). Most vernacular speakers in England, then, do not distinguish, for example, *hair* from *air* or *harm* from *arm*. (Some speakers in fact sometimes use a phonetic [h] in such words, but they use this [h] equally in all of them, without regard to the spelling or the history, so they do not have a phoneme /h/.) The British linguist James Milroy has studied the loss of

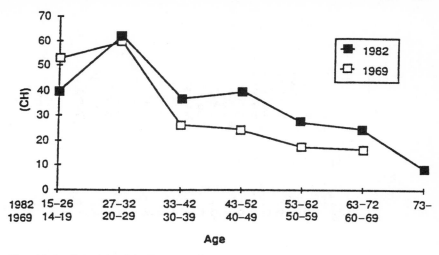

Fig. 10.4 Spanish *ch* in Panama City

prevocalic /h/ (informally known as '*h*-dropping') in various publications, notably Milroy (1983, 1992). Milroy makes the following observations, among others.

(a) Peter Trudgill's work in Norwich shows variable use of /h/ by all speakers, with the familiar correlations with social class and with degree of formality.

(b) In the latter half of the nineteenth century, *h*-dropping is strongly stigmatized by writers on language in England, as it still is today.

(c) There is good evidence that educated speakers in the nineteenth century used /h/-ful and /h/-less pronunciations variably, perhaps as a stylistic device.

(d) The first hostile comments about *h*-dropping in England are found only in the late eighteenth century.

(e) Late sixteenth-century writers like Shakespeare and Marlowe frequently make puns involving words like *air*, *heir* and *hair*, and such puns are put into the mouths of educated characters.

(f) The mid-sixteenth-century *Diary* of Henry Machyn, a carpenter from London and probably a lower-middle-class speaker, uses the letter *h* in such an erratic way that it is clear his speech must have been /h/-less.

(g) Although East Anglia is generally /h/-ful today, some of the most abundant evidence for *h*-dropping in earlier periods comes from East Anglia. Important East Anglian documents like the *Paston Letters* (fifteenth century) and the *Norfolk Gilds* (late fourteenth century), which were written by members of the prosperous middle class, exhibit highly variable use of /h/, with spellings like *alpenie* for 'halfpenny' and *hoke lewes* for 'oak leaves'.

Table 10.9

Age											
	84, 80	71	65	61	54	50	55	46	36	32	
qciyap	-p	-p	-p	-p	-p	-p	-p	-p	-p	-k	'far shore'
ʔiyup	-p	-p	-p	-p	-p	-p	-p	-p	-p	-k	'goshawk'
qatap	-p	-p	-p	-p	-p	-p	-p	-p	-p	-k	'scissors'
tgtap	-p	-p	-p	-p	-p	-p	-k	-p	-p	-k	'fan' (v.)
ghap	-p	-p	-p	-p	-p	-p	-p	-p/-k	-p	-k	'seed'
qurip	-p	-p	-p	-p	-p	-p	-p	-p/-k	-k	-k	'ginger'
hmap	-p	-p	-p	-p	-p	-p	-p	-k	-p	-k	'stab'
pshup	-p	-p	-p	-p	-p	-p	-p	-k	-p	-k	'suck'
hmop	-p	-p	-p	-p	-p	-p	-p	-k	-p	-k	'do magic'
talap	-p	-p	-p	-p	-p	-p	-k	-p	-k	-k	'eaves'
tgiyup	-p	-p	-p	-p	-p	-p	-k	-k	-k	-k	'sink'
miyup	-p	-p	-p	-p	-p	-p	-k	-k	-k	-k	'enter'
qmalup	-p	-p	-p	-p	-p	-p	-k	-k	-k	-k	'hunt'
mgop	-p	-p	-p	-p	-p	-p	-k	-k	-p	-k	'share a cup'
qmuyup	-p	-p	-p	-p	-p	-p	-k	-k	-k	-k	'fold'
kmiyap	-p	-p	-p	-p	-k	-p	-k	-k	-p	-k	'catch'
mnep	-p	-p	-p	-p	-k	-p	-k	-k	-k	-k	'fish' (v.)
msuyap	-p	-p	-p	-p/-k	-k	-p	-k	-k	-k	-k	'yawn'

qom	-m	-m	-m	-m	-m	-m	-ŋ	'anteater'
syam	-m/-ŋ	-m	-m	-m	-m	-m	-ŋ	'pork'
qmtam	-m	-m	-m/-ŋ	-m/-ŋ	-m	-m	-ŋ	'swallow'
rom	-m	-m	-m	-m	-m	-ŋ	-ŋ	'needle'
qinam	-m	-m	-m/-ŋ	-m	-ŋ	-ŋ	-ŋ	'peach'
hmham	-ŋ	-m	-m	-m	-m	-ŋ	-ŋ	'grope'
yuhum	-ŋ	-m	-m/-ŋ	-m	-m	-m	-ŋ	'gall'
prahum	-m	-m	-m/-ŋ	-m	-ŋ	-ŋ	-ŋ	'lips'
trmalam	-m	-ŋ	-ŋ	-m	-ŋ	-ŋ	-ŋ	'taste'
mtlom	-m	-m	-m	-ŋ	-ŋ	-ŋ	-ŋ	'burn'
lmom	-m	-m	-ŋ	-ŋ	-ŋ	-ŋ	-ŋ	'burn'
mktlium	-m	-m	-ŋ	-ŋ	-ŋ	-ŋ	-ŋ	'run'
cmom	-m	-m	-ŋ	-ŋ	-ŋ	-ŋ	-ŋ	'wipe'
mnkum	-ŋ	-m	-ŋ	-ŋ	-ŋ	-ŋ	-ŋ	'dark'

(h) In the late fourteenth century, there is evidence that the Londoner Geoffrey Chaucer, author of *The Canterbury Tales*, had /h/-less speech, and his contemporary, the unknown West Midlands poet who wrote *Sir Gawain and the Green Knight*, regularly alliterates initial *h* with vowels.

(i) Throughout the Middle English period (1066–1500), both literary and non-literary documents show highly variable use of /h/: it is sometimes omitted where we would expect it to be present (thus *ate* for *hate* and *om* for *home*) and sometimes inserted where we would not expect it (thus *halle* for *all* and *his* for *is*). This variation is most prominent in the East Midlands, in East Anglia and in the South; it is much less prominent elsewhere. This was a period when there was no standard English orthography.

Given these observations, suggest a likely sociolinguistic history for *h*-dropping in England.

Now consider the following additional observations.

(j) Today, *h*-dropping is completely unknown in Ireland, which was settled by English-speakers from the sixteenth century onward, in the USA and Canada, which were chiefly settled in the seventeenth and eighteenth centuries, and in Australia, New Zealand and South Africa, which were chiefly settled in the nineteenth century. For the USA, there is contemporary testimony that *h*-dropping was equally unknown in the late nineteenth century, but for Australia there is testimony that *h*-dropping *was* commonplace.

In the light of your conclusions about what has been happening in England, suggest a likely sociolinguistic history for /h/ in these other countries.

A number of very distinguished historians of English, including for example Oliphant and Skeat, who wrote in the late nineteenth century, and Wyld, who wrote in the first half of the twentieth century, noted the historical data summarized above and drew the general conclusion that *h*-dropping first appeared in England only in the late eighteenth century and became commonplace only in the nineteenth; they suggest that the variation observed in the earlier texts results merely from an imperfect command of English, perhaps especially by writers whose first language was Norman French. Do their conclusions agree with yours? If not, why do you suppose they might have drawn such conclusions?

Exercise 10.8

In the southeast of England, in the counties of Kent, Sussex, and Surrey, there is variation between rhotic pronunciations of words like *sort*, *card*, and *bird*, in which an /r/-constriction is present, and non-rhotic pronunciations of the same words, in which no /r/-constriction is present; in non-rhotic pronunciations, *bar* sounds just like *bah*, and so on.

The maps in Figs. 10.5, 10.6, and 10.7 provide some figures on the frequencies of non-rhotic pronunciations. Since these frequencies vary continuously as one travels across the country, the information is presented by means of isopleths. An **isopleth** is a line separating frequencies above and below some reference value. For example, the 75 per cent isopleth separates territory in which the frequency of non-rhotic pronunciations is greater than

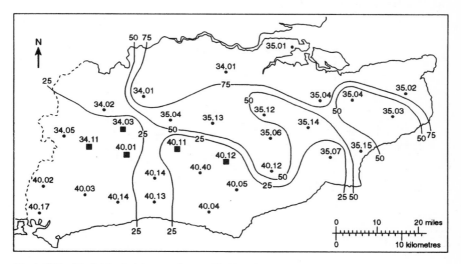

Fig. 10.5 Variable (ar) in southeast England.

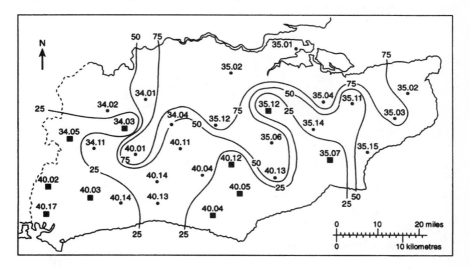

Fig. 10.6 Variable (or) in southeast England.

75 per cent from territory in which that frequency is less than 75 per cent. The small dots with reference numbers are the sampling points from which the data were obtained, and the black squares mark sampling points at which the frequency of non-rhotic pronunciations approaches zero.

Fig. 10.5, marked (ar), shows the frequencies of non-rhotic pronunciations in words like *card* and *start*; Fig. 10.6, marked (or), shows the frequencies in words like *sort* and *cord*; Fig. 10.7, marked (Λr), shows the frequencies in words like *bird*, *hurt*, and *herd*. Fig. 10.8 is a geographical sketch of the area, showing the county boundaries, the chief towns, and the main roads.

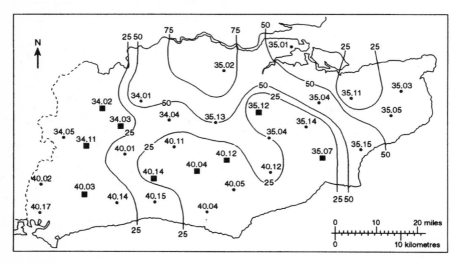

Fig. 10.7 Variable (Λr) in southeast England.

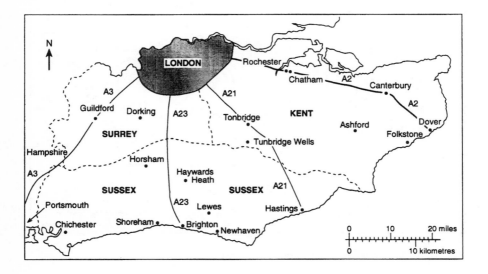

Examine these maps, and explain what appears to be happening in this area. What accounts for the intricate contours of the isopleths? Why do the three maps have different shapes?

These maps include data from speakers of all ages. In fact, in much of this territory – for example, in Brighton, where I work – there is a conspicuous difference between older and younger speakers. What do you suppose that difference is? If the same study were carried out a generation from now, how would you expect the maps to change?

Finally, in this area of England, which appears to be more prestigious: rhotic or non-rhotic speech? How does this compare with New York City?

(These maps were provided by David North and are based upon his own research; I am grateful for his permission to use them here.)

11

Contact and the birth and death of languages

In the last chapter we examined the sociolinguistic approach to language change and found that the processes of change are typically much more complex and variable than we had earlier been inclined to assume. In this chapter we shall be looking further at social factors acting on the history of languages, but this time at large-scale processes which can have profound consequences for the historical development of languages, and even for their very existence.

11.1 Language contact

Only very rarely, if ever, does a language find itself spoken in a completely isolated environment, with no contact at all between its speakers and the speakers of other languages. Far more typically, the speakers of any given language have day-to-day dealings with the speakers of at least one or two other languages, and possibly with a larger number than this. Indeed, for the larger part of human existence, the normal situation was probably for everybody routinely to learn and use two or three or four different languages. This is still what we find today over most of the planet: it is thought that between 70 per cent and 80 per cent of the earth's population are bilingual or multilingual. In the Amazon rainforest, in New Guinea, in much of Africa, in large parts of the Indian subcontinent, multilingualism is still the norm, and the same was true of Australia and of much of North America before the European settlements largely destroyed the indigenous cultures and languages. The state of affairs that we may now think of as typical, with a single language being spoken with some uniformity over hundreds of miles, is a relatively recent development in human affairs, and it is not at all representative of what has been going on during the past few millennia.

This ceaseless contact between speakers of different languages has often had substantial consequences for the historical development of those languages, and historical linguists have perhaps not been as quick as we might have been to appreciate the importance of those consequences.

In Chapter 2, we examined the single most obvious consequence of contact: the borrowing of words. Such borrowing is always with us, and, given sufficient time, its scale can be enormous. Since the Norman Conquest, English has lost at least 60 per cent of the Old English vocabulary in favour of loans from French and Latin, and most of that loss took place in the several centuries after the Conquest. In less than 2000 years Basque has borrowed so many words from the neighbouring Latin and Romance that these loan words now outnumber the indigenous words in the language, and hundreds or thousands of indigenous words have undoubtedly been lost in the process. The Romance language Romanian has borrowed so many Slavic words that scholars for a while believed it was a Slavic language. Albanian seems to have lost more than 90 per cent of its original vocabulary in favour of loans from Latin, Greek, Hungarian, Slavic, Italian, and Turkish. The Arabic spoken in Malta has borrowed so many words from Italian, French, English, and other languages that Maltese is no longer considered by anyone to be a variety of Arabic. Such examples could be multiplied at length.

On occasion, some speakers of a language may take great exception to the presence in their language of a sizeable number of loan words, or of other influences from neighbouring languages, which they regard as a kind of 'contamination' sullying the 'purity' of their language. For example, some conservative speakers of French are deeply disturbed by the huge number of English loans pouring into French, and the French authorities have been making strenuous efforts to stem this tide and to find 'genuine' French replacements for the loan words. This attitude is called **purism**, and purism is not confined to the French. At various times, the Germans, the Hungarians, the Basques, the Bulgarians, and the Turks, to name but a few, have made similar efforts to eliminate loan words from their languages, with variable success. For example, at times of nationalism, German purists have tried to blacklist as foreignisms everyday words which most Germans had never suspected of being anything but German: *Karotte* 'carrot', *Paket* 'package', *Papa* 'daddy', *Insekt* 'insect', *Kilo* 'kilogramme', and so on. Later in this chapter, we shall be considering whether purism is a constructive attitude or not.

In Chapter 2, we also considered some of the consequences of large-scale lexical borrowing, and we saw that a language can acquire new phonemes and new morphological patterns as a result of borrowing. These consequences can have a very substantial effect upon the phonology or the morphology of the borrowing language.

Consider Turkish. Native Turkish words may contain the three phonemes /k/, /g/, and /l/ (among others); these have front allophones [k^j] [g^j] [l^j] next to front vowels and back allophones [k] [g] [l] next to back vowels (a native Turkish word normally contains only front vowels or only back vowels). Thus, typical native words include *kar* 'snow' [kar], *gaga* 'beak' [gaga], *lokum* 'Turkish delight' [lokum], and *yol* 'road' [jol], but *köpek* 'dog' [k^{j}œpek^j], *göz* 'eye' [g^{j}œz], *gelin* 'bride' [g^{j}el^{j}in], and *yel* 'wind' [jel^j]. However, Turkish has borrowed a very large number of words from Arabic, Persian, and French in which the palatalized consonants [k^j], [g^j], and [l^j] occur next to back vowels. Among these are *kâr* 'profit' [k^{j}ar], *mahkûm* 'condemned' [mahk^{j}um], *kâbus* 'nightmare' [k^{j}a:bu:s], *gâvur* 'infidel' [g^{j}a-vur], *gâh* 'moment' [g^{j}ah], *lâle* 'tulip' [l^{j}a:l^{j}e] and *plan* 'plan' [pl^{j}an]. The two sets of consonants now contrast next to back vowels, and there are even minimal pairs like *kar* 'snow' and *kâr* 'profit'. As a result, the overall phonology of Turkish must now be described as having three non-palatalized phonemes /k/, /g/, and /l/ and three palatalized phonemes /k^j/, /g^j/, and /l^j/, which contrast only next to back vowels; only the second set occurs next to front vowels.

Since the new contrast is entirely confined to loan words, some linguists would prefer to say that Turkish has **coexistent phonemic systems** – that is, that it has one set of phonemes in native words and a different set (in this case, larger) in loan words.

This is by no means the entire effect of loans on the phonology of Turkish. In native Turkish words, there are severe constraints upon the possible sequences of vowels: a word may contain only front vowels or only back vowels, an unrounded vowel may not be followed by a rounded vowel, and the two vowels /o/ and /ö/ may only occur in the first syllable. But thousands of loan words violate these constraints: *şoför* 'driver', *lâle* 'tulip', *mümtaz* 'distinguished', *tefevvuk* 'superiority', *emanet* 'deposit', *kale* 'castle', *cami* 'mosque', *radyo* 'radio', *teşekkür* 'thanks', *otobüs* 'bus', *rica* 'request', *vehham* 'apprehensive', *resul* 'envoy', *telâffuz* 'pronunciation', and countless others. The phonology of Turkish has been very strongly altered by the presence of these thousands of loan words.

The morphological consequences of contact can also be profound. Consider Armenian. This Indo-European language has a long literary tradition, and we can see interesting changes in its morphology over the centuries. The Old Armenian of the fifth century AD had a typical IE pattern of case-inflection for nouns, illustrated in Table 11.1. As is usual in the older IE languages, there is no consistent marker of plurality and no consistent marker for any case:

Table 11.1 Old Armenian case-inflection

cer 'old man'	Singular	Plural
Nom	cer	cerk'
Acc, Loc	cer	cers
Gen, Dat, Abl	ceroy	ceroc
Instr	cerov	cerovk'

instead, each ending is an unalysable combination of case and number information. But modern Armenian is very different. Look at Table 11.2. This time the position is very different. There is an invariant plural marker *-er*, and every case is marked by a single invariant suffix in both singular and plural. Now this new pattern is a very unusual one for an IE language. So how does Armenian come to have it? A plausible explanation is contact. Look at the Turkish nominal inflection illustrated in Table 11.3. You can see that the Turkish pattern, which is typical of all the Turkic languages, looks very similar to the Armenian one, except that the actual morphs are all different. Now Armenian has been in contact with Turkish for centuries, and so many scholars have drawn the obvious conclusion that Armenian has remodelled its nominal morphology along Turkish lines. This conclusion is not certain, but it is very plausible.

In this case, although an entire morphological pattern seems to have been acquired by contact, no morphemes were borrowed. But grammatical morphemes can, of course, be borrowed. For example, some dialects of the South American language Quechua have borrowed the plural marker *-s* from Spanish; the Basque participial affix *-tu* was borrowed from Latin *-tum*; a number of Finnish grammatical morphemes, including *-kä* 'negative' and *-ko* 'question', have been borrowed into Sami ('Lappish'); the Persian complementizer

Table 11.2 Modern Armenian case-infection

cer 'old man'	Singular	Plural
Nom, Acc	*cer*	*cerer*
Gen, Dat	*ceri*	*cereri*
Abl	*ceric*	*cereric*
Instr	*cerov*	*cererov*
Loc	*cerum*	*cererum*

Table 11.3 Turkish case-infection

ev 'house'	Singular	Plural
Nom	*ev*	*evler*
Acc	*evi*	*evleri*
Gen	*evin*	*evlerin*
Dat	*eve*	*evlere*
Abl	*evden*	*evlerden*
Loc	*evde*	*evlerde*

ki has been borrowed into Turkish; and many hundreds of such cases are known. An extreme case is the Cushitic language Ma'a, spoken in Tanzania, which has borrowed morphology so extensively from the neighbouring Bantu languages that it now looks like an ordinary Bantu language with an unusual vocabulary. Indeed, some linguists have concluded that Ma'a now *is* a Bantu language, since grammatically it is virtually indistinguishable from any other Bantu language – though most historical linguists find it impossible to accept the suggestion that a language can actually move from one family to another through contact.

A particularly interesting case of a borrowed grammatical morpheme is the Persian complementizer *ki*, which has been borrowed into Turkish. While Persian is an IE language, Turkish is a Turkic language with a very un-IE sentence structure. The borrowed *ki* has introduced Indo-European constructions into Turkish, where they compete with the native constructions. Here are some examples; in each case, the first pattern is the native Turkish one, while the second is the innovating structure.

- *Yarın gel-eceğ-in-e emin-im.*
  tomorrow come-Fut-3Sg-Dat sure-1Sg
  'I'm sure he'll come tomorrow.'

- *Emin-im ki yarın gel-ecek-Ø.*
  sure-1Sg that tomorrow come-Fut-3Sg
  'I'm sure he'll come tomorrow.'

- *Bekle-me-si-ni isti-yor-um.*
  wait-Ger-his-Acc want-Pres-1Sg
  'I want him to wait.'

- *İsti-yor-um ki bekle-sin.*
  want-Pres-1Sg that wait-Juss
  'I want him to wait.'

- *Kapı-yı kapa-mı-yan bir çocuk.*
  door-Acc shut-Neg-Rel a child
  'a child who does not shut the door'

- *Bir çocuk ki kapı-yı kapa-maz-Ø.*
  a child that door-Acc shut-Neg-3Sg
  'a child who does not shut the door'

As pointed out at some length by Lewis (1967: 211–14), the morpheme *ki* has acquired a wide range of idiomatic uses in Turkish, and the existence of the two alternative constructions allows some useful and elegant stylistic variation. The Persian morpheme has not displaced the native constructions; it has instead enriched the language by making possible a wider range of constructions and styles. Here we have a fine example of the positive value of borrowing, and even the Turkish Language Society, an official body which has otherwise displayed notable puristic tendencies, has not attempted to dislodge the 'alien' constructions with *ki*, which in any case are now too firmly embedded in Turkish for anyone to think about removing them.

A particularly striking kind of grammatical borrowing is the borrowing of word-order patterns. The Ethiopian languages provide some especially good examples of this. The majority of these languages are Semitic, but they have long been in contact with the neighbouring Cushitic languages. Now Semitic languages normally have VSO order, with prepositions and postposed genitives and adjectives, while Cushitic languages have just the opposite characteristics: SOV order, with postpositions and preposed genitives and adjectives. The classical Semitic language of Ethiopia, Ge'ez, had typical Semitic characteristics, but the modern Semitic languages show various stages of adjustment towards the Cushitic type, as shown in Table 11.4.

All the modern Semitic languages have moved significantly towards the Cushitic type, though only some of them have gone all the way. It seems clear that these changes in word order result from contact, especially since the particular constellation of properties exhibited by Amharic seems to be extremely rare among the languages of the world and possibly only ever results from contact.

One of the most famous examples of grammatical borrowing is found in the Indian village of Kupwar. Kupwar is located on the boundary between the Indo-Aryan languages of northern India and the unrelated Dravidian languages of the south. Three languages are spoken in Kupwar: Urdu and Marathi (both Indo-Aryan) and Kannada (Dravidian). Everyone speaks all three languages and switches among them constantly depending on the context. Now, as a rule, Indo-Aryan languages and Dravidian languages have very different sentence structures, and elsewhere in the Indian subcontinent this is true of these three languages: a sentence in Kannada looks nothing like a sentence in Urdu or Marathi. In Kupwar, however, things are different. Here are three equivalent sentences in the three languages as spoken in Kupwar:

Urdu:	pala	jəra	kat	ke	le	ke	a		ya
Marathi:	pala	jəra	kap	un	ghe	un	a	l	o
Kannada:	tapla	jəra	khod	i	təgond i		bə		yn
	greens	a.little	cut		having taken		having come	Past	I
	I cut some greens and brought them								

Table 11.4 Word order in Ethiopian Semitic languages

VSO	Prep	NG	NA	Ge'ez
SOV	Prep	NG	AN	Tigre
SOV	Prep	GN	AN	Amharic
SOV	Postp	GN	AN	Harari, Gafat

As you can see, the three sentences are word-for-word equivalents – and this is typical of all sentences in Kupwar. At first glance, you might think you were looking at three dialects of a single language, but this is not so. The three languages have influenced one another so strongly that they have come to have identical sentence structures, structures which are different from what is found in the Urdu, Marathi, and Kannada spoken elsewhere. Indeed, one might almost suggest that the people of Kupwar speak only a single language, but that they speak it with three different vocabularies – and that is exactly what some linguists have suggested.

The linguist Edith Moravcsik (1978) has proposed some universal principles applying to grammatical borrowing. The most interesting of these are given below. (At the cost of some precision, I have reworded her principles for the sake of clarity; Moravcsik is not responsible for my rewordings.)

Universal 1: Grammatical morphemes cannot be borrowed until after some lexical items have been borrowed. This seems to be generally true, though a possible major counterexample is the presence in Russian, Latvian and Lithuanian of a large number of Uralic grammatical features accompanied by almost no loan words; see Thomason and Kaufman (1988: 242–50).

Universal 2: Bound morphemes can be borrowed only as parts of complete words. The idea here is that English *-ette*, as in *kitchenette*, could not have been borrowed directly from French, but rather that English borrowed French words like *cigarette* and *statuette* and then extracted the bound morpheme from these so that it could be attached to other English words like *kitchen*. Again, clear counter-examples are hard to find, though the Finnish loans into Sami mentioned above may be counter-examples.

Universal 3: Verbs cannot be borrowed directly. We saw in Chapter 2 that Turkish and Japanese, among others, normally borrow only nouns and then turn the borrowed nouns into verbs by using an auxiliary verb. Nevertheless, this claim appears to be simply false. English has borrowed innumerable verbs from French (*manœuvre*, *desire*, *acquire*), from Latin (*prevent*, *contend*), and even from Yiddish (*shlep*). Basque borrows verbs from Spanish and French with complete freedom: Basque *erreibindikatu* 'claim' from Spanish *reivindicar*, *kobratu* 'collect (money)' from Spanish *cobrar*, *sentitu* 'feel' from Spanish and French *sentir*, and so on.

Universal 4: Inflectional morphemes cannot be borrowed until after some derivational (word-forming) morphemes have been borrowed. Counterexamples are not common, but the Quechua borrowing of plural *-s* from Spanish appears to be one, since Quechua has borrowed no word-forming affixes from Spanish.

Universal 5: A preposed grammatical item may not be borrowed as a postposed one, and vice versa. This claim prohibits a language from borrowing, say, a preposition and turning it into a postposition. Again, counter-examples are rare, but here is one. The Spanish preposition *contra* 'against' has been borrowed into Basque as a postposition *kontra* (Basque has no prepositions). Thus, 'against John' is *contra Juan* in Spanish but *Jonen kontra* in Basque.

In sum, then, Moravcsik's principles do appear to represent the most typical cases in the borrowing of grammatical morphemes, but they are far from being exceptionless universals, especially number 3.

11.2 *Linguistic areas*

In some cases, centuries of contact between languages can lead to a particularly striking result: several neighbouring but unrelated languages can come to share a number of structural properties with one another, properties which they do not share with their closest genetic relatives elsewhere. A group of languages in which this situation obtains is called a **linguistic area**, or, using the German term, a ***Sprachbund***. A number of such linguistic areas have been identified: the Balkans, the Indian subcontinent, southern Africa, the northwest coast of North America, southeast Asia, and several others.

Southeast Asia is a case in point. Such languages as Chinese, Vietnamese, Thai, Burmese, and the Miao-Yao languages all have tones, and they all have monosyllabic morphemes (and often monosyllabic words). Their closest relatives elsewhere, such as Tibetan, a fairly close relative of Burmese, generally lack these characteristics (though some dialects of Tibetan have acquired tones very recently). Indeed, so distinctive are these languages that it was formerly thought they must all be related, a view now known to be false, and identifying the true relatives of these languages has proved to be an exceedingly difficult problem, because all these languages look far more like one another than they do like their relatives, the more so since Chinese loan words have penetrated deeply into most of the neighbouring languages. In this particular case, it is often thought that the **convergence** among these unrelated languages is chiefly the result of heavy influence from the prestigious Chinese, but no one really knows.

One of the most famous linguistic areas is the Balkans, where the languages participating most strongly in the *Sprachbund* are Bulgarian (Slavic) and the very closely related Macedonian, Romanian (Romance), Greek, and Albanian (the last two both belonging to independent branches of Indo-European); the Slavic language Serbian and the non-IE Turkish are marginal members of the group. Among the distinctive characteristics of the Balkan *Sprachbund* are the following features.

1. The genitive and dative cases are identical (Albanian, Greek, Bulgarian/ Macedonian, Romanian). Other Slavic languages keep them distinct, while other Romance languages have lost their cases altogether.
2. There is a future tense derived from the use of the verb 'want' as an

auxiliary (Bulgarian/Macedonian, Greek, Romanian, southern Albanian, Serbian). Examples: Greek θ*a γrafo*, Romanian *o să scriu*, Albanian *do të shkruaj*, all 'I will write', and all derived historically from 'I want to write'. Neighbouring and related languages have a future derived from 'have' instead, or else they have no future.

3. There is a postposed definite article (Albanian, Rumanian, Bulgarian/ Macedonian). Examples: Bulgarian *voda-ta* 'water-the', Macedonian *mexaničar-ot* 'mechanic-the', Romanian *lupu-l* 'wolf-the', Albanian *shok-u* 'comrade-the'. Note that the morphemes used for the article are different in all the languages. This occurs nowhere else in Europe except in Basque and in the Scandinavian languages.

4. The infinitive has been lost or greatly reduced in function, and 'I want to go' is expressed literally as 'I want that I go' (Greek, Bulgarian/ Macedonian, Serbian, and to some extent Albanian and Romanian). Examples: Greek θ*elo na γrafo*, Serbian *hoću da pisam*, both 'I want to write' and both literally 'I want that I write'. This development is virtually unknown elsewhere in Europe.

5. The comparative of adjectives is formed analytically ('more short') rather than synthetically ('shorter') (Albanian, Bulgarian/Macedonian, Greek, Romanian, Turkish). This pattern is also found in the other Romance languages.

6. An NP used as a direct or indirect object can or must be preceded by a particle marking it as an object (Albanian, Greek, Bulgarian/Macedonian, Romanian). This property is rare elsewhere in Europe.

7. There are distinct verbal forms for reporting events witnessed by the speaker and those being related at second hand (Albanian, Bulgarian/ Macedonian, Turkish, to some extent Romanian). This is unknown elsewhere in Europe.

8. The numerals from 11 to 19 are formed by means of constructions like 'one upon ten' (Albanian, Bulgarian/Macedonian, Romanian). Examples: Albanian *njëm-bë-dhjetë*, Bulgarian *edin-na-deset*, Romanian *un-spre-zece*, all 'eleven' and all literally 'one upon ten'. This feature also occurs in some other Slavic languages and in Hungarian.

9. There is a great deal of common vocabulary. Turkish and Greek loans are numerous in the other languages, and Slavic loans are very numerous in Romanian.

The existence of linguistic areas provides interesting support for the *wave model* of language change discussed in Chapter 7. Just as has occurred with the uvular /r/ of western Europe, various innovations appear to have diffused across language boundaries, into several quite distinct languages which can in no way be regarded as forming a dialect continuum. Some of these features can be attributed to the influence of single languages. For example, feature (7) is almost certainly the result of Turkish influence, while feature (4) is often attributed to Greek influence. For other features, though, it is at present impossible to single out any one language as the source of the innovation.

Linguistic areas perhaps represent a greater than average degree of contact between languages. However, as we shall see in the next section, contact can be more intense still, and it can produce decidedly more dramatic consequences than we have so far seen.

11.3 *Language birth: pidgins and creoles*

We have already seen that new languages commonly arise when a single widespread language splits up into regional dialects which continue to diverge from one another, producing as a result several distinct daughter languages. But this is not the only source of new languages. There is another, very different, way for a new language to come into existence, one which linguists have been very slow to appreciate.

Very many times in human history and prehistory, people speaking different languages, sometimes a number of different languages, have found themselves brought together and obliged to deal with one another. Often the cause has been trade: Europeans trading all round the Mediterranean, west Africans trading along the coast of the continent with one another (and later with Europeans), east Africans doing the same with other Africans (and also with Arabs) – all these and countless other groups have at times been obliged to conduct business without the aid of a common language. Sometimes the causes are more sinister, as with the Africans brought as slaves to North America and the Caribbean, who had no language they could speak with one another or with their European masters. But the possible circumstances are endlessly varied. The thousands of workers, drawn from a dozen Asian and Pacific countries, who went to Hawaii to work in the sugar plantations in the late nineteenth and early twentieth centuries were in the same boat, as, more recently, are the people of Papua New Guinea, now united in a nation speaking hundreds of indigenous languages, each generally confined to a tiny area.

In such circumstances, people almost invariably respond in the same way: they create a pidgin. A **pidgin** is a very basic and crude way of speaking, stitched together from bits and pieces drawn from several different languages, with a tiny vocabulary, a variable phonology, and nothing much in the way of a grammar. Different people speak it differently, and it is a very poor and limited way of communicating, but, for simple purposes, it does work, and pretty much everybody in the community learns to handle it. Most of the pidgins we know something about are the ones created during and after the European expansion of the last several centuries; with these, it seems usually to be the case that a single language, usually the locally important European language, makes the single largest contribution to the vocabulary of the pidgin, though not necessarily to the grammar (in so far as pidgins have any grammar). But this need not always be the case: in Russenorsk, a pidgin used until recently between Norwegian and Russian fishermen, Russian and Norwegian seem to have made about equal contributions to the lexicon.

Now a pidgin, being no one's mother tongue, is not a natural language, and indeed we might think it scarcely deserved to be called a language at all. None the less, a pidgin is much better than nothing, and, if circumstances are favourable, it may persist for generations or even for centuries – and some pidgins used as trade languages have done precisely that. In other circumstances, however, something very different may happen.

If the pidgin is not primarily being used merely for trade, but is instead the sole means of communication between the people in a settled community, then something deeply momentous may occur. The people in the community may get married and have children, and, whatever they may speak at home, the children have only the pidgin to speak with other children. In such a case, the children do what children always do: they take what they hear and turn it into a proper language. They quickly settle on a fixed word order, which pidgins don't have; they begin introducing all sorts of new grammatical elaborations, including things like verbal inflection and subordinate clauses; and they greatly expand the vocabulary, until they can talk easily about anything they like. And, sooner or later, some children in the community will begin acquiring this expanded pidgin as their first language, as their mother tongue. When this occurs, a new natural language has come into existence.

A language derived from a pidgin in this way is called a **creole**. By convention, we usually consider that a creole comes into existence when its first native speakers appear, though naturally the facts, as always, are complex, and some linguists would prefer to distinguish pidgins and creoles in terms of their degree of stabilization. But we can leave this parochial debate to the specialists: the crucial point is that a new natural language can be born out of the intense degree of contact that necessitates the use of a pidgin.

Creoles may be transient creations – for example, the Hawaiian Creole of the sugar plantations is now nearly extinct, its speakers having steadily abandoned it in favour of English, the prestige language of Hawaii. But they can equally endure, perhaps indefinitely. For example, the mother tongue of the entire population of Haiti is the creole created by their mostly African ancestors generations ago, and there is no sign that the creole is likely to be displaced by any other language, not even by French, the official language of the government. Numerous other creoles created in the last several centuries endure today, and many of them show few signs of being abandoned in the near future. Indeed, new creoles are still being created: the English-based pidgin of eastern New Guinea is steadily gaining ground in the new nation of Papua New Guinea, and it has now become the mother tongue of a sizeable number of speakers; the resulting creole, now called Tok Pisin, is one of the country's official languages.

And this fact raises some fascinating questions for historical linguists to ponder. Until not so long ago, most linguists were inclined to dismiss creole formation as a rare and unusual event, perhaps even an aberration; creoles were often thought to be a peculiarity of the modern European expansion, a short-lived idiosyncrasy which could be safely ignored in the study of the history and prehistory of 'real' languages, which arose directly from earlier languages in the familiar way.

But why should we assume this so glibly? We know that countless pidgins have arisen just in the last few centuries, in almost every corner of the globe, and we know that many of these pidgins have undergone creolization and turned into new natural languages. Why could the same thing not have happened any number of times in the more remote past? Why shouldn't any number of the 'real' languages whose histories we are exploring be themselves the offspring of ancient creoles? How can we tell?

In fact, we probably can't tell. Once it exists, a creole is a natural language like any other, and it is subject to the same processes of historical change as any other language. There is absolutely no way of demonstrating that some language or language family is not the the direct descendant of some prehistoric creole, created in circumstances of intense contact between speakers of different languages. Indeed, suggestions along these lines are now beginning to be made. Several linguists have put forward the idea that the genetically isolated Japanese might be the descendant of an ancient creole, perhaps one created by mingling waves of settlers from the Asian mainland to the west and from the Indonesian and Philippine islands to the south. This might even be true, though we have no way of finding out, since the Old Japanese of our earliest records looks no more like a creole than does modern Japanese. For all we know, our beloved Proto-Indo-European itself might have started life as a creole constructed by a mixture of anonymous speakers of several different languages, many thousands of years ago, in circumstances we can only guess at.

If a creole remains in contact with a prestige language from which it is partly derived, it may undergo some degree of **decreolization** – that is, features of the prestige language may be imported into the creole, which therefore comes to resemble the prestige language more closely. This process may go further for some speakers than for others, and the result may be a **creole continuum**: a range of related varieties extending from a very conservative version of the creole at one extreme to something more or less identical to the prestige language at the other. Individual speakers may even modify their own speech along the continuum depending on circumstances.

Here are some examples of English-based creoles. The first is Sranan, spoken in Surinam, where it is the mother tongue of about one-third of the population. Sranan is a very conservative creole and is probably typical of what all Caribbean creoles were like before decreolization.

Ala den bigibigi man de na balkon e wakti en. A kon nanga en buku na ondro en anu. A puru en ati na en ede, en a meki kosi gi den. Dan a waka go na a djari, pe den gansi de.

All the important men were on the balcony waiting for him. He came with his book under his arm. He took off his hat and bowed before them. Then he went to the garden where the geese were.

As you can see, this variety is quite incomprehensible to speakers of standard English: it retains a large non-English element in its vocabulary and in its grammar. Slightly more accessible is Miskito Coast Creole, spoken in eastern Nicaragua; the items *did* and *mi* are past-tense markers:

Wen i pik it op naw, i no kom we a de. I tel mi lay wen i kom naw. Da iyvnin i sey, 'mama', i sey, 'a did tayad an neva kom.' A say 'yu dam lay. Siy yu ay? Yu mi dringkin; das wai yu no mi wahn kom ya.'

When he starts up [drinking] now, he doesn't come where I am. He tells me lies when he comes now. In the evening he says 'Ma'am', he says, 'I was tired and didn't come.' I say 'You damn liar. See your eyes? You've been drinking; that's why you didn't want to come here.'

The creole of Trinidad has undergone more substantial decreolization, and is noticeably easier for us to understand, though it still contains a number of words not found in standard English:

Le mi gi yu a reek. Di oda nait a waz laimin bai Paak Striit Kyafe an a si yu bongsin dong di rood wid yu piki ed in a lat a kɔɔlaz, hoolin haan wid yu maan lov kyaan don.

Let me give you some gossip. The other night I was standing around by Park Street Café and I saw you bouncing down the road with your nappy [tightly curled] hair in a lot of curlers, holding hands with your boyfriend [as though] love couldn't end.

But decreolization is, of course, not the only type of change that can affect a creole. Some of the most interesting work on creoles in recent years has focused on very young creoles which are in the process of acquiring new grammatical features. Here are some examples from Tok Pisin, the English-based creole of Papua New Guinea. In these examples, *bilong* (from English *belong*) is a preposition corresponding roughly to English *of*; *pinis* (from *finish*) and *nau* (from *now*) are grammatical markers of aspect; *i* (from *he*) is a grammatical marker which introduces a predicate. (You can already see here some grammatical formatives derived from lexical items.)

Formerly, Tok Pisin permitted no overt compounds, and circumlocutions were necessary to achieve the same effect:

- *man bilong les* 'lazy fellow'
- *man bilong save* 'expert'
- *meri bilong hambak* 'promiscuous woman'

More recently, however, compounds have come into use and are now favoured:

- *lesman* 'lazy fellow'
- *saveman* 'expert'
- *hambakmeri* 'promiscuous woman'

Earlier, the language permitted only complex predications like the following:

- *Ai bilong mi laik slip.*
  'I'm sleepy.'
- *Yau bilong em i pas.*
  'He's deaf.'
- *Gras bilong mi i wait pinis.*
  'I've got grey hair.'

Now, compounds can function as predicates:

- *Mi aislip nau.*
  'I'm sleepy.'
- *Em i yaupas.*
  'He's deaf.'
- *Mi waitgras pinis.*
  'I've got grey hair.'

Formerly, causatives could only be formed periphrastically, using the auxiliary verb *mekim*, from English *make* plus the suffix *-im* (from *him*), which marks a transitive verb in Tok Pisin:

- *Yu mekim sam wara i boil.*
  'You boil water.'
- *Mi mekim kabora i drai.*
  'I dried the copra.'

Now, synthetic causatives are in use; these are formed with the transitivizing suffix *-im*:

- *Yu boilim wara.*
  'You boil water.'
- *Mi bagarapim haus.*
  'I ruined the house.'

(The delightful verb *bagarapim* derives from English *bugger up*.)

Earlier, habitual action was indicated by placing the verb *save* 'know' before the main verb:

- *Mipela save wokim haus olsem.*
  'We usually build houses like this.'

For modern speakers, however, *save* is reduced to an unstressed particle *se*:

- *Mipela se wokim haus olsem.*
  'We usually build houses like this.'

Earlier, Tok Pisin permitted no complement clauses, and only juxtaposed statements were available:

- *Mi no save. Ol i wokim dispela haus.*
  'I didn't know. They had built this house.'

But modern Tok Pisin allows the adverb *olsem* 'like this, this way' (from *all same*) to be used as a complementizer introducing a complement clause:

- *Mi no save olsem ol i wokim dispela haus.*
  'I didn't know they had built this house.'

(A question to ponder: why should the word *olsem* come to be used in this way? What could have been the intermediate stage leading to its modern use as a complementizer?)

Particularly interesting is the introduction of relative clauses into Tok Pisin, which formerly lacked them. Several different strategies have been devised for making relative clauses. One strategy uses the question word *husat* 'who?' (from *who's that?*) as a relative pronoun; relative clauses are enclosed in brackets:

- *Em man [husat i drawim] em i go lapun tru na em i dai pinis.*
  'The man [who drew (it)] got very old and died.'

- *Em kilim man [husat stilim samting].*
  'He killed the man [who stole something].'

Another strategy uses the question word *we* 'where?' (from *where*) in a similar way:

- *Dispela man i kolim stret man [we em i poisonim long en].*
  'This man named precisely the man [who performed magic on him].'

These two strategies are possibly calques on English. Very different is another strategy, which makes use of the deictic item *ia* 'here' (formerly also *hia*, from *here*). This item can be used like its English counterpart:

- *Yu stap hia.*
  'You stay here.'

But it is very commonly used in Tok Pisin as a generalized deictic item in discourse:

- *dispela haus ia*
  'this house here'

(Compare non-standard English *this here house*.) The frequent use of this item has led to its introduction as yet another marker of relative clauses, but this one behaves differently: it occurs *twice*, once at each end of the relative clause, in what we might call a 'bracketing' strategy:

- *Disla liklik anis ia [em i ben dens waintaim em festaim ia] em go nau.*
  'The little ant [that he danced with the first time] left.'

With a little thought, you can see how this might have come about.

Sometimes two strategies are used together:

- *Man ia [we i maritim wanem meri ia] em . . .*
  'The man who married this girl, he . . . '

Such variation in usage shows that relative-clause formation in Tok Pisin has not yet settled down, and only time will tell whether speakers will finally settle on one particular strategy or whether the language will continue to permit several different constructions. But don't lose sight of the central point: a pidgin which lacked relative clauses entirely has developed into a creole which has acquired them. Just such grammatical elaboration is entirely typical of the development of a creole – and already, perhaps, a hypothetical linguist who was unaware of the existence of English and who encountered Tok Pisin for the first time might conclude that Tok Pisin was just one more indigenous language of New Guinea, descended from a long line of ancestors stretching back into the remote past.

A final note. Some historical linguists have argued that the processes of pidginization and subsequent creolization are so unusual that they could only have happened once, and that all creoles, or at least all creoles based on European languages, are descended ultimately from the Lingua Franca, or Sabir, a pidgin used centuries ago by traders in the Mediterranean, through lines of transmission which involved successive **relexifications** (massive replacements of vocabulary) on the base of the original gram- mar, possibly via the Portuguese-based pidgin used in Africa in the fif- teenth century. This idea is no longer taken seriously, since most linguists are now satisfied that pidgins and creoles can and do spring up wherever and whenever the conditions are right. Nevertheless, some specialists still believe that some particular creoles, such as the Caribbean creoles, may derive from a single common ancestor via relexification. It is open to question, however, just how applicable the genetic model is to pidgins and creoles.

11.4 *Language death*

We have already seen that a language which establishes itself over a wide area may, with the passage of time, break up into a number of distinct daughter languages. We have now also seen that entirely new languages can arise and become established as a result of the kind of intense contact that leads to the formation of pidgins and creoles. Both of these processes, of course, tend to increase the number of different languages spoken on the planet. If there were nothing else going on, then, the number of languages would go on increasing forever. Of course this doesn't happen, because there *is* something else going on: languages are disappearing. In this section we shall be examining the phenomenon of **language death**.

Why should a language disappear? One possibility, of course, is that all its speakers might simply die. And some languages certainly have disappeared in such a way, though rarely if ever from natural causes like plagues or tidal waves. In all known cases, the last speakers of a language were simply killed by more powerful neighbours.

This happened to the Yahi people of California in the nineteenth century, who were massacred – shot to death – by white settlers who coveted their land. The last surviving sixteen Yahis fled into the desert, where all but one of them died from cold, hunger, and disease, still knowing not a word of any language but Yahi. On a larger scale, it happened to the entire indigenous population of Tasmania. After the British arrived on the island in 1803, they found the Tasmanians to be an inconvenient obstacle to their plans for settlement, and so they took vigorous steps. The Tasmanians were ordered out of most of their own territory, and British soldiers were authorized to shoot Tasmanians on sight. By 1830 only 200 Tasmanians remained alive; these were rounded up and placed in a kind of concentration camp, where, denied medical care or adequate food, they eventually died. The last to die was an old woman who reportedly spoke not one word of English.

In the vast majority of cases, however, the death of a language is rather less ghastly. Most often, the speakers of a language simply abandon it in favour of some other language which is seen as more prestigious or more useful, in the process known as **language shift**. Such shifts of language have undoubtedly happened countless times during human history. For example, the first language ever written down, Sumerian, in what is now Iraq, endured for perhaps 2000 years or more before the Sumerians, long since conquered by more powerful neighbours, finally abandoned their ancestral tongue and thereafter spoke only Akkadian, the language of the Assyrian and Babylonian conquerors. Akkadian in turn then disappeared in favour of other languages, chiefly Aramaic, which eventually became the first language of most of the Middle East (it was the mother tongue of Jesus Christ and of the Apostles). More recently still, Aramaic itself has given way to Arabic, the language of the Arab conquerors of the eighth century AD; Arabic is still today the first language of most of the Middle East. Aramaic survives today in corners of Iraq and Iran, but Akkadian and Sumerian are long dead.

We find the same phenomenon almost everywhere where we have records. Several thousand years ago, the chief language of central Asia Minor seems to have been a little-known tongue which we call Hattic. But the rise of a new empire caused Hattic to disappear in favour of the language we call Hittite; Hittite in turn gave way to Greek; many centuries later Greek disappeared in favour of Turkish, the language of the conquering Turks, which is now the first language of almost everybody in central Asia Minor (Greek survives elsewhere, of course). These successive conquests did not result in massacres or expulsions of the earlier population; instead, the local people simply abandoned their traditional language in favour of the new prestige language. The Turks of Asia Minor today look very little like the Turks of central Asia, the ancestral home of the Turkish people, but they look very much like their Greek, Armenian, and Lebanese neighbours, and probably not so different from the Hittites. Indeed, the Turks themselves recognize their complex ancestry. They certainly admire the feats of their Asian forebears, but, when the Turkish Republic decreed in the 1920s that all Turks should adopt surnames, some of them chose the surname *Hitit* in recognition of the Hittite portion of their ancestry.

During the initial peopling of the planet, when our remote ancestors were moving into previously uninhabited stretches of Europe, Australia, and the Americas, it is likely that the number of languages on earth was tending to increase over time, as the combination of language change and geographical separation had its usual effect. (Compare the islands of Polynesia, all settled for the first time within the last 2000 years or so, where we now find a different language on every individual island or archipelago.) Once all the habitable areas were occupied, however, there was probably a very rough equilibrium, with the disappearance of languages more or less balancing the appearance of new ones, so that the total number of languages on the planet remained roughly constant, perhaps between 5000 and 10000. Such an equilibrium probably endured for millennia, but things have changed.

Around 5000 years ago some societies began acquiring enough wealth and technology to raise armies and conquer their neighbours, thus establishing the world's first empires. At least some of these empires succeeded in imposing their chief language upon subjects who had formerly spoken something else (recall the Sumerians). Over time, this imperial tendency to cause language shift became steadily more effective. The Romans managed to establish Latin in most of the western part of their empire, in the process extinguishing any number of earlier languages. Later conquerors like the Arabs and the Turks were even more successful at obliterating a range of earlier languages. But even their efforts were eclipsed by the success of the Europeans.

Beginning in the fifteenth century, the several nations of Europe began to explore the whole world, to establish vast colonial empires and to introduce their European languages into every corner of the globe. Not all of them were equally successful. The Dutch that was introduced into North and South America, the Caribbean, and the East Indies has survived in only a few locales, and German and Italian have had for the most part only a transient effect upon Africa and New Guinea. In great contrast, French, Spanish, Portuguese, Russian, and, above all, English have been successfully transplanted into vast swathes of the globe, where they have become the first languages of hundreds of millions of people on every continent and the everyday second languages of hundreds of millions more. In the process, they have already exterminated many hundreds of indigenous languages, and this process is accelerating all the time. Hundreds of other surviving languages have been reduced to insignificance and are struggling for survival, often vainly.

Some years ago Mrs Laura Fish Somersal was found to be the last surviving speaker of the California language Wappo; when she eventually died, Wappo died with her. Around the same time, the linguist Bob Dixon tracked down Mr Albert Bennett, the last surviving speaker of the Australian language Mbabaram; six months later, Mr Bennett died, and one more language passed into history. This is going on all the time, and only rarely is there a linguist nearby to record the death of another language.

The number of languages currently spoken on earth is usually thought to be between 5000 and 6000, but the majority of these are already in danger of being entirely displaced by more prestigious languages, thanks to our modern development of centralized nation states with their educational and administrative systems and more especially of rapid long-distance transport and the ever-present mass media. Everywhere we look, we see languages in danger of disappearing: Breton in France, Sami ('Lappish') in Norway, Irish in Ireland, Maori in New Zealand, Judaeo-Spanish in Turkey, Manchu in China, Ainu in Japan, and, of course, the whole constellation of surviving indigenous languages in Australia, Canada, the USA, and Brazil.

Consider the case of Irish. Ireland was conquered by the English King Henry II in 1171, and the English at once began settling in Ireland (though many of these settlers were French-speaking Norman nobles). These early settlers, however, adopted the language and the culture of the far more numerous Irish (whence the frequency in Ireland of Norman–Irish surnames like *Fitzpatrick*). Until 1600 Irish remained the normal vehicle of communication for all social classes in Ireland, and English was little known outside the small enclave of Dublin. Soon after this date, the English Protestant leader Oliver Cromwell reinvaded Ireland with a vengeance, and the English (and later the Scots) began to settle in Ireland in significant numbers. Still, by 1800, English was the majority language only in and around Belfast, in Dublin, and in a small area in and around Wexford. But the status of Ireland as a British colony encouraged the spread of English, a trend reinforced by the great famine of the 1840s, which chiefly affected Irish-speakers, many of whom died or emigrated. As a consequence, Irish was by 1851 the majority language only in several discontinuous areas, mainly in Counties Donegal, Mayo, Galway, and Kerry. In that year, the first census of Ireland revealed that, out of 6.5 million inhabitants, there were 320000 Irish monoglots and 1.5 million bilinguals. By the census of 1911, massive emigration had reduced the population to 4.4 million inhabitants, of whom about 600000 spoke Irish, most of these being bilingual. Since the advent of home rule in 1921, followed by full independence for most of the country in 1937, the Irish government has made strenuous efforts to rescue the Irish language: Irish has for decades been a compulsory subject in schools, and new vocabulary is constantly being created to allow Irish to be used in such fields as computing (see the next section). But the effect of official policy has been minimal: there are now no Irish monoglots, apart from a few small children, and recent estimates conclude that only about 8700 people still speak Irish well enough to transmit it to their children, and perhaps only 1100 of these are genuinely more at home in Irish than in English. The apparent position of most Irish people was recently summed up by a commentator as follows: it's fine to keep Irish so long as someone else speaks it.

The case of Irish is entirely typical of hundreds or even thousands of small languages around the world, and it points up an important conclusion: what is good for a minority language as a language is not always what is good for its speakers. Irish has not been openly persecuted for generations, and indeed it has been receiving every kind of official encouragement, but the Irish people are keenly aware that a knowledge of Irish confers few opportunities, and those only in Ireland, while a knowledge of English opens the door to the whole world.

Very recently, linguists have been starting to study dying languages in order to find out what happens to them when they are dying. Their results are interesting, if perhaps not entirely surprising. At the social level, of course, one obvious finding is that some people in a given generation simply fail to learn the language at all, while other people in the same generation acquire it normally. For example, in the Hopi area of the American southwest, there are young people and middle-aged people who speak fluent Hopi living side by side with people of the same age who speak only English; as a result, Hopi-speakers are frequently obliged to speak English to their neighbours and relatives, and important tribal business usually has to be conducted in English so that everyone can take part. This is a common state of affairs. Partly as a consequence of it, though also for other reasons, the occasions on which it is deemed appropriate to speak the dying language become fewer and more circumscribed. Even if everyone in the community can still speak the language, speakers may feel it more appropriate to use the local prestige language for such things as doing business or discussing politics or television programmes. The dying language may be increasingly restricted to certain narrow spheres of conversation, perhaps to the immediate family in the home, then perhaps only to children, then perhaps not even that, and the language may gradually assume little more than a ceremonial role, being entirely confined to certain special occasions. In the end, there may be nothing left apart from a few conventional phrases serving as a badge of identity – for example, many Mexicans have abandoned the Nahuatl language of their Aztec ancestors in favour of Spanish, but they retain a few Nahuatl greetings, and also, amusingly, a few Nahuatl obscenities.

More strikingly, the dying language, even while it continues to be spoken, may undergo substantial changes in structure, especially in the speech of younger speakers. Native lexical items may be increasingly replaced by loan words from the prestige language; when this happens on a massive scale, as it often does, the process is called **relexification**. Irregular forms may be regularized; grammatical alternations may be lost; small inflectional classes of nouns or verbs may be lost, with their members being shifted into larger classes. Those tenses, aspects, and moods of the verb which are less frequent or more complex in formation may drop out of use; case-systems may be greatly reduced and simplified. Synthetic forms may be replaced by analytical (periphrastic) forms. Marked sentence patterns may cease to be used, and syntactically complex constructions may be lost. Regular processes of word-formation may become unproductive, with words being formed instead by borrowing from, or calquing on, the prestige language. Indeed, all of the features characteristic of more formal or elevated styles may be lost, leaving only a single unvarying style available. Even the phonology may change: speakers may lose phonological contrasts not found in the prestige language, or introduce phonological features of the prestige language into the dying language; regular phonological processes like devoicing and nasalization may be disrupted, overgeneralized, or lost. So striking is this **attrition** (as it is known) that some observers have interpreted it as the mirror-image of creolization: in attrition, the language becomes less rich, less expressive, less flexible, less elaborated, and altogether less serviceable as a vehicle of communication.

Here are a few examples. Semi-speakers of the dying Scottish Gaelic of East Sutherland have lost the complex synthetic conjugated prepositions of Gaelic like *riu-m* 'to-me' and *bhu-atha* 'from-them', and replaced them with analytic combinations of free-standing forms, like *ri mis'* 'to me' and *bho aid* 'from them'. Speakers of the Salishan language Flathead under 60 years old no longer know the verb forms with first-plural subject and second-plural object, which are irregular and unusually complex. Semi-speakers of Channel Islands French have lost the contrast between long and short consonants found in that language but absent in English. Semi-speakers of the Mayan language Tuxtla Chico Mam have merged uvular /q/ with velar /k/. American semi-speakers of Finnish have replaced Finnish *takka* 'fireplace' with the compound *tuli-pakka*, literally 'fire-place', a calque on English. Semi-speakers of the Mexican language Pipil retain the Pipil word for 'foot' but use the Spanish words for 'ankle' and 'toe'. Semi-speakers of the SOV language Basque in areas where the language is being lost speak Basque with the SVO order of Spanish. Young semi-speakers of Dyirbal have entirely lost the ergative morphology of that language. Semi-speakers of Breton replace the penultimate stress of Breton with the final stress of French, they use a French-style uvular for /r/ in place of the Breton apical, and they pronounce the Breton phoneme /h/ (absent from French) unsystematically or not at all.

Such examples could be multiplied almost without limit. Languages have been dying for as long as they have existed, but the rate of language death is today greater than ever before. The twentieth century has already seen the deaths of more languages than any preceding century, but that dubious distinction will assuredly pass to the twenty-first century in its turn. Indeed, the linguist Michael Krauss has estimated that perhaps half of the world's languages will disappear in the next century or so, and that in the not too distant future there may be no more than 150 languages still spoken on the planet. The resulting linguistic homogeneity will doubtless carry with it any number of practical advantages, but there will also be a heavy price to pay in terms of loss of individual and group identity – not to mention the catastrophic loss to linguistics.

In linguistics, we normally consider that a language is dead when it no longer has any native speakers. In some cases, though, a dead language may continue to find some use as a ceremonial, literary, scholarly, or, most especially, religious language. Long after Latin had evolved into its several distinct daughters, it continued to be used as a vehicle of scientific and scholarly writing in Europe, and it was also used as a religious language by the Roman Catholic Church, many of whose clergy even learned to speak it. The ancient Egyptian language, whose later forms are called Coptic, died out as a spoken language in the sixteenth century, submerged by Arabic, but Coptic is still in use as a liturgical language by African Christians today.

Such special uses aside, a language that dies stays dead. The occasional attempts at reviving dead languages as spoken tongues have usually been no more than empty exercises. For example, the Cornish language of Cornwall died out around 1800 in favour of English. Since we retain considerable material written in Cornish, some enthusiasts have recently been teaching themselves, and others, to speak Cornish as a second language, and there exists a Cornish Language Society to promote this end. But there appears to be no possibility that we will see a new generation of native speakers of Cornish: few Cornish people can see the point in learning a dead language with no conceivable function beyond that of reinforcing a Cornish identity.

Only a single case is known of a dead language which has truly been brought back to life as a mother tongue. This is Hebrew. As a result of repeated conquests of their ancient Mediterranean homeland, the Jews became scattered to the corners of the earth; obliged to learn the local languages in order to live, they eventually abandoned Hebrew speech altogether, and the language died out as a mother tongue – though it always retained a variety of religious and ceremonial uses, and there were always people who could read it and, to some extent, speak it as a second language. When, in the late nineteenth and early twentieth centuries, the Zionist movement brought many members of the Jewish diaspora back to Palestine, where they established the settlements that eventually became the state of Israel, they no longer had a common spoken language. The largest single group spoke Yiddish, a distinctive offshoot of German with heavy influence from Slavic and Hebrew, while other sizeable groups spoke Judaeo-Spanish or Arabic as their first language; most Jews in any case were bilingual or multilingual, and there were speakers of Russian, Polish, Hungarian, Turkish, Italian, French, English, and a dozen other languages.

Faced with a major linguistic problem, the settlers settled on the bold solution of reviving Hebrew as their common language. Painfully they taught themselves to read Hebrew and to speak it as best they could; crucially, they taught Hebrew to their children. Their efforts were eventually successful, and today Hebrew is the first language of almost all native-born Jews in Israel. So the revival of a dead language is not quite impossible, but it is most unlikely that we will ever see another such instance. The circumstances in which the Zionist settlers found themselves were extraordinary, and they are unlikely to be repeated in other cases. In all likelihood, the case of Hebrew will remain unique.

Of course, biblical Hebrew was scarcely adequate to serve as the principal language of a modern technological society, and the Israelis have been obliged to make strenuous efforts to develop the language into a suitable vehicle for all purposes. Efforts of this sort are the subject of the next section.

11.5   *Language planning*

In most of this book we have been discussing the various types of change which, intuitively, just 'happen' to a language, with no conscious or deliberate decisions by its speakers. But not all changes are like this. It is quite possible for speakers to make deliberate decisions about the future of their language, and sometimes even to succeed in imposing decisions made by official bodies upon the speech and writing at least of educated speakers.

To some extent, this is always happening, particularly in literate societies in which the language is used for a wide variety of purposes. English writers like Spenser, Shakespeare, and Milton often deliberately introduced new words into their writing, words which have since taken root in the language, such as Spenser's *derring-do* (which was apparently more of a misunderstanding than a conscious coinage) and Shakespeare's *multitudinous* (a loan from Latin). As we saw in Chapter 2, this activity is still very much with us: such modern coinages as *blurb*, *user-friendly*, *ecosystem*, *sexism*, and *biodiversity* are now so familiar that we are hardly aware we once did without them.

Decisions can be more official than this. The opposite of *starboard* (on a ship) used to be *larboard*, but these two terms can easily be confused in noisy conditions at sea, with possibly catastrophic results, and so in 1844 the British Admiralty decreed that *larboard* should be abandoned in favour of *port*, a decision now universally accepted in English.

Historical linguistics itself provides a particularly fine example of self-conscious and successful coinage. In the nineteenth century, historical linguistics was developed in Germany, and almost all important work was published in German; consequently, German-speaking linguists deliberately coined large numbers of new technical terms for their purposes. When English-speaking linguists began to use their own language, around the beginning of the twentieth century, they were forced to find English equivalents for all these terms, and it wasn't easy: for example, the English translator of Brugmann's famous book on IE grammar complains in his introduction of the difficulty of finding suitable English terms. Equivalents were eventually found, of course, and today it rarely occurs to us that our everyday technical terms were once absent from the language and exist today because our predecessors sweated blood to construct them.

But it's not only vocabulary that's affected by self-conscious coinages: new grammatical constructions can be introduced as well. All educated speakers of English are familiar with the *respectively* construction, as in *Esther and Larry drank whisky and brandy, respectively*. But tests have shown that this construction is not used by uneducated people and is moreover usually not even understood by them. It thus appears to be a deliberate introduction into the language, acquired only through formal education, rather than a 'natural' development in English – though my use of 'natural' here is perhaps not entirely appropriate.

The linguistic case is particularly interesting. At the time, English was already widely used for most purposes, but it wasn't much used for historical linguistics, and so we had to construct a whole terminology rather quickly before we could make satisfactory use of our language in this particular field. But many other languages have found themselves in the position of suddenly needing technical vocabulary for *everything*, and sometimes not just technical vocabulary but even an agreed set of standard forms for ordinary words and for grammatical inflections. Most obviously, this happens when a country or a people has long been under foreign domination and then achieves its independence.

For example, Finland achieved its independence from Russia only in 1918, and the Finns, naturally, decided that Finnish would henceforth be their national language for all purposes, instead of Russian. But Finnish had never before been used even for education or government, let alone for linguistics or physics, and moreover there wasn't even an agreed standard form of the language: there were merely innumerable local varieties of Finnish, differing somewhat in vocabulary, in the forms of words, and in grammatical inflections. The Finns therefore set out to construct both a single standard form of Finnish, to be learned and used by everyone, as well as a simply gigantic number of new abstract and technical terms, in order to allow Finns to speak and write about any subject in their language. This process is called **language planning**, and you will appreciate that, in such circumstances, it is a colossal enterprise.

In the Finnish case, the task was eventually carried out to general satisfaction, and today there is an agreed standard form of Finnish, used by all educated speakers, complete with a massive technical vocabulary. But the work is never done. Today most work in such fields as physics and linguistics is carried out in other languages, most usually in English, and the Finns still have to keep finding Finnish equivalents for the annual flood of new technical terms. In Finland, this is done centrally. Committees of specialists have been set up to coin the required new words, and their decisions are official. I used to know a Finnish physicist who was on the physics committee. Twice a year the members would meet to agree on Finnish equivalents for the latest crop of new technical terms in their field. For example, after deliberation, they agreed that the Finnish word for *quark* (a recently coined term in particle physics) would be *kvarkki*, which is at least pronounceable in Finnish.

Many other languages are in a similar position, but the Finnish solution is not always available. Arabic is the chief language of eighteen separate countries, and there is no official body with the power to legislate for the whole language, and even individual Arab countries rarely have such bodies. Consequently, Arabs writing about technical subjects in their own language simply have to coin their own terms, with predictable results: enormous regional variation in technical terms and even in everyday terms. Recent bilingual dictionaries and other sources show eleven different Arabic words for 'mineralogy', eighteen for 'metallurgy', twenty-three for 'geology', and even twenty-three for 'linguistics', all of them currently in use somewhere in the Arab world. As the Arabs themselves would be the first to agree, this is hardly an ideal approach.

But a lack of political unity is not the only obstacle to successful language planning. Consider the case of Norwegian. When Norway obtained its independence from Denmark in 1814, all Norwegians were agreed that Norwegian should be the national language of the new country, replacing Danish, which had been used there for centuries. But they immediately faced a big problem: *what sort* of Norwegian?

In the populous south of the counry, just across the strait from Denmark, educated Norwegians spoke a variety of Norwegian that was much influenced by Danish and very close to it. In the remote and rural west of the country, however, the influence of Danish had been minimal. Hence the educated Norwegian of the capital city was actually more similar to Danish in many respects than it was to rural Norwegian: for example, southern Norwegian, like Danish, had only two grammatical genders, while western Norwegian had three.

So what was to be done? Some Norwegians argued as follows: 'All educated people speak a form of Norwegian which is close to Danish. Let us therefore make this Dano-Norwegian our national language, since doing so will minimize the disruption.' Others, however, took a very different view: 'Dano-Norwegian is a corrupt form of Norwegian, little more than bad Danish. The *real* Norwegian is what they speak in the west, which has been little affected by Danish and which is the purest form of the language. This must therefore be our national language.'

The second position, of course, illustrates the force of purism, discussed above. But it also demonstrates a second factor: the desire for **Abstand**. This German word means 'linguistic distance', and the point is that the second group of Norwegians were fearful that outsiders might continue to regard Norwegian as little more than an eccentric dialect of the closely related Danish.

In Norway, neither side succeeded in gaining the upper hand, with the result that Norway, a nation of four million people, today has *two* standard forms of Norwegian. Everybody is required to learn both in school; government documents have to be printed in both forms; and so on. Both forms have been revised at intervals, and for a while an exasperated government was hoping to merge the two into a compromise single standard, but this has not worked out so far. Part of the problem is that those who prefer to use Dano-Norwegian, today called *Riksmål* (a small minority in 1814 but a large majority today), deeply resent the continued efforts to get them to accept, as standard, forms which they regard as colloquial or even as illiterate. Imagine how you would feel if, now that you have (perhaps painfully) acquired a good command of standard English, you were suddenly told that you should henceforth accept forms like *I ain't got none* and *We was there* as standard English. At present, no official solution appears to be in sight, and the Norwegians will apparently just have to wait for future generations to resolve the problem by opting overwhelmingly for one choice or the other.

But at least the Norwegians were agreed from the start that their national language should be some variety of Norwegian. Sometimes even that degree of consensus is wanting.

In seventeenth-century Germany, the position was even worse, since most educated people refused even to consider using German as their national language. Latin was the language of scholarship, while French was the language of polite society, including government and diplomacy, and most educated Germans despised the German language as the language of peasants, reeking of cabbage and onions and far too boorish to be used for educated discourse. For two centuries, scholars like Dürer, Kepler, Luther, and Leibniz had fought to raise the status of German, but with little effect. Leibniz even found it necessary to publish his polemics in French or Latin, in order to reach his audience, since most educated Germans could not or would not read anything written in German. There were repeated attempts at coining the necessary German technical terms: *Zwerchlinie* 'cross-line' for 'diameter', *Eierlinie* 'egg-line' for 'ellipse', *Schnitz* 'splinter, chunk' for 'segment', *Anstreicher* 'on-striker' for 'tangent', and so on. Almost none of these efforts has survived.

Lectures in German universities were delivered in Latin, and the use of German was expressly forbidden in many of them. When, in 1687, the academic Thomasius at the august University of Leipzig pinned up a notice (in German) announcing that he would be giving a lecture in German, there was an uproar; the very notice itself was considered to be such an abomination that Thomasius was fearful it might be doused in holy water. Thomasius gave his lecture, but soon after he was obliged to leave Leipzig for a less traditional university.

Such efforts eventually had an effect: by 1800 only 4 per cent of printed material was still in Latin, and German was routinely being used for scholarly publication, just in time for the pioneering work of Rask, Bopp, and Grimm in historical linguistics to be written in German. Even half a century earlier, this work might have appeared in Latin instead. But German did not replace

French as the language of government in Germany until the early nineteenth century.

Language planning is a formidable undertaking. Consider the case of Basque. Though Basque has been regularly written since the sixteenth century, there was no standard form of the language before the 1960s, and there was, of course, a great dearth of technical terms. Only in 1964 did the Basque Language Academy promulgate a standard orthography, followed a few years later by a standard morphology, standard forms of place names, and standard forms of some hundreds of common words. (Neither the pronunciation nor the syntax has yet received any significant degree of standardization.) But even these basic decisions proved to be difficult and controversial.

The standard orthography included half a dozen digraphs, such as *tx*, *tt*, and *ll*, all of which represent single consonants in Basque. But were these digraphs meant to be single letters, following the example of Spanish, in which digraphs like *ch* and *ll* are distinct letters with their own place in the alphabet, or were they meant to be only sequences of letters, like the French digraphs *ch* and *gn*? The Academy neglected to say, and so there ensued a period of confusion, with some dictionaries adopting the first policy and others the second, before the Academy belatedly settled on the second.

The Basque town called *Rentería* in Spanish is variously known in Basque as *Errenteria*, *Errenteri*, or *Errenderi*, and moreover a medieval document reveals that the town was formerly known in Basque as *Orereta*, a name which has dropped out of use. The Academy's choice of *Errenteria* upset many of the town's inhabitants, who campaigned for reviving the lost medieval name, and for some years visitors to the town were greeted with banners, posters, and graffiti demanding the old name.

Loan words presented a particular problem, because of the political frontier running through the country. For 'judge', French Basques used *juje*, a loan from French *juge*, while Spanish Basques used *juez*, a loan from Spanish. In this case, the neologism *epailari* was coined, from *epai* 'judgement, sentence' and the suffix *-lari* 'one who performs'. But 'crocodile' was more difficult, since French Basque *krokodila* and Spanish Basque *kokodrilo*, both loans, were substantially different; the Academy's curious choice was the compromise *krokodilo*, a form used by no one. For 'car', no solution has yet been found: French Basque *boitura* (from French *voiture*) and Spanish Basque *kotxe* (from Spanish *coche*) both remain in use.

Neologisms, of course, were coined in their thousands, taking advantage of the language's abundant supply of word-forming suffixes: *hozkailu* 'refrigerator' (from *hotz* 'cold' and *-gailu* 'apparatus'), *adabegi* 'node' (in a syntactic tree') (an extension of *adabegi* 'node, knot' (in a botanical tree), itself a compound of *adar* 'branch' and *begi* 'eye'), *aurrerakuntza* 'progress' (from *aurrera* 'forward' and *-kuntza* 'abstract action'), *ikerketa* 'research' (from *iker-* 'investigate' plus *-keta* 'activity'), *iragankor* 'transitive' (from *iragan* 'put through' plus *-kor* 'tending to'), *kutsadura* 'pollution' (from *kutsa-* 'contaminate' plus *-dura* 'effect of an action'), *iraultza* '(political) revolution' (from *irauli* 'turn over' plus *-tza* 'action'), *ortzune* 'cosmos' (from *ortzi* 'sky' plus *-une* 'place'), and so on.

A particular problem has been to find a way of rendering the numerous prefixes found in other European languages, since Basque has no prefixes of its own. Latin and Greek prefixes like *con-*, *pre-*, *anti-*, *post-*, *syn-*, *dis-*, *dia-*, *trans-*, *meta-*, *contra-*, and *in-* have no straightforward counterparts in Basque, and international words like *transcontinental, antisocial, hyperventilation, subsection, supersonic,* and *synchronic* therefore present considerable difficulties. Various devices have been pressed into service to obtain Basque equivalents for such words. In some cases, traditional means of word-formation can be employed. Thus, 'posthumous' is rendered as *hilondoko*, from *hil* 'die' plus *ondo* 'after' plus the adjective-forming suffix *-ko*; the resulting formation is entirely parallel to long-established words like *afalondoko* 'after-dinner'. Other cases are more difficult. For 'prehistory', the closest Basque equivalent to the prefix is the noun *aurre* 'front'. Some writers have attempted to use this noun as a prefix, producing *aurrehistoria*, a word whose formation is decidedly un-Basque. Others have preferred *historiaurre*, which at least conforms to the normal rules of word-formation.

At present there is something of a tendency to use the first pattern, producing words like *kontraeraso* 'counteroffensive' (*eraso* 'attack'; the postposition *kontra* 'against' has been in the language for centuries) and *gainjarri* 'superimpose' (*gain* 'top' plus *jarri* 'put'). In this way, as a result of the extensive and self-conscious creation of neologisms, Basque is apparently acquiring a new set of word-forming prefixes derived from native materials which historically never functioned as prefixes. If this pattern proves to be an enduring one, the new prefixes will represent a paradigm case of the way in which a language can be deliberately engineered by its speakers to meet their needs.

Of course, the business of language planning involves a good deal more than official decisions and lists of new words: the decisions have to be accepted by the community, and the official forms and the new words have to be used by speakers and writers. In the Basque case, this has now, after some initial resistance, largely happened, and the new forms are widely used. Naturally, not every proposal has been accepted. The suggested neologisms *beroneurkin* 'thermometer' (from *bero* 'heat' plus *neur-* 'measure' plus *-kin* 'instrument') and *suomitar* 'Finn' (from Finnish *Suomi* 'Finland' plus Basque *-tar* 'who is from') have never left the pages of the dictionaries in which they were proposed, and all Basques continue to use the established forms *termometro* and *finlandes*.

A good example of the pitfalls involved in language planning is provided by Turkish. During the Ottoman Empire, official Turkish was heavily influenced by Arabic and Persian and was incomprehensibly remote from ordinary speech. After the establishment of the Turkish Republic in 1923, the authorities determined to reform the standard language, in order to bring it closer to ordinary people. This was a wise decision, and the Turkish Language Society has been very successful in carrying through the needed reforms. But not all their decisions have found favour with the Turkish people.

The Ottoman word for 'international' was the impossibly clumsy *beyn-el-milel*, a complete Arabic phrase meaning 'between the nations'. This structure is utterly alien to Turkish, and so the planners replaced it with *milletlerarası*, a perfectly normal Turkish formation. But the planners were not satisfied with this, because it was still based on the Arabic loan *millet* 'nation'. They therefore combed the Turkic languages of central Asia for a native Turkic word for 'nation'. Finally they came across *ulus* 'tribe, people', and pressed this into service to create *uluslararası*, their final choice for 'international'. Satisfied, they turned their attention to the next problem.

And so, if you go to Turkey today, you will find that the universal Turkish word for 'international' is in fact *enternasyonal* – which is, of course, a loan from French. Language planning can be tough work.

This example brings me to my final point. Regardless of the planning policies (if any) adopted by the nations which speak them, the languages of the world, particularly those which are important enough to be used for a wide range of purposes, are seeing their vocabularies increasingly subject to what we might call **internationalization**: the spread into all of them of a body of common words. This is most obvious with technical terms: for centuries, words like *thermometer*, *gas*, *radio*, *telephone*, *jet*, *plutonium*, and *gene*, of whatever origin, have been accepted into countless languages with no more than minimal phonological adaptation. But technical terms are not the only international words: *coffee*, *tomato*, *ski*, *yogurt*, *pizza*, *jazz*, *rock* (music), *hobby*, *striptease*, and *football* have spread just as widely.

Such international spread of words has been going on for a very long time (in Chapter 13 we will consider the possibility that the word *wheel* might represent a prehistoric example), but it has been steadily gaining momentum in the last several centuries and especially in the last few decades. Consider Table 11.5, which lists the names of four chemical elements in six languages.

Gold occurs free in nature and has been known for thousands of years, and so every language has its own native name for the metal. Oxygen was discovered only in 1774 and baptized with a Greek-derived name meaning 'acid-former' (it was wrongly believed at the time that oxygen was the

Table 11.5 The names of four chemical elements

Greek	Italian	English	German	Japanese	Chinese
málama	*oro*	*gold*	*Gold*	*kin*	*jin*
oxygónon	*ossigeno*	*oxygen*	*Sauerstoff*	*sanso*	*yǎng*
ouránion	*uranio*	*uranium*	*Uran*	*uran*	*yóu*
samárion	*samario*	*samarium*	*Samarium*	*samarium*	*shān*

essential component of acids). This name has been widely borrowed, but German chose to form a calque instead: *Sauerstoff* means 'acid-stuff'. The German name was in turn calqued into Japanese, using the elements *san* 'acid' and *so* 'simple'. Chinese preferred to coin its own name for the element. Uranium was discovered in 1789, though it became important only in the twentieth century; its newly bestowed name, also derived ultimately from Greek, has been accepted into all six languages, but not without modification: German has shortened the name, Japanese has borrowed the German form, and Chinese has taken only the first syllable and dropped the rest. Finally, samarium was isolated only in 1879, and its new name has passed into all six languages with a bare minimum of modification, except that Chinese has once again contracted it.

This sharing of technical terms has obvious advantages. A physicist doesn't have to know much Basque to realize that Basque *erresonantzia* means 'resonance', that *bapore-presio* means 'vapour pressure', or that *momentu dipolar magnetiko* means 'magnetic dipole moment'; he might even spot that *ultramore* is 'ultraviolet', or that *higidura browndar* is 'Brownian movement'. In the same way, a Scot, a Norwegian, or a Pole reading an Italian popular magazine is unlikely to be troubled by Italian words like *sex-symbol*, *floppy*, *happy-end*, *massage parlour*, *T-shirt*, *jogging*, *gay*, or *look* (in a fashion article), since these English words have become part of the common currency of most European languages. The linguistic homogenization of the planet does not result only from the spread of a few large languages and the death of hundreds of smaller ones.

Further reading

The classic work on language contact is Weinreich (1953); this is still very readable. A more recent brief introduction is Lehiste (1988). A much more substantial, but still very approachable, book dealing with contact and creolization is Thomason and Kaufman (1988); this is particularly recommended. Mackey and Ornstein (1979) includes a number of essays on language contact in various parts of the world. Chapter 6 of Harris and Campbell (1995) is a valuable survey of the borrowing of grammatical morphemes and patterns. Masica (1976) is a major study of the linguistic area of India, and Emeneau (1980) includes a number of essays on the same topic. The Kupwar case is described in Gumperz and Wilson (1971). There is now a substantial literature on pidgins and creoles. A good brief introduction is Foley (1988), which has a good deal to say about grammatical elaboration. The most comprehensive survey is Holm (1988, 1989); the first volume concentrates on structural factors, while the second deals with sociolinguistic factors and includes a review of all known pidgins and creoles, past and present. Dressler (1988) and Lyle Campbell's article in Asher (1994) are good brief introductions to language death with references. Krauss's estimates on the death rate of languages can be found in Hale *et al.* (1992). Two collections of articles on language death are Dressler and Wodak-Leodolter (1977) and Dorian (1989); some of the articles in Seliger and Vago (1991) deal with attrition in language death. Book-length studies of particular languages include Dorian (1981) for Scottish Gaelic, A. Schmidt (1985) for Dyirbal, and Hindley (1990) for Irish. The classic work on language planning is Haugen (1966); a recent survey with references is Christian (1988). Edwards (1994) is a popular book on multi-lingualism which deals with some of the issues discussed in this chapter.

Exercises

Exercise 11.1

The pidgin ancestor of Tok Pisin contained the lexical item *baimbai* 'later, after a while, in the future', a loan from English *by and by*. This was an adverb, and its position was rather free:

> *Baimbai mi kom long haus.* **or**
> *Mi kom long haus baimbai.*
> 'I'll come to the house later.'

There was a marked tendency to prefer sentence-initial position for this item, and it was phonologically reduced to *bai*:

> *Bai mi kom long haus.*

In this position *bai* received full stress, like every word in the pidgin. In modern Tok Pisin, however, two further things have happened: the item *bai* now almost invariably occurs immediately before the verb, and it receives less than full stress:

> *Mi bai kom long haus.*
> 'I'll come to the house.'

Describe in grammatical terms what has happened to the word *baimbai*.

Exercise 11.2

The distinguished Russian linguist Nikolai Trubetzkoy once suggested that a non-Indo-European language could become Indo-European by acquiring a sufficient number of IE features through contact (or otherwise), while an IE language could equally cease to be IE by losing a sufficient number of IE features through contact (or otherwise). This notion has generally been ridiculed by historical linguists on the ground that the ancestry of a language is a matter of unalterable historical fact. In your view, does Trubetzkoy have a serious point, or is he talking nonsense? Why? (In considering your answer, bear in mind the observations in the chapter on the Bantuized Cushitic language Ma'a and on the three languages of Kupwar.)

Exercise 11.3

Basque has no relative pronouns, and relative clauses are constructed in a very different way from those found in Indo-European languages: the relative clause precedes its head, and the verb in the relative clause is final and bears the subordination marker *-(e)n*:

> [*Eman didazun*] *liburua interesgarria da.*
> gave Aux-me-you-Sub book-Det interesting is
> 'The book (which) you gave me is interesting.'

This pattern of relative-clause formation makes it difficult or impossible to relativize upon obliques and genitives. That is, this pattern cannot express structures equivalent to English relative clauses like *the book in which I found this example, the tree under which she was sitting, the children whose parents are present*, and *the magazine on the cover of which there is a picture of a fox*.

Some Basque-speakers have introduced a new relative clause construction of the IE type: the question word *zein* 'which?' is pressed into service as a relative pronoun, and it takes any required case-ending or postposition within the relative clause:

> *umeak* [*zeinen gurasoak hemen dauden*]
> child-Det-Pl *zein*-Gen parents here are-Sub
> 'the children whose parents are here'

> *gizona* [*zeinekin etorri naizen*]
> man-Det *zein*-with came I-Aux-Sub
> 'the man with whom I came'

This construction has occasionally been used in writing since the eighteenth century, but it is also found in the spontaneous speech of some uneducated speakers. It has often been condemned by purists as a barbarism resulting from the influence of Spanish. Nevertheless, it is now widely used in writing, especially in technical writing:

> *aldizkaria* [*zeinen azalean azeriaren irudia dagoen*]
> magazine-Det *zein*-Gen cover-Det-on fox-Det-Gen picture-Det is-Sub]
> 'the magazine on the cover of which there is a picture of a fox'

What pressures would have led to the use of the *zein*-construction (a) by uneducated native speakers and (b) by well-educated professional writers? Why should the construction be particularly frequent in technical writing? Do the purists have a good case for dismissing this construction as an ignorant barbarism?

Exercise 11.4

As is widely known, the French are notoriously sensitive to the presence of English loans in their language and make strenuous efforts to replace them with newly coined French words. The Germans, in contrast, usually take a much more relaxed view of loan words: look at any issue of a popular German magazine. But things are not always so simple.

I have a friend who works in the packaging industry in Britain, and she has extensive business dealings with both France and Germany. Now the packaging industry, like any business, has its own technical terminology: there are hundreds of words for different types of cardboard, different techniques for printing and embossing, different ways of cutting and gluing packages, and so on. All three languages have their own terms for all of these. However, my friend tells me that her French customers invariably use the English terms when speaking French: not only do they not use the 'official' French words, they don't even understand these when she uses them. The Germans, in contrast, invariably use their own German terms when speaking German and profess not to understand the English words.

Do you have any idea why my friend's French and German clients behave (a) so differently from each other and (b) so differently from the perceived stereotypes of the two nations? If this attitude to English loans proves to be widespread in France outside the packaging business, what do you suppose will be the consequences for French? Will this be a good thing or a bad thing?

Exercise 11.5

Before 1979, Basque had no standing in the Spanish Basque Country, and Spanish was used exclusively for all official purposes. Since that date, the new Basque Autonomous Government (BAG) has administered most of the region, and both the BAG and the various provincial and municipal authorities have taken steps to protect the future of the language, which, like all minority languages, is under serious threat. These steps have often induced outrage among the very large number of monoglot Spanish-speakers in the region, the majority of whom are immigrants from elsewhere in Spain who came to the industrialized Basque Country decades ago to find work and who have not bothered to learn Basque. Here is a typical example.

Several years ago, the Basque-speaking majority on the municipal council of the town of Arrasate (Spanish *Mondragón*) decreed that, henceforth, all of the council's proceedings would be conducted exclusively in Basque. Naturally, this decision infuriated the large minority of non-Basque-speaking councillors (most of them immigrants). The Basque-speakers point out that Basque is the mother tongue of the great majority of the indigenous inhabitants, and that immigrants can therefore be reasonably expected to learn it, just as Spanish immigrant workers in France have to learn French. The Spanish-speakers retort that this is ridiculous, since Spanish is the national language of Spain and since all the Basque-speakers in fact speak Spanish perfectly well.

In your view, then, is the decision of the Arrasate council a fair and reasonable one? Why or why not? Is it likely that such policies will have a significant effect in preserving the use of Basque? If Basque should finally be lost, will the Basques be better off as a result or worse off?

In considering your answer, you might like to note the following points and to explain how they influence your answer, if at all.

- Until recently, facilities and materials for teaching Basque were poor and limited, but there are now good textbooks, inexpensive evening classes, and abundant Basque-language publication and broadcasting, including a Basque TV station.
- Basque is of virtually zero usefulness outside the Basque Country.
- Many Basques are still deeply resentful of the ferocious persecution they suffered during the thirty-eight years of Fascist government under the Spanish dictator General Franco, and believe they have a right to try to repair some of the damage to their culture and their language by means of positive discrimination.
- When the Spanish immigrants arrived, they had every reason to believe that they were merely moving to a different part of Spain and that they would be able to carry on speaking Spanish as usual.

Exercise 11.6

Like the other Celtic languages, Breton exhibits several types of *mutation*, in which the initial consonant of a word is changed in certain grammatical and lexical environments. Breton has three mutations, each of which occurs in different circumstances:

- Spirantization: initial /p t k/ change to /f z h/, as in *penn* 'head' but *va fenn* 'my head'.
- Fortition: initial /b d g/ change to /p t k/, as in *belo* 'bike' but *o pelo* 'your bike'.
- Lenition: initial /p t k b d g m/ change to /b d g v z h v/, as in *penn* 'head' but *e benn* 'his head' and *belo* 'bike' but *e velo* 'his bike'.

As you can see, lenition applies to a larger set of consonants than the other two, and it also applies in a much wider range of circumstances. These mutations tend to be lost by semi-speakers of Breton, but not all are lost at once or in the same way. Investigation shows that loss of mutations typically proceeds more or less as follows:

- First, spirantization is lost and replaced by lenition, so that *va fenn* 'my head' is replaced by *va benn*.
- Second, the consonants subject to lenition are reduced to /p t k/, so that *e*

benn 'his head' remains but *e velo* 'his bike' is replaced by unmutated *e belo*.

- Third, fortition is lost and replaced by lenition, so that *o pelo* 'his bike' is replaced by *o velo*.
- During all this time, the range of circumstances in which any mutation occurs is steadily reduced; in the final stages, the mutations may be lost altogether.

Can you see any principled reasons why the loss of the mutations should proceed in this manner and not in some other way? In particular, why should the other two mutations be replaced by lenition instead of merely disappearing? (Data from Dressler 1991.)

Exercise 11.7

English has no third-singular pronoun which is unmarked for sex, a fact which is highly inconvenient: traditionally, we have been obliged to say things like *Someone has forgotten his umbrella* even when addressing a mixed group. Such usages are greatly annoying to women, and recently there have been efforts to find a solution. On the one hand, some people have proposed the invention of a new pronoun, unmarked for sex, such as *herm* (a blend of *her* and *him*) or *han* (borrowed from Finnish), and a few of these proponents actually use one of these creations in their own English. On the other hand, popular speech has usually preferred to turn plural *they* into a singular: *Someone has forgotten their umbrella*. Both of these solutions are felt by many speakers to be unsatisfactory; even the second choice runs into difficulty in cases like *Any candidate who considers themself adequately prepared is requested to present themself to their personal tutor for their examination.*

What, if anything, can be done about this? Should we attempt to impose a solution by legislation or by public pressure? (There is precedent for this: the Swedes and the Italians, among others, have consciously attempted to reform their pronoun systems in certain respects, with mixed success.) Should we merely wait to see if a solution emerges of its own accord? Is either of the solutions mentioned above likely to prove satisfactory in the long run?

Exercise 11.8

The following extracts are taken from an article by the distinguished British sociolinguist and creolist Robert Le Page (1993); the article deals with the manner in which an identifiable and more-or-less standardized language may emerge from a very complex linguistic situation.

> I went to Jamaica in 1950 to be the first lecturer in English language in the newly-founded University College of the West Indies. I became involved in a spectrum of language studies ranging from the very highly reified and focused concept of something called Old English, which I had to teach because it was in the London

University syllabus, to something at the other end of the spectrum, the vernacular usage of the people around me in the streets and markets, which local teachers denied the dignity of even a name, dismissing it as as 'broken talk' or 'bungo talk' or 'patois', as having no grammar, something to be stamped out by teachers for whom 'grammar' was the Holy Grail. When I first proposed to London University that the study of West Indian vernaculars should form part of our English language syllabus I was told that this was impossible: there were no grammars, no books about it, nobody at London University knew anything about it and therefore would not be able [*sic*] to mark examination questions on it, whereas Old English was a familiar object of study with a primer and a normalized grammar and well-edited texts about which examination questions could reasonably be asked and the answers marked. Notice I say an object rather than a subject of study. The Old English I was taught at Oxford came from Henry Sweet's *Anglo-Saxon Primer* and *Reader*, with standardized spellings and only a few short extracts to indicate that there had been five centuries of Germanic language use in Britain before late West Saxon, many different centres of culture before Wessex, that it had been a slave-owning society with only a clerical elite having any sort of formal education, and that education normally meaning learning Latin, that the Vikings had imposed a different kind of culture on the north and east of Britain from the ninth century on, and so on. Sweet's Anglo-Saxon was just one possible abstraction from several highly dynamic sets of linguistic circumstances, just as Standard English is today, but it was Sweet's Anglo-Saxon which we were all taught to use as a base for an edifice known as the history of the English language, a set of stereotypes shaped at least in part by the desire of Germanic scholars in the nineteenth century to have the same kind of animal to study with the same kind of genetic pedigree as the Romance scholars and the Sanskritists and the classicists had. It was for this reason that they changed the name 'Anglo-Saxon' to 'Old English'. I myself had learned to read and pronounce Sweet's texts from scholars who had been taught by scholars who had been taught by Henry Sweet, and I taught my West Indian students in the same way, so that when one of them went on to do graduate work at Oxford and was interviewed by Neville Coghill and read *Beowulf* to him as he had read it to me, she was admitted without further question. This is an example of focusing a stereotype. . . .

Something called a 'language' may be reified and totemized out of complex and even chaotic human activities. In many cases there is a multiple linguistic input to and, initially at least, a multiple linguistic output from the community, a range of idiolects, each itself complex, from which more focused behaviour emerges. The reality of a focused reified language is one toward which groups work rather than their inherited starting point, something which linguists easily forget. At any given time a complex dynamic of interacting systems is in use, each socially marked, the rules for the outcome of the interaction more like those of cloud-formation than of clockwork. The nature of the system is sociolinguistic, though linguistic abstractions are imposed upon it.

Some historical linguists might find Le Page's views radical, heretical, even outrageous or shocking. What do you think? Is Le Page right to compare the

origins of modern standard English, and even the origins of the literary Old English used in King Alfred's Wessex, to the complex and bewildering linguistic state of affairs found in contemporary Jamaica and in the rest of the West Indies? In particular, is he right to maintain that what we call 'English' is an idealization, perhaps even a goal, rather than a contemporary or a historical reality? In considering these questions, bear in mind what you've learned in the earlier chapters of this book.

12

Language and prehistory

12.1 *Etymology*

The name **etymology** is given to the study of the origins and histories of individual words, and also to the history of a particular word. The study of word origins has a certain obvious appeal, and a number of popular books and newspaper columns (of varying degrees of reliability) are devoted to the subject; consequently, beginning students often expect that etymology will form a prominent part of the subject of historical linguistics. They will be disappointed. I know of no other textbook which devotes any space to the subject, nor do I know of a single textbook of etymology. There is probably a reason for this. In etymology, more than anywhere else in linguistics, we are forced to get to grips with the individual and the particular, and general principles are accordingly difficult to identify. Most linguists prefer principles to miscellaneous details, and etymology is therefore commonly relegated to a very peripheral position in the discipline. Major journals of linguistics, even of historical linguistics, rarely carry articles on etymology, and indeed etymologists have not infrequently complained that they find their studies difficult to publish at all.

This is a pity, since etymology is undoubtedly a fascinating subject, and one that beginning students particularly enjoy, since it is full of surprises. Let's look at a few cases. You are advised to have a good dictionary by your side while you're reading this section. Ideally, you ought to have one of the serious etymological dictionaries of English: Partridge (1958), Onions (1966), or Klein (1971). If that's not possible, any good dictionary of English will provide some etymological information; outstanding in this respect is the *American Heritage Dictionary*, published outside the USA as the *Heritage Dictionary*, which traces words wherever possible all the way back to Proto-Indo-European.

Take the words *cook* and *cookie*. These look as if they are obviously related, but take a minute to look up their etymologies before you read further. You will find that the verb *cook* derives from the noun *cook* 'one who cooks', and that this noun is descended from Old English *cōc*. This in turn is thought to be borrowed from an unattested late Latin *$c\bar{o}cus$*, an alteration of classical Latin *coquus*, which in turn is a derivative of the Latin verb *coquere* 'cook'. And this verb derives from a pre-Latin *$*kwekw-$* or *$*kwokw-$*, an assimilated form of a PIE root *$*pekw-$* 'cook, ripen'. The same Latin root appears, often well disguised, in other English words derived from Latin or Romance, such as *cuisine, kiln, kitchen, apricot, biscuit, concoct, precocious*, and *ricotta* (the name of a type of cheese), among others. (Try looking these words up.) Moreover, the same PIE root *$*pekw-$* developed into *pep-* in Greek, and this underlies Greek *peptein* 'cook, ripen, digest', from which source we get our words *peptic, dyspepsia*, and (surprisingly) *pumpkin*, among others. Finally, the same PIE root yields Sanskrit *pakva* 'ripe', which is the source of our word *pukka*.

But *cookie* has nothing to do with any of these words. It is a loan from Dutch *koekje* 'small cake', a diminutive of *koek* 'cake'. This can be traced back to a Proto-Germanic root *$*kak-$* 'round thing', which has no known Indo-European source; its Old Norse derivative *kaka* 'cake' is the source of our word *cake*, which was borrowed from Old Norse. This same Germanic word, borrowed into French, is the ultimate source of our word *quiche*, borrowed from French. Thus *cookie* is related to *cake* and to *quiche*, but not to *cook*: the resemblance in form between *cook* and *cookie* is purely accidental. This is probably not what you were expecting, but etymological studies very frequently lead to such surprises.

How do we know these things are true? Only because generations of patient and careful scholarly work have gone into teasing out these various strands. Sometimes we have documentary evidence for earlier words and forms, but sometimes we don't (as with the unattested Latin *$*c\bar{o}cus$*), and we have to fill in the gaps as best we can. But we don't fill in the gaps with flights of sheer fancy, to obtain conclusions that appeal to us. The reduction of classical *coquus* to *$*c\bar{o}cus$* is not only phonologically understandable but parallelled by other, similar, cases in the history of Latin. In the same way, the development of PIE *$*pekw-$* to Greek *pep-* is a regular change in the prehistory of Greek: compare the development of PIE *$*kwel-$* ~ *$*kwol-$* 'revolve' into Greek *polos* 'axis', the source of our word *pole* (as in *north pole*).

Perhaps more than any other branch of linguistics, etymology is an art. Its pursuit requires a certain degree of erudition, in the form of knowledge of the languages which are or may be relevant to the problems at hand, and also a talent for sniffing out useful evidence and the ability to do a little lateral thinking now and again. Let's consider an example from Basque.

Spoken on the Atlantic coast, along the Bay of Biscay, Basque is a genetically isolated language, but it has been borrowing words extensively from its Latin and Romance neighbours for 2000 years. Like any language, Basque presents a number of intriguing etymological puzzles. One of those puzzles is the word *gorotz* 'animal dung', which has a very widespread variant *korotz(a)*. This word is quite opaque in Basque, and we might wonder where it comes from. Here I shall consider two approaches to the problem.

One approach is to scour the languages of the world looking for similar words. Several linguists have done this, and they have noted that specialists in North Caucasian languages have reconstructed a word *$k'urč'V$ 'dung', and that Burushaski, another genetic isolate spoken in the Himalayas, has a word $\gamma urA\check{s}$ 'dung'. Since these linguists believe they have found other connections among Basque, Burushaski, and North Caucasian, they therefore declare that all three words for 'dung' must be related in some way. They might have proposed an ancient loan word which somehow made its way into all these languages, but in fact they are bolder and want to interpret the matches as evidence of a (very remote) genetic relationship linking the languages, with the word for 'dung' being a survivor in all the languages of some word in a remote ancestral language. Ignoring here the proposal of a genetic link, is it really plausible to link the Basque word with the words in Caucasian and Burushaski?

Let me turn to the second approach. Specialists in Basque have long been aware that native Basque words of any antiquity do not normally begin with /k/ (or indeed with any voiceless plosive), and hence the widespread existence of the variant *korotz* strongly suggests that we are looking at a loan word of some sort, most likely from Latin or Romance, virtually the only source of loan words in Basque. But no such word as *korotz ~ gorotz* is attested anywhere in Latin or Romance with the sense of 'dung'. So what can we do?

This problem has been addressed by the distinguished Catalan etymologist Joan Coromines (who writes in Spanish as Juan Corominas). Coromines notes that Latin had a word *crocea* meaning 'saffron-coloured'. If this had been borrowed into Basque, the result would have been the non-existent *$*goroke(a)$ – not very helpful. But late Latin underwent a very well-known change by which /k/ was converted to an affricate /ts/ before a front vowel, and hence the early Romance continuation of the Latin word must have been (roughly) *$*crotsea$. In fact, the word is attested in Old Spanish as *croça*, which represents a pronunciation [krotsa]. And *this*, if borrowed into Basque, would have produced *$*gorotz(a) ~ *korotz(a)$: Latin and Romance /k/ is borrowed as both Basque /g/ and Basque /k/ (compare Basque *gatu ~ katu* 'cat', from Latin *cattu*, or Basque *gatea ~ katea* 'chain', from Latin *catena*), and early Basque always broke up word-initial consonant clusters (compare Basque *garau* 'grain', from Latin *granu*, or Basque *boronde* 'forehead', from Latin *fronte*). Phonologically, then, *crocea* is a perfect source for the Basque word. But what about the meaning? The Latin word doesn't mean 'dung', or anything similar.

Here Coromines displays the result of the sort of painstaking investigations in which etymologists specialize. First he observes that Latin *crocea* is attested in post-classical times in the sense of 'saffron-coloured garment' (this is in the Vulgate, the first Latin Bible). Next he notes that the various Romance descendants of Latin *crocea* have long been applied in northern Spain (near the Basque Country) to various types of dun-coloured (dull yellow) coverings, always in a rustic context. For example, Old Spanish *croça* and related forms were applied to several rude types of yellowish cap, hood, cloak, or overcoat traditionally worn by farmers in the area, perhaps originally to a kind of broad straw hat worn against the rain. More significantly, the same word was formerly applied to the covering placed over a haystack to keep it dry – and what were such coverings made of? They were made of dung, mixed with straw.

Coromines therefore proposes that the Romance word, already in use to denote various sorts of yellowish coverings, including dung coverings for haystacks, was borrowed into Basque, and that the Basque-speakers merely generalized the meaning of the word from 'dung used to cover a haystack' to 'dung' in general – not a very dramatic shift of meaning, after all.

Is Coromines's etymology obviously and certainly correct? No, it is not, as he himself admits: he declares that the question 'needs further study'. It is very plausible, and it is supported by a certain amount of evidence, but that is all. There is always a possibility that somebody, one day, will come up with a more persuasive source for Basque *gorotz*. That's the way things often are in etymology: at the moment, Coromines's proposal is merely the best explanation we have.

Or is it? Should we dismiss Coromines's account as fanciful, and prefer the link with Caucasian and Burushaski favoured by the other group of linguists? Well, what do you think? Ponder this question for a moment, before you read on. What kinds of considerations might move you to prefer one explanation to the other?

Clearly, if the proponents of the first explanation could produce overwhelmingly persuasive evidence that Basque is indeed connected somehow to Caucasian and to Burushaski, we would then have to take their etymology seriously (though it might still be wrong, even then). But no such evidence has been forthcoming, and the proposed three-way link remains a fanciful notion, supported by no more than hopeful guesses which, moreover, utterly fail to take into account the well-established phonological prehistory of Basque.

On the other hand, Coromines's etymology has a great deal going for it. First, the form of the Basque word is out of line with what native Basque words look like: the word just looks like a loan word. Second, the phonology is perfect: Basque *gorotz* doesn't merely bear a vague resemblance to the Romance word: it has *exactly* the form we would expect it to have if it had been borrowed as Coromines proposes. Third, we already know that Basque has borrowed thousands of words from Latin and Romance, and so finding one more is hardly going to raise any eyebrows. This point illustrates very well an old dictum in etymology: 'Look for Latin etymologies on the Tiber.' (The Tiber is the river upon which Rome stands.) That is, a source close to home is generally to be preferred to a source thousands of miles away. While not necessarily correct, therefore, Coromines's proposal is vastly preferable to an unsubstantiated link with languages as far away as the Caucasus and the Himalayas.

Finally, Coromines's etymology offers one more interesting point. The chief difficulty he had to address, in order to make his etymology go through, was the semantic one: how to get from 'saffron-coloured' to 'dung'. He succeeded in finding a solution to the problem by discovering the former practice, in and around the Basque Country, of covering haystacks with dung. Without this crucial information, his explanation would be little better than a wild guess. In other words, to solve a linguistic problem, he had to turn to non-linguistic information – in this case, the former practice of farmers. Such appeals to non-linguistic information about the community in which a language is spoken are very often necessary in etymological work. (Recall from Chapter 2 the case of *southpaw*, whose origin can only be understand in terms of the game of baseball, in which it originated.)

The connection between linguistic and non-linguistic information can also be used in the opposite direction: we can sometimes use linguistic information to draw conclusions about the nature of a society in which the language was spoken. This procedure has been called the **Wörter und Sachen** approach (this German phrase means 'words and things'); it was initiated by the great German linguist Jacob Grimm, and it has been particularly influential in Germany and France, and perhaps especially among Indo-Europeanists. To take a very simple example, Old English had a word *wergeld*, literally 'man-payment', denoting the fine paid by a killer to the family or the lord of his victim. The existence of such a word immediately suggests that the Anglo-Saxons had an institutionalized system of such fines for dealing with violent crime, in place of the kinds of punishments (jail, flogging, execution) with which we are perhaps more familiar. In this case, we have abundant documentation that such a system existed: the greater the importance of the victim, the larger the fine the killer had to pay in order to free himself from further punishment or obligation.

A more elaborate case is provided by early IE terms pertaining to social organization (here I follow Lehmann 1993: 251–2). There are two PIE roots used for constructing terms for social groups: **dem-* ~ **dom-* and **weik-* ~ **woik-*. Examples of the first are Sanskrit *dám-* and *damá-*, Avestan *dam*, Greek *dómos*, Latin *domus*, Old Church Slavic *domŭ*, and possibly Greek *dô*, all meaning 'house' or 'household'. Derived from the same root are Sanskrit *dám-pati-* and Greek *des-pótēs* < **dem-s-poti-s*, both originally meaning 'master of the house'. Examples of the second are Sanskrit *víš-* 'dwelling, village', Greek *oîkos* 'house, household', Latin *vīcus* 'village', Old Church Slavic *visi* 'village', and Avestan *vīsəm* and Old Persian *viþəm* 'house, village, clan'. From the same root are derived Latin *villa* 'estate' < **weiks-la-*, Sanskrit *viś-pátis* 'head of a house/community', and Lithuanian *viеš-pat(i)s* 'God'.

On the whole, the **dem-* ~ **dom-* words seem to denote a smaller unit, probably a single house or household, a conclusion reinforced by the observation that the central sense of the root appears to be 'build'. In contrast, the **weik-* ~ **woik-* words seem to denote some kind of larger unit, perhaps an extended family or a small clan, or at most a village; the original sense of the root is not known. We may therefore tentatively conclude that the early Indo-Europeans knew at least two levels of social organization, the individual household and the clan or village.

But we can reconstruct no IE words for any larger units. All names for larger units, and in particular all words meaning 'people, nation', are late formations found only in particular branches of the IE family, and the same is true of words for high-level rulers or leaders, such as the words for 'king'. Naturally, negative evidence can never be conclusive, but it does rather look as though larger social units were unknown to the early Indo-Europeans, and that such larger units developed only later, after the division of the ancestral language into its various daughters. This conclusion is reinforced by the observation that some of the older words, or later derivatives of them, seem to have extended their meaning at a late stage. For example, Greek *despótēs*, originally 'master of the house', denoted in classical times the ruler of a city, and Latin *dominus*, a late formation from *domus* 'house', meant 'lord'. Some scholars have concluded, therefore, that we have linguistic evidence for the development of an originally clan-based social structure into one with larger social units like cities and nations.

12.2   *Place names*

The particular branch of etymology dealing with the origins and histories of proper names is called **onomastics**. Various types of proper names may be studied: personal names (both given names and surnames), habitation names, hydronyms (names of rivers and other bodies of water), and so on. As with all etymological work, onomastics is a painstaking and often frustrating endeavour, but a very satisfying one when it works. Here I can do no more than give a brief sample of such work, just to provide some of the flavour, and I have chosen to look at the study of place names, or **toponyms**.

Much more than ordinary words, place names (and indeed names in general) tend to suffer from the vagaries of history: they frequently undergo highly irregular phonological alterations, and they may be modified in a seemingly capricious manner, as a result of contamination, from folk etymology, or seemingly for no good reason at all. As a result, the modern forms of place names are frequently not a reliable guide to their origins, and a primary requirement for specialists is to track down and scrutinize the greatest possible number of early documents recording the names they are interested in. To take a simple example, the town of *Bridgwater* in the English county of Somerset has a name which seems transparent enough, even if the motivation is obscure, but a document from 1194 reveals that it was originally named *Brigewaltier*, that is, '(place at) the bridge (held by a man named) Walter'.

Slightly more difficult is the name of the English town of *Shrewsbury*, pronounced Shroze-bury (except locally). This name has nothing to do with shrews, or even with Shrove Tuesday, even though a much earlier form *Shrovesbury* is in fact recorded. Our earliest documents give the name as *Scrobbesbyrig*. While this plainly contains the very frequent Old English element *byrig* 'fortified place', the origin of the first element is disputed. A few scholars have interpreted the name as 'Scrobb's fortified place', and thus as preserving a record of a now-forgotten local magnate who rejoiced in the name of *Scrobb*, even though no such personal name is otherwise recorded. Most specialists, however, prefer to see the first element as nothing other than Old English *scrybb* 'scrubland', the ancestor of modern English *shrub* and its variant *scrub*; this yields the etymology 'fortified place of the scrubland'.

But let's look in a little detail at the name *Pimlico*, whose origin has recently been uncovered by Richard Coates (1995). Though a fairly representative example of the onomastician's art, the story of *Pimlico* is exceptionally interesting.

Pimlico is today the name of a well-known district in southwest London, located within the borough of Westminster. The name is also found elsewhere in Britain and Ireland, but these other occurrences are all first recorded considerably later than that of the Westminster Pimlico, and are presumably derived from it. The name *Pimlico* is first recorded for the place in Westminster in 1626, but this is not the earliest occurrence of the name.

Quite a few years earlier, we find the name *Pimlico* attached to a small district in a northern part of London called Hoxton. In particular, it was given to a celebrated and exceedingly popular ale-house located there. This ale-house was located close to a couple of theatres, and it is repeatedly mentioned in literary and theatrical works written between 1609 and about 1658, including Ben Jonson's famous play *The Alchemist*, written in 1610. As long ago as 1849, it was established that the earliest recorded reference to the name occurs in a tract published in 1598, called *Newes from Hogsdon* [i.e. Hoxton], which contains the line 'Have at thee, then, my merrie boyes, and hey for old Ben Pimlico's nut browne.' This allows scholars to conclude that *Ben Pimlico* was the name of the publican, and that his surname was transferred in turn to his ale, to his establishment, and to his house and a neighbouring alley. So far, so good, but now we run into a blank wall: no such surname as *Pimlico* is recorded anywhere else at all, and its formation is totally opaque. There the matter rested for a century and a half, until Coates took up the chase.

Coates begins by noting that the name is sometimes given in early sources as *Pemlico*, a fact which will be important. Then, finding no joy in Britain, he directs his inquiries to North America. His attention is immediately drawn to North Carolina, where the stretch of water lying between the Outer Banks and the coast proper is called *Pamlico Sound*. This sound takes its name from a river flowing into it, today called the *Tar-Pamlico*, but formerly, the records confirm, named simply the *Pamlico*. And the river in turn takes its name from a now vanished native American people who lived along its banks; their Algonquian name would more typically have been *Pamticough*, but either the local pronunciation was different or English-speaker settlers merely altered this to *Pamlico*. And this *Pamlico* is exceedingly similar to the early variant *Pemlico* of the name we are interested in.

So does Coates immediately declare that he has found the origin of *Pimlico*? Certainly not, because that would be deeply unprofessional. For all anyone knows, there might be dozens of names resembling *Pimlico* in locations from Montevideo through Mozambique to Mongolia. It is a constant error of linguistic amateurs and cranks to assume that, because they have uncovered a resemblance, they have identified the origin of the name they are playing with. The crucial part is to provide a *pathway*: to show how the name could reasonably have travelled from North Carolina to London, especially at a time when no permanent English-speaking settlement had yet been founded in North America (that first permanent settlement was Jamestown, in Virginia, not founded until 1607).

However, Pamlico Sound is by no means a totally insignificant locale in the English settlement of North America, for, at its northern end, there lies the island of Roanoke, the site of Sir Walter Raleigh's abortive first attempts at establishing a colony, in 1585 and 1587. This is just early enough to pre-date that reference to Ben Pimlico in 1598, and so Coates turns his attention to the Roanoke settlers, noting first that a 1747 map of London records a street called *Virginia Row* not far from Pimlico's ale-house, which perhaps reinforces the suspicion that some of the returned Roanoke colonists might have settled in Hoxton.

And some of those colonists did indeed return from Roanoke to England; this occurred in 1586, when Sir Francis Drake brought them back on his returning ship. The names of some of the returning colonists are recorded (the keeping of records is a wonderful thing), and, fascinatingly, two of them were named *Bennet Chappell* and *Bennet Harrye*. Coates therefore wonders whether one of these men, as a result of some unrecorded incident while he was living at Roanoke, might have acquired the nickname 'Pemlico' or 'Pimlico', and whether he might have brought this nickname back to England with him and used it as a surname, perhaps out of pride or whimsy. Coates notes further that one of the reasons for the great popularity of Pimlico's ale-house seems to have been the availability there of a novel pleasure, that most famous product of Virginia and North Carolina, tobacco. Possibly Ben Pimlico, having become acquainted with the weed while at Roanoke, had taken steps to obtain a supply for his establishment.

That would seem to be that, but things are rarely so simple in this line of work. Just about to submit his account for publication, Coates stumbled across two more instances of *Pimlico*, instances which cast doubt upon his conclusions. First, there is a *Pimlico Island* near Bermuda, a name for which we have no information whatever about its earliest use (the absence of records is not wonderful at all). Second, there are several early references to a bird called the *pemblico*, found all along the Atlantic Coast and, according to the 1624 account of John Smith, leader of the Jamestown settlement, so called because that's what the bird's cry sounds like. (This bird is now known as Audubon's shearwater.) Could it be, then, that Coates's account is a hopeless fabrication, and that all the Pimlicos in fact take their names from nothing more than the imitative name given to this noisy bird?

Nothing for it, then, but to go back to the documents. This time Coates finds an account of the history of the Bahamas, of uncertain authorship but dating from around 1630. And this account contains the following illuminating passage: 'Another smale Birde ther is, the which, by some Ale-banters of London sent ouer hether, hath bin tearmed pimplicoe, for so they Imagine (and a little resemblance putts them in mind of a place so dearely beloued) her note articulates.' In other words, the name was given to the bird by a group of Londoners arriving in the Bahamas merely because its cry reminded them of the name of their favourite ale-house, the celebrated and fashionable Ben Pimlico's of Hoxton. Having originated in North America, the name *Pimlico* was carried to London, where it became a famous name, later to be transferred to a district of Westminster and elsewhere, and, scarcely two decades after its successful establishment in London, back to North America.

Coates therefore concludes that *Pimlico* is probably the first native American place name to be carried to Britain, and certainly the first name derived from a native American language to take root in Britain. The origin of the Algonquian name *Pamticough* is unknown, though it may be a derivative of an earlier name of the river.

This vignette well illustrates most of the central requirements of good onomastic work:

- the importance of locating and consulting all available documentation, especially the earliest documentation;
- the importance of taking into account *all* the available information;
- the importance of ensuring that dates tally, so that names are not obliged to travel backwards in time;
- the importance of providing a plausible pathway by which the name could have got to where it is attested by the time it is attested;
- the importance of being prepared to consider alternative accounts to the one you have already settled on as the likeliest.

To these I might add one more which did not happen to feature prominently in our case: the importance of evaluating the reliability of your sources. Just as you can't believe everything you read in the newspaper, you can't believe everything you read in even the most impressively dusty piece of parchment or vellum. Four hundred years ago, people were making just as many mistakes as we make today, and they were telling just as many lies.

And what happened to the Pamticough, or Pamlico, people, whose name has travelled so far and wide? Sadly, they were massacred in 1711 by the Tuscarora allies of the English, with whom they were at war at the time.

12.3 *Linguistic palaeontology*

The name **linguistic palaeontology** is given to the technique of drawing conclusions about the material and non-material cultures of ancient peoples by extracting evidence from their languages. Such evidence is almost exclusively lexical. If we can show that an ancient people had a word for a particular object or practice, then it is (possibly!) safe to conclude that they were familiar with that object or practice.

Here is a simple example. Since the arrival of the Romans in the Basque Country just over 2000 years ago, Basque has borrowed thousands of words from Latin and Romance. However, the cereal names *gari* 'wheat', *garagar* 'barley', and *olo* 'oats' bear no relation to anything in Latin or Romance, and must be indigenous; we may therefore assume that these cereals were already known to the Basques before the Romans arrived. But we must be careful. Basque *arto* 'maize, sweet corn' is also an indigenous word, and a rash investigator might therefore conclude that maize too was known to the ancient Basques. But this is absurd, since maize is native to the Americas and was introduced into Europe only in the sixteenth and seventeenth centuries. In this case, our historical records of Basque are adequate to explain what has happened. The word *arto* originally meant 'millet', which was formerly a major food crop among the Basques; since the newly introduced maize proved to be much more suitable for the damp Basque climate than millet, the new crop virtually displaced the old one, and the name was transferred from millet to the somewhat similar-looking maize. Today the Basques call millet *artatxiki* 'little *arto*'. But it is none the less millet, and not maize, which is the indigenous cereal. Such transfer of words from one referent to another is a constant stumbling block in evaluating lexical evidence for ancient cultures.

On the other hand, the universal Basque word for 'plough' is *golde*, which appears to be a borrowing from Latin *culter* 'ploughshare'. We might therefore surmise that the pre-Roman Basques lacked the plough, but this would be dangerously rash, not to mention highly implausible: it hardly seems likely that the ancient Basques would have been growing all these cereals without ploughs, and anyway the plough is a very ancient invention, attested in the fourth millennium BC in most of Europe. It is far more likely that the Latin word simply displaced the indigenous word, perhaps for reasons of prestige, just as Norman French *face* long ago displaced the native English word *anleth*. Negative evidence is very treacherous in linguistic palaeontology, and only in certain special circumstances can we attach any weight to our failure to find a word for something.

Beyond any doubt the most famous case of linguistic palaeontology is that involving the speakers of PIE. Since we have so many different branches of IE to consult, since there are so many surviving and attested languages in the family, and since a few of these are thousands of years old, historical linguists have been highly successful at reconstructing the vocabulary of PIE. Since we don't know where PIE was spoken, we have scoured this reconstructed vocabulary for possible clues, in the purely linguistic contribution to the **Indo-European homeland problem**. At first glance, the PIE vocabulary seems to present a very clear picture. We find PIE words for temperate plants and animals, such as 'beech', 'birch', 'pine', 'ash', 'bear', 'deer', 'salmon', but none for subtropical plants and animals, like 'olive', 'palm', 'camel'. We also find a PIE word for 'snow', but apparently none for 'sea'. This kind of evidence has convinced any number of linguists that PIE must have been spoken in a temperate region, probably well wooded and teeming with animal life, and possibly some distance from the sea. But things are not so simple.

For example, the apparent existence of the IE word *$laks$-* 'salmon' appears to require the homeland to have been in a location inhabited by salmon, a creature found in Europe only in and around the Baltic Sea. Unfortunately, this word is applied in places to one or another species of trout, a creature which is ubiquitous in Europe, and it may be that 'trout' is the original sense of the term, rather than 'salmon'. If so, there is no reason to assume that the IE homeland was in an area inhabited by salmon: the name may simply have been transferred from one fish to the other by people moving to a new location with different fauna. (Compare English *robin*, which in Britain denotes a small, friendly bird with a red breast. English-speaking settlers in North America did not find the familiar bird there, but they did find a new bird, unrelated to the British one but also having a red breast, and so they simply transferred the name.)

More encouraging, perhaps, is the PIE tree name *$bhergo$-*. This word is applied to the birch tree in Indic (Sanskrit *bhurja-*), Iranian (Ossetic *bärz*), Germanic (English *birch*), Baltic (Latvian *berzs*), and Slavic (Russian *berëza*). In Latin, however, the reflex *fraxinus* denotes the ash tree, not the birch, while the word is absent altogether from Greek. Now the birch is very common in northern and eastern Europe, but rare or absent in the Mediterranean. It therefore seems plausible that the original meaning of the word was 'birch', that this sense has been retained in languages spoken where the birch is common, but that IE-speakers moving to the Mediterranean, finding no birches, either shifted the word to a different kind of tree (as in Latin) or lost it completely (as in Greek). This conclusion reinforces the idea that the IE homeland must have been in the temperate forests of northern or eastern Europe.

The problem of IE origins remains a thorny and controversial one, and we'll be returning to it in the next section to consider it from a different point of view. For now, though, I should point out that linguistic palaeontology has led to some considerable success in characterizing the material culture of the PIE-speakers. We have managed to reconstruct a number of PIE names for domesticated animals, including *owi-* 'sheep', *$agwhno$-* 'lamb', *aig-* and *$ghaido$-*, both 'goat', *$kapro$-* '(male) goat', *su-* 'pig', *$porko$-* '(young) pig', *$gwou$-* 'cow, bull, ox', and *$kwon$-* 'dog', as well as *$peku$-* 'cattle, wealth'. It thus appears indisputable that animal husbandry was important among the PIE-speakers. Further, we also reconstruct $*gr_Hno-$, $*yewo-$, and $*p\bar{u}ro-$, all 'cereal, grain, corn', $*wrughyo-$ 'rye', $*bhares-$ 'barley', $*al-$ and $*mel_H-$, both 'grind', $*s\bar{e}-$ 'sow', $*ar_H-$ 'plough' (verb), $*wogwhni-$ 'plough-share', $*perk-$ and $*selk-$ 'furrow', $*yeug-$ 'yoke', $*serp-$ 'sickle', $*kerp-$ 'gather, harvest', and $*gw_Hr_Hn-$ 'hand mill', all of which points to the existence of agriculture. There is also a PIE word $*ekwo-$ 'horse', as well as $*wegh-$ 'convey, go in a vehicle', $*kwekwlo-$ 'wheel', $*aks-$ 'axle', and $*nobh-$ 'hub of a wheel'. This has led some scholars to conclude that the PIE-speakers not only rode horses but had wagons and chariots as well. This is debatable, however, since everyone places PIE at least 6000 years in the past, while hard evidence for wheeled vehicles is perhaps no earlier than 5000 years ago. Watkins (1969) considers that these terms pertaining to wheeled vehicles were chiefly metaphorical extensions of older IE words with different senses ($*nobh-$, for example, meant 'navel'). The word $*kwekwlo-$ 'wheel' itself is derived from the PIE root $*kwel-$ 'turn, revolve'. Nevertheless, the vision of fierce IE warriors, riding horses and driving chariots, sweeping down on their neighbours brandishing bloody swords, has proved to be an enduring one, and scholars have found it difficult to dislodge from the popular con-sciousness the idea of the PIE-speakers as warlike conquerors in chariots. In fact, as we shall see in the next section, there are scholars who actively defend such an interpretation.

12.4   *Links with archaeology*

Archaeology is the science of prehistory, and naturally archaeologists and historical linguists have often been interested in comparing their findings, in the hope of finding links between linguistic and archaeological evidence. Nowhere have these links been pursued more vigorously than in connection with the IE homeland problem discussed in the last section. Since we find IE speech established many centuries ago in a broad swathe extending from Ireland in the west to India and central Asia in the east, it is a plausible surmise (though not necessarily a correct one!) that the ancestral speakers of PIE must have spread out widely from some original homeland, and that we might therefore be able to find some traces of such movements in the archaeological record.

In order to compare notes with the archaeologists, of course, we first need to have some idea what kind of time and place we want to look at. The time is easier: most specialists consider that the degree of linguistic divergence among the IE languages points to a date of roughly 6000 years ago for the ancestral language – though see below for a dissenting view even on this. That is, a date of 4000 years ago would be too late to allow the development of the differences we can see in the first millennium BC between Greek, Sanskrit, and

Latin, while a date of 8000 years ago would probably have allowed the development of much greater differences than we see in the daughter languages.

There are ways of cross-checking estimated dates. The Uralic languages sprawl across much of northern Eurasia, and they exhibit a number of loan words from IE. One of these is the word for 'pig', which appears as *porsas* in Finnish and as *pars* in Udmurt (formerly called Votyak). These two Uralic languages are spoken at least 600 kilometres apart, and they are not closely related. Uralic specialists believe they must have separated from their common ancestor no later than 1500 BC. Now, the word for 'pig' cannot possibly, on phonological grounds, have been borrowed from PIE *porkos*: instead, it must have been borrowed from Indo-Iranian *parsa* (the regular development of *porkos* in Indo-Iranian). But that means that Indo-Iranian must already have been in existence before 1500 BC, complete with its distinctive phonological developments, and hence that it must already have undergone many centuries of individual evolution by that date – confirming that PIE must have begun breaking up significantly earlier than 4000 years ago.

The place is more difficult, and of course the whole point of the homeland problem is to find the place. In practice, all we can do is either to make what we hope is a plausible guess and then ask the archaeologists if they have any evidence for migrations out of that area at something like the right time, or else to ask the archaeologists what interesting migrations they've turned up and then see if we can make the linguistic data fit.

Unfortunately, none of this has yet led to any kind of consensus. Even though, as we saw in the last section, most linguists favour a homeland in northern or eastern Europe for purely linguistic reasons, the number of diverse proposals on the table is startlingly large. Fig. 12.1 shows the various locations proposed for the IE homeland just since 1960, and it excludes some

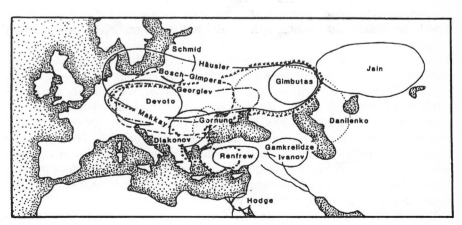

Fig. 12.1 Proposals for the Indo-European homeland

rather less plausible locations defended in the past, such as Africa, the Pacific coast, and the North Pole!

As you can see, the recent proposals extend from southern Scandinavia (Häusler) or Lithuania (Schmid) through central Asia (Jain) to Egypt (Hodge), demonstrating that the homeland problem is still very far from being solved. But you can also see that the majority of proposals cluster around eastern Europe. This makes sense: since IE speakers seem to have been so phenomenally successful at spreading their languages across much of Eurasia, we might guess that they started somewhere near the middle of the territory that eventually became IE-speaking and spread out both east and west. It would be less easy to understand how they might have started out near one edge of what is now IE-speaking territory and spread out only in one direction. Moreover, the IE languages of Europe show much greater diversity than those of Asia, where a single, and relatively homogeneous, Indo-Iranian branch occupies a vast stretch of territory running from the Caucasus almost to Burma. It is a principle of historical linguistics that a language family exhibits the greatest diversity in the area where it has been established longest, and the least diversity where it has arrived most recently.

Observe also that most of the proposals posit an original area for PIE of between 250000 and 1000000 square kilometres. This is in line with other research which suggests that, before the rise of nation states several millennia ago, this was about the largest area that could be occupied by a single language: anything much larger, and communication would become impossible among widely separated speakers, so that the ordinary processes of linguistic change would rapidly splinter the language into several divergent daughters.

We shall therefore assume that the speakers of PIE occupied only such a modest area something like 6000 years ago, and that they spread out from there over what eventually became the vast IE-speaking area of recorded history. We know this scenario is possible in principle, because we have comparatively modern parallels. In the sixth century AD, the speakers of Turkic languages occupied only a small area in central Asia; by the ninth century, they had abruptly expanded over about 2.5 million square kilometres; by the thirteenth century, they occupied nearly 5 million square kilometres, including a large extent of territory that had formerly been IE-speaking. Of course, the Turks, with their mobile, nomadic lifestyle, were ideally placed for this sort of rapid expansion. As we saw in the preceding section, the first stages of the IE dispersal may have taken place before wheeled vehicles existed, but then that dispersal probably took 3000 or 4000 years to complete: for example, the archaeological evidence suggests that the Celts did not reach Britain and Ireland before the first millennium BC, and much of modern France, Spain, and Portugal were still occupied by non-IE languages when the Romans arrived in the first century BC.

However slow the IE dispersal was, it was certainly thorough. By about AD 1000, the sole surviving pre-IE language in western Europe was, as it is today,

Basque. In Spain and Portugal, intrusive IE speech had obliterated earlier languages like Iberian, Tartessian, and Punic, and probably others whose names we don't even know; the same had happened to Pictish in Scotland and Etruscan in Italy. These languages are among the last faint traces of what must have been an extraordinarily diverse linguistic map in Europe before the arrival of Indo-European speech.

Now: can we find any archaeological traces of the IE dispersal? Well, there are undoubtedly some plausible candidates for certain stages of that dispersal. For example, in the third millennium BC, a time when the linguists would reckon that PIE had already begun to break up into daughter languages, the archaeologists have abundant evidence in northeastern Europe for a culture they call the 'Corded Ware' culture, after its distinctive pottery. Some scholars suggest that the Corded Ware people probably represented a northern branch of IE, possibly the linguistic ancestors of the Celts, the Germans, the Balts, and the Slavs. But can we find something earlier, some physical remnants of a people who might have been the speakers of PIE itself?

One proposal stands out. In the fifth and early fourth millennia BC, we find a distinctive culture appearing in the region of the Volga River, north of the Caspian Sea, and spreading westwards across the steppes and forests of southern Russia and Ukraine. These people were apparently nomadic pastoralists who rode horses and used wheeled vehicles. They built few settlements, and we know them primarily by their highly conspicuous burial practices: they buried their important dead in tombs which were often covered by an artificial mound called in Russian a *kurgan*, and it is their grave goods which provide most of the evidence for the nature of their society.

This **Kurgan culture** has for decades been the favourite candidate for the PIE-speakers. The Kurgan identification was pursued in particular by the late Lithuanian–American archaeologist Marija Gimbutas, who spent nearly thirty years developing and defending this identification of Kurgan and PIE. She finds evidence that the Kurgan people, some time after 4000 BC, spread out eastwards into central Asia, Persia, and India, westwards into central Europe and the Balkans, and southwards across the Caucasus into Anatolia – more or less the attested IE territory.

Gimbutas devotes particular attention to the Kurgan intrusion into Europe. In her view, Europe before the Kurgan people was settled, primarily agricultural, and seemingly peaceful; horses and wheeled vehicles were unknown; fine ceramics were produced and often painted; there was a major copper industry in the Balkans; clay female figurines were produced in thousands, suggesting a society, and perhaps a religion, in which women played an important part. The Kurgan invasion changed all this: settlements were abandoned in numbers; agriculture collapsed and was replaced by pastoralism; horses and wheeled vehicles were introduced; the copper industry collapsed; the fine ceramics disappeared and were replaced by much cruder ones; fortified strongholds appeared for the first time; Kurgan-style burials appeared; the production of female figurines ceased abruptly, and instead we find stone stelae decorated with sunbursts, horses, wagons, and, above all, weapons; a new physical type appeared, very different from the earlier European skeletons but identical to those found in the steppes.

All this Gimbutas takes as evidence that a quiet, matriarchal, agricultural society was invaded from the steppes by warlike pastoralists with a cult of sky gods and sun worship, a strongly patriarchal organization, and a great love of horses and weapons. This perhaps somewhat colourful picture has attracted a good deal of support from both archaeologists and linguists. Its proponents see the Kurgan solution as an elegant and economical one which simultaneously accounts for a wide range of observations, and more than a few reference books present the Kurgan–PIE equation as gospel.

But the hypothesis also has its critics, lots of them. It's not that the archaeologists have better candidates for the PIE-speakers – they don't. It's rather that the critics consider Gimbutas's seductive picture to be the result of very selective reading of the evidence: they argue that most of the physical evidence she adduces either has other explanations or is simply contradicted by further evidence which is silently ignored. The argument continues today, and it would be too much to claim that the Kurgan solution is accepted even by a majority of specialists in either field. None the less, it is still the best solution we have, and it refuses to go away. We must keep our heads and look at the evidence and counter-evidence with cold scientific eyes. But even the severest critics would probably be secretly delighted to be persuaded, in the end, that those evocative mounds we can still see today in the Russian steppes once covered the mortal remains of people who were native speakers of that most romantic of all languages, Proto-Indo-European.

Recently, however, the British archaeologist Colin Renfrew has rejected every aspect of Gimbutas's interpretation and of every similar proposal. He puts forward a view of the IE dispersal that could hardly be more different. Renfrew argues that the whole conception of IE-speakers overrunning huge tracts of territory by military force is anachronistic: at a time when states and even cities did not yet exist, Renfrew considers that no group of people could have possessed the economic and technological resources necessary to launch large-scale invasions and to overrun already populated lands. He therefore advances a very different scenario: IE speech must have diffused slowly and peacefully across Eurasia in conjunction with some economic or technological advance. And he can find only one such advance which is sufficiently widespread and important to be the vehicle of such linguistic spread: the development and spread of agriculture. Now there is no doubt that agriculture spread out slowly across much of Europe and Asia from a very few small sites at which it was first developed – for our purposes, principally in the Middle East. The difficulty, of course, is that the spread of agriculture began, not 6000 years ago, but over 10000 years ago, in the period we call the Neolithic, or the Late Stone Age. And, as we saw above, this date is quite unacceptable to most linguists: such an early date would require IE speech to have diffused over a vast area during thousands of years while hardly changing at all, something which historical linguists consider impossible. Remember what I said in Chapter 1 about the remorselessness of language change, and in Chapter 7 about the dramatic consequences of the geographical dispersion of a language.

On the other hand, Renfrew's bold conception has certain advantages from the archaeological point of view. While an earlier generation of archaeologists was often inclined to see every change in the style of pottery as evidence of an invasion, contemporary archaeologists are now generally suspicious of such ceaseless appeals to hypothetical invasions, and are far more inclined to view changes in material culture as representing only the diffusion of new ideas from one population to a neighbouring population. Renfrew's hypothesis therefore makes considerable sense to some archaeologists, even if the linguists don't like it.

Observe that Renfrew's idea doesn't actually require any people to move at all, at least not more than a few kilometres. He proposes that, as knowledge of agriculture spread slowly across Europe and western Asia, the non-farmers along the edge of the wave simply accepted IE speech from their neighbours along with a knowledge of the new agricultural techniques.

Renfrew's hypothesis, which, among its other novelties, posits Anatolia (modern Turkey) as the IE homeland, remains deeply controversial, and linguists in particular mostly find it too much to swallow. Only time will tell whether some way can be found of reconciling Renfrew's economic view of the IE dispersal with the linguists' understanding of language change. But Renfrew has not stopped with IE; in the next chapter we'll encounter an even bolder hypothesis from the same source.

12.5 *Statistical methods*

As we move further back in time, the evidence available to us becomes ever scantier. On the one hand, what written evidence there is becomes sparser and finally disappears. On the other hand, the internal linguistic evidence for genetic relationships becomes increasingly faint as the languages in question become further separated in time. Eventually, of course, we must reach a point at which two originally related languages have diverged for so long that we can no longer find any evidence at all of their common origin, at least with standard techniques: the last faint traces of a common origin just disappear into the background noise of chance resemblances. But fields other than linguistics have developed useful techniques for extracting faint 'signals' from 'noise', and these techniques are mathematical in nature, chiefly statistical.

There have been several attempts to bring statistical methods to bear upon various aspects of historical linguistics. The earliest and simplest of these is **lexicostatistics**. This is in fact a very general label for any kind of statistical analysis of vocabularies, but it is most particularly applied to a simple procedure for estimating the degree of linguistic distance between genetically related languages. The central idea is that individual words in any language are steadily replaced over time. Thus, if we have several languages which we know are related, then we can choose a representative sample of the vocabularies of all of them and calculate the percentage of shared vocabulary items. Languages which share a larger proportion of their vocabularies are presumably more closely related than those sharing a smaller proportion. Thus, if among the three related languages A, B, and C, we find that A and B share 62 per cent of their vocabulary, A and C share 54 per cent, and B and C share 83 per cent, we might conclude that B and C are more closely related to each other than either is to A. This is admittedly a rather crude approach, but it may sometimes yield results of interest.

Note, however, that lexicostatistics of this kind can be applied only *after* the languages of interest have been shown to be related and *after* cognate words have been securely identified. In defiance of this plain fact, some linguists have on occasion tried to apply the technique to languages which are not known to be related, often in the very hope of finding evidence for a genetic link. Thus, for example, Tovar *et al.* (1961) attempt a lexicostatistical comparison of Basque with several other languages, including the North and South Caucasian languages and Berber, and they solemnly report a figure of 10 per cent 'cognates' for Basque and Berber and a 7.5 per cent figure for Basque and Kartvelian. But Basque has never been shown to be related to these other languages (or indeed to any other living languages at all), and all that these pretty numbers represent is the proportion of arbitrary resemblances between the languages by which the authors are prepared to be impressed. Such work constitutes an abuse of lexicostatistics: guesswork wrapped up in numbers expressed to any number of decimal places is still guesswork, and it should not be presented as something better. I return to this point below.

In the 1940s the American linguist Morris Swadesh introduced a dramatic new factor into lexicostatistics: a time element. His reasoning was as follows: *if* we assume that the rate of vocabulary replacement is roughly constant, and *if* we can assign a value to the rate of replacement (so many words replaced per thousand years), then we can calculate an absolute date for the separation of any two related languages. This modified and far more ambitious version of lexicostatistics is called **glottochronology** (some people in fact use these two terms interchangeably, but this is not good practice). In the 1950s the American linguist Robert Lees derived an equation which expresses Swadesh's idea (Lees 1953):

$$t = \frac{\log c}{2 \log r}$$

Here t is the *time depth*, the time which has elapsed since the two languages separated, expressed in thousands of years; c is the percentage of cognates (shared vocabulary) found in the two languages today (expressed as a decimal); r is the *glottochronological constant*, the (supposedly constant) percentage of ancestral words retained by any given language after 1000 years has elapsed (also expressed as a decimal); and *log* stands for the logarithm to base 10.

Assuming that this idea has some validity, we need three things to make glottochronology a practical proposition. First, as I explained above, we need to be certain that the languages we are comparing really are genetically related, and we need to identify the cognate words before we begin any calculations. For example, English *foot* and Spanish *pie* 'foot' really are cognate, even though they scarcely look it, while English *day* and Spanish *día* 'day' are not cognate at all, in spite of their great similarity. Just like lexicostatistics, glottochronology must be based upon a firm foundation of good comparative work, or else it is a waste of time.

Second, we need a standardized set of vocabulary items to work with. This issue was addressed by Swadesh himself, who prepared several such standard lists. Two of these are still in use; they are known as the **Swadesh 100-word list** and the **Swadesh 200-word list**. The 200-word list is given in the appendix to this book; there are several slightly different versions of it, and my composite list in fact includes 207 items. The 100-word list can be found in Exercise 7 at the end of this chapter. The items in the list are all (supposedly) of the sort I called *basic vocabulary* in Chapter 2. That is, they are words which change more slowly than vocabulary in general: pronouns, low numerals, body-part names, simple verbs and adjectives, and so on. You will see that the list contains words like *mother*, *foot*, *we*, *two*, *red*, and *sit*, but not words like *king*, *shoe*, *lord*, *teach*, or *above*.

In using the Swadesh lists, it is essential that we should not go searching for cognates. For example, one item in the list is the word for 'head' in the anatomical sense. The English word is, of course, *head*, while the German and French words are *Kopf* and *tête*, respectively, neither of them cognate with the English word. As it happens, both the other languages do have cognates of the English word: German *Haupt* and French *chef*. At some ancient stage, these really were the words for 'head' in these languages, but today they have quite different meanings only metaphorically related to the anatomical head: they mean 'central figure', 'chief person', 'leader', 'director'. Hence we don't count these words, and the words for 'head' would be tabulated as non-cognate in all three languages.

Finally, and critically, we need a value for that constant *r*. This we can estimate by looking at languages for which we already have, on independent grounds, a good idea of their date of separation (that is, we already have a value for *t*) and then by counting the number of cognates which they share (so that we can find *c*). Most attempts at calculating *r* in this way give a value between 76 per cent and 86 per cent – that is, a given language allegedly retains 76–86 per cent of its ancestral vocabulary after 1000 years, having replaced the remaining 14–24 per cent. Consequently, many people take the median value of 81 per cent, sometimes rounded off to 80 per cent, as a reasonable value for *r*.

Let's do a sample calculation. The 200-word list applied to English and German yields 59 per cent shared cognates; this is our value for c in this case. If we take r as 80 per cent, we can calculate as follows:

$$t = \frac{\log c}{2 \log r} = \frac{\log 0.59}{2 \log 0.80} = \frac{-0.229}{2(-0.097)} = \frac{-0.229}{-0.194}$$

$$= 1.180 \text{ kiloyears}$$

We calculate that English and German separated 1180 years ago, or in about AD 815. This is too late, however: by this date the Anglo-Saxons had been settled in England for centuries, and a more realistic result would have been 1600 years ago or even earlier. Naturally, even the most enthusiastic proponents of glottochronology do not insist that their calculated dates are better than reasonable estimates; in practice, proponents normally try to estimate likely margins of error, and they cite results like the 2200 years ± 200 years reported by Sarah Gudschinsky (1956) as the time depth for the separation of the Mexican languages Ixcatec and Mazatec.

But a number of calculated time depths have proved to be wildly inaccurate. On the one hand, the 83 per cent shared cognates of French and Italian yield a separation date of AD 1586, which is absurd: by this date, these two languages had been distinct for perhaps a thousand years, and both already possessed centuries-old literary traditions. On the other hand, the tiny number of shared cognates between Latin and Old Irish puts their separation as far back as 3700 BC, a time when most specialists believe that PIE was still being spoken and that the major daughter languages had yet to emerge.

There are obvious difficulties with glottochronology. For one thing, as we saw in Chapter 7, it is clearly too simplistic to assume that an ancestral language suddenly splits into two (or more) daughters which thereafter have no contact with each other: a split into daughter languages is typically much slower and much more gradual than this, and the time depths coming out of the equation can rarely represent a genuine historical event with a hard date on it. At best, it can only be a compromise between the time when significant dialectal differences began to appear and the time when the new regional varieties were indisputably distinct languages.

More significantly, it has now been established that the supposed 'constant' r is not constant at all: some languages unquestionably change their vocabularies much faster than others. At one extreme, Icelandic has scarcely replaced any ancestral words at all since Iceland was first settled over a thousand years ago. At the other extreme, there was until recently a Gypsy variety of Armenian which, in spite of preserving the Armenian grammatical structure almost intact, had virtually no Armenian words left in it. These differences are easy to understand. Icelandic is spoken on a remote island and, until recently, its speakers had minimal contact with anyone else. Gypsies, however, being wanderers, are obliged to learn and use the languages of the countries in which they travel, and hence their languages suffer unusually intense pressure from more prestigious neighbours.

Some practitioners of glottochronology have attempted to get to grips with such variation by converting the 'constant' r to a parameter which has different values in different circumstances or even in different language families. Naturally, there is a danger that such manœuvres might render glottochronology vacuous, that proponents might be reduced merely to sticking in whatever value of r is required to yield the desired result. There is as a consequence no shortage of critics, especially among those linguists with a good grounding in statistics who argue that glottochronology is little more than an empty exercise in computing impressive-looking but essentially meaningless numbers. As a case in point, some critics have pointed out that a glottochronological comparison of English and the English-based pidgin Tok Pisin of Papua New Guinea yields the result that they apparently separated about 2000 years ago – and yet Tok Pisin is less than 200 years old. Nevertheless, a significant number of linguists continue to believe that the difficulties, while real, are tractable, and that the method, used thoughtfully and carefully, can still afford us some valuable results.

Fig. 12.2 gives a nomograph of the Lees equation, using $r = 80\%$. If you're not very comfortable with logarithms, you can use this nomograph to read off an approximate value of t for any given value of c. (Remember, once you have t, you must count back that many years from the present to get the date of separation.)

Above I declared that lexicostatistical (and therefore glottochronological)

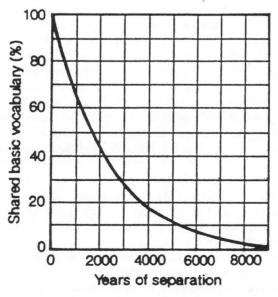

Fig. 12.2 A nomagraph of the Lees equation

methods cannot sensibly be applied to languages which have not been shown to be related and between which cognates have therefore not been identified, on the reasonable ground that such attempts can involve nothing but sheer blind guesswork as to which words might possibly be cognates *if* the languages are indeed related. On the one hand, genuine cognates can be impossible to recognize without a solid basis in comparative work: recall the case of English *head* and French *chef*. On the other hand, such guesswork runs straight into the problem of spotting spurious 'cognates' involving nothing more than chance resemblances: recall the cases like English *much* and Spanish *mucho* 'much', and English *bad* and Persian *bad* 'bad', which are not cognate even though all three languages are in fact distantly related.

In Chapter 8 I briefly pointed out the existence of such chance resemblances in form and meaning as a potential stumbling block if the comparative method is not applied with scrupulous care. None the less, a number of linguists have chosen to reject the comparative method and to appeal instead to the simpler technique of merely looking for resemblances of form and meaning between languages that interest them, in an approach often called *mass comparison*; if they find enough such resemblances, they declare that they have identified a genetic link. (Recall the words for 'dung' in Basque, North Caucasian, and Burushaski, discussed above.) When challenged on the issue of chance resemblances, they typically appeal to the *number* of resemblances they have found, and assert that this number is surely too large to result from chance alone. It is therefore a matter of some importance to try to estimate the likely number of chance resemblances we might reasonably expect to find between arbitrary languages which are not discoverably related.

The American linguist Don Ringe has tackled this problem using ordinary probability theory. To start with, Ringe is able to show that the likelihood of finding resemblances of form and meaning between arbitrary languages is considerably higher than our naïve expectations might have suggested. Naturally, the frequency of chance resemblances depends crucially on just how much resemblance in form and in meaning we want to insist on, but Ringe adheres to a very narrow and restrictive definition of resemblance, and yet he still finds that chance resemblances are bound to be almost startlingly common. Most of the linguists whose work he is evaluating in fact adopt far laxer criteria about what to count as a resemblance, and they accordingly find very many resemblances.

Much of Ringe's work is based upon pairwise comparisons of languages – that is, on languages compared only two at a time. The proponents of mass comparison frequently protest about this. They agree that chance resemblances may be reasonably frequent between any two languages, but point out that they themselves don't work that way: instead, they typically compare six languages at once, or ten languages, or even more. They argue that increasing the number of languages in this way must necessarily reduce the likelihood of chance resemblances to insignificance, and hence that their findings must in most cases represent genuine cognates.

This line of argument sounds seductive, but Ringe is easily able to dispose of it. The key point here is that the mass comparativists do not in practice insist that every single word should match up in every one of the languages they are comparing. Instead, they are satisfied if the words for, say, 'liver' resemble one another in three or four out of ten languages, while the words for 'day' resemble one another in a *different* three or four languages, and so on. Statistically speaking, the consequences of this policy are quite dramatic, as Ringe is able to show.

To see this, consider a simple example. Suppose, for the sake of argument, that the overall probability that any given word might be judged a satisfactory member of some comparison is 20 per cent, or 0.20, which is in fact a rather conservative estimate, given the established practice of those linguists who adopt mass comparison as their approach. Now, if we are comparing just six languages, the probability that any single word in one language will prove to have satisfactory matches in all six languages is clearly $(0.20)^6$, or 0.00032 – less than one in 3000. But suppose we increase the number of languages to ten. What is now the probability that we will find a satisfactory match among exactly six languages by chance alone? Well, the probability of finding an acceptable six-way match-up among any given six languages is still $(0.20)^6$, as before. Since the probability of *not* finding an acceptable match in any one language is obviously $(1 - 0.20) = 0.80$, the probability of not finding any match-ups in the remaining four languages is $(0.80)^4$. Therefore the overall probability of finding suitable matches by chance alone in *any given* six languages is $(0.20)^6 \times (0.80)^4$. But, with ten languages to play with, there are no fewer than 210 different ways of choosing exactly six languages, and any one of these 210 arrangements has exactly the same likelihood of producing a six-way match-up by chance alone. Thus the *overall* probability of finding chance match-ups in exactly six of the ten languages is $(0.20)^6 \times (0.80)^4 \times 210 = 0.005505$, or roughly one in 180.

So, if we examine the Swadesh 200-word lists for ten arbitrary languages, we will certainly expect to find at least one six-way match by chance alone. But we're not done yet, because we also have to consider the probability of finding seven-way, eight-way, nine-way, and ten-way matches by chance alone, plus the probability of five-way matches, four-way matches, and so on, down to whatever minimal number of matches is considered interesting. Once we've done all this, we are left with the result that the probability of finding a number of matches resulting from chance resemblance alone is not small at all: unless we are very unlucky, we will find an impressive number of chance matches among any ten arbitrary languages we happen to pick, even if we stick to the 200-word list. That is, increasing the number of languages most emphatically does *not* reduce the likelihood of chance matches: instead, it greatly increases that likelihood. The reason for this is simple: the more languages we add, the more opportunities we are providing for chance resemblances to appear. In short, Ringe has demonstrated that chance resemblances constitute a serious problem for the mass comparativists, one which they have completely failed to deal with or even to recognize.

To make matters still worse, the proponents of mass comparison do not in practice confine their attentions to the Swadesh word lists. Instead, they trawl dictionaries in search of *any* resemblances they can find anywhere: words for 'otter', 'heifer', 'fruitstone', 'moth', 'eyelash', 'room', 'old man', 'armpit', 'membrane', 'mushroom', 'shaman', 'strap', 'clumsy person' – anything at all will do, if it offers a resemblance. Worse still, they make no reasonable attempt to control the semantics, and so they routinely match a word for 'bear' with a word for 'hamster', they match 'hear' with 'earrings', they match 'blood' with 'contents of an egg', and they match any or all of 'trough', 'spoon', 'basket', 'plate', and 'measure of grain', as long as the phonological resemblance is adequate for their purposes. This policy, of course, guarantees that they will find vast numbers of match-ups resulting from chance alone, and they most certainly do find them, but they none the less remain convinced that their findings must be significant because their match-ups are so numerous. In historical linguistics, as elsewhere, ignorance of the laws of probability leads to appalling misjudgements of the likelihood of coincidences. I return to mass comparison in the next chapter.

A simpler, and quite ingenious, approach to the problem of ascertaining the likelihood of chance resemblances between arbitrary languages has recently been proposed by Robert Oswalt. This is the **shift test**, and it works like this. We take, say, the Swadesh 100-word lists for two languages A and B. We then compare word 1 in language A with word 2 in language B, word 2 in A with word 3 in B, and so on, until we have matched word 100 in A with word 1 in B. Now, using any criteria for phonological resemblance we like, we can calculate the number of resemblances we have found between words which are virtually certain not to be cognates: *all* in A and *ashes* in B, *ashes* in A and *bark* in B, and so on. For best results, we do this 99 times: on the second pass, we compare word 1 in A with word 3 in B, and so on; on the third pass, word 1 in A with word 4 in B, and so on. The combined result is the *background score*, an estimate of the likelihood of chance resemblances between arbitrary words in the languages in question. We then go ahead and apply the same criteria of similarity to the lists in the normal way: word 1 in A with word 1 in B, and so on. If the result is not significantly better than the background score, we may rest assured that we have found nothing but chance resemblances; if, using standard statistical tests, we find that the result is significantly better than the background score, we have reason to suppose that we may be looking at some genuine cognates.

Recently Ringe and his colleagues have been developing a new methodology for determining the family trees of language families. The technique uses linguistic information encoded as qualitative characters. A single character consists of the presence or absence of a particular lexical item or of a particular phonological or grammatical innovation, and the characters used have to be chosen with some care. A computer program is then used to find the optimal family tree, the one that, so far as possible, puts each innovation into a single branch of the tree. The method has been tested on IE, with each established branch of the family being represented by its earliest well-attested member; the languages used were Old Church Slavonic, Lithuanian, Old English, Vedic Sanskrit, Avestan, Armenian, Greek, Latin, Tocharian B, Old Irish, and Hittite.

This is an interesting exercise, for several reasons. For one thing, the conventional split of PIE into ten or more daughter languages, as seen in the familiar illustrations, is most unrealistic: it is difficult to imagine that a single language could split simultaneously into ten or more daughters. Almost certainly the family tree ought to have a lot more structure, but so far we haven't been able to find any principled way of grouping some of the ten branches into larger branches. A second point is the **Indo-Hittite hypothesis**, proposed a century ago by the American linguist Edgar Sturtevant. Sturtevant's idea was that the Anatolian branch, whose best-known member is Hittite, might not be a daughter of PIE at all, but rather a *sister* of it, so that the family tree ought to show two main branches: Anatolian and everything else. Again, no one had previously found a realistic way of testing this hypothesis.

The result of the exercise is shown in Fig. 12.3. You can see at once how different this tree looks from the conventional one: this time, every single branching is binary. You can also see that the results of the test confirm the Indo-Hittite hypothesis: Anatolian (represented here by Hittite) comes out as the sister of just one other group containing the whole rest of the family.

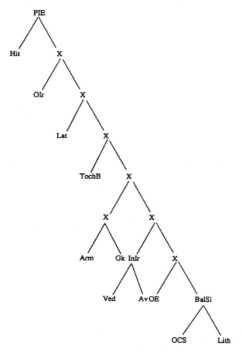

Fig 12.3 A revised tree for Indo-European

The position of Germanic, represented here by Old English, looks very odd: it comes out closer to Balto-Slavic than to anything else. Here Ringe and his colleagues report a curious finding: uniquely, Germanic appears to belong in two different positions in the tree. In terms of its morphology, it belongs with Balto-Slavic, as shown, but in terms of its vocabulary it belongs between the Western languages Latin and Old Irish. They interpret this result as meaning that Germanic indeed began to evolve in the east, along with Balto-Slavic, but that its speakers then migrated westwards, coming into contact with the ancestors of Celtic and Latin, and borrowing from them a large amount of Western vocabulary which is now no longer distinguishable from native Germanic words.

This new method is still in is infancy, but it looks extremely interesting. If it proves to be as reliable as the authors suggest, we may reasonably expect it to become a standard tool in the field. Computer programming may well be a necessary skill for the next generation of historical linguists.

Further reading

Thee are no textbooks of etymology, but you might like to read Alan Ross (1965), which, though brief, is somewhat technical, Bammesberger (1984), or Malkiel (1993), which is a personal account of etymological work in Europe. There are very many good books on British place names, including Cameron (1988), Gelling (1984, 1988) and Mills (1991). Watkins (1969) is a convenient brief summary of linguistic palaeontology with the Indo-Europeans. For the IE problem in general, the best introduction is Mallory (1989); Mallory (1973) is much briefer and less up to date. See also Cardona *et al.* (1970), Puhvel (1970), and Benveniste (1973). A brief overview of the issues can be found in the last two chapters of Lehmann (1993). Renfrew's ideas are laid out in Renfrew (1987) and given a popular treatment in Renfrew (1989). Glottochronology is presented in Swadesh (1955, 1971: 271–84); the equation is derived in Lees (1953); Gudschinsky (1956) is the most approachable introduction, but see also the article in Asher (1994). If you can read German, Tischler (1973) is an excellent account of the application of the method to IE languages; Bergsland and Vogt (1962) is a vigorous critique of the whole approach. The chief presentation of Don Ringe's analysis is Ringe (1992); in further publications (Ringe 1993, 1995, 1996, forthcoming) he extends his work, applies it to some particular cases of interest, and replies to his critics. Robert Oswalt's shift test is described in Oswalt (1991). Embleton (1986) is a handbook of statistical methods in historical linguistics. The new method for constructing family trees is presented in Warnow *et al* (1995).

Exercises

Exercise 12.1

You will need to consult a good etymological dictionary here. For each of the following groups of words and names, identify the ones which are ultimately derived from a single common origin and which ones are unrelated. You might find it helpful to draw a tree showing how the related items are derived from their common source.

(a) east, Easter, aster, Esther, Austria, Ostrogoth
(b) hell, hall, holly, holster, Valhalla, helmet, occult, clandestine, eucalyptus (comment here on the variation between /h/ and /k/)
(c) yellow, gold, chlorine, guild, guilder, cholera, gleam, glass

Exercise 12.2

The origin of the name of the Basque city of *Baiona* (French *Bayonne*) is disputed. At least three suggestions have been put forward:

(a) The name derives from Basque *ibai* 'river' plus *on* 'good' plus the article -*a*, and it thus means 'the good river'.
(b) The name derives from a personal name *Baio*, again plus *on* and -*a*, and it thus means '(place of) Baio the Good'.
(c) The name derives from the same personal name *Baio* plus an unrecorded Latin word **onna* meaning 'stream, watercourse', and it thus means 'Baio's stream'.

What sort of evidence would you look for in trying to evaluate each of these proposals? Try to consider every possible type of evidence: phonological, morphological, textual, geographical, and anything else you can think of.

Exercise 12.3

Suggest a plausible historical explanation for each of the following observations:

(a) In Bronze Age Greece, the word *wanax* meant 'king', while the word *basileus* denoted some kind of local official, a governor. The Bronze Age civilization underwent some kind of disastrous collapse, and all knowledge of writing was lost. After writing was re-introduced centuries later, the word *wanax* had disappeared, and the word *basileus* had come to mean 'king'.
(b) The Greeks call themselves *Hellenes*. Most other European languages, including English, give them a name derived from Latin *Graecus*, which in turn derives from the name of the *Graikoi*, a particular Greek tribe in western Greece. But the Turkish word for 'Greek' is *Yunan*, which derives from *Ionia*, the old name for western Asia Minor.
(c) In southern Greece and Crete, there are a number of place names in -*nthos* and -*ssos*, such as *Korinthos*, *Zakynthos*, *Knossos* and *Tylissos*. These names are of odd formation and have no etymologies.

Exercise 12.4

Whatever one may think of the evidence for the Kurgan hypothesis of Indo-European origins, defenders of the hypothesis are clearly obliged to provide answers to at least two questions:

(a) Why should the Kurgan people have moved out of the Russian steppes in the first place, into terrain that was often less suitable for a pastoral way of life?

(b) How could they have been so successful at imposing themselves over such a huge area which was already inhabited, mostly by farmers?

Suggest answers to these questions. Bear in mind that an agricultural economy typically supports a much higher population density than a pastoral economy.

Exercise 12.5

Almost all of the northern part of the Indian subcontinent is occupied by languages belonging to the Indo-Aryan branch of Indo-European, while the (non-IE) Dravidian family of languages occupies most of southern India. There is one Dravidian outlier, Brahui, spoken in northern Pakistan, some 1500 kilometres from the rest of the family. In the second millennium BC, there was a flourishing and prosperous urban civilization, the Harappan culture, located in the Indus valley, in what is now Pakistan. That civilization collapsed and disappeared abruptly and completely, and its cities were never rebuilt. A number of scholars have proposed that the Harappan civilization was Dravidian-speaking and that it was destroyed by the invading Indo-Aryans, whose language displaced Dravidian speech. Apart from the existence of Brahui, what *linguistic* evidence might you look for to evaluate this scenario?

Exercise 12.6

Below are the percentages of cognates shared between certain pairs of languages. In each case, apply glottochronology to calculate the date at which the languages separated. If at all possible, use the Lees equation; use the nomograph only if you have no command of algebra.

(a) Nootka and Kwakiutl, two Wakashan languages of British Columbia: 30%;

(b) Georgian and Zan, two Kartvelian languages of the Caucasus: 44%;

(c) Spanish and Romanian, two Romance languages of Europe: 61%.

Exercise 12.7

Table 12.1 gives the Swadesh 100-word lists for English, French, and Basque, in phonemic transcription. English and French are generally believed to be

Table 12.1

		English	French	Basque
1.	'all'	ɔːl	tu	gusti
2.	'ashes'	æʃəz	sãdʀ	hautś
3.	'bark'	bɑːk	ekɔʀs	asal
4.	'belly'	beli	vãtʀ	śabel
5.	'big'	bɪg	gʀã	handi
6.	'bird'	bɜːd	wazo	tʃoɾi
7.	'bite'	baɪt	mɔʀdʀ	horskatu
8.	'black'	blæk	nwaʀ	belts
9.	'blood'	blʌd	sã	odol
10.	'bone'	bəʊn	ɔs	hesur
11.	'breast'	brest	pwatrin	bular
12.	'burn'	bɜːn	bʀyle	ere
13.	'claw'	klɔː	gʀif	askasal
14.	'cloud'	klɑʊd	nyaʒ	hodei
15.	'cold'	kəʊld	fʀwa	hots
16.	'come'	kʌm	vniʀ	etori
17.	'die'	daɪ	muʀiʀ	hil
18.	'dog'	dɒg	ʃjɛ̃	sakur
19.	'drink'	drɪŋk	bwaʀ	edan
20.	'dry'	draɪ	sɛk	agor
21.	'ear'	ɪə	ɔʀɛj	belari
22.	'earth'	ɜːθ	tɛʀ	lur
23.	'eat'	iːt	mãʒe	jan
24.	'egg'	eg	œf	araultsa
25.	'eye'	aɪ	œj	begi
26.	'fat'	fæt	gʀa	gants
27.	'feather'	feðə	plym	luma
28.	'fire'	faɪə	fø	śu
29.	'fish'	fɪʃ	pwasɔ̃	arain
30.	'fly'	flaɪ	vɔle	hegas [egin]
31.	'foot'	fʊt	pje	oin
32.	'full'	fʊl	plɛ̃	bete
33.	'give'	gɪv	dɔne	eman
34.	'good'	gʊd	bɔ̃	on
35.	'green'	griːn	vɛʀ	berde
36.	'hair'	hɛə	ʃvø	ile
37.	'hand'	hænd	mɛ̃	eśku
38.	'head'	hed	tɛt	buɾu
39.	'hear'	hɪə	ãtãdʀ	entsun
40.	'heart'	hɑːt	kœʀ	bihots
41.	'horn'	hɔːn	kɔʀn	adar
42.	'I'	aɪ	ʒə	ni
43.	'kill'	kɪl	tye	hil
44.	'knee'	niː	ʒnu	belaun
45.	'know'	nəʊ	savwaʀ	jakin
46.	'leaf'	liːf	fœj	ori
47.	'lie'	laɪ	alɔ̃ʒe	etsan
48.	'liver'	lɪvə	fwa	gibel
49.	'long'	lɒŋ	lɔ̃	luse
50.	'louse'	lɑʊs	pu	sori

Table 12.1 Continued

		English	French	Basque
51.	'man'	mæn	ɔm	gison
52.	'many'	menɪ	boku	aśko
53.	'meat'	miːt	vjãd	haɾagi
54.	'moon'	muːn	lyn	ilargi
55.	'mountain'	mɑʊntən	mõtaɲ	mendi
56.	'mouth'	mɑʊθ	buʃ	aho
57.	'name'	neɪm	nõ	isen
58.	'neck'	nek	ku	lepo
59.	'new'	njuː	nuvo	beri
60.	'night'	naɪt	nɥi	gau
61.	'nose'	nəʊz	ne	śudur
62.	'not'	nɒt	pa	es
63.	'one'	wʌn	œ̃	bat
64.	'person'	pɜːsən	pɛRsɔn	gisaki
65.	'rain'	reɪn	plɥi	euɾi
66.	'red'	red	Ruʒ	gori
67.	'road'	rəʊd	Rut	bide
68.	'root'	ruːt	Rasin	ero
69.	'round'	rɑʊnd	Rõ	biɾibil
70.	'sand'	sænd	sabl	hondar
71.	'say'	seɪ	diR	eśan
72.	'see'	siː	vwaR	ikuśi
73.	'seed'	siːd	gRɛn	ale
74.	'sit'	sɪt	aswaR	jari
75.	'skin'	skɪn	po	asal
76.	'sleep'	sliːp	dɔRmiR	lo [egin]
77.	'small'	smɒl	pti	tʃiki
78.	'smoke'	sməʊk	fyme	ke
79.	'stand'	stænd	[ɛtR] dəbu	sutik [egon]
80.	'star'	stɑː	etwal	isar
81.	'stone'	stəʊn	pjɛR	hari
82.	'sun'	sʌn	sɔlɛj	eguski
83.	'swim'	swɪm	naʒe	igeɾi [egin]
84.	'tail'	teɪl	kø	bustan
85.	'that'	ðæt	səla	huɾa
86.	'this'	ðɪs	səsi	hau
87.	'thou'	juː	ty	hi
88.	'tongue'	tʌŋ	lãg	min
89.	'tooth'	tuːθ	dã	horts
90.	'tree'	triː	aRbR	suhaits
91.	'two'	tuː	dø	bi
92.	'walk'	wɒk	maRʃe	ibili
93.	'warm'	wɔːm	ʃo	beɾo
94.	'water'	wɒtə	o	ur
95.	'we'	wiː	nu	gu
96.	'what'	wɒt	kwa	ser
97.	'white'	waɪt	blã	suɾi
98.	'who'	huː	ki	nor
99.	'woman'	wʊmən	fam	emakume
100.	'yellow'	jeləʊ	ʒon	hoɾi

distantly related, while English and Basque are generally believed not to be discoverably related. Apply Oswalt's shift test to English and French, and again to English and Basque. Unless you are very ambitious, make just one pass, not 99. You may use any criteria of phonological similarity you like, but I advise you to choose something simple. For example, you might count words as similar if they both begin with labial consonants, or both begin with coronal/palatal consonants, or both begin with back consonants, or both begin with vowels. Evaluate your results. (Basque /ś/ and /s/ represent contrasting apical and laminal sibilants, respectively.)

13

Very remote relations

13.1 *The mainstream view*

Linguists have been highly successful at grouping the world's languages into genetic families, some of them very large. The great majority of the languages of the Old World have been grouped into fewer than two dozen families, almost all of them regarded as secure constructs, with only half a dozen or so isolates and a few problem areas, such as New Guinea, southeast Asia, and the Caucasus. The position in the Americas is at present much less satisfactory, with 140 or more distinct families being generally recognized, but this number is being steadily reduced by continuing research, especially in South America, still perhaps the least well investigated area on earth.

Even in the Old World, however, there is an obvious question to be asked: are any of the recognized families themselves genetically related? The answer to this question must surely be 'yes'. It is inconceivable that every major language family we have so far been able to identify is completely unrelated to every other family. The ancestors of at least some of these families must undoubtedly have diverged from some much more remote common ancestor, in the familiar way. But which of our families are so related? How can we find out? *Can* we find out?

In considering these questions, the conventional position among historical linguists is a decidedly pessimistic one. What we may safely call the 'mainstream' view can be briefly summarized as follows:

- Human languages have been spoken for many tens of thousands of years, probably for at least 100000 years, and possibly for much longer.
- The rate of linguistic change, while quite variable, is great enough for a few thousand years of divergent development of languages to be generally sufficient to obliterate all but the faintest traces of a common origin.
- Hence the familiar and reliable historical methods can be invoked to identify only a common ancestry which is not more than a few thousand years earlier than our oldest substantial information.

- But written records are a very recent development in comparison with speech. No known written text is more than about 5000 years old. Only for a tiny handful of languages do we have texts as old as 2000 years. The vast majority of languages were never written down at all before the European expansion of the modern era, and most are still not normally written today.
- Consequently, we cannot hope to identify any ancestral languages which were spoken more than a few thousand years ago – perhaps 6000–8000 years ago in a few particularly favourable cases, probably not more than 3000–4000 years ago in most cases. Older genetic links than this undoubtedly exist, but they will remain forever beyond our reach.

This mainstream position has been the view of most historical linguists for generations, and it is still unquestionably the majority view today. However, there have always been a few dissenters prepared to argue that things are not nearly so bleak as the mainstream position would imply. Today these dissenters are more numerous, more vociferous, and more determined than ever before. In this chapter we shall examine the often deeply controversial proposals of the dissenters.

13.2 *A brief history of remote proposals*

Suggestions of remote relationships have been made for centuries. For example, Martin Frobisher suggested a connection between Uralic and Eskimo as early as 1576, or long before the existence of IE was established (or, for that matter, before the genetic unity of Uralic itself was established). Indeed, it is often only with the advantage of hindsight that we can decide whether a proposal should be regarded as 'remote' and 'speculative' or rather as 'perceptive' and 'mainstream'. For example, the suggestion of Francis Newman (1844) that the Chadic languages of West Africa were related to Afro-Asiatic remained deeply controversial for decades and was flatly rejected by many scholars; only in the 1950s was this connection finally accepted by everyone, and it is now a pillar of orthodoxy. On the other hand, the suggestion of Vilhelm Thomsen (1869) that IE was related to Uralic was and still is rejected as unsubstantiated by the great majority of linguists (though not by all, as we shall soon see), and Thomsen's proposal is therefore confined to the outer darkness of speculations about remote relations.

In view of the mainstream position described above, the only thing that distinguishes a remote relation from a non-remote one is the time depth involved, but of course a linguist who proposes a genetic link does not usually know in advance what time depth might be implicated. In practice, all the linguist can do is to draw attention to what looks like evidence and hope that other linguists are impressed. The potential for frustration is very great, as is illustrated by the career of Edward Sapir.

Sapir was a brilliant and influential linguist who, among his other achievements, championed the phoneme principle at a time when it was still highly controversial; he also wrote important descriptions of several North American languages. In 1913 he announced that he had found a genetic link between Wiyot and Yurok, two otherwise isolated languages of California, and the great Algonquian family of northeastern North America, at the other end of the continent. Sapir's conclusion was bitterly denounced by some distinguished Algonquianists, who rejected it out of hand, to Sapir's considerable exasperation. This dismissal continued for nearly half a century – and yet today Sapir's proposal is universally accepted. Undeterred by the rebuff, Sapir went on in 1915 to make a further proposal: that the Alaskan languages Haida and Tlingit were remotely related to the great Athabaskan family of western Canada and the southwestern USA in a family for which Sapir proposed the name 'Na-Déné'. This proposal too stirred up a storm of controversy, complete with more fulminations from leading Athabaskanists. Today Na-Déné is almost universally accepted as a valid genetic grouping, though there remains some disagreement over the details. But Sapir did not stop with Na-Déné. In a series of private letters written in the 1920s, he claimed that he had discovered ample evidence of a genetic link between Na-Déné and – wait for it – the Sino-Tibetan languages of Asia. But, perhaps discouraged by the frosty reception accorded his earlier more modest proposals, Sapir never published his evidence, which still today remains buried in his notebooks. Unsurprisingly, the Na-Déné–Sino-Tibetan proposal, spanning as it does the Old and New Worlds, is dismissed by nearly everyone as unbridled speculation or even hallucination. Nearly everyone – but not quite everyone: see below.

These few but typical examples suffice to show that new proposals of distant genetic connections are very frequently greeted with indifference, with outright rejection, and even with considerable hostility, sometimes spilling over into what comes alarmingly close to personal abuse. Why should this be so? There are several reasons. For one thing, not a few such proposals are undeniably bad. Even the most enthusiastic and open-minded linguist is sometimes forced to conclude, after looking at some proposal, that it is little better than garbage. Data are sometimes grotesquely in error or manipulated in a manner that is transparently irresponsible and occasionally even downright deceptive. Some proposals come from the pens of obvious cranks, and can be dismissed as frankly crazy. But there must be more to it than that, since there are so many instances of proposed relations which were furiously rejected at first and for decades after, only to pass quietly into the body of received knowledge some time later.

Some of these other reasons are ones which are all too human and familiar from other disciplines than linguistics. Nearly a century ago, the great phonetician Henry Sweet wrote the following words (1901):

In philology, as in all branches of knowledge, it is the specialist who most strenuously opposes any attempt to widen the field of his methods. Hence the advocate of affinity between the Aryan [IE] and the Finnish [Finno-Ugric] languages need not be alarmed when he hears that the majority of Aryan philologists reject the hypothesis. In many cases this rejection merely means that our specialist has his hands full already, and shrinks from learning a new set of languages. . . . Even when this passively agnostic attitude develops into aggressive antagonism, it is generally little more than the expression of mere prejudice against dethroning Aryan from its proud isolation and affiliating it to the languages of yellow races; or want of imagination and power of realizing an earlier morphological stage of Aryan; or, lastly, that conservatism and caution which would rather miss a brilliant discovery than run the risk of having mistakes exposed.

Sweet here puts his finger on several important points. First, specialization. A linguist who chooses to become a top-flight specialist in one family of languages usually pays the price of knowing little about other families: life is too short for one person to master even three or four sizeable families. Consequently, few linguists are in a position to undertake a magisterial examination of far-flung families which, superficially at least, often appear very different. Moreover, such a specialist is often less than eager to be told that his area of expertise is no more than one corner of a much vaster linguistic edifice, and may thus be apathetic towards, or even resentful of, proposals to incorporate his specialist family into a larger grouping. Second, racism. It is clear, for example, that one of the reasons for the long resistance to the inclusion of Chadic in Afro-Asiatic was that Chadic speakers are incontrovertibly black, while speakers of the best-known Afro-Asiatic languages are white. The nineteenth-century prejudice that regarded language as intimately bound up with culture and with race – a prejudice which has perhaps not entirely disappeared – made it hard for the linguists of the time to accept 'black' languages in a 'white' family. Third, fear. Anyone who puts forward a sweeping proposal to relate distant families of languages – often languages of which he can have little or no specialist knowledge – runs the risk of being found embarrassingly wrong, if not in the main lines, then surely in many of the details. Even if he's right, he will often, as we have already seen, encounter professional scorn and hostility from his fellow linguists, resulting at least in damage to the ego and possibly even in more tangible penalties, such as difficulty in obtaining jobs, promotions, or research grants. It is far safer to be a solid, distinguished specialist in a small area than to whip up controversy with bold hypotheses.

Such human factors, combined with the undoubtedly real difficulty of finding adequate evidence to support a remote relation, have largely had the effect of relegating the search for remote genetic links to the periphery of historical linguistics. Very many reputable linguists are inclined to think that the search for remote relations is not quite respectable, that it must intrinsically be the preserve, if not of outright cranks, then of misguided linguists who waste their talents in chasing will-o'-the-wisps, in deluding themselves into seeing a handful of chance resemblances as evidence, instead of doing serious work. Consequently, most other textbooks of historical linguistics say nothing about the search for remote relations, or merely cite one or two examples in order to dismiss them.

Such caution is understandable enough, if only because so many conflicting remote genetic links have been proposed that it would seem they can't possibly all be right, and it is often very hard to see that some such proposals deserve to be taken more seriously than others. Nevertheless, it is a fact that a greater number of serious and capable linguists than ever before are now pursuing the search for remote relations: this search is now very definitely on the table, and it is steadily growing in respectability – though it is still a long way from being accepted into the linguistic mainstream.

Here is a tiny but representative sample of the remote relations which have been proposed: Niger-Kordofanian and Nilo-Saharan (Gregersen 1972; Boyd 1978; Bender 1981); IE and Semitic (Levin 1971); Dravidian and Uralic; Dravidian and Australian; Dravidian and Nilo-Saharan; Sino-Tibetan and Mon-Khmer; Sino-Tibetan and Austronesian; Australian and Papuan (Wurm 1982); Na-Déné and Sino-Tibetan (Sapir 1925; Shafer 1952, 1957; Swadesh 1952); Japanese and Altaic (Miller 1971; Starostin 1991); Sino-Tibetan and IE (Pulleyblank 1978); IE, Afro-Asiatic, and Sino-Tibetan (Modini 1991); IE and Uralic (Thomsen 1869); Sino-Tibetan, North Caucasian and Yeniseian (Starostin 1984); Basque and North Caucasian (Čirikba 1985); Basque and Kartvelian (Lafon 1948); Na-Déné, Sino-Tibetan, and North Caucasian (Nikolaev 1986); Japanese and Austronesian (Benedict 1990); Hurrian and North Caucasian (Diakonov and Starostin 1986); Austroasiatic and Austronesian (W. Schmidt 1906); North Caucasian and Etruscan (Orël and Starostin 1990). Though one or two of these are little more than suggestions, most of them have been defended in the literature with some vigour. Perhaps even this small sample is enough to demonstrate why so many linguists recoil in horror from what looks to them like a gigantic morass of confused and unconstrained speculation.

And these are only a few of the more modest proposals, involving just two or three families each. They are almost unambitious in comparison with some of the more audacious proposals that have been put forward. For example, Collinder (1965) proposes a super-family including all of IE, Uralic–Yukaghir, Altaic, Korean, Chukchi-Kamchatkan, and Eskimo–Aleut. Benedict (1942) suggests another super-family (dubbed **Austric**) including Miao-Yao, Austroasiatic, Tai, Kadai, and Austronesian. Bengtson (1991) and Ruhlen (1991) propose still another vast family, including Basque, North Caucasian, Burushaski, Sumerian, Nahali, Sino-Tibetan, Yeniseian, and Na-Déné; this construct is called **Déné-Caucasian**. Among these very large-scale proposals are a few which have, for one reason or another, attracted particular attention, and a correspondingly great degree of controversy. To these exceptionally interesting proposed super-families we now turn, beginning with the one which has perhaps the most impressive support.

13.3 *The Nostratic hypothesis*

In 1903 the Danish linguist Holger Pedersen suggested a genetic relation linking all of IE, Uralic, Altaic, Afro-Asiatic, and Kartvelian; this super-family he dubbed **Nostratic**, from the Latin word *nostras* 'our countryman'. Pedersen did little work on his idea, and the Nostratic proposal languished half-forgotten in the literature for decades. In the 1960s, however, two Russian linguists, V. M. Illich-Svitych and A. Dolgopolsky, independently began to work seriously on Pedersen's proposal. Only after several years did they discover their common interest and begin a collaboration on Nostratic, to which Illich-Svitych had added a sixth family, Dravidian. Illich-Svitych in particular chose to make the reconstruction of Proto-Nostratic (PN) his life's work, and he undertook an ambitious programme of sifting through the available materials for all six of his families. Reportedly, he was able to reconstruct some 700 PN lexical items to his own satisfaction, as well as a fairly complete PN phonological system and a few aspects of PN grammar. Tragically, however, he was killed in a traffic accident in 1966, before he had been able to publish his findings. Since his death, a number of his students and colleagues have collaborated on editing and publishing his papers, and three volumes have so far appeared, allowing us to look at a fairly substantial sample of Illich-Svitych's results. Meanwhile, Dolgopolsky (who now works in Israel) and others (notably Mark Kaiser, Vitaly Shevoroshkin, and Alexis Manaster-Ramer, and also Allan Bomhard, whose version of Nostratic is, however, very substantially different from the 'Moscow/Ann Arbor' inter-pretation of the other scholars) have also been contributing to the PN research programme, and, of all the proposed super-families, Nostratic is unquestion-ably the one which has received the greatest amount of detailed work. (Some workers have proposed extending Nostratic to include such additional families as Chukchi-Kamchatkan, Eskimo-Aleut, Sumerian, Nilo-Saharan and Niger-Congo, but these additions are somewhat controversial even among Nostraticists, and we ignore them here.)

In contrast with the proposed remote relations which we shall be examining below, the proponents of Nostratic, and Illich-Svitych in particular, have tried to adhere firmly to conventional methods in their research. They have worked with reconstructed proto-forms for their six families (in so far as these are available), they have looked for rigorous systematic correspondences among the forms of these proto-languages, they usually assign full value only to items which appear to be attested in at least three of their six families, they have reconstructed a phonological system for PN, and they have tried to identify regular phonological developments leading from PN to each of the six daughter languages.

Here is a sample of Illich-Svitych's Nostratic work taken from Kaiser and Shevoroshkin (1988). Table 13.1 illustrates the proposed systematic corre-spondences involving the four velar and uvular plosives reconstructed for PN:

Table 13.1 Some Nostratic correspondences

PN	PIE	PAA	PK	PU	PD	PAlt	[PTk	PM	PTg]
$**q'$	$*k/*k^j/*k^w$	$*k'$	$*q'$	$*k$	$*k$	$*k^h$	$*k^h$	$*k$	$*x$
$**k'$	$*k/*k^j/*k^w$	$*k'$	$*k'$	$*k$	$*k$	$*k^h$	$*k^h$	$*k$	$*x$
$**k$	$*g/*g^j/*g^w$	$*k$	$*k$	$*k$	$*k$	$*k$	$*k$	$*k$	$*k$
$**g$	$*g^h/*g^{hj}/*g^{hw}$	$*g$	$*g$	$*k$	$*k$	$*g$	$*k^h$	$*g$	$*g$

$**q'$, $**k'$, $**k$, and $**g$. (The double asterisk marks a reconstruction itself based on reconstructions for the direct ancestors of the six daughter languages; a prime marks an ejective ('glottalized') consonant). Observe that Illich-Svitych works with a very traditional version of PIE phonology, one which precedes the 'glottalic' hypothesis, which includes no laryngeals, and which recognizes a distinct 'palatal' series of obstruents for PIE, such as $*k^j$; this palatal series has been traditionally recognized in the standard handbooks but it is rejected by many specialists today on the ground that the evidence for it is scanty. The table also includes the reflexes in the three main daughters of Proto-Altaic. The languages cited are P(roto)–I(ndo)-E(uropean), P(roto)–A(fro)-A(siatic), P(roto)-K(artvelian), P(roto)-U(ralic), P(roto)-D(ravidian), P(roto)-Alt(aic), and the three daughters of this last, P(roto)-T(ur)k(ic), P(roto)-M(ongolian), and P(roto)-T(un)g(usic).

The reason for the three reflexes in each case in PIE Illich-Svitych argues, is as follows. The PN vowel system collapsed in PIE, but certain qualities of the old vowels were retained in a preceding velar plosive, as follows: before a front vowel, an ancestral velar (or uvular) became a palatalized plosive (such as $*k^j$) in PIE; before a rounded vowel, an ancestral velar (or uvular) became a labialized plosive (such as $*k^w$); before $**a$, an ancestral velar (or uvular) became a plain plosive (such as $*k$). Schematically, then, using K as a cover symbol for any back plosive, and E and U as cover symbols for front vowels and rounded vowels, respectively, PIE supposedly developed as follows: $**KU- > PIE *K^we-$, $**KE- > PIE *K^je-$, and $**Ka- > PIE *Ke-$.

Here now are some examples of putative cognates exhibiting these systematic correspondences:

- PN $**q'-$:

  PN $**q'[iw]lV$ 'hear': PIE $*k^jleu-$ 'hear'; PK $*q'ur-$ 'ear'; PAlt $*[k^h]ul-$ 'ear'; PU $*kūle$ 'hear'; PD $*kēl-$ 'hear'.

  PN $**q'arV$ 'smell, reek': PIE $*ker-m-$ 'reeking plant'; PAA $*k'r-$ 'smell'; PK $*q'(a)r-$ 'reek'.

- PN $**k'-$:

  PN $**k'udi$ 'tail': ? PIE $*kaud-$ 'tail'; ? PAA $*k'dr$ 'tail'; PK $*k'wad-/$ $*k'ud-$ 'tail'; PAlt $*k^hudi-rga$ 'tail'.

PN **$k'olV$ 'round': PIE *k^wel- 'round, revolve'; PAA *$k'(w)l$ 'round, revolve'; PK *k^wwer-/*k^wwal- 'round'; PAlt *$KolV$- 'mix, rotate'; ? PU *$kola$ 'circle'; ? PD *$ku/ūl$- 'round, whirl'.

PN **$k'äćä$ 'cut': PIE *k^jes- 'cut'; PAA *$k's$ 'cut, beat, break'; PK *$k'ać$- 'cut'; PAlt *$k^häsä$ 'cut'; PU *$käćV/$*$kećä$ 'knife, sharp point'; ? PD *$kacc$- 'bite, sting'.

PN **$k'adV$ 'weave': PIE *ket- (Slavic *$koti$- 'wicker, wattle'); PAA *$k'd$- 'build'; PK *$k'ed$- 'build'; PD *$katt$- 'tie together, build; woven thing, vessel'.

• PN **k-:

PN **$küni$ 'wife, woman': PIE *g^wen- 'wife, woman'; PAA *$k(w)n/$*knw 'wife, woman'; PTk *$küni$ 'one of the wives (in polygamy)'.

PN **$kälU$ 'female in-law': PIE *$g^jlōu$- 'brother's wife'; PAA *$kl(l)$ 'sister-in-law, bride'; ? PK *kal- 'woman'; PAlt *$käli(n)$ 'wife of younger brother or son; sister's husband'; PD *kal- 'father's brother's wife'.

PN **$kamu$ 'grasp, grab, squeeze': PIE *gem- 'grab, take, squeeze'; PAA *km- 'grab, take, squeeze'; PAlt *$kamu$- 'seize, take, squeeze'; PU *$kamo$- > *$kama-lV$, *$koma-rV$ 'handful'; PD *$kamV$- 'grab, take, hold'.

• PN **g-:

PN $gUrV$ 'live coals': PIE *$g^{hw}er$- 'burn, hot, live coals'; PAA *$g(w)r$ 'fire coals'; ? PAlt *$gur(V)$- 'live coals; catch fire'.

PN **$gilV$ 'sickly; bad state, grief': PIE *$g^{hj}[e]l$- 'illness, damage'; ? South Arabian (AA) *gjl 'illness'; PK *gl- 'grief'; ? PTg *$gil(a)$- 'be sad, grieve'.

PN **$gara$ 'thorn, thorny branch': PIE *g^her-/*g^herH-/*g^hreH- 'thorn, sharp point, branch/twig'; PAlt *$gara$ 'sharp point, branch, conifer'; PU *$kara$ 'thorn, branch, twig, conifer'; PD *$kar(a)$- 'thorn, sharp point'.

This small sample can do no more than to provide some of the flavour of Nostratic work. Nevertheless, it should be obvious that such work lies solidly within the mainstream of comparative methodology, and that it is not riddled with wild speculations or outrageous assumptions. Consequently, one might have expected that the Nostratic hypothesis would have received a certain amount of interest, and even enthusiasm, from the linguistic establishment. This, however, has not been the case.

For one thing, until very recently, nearly all the relevant work was published in Russian, a language which few Western linguists can read comfortably. Moreover, the Western linguists who could read the work were often those who were by training and inclination most deeply suspicious of proposed remote relations. On top of this, several fairly distinguished Russian linguists fiercely attacked the Nostratic work, which did little to encourage its dissemination to the West. As a result, the Nostratic hypothesis for some years remained, for most Western linguists, little more than a rumour. Curiously, what finally seems to have broken the logjam was two articles in popular American magazines dealing with remote relations generally (P. E. Ross 1991 and Wright 1991), in which the Nostratic hypothesis was mostly discussed by linguists who were critical of it.

Since the early 1990s the Nostratic hypothesis has become far more prominent than formerly. Translations, reviews, and original articles are beginning to appear in English in some numbers. Manaster-Ramer (1993) has provided the first detailed review in English of the three volumes based on Illich-Svitych's work; the review is critical but supportive, and Manaster-Ramer pleads with his fellow linguists to accord Nostratic a more respectful and sympathetic reception than it has so far managed to obtain.

Most linguists have apparently adopted a 'wait-and-see' attitude to the Nostratic hypothesis, while some are openly sceptical or even hostile. A particularly interesting critique of Nostratic has been advanced by the mathematical linguist Don Ringe, who argues that the statistical distribution of putative cognates across the six branches of the proposed family is indistinguishable from a chance distribution and hence that Illich-Svitych's putative cognates might be nothing more than chance resemblances (Ringe 1995); Ringe compares the distribution of cognates within the IE family and shows that this is very different from a chance distribution. (See Exercise 13.1.) The proponents of Nostratic have promised a rebuttal to Ringe's work, but at the time of writing it has not yet appeared.

Only time will tell, of course, whether the Nostratic family will ever achieve even the measure of support enjoyed by, say, the controversial Altaic family, let alone IE. If Nostratic does finally win widespread support, though, one thing is clear: the time depth tolerated by the mainstream view described at the beginning of this chapter will have to be significantly increased. If there ever was a PN language, it must have been spoken at least 10000 years ago, and those who have considered the question seem inclined to suggest a date of 15000 years ago.

The Nostratic hypothesis is conspicuously controversial, to be sure. But the controversy over Nostratic is as nothing in comparison with the reception afforded to another set of proposed super-families, to which we now turn our attention.

13.4   *Greenberg's multilateral comparisons*

The Nostraticists, as we have seen, have clung firmly to the established historical methods, in which systematic correspondences are identified, proto-languages are reconstructed, and regular phonological developments are worked out for each daughter. Not everyone is convinced, however, that this painstaking procedure is the only useful way of identifying genetic linkages. There have always been a few linguists who were prepared to adopt the quite different approach called **mass comparison**. The idea of mass comparison is simple: you collect some hundreds or thousands of words from whichever languages you are interested in, you put those words side by side to see if any languages seem to show an unusual number of resemblances, and, if any do, you declare a genetic relationship between those languages. This, of course, is exactly the approach which I dismissed as unworkable in Chapter 8. The overwhelming majority of historical linguists similarly reject this approach; it has never in modern times been regarded as respectable, and the occasional linguist who has tried to employ it has invariably found himself dismissed as a crank. A prominent example is the early twentieth-century Italian linguist Alfredo Trombetti, whose enthusiastic embrace of large-scale mass comparisons led to a storm of abuse aimed in his direction: as one modern sympathizer remarks, 'They practically ran him out of the linguistics community.'

In spite of such depressing precedents, one contemporary linguist has firmly championed the method of mass comparison, now renamed **multilateral comparison**. This is the American linguist Joseph Greenberg, whose comment about Trombetti I have just quoted. Greenberg is, by any standard, a distinguished and influential linguist: for example, in the early 1960s, he almost single-handedly touched off the explosion of interest in linguistic typology and universals which is now such a prominent feature of our linguistic landscape. But Greenberg has also, throughout his career, been deeply interested in genetic relationships.

Greenberg began his genetic work in the 1950s with a comparatively brief examination of the languages of Australia, at the time almost *terra incognita*. With only a few fragmentary and unreliable sources at his disposal, he sketched out in Greenberg (1953) a classification of Australian languages which has stood up surprisingly well: in its main lines, at least, it compares favourably with the recent classification of Dixon (1980), which is based on far more comprehensive and reliable data. He then turned his attention to the troubled area of African languages. In a series of publications, culminating in his brilliant 1963 book (Greenberg 1963b), he substantially reorganized some recognized families (most notably, by scrapping the venerable but clearly creaky 'Hamito-Semitic' family in favour of an Afro-Asiatic family with at least five coordinate branches), he moved some languages out of one family and into another, and, most dramatically, he reduced all the 1500 or so African languages to just four families. He did this by applying multilateral comparison – that is, by the rapid inspection of hundreds of words and grammatical forms from each of hundreds of languages, with languages showing sizeable numbers of resemblances being grouped together. In spite of his suspect methodology, Greenberg's new language map of Africa was so obviously a great improvement on previous conceptions that it rapidly gained something approaching total acceptance. Today, while many of the details naturally remain controversial, there is almost no serious opposition to Greenberg's four families. Greenberg's method was nothing short of heresy, but, to the astonishment of the community of linguists, it appeared to work.

Greenberg next turned his attention to New Guinea and the surrounding area, a region whose languages had long proved difficult to classify. Throughout the 1960s he applied his method to an ever greater number of languages, and finally in 1971 he published his findings. He concluded that virtually all of the non-Austronesian (Papuan) languages of New Guinea and of the surrounding islands were genetically related, and he proposed a number of subgroupings. To his new family he added the language of the Andaman Islands, some three thousand kilometres away, and, surprisingly, the extinct languages of Tasmania, on the far side of the Australian continent. This new super-family he dubbed **Indo-Pacific**.

The Indo-Pacific hypothesis has had a mixed reception. Several specialists have greeted it with enthusiasm: for example, Blust (1978) finds it 'bold and brilliant', showing Greenberg 'at his best'. Others, however, have been far from impressed. The inclusion of the Tasmanian languages has been particularly controversial; for example, the Australian specialists Crowley and Dixon (1981) consider this move 'outrageous'. It seems fair to conclude that Indo-Pacific has already attained the status of, say, Altaic: accepted unhesitatingly as valid by many distinguished specialists, but rejected by other equally distinguished specialists as unsubstantiated speculation.

This mild scholarly controversy, however, provided only the slightest taste of what was to happen to Greenberg's next proposal. At the same time as his Indo-Pacific investigations, Greenberg began turning his attention to the largest outstanding problem on earth: the languages of the Americas. Generations of patient work had already succeeded in establishing a number of fairly large families, especially on the better-investigated North American continent, as well as innumerable smaller groupings, but most Americanists were still recognizing at least 140 distinct families in the New World, and possibly as many as 200 – a surprisingly large number, considering that the total number of surviving American languages is probably only about 650. This, of course, was a situation tailor-made for Greenberg, and he spent nearly three decades working across the two continents with his multilateral comparisons. After a series of preliminary reports, he finally published his definitive conclusions in his 1987 book.

Whatever else one may think of Greenberg's American classification, it is certainly revolutionary. The established Eskimo–Aleut family he accepts as valid and distinct, and Sapir's Na-Déné is likewise classified as a separate family. There is nothing controversial about this (though there once was, remember). But these two recognized families account for no more than fifty languages. The stunning part of Greenberg's conclusions is what he does with the remaining 600 languages: he places *all* of them, without exception, in a single vast family which he calls **Amerind**. That's right: all the remaining languages of North America, all the languages of South America, and all the languages of the Caribbean, in just one family.

If I told you that the Amerind hypothesis was controversial, I would hardly be doing justice to the facts. The truth is that a storm of outraged protest and furious condemnation broke over Greenberg's head, the like of which has rarely been seen in linguistics. If the general public think of historical linguists at all, they probably think of us as quiet, meek, bespectacled eccentrics poring over mouldering books in cluttered studies and rarely venturing any comment more offensive than a polite modification of somebody's proposed Proto-Dravidian word for 'elbow'. This is not the way it looks to Greenberg.

Greenberg's critics – who are numerous and often very distinguished – apply to his work such phrases as 'worthless', 'illusory', 'unsupported', 'deeply flawed', 'distressing', 'crude and puerile', 'irrelevant nonsense', 'misguided and dangerous', and 'completely unscientific'. One critic has described the attention given to Greenberg's ideas as 'really depressing' and has suggested that Greenberg should be 'shouted down', while another inventive critic has coined a new term of abuse just to throw it at Greenberg: he accuses Greenberg of *columbicubiculomania*, or an obsession with putting things into pigeon-holes. At the same time, Greenberg is not without his – equally distinguished – supporters, who have praised his boldness and imagination, declared his Amerind grouping 'obviously correct', and, on occasion, attacked the critics for what they see as unfair distortions and misrepresentations of Greenberg's work.

Quite apart from their contempt for the very method of multilateral comparison, Greenberg's critics make a number of more substantial points: they complain that Greenberg has often ignored reliable and up-to-date sources of information in favour of antiquated and defective ones, they complain that he has sometimes neglected the best-studied languages altogether, and, most importantly, they complain that his data contain a simply enormous number of errors. In reply, Greenberg takes the rather unexpected line that his method is so powerful, so effective at finding genetic links, that none of this matters: scanty and defective materials, he argues, will reveal a relationship just as well as abundant materials of good quality. Few critics have found this response reassuring.

On the other hand, Greenberg's evidence includes the identification of what appear to be virtually identical grammatical alternations in a number of widely dispersed American languages not previously known to be related, and, as we saw in Chapter 8, shared grammatical alternations are commonly taken as powerful evidence for a genetic link. But perhaps the most startling support for Greenberg has come from some quite unexpected quarters: from genetics and from physical anthropology. Entirely independently of Greenberg, the geneticist Luigi Luca Cavalli-Sforza has published a map of genes in the cell nucleus for native American populations; he reports three distinct population groups whose distribution corresponds remarkably well to the distribution of Greenberg's three language families, with the Eskimo-Aleut and Na-Déné speakers being genetically noticeably distinct from the comparatively homogeneous remainder: Greenberg's Amerinds (Cavalli-Sforza *et al.* 1988). At the same time, the physical anthropologist Christy Turner has made a study of the dental anatomy of native Americans, and he too finds three anatomically distinct groups corresponding reasonably well to Greenberg's three language families (Turner 1983, 1985, 1986) – though the match with Na-Déné is decidedly poor. As a result, Greenberg, Turner, and another geneticist, Stephen Zegura, have jointly put forward the hypothesis that what we are looking at is the result of three separate peoplings of the Americas from the Old World: an early Amerind invasion, a much later Na-Déné settlement, and a rather recent Eskimo-Aleut settlement, with each group being internally rather homogeneous in genes, teeth, and language, but different in all respects from the other groups (Greenberg *et al.* 1986).

Such coincidence between the findings of historical linguists and those of other disciplines is unprecedented, and many linguists have reacted with astonishment, disbelief, and suspicion. While nineteenth-century linguists were inclined to see language as part and parcel of culture and race, modern linguists have, in complete contrast, generally regarded it as a central tenet that languages show no particular tendency to correspond to genetic or physical differences – recall the black Chadic speakers in the 'white' Afro-Asiatic family, and note the widespread imposition of European languages on Africans, Asians, Australians, and native Americans in the last few centuries. There is a widespread feeling, therefore, that these results are just too good to be true, and some critics have had harsh words to say, particularly about Cavalli-Sforza, who, they suggest, has been unnecessarily vague about his data and his methods.

A further difficulty is that the 'three-invasions' picture drawn by Greenberg and his supporters requires that the first of those invasions should not have occurred more than about 13000 years ago. Until recently, this was indeed the approximate date for the first peopling of the Americas preferred by most anthropologists, but things have changed. Evidence for much earlier human habitation of the Americas, while still controversial, has been steadily mounting, and an increasing number of archaeologists and anthropologists are convinced that we have evidence for settlement 20000, 35000, perhaps even 50000 years ago – far too early to allow the presence of only three language families in the New World, let alone only three ethnic groups. Moreover, the linguist Johanna Nichols has recently concluded that the degree of structural diversity among American languages is so vast as to require a dozen or more separate settlements dating back at least 36000 years and perhaps 50000 years (Nichols 1990). In terms of our ideas about the settlement of the Americas, the tide now seems to be running very much against Greenberg.

The debate over the Amerind hypothesis will no doubt continue for some time, though the initial burst of outrage and hostility seems to have died down a bit into a kind of smouldering resentment. It is certainly unfortunate that the debate has become so heated, and that so many hard words have been uttered in print. One might hope that Greenberg's next proposal would be debated with a modicum of good-natured courtesy.

This is unlikely to happen, however. Greenberg has already indicated that his next major publication will be yet another proposed super-family, this time called **Eurasiatic**, embracing all of IE, Uralic-Yukaghir, Altaic, Korean, Japanese, Ainu, Gilyak, Chukchi-Kamchatkan, and Eskimo-Aleut. The method, of course, will be multilateral comparison, and the response, of course, will be a predictably furious one from most of the specialists in the relevant families. (Note that this Eurasiatic construct, as so far described, largely overlaps the Nostratic proposal but is by no means identical to it.)

What are we to make of all this? Can Greenberg's seemingly simple-minded method really be so devastatingly effective at uncovering genetic relationships, even at astounding time depths? Even, as he himself claims, with only scanty and defective materials to work with? Or is he, as his numerous critics claim, merely deluding himself by collecting fistfuls of the meaningless chance resemblances to be found everywhere and arranging them into pretty patterns to suit himself, like a child playing with a big box of buttons?

There seem to me, broadly speaking, to be three possible responses to Greenberg's work:

1. Mass comparison is, all by itself, adequate to establish previously undetected genetic groupings.
2. Mass comparison is not, of itself, adequate to establish genetic links, but it is none the less valuable in throwing up promising hypotheses for further investigation by conventional methods.
3. Mass comparison is worthless for any purpose, and is indeed pernicious and obstructive of serious work.

What strikes me most forcibly about the discussion to date is that the eminently plausible and reasonable position (2) has hardly been taken up by anyone. Indeed, the closest thing I have found to an explicit defence of this middle way is, surprisingly, in Greenberg's own writings (Greenberg 1987: 37), though elsewhere, of course, this same work defends position (1) with some vigour. Virtually everyone else who has ventured into print has opted either for Position (1) ('Greenberg is obviously right, so stop carping') or for Position (3) ('Greenberg is a dangerous madman, and you should steer clear of him'). This extreme polarization of opinion can hardly be either rational or healthy.

One possible approach to the evaluation of multilateral comparison might be to apply it to an area which has already been well mapped out by conventional methods to see if we get the same result. We might, for example, look at Europe, in order to ascertain whether the recognized IE and Uralic families, together with their main branches, emerge from the method. However, unless one counts Greenberg's work on African languages, this seems not to have been attempted on a large scale, though Greenberg has briefly considered the point in his various publications.

Finally, methodological controversies aside, is Greenberg right or wrong about Amerind? Only time will tell, but, as one fairly neutral commentator recently put it: 'If you were forced to bet, you'd just have to bet on Greenberg. He's been right so often.' It must be said, though, that not many linguists share even this cautious degree of optimism.

13.5   *Towards an evaluation of the macro-families*

What are we to make of this flurry of activity? How successfully have the proponents of the super-families made their case?

To begin with, there is no doubt at all that Nostratic represents far and away the most plausible of all these proposals. For one thing, all but one of the six stocks assigned to Nostratic are believed to have originated somewhere near the centre of the Eurasian land mass, making it *a priori* likely that at least some of them might share a common ancestor (the exception is Afro-Asiatic, which is usually thought to have spread out from north Africa). More importantly, the defenders of Nostratic, almost uniquely among the proponents of super-families, have at least attempted to stick rigorously to conventional historical methodology and conventional standards of evidence. Rejecting all appeals to casual resemblances, no matter how numerous, they accept as data only the best available reconstructions for items in the six proto-languages which they regard as daughters of PN; they usually posit PN etyma only for forms found in at least three of those six (this is called **Meillet's principle**, after the great French linguist who proposed it); and, most importantly, they insist upon the identification of systematic correspondences and of regular phonological developments in all branches. Even so, they have still managed to come up with some hundreds of PN roots and affixes. Their work clearly deserves to be taken seriously.

So far, however, it has been largely greeted with a mixture of apathy and hostility. In part, this reaction derives from the fact that the work is only slowly becoming available in languages other than Russian. In part, though, it surely reflects the human inertia identified by Henry Sweet in the passage quoted earlier. None the less, the number of Western linguists taking an interest in Nostratic is slowly growing, and it is possible that, within a decade or so, the Nostratic hypothesis may succeed in winning, if not general acceptance, at least general respect.

Of course, it is also possible that the hypothesis may collapse. If it does so, that outcome will occur because the hypothesis is *falsifiable*. Reliance upon stringent standards of evidence carries with it the consequence that one's evidence can be objectively evaluated and hence the possibility that it may be found wanting. As Alexis Manaster-Ramer has stressed (quoted in Lewin 1988: 1129), it is possible to show that a given language or family *cannot* belong to Nostratic. The Nostratic hypothesis is testable.

The evidence for the other proposed super-families, however, is far less impressive – so far, at least. For Sino-Caucasian, or Déné-Caucasian, we now have a flurry of publications, highly variable in quality (see, for example, the papers collected in Shevoroshkin 1991). Some work on this putative super-family looks interesting, at least to a non-specialist, while other work is clearly characterized by a shocking ignorance of the languages concerned and by a proliferation of errors so numerous as to render the work devoid of value. Nor is it encouraging that there seems to be almost no agreement as to the membership of this supposed family, or that some of its proponents seem inclined to toss every language isolate they can find into the cauldron.

In the case of Amerind, it will almost certainly be a long time before we will be able to make any confident judgements. Amerind is probably best regarded as a research programme for the next few generations of linguists.

13.6 *Towards Proto-World?*

In Section 13.2 above, I pointed out that many of the remote relations that have been proposed are overlapping and seemingly incompatible: Japanese, for example, has been variously linked with Korean, with Altaic, with Austronesian, with Dravidian, with Sino-Tibetan, and with a large group including IE, Uralic, and Eskimo-Aleut, and many other proposals overlap just as confusingly. This might appear a good reason for abandoning remote relations altogether, and to the critics of remote relations that is exactly how it does appear. But there is, of course, one way in which all of these conflicting proposals could be at least partly correct: if *all* the languages of the world are genetically related.

We apply the label **monogenesis** to the conjecture that human language evolved only once, and that all the languages that have ever been spoken are descended from that single ancestor. The slightly facetious term **Proto-World** is similarly applied to a hypothetical proto-language which is the ancestor of all languages spoken today or attested. Strictly speaking, the hypotheses of monogenesis and Proto-World are not identical, since it is perfectly conceivable that human language might have evolved independently in several places (thus falsifying monogenesis), but that all these strains died out except one, which is therefore the ancestor of all known languages (confirming Proto-World). Since, however, we will never be in a position to distinguish between these two conjectures, I shall simply speak of Proto-World from now on.

If the majority of historical linguists are enraged by the suggestion of Amerind, they are rendered almost speechless by the vastly more ambitious suggestion that all human languages can be shown to be related, whether by mass comparison or in any other way. Even most of those linguists who have welcomed Greenberg's bold constructions tend to shudder and turn away when Proto-World is mentioned. Those few linguists who are actually championing the Proto-World hypothesis find that other linguists cross the road to avoid meeting them. In fact, I can cite only four linguists who are prepared to declare openly that finding traces of Proto-World is a realistic possibility: the Americans Merritt Ruhlen and John Bengtson, the Czech Václav Blažek, and the Russian Vitaly Shevoroshkin, who now works in the USA. (Greenberg has often been described as another, but he has not so far committed himself in print.) Of these four, only Shevoroshkin holds an academic post. As I remarked earlier, breathtaking hypotheses do not usually constitute the shrewdest career move.

Questions of methodology aside, what makes the quest for Proto-World so hopeless in the eyes of even the most enthusiastic seekers after remote relations is the time depth. If Proto-World ever existed (and very many linguists are quite happy to concede that it probably did), it must have been spoken at least 100000 years ago, and possibly earlier still. That, most linguists would say, is more than enough time for the ordinary processes of lexical replacement and phonological change to obliterate all traces of the first language in every daughter, many times over.

Naturally, the Proto-Worlders are obliged to deny this, and deny it they most certainly do. They maintain that, statistically speaking, a small proportion of items in every daughter language can be expected to avoid replacement or phonological deformation into unrecognizability: Ruhlen (1991) cites the example of PIE *nepot-* 'nephew', which survives virtually unchanged today as Romanian *nepot* 'nephew', some 6000 years later. More importantly, however, they maintain that certain lexical items are intrinsically highly resistant to replacement – a point which is stressed also by Greenberg and more particularly by the Nostraticists. Among these are such items as personal pronouns, the lower numerals, and the names of certain body parts. And they have undertaken a search for these supposed refractory remnants of our ancestral tongue.

In reporting their findings, the Proto-Worlders cannot be said to be retiring or cautious. Here, for example, is an extract from an article by Shevoroshkin (1990: 27):

> Naturally, proto-World was a rather basic language. The most common term was, as it is today, the word for I, *ngai*, followed by the word for two. . . . Among the most accurately reconstructed words are those for body parts – *eye, ear, finger, heart* and even *nihwa* and *hwina*, terms referring at once to blood, breath and life. Fleas, lice and in-laws were also common topics of discussion among early humans. Curiously, no words in proto-World . . . refer specifically to emotions. . . . In the earliest state of our language, consonants were the sole bearers of meaning: words such as

changa and *sanga* meant, at once, nose, odor and the act of smelling. Apparently there was only one vowel, *a*.

The confidence expressed here almost beggars belief.

Taking up a suggestion first made by Greenberg, Merritt Ruhlen has argued in a series of publications that the Proto-World roots *tik* 'one, finger, point' and *pal* 'two' can be identified in language families all over the world. Table 13.2 lists a few of the 100 or so forms assigned by Ruhlen to *tik* (Ruhlen obviously admits more than one vowel into Proto-World); the list is taken from Ruhlen (1991: 261), with a few additions from the much longer list given in Ruhlen (1994: 322–3).

The critics understandably respond by declaring that Ruhlen has found nothing but the chance similarities that exist between all languages. With entire families of languages to play with, they argue, he was bound to find something like this, especially since he admits such phonetically marginal forms as *tong* and such semantically questionable items as 'arm'. Ruhlen replies that, if his critics were right, it should be just as easy to adduce forms like *tik* meaning 'two' and forms like *pal* meaning 'one'. Having done the spade work, he denies that any such patterns exist, and challenges the critics to find any evidence for the opposite match. No one has yet accepted the

Table 13.2 Reflexes of Ruhlen's Proto-World *tik* 'one, finger'

Phylum	Form(s)	Meaning
Nilo-Saharan	*tok~tek~dik*	'one'
Kartvelian	*tit-i*	'finger'
Kartvelian	*tito*	'single'
Indo-European	**d(e)ik*	'to point'
Uralic	*ik~odik~ɣtik*	'one'
Ainu	*tek*	'hand'
Japanese	*te*	'hand'
Eskimo-Aleut	*tik(-eq)*	'index finger'
Eskimo-Aleut	*tik(-laq)*	'middle finger'
Sino-Tibetan	**tik*	'one'
Yeniseian	**tok*	'finger'
Miao-Yao	**ntoʔ*	'finger'
Austroasiatic	**tiʔ*	'hand, arm'
Austro-Tai	**dia*	'finger, point'
Indo-Pacific	*tong~tang~teng*	'finger, hand, arm'
Na-Déné	*t'ek~tikhi~łaq*	'one'
Na-Déné	*(ka-)tleek-~tłʔeq~ (ka-)tliki*	'finger'
Amerind	**tik*	'finger'
Afro-Asiatic	**tak*	'one'
Turkish	*tek*	'only'
Korean	*(t)tayki*	'one, thing'
Gilyak	*r̃ak*	'once'
Kamchadal	*itygin*	'foot, paw'

challenge, and no one is likely to. This is not because of fear. A linguist who believes deep down that the Proto-World enterprise is a massive waste of time (and that's most linguists) is not going to devote a sizeable chunk of his career to trying to demonstrate that it's a waste of time, for essentially the same reason that few scientists consider it worth their while to devote years of work to the debunking of the ever-present claims of flying saucers, ESP, telekinesis, fork-bending, divining rods, perpetual-motion machines, or astrology. It's a pity, though, that at least one neutral linguist has not been tempted to pick up Ruhlen's gauntlet, since we might then be able to establish something, one way or the other.

At least one linguist, however, has undertaken a detailed scrutiny of Ruhlen's work, and more particularly of his alleged **tik*. Salmons (1992), having examined all of Ruhlen's materials which are publicly available, puts forward a number of telling criticisms of Ruhlen's procedures. I cite here the most interesting of these criticisms.

- In many cases, alleged reflexes of **tik* are found only in one branch of a family, but are unhesitatingly projected by Ruhlen back to the ancestor of the entire family. For example, forms found only in Finno-Ugric are assumed to have existed in Proto-Uralic, while forms occurring only in Tibeto-Burman are projected all the way back to the ancestor of the entire vast Sino-Tibetan family. This is clearly illegitimate.

- In many cases, alleged reflexes of **tik* are found in only a handful of languages in a large family or putative family, but again these are assumed by Ruhlen to have been present in the ancestor of the whole family. For example, among the 600 or so surviving languages assigned by Greenberg to his vast Amerind construct, only nineteen are reported as showing reflexes of **tik*, and all but two of these are found in a single area, the Caribbean and the adjoining coast of South America, but this is enough for Ruhlen to posit **tik* for Proto-Amerind. Likewise, only eighteen languages of the more than 1000 assigned to the Austro-Tai grouping have been found to exhibit alleged reflexes of **tik*, but again the word is immediately projected by Ruhlen back to Proto-Austro-Tai. This is even more clearly illegitimate.

- In families in which plenty of data are available, the semantics are often not obviously supportive. Ruhlen includes PIE **deik-* in his evidence, but this root is variously attested in the branches of IE as meaning all of 'say, tell', 'proclaim', 'teach, instruct', 'show', ' point', 'finger', 'sign, mark', 'throw', and possibly 'toe'. Of these, 'finger' is attested only in Latin, and 'point' only in Sanskrit. It therefore takes a considerable act of faith to conclude that 'finger' or 'point' was the original meaning of this root, and most specialists in fact conclude that it must have meant something like 'show' or 'direct'.

- Phonologically, Ruhlen is very generous in recognizing supposed reflexes of **tik*. For the final k alone, he allows any of k, g, kh, q, η,

$?$, t, and zero as a match. Reasoning from Maddieson's (1984) data on consonant systems and frequencies, Salmons concludes that fully 6 per cent of *all* the CVC forms in any language would be accepted by Ruhlen as constituting a match in form for **tik*. And this figure doesn't even make allowance for Ruhlen's policy of also admitting CV and VC forms like Japanese *te* and Finno-Ugric *ik*, or of his further policy of admitting forms containing additional segments, such as *tXVk* and *tVkX*: note Aleut *tiklaq* and Na-Déné *katleek*, for example. This additional latitude, naturally, will make it that much easier to find 'matches' for **tik*.

- Ruhlen treats on an equal footing forms of four different time depths: attested forms in particular languages, including isolates; shallow reconstructions in tiny families like Eskimo-Aleut; remote reconstructions in large and well-studied languages like IE; and forms posited for the ancestors of vast and highly speculative constructs like Amerind. This effectively multiplies still further his chances of finding a match somewhere.

- Ruhlen's results appear to point to a bizarre conclusion: languages which are isolated or which belong to families that are small or poorly studied frequently show forms that are virtually identical to **tik*, while languages belonging to large and well-studied families usually do not do this, exhibiting instead only complex developments of reconstructed ancestral forms resembling **tik*, such as English *teach* and French *doigt* /dwa/ 'finger'. It would seem, then, that speakers of Ainu, Aleut, Yupik, and Svan have retained Proto-World **tik* virtually unchanged, while speakers of IE, Sino-Tibetan, and Uralic have altered it drastically. This is hardly an acceptable conclusion.

- Ruhlen's **tik* is out of line with more conventional work in historical linguistics. In particular, the proponents of Nostratic do not recognize a root of this form, with a relevant meaning, in their reconstructions of PN, even though Ruhlen claims to have found reflexes of **tik* in some of the language families assigned to Nostratic.

- Finally, Salmons maintains that Ruhlen's claim is virtually unfalsifiable. Since Ruhlen recognizes no systematic correspondences, there is no way of checking the validity of proposed instances of **tik*, and there can be no such thing as counter-evidence. Instead, there are only confirming instances: finding one language that presents a suitable word counts as evidence, while finding 100 languages that fail to do so counts for nothing.

Taken together, Salmons's points amount, in my opinion, to a devastating critique. In essence, Salmons has demonstrated that Ruhlen's materials have exactly the characteristics we would expect them to have if they were nothing more than an assembly of random similarities. The only possible way of falsifying Ruhlen's collection of confirming instances would be to take up his challenge to collect just as many words of the form **tik* but meaning 'two'. Until someone is moved to undertake this task, it is highly likely that the proponents of Proto-World will continue to be able to hold their congresses in a very small room.

13.7   *The early spread of people and languages*

Palaeoanthropologists are agreed that the genus *Homo*, to which our species belongs, arose in Africa around two and a half million years ago. The majority of them also agree that our own species, *Homo sapiens*, itself originated in Africa somewhat more than 100000 years ago, though a sizeable minority argue for a somewhat more complex scenario. Our best guess, then, is that human beings once lived only in Africa but then spread out from there to settle all the habitable areas of the earth. Apart from Africa, we find the earliest evidence of our species in southeast Asia, and then in southern Europe, the Middle East, and Australia; most of the rest of Asia and Europe seem to have been settled a little later; the Americas were reached (from Asia) somewhere between 50000 and 13000 years ago (this is still being debated); the islands of the Pacific began to be settled little more than 2000 years ago.

Most (though not all) scholars agree that our species has been able to speak throughout its history, and hence that the peopling of the earth must also represent the introduction of human language to all parts of the earth. In recent years, some people have begun to wonder whether some evidence for this original spread of human beings might still be recoverable in one way or another, but particularly from the distribution of languages. At least four major attempts to do this have been offered, two by linguists, one by an archaeologist, and one by a geneticist.

The American linguist Morris Swadesh (1909–67) throughout his career made strenuous attempts to find links between far-flung languages and families. To this end he developed the techniques of lexicostatistics and glottochronology discussed in Chapter 12, and of course he compiled the Swadesh word list. In his posthumous 1971 book he offers a breathtaking synthesis of his ideas, in which he attempts to trace the origin of language all the way back to the calls of non-human animals, a view of language origin which is almost universally rejected today. More to the point here, he offers a sweeping reconstruction of the spread of language families in terms of what he calls the 'Bulging Hub Principle', according to which language families have repeatedly spread out in waves from an epicentre located roughly in west-central Asia. Fig. 13.1 illustrates Swadesh's conception of the world language map around 25000 years ago.

Swadesh's synthesis was based on very scanty data, much of it collected by people with no linguistic training. It is, of course, speculative in the extreme. Note, for example, that Swadesh posits a connection between Basque and the Na-Déné languages of North America, a position recently revived by Bengt-

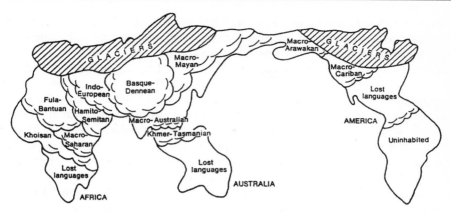

Fig. 13.1 Swadesh's wave model, 25 000 BC

son and Ruhlen, as we saw above (though Swadesh's map seems to require the Basques to have leapfrogged over the entire IE family in order to reach their present position in western Europe). It is probably fair to say that Swadesh's ideas have been almost universally dismissed by linguists as unsubstantiated fantasies.

Since Swadesh's work, we have managed to collect vastly more information about the languages of the world, and our understanding of linguistic structures and systems has increased substantially (or so we would like to think). A few people are now once again beginning to think that we might be in a position to recover, purely by the examination of languages, some information about their ancient spread.

In her 1992 book, the linguist Johanna Nichols approaches this issue from the point of view of typology. Eschewing any appeal either to words, which change very rapidly, or to such traditional typological characteristics as the presence of tones, which we know can appear rather suddenly in a language that formerly lacked them, she concentrates upon grammatical characteristics, which, she argues, are comparatively resistant to change and hence constitute a more reliable guide to linguistic history. Among the features she singles out for attention are head-marking versus dependent-marking, ergativity, inclusive/exclusive oppositions, alienable and inalienable possession, noun classes, and numeral classifiers. Using a carefully selected sample of 174 languages, she plots the distribution around the globe of the various grammatical characteristics and then looks for clear distributional patterns.

To begin with, she distinguishes *residual zones* from *spread zones*. A residual zone is an area characterized by very great linguistic diversity in a small territory, such as New Guinea or the Caucasus. In these areas, languages survive for millennia, giving rise to families of some considerable depth; languages are not displaced by others, but new arrivals may introduce further languages, so that the linguistic diversity of the area increases with time.

There are usually strong areal features, but there is no identifiable centre of innovation, and no single language enjoys any position of dominance. A spread zone is utterly different. A spread zone is large but shows little linguistic diversity; it is dominated by a single language family and often by a single language (for example, the Eurasian steppes, western Europe, or central Australia). This language serves as a prestige language throughout the area; it has a political, economic, or cultural centre from which innovations spread, and the area shows a classic dialect-geographical form, with an innovating centre and a conservative periphery. At fairly frequent intervals, the prestige language is displaced and more or less obliterated by an intrusive language, which then becomes the new prestige language.

Nichols then goes on to construct an interpretation of her maps. Briefly, what she concludes is that the geographical distribution of typological features is consistent with a settlement of the world that took place in four waves, all of them spreading out from Africa and later from Asia in a broadly west-to-east direction. Each new wave of people, she proposes, pushed the earlier waves further to the east. The survivors of the first wave are now to be found chiefly in Australia and southern South America, while the second wave is mostly attested now in New Guinea and central North America. The third wave occupies most of the Pacific coasts of Asia and the Americas, while the fourth and most recent wave consists only of Eskimo-Aleut in the Arctic. The rest of Eurasia and Africa are too complex to interpret in terms of these waves. See Fig. 13.2.

Nichols sees the residual areas as regions of refuge, in which the remnants of earlier waves have not been displaced by later waves. She also offers some more specific conclusions: she reckons, for example, that the first wave of

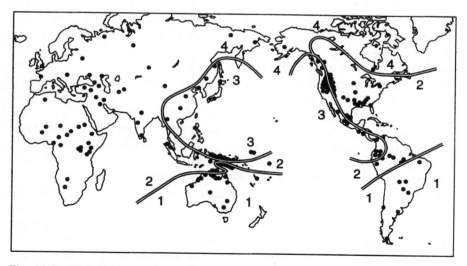

Fig. 13.2 Nichol's four waves of settlement

settlers in the Americas must have arrived at least 35000 years ago, a date that falls at the very beginning of the time that most archaeologists are remotely inclined to consider, and must have consisted of at least ten different linguistic groups, with further groups arriving later in the succeeding waves. Her results, she says, demonstrate such considerable linguistic diversity in the Americas that Greenberg's Amerind hypothesis is out of the question (Nichols 1990).

So far, a few linguists have expressed interest in Nichols's work, but most are remaining cautious, and some have been openly critical. Not everyone is convinced that typological features of grammar are anything like as stable as Nichols would have us believe: such languages as Amharic and Armenian, for example, have undergone substantial changes in their grammatical systems as a result of intense contact with typologically different neighbours.

Somewhat similar to Nichols's work in conception, but differing greatly in motivation and details, is the recent proposal of the archaeologist Colin Renfrew (1992, 1994, 1995). Like many contemporary archaeologists, Renfrew rejects the hoary tradition that sees every innovation in culture or language as evidence of an 'invasion'. Instead, he prefers to see the mosaic of languages in terms of economic, ecological, and technological factors, chief among which is the spread of farming.

In Renfrew's view, the distribution of languages is best understood in terms of four periods of dispersal, each occurring in different circumstances and for different reasons, and only the most recent involving identifiable invasions.

First, he assumes that people, and hence languages, began spreading out from the African homeland around 100000 years ago, eventually reaching all the habitable areas of the earth except the Pacific islands: this he calls the *initial migration*. In some parts of the world, both large and small, he assumes that the direct descendants of these first languages are still in place. These are, by and large, the areas of enormous linguistic diversity: most of North and South America, the Caucasus, southeast Asia, New Guinea, and Australia. That diversity, he argues, exists because no later languages have ever displaced the original ones, and hence tens of millennia of ordinary language change have brought about the inevitable splintering into large numbers of descendants. (Australia, he admits, is something of a problem, since only the northwest of the continent shows the expected degree of diversity, with the rest of it occupied by what is transparently a single large family, Pama-Nyungan.) Renfrew also includes Basque, the Nilo-Saharan languages of north central Africa, and the Khoisan languages of southern Africa among the survivors of this ancient first settling.

Second, and most crucially in his scheme of things, Renfrew argues that this initial distribution of first languages was seriously disturbed only by the invention of agriculture around 10000 years ago. As the knowledge of farming slowly spread out from the several locations in which it was invented, Renfrew proposes, the languages of the inventors went with it, in what he calls the *farming dispersal*. Recall from Chapter 12 Renfrew's controversial suggestion that IE began spreading across Eurasia as much as 10000 years ago along with agriculture. In fact, Renfrew sees the spread of farming as carrying with it, in different directions, several ancient languages, each of which consequently came to be the ancestor of a vast and widespread family: IE, Afro-Asiatic, Niger-Kordofanian, Elamo-Dravidian, Sino-Tibetan, and Austronesian. The great language families of the Old World, then, are for Renfrew testimony to the spread of agriculture thousands of years ago. (Note carefully that Renfrew is proposing that the *languages* spread to new regions along with farming: he expressly denies that any significant numbers of farmers invaded and settled the territory of their neighbours who had not yet acquired the new technology.)

Third, Renfrew recognizes what he calls a *late climate-related dispersal*. What happened here, also beginning perhaps about 10000 years ago, is that continued global warming caused the ice sheets to retreat, opening up much of the Arctic to human settlement for the first time. Hence the speakers of what later became Uralic, Chukchi-Kamchatkan, Eskimo–Aleut, and Na-Déné moved north and east into the now barely habitable tundra of Europe, Asia, North America, and Greenland.

Finally, and only in comparatively modern times, Renfrew concludes, the development of complex societies backed up by a significant degree of wealth and technological sophistication made it possible for the first time for one people to conquer their neighbours by force and to impose their own language on those neighbours. The Roman Empire, the medieval empires of the Mongols and the Turks, and the modern-day empires of the several European powers are all examples of what he terms *élite dominance*.

Renfrew's interpretation is principally based upon factors which make archaeological sense: climate and technology. From a linguist's point of view, it is noticeably *a priori*: he first works out what *should* have happened, and then tries to fit the world's linguistic map into his scheme. Linguistic evidence is subordinated to other considerations, such as when he pushes the IE expansion 4000 years further back than the linguists are willing to countenance, in order to fit that expansion into his archaeological framework. For this reason, few linguists have yet been persuaded, though many find Renfrew's ideas interesting.

(Interestingly, the anthropologist Grover Krantz has independently argued (1988) along much the same lines as Renfrew, but only for the continent of Europe; his reconstruction of European linguistic history from an economic and technological perspective likewise leads to conclusions which are unacceptable to linguists, such as his conclusion that the cradle of the Uralic family was the plain of Hungary.)

Clearly, the work of scholars like Nichols and Renfrew is highly speculative, and it is certainly deeply controversial. More than a few linguists would argue that trying to do any linguistic work at all at this kind of time depth, let alone constructing such ambitious grand schemes, is a simple waste of time. The critics may well be right. Still, as always, it would be wise not to be too hasty with our criticism: if it *is* possible to extract from the language map of the world any information about the peopling of the planet, then we certainly want to find that information, and we won't find it unless somebody looks for it.

Very different is the work of the geneticist Luigi Luca Cavalli-Sforza. Cavalli-Sforza has taken samples of the genes of groups of people all over the planet. From his data, he has attempted to construct a *phylogenetic tree* – that is, by assuming that populations that are genetically similar must have a recent common ancestor, while people who are genetically different must have separated much earlier from their last common ancestor, he has produced a tree which purports to show how our earliest ancestors spread out over the world, splitting into distinct populations as they spread. This genetic tree he has compared with an inventory of recognized and postulated language families, to see if they match up at all well. His result is shown in Fig. 13.3.

Of the linguistic phyla listed, most are generally accepted, but Altaic is controversial, Austric and Indo-Pacific are very controversial, and Amerind, as we have seen, is angrily rejected by most specialists; the Nostratic and Eurasiatic superphyla, of course, remain conjectures. Cavalli-Sforza and his colleagues conclude that the match-up is impressive; they declare that 'every linguistic phylum corresponds to only one of the six major genetic clusters defined by the [genetic] tree' – though they later qualify this statement. They

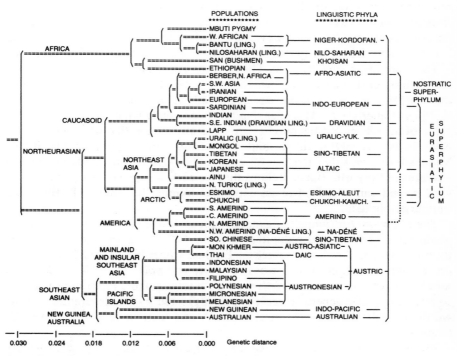

Fig. 13.3 Cavalli-Sforza's trees for genes and languages

therefore propose that the distribution of language families on the planet, in large measure, directly reflects the original peopling of the planet.

This work, and these conclusions, have been fiercely attacked, from every quarter and for every possible reason. Among other things, the critics declare that Cavalli-Sforza's methodology is unsatisfactory, that his data are inadequate, that a number of contrary cases are ignored or glossed over, and, most damningly of all, that the claimed match is illusory. (This last point is dealt with in one of the exercises.) While some biologists and anthropologists have pronounced themselves impressed by Cavalli-Sforza's findings, most other scholars, including practically all linguists who have expressed an opinion, have taken an extremely negative view: they consider that Cavalli-Sforza has established nothing.

In sum, then, the various attempts at seeing a record of the original peopling of the earth in the modern distribution of language families are all controversial at best, and some of them have attracted some very harsh words.

13.8   *Worldwide loan words?*

As we saw in Chapter 2, it is possible for a loan word to spread over a phenomenal portion of the planet: such words as *whisky*, *bus*, *telephone*, *spaghetti*, and *tobacco*, of various origins, can now be found in languages on every continent. These, however, are modern loan words. Is it possible that some loans might have enjoyed a comparable success thousands of years ago?

There are those who think so. The obvious candidates, of course, are words for technological innovations which were created in one locality but which then spread over much of the world, possibly taking their names with them.

Robert Bauer (1993–4) argues that this is precisely what happened with the name of the wheel. Archaeologists are generally agreed that wheeled vehicles were invented only once (around 5000–6000 years ago, probably in the Middle East), and that the use of wheels then spread out gradually over a vast area of the earth. Bauer reckons that the earliest name of the wheel spread with it, and can be found in an enormous number of languages. Here is a sample of his data.

The PIE word for 'wheel' is generally reconstructed as $*k^w elo\text{-}s$, with an *o*-grade form $*k^w olo\text{-}s$ and reduplicated forms $*k^w ek^w lo\text{-}s$ and $*k^w ok^w lo\text{-}s$. The third of these is the direct source of English *wheel* (Old English *hweowol*); others yield (via Greek) such words as *cycle* and *pole*. The PIE words are in turn derived from a root $*k^w el\text{-}$ 'revolve', 'move round'. From the same PIE source, it is either generally accepted or suggested by Bauer, are derived the words for 'wheel', 'round', 'circle', 'ball', and 'cart' in a wide range of IE languages.

But Bauer's point is that words of similar form and meaning occur widely outside IE. He cites (from various sources) such forms as Proto-Uralic *kola* 'circle', Proto-North-Caucasian *$gw\bar{e}lgV$ 'round', Proto-Kartvelian *$k'wer$-/ *$k'wal$- 'round', Proto-Dravidian *$ku/\bar{u}l$- 'round, whirl', Proto-Afro-Asiatic *$k'(w)l$ 'round, revolve', Proto-Sino-Tibetan *$k^w(r)e\dagger$ 'roll, wind', Proto-Mongolian *$koli$- 'cause to revolve', and Proto-Tungisic *$xolo$- 'rotate, revolve', as well as words in individual languages such as Korean *kulda* 'roll' (intr.), Japanese *kuruma* 'wheel, cart, wagon', Malay *golek* 'round', and Muong (Austro-Asiatic) *kwal* 'revolve', among many others. (Note, however, that many of these items are among those assigned by Illich-Svitych to a single PN etymon.)

Bauer's proposal is by no means implausible. There seems to be no reason why the name of the wheel should not have accompanied the object itself, just as the name of the telephone has done in modern times. Nevertheless, we cannot immediately rule out coincidence as the source of at least some of Bauer's data. A useful control would be to check the languages spoken in regions into which knowledge of the wheel never spread before modern times, to see if they too show a comparable frequency of words for 'round' or 'revolve' of the same general form. Such regions exist: Australia and the Americas. In fact, Bauer himself cites a few words from North American and Australian languages, apparently unaware of the absence of the wheel on those continents, such as Tunica *kúra* 'turn' and Pandjima *kuru kuru* 'round'. Clearly no firm conclusions can be drawn without a great deal more evidence, and there is at least some danger that such investigations will fall foul of the same problem as Ruhlen's Proto-World etymologies: the problem of noting only confirming instances.

Further reading

Ruhlen (1991) provides a historical survey of the efforts at identifying and characterizing language families, including many proposals of remote relations. Ruhlen (1994) presents a reasonable sample of recent work on remote relations, but all this work is by enthusiasts and there are no attempts at criticism. Trask (1995) is a deeply critical look at certain aspects of the Déné-Caucasian hypothesis. Kaiser and Shevoroshkin (1988) is an approachable introduction to the Nostratic hypothesis, and Manaster-Ramer (1993) provides a critical but sympathetic review of the hypothesis. Bomhard's very different version of Nostratic is presented in Bomhard (1990) and in the massive Bomhard and Kerns (1994). The Amerind hypothesis is presented in Greenberg (1987), while Greenberg *et al.* (1987) is a briefer presentation followed by a panel discussion with critics, and Greenberg and Ruhlen (1992) is a brief popular account. Reviews (mostly hostile) of Greenberg's work include Campbell (1988), Adelaar (1989), and Matisoff (1990). Greenberg (1989) is a reply to Campbell. The confluence of the linguistic, dental, and genetic evidence is presented in Greenberg *et al.* (1986), which is also a panel discussion involving a number of critics. Popular accounts of all these controversies are P. E. Ross (1991) and Wright (1991), while the much briefer Lewin (1990) deals only with Greenberg. Cavalli-Sforza's correlations are presented in Cavalli-Sforza *et al.* (1988) and briefly summarized in popular form in Cavalli-Sforza (1991); this work is critically discussed in O'Grady *et al.* (1989) (very brief) and in Bateman *et al.* (1990) (long and detailed). The entire Amerind issue is critically surveyed in McMahon and McMahon (1995). Johanna Nichols's typological approach is presented in Nichols (1992), and a discussion of the Americas in particular in Nichols (1990). Colin Renfrew's interpretation of the IE spread is developed in Renfrew (1987) and summarized in Renfrew (1989), while his global hypothesis is presented in Renfrew (1992, 1995) and given a popular presentation in Renfrew (1994). A brief popular account of Proto-World, by one of its proponents, is Shevoroshkin (1990); the notion is criticized in Salmons (1992) and Picard (1995a). The global loan words for 'wheel' are presented in R. S. Bauer (1993–4), while R. S. Bauer (1992) does the same for 'soap'.

Exercises

Exercise 13.1

The mathematical linguist Donald Ringe has drawn attention to the distribution of proposed cognates in Nostratic and in IE (Ringe 1995). His procedure is as follows. First, he consults the standard dictionary of PIE roots (which contains 2008 roots) to find out, for each proposed PIE root, how many of the fourteen recognized branches of IE that root is attested in: a minimum of two (since a root found in only one branch is not assigned to PIE) and a maximum of fourteen. Then, using standard procedures in probability theory, he asks the following question: by chance alone, how many apparently acceptable matches would we expect to find that are shared between exactly two branches, between exactly three branches, and so on, up to exactly fourteen branches. This, of course, depends upon the initial probability that a given item in one branch will be judged to have a satisfactory match in another branch. By trial and error, he settles on a figure of 0.2 probability, because this gives the best available match to the empirical data. For the 2008 roots, he then calculates how many chance matches we would expect between just two languages, between just three languages, and so on. The distribution that results is what mathematicians call the **binomial distribution**. Table 13.3 shows the number of matches expected from the binomial distribution (that is, by chance) and the actual number of matches found in the dictionary. The symbol '≈ 0' means 'virtually nil'. Plot these results on a graph. How well does the empirical distribution match the binomial distribution?

Ringe now does the same thing for the 205 proposed Proto-Nostratic roots recognized in Illich-Svitych's dictionary as found in at least two branches, excluding additional roots marked as doubtful by the editor. Here he finds that the binomial distribution gives the best match with the empirical data when the initial probability is set at 0.4. Table 13.4 shows the results (Nostratic has only six branches). Plot these results in the same way. How well does the empirical distribution match the binomial distribution?

Compare and discuss the two results. Do these results, in your view, lead to any conclusions? Does it matter that Ringe has used a figure of 0.4 (40 per cent) for the probability that Illich-Svitych might, for a given item, be prepared to accept some item in another branch as a cognate?

The last line of the Nostratic table shows that we would expect only one match among all six branches by chance alone, whereas Illich-Svitych recognizes five – that is, five times as many as would be expected by chance alone. Here are those five putative PN roots: *$calu$ 'split, cut', *da (locative particle), *$?i$ ~ *$?e$ (demonstrative pronoun), *ja 'which' (interrogative and relative) and *$kaba$ ~ *$ka'pa$ 'grasp'. Does anything strike you about these five roots? What obvious question might you ask about the remaining 200

Table 13.3

Number of matches found in a given number of branches	Binomial (chance)	Empirical
2	440	440
3	440	407
4	303	297
5	151	221
6	57	151
7	16	146
8	3.5	112
9	0.5	85
10	≈ 0	76
11	≈ 0	36
12	≈ 0	28
13	≈ 0	8
14	≈ 0	1

Table 13.4

Number of matches found in a given number of branches	Binomial (chance)	Empirical
2	84	84
3	75	70
4	37	37
5	10	9
6	1	5

roots? What different answers are possible, and how would you interpret each?

Exercise 13.2

Take a close look at Figure 13.5, showing Cavalli-Sforza's proposed matchup between genetic and linguistic trees. Note the following points:

(a) The Mbuti Pygmies no longer have a language of their own; they speak the languages of their Bantu neighbours, for whom they work.

(b) The populations marked 'ling.' are in fact defined by their languages, and not by their genes.

(c) The Altaic, Austric, and Indo-Pacific phyla are all controversial or worse among linguists; Amerind is *extremely* controversial; Nostratic is generally regarded as no more than a hypothesis; no evidence has yet been published in support of Eurasiatic.

(d) A number of potentially important populations are absent from the tree: the Uralic-speaking Hungarians (in Europe), the Austronesian-speakers of New Guinea, the Sino-Tibetan-speakers of north China, and others.

Now ask yourself the following questions:

(a) How well does each of the following linguistic families match the genetic tree: Niger-Kordofanian; Afro-Asiatic; Indo-European; Uralic; Altaic; Sino-Tibetan (note this one especially); Austronesian?

(b) Eight linguistic families are each connected with only a single bottom-most branch of the genetic tree: Nilo-Saharan, Khoisan, Dravidian, Eskimo-Aleut, Chukchi-Kamchatkan, Na-Déné, Indo-Pacific, and Australian. If we ignore the Austric hypothesis, we can add Austro-Asiatic and Daic to this list. Is it reasonable to conclude that an observation that a single language family is spoken by a single population constitutes an interesting correlation?

In view of your answers, how well would you say the genetic groupings correlate with the linguistic ones? Has Cavalli-Sforza made a strong case?

Exercise 13.3

Greenberg and Ruhlen (1992) argue that a Proto-Amerind root *maliq'a* 'swallow, throat' is widely attested throughout the Americas, and they present the data in Table 13.5 as evidence. The authors argue as follows. They ask: what is the probability that a word of the form $m \ldots L \ldots K$, with a suitable meaning, will occur purely by chance in six different families, where L is /l/ or /r/ and K is any velar or uvular consonant? Making some simple assumptions, they estimate this probability at about one in ten billion. They therefore conclude that their data cannot consist of chance resemblances and

Table 13.5

Family	Language	Form	Meaning
Almosan	Halkomelem	*məlqw*	'throat'
	Kwakwala	*m'lχw-'id*	'chew food for a baby'
	Kutenai	*u'mqolh*	'swallow'
Penutian	Chinook	*mlqw-tan*	'cheek'
	Takelma	*mülk'*	'swallow'
	Tfaltik	*milq*	'swallow'
	Mixe	*amu'ul*	'suck'
Hokan	Mohave	*mal^{y}aqé*	'throat'
	Walapei	*malqi'*	'throat, neck'
	Akwa'ala	*milqi*	'neck'
Chibchan	Cuna	*murki-*	'swallow'
Andean	Quechua	*malq'a*	'throat'
	Aymara	*mal^{y}q'a*	'swallow; throat'
Macro-Tucanoan	Iranshe	*moke'i*	'neck'
Equatorial	Guamo	*mirko*	'drink'
Macro-Carib	Surinam	*e'mōkï*	'swallow'
	Faai	*mekeli*	'nape of the neck'
	Kaliana	*imukulali*	'throat'

must represent genuine cognates, and that these data therefore support the Amerind hypothesis.

Assuming that the authors' data are impeccable, try to evaluate their argument as critically as you can. Does their case look persuasive, or can you see serious holes in it?

The authors then go on to suggest that their posited root also occurs widely in other language families: as evidence, they cite Central Yupik (Eskimo-Aleut family) *melug-* 'suck', Proto-Afro-Asiatic **mlg* 'suck, breast, udder', Proto-Indo-European **melg-* 'milk', Proto-Finno-Ugric **mälke* 'breast', Tamil (Dravidian) *melku* 'chew', Malayalam (Dravidian) *melluka* 'chew', and Kurux (Dravidian) *melkhā* 'throat'. Are you persuaded that these words must represent the same root as before? Why or why not?

Not cited by the authors is Basque *milika* 'act of licking, act of tasting' (Basque is genetically isolated). Is this word likely to be relevant to the authors' case?

Appendix: The Swadesh 200-word list

Note: Items in the 100-word list are listed in boldface, including seven words not included in the 200-word list. Source: Gudschinsky (1956).

1. **all**
2. and
3. animal
4. **ashes**
5. at
6. back
7. bad
8. **bark**
9. because
10. **belly**
11. **big**
12. **bird**
13. **bite**
14. **black**
15. **blood**
16. blow (v.)
17. **bone**
18. breathe
19. **burn**
20. child
21. **cloud**
22. **cold**
23. **come**
24. count
25. cut (v.)
26. day
27. **die**
28. dig
29. dirty
30. **dog**
31. **drink**
32. **dry**
33. dull (blunt)
34. dust
35. **ear**
36. **earth**
37. **eat**
38. **egg**
39. **eye**
40. fall (v.)
41. far
42. **fat**/grease
43. father
44. fear (v.)
45. **feather**
46. few
47. fight (v.)
48. **fire**
49. **fish**
50. five
51. float
52. flow
53. flower
54. **fly** (v.)
55. fog
56. **foot**
57. four
58. freeze
59. fruit
60. **give**
61. **good**
62. grass
63. **green**
64. guts
65. **hair**
66. **hand**
67. he
68. **head**
69. **hear**
70. **heart**
71. heavy
72. here
73. hit
74. hold/take
75. how
76. hunt
77. husband
78. **I**
79. ice
80. if
81. in
82. **kill**
83. **know**
84. lake
85. laugh
86. **leaf**
87. left (side)
88. leg
89. **lie** (recline)
90. live
91. **liver**
92. **long**
93. **louse**
94. **man/male**
95. **many**
96. **meat/flesh**
97. mother
98. **mountain**
99. **mouth**
100. **name**
101. narrow
102. near
103. **neck**
104. **new**
105. **night**
106. **nose**
107. **not**
108. old
109. **one**
110. other
111. **person**
112. play
113. pull
114. push
115. **rain**
116. **red**

117. right (correct)
118. right (side)
119. river
120. **road**
121. **root**
122. rope
123. rotten
124. rub
125. salt
126. **sand**
127. **say**
128. scratch
129. sea
130. **see**
131. **seed**
132. sew
133. sharp
134. short
135. sing
136. **sit**
137. **skin**
138. sky
139. **sleep**

140. **small**
141. smell (v.)
142. **smoke**
143. smooth
144. snake
145. snow
146. some
147. spit
148. split
149. squeeze
150. stab/pierce
151. **stand**
152. **star**
153. stick
154. **stone**
155. straight
156. suck
157. **sun**
158. swell
159. **swim**
160. **tail**
161. **that**
162. there

163. they
164. thick
165. thin
166. think
167. **this**
168. **thou**
169. three
170. throw
171. tie
172. **tongue**
173. **tooth**
174. **tree**
175. turn
176. **two**
177. vomit
178. **walk**
179. **warm**
180. wash
181. **water**
182. **we**
183. wet
184. **what**
185. when

186. where
187. **white**
188. **who**
189. wide
190. wife
191. wind
192. wing
193. wipe
194. with
195. **woman**
196. woods
197. worm
198. ye
199. year
200. **yellow**
201. **breast**
202. **claw**
203. **full**
204. **horn**
205. **knee**
206. **moon**
207. **round**

References

Adelaar, Willem F. H. 1989: Review of Greenberg (1987). *Lingua* 78, 249–55.

Adams, Valerie 1973: *An introduction to modern English word-formation*. London: Longman.

Aitchison, Jean 1980: Review of Lightfoot (1979). *Linguistics* 18, 137–46.

Allen, W. Sidney 1968: *Vox Graeca: a guide to the pronunciation of classical Greek*. Cambridge: Cambridge University Press.

Anderson, James M. 1973: *Structural aspects of language change*. London: Longman.

Anderson, Stephen 1977: On mechanisms by which languages become ergative. In Li (1977), 317–63.

Anttila, Raimo 1973: Internal reconstruction and Finno-Ugric (Finnish). In Thomas A. Sebeok (ed.), *Current trends in linguistics*. The Hague: Mouton, XI, pp. 317–53.

—— 1977: *Analogy*. The Hague: Mouton.

—— 1988: *An introduction to historical and comparative linguistics*. 2nd edn. New York: Macmillan.

Ash, S. and Myhill, J. 1986: Linguistic correlates of inter-ethnic contact. In David Sankoff (ed.), *Diversity and diachrony*. Amsterdam: John Benjamins, 33–44.

Asher, R. E. (ed.) 1994: *The encyclopedia of language and linguistics*. 10 vols. Oxford: Pergamon Press.

Atwood, E. Bagby 1953: *A survey of verb forms in the eastern United States*. Ann Arbor: University of Michigan Press.

Baldi, Philip 1983: *An introduction to the Indo-European Languages*. Carbondale, IL: Southern Illinois University Press.

—— (ed.) 1990: *Linguistic change and reconstruction methodology*. Berlin: Mouton de Gruyter.

—— (ed.) 1991a: *Patterns of change, change of patterns: linguistic change and reconstruction methodology*. Berlin: Mouton de Gruyter.

—— 1991b: Introduction: the comparative method. In Baldi (1991a), 1–13.

Bammesberger, A. 1984: *English etymology*. Heidelberg: Carl Winter.

Bateman, Richard, Goddard, Ives, O'Grady, Richard, Funk, V. A., Mooi, Rich, Kress, W. John, and Cannell, Peter 1990: Speaking of forked tongues: the feasibility of reconciling human phylogeny and the history of language. *Current Anthropology* 31, 1–183.

Bauer, Laurie, 1983: *English word-formation*. Cambridge: Cambridge University Press.

—— 1988: *Introducing linguistic morphology*. Edinburgh: Edinburgh University Press.

—— 1994: *Watching English change*. London: Longman.

Bauer, Robert S. 1992: *SOAP* rings the globe. *Linguistics of the Tibeto-Burman Area* 15(1), 125–37.

—— 1993–4: Global etymology of *KOLO 'wheel'. *Dhumbadji!* 1(3), 3–17.

Baugh, Albert C. and Cable, Thomas 1993: *A history of the English language*. 4th edn. London: Routledge.

Beekes, Robert S. 1984: Laryngeal developments: a survey. In Alfred Bammesberger (ed.), *Die Laryngealtheorie und die Rekonstruktion des indogermanischen Laut- und Formensystems*. Heidelberg: Winter, 59–105.

—— 1989: The nature of the Proto-Indo-European laryngeals. In Theo Vennemann (ed.), *The new sound of Indo-European: essays in phonological reconstruction*. Berlin: Mouton de Gruyter, 23–33.

Bender, M. Lionel 1981: Some Nilo-Saharan isoglosses. In Thilo C. Schadeberg and M. Lionel Bender (eds), *Nilo-Saharan*. Dordrecht: Foris.

Benedict, Paul 1942: Thai, Kadai, and Indonesian: a new alignment in southeastern Asia. *American Anthropologist* 44, 576–601.

—— 1990: *Japanese-Austro-Tai*. Ann Arbor: University of Michigan Press.

Bengtson, John 1991: Macro-Caucasian phonology (part I). In Shevoroshkin (1991), 142–61.

Bennett, Paul 1979: Observations on the transparency principle. *Linguistics* 17, 843–61.

Benveniste, Émile 1954: Problèmes sémantiques de la réconstruction. *Word* 10, 251–64. English translation Semantic problems in reconstruction in Émile Benveniste (1971), *Problems in general linguistics*. Coral Gables: University of Miami Press, 249–64.

—— 1973: *Indo-European language and society*. Coral Gables: University of Miami Press.

Bergsland, Knut and Vogt, Hans 1962: On the validity of glottochronology. *Current Anthropology* 3, 115–53.

Bloomfield, Leonard 1925: On the sound system of central Algonquian. *Language* 1, 130–56.

—— 1933: *Language*. New York: Holt, Rinehart & Winston.

—— 1946: Algonquian. In Henry Hoijer *et al.* (eds), *Linguistic structures of native America*. Viking Fund Publications in Anthropology 6. New York: Viking, 85–129.

Blust, Robert 1978: Review of Thomas A. Sebeok (ed.), *Current trends in linguistics VIII: linguistics in Oceania. Language* 54, 467–80.

Bolton, W. F. and Crystal, David (eds) 1987: *The Penguin history of literature, x. The English language*. London: Penguin.

Bomhard, Allan R. 1990: A survey of the comparative phonology of the so-called 'Nostratic' languages. In Philip Baldi (ed.), *Linguistic change and reconstruction methodology*. The Hague: Mouton de Gruyter, 331–58.

—— Kerns, John C. 1994: *The Nostratic macrofamily: a study in distant linguistic relationship*. The Hague: Mouton de Gruyter.

Bonaparte, Prince Louis-Lucien 1869: *Deux cartes des sept provinces basques*. London: privately printed.

Borgström, Carl Hj. 1954: Internal reconstruction of Pre-Indo-European word-forms. *Word* 10, 275–87.

Boyd 1978: À propos des ressemblances lexicales entre langues niger-congo et nilo-sahariennes, in *Études comparatives*. Paris.

Bright, William (ed.) 1992: *International encyclopedia of linguistics*. 4 vols. Oxford: Oxford University Press.

Buck, Carl Darling 1949: *A dictionary of selected synonyms in the principal Indo-European languages: a contribution to the history of ideas*. Chicago: University of Chicago Press.

Bybee, Joan, Perkins, Revere, and Pagliuca, William 1994: *The evolution of grammar:*

tense, aspect and modality in the languages of the world. Chicago: University of Chicago Press.

Bynon, Theodora 1977: *Historical linguistics*. Cambridge: Cambridge University Press.

Cameron, Kenneth 1961: *English place-names*. London: Methuen.

——1988: *English place-names*. 4th edn. London: Methuen.

Campbell, Lyle 1988: Review of Greenberg (1987). *Language* 64, 591–615.

——Mithun, Marianne (eds) 1979: *The languages of native America*. Austin: University of Texas Press.

——1980: Syntactic reconstruction: priorities and pitfalls. *Folia Linguistica Historica* 1, 19–40.

Cardona, George, Hoenigswald, Henry M., and Senn, Alfred (eds) 1970: *Indo-European and Indo-Europeans*. Philadelphia: University of Pennsylvania Press.

Cavalli-Sforza, Luigi Luca 1991: Genes, peoples and languages. *Scientific American* (November), 72–8.

——Piazza, Alberto, Menozzi, Paolo, and Mountain, Joanna 1988: Reconstruction of human evolution: bringing together genetic, archaeological, and linguistic data. *Proceedings of the National Academy of Sciences of the USA* 85, 6002–6.

Cedergren, Henrietta 1973: The interplay of social and linguistic factors in Panama. Ph.D. dissertation, Cornell University.

——1984: Panama revisited: sound change in real time. Paper given at NAVE, Philadelphia.

Chafe, Wallace L. 1959: Internal reconstruction in Seneca. *Language* 35, 477–95.

Chambers, J. K. 1995: *Sociolinguistic theory*. Oxford: Blackwell.

——Trudgill, Peter 1980: *Dialectology*. Cambridge: Cambridge University Press.

Chen, Matthew and Wang, William 1975: Sound change: actuation and implementation. *Language* 51, 255–81.

Christian, Donna, 1988: Language planning: the view from linguistics. In Newmeyer (1988), IV, pp 193–209.

Chung, Sandra,1978: *Case marking and grammatical relations in Polynesian*. Austin: University of Texas Press.

Čirikba, Vjačeslav A. 1985: Baskskij i severokavkazskie jazyki [Basque and the North Caucasian languages]. In B. B. Pietrovskij (ed.), *Drevnjaja Anatolija* [*Ancient Anatolia*]. Moscow: Nauka, 95–105.

Coates, Richard A. 1995: The first American placename in England: *Pimlico*. *Names* 43, 213–27.

Collinder, Björn 1965: *An introduction to the Uralic languages*. Berkeley: University of California Press.

Comrie, Bernard 1978: Ergativity. In W. P. Lehmann (ed.), *Syntactic typology: studies in the phenomenology of language*. Austin: University of Texas Press, 329–74.

——1989: *Language universals and linguistic typology*. 2nd edn. Oxford: Basil Blackwell.

Corominas, Juan and Pascual, José A. 1980: *Diccionario crítico etimológico Castellano e Hispánico*. 6 vols. Madrid: Gredos.

Croft, William 1990: *Typology and universals*. Cambridge: Cambridge University Press.

Crothers, John 1978: Typology: universals of vowel systems. In Greenberg *et al.* (1978), II, pp. 93–152.

Crowley, Terry 1992: *An introduction to historical linguistics*, 2nd edn. Oxford: Oxford University Press.

——Dixon, Robert M. W. 1981: Tasmanian. In R. M. W. Dixon and Barry J. Blake (eds), *Handbook of Australian languages* 2. Amsterdam: John Benjamins, and Canberra: Australian National University Press.

Crystal, David 1987: *The Cambridge encyclopedia of language*. Cambridge: Cambridge University Press.
—— 1988: *The English language*. London: Penguin.
—— 1995: *The Cambridge encyclopaedia of the English language*. Cambridge: Cambridge University Press.
Davis, Lawrence M. 1983: *English dialectology: an introduction*. University, AL: University of Alabama Press.
Dauzat, Albert 1922: *La géographie linguistique*. Paris: Flammarion.
Denison, David 1993: *English historical syntax*. London: Longman.
Diakonov, Igor M. and Starostin, Sergei 1986: *Hurro-Urartian as an eastern Caucasian language*. Munich: Kitzinger.
Dillard, J. L. 1992: *A history of American English*. London: Longman.
Dixon, Robert M. W. 1979: Ergativity. *Language* 55, 59–138.
—— 1980: *The languages of Australia*. Cambridge: Cambridge University Press.
—— (ed.) 1987: *Studies in ergativity*. Amsterdam: North Holland.
—— 1994: *Ergativity*. Cambridge: Cambridge University Press.
Dorian, Nancy C. 1981: *Language death: the life cycle of a Scottish Gaelic dialect*. Philadelphia: University of Pennsylvania Press.
—— (ed.) 1989: *Investigating obsolescence: studies in language contraction and death*. Cambridge: Cambridge University Press.
Dressler, Wolfgang U. 1985a: *Morphonology*. Ann Arbor: Karoma.
—— 1985b: On the predictiveness of natural morphology. *Journal of Linguistics* 21, 321–37.
—— 1988: Language death. In Newmeyer (1988), IV, pp. 184–92.
—— 1991: The sociolinguistic and patholinguistic attrition of Breton phonology, morphology and morphonology. In Seliger and Vago (1991), 99–112.
Dressler, Wolfgang U. and Wodak-Leodolter, R. (eds) 1977: *Language death*. Special number of *International Journal of the Sociology of Language* 12.
Edwards, John 1994: *Multilingualism*. London: Routledge.
Emeneau, Murray B. 1980: *Language and linguistic area: essays*, ed. Anwar S. Dil. Stanford: Stanford University Press.
Embleton, Sheila 1986: *Statistics in historical linguistics*. Bochum: Brockmeyer.
Ernout, A. and Meillet, Antoine 1959: *Dictionnaire etymologique de la langue latine: histoire des mots*. Paris: Klincksieck.
Foley, William A. 1988: Language birth: the processes of pidginization and creolization. In Newmeyer (1988), IV, pp. 162–83.
Fox, Anthony 1995: *Linguistic reconstruction: an introduction to theory and method*. Oxford: Oxford University Press.
Francis, W. N. 1983: *Dialectology*. London: Longman.
Freeborn, Dennis 1992: *From Old English to standard English*. Houndmills, Basingstoke, Hants: Macmillan.
Gamkrelidze, Thomas V. and Ivanov, Vyacheslav V. 1973: Sprachtypologie und die Rekonstruktion der gemeinindg. Verschlüsse. *Phonetica* 27, 150–6.
—— 1990: The early history of the Indo-European languages. *Scientific American* 262 (March), 82–9.
Gelling, Margaret 1984: *Place-names in the landscape*. London: J. M. Dent & Sons.
—— 1988: *Signposts to the past: place-names and the history of England*. 2nd edn. Chichester: Phillimore.
George, Ken 1993: Alternative French. In Sanders (1993), pp. 155–70.
Gildea, Spike 1993: The development of tense markers from demonstrative pronouns in Panare (Cariban). *Studies in language* 17, 53–73.
Gilliéron, Jules 1902–10: *Atlas linguistique de France*. 13 vols. Paris: Champion.
Givón, Talmy 1977: The drift from VSO to SVO in biblical Hebrew: the pragmatics of tense-aspect. In Li (1977), 181–254.

Greenberg, Joseph H. 1953: Historical linguistics and unwritten languages. In A. L. Kroeber (ed.), *Anthropology Today*. Chicago: University of Chicago Press.

—— 1963a: Some universals of grammar with particular reference to the order of meaningful elements. In Joseph H. Greenberg (ed.), *Universals of Language*. Cambridge, MA: MIT Press, 73–113.

—— 1963b: *The languages of Africa*. Bloomington: Indiana University Press.

—— 1971: The Indo-Pacific hypothesis. In Thomas A. Sebeok (ed.), *Current trends in linguistics VIII: linguistics in Oceania*. The Hague: Mouton, 807–71.

—— 1987: *Language in the Americas*. Stanford: Stanford University Press.

—— 1989: Classification of American Indian languages: a reply to Campbell. *Language* 65, 107–14.

——Ruhlen, Merritt 1992: Linguistic origins of native Americans. *Scientific American* (November), 60–5.

——Ferguson, Charles A. and Moravcsik Edith, (eds) 1978: *Universals of human language*. 4 vols. Stanford: Stanford University Press.

——Turner, Christy G., II, and Zegura, Stephen L. 1986: The settlement of the Americas: a comparison of the linguistic, dental, and genetic evidence. *Current Anthropology* 27, 477–97.

——*et al.* 1987: Review and discussion of Greenberg (1987). *Current Anthropology* 28, 647–67.

Gregersen, Edgar A. 1972: Kongo-Saharan. *Journal of African Languages* 11, 69–89.

Gregerson, Kenneth and Hartzler, Margaret 1987: Towards a reconstruction of Proto-Tabla-Sentani phonology. *Oceanic Linguistics* 26, 1–29.

Grimes, B. F. 1992: *Ethnologue: languages of the world*. 12th edn. Dallas: Summer Institute of Linguistics.

Gudschinsky, Sarah C. 1956: The ABC's of lexicostatistics (glottochronology). *Word* 12, 175–220.

Gumperz, John and Wilson Robert, 1971: Convergence and creolization: a case from the Indo-Aryan/Dravidian border in India. In Dell Hymes (ed.), *Pidginization and creolization of languages*. Cambridge: Cambridge University Press, 151–67.

Hahn, Reinhard 1991: Diachronic aspects of regular disharmony in modern Uyghur. In William G. Boltz and Michael C. Shapiro (eds), *Studies in the historical phonology of Asian languages*. Amsterdam: John Benjamins, 68–101.

Hale, Kenneth 1976: Phonological developments in particular northern Paman languages. In Peter Sutton (ed.), *Languages of Cape York*. Canberra: Australian Institute of Aboriginal Studies, 7–40.

Hale, Ken *et al.* 1992: Endangered languages. *Language* 68, 1–42.

Hall, Robert A. 1950: The reconstruction of Proto-Romance. *Language* 26, 63–85. Reprinted in Martin Joos (ed.) (1957), *Readings in linguistics I*. Chicago: University of Chicago Press, 303–14.

—— 1976: *Proto-Romance phonology*. New York: Elsevier.

Halle, Morris 1962: Phonology in generative grammar. *Word* 18, 54–72. Reprinted in Jerry A. Fodor and Jerrold J. Katz (eds) (1964), *The structure of language: readings in the philosophy of language*. Englewood Cliffs, NJ: Prentice-Hall, 334–52.

Harris, Alice C. and Campbell, Lyle 1995: *Historical syntax in cross-linguistic perspective*. Cambridge: Cambridge University Press.

Harris, Martin 1978: *The evolution of French syntax: a comparative approach*. London: Longman.

Haugen, Einar 1966: Dialect, language, nation. *American anthropologist* 68, 922–35. Reprinted in J. B. Pride and J. Holmes (eds) (1972), *Sociolinguistics*. Harmondsworth, Middx: Penguin, 97–112.

Hawkins, John 1983: *Word order universals*. New York: Academic Press.

Heine, Bernd 1992: Grammaticalization chains. *Studies in language* 16, 335–68.

Hindley, Reg 1990: *The death of the Irish language: a qualified obituary*. London: Routledge.

Hock, Hans Henrich 1986: *Principles of historical linguistics*. The Hague: Mouton de Gruyter.

Hockett, Charles F. 1955: *A manual of phonology*. Baltimore: Waverley Press.

Hoenigswald, Henry M. 1944: Internal reconstruction. *Studies in linguistics* 2, 78–87.

—— 1950: The principal step in comparative grammar. *Language* 22, 138–143. Reprinted in Martin Joos (ed.) (1957), *Readings in linguistics I*. Chicago: University of Chicago Press, 298–302.

—— 1960: *Language change and linguistic reconstruction*. Chicago: University of Chicago Press.

—— 1973: The comparative method. In Thomas A. Sebeok, *Current trends in linguistics*. The Hague: Mouton, III, p. 51–62.

Holm, John 1988: *Pidgins and Creoles*, i. *Theory and structure*. Cambridge University Press.

—— 1989: *Pidgins and creoles*, ii. *Reference survey*. Cambridge: Cambridge University Press.

Holmes, Janet 1992: *An introduction to sociolinguistics*. London: Longman.

Hopper, Paul J. 1973: Glottalized and murmured occlusives in IE. *Glossa* 7, 141–66.

—— Traugott, Elizabeth Closs 1993: *Grammaticalization*. Cambridge: Cambridge University Press.

Horne, Kibbey M. 1966: *Language typology, 19th and 20th century views*. Washington: Georgetown University Press.

Howard, Philip 1977: *New words for old*. London: Hamish Hamilton.

Hudson, Richard A. 1980: *Sociolinguistics*. Cambridge: Cambridge University Press.

Hughes, Arthur and Trudgill, Peter 1979: *English accents and dialects*. London: Edward Arnold.

Jeffers, Robert J. and Lehiste, Ilse 1979: *Principles and methods for historical linguistics*. Cambridge, Mass.: MIT Press.

Jonsson, H. 1978: *The laryngeal theory: a critical survey*. Lund: Gleerup.

Kaiser, Mark and Shevoroshkin, Vitaly 1988: Nostratic. *Annual Review of Anthropology* 17, 309–29.

Katamba, Francis 1994: *English words*. London: Routledge.

Keiler, Allan R. 1970: *A phonological study of the Indo-European laryngeals*. The Hague: Mouton.

Keller, R. E. 1978: *The German language*. London: Faber & Faber.

King, Robert D. 1969: *Historical linguistics and generative grammar*. Englewood Cliffs, NJ: Prentice-Hall.

Kiparsky, Paul 1968a: Linguistic universals and language change. In Emmon Bach and Robert T. Harms (eds), *Universals in linguistic theory*. New York: Holt, Rinehart & Winston, 171–202.

—— 1968b: *How abstract is phonology?* Bloomington, IN: Indiana University Linguistics Club. Reprinted in O. Fujimura (ed.) (1974), *Three dimensions of linguistic theory*. Tokyo: TEC, 5–56.

—— 1971: Historical linguistics. In William Orr Dingwall (ed.), *A survey of linguistic science*. College Park: University of Maryland, 576–649.

—— 1973: *Abstractness, opacity and global rules*. Bloomington, IN: Indiana University Linguistics Club. Reprinted in O. Fujimura (ed.) (1974), *Three dimensions of linguistic theory*. Tokyo: TEC, 57–86.

—— 1988: Phonological change. In Newmeyer (1988), I, pp. 363–15.

Kirk, John M., Sanderson, Stewart and Widdowson, J. D. A. (eds) 1985: *Studies in linguistic geography: the dialects of English in Britain and Ireland*. London: Croom Helm.

Klein, E. 1971: *A comprehensive etymological dictionary of the English language.* Amsterdam: Elsevier.

Kleiner, Kurt 1994: Echoes of ancient Africa in our speech? *New Scientist* (23 April), p. 10.

Krantz, Grover S. 1988: *Geographical development of European languages.* New York: Peter Lang.

Kurath, Hans 1949: *Word geography of the eastern United States.* Ann Arbor: University of Michigan Press.

Kurath, Hans and McDavid, Raven I. 1961: *The pronunciation of English in the Atlantic states.* Ann Arbor: University of Michigan Press.

Kuryłowicz, Jerzy 1927: ə indoeuropéen et ḫ hittite. In [no editor], *Symbolae grammaticae in honorem Ioannis Rozwadoswki*, Krakow: Gebethner & Wolff, I, pp. 95–104.

—— 1947: La nature des procès dits analogiques. *Acta linguistica* 5, 121–38. Reprinted in Eric P. Hamp, Fred W. Householder, and Robert Austerlitz (eds), *Readings in linguistics II.* Chicago: University of Chicago Press, 158–74.

Labov, William 1966: *The social stratification of English in New York City.* Washington: Center for Applied Linguistics.

—— 1972: *Sociolinguistic patterns.* Philadelphia: University of Pennsylvania Press.

—— 1994: *Principles of linguistic change, i. Internal factors.* Oxford: Blackwell.

Lafon, René 1948: Correspondances basques-caucasiques. *Eusko-Jakintza* 2, 359–70.

Langacker, Ronald W. 1977: Syntactic reanalysis. In Li (1977), 57–139.

Lass, Roger 1975: Internal reconstruction and generative phonology. *Transactions of the Philological Society*, 1–26.

—— 1984: *Phonology.* Cambridge: Cambridge University Press.

—— 1994: *Old English: a historical linguistic companion.* Cambridge: Cambridge University Press.

Lees, Robert B. 1953: The basis of glottochronology. *Language* 29, 113–27.

Lehmann, Winfred P. 1952: *Proto-Indo-European phonology.* Austin: University of Texas Press.

—— 1992: *Historical linguistics.* 3rd edn. London: Routledge.

—— 1993: *Theoretical bases of Indo-European linguistics.* London: Routledge.

Lehiste, Ilse 1988: *Lectures on language contact.* Cambridge, MA: MIT Press.

Leith, Dick 1983: *A social history of English.* London: Routledge.

Le Page, Robert B. 1993: Conflicts of metaphors in the discussion of language and race. In Ernst Håkon Jahr (ed.), *Language conflict and language planning.* Berlin: Mouton de Gruyter, 143–64.

Levin, Saul 1971: *The Indo-European and Semitic languages.* Albany: State University of New York.

Lewin, Roger 1988: Linguists search for the mother tongue. *Science* 242 (25 November), 1128–9.

—— 1990: Ancestral voices at war. *New Scientist* (16 June), 42–7.

Lewis, G. L. 1967: *Turkish grammar.* Oxford: Clarendon Press.

Li, Charles N. (ed.) 1975: *Word order and word order change.* Austin: University of Texas Press.

—— (ed.) 1977: *Mechanisms of syntactic change.* Austin: University of Texas Press.

Li, Charles N. and Thompson, Sandra 1974: An explanation of word order change SVO → SOV. *Foundations of Language* 12, 201–14.

—— 1977: A mechanism for the development of copula morphemes. In Li (1977), 419–4.

Li, Paul Jen-Kuei 1982: Linguistic variations of different age groups in the Atayalic dialects. *The Tsing Hua Journal of Chinese Studies* (new series) 14, 167–91.

Lichtenberk, Frantisek 1985: Syntactic-category change in Oceanic languages. *Oceanic Linguistics* 24, 1–84.

Lightfoot, David 1974: The diachronic analysis of the English modals. In John M. Anderson and Charles Jones (eds), *Historical linguistics: proceedings of the First International Conference on Historical Linguistics*. Amsterdam: North Holland, I, pp. 219–49.

—— 1979: *Principles of diachronic syntax*. Cambridge: Cambridge University Press.

—— 1981: Explaining syntactic change. In Norbert Hornstein and David Lightfoot (eds), *Explanation in linguistics: the logical problem of language acquisition*. London: Longman, 209–40.

—— 1988: Syntactic change. In Newmeyer (1988), I, pp. 303–23.

Lindblom, Björn 1986: Phonetic universals in vowel systems. In John J. Ohala and Jeri J. Jaeger (eds), *Experimental phonology*, Orlando: Academic Press, 13–44.

Lindeman, Fredrik O. 1987: *Introduction to the ' laryngeal theory'*. Oslo: Norwegian University Press/The Institute for Comparative Research in Human Culture.

Lockwood, W. B. 1965: *An informal history of the German language: with chapters on Dutch and Afrikaans, Frisian and Yiddish*. Cambridge: Heffer.

—— 1969: *Indo-European philology*. London: Hutchinson.

—— 1972: *A panorama of Indo-European languages*. London: Hutchinson.

Lodge, R. Anthony 1993: *French: from dialect to standard*. London: Routledge.

McCrum, Robert, Cran, William and MacNeil, Robert 1992: *The Story of English*. London: Faber & Faber/BBC Books.

Mackey, W. F. and J. Ornstein (eds) 1979: *Sociolinguistic studies in language contact: methods and cases*. The Hague: Mouton.

McMahon, April M. S. 1994: *Understanding language change*. Cambridge: Cambridge University Press.

——McMahon, Robert 1995: 'Linguistics, genetics and archaeology: internal and external evidence in the Amerind controversy'. *Transactions of the Philological Society* 93, 125–225.

Maddieson, Ian 1980a: A survey of liquids. *UCLA Working Papers in Phonetics* 50, 93–112.

—— 1980b: Vocoid approximants in the world's languages. *UCLA Working Papers in Phonetics* 50, 113–9.

—— 1984: *Patterns of sounds*. Cambridge: Cambridge University Press.

Maiden, Martin 1995: *A linguistic history of Italian*. London: Longman.

Malkiel, Yakov 1993: *Etymology*. Cambridge: Cambridge University Press.

Mallory, J. P. 1973: A short history of the Indo-European problem. *Journal of Indo-European Studies* 1, 21–65.

—— 1989: *In search of the Indo-Europeans: language, archaeology and myth*. London: Thames & Hudson.

Manaster-Ramer, Alexis 1993: On Illič-Svityč's Nostratic theory. *Studies in Language* 17, 205–50.

Mańczak, Witold 1958: Tendances générales des changements analogiques. *Lingua* 7, 298–325, 387–420.

Manser, Martin 1988: *The Guinness book of words*. Enfield, Middx: Guinness Books.

Marchand, James W. (1956): Internal reconstruction of phonemic split. *Language* 32, 245–53.

Martinet, André 1953: Remarques sur le consonantisme sémitique. *Bulletin de la Société de Linguistique de Paris* 49, 67–78.

—— 1955: *Économie des changements phonétiques*. Berne: A. Francke.

Masica, Colin P. 1976: *Defining a linguistic area: South Asia*. Chicago: University of Chicago Press.

Matisoff, James A. 1990: On megalocomparison. *Language* 66, 106–20.

Mattoso Camara, Joaquim 1972: *The Portuguese language*. Chicago: University of Chicago Press.

Meillet, Antoine 1926–8: *Linguistique historique et linguistique générale*. Paris: Champion.

——Cohen, Marcel 1952: *Les langues du monde*. 2 vols. Paris: CNRS.

Meyer-Lübke, Wilhelm 1935: *Romanisches etymologisches Wörterbuch*. 3rd edn. Heidelberg: Carl Winter.

Michelena, Luis 1977: *Fonética histórica vasca*. 2nd edn. [1st edn. 1961]. San Sebastián: Publicaciones del Seminario de Filología Vasca 'Julio de Urquijo'.

Miller, Roy 1971: *Japanese and the other Altaic languages*. Chicago: University of Chicago Press.

Mills, A. D. 1991: *A dictionary of English place-names*. Oxford: Oxford University Press.

Milroy, James 1983: On the sociolinguistic history of /h/-dropping in English. In M. Davenport, E. Hansen, and H.-F. Nielsen (eds), *Current topics in English historical linguistics*. Odense: Odense University Press, 37–53.

——1992: *Linguistic variation and change*. Oxford: Blackwell.

Harris, J. 1980: When is a merger not a merger?: the MEAT/MATE problem in a present-day English vernacular. *English World Wide* 1, 199–210.

Miranda, Rocky V. 1975: Internal reconstruction: scope and limits. *Lingua* 36, 289–306.

Modini, Paul 1991: PIE-AA-ST: a genetic link between Indo-European, Afro-Asiatic and Sino-Tibetan. *Folia Linguistica Historica* 12, 89–106.

Moravcsik, Edith 1978: Language contact. In Greenberg *et al.* (1978), I, pp. 93–123.

Moseley, C. and Asher, R. E. (eds) 1994: *Atlas of the world's languages*. London: Routledge.

Munro, Pamela 1977: From existential to copula: the history of Yuman *BE*. In Li (1977), 445–90.

Nartey, J. N. A. 1979: A study in phonemic universals – especially concerning fricatives and stops. *UCLA Working Papers in Phonetics* 46.

Newman, Francis 1844: *On the structure of the Berber language*. London.

Newmeyer, Frederick J. (ed.) 1988: *Linguistics: the Cambridge survey*. 4 vols. Cambridge: Cambridge University Press.

Nichols, Johanna 1990: Linguistic diversity and the first settlement of the New World. *Language* 66, 475–521.

——1992: *Linguistic diversity in space and time*. Chicago: University of Chicago Press.

Nikolaev, Sergei L. 1986: Sino-kavkazkie jazyki v Amerike. Unpublished manuscript. English translation Sino-Caucasian languages in America, in Shevoroshkin (1991), 42–66.

Noreiko, Stephen 1993: New words for new technologies. In Sanders (1993), 171–84.

O'Connor, J. D. 1973: *Phonetics*. Harmondsworth, Middx: Penguin.

O'Grady, Richard T., Goddard, Ives, Bateman, Richard M., DiMichele, William A., Funk, V. A., Kress, W. John, Mooi, Rich, and Cannell, Peter F. 1989: Genes and tongues. *Science* 243, 1651.

Onions, C. T. (ed.) 1966: *The Oxford dictionary of English etymology*. Oxford: Clarendon Press.

Orël, Vladimir E. and Starostin, Sergei 1990: Etruscan as an East Caucasian language. In Vitaly Shevoroshkin (ed.), *Proto-languages and proto-cultures*. Bochum: Brockmeyer, 60–6.

Orton, Harold and Wright, N. 1974: *A word geography of England*. London: Seminar Press.

——Sanderson, S., and Widdowson, J. 1978: *Linguistic atlas of England*. London: Croom Helm.

——*et al.* 1962–71: *Survey of English dialects: the basic material*. Leeds: E. J. Arnold.

Oswalt, Robert 1991: A method for assessing distant linguistic relationships. In Sydney M. Lamb and E. Douglas Mitchell (eds), *Sprung from some common source: investigations into the prehistory of languages.* Stanford: Stanford University Press, 389–404.

Oxford English Dictionary. 2nd edn. 20 vols. Edition eds. J. A. Simpson and E. S. C. Weiner. Oxford: Clarendon Press.

Partridge, Eric 1958: *Origins: an etymological dictionary of modern English.* London: Routledge.

—— 1966: *Origins: an etymological dictionary of modern English.* 4th edn. London: Routledge.

Pasau, Georges 1994: Éditorial. *Singuliers: Revue des parlers romans de la province de Luxembourg* 4, 4–5.

Pedersen, Holger 1903: Türkische Lautgesetze. *Zeitschrift der deutschen morgenländischen Gesellschaft* 57, 535–61.

—— 1931: *The discovery of language: linguistic science in the 19th century.* Cambridge, MA: Harvard University Press.

Penny, Ralph 1991: *A history of the Spanish language.* Cambridge: Cambridge University Press.

Petyt, K. M. 1978: *The study of dialect.* London: André Deutsch.

Picard, Marc 1995a: On the nature of the Algonquian evidence for global etymologies. *Mother Tongue* 24, 50–4.

—— Arapaho, Blackfoot and Basque: a 'snow' job. *Mother Tongue* 24, 71–2.

Pinker, Steven 1994: *The language instinct: the new science of language and mind.* London: Allen Lane/Penguin.

Plank, Frans (ed.) 1979: *Ergativity: towards a theory of grammatical relations.* London: Academic Press.

Pokorny, Julius 1959: *Indogermanisches Etymologisches Wörterbuch,* vol. 1. Bern: Francke.

—— 1969: *Indogermanisches Etymologisches Wörterbuch,* II. Bern: Francke.

Polomé, Edgar C. (1965) The laryngeal theory so far. In Werner Winter (ed.), *Evidence for laryngeals.* The Hague: Mouton, 9–78.

Price, Glanville 1971: *The French language: present and past.* London: Edward Arnold.

Puhvel, Jaan (ed.) 1970: *Myth and law among the Indo-Europeans: studies in Indo-European comparative mythology.* Berkeley and Los Angeles: University of California Press.

Pulleyblank, Edwin G 1978: Sino-Tibetan and Indo-European: the case for a genetic comparison. Paper delivered at the Conference on the Origin of Chinese Civilization, Berkeley, CA, June 1978.

Pyles, Thomas and Algeo, John 1993: *The origins and development of the English language.* 4th edn. Fort Worth, TX: Harcourt Brace & World.

Quirk, Randolph 1995: *Grammatical and lexical variance in English.* London: Longman.

Renfrew, Colin 1987: *Archaeology and language: the puzzle of Indo-European origins.* London: Jonathan Cape.

—— 1989: The origins of Indo-European languages. *Scientific American* (October), 82–90.

—— 1992: World languages and human dispersals: a minimalist view. In John A. Hall and I. C. Jarvie (eds), *Transition to modernity: essays on power, wealth and belief.* Cambridge: Cambridge University Press, 11–68.

—— 1994: World linguistic diversity. *Scientific American* (January), 104–110.

—— 1995: Language families as evidence of human dispersals. In Sidney Brenner and Kazuro Hanihara (eds), *The origin and past of modern humans as viewed from DNA.* Singapore: World Scientific, 285–306.

Rijk, Rudolf P. G. de 1995: 'Nunc' vasconice. In José Ignacio Hualde, Joseba Lakarra, and R. L. Trask (eds), *Towards a history of the Basque language: studies in Basque historical linguistics*. Amsterdam: John Benjamins, 295–311.

Ringe, Donald A. 1992: On calculating the factor of chance in language comparison. *Transactions of the American Philosophical Society* 82, 1–110.

—— 1993: A reply to Professor Greenberg. *Proceedings of the American Philosophical Society* 137, 91–109.

—— 1995: 'Nostratic' and the factor of chance. *Diachronica* 12, 55–74.

—— 1996: The mathematics of 'Amerind'. To appear in *Diachronica*.

——forthcoming. 'Internal reconstruction'. To appear in a volume edited by Brian Joseph, from Blackwell.

Robinson, Orrin W 1992: *Old English and its closest relatives*. London: Routledge.

Romaine, Suzanne 1994: *Language in society: an introduction to sociolinguistics*. Oxford: Oxford University Press.

Ross, Alan S. C. 1965: *Etymology, with especial reference to English*. London: Methuen.

Ross, Philip E. 1991: Hard words. *Scientific American* (April), 70–9.

Ruhlen, Merritt 1991: *A guide to the world's languages, i. Classification*. Expanded edn. London: Edward Arnold.

—— 1994: *On the origin of languages: studies in linguistic taxonomy*. Stanford: Stanford University Press.

Salmons, Joseph 1992: A look at the data for a global etymology: **tik* 'finger'. In Garry W. Davis and Gregory K. Iversen (eds), *Explanation in Historical Linguistics*. Amsterdam: John Benjamins, 207–28.

Sanders, Carol (ed.) 1993: *French today: language in its social context*. Cambridge: Cambridge University Press.

Sapir, Edward 1913: Wiyot and Yurok, Algonkin languages of California. *American Anthropologist* 15, 617–46.

—— 1915: The Na-Déné languages: a preliminary report. *American Anthropologist* 17, 534–58.

—— 1925: The similarity of Chinese and Indian languages. *Science* 62, 1607.

Saussure, Ferdinand de 1879: *Mémoire sur le système primitif des voyelles dans les langues indo-européennes*. Leipzig: Teubner.

Schleicher, August 1871: *Compendium der vergleichenden Grammatik der indogermanischen Sprachen*. 3rd edn. Weimar: Böhlau.

Schmidt, Alice 1985: *Young people's Dyirbal: an example of language death from Australia*. Cambridge: Cambridge University Press.

Schmidt, Wilhelm 1906: *Die Mon-Khmer-Völker, ein Bindeglied zwischen Völkern Zentralasiens und Austronesians*. Braunschweig.

Sedlak, P. 1969: Typological considerations of vowel quality systems. *Stanford Working Papers on Language Universals* 1.

Seliger, Herbert W. and Vago, Robert M. (eds) 1991: *First language attrition*. Cambridge: Cambridge University Press.

Shafer, Robert 1952: Athabascan and Sino-Tibetan. *International Journal of American Linguistics* 18, 12–19.

—— 1957: Note on Athabascan and Sino-Tibetan. *International Journal of American Linguistics* 23, 116–17.

Sheard, J. A. 1966: *The words of English*. New York: W. W. Norton.

Shevoroshkin, Vitaly 1990: The mother tongue. *The Sciences* (May/June), 20–7.

—— (ed.) 1991: *Déné-Sino-Caucasian languages*. Bochum: Brockmeyer.

Sommerfelt, Alf 1962: *Diachronic and synchronic aspects of language*. The Hague: Mouton.

Starostin, Sergei 1984: Gipoteza o geneticheskix svjazjax sinotibetskix jazykov s enisejskimi i severokavkazskimi jazykami. English translation 'On the hypothesis of a genetic connection between the Sino-Tibetan languages and the Yeniseian and North-Caucasian languages', in Shevoroshkin (1991), 12–41.

—— 1991: *Altajskaja Problema i Proisxozhdenije zhaponskogo jazyka* [*The Altaic problem and the origin of the Japanese language*]. Moscow: Nauka.

Stern, Gustaf 1931: *Meaning and change of meaning*. Bloomington, IN: Indiana University Press.

Strang, Barbara 1970: *A history of English*. London: Methuen.

Swadesh, Morris 1952: Review of Shafer (1952). *International Journal of American Linguistics* 18, 178–81.

—— 1955: 'Towards greater accuracy in lexico-statistic dating'. *International Journal of American Linguistics* 21, 121–37.

—— 1971: *The origin and diversification of language*, ed. Joel Sherzer. London: Routledge.

Sweet, Henry 1901: *The history of language*. London.

Szemerényi, Oswald 1973: La théorie des laryngales de Saussure à Kuryłowicz et à Benveniste. Essai de réévaluation. *Bulletin de la Société de Linguistique de Paris* 68, 1–25.

Thieme, Paul 1964: The comparative method for reconstruction in linguistics. In Dell H. Hymes (ed.), *Language in culture and society*, New York: Harper & Row, 585–98.

Thomason, Sarah Grey and Kaufman, Terrence 1988: *Language contact, creolization, and genetic linguistics*. Berkeley and Los Angeles: University of California Press.

Thomsen, Vilhelm L. P. 1869. *Den gotiske sprogklasses indflydelse på den friske.* Copenhagen: Den Gyldendalske boghandel.

Tischler, J. 1973: *Glottochronologie und Lexikostatistik*. Innsbrücker Beiträge zur Sprachwissenschaft 11.

Tovar, Antonio, Bouda, Karl, Lafon, René, Michelena, Luis, Swadesh, Morris, and Vycichl, W. 1961: El método léxico-estadístico y su aplicación a las relaciones del vascuence. *Boletín de la Real Sociedad Vascongada de los Amigos del País* 17, 249–81.

Trask, R. L. 1995: Basque and Déné-Caucasian: a critique from the Basque side. *Mother Tongue* NS 1, 3–82.

Traugott, Elizabeth Closs 1972: *The history of English syntax*. New York: Holt, Rinehart & Winston.

—— 1982: 'From propositional to textual and expressive meanings: some semantic-pragmatic aspects of grammaticalization'. In Winfred P. Lehmann and Yakov Malkiel (eds), *Perspectives on Historical Linguistics*. Amsterdam: John Benjamins, 245–71.

—— 1989: 'On the rise of epistemic meanings in English: an example of subjectification in semantic change'. *Language* 65, 31–55.

Trubetzkoy, Nikolai 1939: *Gründzüge der Phonologie*. Travaux du Cercle Linguistique de Prague VII. English translation (1969), *Principles of phonology*, Berkeley and Los Angeles: University of California Press.

Trudgill, Peter 1974: *The social differentiation of English in Norwich*. Cambridge: Cambridge University Press.

—— 1986: *Dialects in contact*. Oxford: Blackwell.

—— 1990: *The dialects of England*. Oxford: Blackwell.

—— 1994: *Dialects*. London: Routledge.

—— 1995: *Sociolinguistics*. 2nd edn. London: Penguin.

——Chambers, J. K. (eds) 1991: *Dialects of English*. London: Longman.

——Hannah, Jean 1994: *International English: a guide to the varieties of standard English*. 3rd ed. London: Edward Arnold.

Turner, Christy G. 1983: Dental evidence for the peopling of the Americas. In R. Shutler (ed.), *Early man in the new world*, Beverly Hills: Sage, 147–57.

Turner, Christy G. 1985: The dental search for native American origins. In R. L. Kirk and E. Szathmary (eds), *Out of Asia: peopling the Americas and the Pacific*. Canberra: Journal of Pacific History, 31–78.

—— 1986: The first Americans: the dental evidence. *National Geographic Research* 2: 37–46.

Ullmann, Stephen 1961: *The Principles of Semantics*. 2nd edn. Glasgow: Jackson.

Upton, Clive, Sanderson, Stewart, and Widdowson, John 1987: *Word maps: a dialect atlas of England*. London: Croom Helm.

Vennemann, Theo, and Wilbur, Terence H., 1972: *Schuchardt, the Neogrammarians, and the transformational theory of phonological change: four essays*. Frankfurt/Main: Athenäum.

Voegelin, C. F. and Voegelin, F. M. 1977: *Classification and index of the world's languages*. New York: Elsevier.

Walter, Henriette 1994: *French inside out*. London: Routledge. English translation by Peter Fawcett of *Le français dans tous le sens*, 1988, Paris: Éditions Robert Laffont.

Wang, William 1969: Competing changes as a cause of residue. *Language* 45, 9–25.

Warner, Anthony 1983: Review of Lightfoot (1979). *Journal of Linguistics* 19, 187–209.

Warnow, Tandy, Ringe, Donald, and Taylor, Ann 1995: *Reconstructing the evolutionary history of natural languages*. Institute for Research in Cognitive Science, IRCS Report 95–16. Philadelphia: University of Pennsylvania.

Waterman, J. T. 1966: *A history of the German language, with special reference to the cultural and social forces that shaped the literary language*. Rev. edn. Seattle: University of Washington Press.

Watkins, Calvert 1969: Indo-European and the Indo-Europeans. Appendix to the *American heritage dictionary*. Boston: American Heritage Publishing Co./Houghton Mifflin Company, 1496–1502.

Weinreich, Uriel 1953: *Languages in contact: findings and problems*. The Hague: Mouton.

—— Labov, William, and Herzog, Marvin I., 1968: Empirical foundations for a theory of language change. In W. P. Lehmann and Yakov Malkiel (eds), *Directions for Historical Linguistics*. Austin: University of Texas Press, 95–195.

Wells, C. J. 1987: *German: a linguistic history to 1945*. Oxford: Clarendon Press.

Wells, John C. 1982: *Accents of English*. 3 vols. Cambridge: Cambridge University Press.

Williams, Joseph M. 1975: *Origins of the English language: a social and linguistic history*. London: Collier Macmillan.

Winter, Werner (ed.) 1965: *Evidence for Laryngeals*. The Hague: Mouton.

Wright, Robert 1991: Quest for the mother tongue. *Atlantic Monthly* (April), 39–68.

Wurm, Stephen 1982: *Papuan languages of Oceania*. Tübingen: Gunter Narr.

Wurzel, Wolfgang U. 1989: *Inflectional morphology and naturalness*. Dordrecht: Kluwer.

Index